ANDERSON'S
Law School Publications

Administrative Law Anthology
Thomas O. Sargentich

Administrative Law: Cases and Materials
Daniel J. Gifford

An Admiralty Law Anthology
Robert M. Jarvis

Alternative Dispute Resolution: Strategies for Law and Business
E. Wendy Trachte-Huber and Stephen K. Huber

The American Constitutional Order: History, Cases, and Philosophy
Douglas W. Kmiec and Stephen B. Presser

American Legal Systems: A Resource and Reference Guide
Toni M. Fine

Analytic Jurisprudence Anthology
Anthony D'Amato

An Antitrust Anthology
Andrew I. Gavil

Appellate Advocacy: Principles and Practice, *Third Edition*
Ursula Bentele and Eve Cary

Arbitration: Cases and Materials
Stephen K. Huber and E. Wendy Trachte-Huber

Basic Accounting Principles for Lawyers: With Present Value and Expected Value
C. Steven Bradford and Gary A. Ames

Basic Themes in Law and Jurisprudence
Charles W. Collier

A Capital Punishment Anthology (and Electronic Caselaw Appendix)
Victor L. Streib

Cases and Materials on Corporations
Thomas R. Hurst and William A. Gregory

Cases and Materials on the Law Governing Lawyers
James E. Moliterno

Cases and Problems in California Criminal Law
Myron Moskovitz

Cases and Problems in Criminal Law, *Fourth Edition*
Myron Moskovitz

The Citation Workbook: How to Beat the Citation Blues, *Second Edition*
Maria L. Ciampi, Rivka Widerman, and Vicki Lutz

Civil Procedure Anthology
David I. Levine, Donald L. Doernberg, and Melissa L. Nelken

Civil Procedure: Cases, Materials, and Questions, *Second Edition*
Richard D. Freer and Wendy Collins Perdue

Clinical Anthology: Readings for Live-Client Clinics
Alex J. Hurder, Frank S. Bloch, Susan L. Brooks, and Susan L. Kay

Commercial Transactions Series: Problems and Materials
Louis F. Del Duca, Egon Guttman, Alphonse M. Squillante, Fred H. Miller,
    Linda Rusch, and Peter Winship
        Vol. 1: Secured Transactions Under the UCC
        Vol. 2: Sales Under the UCC and the CISG
        Vol. 3: Negotiable Instruments Under the UCC and the CIBN

Communications Law: Media, Entertainment, and Regulation
Donald E. Lively, Allen S. Hammond, Blake D. Morant, and Russell L. Weaver

A Conflict-of-Laws Anthology
Gene R. Shreve

Constitutional Conflicts
Derrick A. Bell, Jr.

A Constitutional Law Anthology, *Second Edition*
Michael J. Glennon, Donald E. Lively, Phoebe A. Haddon, Dorothy E. Roberts,
    and Russell L. Weaver

Constitutional Law: Cases, History, and Dialogues, *Second Edition*
Donald E. Lively, Phoebe A. Haddon, Dorothy E. Roberts, Russell L. Weaver,
and William D. Araiza

The Constitutional Law of the European Union
James D. Dinnage and John F. Murphy

The Constitutional Law of the European Union: Documentary Supplement
James D. Dinnage and John F. Murphy

Constitutional Torts
Sheldon H. Nahmod, Michael L. Wells, and Thomas A. Eaton

A Contracts Anthology, *Second Edition*
Peter Linzer

Contract Law and Practice
Gerald E. Berendt, Michael L. Closen, Doris Estelle Long, Marie A. Monahan,
    Robert J. Nye, and John H. Scheid

Contracts: Contemporary Cases, Comments, and Problems
Michael L. Closen, Richard M. Perlmutter, and Jeffrey D. Wittenberg

A Copyright Anthology: The Technology Frontier
Richard H. Chused

Corporate Law Anthology
Franklin A. Gevurtz

Corporate and White Collar Crime: An Anthology
Leonard Orland

A Criminal Law Anthology
Arnold H. Loewy

Criminal Law: Cases and Materials, *Second Edition*
Arnold H. Loewy

A Criminal Procedure Anthology
Silas J. Wasserstrom and Christie L. Snyder

Criminal Procedure: Arrest and Investigation
Arnold H. Loewy and Arthur B. LaFrance

Criminal Procedure: Trial and Sentencing
Arthur B. LaFrance and Arnold H. Loewy

Economic Regulation: Cases and Materials
Richard J. Pierce, Jr.

Elder Law: Readings, Cases, and Materials
Thomas P. Gallanis, A. Kimberley Dayton, and Molly M. Wood

Elder Law: Statutes and Regulations
Thomas P. Gallanis, A. Kimberley Dayton, and Molly M. Wood

Elements of Law
Eva H. Hanks, Michael E. Herz, and Steven S. Nemerson

Ending It: Dispute Resolution in America
  Descriptions, Examples, Cases and Questions
Susan M. Leeson and Bryan M. Johnston

An Environmental Law Anthology
Robert L. Fischman, Maxine I. Lipeles, and Mark S. Squillace

Environmental Law Series
  Environmental Decisionmaking, *Third Edition*
  Robert L. Fischman and Mark S. Squillace

  Water Pollution, *Third Edition*
  Jackson B. Battle and Maxine I. Lipeles

  Air Pollution, *Third Edition*
  Mark S. Squillace and David R. Wooley

  Hazardous Waste, *Third Edition*
  Maxine I. Lipeles

Environmental Protection and Justice
  Readings and Commentary on Environmental Law and Practice
Kenneth A. Manaster

European Union Law Anthology
Karen V. Kole and Anthony D'Amato

An Evidence Anthology
Edward J. Imwinkelried and Glen Weissenberger

Family Law in Action: A Reader
Margaret F. Brinig, Carl E. Schneider, and Lee E. Teitelbaum

Federal Antitrust Law: Cases and Materials
Daniel J. Gifford and Leo J. Raskind

Federal Income Tax Anthology
Paul L. Caron, Karen C. Burke, and Grayson M.P. McCouch

Federal Rules of Civil Procedure
Publisher's Staff

Federal Rules of Evidence Handbook
Publisher's Staff

Federal Rules of Evidence: Rules, Legislative History, Commentary and Authority
Glen Weissenberger

Federal Wealth Transfer Tax Anthology
Paul L. Caron, Grayson M.P. McCouch, Karen C. Burke

First Amendment Anthology
Donald E. Lively, Dorothy E. Roberts, and Russell L. Weaver

The History, Philosophy, and Structure of the American Constitution
Douglas W. Kmiec and Stephen B. Presser

Individual Rights and the American Constitution
Douglas W. Kmiec and Stephen B. Presser

International Environmental Law Anthology
Anthony D'Amato and Kirsten Engel

International Human Rights: Law, Policy, and Process, *Second Edition*
Frank C. Newman and David Weissbrodt

**Selected International Human Rights Instruments and
   Bibliography for Research on International Human Rights Law,** *Second Edition*
Frank C. Newman and David Weissbrodt

International Intellectual Property Anthology
Anthony D'Amato and Doris Estelle Long

International Law Anthology
Anthony D'Amato

International Law Coursebook
Anthony D'Amato

International Taxation: Cases, Materials, and Problems
Philip F. Postlewaite

Introduction to the Study of Law: Cases and Materials, *Second Edition*
John Makdisi

Judicial Externships: The Clinic Inside the Courthouse, *Second Edition*
Rebecca A. Cochran

A Land Use Anthology
Jon W. Bruce

Law and Economics Anthology
Kenneth G. Dau-Schmidt and Thomas S. Ulen

The Law of Disability Discrimination, *Second Edition*
Ruth Colker and Bonnie Poitras Tucker

The Law of Disability Discrimination Handbook: Statutes and Regulatory Guidance
   Second Edition
Ruth Colker and Bonnie Poitras Tucker

Lawyers and Fundamental Moral Responsibility
Daniel R. Coquillette

Mediation and Negotiation: Reaching Agreement in Law and Business
E. Wendy Trachte-Huber and Stephen K. Huber

Microeconomic Predicates to Law and Economics
Mark Seidenfeld

Natural Resources: Cases and Materials
Barlow Burke

Patients, Psychiatrists and Lawyers: Law and the Mental Health System, *Second Edition*
Raymond L. Spring, Roy B. Lacoursiere, and Glen Weissenberger

Preventive Law: Materials on a Non Adversarial Legal Process
Robert M. Hardaway

Principles of Evidence, *Fourth Edition*
Irving Younger, Michael Goldsmith, and David A. Sonenshein

Problems and Simulations in Evidence, *Second Edition*
Thomas F. Guernsey

A Products Liability Anthology
Anita Bernstein

Professional Responsibility Anthology
Thomas B. Metzloff

A Property Anthology, *Second Edition*
Richard H. Chused

Public Choice and Public Law: Readings and Commentary
Maxwell L. Stearns

The Question Presented: Model Appellate Briefs
Maria L. Ciampi and William H. Manz

Readings in Criminal Law
Russell L. Weaver, John M. Burkoff, Catherine Hancock, Alan Reed, and Peter J. Seago

Science in Evidence
D.H. Kaye

A Section 1983 Civil Rights Anthology
Sheldon H. Nahmod

Sports Law: Cases and Materials, *Fourth Edition*
Ray L. Yasser, James R. McCurdy, C. Peter Goplerud, and Maureen A. Weston

A Torts Anthology, *Second Edition*
Julie A. Davies, Lawrence C. Levine, and Edward J. Kionka

Trial Practice
Lawrence A. Dubin and Thomas F. Guernsey

Unincorporated Business Entities
Larry E. Ribstein

FORTHCOMING PUBLICATIONS

Cases and Materials in Juvenile Law
J. Eric Smithburn

Elements of Laʌ, *Second Edition*
Eva H. Hank, Michael E. Herz, and Steven S. Nemerson

First Amendment Law: Cases, Comparative Perspectives, and Dialogues
Donald E. Lively, Phoebe A. Haddon, John C. Knechtle, and Dorothy E. Roberts

Property Law: Cases, Materials, and Questions
Edward E. Chase

State and Local Government Law
John Martinez and Michael E. Libonati

Taxation: A Skills Approach
Michael A. Livingston

BASIC THEMES IN LAW AND JURISPRUDENCE

CHARLES W. COLLIER

Professor of Law and Philosophy
University of Florida

ANDERSON PUBLISHING CO.
CINCINNATI, OHIO

BASIC THEMES IN LAW AND JURISPRUDENCE
CHARLES W. COLLIER

© 2000 by Anderson Publishing Co.

Anderson Publishing Co.
2035 Reading Road / Cincinnati, Ohio 45202
800-582-7295 / e-mail lawschool@andersonpublishing.com / Fax 513-562-5430
www.andersonpublishing.com

ISBN: 1-58360-763-3

Library of Congress Cataloging-in-Publication Data

Collier, Charles W., 1950-
    Basic themes in law and jurisprudence / Charles W. Collier.
        p. cm.
    Includes index.
    ISBN 1-58360-763-3 (hard cover)
    1. Law--United States--Cases. 2. Jurisprudence--United States--Cases. I. Title.

KF379 .C65 2000
349.73--dc21   99-087576

Contents

Part III
The Reach of the Law

Part IV
The Legal and the Non-Legal

Part V
Law and Morality

Preface

This book is an introduction to law and jurisprudence. Instead of presenting these subjects as they happened to unfold historically, or as they have been advanced by various "schools," this book pursues five basic themes that inevitably emerge in the study of law and jurisprudence:

Law and Society
Freedom and Necessity
The Reach of the Law
The Legal and the Non-Legal
Law and Morality

While these themes do not exhaust the study of either law or jurisprudence, they do focus attention on the most important issues.

In preparing this collection of readings I have tried to bring together original sources that compellingly present concrete legal conflicts. These are also, I have found, the kinds of readings that provoke the most interesting and important classroom discussions.

Jurisprudential issues arise in the context of concrete legal conflicts, and they can most readily be grasped (at least initially) in such contexts. *Ex facto jus oritur* (law arises out of facts). Indeed, it is hard to imagine a genuine legal issue that could not, in principle, be the subject of an actual legal case. I therefore make one major assumption about jurisprudence, and it is this: Any jurisprudential principle that has not been, or cannot be, found embedded in a legal case is not a real jurisprudential principle. Where it can be so found, however, I prefer to read the case or cases themselves rather than theories about the principle. These readings are organized around the thesis that jurisprudence is most revealingly on display *in case law*. The "facts" of law cannot be irrelevant to jurisprudential "theory."

These readings can and should be taught and learned in many ways and on many levels. I have therefore provided only limited guidance for—or constraints on—their use. In order to accommodate many different styles of teaching and learning, I have included more material than can normally be used in any one-semester course. A considerable amount of picking and choosing among the selections is thus to be encouraged. Thoughtful and independent-minded teachers and students alike will, I trust, make these materials their own.

Editorial note. In edited selections, citations and footnotes have generally been omitted or renumbered without notice. Other deletions are indicated by ellipses or brackets.

General Introduction

In early English usage the word "jurisprudence" referred to legal systems generally and to the study of them.[1] Since the nineteenth century jurisprudence has also come to mean the philosophy of law or legal theory.[2] Jurisprudence focuses on the more general or abstract aspects of concrete legal problems and their institutional solutions.

Since jurisprudence is defined partly in terms of "law," it will be useful to consider the concept of law itself; and here we encounter an even wider variety of notions. Consider, for example, the following:

> [T]he creator . . . has laid down only such laws as were founded in those relations of justice, that existed in the nature of things antecedent to any positive precept. These are the eternal, immutable laws of good and evil.[3]

> The first requirement of a sound body of law is, that it should correspond with the actual feelings and demands of the community, whether right or wrong.[4]

> A law . . . may be said to be a rule laid down for the guidance of an intelligent being by an intelligent being having power over him.[5]

> [T]he only method of proving, that this or that maxim is a rule of the common law, is by shewing that it hath been always the custom to observe it.[6]

> The law . . . is not simply a chart of do's and don'ts; it is a program for living together.[7]

---

[1]   8 Oxford English Dictionary 321 (2d ed. 1989); cf. Grant Gilmore, The Ages of American Law 113 n.2 (1977). This is the sense, for example, in which "[i]t would be a reproach to the jurisprudence of the country" if one could recover insurance proceeds by murdering the insured. Riggs v. Palmer, 115 N.Y. 506, 512 (1889).

[2]   The earliest example of usage in the first sense given by the *Oxford English Dictionary* predates by 100 years (1656 to 1756) the earliest example of the second sense.

[3]   1 William Blackstone, Commentaries on the Laws of England *40.

[4]   O.W. Holmes, The Common Law 36 (Howe ed. 1963).

[5]   John Austin, The Province of Jurisprudence Determined, Lecture I (1832).

[6]   1 William Blackstone, Commentaries on the Laws of England *68.

[7]   Lon L. Fuller, Human Interaction and the Law, in The Principles of Social Order 222 (Kenneth I. Winston ed. 1981).

A social norm is legal if its neglect or infraction is regularly met, in threat or in fact, by the application of physical force by an individual or group possessing the socially recognized privilege of so acting.[8]

[T]he people who have the doing in charge, whether they be judges or sheriffs or clerks or jailers or lawyers, are officials of the law. *What these officials do about disputes is, to my mind, the law itself.*[9]

The prophecies of what the courts will do in fact, and nothing more pretentious, are what I mean by the law.[10]

Each of these definitions has had its distinguished proponents, and none of them is (given certain assumptions) obviously unintelligible. Yet this extreme diversity among competing conceptions of law itself suggests the need for a background understanding of law, before various definitions of it can be meaningfully considered and compared. This book attempts to provide the materials for developing a personal philosophy of law.

The book is organized around a few basic themes in law and jurisprudence: law and society, freedom and necessity, the reach of the law, the legal and the non-legal, law and morality. These themes are best explored, at least initially, in the concrete contexts in which they arise. Note, however, that the themes are overlapping categories, and some of the readings involve more than one theme. (The *Katz* case, for example, could arguably have been put in any of the five categories.)

---

8   E. Adamson Hoebel, The Law of Primitive Man 28 (1954).

9   K.N. Llewellyn, The Bramble Bush 3 (1930).

10   O.W. Holmes, The Path of the Law, 10 Harvard Law Review 457, 461 (1897).

Part I
Law and Society

Law reflects but in no sense determines the moral worth of a society. The values of a reasonably just society will reflect themselves in a reasonably just law. . . . The values of an unjust society will reflect themselves in an unjust law.[1]

Law and society is perhaps the most general theme in law and jurisprudence. The basic idea is that one cannot advance very far in understanding law without also understanding the society in which it arises. In fact, it might be argued that one must know a great deal about a society in order to understand its law.

1.   Communities in Crisis

The theme of law and society introduces what has been termed "cultural relativism" into the study of law and jurisprudence. Carried to an extreme, cultural relativism suggests that different societies and cultures are unique and incommensurable. And if legal systems are derived from and "relative to" such incomparable settings, then they too may be thought of as unique and incommensurable.

The truth of cultural relativism is most dramatically and jarringly revealed when our settled expectations about a legal system are forcibly wrenched (as in *The Lottery*) out of their usual social and cultural moorings. As Oliver Wendell Holmes once remarked, "It is perfectly proper to regard and study the law simply as a great anthropological document . . . as an exercise in the morphology and transformation of human ideas."[2] To some extent—at least at the stage of gathering evidence and understanding—it is necessary to be a cultural relativist in order to be a good student of jurisprudence.

Law may be understood functionally as the social process of defining deviations (literally, "outlaws") from its norms. In this sense, a social group's legal definitions and its exclusions are simply complementary aspects of the same phenomenon. We may consider what kind of society we are in terms of who—by definition—we would exclude.

---

[1]   Grant Gilmore, The Ages of American Law 110-11 (1977).

[2]   Law in Science and Science in Law, 12 Harvard Law Review 443, 444 (1899).

2.   From Community to Society

A "community" may provisionally be defined as a relatively small group in which shared values may be assumed; communities in this sense range in size from the family to the Greek city-state. A "society" may provisionally be defined as a relatively large group in which shared values cannot be assumed.

According to Sir Henry Maine, "the movement of the progressive societies has hitherto been a movement *from Status to Contract.*" In other words, the movement has been from communal norms to social laws. If this analysis is correct, legal standards that retain a basis in community norms must be closely examined to see whether—as a number of the reading selections suggest—communal standards have been inappropriately generalized at the social level.

Our view of law would remain incomplete if it did not include an account of the ways that law facilitates human interaction, even while effecting social control. To take a familiar example: Traffic laws are prohibitions and restrictions on individual freedom, complete with sanctions. They define outer limits on what may be done in an area of human conduct. But they also give effect to the desirable social end of facilitating an orderly system of transportation; and in this sense the restrictions on us as individuals are completely consistent with our common ends. We—as individuals, and as a society—would not want to live under circumstances permitting absolutely no regulation of vehicular traffic. But, again (as the vagrancy cases emphasize), we would also not want to live in a society that restricted our individual freedom of movement in an unnecessarily draconian or totalitarian way.

Chapter 1
Communities in Crisis

The Lottery[*]
Shirley Jackson

The morning of June 27th was clear and sunny, with the fresh warmth of a full-summer day; the flowers were blossoming profusely and the grass was richly green. The people of the village began to gather in the square, between the post office and the bank, around ten o'clock; in some towns there were so many people that the lottery took two days and had to be started on June 26th, but in this village, where there were only about three hundred people, the whole lottery took less than two hours, so it could begin at ten o'clock in the morning and still be through in time to allow the villagers to get home for noon dinner.

The children assembled first, of course. School was recently over for the summer, and the feeling of liberty sat uneasily on most of them; they tended to gather together quietly for a while before they broke into boisterous play, and their talk was still of the classroom and the teacher, of books and reprimands. Bobby Martin had already stuffed his pockets full of stones, and the other boys soon followed his example, selecting the smoothest and roundest stones; Bobby and Harry Jones and Dickie Delacroix—the villagers pronounced this name "Dellacroy"—eventually made a great pile of stones in one corner of the square and guarded it against the raids of the other boys. The girls stood aside, talking among themselves, looking over their shoulders at the boys, and the very small children rolled in the dust or clung to the hands of their older brothers or sisters.

Soon the men began to gather, surveying their own children, speaking of planting and rain, tractors and taxes. They stood together, away from the pile of stones in the corner, and their jokes were quiet and they smiled rather than laughed. The women, wearing faded house dresses and sweaters, came shortly after their menfolk. They greeted one another and exchanged bits of gossip as they went to join their husbands. Soon the women, standing by their husbands, began to call to their children, and the children came reluctantly, having to be called four or five times. Bobby Martin ducked under his mother's grasping hand and ran, laughing, back to the pile of stones. His father spoke up sharply, and Bobby came quickly and took his place between his father and older brother.

The lottery was conducted—as were the square dances, the teen-age club, the Halloween program—by Mr. Summers, who had time and energy to devote to civic activities. He was a round-faced, jovial man and he ran the coal business, and people were sorry for him, because he had no children and his wife was a scold. When he arrived in the square, carrying the black wooden box, there was a murmur of conversation among the villagers, and he waved and called, "Little late today, folks." The postmaster, Mr. Graves, followed him, carrying a three-legged stool, and the stool was put in the center of the square and Mr. Summers set the black box down on it. The villagers kept their distance, leaving a space between themselves and the stool, and when Mr. Summers said, "Some of you fellows want to give me a hand?" there was a hesitation before two men, Mr. Martin and his oldest son, Baxter, came forward to hold the box steady on the stool while Mr. Summers stirred up the papers inside it.

The original paraphernalia for the lottery had been lost long ago, and the black box now resting on the stool had been put into use even before Old Man Warner, the oldest man in town, was born. Mr. Summers spoke frequently about making a new box, but no one liked to upset even as much tradition as was represented by the black box. There was a story that the present box had been made with some pieces of the box that had preceded it, the one that had been constructed when the first people settled down to make a village here. Every year, after the lottery, Mr. Summers began talking again about a new box, but every year the subject was allowed to fade off without anything's being done. The black box grew shabbier each year; by now it was no longer completely black but splintered badly along one side to show the original wood color, and in some places faded or stained.

Mr. Martin and his oldest son, Baxter, held the black box securely on the stool until Mr. Summers had stirred the papers thoroughly with his hand. Because so much of the ritual had been forgotten or discarded, Mr. Summers had been successful in having slips of paper substituted for the chips of wood that had been used for generations. Chips of wood, Mr. Summers had argued, had been all very well when the village was tiny, but now that the population was more than three hundred and likely to keep on growing, it was necessary to use something that would fit more easily into the black box. The night before the lottery, Mr. Summers and Mr. Graves made up the slips of paper and put them in the box, and it was then taken to the safe of Mr. Summers' coal company and locked up until Mr. Summers was ready to take it to the square next morning. The rest of the year, the box was put away, sometimes one place, sometimes another; it had spent one year in Mr. Graves' barn and another year underfoot in the post office, and sometimes it was set on a shelf in the Martin grocery and left there.

There was a great deal of fussing to be done before Mr. Summers declared the lottery open. There were the lists to make up—heads of families, heads of households in each family, members of each household in each family. There was the proper swearing-in of Mr. Summers by the postmaster, as the official of the lottery; at one time, some people remembered, there had been a recital of some sort, performed by the official of the lottery, a perfunctory, tuneless chant that had been rattled off duly each year; some people believed that the official of the lottery used to stand just so when he said or sang it, others believed that he was supposed to walk among the people, but years and years ago this part of the ritual had been allowed to lapse. There had been, also, a ritual salute, which the official of the lottery had had to use in addressing each person who came up to draw from the box, but this also had changed with time, until now it was felt necessary only for the official to speak to each person approaching. Mr. Summers was very good at all this; in his clean white shirt and blue jeans, with one hand resting carelessly on the black box, he seemed very proper and important as he talked interminably to Mr. Graves and the Martins.

Just as Mr. Summers finally left off talking and turned to the assembled villagers, Mrs. Hutchinson came hurriedly along the path to the square, her sweater thrown over her shoulders, and slid into place in the back of the crowd. "Clean forgot what day it was," she said to Mrs. Delacroix, who stood next to her, and they both laughed softly. "Thought my old man was out back stacking wood," Mrs. Hutchinson went on, "and then I looked out the window and the kids was gone, and then I remembered it was the twenty-seventh and came a-running." She dried her hands on her apron, and Mrs. Delacroix said, "You're in time, though. They're still talking away up there."

Mrs. Hutchinson craned her neck to see through the crowd and found her husband and children standing near the front. She tapped Mrs. Delacroix on the arm as a farewell and began to make her way through the crowd. The people separated good-humoredly to let her through; two or three people said, in voices just loud enough to be heard across the crowd, "Here comes your Missus, Hutchinson," and "Bill, she made it after all." Mrs. Hutchinson reached her husband, and Mr. Summers, who had been waiting, said cheerfully, "Thought we were going to have to get on without you, Tessie." Mrs. Hutchinson said, grinning, "Wouldn't have me leave m'dishes in the sink, now, would you, Joe?," and soft laughter ran through the crowd as the people stirred back into position after Mrs. Hutchinson's arrival.

"Well, now," Mr. Summers said soberly, "guess we better get started, get this over with, so's we can go back to work. Anybody ain't here?"

"Dunbar," several people said. "Dunbar, Dunbar."

Mr. Summers consulted his list. "Clyde Dunbar," he said. "That's right. He's broke his leg, hasn't he? Who's drawing for him?"

"Me, I guess," a woman said, and Mr. Summers turned to look at her. "Wife draws for her husband," Mr. Summers said. "Don't you have a grown boy to do it for you, Janey?" Although Mr. Summers and everyone else in the village knew the answer perfectly well, it was the business of the official of the lottery to ask such questions formally. Mr. Summers waited with an expression of polite interest while Mrs. Dunbar answered.

"Horace's not but sixteen yet," Mrs. Dunbar said regretfully. "Guess I gotta fill in for the old man this year."

"Right," Mr. Summers said. He made a note on the list he was holding. Then he asked, "Watson boy drawing this year?"

A tall boy in the crowd raised his hand. "Here," he said. "I'm drawing for m'mother and me." He blinked his eyes nervously and ducked his head as several voices in the crowd said things like "Good fellow, Jack," and "Glad to see your mother's got a man to do it."

"Well," Mr. Summers said, "guess that's everyone. Old Man Warner make it?"

"Here," a voice said, and Mr. Summers nodded.

A sudden hush fell on the crowd as Mr. Summers cleared his throat and looked at the list. "All ready?" he called. "Now, I'll read the names—heads of families first—and the men come up and take a paper out of the box. Keep the paper folded in your hand without looking at it until everyone has had a turn. Everything clear?"

The people had done it so many times that they only half listened to the direction; most of them were quiet, wetting their lips, not looking around. Then Mr. Summers raised one hand high and said, "Adams." A man disengaged himself from the crowd and came forward. "Hi, Steve," Mr. Summers said, and Mr. Adams said, "Hi, Joe." They grinned at one another humorlessly and nervously. Then Mr. Adams reached into the black box and took out a folded paper. He held it firmly by one corner as he turned and went hastily back to his place in the crowd, where he stood a little apart from his family, not looking down at his hand.

"Allen," Mr. Summers said. "Anderson . . . Bentham."

"Seems like there's no time at all between lotteries any more," Mrs. Delacroix said to Mrs. Graves in the back row. "Seems like we got through with the last one only last week."

"Time sure goes fast," Mrs. Graves said.

"Clark . . . Delacroix."

"There goes my old man," Mrs. Delacroix said. She held her breath while her husband went forward.

"Dunbar," Mr. Summers said, and Mrs. Dunbar went steadily to the box while one of the women said, "Go on, Janey," and another said, "There she goes."

"We're next," Mrs. Graves said. She watched while Mr. Graves came around from the side of the box, greeted Mr. Summers gravely, and selected a slip of paper from the box. By now, all through the crowd there were men holding the small folded papers in their large hands, turning them over and over nervously. Mrs. Dunbar and her two sons stood together, Mrs. Dunbar holding the slip of paper.

"Harburt . . . Hutchinson."

"Get up there, Bill," Mrs. Hutchinson said, and the people near her laughed.

"Jones."

"They do say," Mr. Adams said to Old Man Warner, who stood next to him, "that over in the north village they're talking of giving up the lottery."

Old Man Warner snorted. "Pack of crazy fools," he said. "Listening to the young folks, nothing's good enough for *them*. Next thing you know, they'll be wanting to go back to living in caves, nobody work any more, live *that* way for a while. Used to be a saying about 'Lottery in June, corn be heavy soon.' First thing you know, we'd all be eating stewed chickweed and acorns. There's *always* been a lottery," he added petulantly. "Bad enough to see young Joe Summers up there joking with everybody."

"Some places have already quit lotteries," Mrs. Adams said.

"Nothing but trouble in *that,*" Old Man Warner said stoutly. "Pack of young fools."

"Martin." And Bobby Martin watched his father go forward. "Overdyke . . . Percy."

"I wish they'd hurry," Mrs. Dunbar said to her older son. "I wish they'd hurry."

"They're almost through," her son said.

"You get ready to run tell Dad," Mrs. Dunbar said.

Mr. Summers called his own name and then stepped forward precisely and selected a slip from the box. Then he called, "Warner."

"Seventy-seventh year I been in the lottery," Old Man Warner said as he went through the crowd. "Seventy-seventh time."

"Watson." The tall boy came awkwardly through the crowd. Someone said, "Don't be nervous, Jack," and Mr. Summers said, "Take your time, son."

"Zanini."

After that, there was a long pause, a breathless pause, until Mr. Summers, holding his slip of paper in the air, said, "All right, fellows." For a minute, no one moved, and then all the slips of paper were opened. Suddenly, all the women began to speak at once, saying, "Who is it?," "Who's got it?," "Is it the Dunbars?," "Is it the Watsons?" Then the voices began to say, "It's Hutchinson. It's Bill," "Bill Hutchinson's got it."

"Go tell your father," Mrs. Dunbar said to her older son.

People began to look around to see the Hutchinsons. Bill Hutchinson was standing quiet, staring down at the paper in his hand. Suddenly, Tessie Hutchinson shouted to Mr. Summers, "You didn't give him time enough to take any paper he wanted. I saw you. It wasn't fair!"

"Be a good sport, Tessie," Mrs. Delacroix called, and Mrs. Graves said, "All of us took the same chance."

"Shut up, Tessie," Bill Hutchinson said.

"Well, everyone," Mr. Summers said, "that was done pretty fast, and now we've got to be hurrying a little more to get done in time." He consulted his next list. "Bill," he said, "you draw for the Hutchinson family. You got any other households in the Hutchinsons?"

"There's Don and Eva," Mrs. Hutchinson yelled. "Make *them* take their chance!"

"Daughters draw with their husbands' families, Tessie," Mr. Summers said gently. "You know that as well as anyone else."

"It wasn't *fair*," Tessie said.

"I guess not, Joe," Bill Hutchinson said regretfully. "My daughter draws with her husband's family, that's only fair. And I've got no other family except the kids."

"Then, as far as drawing for families is concerned, it's you," Mr. Summers said in explanation, "and as far as drawing for households is concerned, that's you, too. Right?"

"Right," Bill Hutchinson said.

"How many kids, Bill?" Mr. Summers asked formally.

"Three," Bill Hutchinson said. "There's Bill, Jr., and Nancy, and little Dave. And Tessie and me."

"All right, then," Mr. Summers said. "Harry, you got their tickets back?"

Mr. Graves nodded and held up the slips of paper. "Put them in the box, then," Mr. Summers directed. "Take Bill's and put it in."

"I think we ought to start over," Mrs. Hutchinson said, as quietly as she could. "I tell you it wasn't *fair*. You didn't give him time enough to choose. *Every*body saw that."

Mr. Graves had selected the five slips and put them in the box, and he dropped all the papers but those onto the ground, where the breeze caught them and lifted them off.

"Listen, everybody," Mrs. Hutchinson was saying to the people around her.

"Ready, Bill?" Mr. Summers asked, and Bill Hutchinson, with one quick glance around at his wife and children, nodded.

"Remember," Mr. Summers said, "take the slips and keep them folded until each person has taken one. Harry, you help little Dave." Mr. Graves took the hand of the little boy, who came willingly with him up to the box. "Take a paper out of the box, Davy," Mr. Summers said. Davy put his hand into the box and laughed. "Take just *one* paper," Mr. Summers said. "Harry, you hold it for him." Mr. Graves took the child's hand and removed the folded paper from the tight fist and held it while little Dave stood next to him and looked up at him wonderingly.

"Nancy next," Mr. Summers said. Nancy was twelve, and her school friends breathed heavily as she went forward, switching her skirt, and took a slip daintily from the box. "Bill, Jr.," Mr. Summers said, and Billy, his face red and his feet overlarge, nearly knocked the box over as he got the paper out. "Tessie," Mr. Summers said. She hesitated for a minute, looking around defiantly, and then set her lips and went up to the box. She snatched a paper out and held it behind her.

"Bill," Mr. Summers said, and Bill Hutchinson reached into the box and felt around, bringing his hand out at last with the slip of paper in it.

The crowd was quiet. A girl whispered, "I hope it's not Nancy," and the sound of the whisper reached the crowd.

"It's not the way it used to be," Old Man Warner said clearly. "People ain't the way they used to be."

"All right," Mr. Summers said. "Open the papers. Harry, you open little Dave's."

Mr. Graves opened the slip of paper and there was a general sigh throughout the crowd as he held it up and everyone could see that it was blank. Nancy and Bill, Jr., opened theirs at the same time, and both beamed and laughed, turning around to the crowd and holding their slips of paper above their heads.

"Tessie," Mr. Summers said. There was a pause, and then Mr. Summers looked at Bill Hutchinson, and Bill unfolded his paper and showed it. It was blank.

"It's Tessie," Mr. Summers said, and his voice was hushed. "Show us her paper, Bill."

Bill Hutchinson went over to his wife and forced the slip of paper out of her hand. It had a black spot on it, the black spot Mr. Summers had made the night before with the heavy pencil in the coal-company office. Bill Hutchinson held it up, and there was a stir in the crowd.

"All right, folks," Mr. Summers said. "Let's finish quickly."

Although the villagers had forgotten the ritual and lost the original black box, they still remembered to use stones. The pile of stones the boys had made earlier was ready; there were stones on the ground with the blowing scraps of paper that had come out of the box. Mrs. Delacroix selected a stone so large she had to pick it up with both hands and turned to Mrs. Dunbar. "Come on," she said. "Hurry up."

Mrs. Dunbar had small stones in both hands, and she said, gasping for breath, "I can't run at all. You'll have to go ahead and I'll catch up with you."

The children had stones already, and someone gave little Davy Hutchinson a few pebbles.

Tessie Hutchinson was in the center of a cleared space by now, and she held her hands out desperately as the villagers moved in on her. "It isn't fair," she said. A stone hit her on the side of her head.

Old Man Warner was saying, "Come on, come on, everyone." Steve Adams was in the front of the crowd of villagers, with Mrs. Graves beside him.

"It isn't fair, it isn't right," Mrs. Hutchinson screamed, and then they were upon her.

A Trial of Witches[*]
Taken by a Person then Attending the Court

TO THE READER

This trial of witches hath lain a long time in a private gentleman's hands in the country, it being given to him by the person that took it at the court for his own satisfaction; but it came lately to my hands, and having perused it, I found it a very remarkable thing, and fit to be published; especially in these times, wherein things of this nature are much controverted, and that by persons of much learning on both sides. I thought that so exact a relation of this trial would probably give more satisfaction to a great many persons, by reason that it is pure matter of fact, and that evidently demonstrated; than the arguments and Reasons of other very Learned Men, that probably may not be so Intelligble to all Readers; especially this being held before a Judge, whom for his Integrity, Learning, and Law, hardly any Age, either before or since could parallel; who not only took a great deal of paines, and spent much time in this Tryal himself: but had the Assistance and Opinion of several other very Eminent and Learned Persons: So that this being the most perfect Narrative of any thing of this Nature hitherto Extant, made me unwillingly to deprive the World of the Benefit of it: which is the sole Motive that induced me to Publish it.

Farewel.

A TRYAL OF WITCHES

At the Assizes and General Gaol delivery, held at Bury St. Edmonds for the County of Suffolk, the Tenth day of March, in the Sixteenth Year of the Reign of our Sovereign Lord King Charles II: before *Matthew Hale,* Knight, Lord Chief Baron of His Majesties Court of Exchequer: *Rose Cullender and Amy Duny,* Widows, both of Leystoff in the County aforesaid, were severally indicted for Bewitching *Elizabeth and Ann Durent, Jane Bocking, Susan Chandler, William Durent, Elizabeth and Deborah Pacey:* And the said Cullender and Duny, being arraigned upon the said Indictments, pleaded *Not Guilty:* And afterwards, upon a long Evidence, were found *Guilty,* and thereupon had Judgment to dye for the same.

The Evidence whereupon these Persons were convicted of Witchcraft, stands upon divers particular Circumstances.

I. Three of the Parties above-named, viz. Anne Durent, Susan Chandler, and Elizabeth Pacy were brought to Bury to the Assizes and were in reasonable good condition: But that Morning they came into the Hall to give Instructions for the drawing of their Bills of Indictments, the Three Persons fell into strange and violent fits, screeking out in a most sad manner, so that they could not in any wise give any Instructions in the Court who were the Cause of their Distemper. And although they did after some certain space recover out of

---

[*]   Reprinted from Gilbert Geis & Ivan Bunn, A Trial of Witches: A Seventeenth-Century Witchcraft Prosecution, Appendix (1997), with the generous assistance of, and by special arrangement with, the authors.

their fits, yet they were every one of them struck Dumb, so that none of them could speak neither at that time, nor during the Assizes until the Conviction of the supposed Witches.

As concerning William Durent, being an Infant, his Mother Dorothy Durent sworn and examined deposed in open Court, That about the Tenth of March, Nono Caroli Secundi, she having a special occasion to go from home, and having none in her House to take care of her said Child (it then sucking) desired Amy Duny her Neighbour, to look to her child during her absence, for which she promised her to give her a Penny: but the said Dorothy Durent desired the said Amy not to Suckle her Child, and laid a great charge upon her not to do it. Upon which it was asked by the Court, why she did give that direction, she being an old Woman and not capable of giving Suck? It was answered by the said Dorothy Durent, that she very well knew that she did not give suck, but that for some years before, she had gone under the Reputation of a Witch, which was one cause made her give the caution: Another was, That it was customary with old Women, that if they did look after a sucking Child, and nothing would please it but the Breast, they did use to please the Child, to give it the breast, and it did please the Child, but it sucked nothing but Wind, which did the Child hurt. Nevertheless after the departure of this Deponent, the said Amy did Suckle the Child: And after the return of the said Dorothy, the said Amy did acquaint her, *That she had given Suck to the Child* contrary to her command. Whereupon the Deponent was very angry with the said Amy for the same; at which the said Amy was much discontented, and used many high Expressions and Threatening Speeches towards her; telling her, *That she had as good to have done otherwise than to have found fault with her, and so departed out of her House:* And that very Night her Son fell into strange fits of swounding, and was held in such terrible manner, that she was much affrighted therewith, and so continued for divers weeks. And the said Examinant farther said, that she being exceedingly troubled at her Childs Distemper, did go to a certain Person named Doctor Jacob, who lived at Yarmouth, who had the reputation in the Country, to help children that were Bewitch'd: who advis'd her to hang up the Childs Blanket in the Chimney-corner all day, and at night when she put the Child to Bed, to put it into the said blanket, and if she found any thing in it, she should not be afraid, but to throw it into the Fire. And this Deponent did according to his direction; and at night when she took down the Blanket with an intent to put her Child therein, there fell out of the same a great Toad, which ran up and down the hearth, and she having a young youth only with her in the House, desired him to catch the Toad, and throw it into the Fire, which the youth did accordingly, and held it there with the Tongs; and as soon as it was in the Fire it made a great and horrible Noise, and after a space there was a flashing in the Fire like Gun-powder, making the noise like the discharge of a Pistol, and thereupon the Toad was no more seen nor heard. It was asked by the Court, if that after the noise and flashing, there was not the Substance of the Toad to be seen to consume in the fire? And it was answered by the said Dorothy Durent, that after the flashing and noise, there was no more seen than if there had been none there. The next day there came a young Woman a Kinswoman of the said Amy, and a neighbour of this Deponent, and told this Deponent, that her Aunt (meaning the said Amy) was in a most lamentable condition having her face all scorched with fire, and that she was sitting alone in her House, in her smock without any fire. And thereupon this Deponent went into the House of the said Amy Duny to see her, and found her in the same condition as was related to her; for her Face, her Leggs, and Thighs, which this Deponent saw, seemed very much scorched and burnt with Fire, at which this Deponent seemed much to wonder. And asked the said Amy how she came into that sad condition? and the said Amy replied, she might thank her for it, for that she this Deponent was the cause thereof, but that she should live to see some of her Children dead, and she upon Crutches. And this Deponent farther saith, that after the burning of the said Toad, her Child recover'd, and was well again, and was living at the time of the Assizes. And this Deponent farther saith, That about the 6th of March, 11 Car. 2. her Daughter Elizabeth Durent, being about the Age of Ten Years, was taken in a like manner as her first Child was, and in her fits complained much of Amy Duny, and said, That she did appear to her, and Afflict her in such manner as the former. And she this Deponent going to the Apothecaries for some thing for her said Child, when she did return to her own House, she found the said Amy Duny there, and asked her what she did do there? and her answer was, *That she came to see her Child, and to give it some water.* But she this Deponent was very angry with her, and thrust her forth of her doors, and when she was out of doors, she said, *You need not be so angry, for your Child will not live long:* and this was on a Saturday, and the Child dyed on the Monday following. The cause of whose Death this Deponent verily believeth was occasion'd by the Witchcraft of the said Amy Duny: for that the said Amy hath been long reputed to be a Witch, and a person of very evil behaviour, whose Kindred and Relations have been many of them accused for Witchcraft, and some of them have been Condemned.

The said Deponent further saith, that not long after the death of her Daughter Elizabeth Durent, she this Deponent was taken with a Lameness in both her Leggs, from the knees downward, that she was fain to go upon Crutches, and that she had no other use of them but only to bear a little upon them till she did remove her Crutches, and so continued till the time of the Assizes, that the Witch came to be Tryed, and was there upon her Crutches, the Court asked her, *That at the time she was taken with this Lameness, if it were with her according to the Custom of Women?* Her Answer was, that it was so, and that she never had any stoppages of those things, but when she was with Child.

This is the Substance of her Evidence to this Indictment.

There was one thing very remarkable, that after she had gone upon Crutches for upwards of Three Years, and went upon them at the time of the Assizes in the Court when she gave her Evidence, and upon the Juries bringing in their Verdict, by which the said Amy Duny was found Guilty, to the great admiration of all Persons, the said Dorothy Durent was restored to the use of her Limbs, and went home without making use of her Crutches.

II. As concerning Elizabeth and Deborah Pacy, the first of the Age of Eleven Years, the other of the age of Nine Years or thereabouts: as to the Elder, she was brought into the Court at the time of the Instructions given to draw up the Indictments, and afterwards at the time of Tryal of the said Prisoners, but could not speak one Word all the time, and for the most part she remained as one wholly senseless as one in a deep Sleep, and could move no part of her body, and all the Motion of Life that appeared in her was, that as she lay upon Cushions in the Court upon her back, her stomack and belly by the drawing of her breath, would arise to a great height: and after the said Elizabeth had lain a long time on the Table in the Court, she came a little to her self and sate up, but could neither see nor speak, but was sensible of what was said to her, and after a while she laid her Head on the Bar of the Court with a Cushion under it, and her hand and her Apron upon that, and there she lay a good space of time: and by the direction of the Judg, Amy Duny was privately brought to Elizabeth Pacy, and she touched her hand; whereupon the Child without so much as seeing her, for her Eyes were closed all the while, suddenly leaped up, and catched Amy Duny by the hand, and afterwards by the face; and with her nails scratched her till Blood came, and would by no means leave her till she was taken from her, and afterwards the Child would still be pressing towards her, and making signs of Anger conceived against her.

Deborah the younger Daughter was held in such extream manner, that her Parents wholly despaired of her life, and therefore could not bring her to the Assizes.

The Evidence which was given concerning these Two Children was to this Effect.

Samuel Pacy a Merchant of Leystoff aforesaid, (a man who carried himself with much soberness during the Tryal, from whom proceeded no words either of Passion or Malice, though his Children were so greatly Afflicted,) Sworn and Examined, Deposeth, That his younger Daughter Deborah, upon Thursday the Tenth of October last, was suddenly taken with a Lameness in her Leggs, so that she could not stand, neither had she any strength in her Limbs to support her, and so she continued until the Seventeenth day of the same Month, which day being fair and Sunshiny, the Child desired to be carryed on the East part of the House, to be set upon the Bank which looketh upon the Sea; and whil'st she was sitting there, Amy Duny came to this Deponents House to buy some Herrings, but being denied she went away discontented, and presently returned again, and was denied, and likewise the third time and was denied as at first; and at her last going away, she went away grumbling; but what she said was not perfectly understood. But at the very same instant of time, the said Child was taken with most violent fits, feeling most extream pain in her Stomach, like the pricking of Pins, and Shreeking out in a most dreadful manner like unto a Whelp, and not like unto a sensible Creature. And in this extremity the Child continued to the great grief of the Parents until the Thirtieth of the Same Month. During this time this Deponent sent for one Dr. Feavor, a Doctor of Physick, to take his advice concerning his Childs Distemper: the Doctor being come, he saw the Child in those fits, but could not conjecture (as he then told this Deponent, and afterwards affirmed in open Court, at this Tryal) what might be the cause of the Childs Affliction. And this Deponent farther saith, That by reason of the circumstances aforesaid, and in regard Amy Duny is a Woman of an ill Fame, & commonly reported to be a Witch & Sorceress, and for that the said Child in her fits would cry out of Amy Duny as the cause of her Malady, and that she did affright her with Apparitions of her Person (as the Child in the intervals of her fits related) he this Deponent did suspect the said Amy Duny for a Witch, and charged her with the injury and wrong to his Child, and caused her to be set in the Stocks on the Twenty eighth of the same October: and during the time of her continuance there, one Alice Letteridge and Jane Buxton demanding of her (as they also affirmed in Court upon their Oathes) what should be the reason of Mr. Pacy's Childs Distemper? telling her, That she was suspected to be the cause thereof; she replyed, *Mr. Pacy keeps a great stir about his Child, but let him stay until he hath done as much by his Children, as I have done by mine.* And being further examined, what she had done to her Children? She answered, *That she had been fain to open her Child's Mouth with a Tap to give it Victuals.*

And the said Deponent further desposeth, That within two days after speaking of the said words being the Thirtieth of October, the eldest Daughter Elizabeth, fell into extream fits, insomuch, that they could not open her Mouth to give her breath, to preserve her Life without the help of a Tap which they were enforced to use; and the younger Child was in the like manner Afflicted, so that they used the same also for her Relief.

And further the said Children being grievously afflicted would severally complain in their extremity, and also in the intervals, That Amy Duny (together with one other Woman whose person and Cloathes they described) did thus Afflict them, their Apparitions appearing before them, to their great terrour and affrightment: And sometimes they would cry out, saying, *There stands Amy Duny, and there Rose Cullender;* the other Person troubling them.

Their fits were various, sometimes they would be lame on one side of their Bodies, sometimes on the other: sometimes a soreness over their whole Bodies, so as they could endure none to touch them: at other times they would be restored to the perfect use of their Limbs, and deprived of their Hearing; at other times of their Sight, at other times of their Speech; sometimes by the space of one day, sometimes for two; and once they were wholly deprived of their Speech for Eight days together, and then restored to their Speech again. At other times they would fall into Swounings, and upon the recovery to their Speech they would Cough extreamly, and bring up much Flegme, and with the same crooked Pins, and one time a Two-penny Nail with a very broad head, which Pins (amounting to Forty or more) together with the Two-penny Nail were produced in Court, with the affirmation of the said Deponent, that he was present when the said Nail was Vomited up, and also most of the Pins. Commonly at the end of every fit they would cast up a Pin, and sometimes they would have four or five fits in one day.

In this manner the said Children continued with this Deponent for the space of two Months, during which time in their Intervals this Deponent would cause them to Read some Chapters in the New Testament. Whereupon this Deponent several times observed, that they would read till they came to the Name of Lord, or Jesus, or Christ; and then before they could pronounce either of the said Words they would suddenly fall into their fits. But when they came to the Name of Satan, or Devil, they would clap their Fingers upon the Book, crying out, *This bites, but makes me speak right well.*

At such time as they be recovered out of their fits (occasion'd as this Deponent conceives upon their naming of Lord, or Jesus, or Christ,) this Deponent hath demanded of them, what is the cause they cannot pronounce those words, They reply and say, *That Amy Duny saith, I must not use that name.*

And farther, the said Children after their fits were past, would tell, how that Amy Duny, and Rose Cullender would appear before them, holding their Fists at them, threatning, *That if they related either what they saw or heard, that they would Torment them Ten times more than ever they did before.*

In their fits they would cry out, *There stands Amy Duny, or Rose Cullender;* and sometimes in one place and sometimes in another, running with great violence to the place where they fancied them to stand, striking at them as if they were present; they would appear to them sometimes spinning, and sometimes reeling, or in other postures, deriding or threatning them.

And this Deponent farther saith, That his Children being thus Tormented by all the space aforesaid, and finding no hopes of amendment, he sent them to his Sisters House, one Margaret Arnold, who lived at Yarmouth, to make tryal, whether the change of the Air might do them any good. And how, and in what manner they were afterwards held, he this Deponent refers himself to the Testimony of his said Sister.

Margaret Arnold, Sworn and Examined, saith, That the said Elizabeth and Deborah Pacy came to her House about the Thirtieth of November last, her Brother acquainted her, that he thought they were Bewitch'd, for that they vomited Pins; and farther Informed her of the several passages which occurred at his own House. This Deponent said, that she gave no credit to that which was related to her, conceiving possibly the Children might use some deceit in putting Pins in their mouths themselves. Wherefore this Deponent unpinned all their Cloathes, and left not so much as one Pin upon them, but sewed all the Clothes they wore, instead of pinning of them. But this Deponent saith, that notwithstanding all this care and circumspection of hers, the Children afterwards raised at several times at least Thirty Pins in her presence, and had most fierce and violent Fitts upon them.

The Children would in their Fitts cry out against Rose Cullender and Amy Duny, affirming that they saw them; and they threatned to Torment them Ten times more, if they complained of them. At some times the Children (only) would see things run up and down the House in the appearance of Mice; and one of them suddainly snapt one with the Tongs, and threw it into the fire, and it screeched out like a Rat.

At another time, the younger Child being out of her Fitts went out of Doors to take a little fresh Air, and presently a little thing like a Bee flew upon her Face, and would have gone into her Mouth, whereupon the Child ran in all haste to the door to get into the House again, screeking out in a most terrible manner; whereupon, this Deponent made haste to come to her, but before she could get to her, the Child fell into her swooning Fitt, and at last with much pain straining herself, she vomited up a Two-penny Nail with a broad Head; and after that the Child had raised up the Nail she came to her understanding; and being demanded by this Deponent, how she came by this Nail? she Answered, *That the Bee brought this Nail and forced it into her Mouth.*

And at other times, the Elder Child declared unto this Deponent, that during the time of her Fitts, she saw Flies come unto her, and bring with them in their Mouthes crooked Pins; and after the Child had thus declared the same, she fell again into violent Fits, and afterwards raised several Pins.

At another time, the said Elder Child declared unto this Deponent, and sitting by the Fire suddainly started up and said, *she saw a Mouse,* and she crept under the Table looking after it, and at length, she put something in her Apron, saying, *she had caught it;* and immediately she ran to the Fire and threw it in, and there did appear upon it to this Deponent, like the flashing of Gunpowder, though she confessed she saw nothing in the Childs Hand.

At another time the said Child being speechless, but otherwise of perfect understanding, ran round about the House holding her Apron, crying *hush, hush,* as if there had been some Poultrey in the House; but this Deponent could perceive nothing: but at last she saw the Child stoop as if she had catch't at something, and put it into her Apron, and afterwards made as if she had thrown it into the Fire: but this Deponent could not discover anything: but the Child afterwards being restored to her speech, she this Deponent demanded of her what she saw at the time she used such a posture? who answered, *That she saw a Duck.*

At another time, the Younger daughter being recovered out of her Fitts, declared, *That Amy Duny had been with her, and that she tempted her to Drown her self, and to cut her Throat, or otherwise to Destroy her self.*

At another time in their Fitts they both of them cryed out upon Rose Cullender and Amy Duny, complaining against them; *Why do not you come your selves, but send your Imps to Torment us?*

These several passages as most remarkable, the said Deponent did particularly set down as they daily happen'd, and for the reasons aforesaid, she doth verily believe in her conscience, that the Children were bewitched, and by the said Amy Duny, and Rose Cullender; though at first she could hardly be induced to believe it.

As concerning Ann Durent, one other of the Parties, supposed to be bewitched, present in Court.

Edmund Durent her Father Sworn and Examined: said, That he also lived in the said, Town of Leystoff, and that the said Rose Cullender, about the latter end of November last, came into this Deponents House to buy some Herrings of his Wife, but being denyed by her, the said Rose returned in a discontented manner; and upon the first of December after, his Daughter Ann Durent was very sorely Afflicted in her Stomach, and felt great pain, like the pricking of Pins, and then fell into swooning fitts, and after the Recovery from her Fitts, she declared, *That she had seen the Apparition of the said Rose, who threatned to Torment her.* In this manner she continued from the first of December, until this present time of Tryal; having likewise vomited up divers Pins (produced here in Court). This Maid was present in Court, but could not speak to declare her knowledge, but fell into most violent fits when she was brought before Rose Cullender.

Ann Baldwin Sworn and Examined, Deposeth the same thing as touching the Bewitching of the said Ann Durent.

As concerning Jane Bocking who was so weak, she could not be brought to the Assizes.

Diana Bocking Sworn and Examined, Deposed, That she lived in the same Town of Leystoff, and that her said Daughter having been formerly Afflicted with swooning fitts recovered well of them, and so continued for a certain time; and upon the First of February last, she was taken also with great pain in her Stomach, like pricking with Pins; and afterwards fell into swooning fitts and so continued till the Deponents coming to the

Assizes, having during the same time taken little or no food, but daily vomited crooked Pins; and upon Sunday last raised Seven Pins. And whilst her fits were upon her she would spread forth her Arms with her hands open, and use postures as if she catched at something, and would instantly close her hands again; which being immediately forced open, they found several Pins diversly crooked, but could neither see nor perceive how or in what manner they were conveyed thither. At another time, the same Jane being in another of her fitts, talked as if she were discoursing with some persons in the Room, (though she would give no answer nor seem to take notice of any person then present) and would in like manner cast abroad her Arms, saying, *I will not have it, I will not have it;* and at last she said, *Then I will have it,* and so waving her Arm with her hand open, she would presently close the same, which instantly forced open, they found in it a Lath-Nail. In her fitts she would frequently complain of Rose Cullender and Amy Duny, saying, That *now she saw Rose Cullender standing at the Beds feet, and another time at the Beds-head, and so in other places.* At last she was stricken Dumb and could not speak one Word, though her fitts were not upon her, and so she continued for some days, and at last her speech came to her again, and she desired her Mother to get her some Meat; and being demanded the reason why she could not speak in so long time? She answered, *That Amy Duny would not suffer her to speak.* This Lath-Nail, and divers of the Pins were produced in Court.

As concerning Susan Chandler, one other of the Parties supposed to be Bewitched and present in Court.

Mary Chandler Mother of the said Susan, Sworn and Examined, Deposed and said, That about the beginning of February last past, the said Rose Cullender and Amy Duny were Charged by Mr. Samuel Pacy for Bewitching of his Daughters. And a Warrant being granted at the request of the said Mr. Pacy, by Sir Edmund Bacon Baronet, one of the Justices of the Peace for the County of Suffolk to bring them before him, and they being brought before him were Examined, and Confessed nothing. He gave order that they should be searched; whereupon this Deponent with five others were appointed to do the same: and coming to the House of Rose Cullender, they did acquaint her with what they were come about, and asked whether she was contented that they should search her? she did not oppose it, whereupon they began at her Head, and so stript her naked, and in the lower part of her Belly they found a thing like a Teat of an Inch long, they questioned her about it, and she said, *That she had got a strain by carrying of water which caused that Excrescence.* But upon narrower search, they found in her Privy Parts three more Excrescencies or Teats, but smaller than the former: This Deponent farther saith, That in the long Teat at the end thereof there was a little hole, and it appeared unto them as if it had been lately sucked, and upon the straining of it there issued out white milkie Matter.

And this Deponent farther saith, That her said Daughter (being of the Age of Eighteen Years) was then in Service in the said Town of Leystoff, and rising up early the next Morning to Wash, this Rose Cullender appeared to her, and took her by the hand, whereat she was much affrighted, and went forthwith to her Mother, (being in the same town) and acquainted her with what she had seen; but being extreamly terrified, she fell extream sick, much grieved at her Stomach; and that Night after being in Bed with another young

Woman, she suddenly scrieked out, and fell into such extream fits as if she were distracted, crying against Rose Cullender; saying, *she would come to bed to her.* She continued in this manner beating and wearing her self, insomuch, that this Deponent was glad to get help to attend her. In her Intervals she would declare, *That some time she saw Rose Cullender, at another time with a great Dog with her:* She also vomited up divers crooked Pins; and sometimes she was stricken with blindness, and at another time she was Dumb, and so she appeared to be in Court when the Tryal of the Prisoners was; for she was not able to speak her knowledge; but being brought into the Court at the Tryal, she suddenly fell into her fits, and being carried out of the Court again, within the space of half an hour she came to her self and recovered her speech, and thereupon was immediately brought into the Court, and asked by the Court, whether she was in condition to take an Oath, and to give Evidence, she said she could. But when she was Sworn, and asked what she could say against either of the Prisoners? before she could make any answer, she fell into her fits, screeking out in a miserable manner, crying *Burn her, burn her,* which were all the Words she could speak.

Robert Chandler father of the said Susan gave in the same Evidence, that his Wife Mary Chandler had given, only as to the searching of Rose Cullender as aforesaid.

This was the sum and Substance of the Evidence which was given against the Prisoners concerning the Bewitching of the Children before mentioned. At the hearing this Evidence there were divers known persons, as Mr. Serjeant Keeling, Mr. Serjeant Earl, and Mr. Serjeant Barnard, present. Mr Serjeant Keeling seemed much unsatisfied with it, and thought it not sufficient to Convict the Prisoners: for admitting that the Children were in Truth Bewitched, yet said he, it can never be applyed to the Prisoners, upon the Imagination only of the Parties Afflicted; For if that might be allowed, no person whatsoever can be in safety, for perhaps they might fancy another person, who might altogether be innocent in such matters.

There was also Dr. Brown of Norwich, a Person of great knowledge; who after this Evidence given, and upon view of the three persons in Court, was desired to give his Opinion, what he did conceive of them: and he was clearly of Opinion, that the persons were Bewitched; and said, That in Denmark there had been lately a great Discovery of Witches, who used the very same way of Afflicting Persons, by conveying Pins into them, and crooked as these Pins were, with Needles and Nails. And his Opinion was, That the Devil in such cases did work upon the Bodies of Men and Women, upon a Natural Foundation, (that is) to stir up, and excite such humours super-abounding in their Bodies to a great excess, whereby he did in an extraordinary manner Afflict them with such Distempers as their Bodies were most subject to, as particularly appeared in these Children; for he conceived, that these swouning Fits were Natural, and nothing else but that they call the Mother, but only heightned to a great excess by the subtilty of the Devil, co-operating with the Malice of these which we term Witches, at whose Instance he doth these Villanies.

Besides the particulars above-mention'd touching the said persons Bewitched, there were many other things Objected against them for a further proof and manifestation that the said Children were Bewitched.

As First, during the time of the Tryal, there were some experiments made with the Persons Afflicted, by bringing the Persons to touch them; and it was observed, that when they were in the midst of their Fitts, to all Mens apprehension wholly deprived of all sense and understanding, closing their Fists in such manner, as that the strongest Man in the Court could not force them open; yet by the least touch of one of these supposed Witches, Rose Cullender by Name, they would suddenly shriek out opening their hands, which accident would not happen by the touch of any other person,

And least they might privatly see when they were touched, by the said Rose Cullender, they were blinded with their own Aprons, and the touching took the same Effect as before.

There was an ingenious person that objected, there might be a great fallacy in this experiment, and there ought not to be any stress put upon this to Convict the Parties, for the Children might counterfeit this their Distemper, and perceiving what was done to them, they might in such manner suddenly alter the motion and gesture of their Bodies, on purpose to induce persons to believe that they were not natural, but wrought strangely by the touch of the Prisoners.

Wherefore to avoid this scruple it was privatly desired by the Judge, that the Lord Cornwallis, Sir Edmund Bacon, and Mr. Serjeant Keeling, and some other Gentlemen there in Court, would attend one of the Distempered persons in the farther part of the Hall, whilst she was in her fits, and then to send for one of the Witches, to try what would then happen, which they did accordingly: and Amy Duny was conveyed from the Bar and brought to the Maid: they put an Apron before her Eyes, and then one other person touched her hand, which produced the same effect as the touch of the Witch did in the Court. Whereupon the Gentlemen returned, openly protesting, that they did believe the whole transaction of this business was a meer Imposture.

This put the Court and all persons into a stand. But at length Mr. Pacy did declare, That possibly the Maid might be deceived by a suspition that the Witch touched her when she did not. For he had observed divers times, that although they could not speak, but were deprived of the use of their Tongues and Limbs, that their understandings were perfect, for that they have related divers things which have been when they were in their fits, after they were recovered out of them. This saying of Mr. Pacy was found to be true afterwards, when his Daughter was fully recovered (as she afterwards was) as shall in due time be related: For she was asked, whither she did hear and understand any thing that was done and acted in the Court, during the time that she lay as one deprived of her understanding? and she said, *she did:* and by the Opinions of some, this experiment, (which others would have a Fallacy) was rather a confirmation that the Parties were really Bewitched, than otherwise: for say they, it is not possible that any should counterfeit such Distempers, being accompanied with such various Circumstances, much less Children; and for so long time, and yet undiscovered by their Parents and Relations: For no man can suppose that they should all Conspire together, (being out of several families, and, as they Affirm, no way related one to the other, and scarce of familiar acquaintance) to do an Act of this nature whereby no benefit or advantage could redound to any of the Parties, but a guilty Conscience for Perjuring themselves in taking the Lives of two poor simple Women away, and there appears no

Malice in the Case. For the Prisoners themselves did scarce so much as Object it. Wherefore, say they, it is very evident that the Parties were Bewitched, and that when they apprehend or understand by any means, that the persons who have done them this wrong are near, or touch them; then their spirits being more than ordinarily moved with rage and anger at them being present, they do use more violent gestures of their Bodies, and extend forth their hands, as desirous to lay hold upon them; which at other times not having the same occasion, the instance there falls not out the same.

2ly. One John Soam of Leystoff aforesaid, Yeoman, a sufficient Person, Deposeth, That not long since, in harvest time he had three Carts which brought home his Harvest, and as they were going into the field to load, one of the Carts wrenched the Window of Rose Cullenders House, whereupon she came out in a great rage and threatned this Deponent for doing that wrong, and so they passed along into the Fields and loaded all the Three Carts, the other two Carts returned safe home, and back again, twice loaded that day afterwards; but as to this Cart which touched Rose Cullenders House, after it was loaded it was overturned twice or thrice that day; and after that they had loaded it again the second or third time, as they brought it through the Gate which leadeth out of the Field into the Town, the Cart stuck so fast in the Gates-head, that they could not possibly get it through, but were inforced to cut down the Post of the Gate to make the Cart pass through, although they could not perceive that the Cart did of either side touch the Gate-posts. And this Deponent further saith, That after they had got it through the Gate-way, they did with much difficulty get it home into the Yard; but for all that they could do, they could not get the Cart near unto the place where they should unload the Corn, but were fain to unload it at a great distance from the place, and when they began to unload they found much difficulty therein, it being so hard a labour that they were tired that first came; and when others came to assist them, their Noses burst forth a bleeding: so they were fain to desist and leave it until the next Morning; and then they unloaded it without any difficulty at all.

Robert Sherringham also Deposeth against Rose Cullender, That about Two Years since, passing along the Street with his Cart and Horses, the Axletree of his Cart touched her House, and broke down some part of it, at which, she was very much displeased, threatning him, that his Horses should suffer for it; and so it happen'd, for all those Horses, being Four in Number, died within a short time after: since that time he hath had great Losses by the suddain dying of his other Cattle; so soon as his Sows pigged, the Pigs would leap and caper, and immediately fall down and dye. Also, not long after, he was taken with a Lameness in his Limbs that he could neither go nor stand for some days. After all this, he was very much vexed with great Number of Lice of an extraordinary bigness, and although he many times shifted himself, yet he was not anything the better, but would swarm again with them; so that in the Conclusion he was forc'd to burn all his Clothes, being two suits of Apparel, and then was clean from them.

As concerning Amy Duny, one Richard Spencer Deposeth, That about the first of September last, he heard her say at his House, *That the Devil would not let her rest until she were Revenged on one Cornelius Sandeswell's Wife.*

Ann Sandeswel Wife unto the above-said Cornelius, Deposed, That about Seven or Eight Years since, she having bought a certain number of Geese, meeting with Amy Duny, she told her, *If she did not fetch her Geese home they would all be Destroyed:* which in a few days after came to pass.

Afterwards the said Amy became Tenant to this Deponents Husband for a House, who told her, *That if she looked not well to such a Chimney in her House, that the same would fall:* Whereupon this Deponent replyed, That it was a new one; but not minding much her Words, at that time they parted. But in a short time the Chimney fell down according as the said Amy had said.

Also this Deponent farther saith, That her Brother being a Fisherman, and using to go into the Northern Seas, she desired him to send her a Firkin of Fish, which he did accordingly; and she having notice that the said Firkin was brought into Leystoff-Road, she desired a Boatman to bring it ashore with the other Goods they were to bring; and she going down to meet the Boat-man to receive her Fish, desired the said Amy to go along with her to help her home with it; Amy Replyed, *She would go when she had it.* And thereupon this Deponent went to the Shoar without her, and demanded of the Boat-man the Firkin, they told her, That they could not keep it in the Boat from falling into the Sea, and they thought it was gone to the Divel, for they never saw the like before. And being demanded by this Deponent, whether any other Goods in the Boat were likewise lost as well as hers? They answered, *Not any.*

This was the substance of the whole Evidence given against the Prisoners at the Bar; who being demanded, what they had to say for themselves? They replyed, *Nothing material to any thing that was proved against them.* Whereupon, the Judge in giving his direction to the Jury, told them, That he would not repeat the Evidence unto them, least by so doing he should wrong the Evidence on the one side or on the other. Only this acquainted them, That they had Two things to enquire after. *First,* Whether or no these Children were Bewitched? *Secondly,* Whether the Prisoners at the Bar were Guilty of it?

That there were such Creatures as Witches he made no doubt at all; For *First,* the Scriptures had affirmed so much. *Secondly,* The wisdom of all Nations had provided Laws against such Persons, which is an Argument of their confidence of such a Crime. And such hath been the judgment of this Kingdom, as appears by that Act of Parliament which hath provided Punishments proportionable to the quality of the Offence. And desired them, strictly to observe their Evidence; and desired the great God of Heaven to direct their Hearts in this weighty thing they had in hand: *For to Condemn the Innocent, and to let the Guilty go free, were both an Abomination to the Lord.*

With this short Direction the Jury departed from the Bar, and within the space of half an hour returned, and brought them in both *Guilty* upon the several Indictments, which were Thirteen in Number, whereupon they stood Indicted.

This was upon Thursday in the Afternoon, March 13. 1662.

The next Morning, the Three Children with their Parents came to the Lord Chief Baron Hale's Lodging, who all of them spake perfectly, and were as in good Health as ever they were; only Susan Chandler, by reason of her very much Affliction, did look very thin and wan. And their friends were asked, At what time they were restored thus to their Speech and Health? And Mr. Pacy did Affirm, That within less than half an hour after the Witches were Convicted, they were all of them Restored, and slept well that Night, feeling no pain; only Susan Chandler felt a pain like pricking of Pins in her Stomach.

After, they were all of them brought down to the Court, but Ann Durent was so fearful to behold them, that she desired she might not see them. The other Two continued in the Court, and they Affirmed in the face of the Country, and before the Witches themselves, what before hath been Deposed by their Friends and Relations; the Prisoners not much contradicting them. In Conclusion, the Judge and all the Court were fully satisfied with the Verdict, and thereupon gave Judgment against the Witches that they should be Hanged. They were much urged to confess, but would not.

That Morning we departed for Cambridge, but no Reprieve was granted: And they were Executed on Monday, the Seventeenth of March following, but they Confessed nothing.

The Vigilantes of Montana
Prof. Thomas J. Dimsdale

Preface

The object of the writer in presenting this narrative to the public is twofold. His intention is, in the first place, to furnish a correct history of an organization administering justice without the sanction of constitutional law; and secondly, to prove not only the necessity for their action, but the equity of their proceedings.

Having an intimate acquaintance with parties cognizant of the facts related, and feeling certain of the literal truth of the statements contained in this history, he offers it to the people of the United States, with the belief that its perusal will greatly modify the views of those even who are most prejudiced against the summary retribution of mountain law, and with the conviction that all honest and impartial men will be willing to admit both the wisdom of the course pursued and the salutary effect of the rule of the Vigilantes in the Territory of Montana.

It is also hoped that the history of the celebrated body, the very mention of whose name sounded as a death-knell in the ears of the murderers and Road Agents, will be edifying and instructive to the general reader. The incidents related are neither trivial in themselves, nor unimportant in their results; and, while rivalling fiction in interest, are unvarnished accounts of transactions, whose fidelity can be vouched by thousands.

As a literary production, the author commits it to the examination of the critical without a sigh. If any of these authorslayers are inclined to be more severe in their judgment than he is himself, he trusts they will receive the reward to which their justice entitles them; and if they should pass it by he cannot but think that they will exercise a sound discretion, and avoid much useless labor. With all its imperfections, here it is.

Introductory:
Vigilance Committees

"The teeth that bite hardest are out of sight."—Prov.

The end of all good government is the safety and happiness of the governed. It is not possible that a high state of civilization and progress can be maintained unless the tenure of life and property is secure; and it follows that the first efforts of a people in a new country for the inauguration of the reign of peace, the sure precursor of prosperity and stability, should be directed to the accomplishment of this object. In newly settled mining districts, the necessity for some effective organization of a judicial and protective character is more keenly felt than it is in other places, where the less exciting pursuits of agriculture and commerce mainly attract the attention and occupy the time of the first inhabitants.

There are good reasons for this difference. The first is the entirely dissimilar character of the populations; and the second, the possession of vast sums of money by uneducated and unprincipled people, in all places where the precious metals may be obtained at the cost of the labor necessary to exhume them from the strata in which they lie concealed.

In an agricultural country, the life of the pioneer settler is always one of hard labor, of considerable privation, and of more or less isolation; while the people who seek to clear the farm in the wild forest, or who break up the virgin soil of the prairies are usually of the steady and hard-working classes, needing little assistance from courts of justice to enable them to maintain rights which are seldom invaded; and whose differences, in the early days of the country are, for the most part, so slight as to be scarcely worth the cost of a litigation more complicated than a friendly and, usually, gratuitous arbitration—submitted to the judgment of the most respected among the citizens.

In a marked contrast to the peaceful life of the tiller of the soil, and to the placid monotony of his pursuits are the turbulent activity, the constant excitement, and the perpetual temptations to which the dweller in a mining camp is subject, both during his sojourn in the gulches, or, if he be given to prospecting, in his frequent and unpremeditated change of location, commonly called a "stampede." There can scarcely be conceived a greater or more apparent difference than exists between the staid and sedate inhabitants of rural districts, and the motley group of miners, professional men and merchants, thickly interspersed with sharpers, refugees, and a full selection from the dangerous classes that swagger, armed to the teeth, through the diggings and infest the roads leading to the newly discovered gulches, where lies the object of their worship—Gold.

Fortunately the change to a better state of things is rapid, and none who now walk the streets of Virginia would believe that, within two years of this date, the great question to be decided was, which was the stronger, right or might?

And here it must be stated, that the remarks which truth compels us to make, concerning the classes of individuals which furnish the law defying element of mining camps, are in no wise applicable to the majority of the people, who, while exhibiting the characteristic energy of the American race in the pursuit of wealth, yet maintain, under every disadvantage, an essential morality, which is the more creditable since it must be sincere, in order to withstand the temptations to which it is constantly exposed. "Oh, cursed thirst of gold," said the ancient, and no man has even an inkling of the truth and force of the sentiment, till he has lived where gold and silver are as much the objects of desire, and of daily and laborious exertion, as glory and promotion are to the young soldier. Were it not for the preponderance of this conservative body of citizens, every camp in remote and recently discovered mineral regions would be a field of blood; and where this is not so, the fact is proof irresistible that the good is in sufficient force to control the evil, and eventually to bring order out of chaos.

Let the reader suppose that the police of New York were withdrawn for twelve months, and then let them picture the wild saturnalia which would take the place of the order that reigns there now. If, then, it is so hard to restrain the dangerous classes of old and settled communities, what must be the difficulty of the task, when, tenfold in number, fearless in character, generally well armed, and supplied with money to an extent unknown among their equals in the east, such men find themselves removed from the restraints of civilized society, and beyond the control of the authority which there enforces obedience to the law?

Were it not for the sterling stuff of which the mass of miners is made, their love of fair play, and their prompt and decisive action in emergencies, this history could never have been written, for desperadoes of every nation would have made this country a scene of bloodshed and a sink of iniquity such as was never before witnessed.

Together with so much that is evil, nowhere is there so much that is sternly opposed to dishonesty and violence as in the mountains; and though careless of externals and style, to a degree elsewhere unknown, the intrinsic value of manly uprightness is nowhere so clearly exhibited and so well appreciated as in the Eldorado of the west. Middling people do not live in these regions. A man or a woman becomes better or worse by a trip towards the Pacific. The keen eye of the experienced miner detects the imposter at a glance, and compels his entire isolation, or his association with the class to which he rightfully belongs.

Thousands of weak-minded people return, after a stay in the mountains, varying in duration from a single day to a year, leaving the field where only the strong of heart are fit to battle with difficulty, and to win the golden crown which is the reward of persevering toil and unbending firmness. There is no man more fit to serve his country in any capacity requiring courage, integrity, and self-reliance, than an "honest miner," who has been tried and found to be true by a jury of mountaineers.

The universal license that is, at first, a necessity of position in such places, adds greatly to the number of crimes, and to the facilities for their perpetration. Saloons, where poisonous liquors are vended to all comers, and consumed in quantities sufficient to drive excitable men to madness and to the commission of homicide, on the slightest provocation, are to be found in amazing numbers, and the villainous compounds there sold, under the generic name of whiskey, are more familiarly distinguished by the cognomens of "tangle-leg," "Forty-rod," "Lightning," "Tarantula-juice," etc., terms only too truly describing their acknowledged qualities.

The absence of good female society, in any due proportion to the numbers of the opposite sex, is likewise an evil of great magnitude; for men become rough, stern and cruel, to a surprising degree, under such a state of things.

In every frequent street, public gambling houses with open doors and loud music, are resorted to, in broad daylight, by hundreds—it might almost be said—of all tribes and tongues, furnishing another fruitful source of "difficulties," which are commonly decided on the spot, by an appeal to brute force, the stab of a knife, or the discharge of a revolver. Women of easy virtue are to be seen promenading through the camp, habited in the gayest and most costly apparel, and receiving fabulous sums for their purchased favors. In fact, all the temptations to vice are present in full display, with money in abundance to secure the gratification of the desire for novelty and excitement, which is the ruling passion of the mountaineer. . . .

One marked feature of social intercourse, and (after indulgence in strong drink) the most fruitful source of quarrel and bloodshed is the all-pervading custom of using strong language on every occasion. Men will say more than they mean and the unwritten code of the miners, based on a wrong view of what constitutes manhood, teaches them to resent by force what should be answered by silent contempt.

Another powerful incentive to wrong-doing is the absolute nullity of the civil law in such cases. No matter what may be the proof, if the criminal is well liked in the community, "Not Guilty" is almost certain to be the verdict of the jury, despite the efforts of the Judge and prosecutor. If the offender is a moneyed man, as well as a popular citizen, the trial is only a farce—grave and prolonged, it is true, but capable of only one termination—a verdict of acquittal. In after days, when police magistrates in cities can deal with crime, they do so promptly. Costs are absolutely frightful, and fines tremendous. An assault provoked by drunkenness frequently costs a man as much as thrashing forty different policemen would do, in New York. A trifling "tight" is worth from $20 to $50 in dust, all expenses told, and so on. One grand jury that we wot of presented that it would be better to leave the punishment of offenders to the Vigilantes, who always acted impartially, and who would not permit the escape of proved criminals on technical and absurd grounds—than to have justice defeated, as in a certain case named. The date of that document is not ancient, and though, of course, refused and destroyed, it was the deliberate opinion, on oath, of the Grand Inquest, embodying the sentiment of thousands of good citizens in the community.

Finally, swift and terrible retribution is the only preventive of crime, while society is organizing in the far West. The long delay of justice, the wearisome proceedings, the remembrance of old friendships, etc., create a sympathy for the offender, so strong as to cause a hatred of the avenging law, instead of inspiring a horror of the crime. There is something in the excitement of continued stampedes that makes men of quick temperaments, uncontrollably impulsive. In the moment of passion, they would slay all around them; but let the blood cool, and they would share their last dollar with the men whose life they sought a day or two before.

Habits of thought rule communities more than laws, and the settled opinion of a numerous class is, that calling a man liar, a thief, or a son of a b___h, is provocation sufficient to justify instant slaying. Juries do not ordinarily bother themselves about the lengthy instructions they hear read by the court. They simply consider whether the deed is a crime against the Mountain Code; and if not, "not guilty" is the verdict, at once returned. Thieving, or any action which a miner calls *mean,* will surely be visited with condign punishment, at the hands of a Territorial jury. In such cases mercy there is none; but, in affairs of single combats, assaults, shootings, stabbings, and highway robberies, this civil law, with its positively awful expense and delay, is worse than useless.

One other main point requires to be noticed. Any person of experience will remember that the universal story of criminals, who have expiated their crimes on the scaffold, or who are pining away in the hardships of involuntary servitude—tells of habitual Sabbath breaking. This sin is so general in newly discovered diggings in the mountains that a remonstrance usually produced no more fruit than a few jocular oaths and a laugh. Religion is said to be "played out," and a professing Christian must keep straight, indeed, or he will be suspected of being a hypocritical member of a tribe, to whom it would be very disagreeable to talk about hemp.

Under these circumstances, it becomes an absolute necessity that good, law-loving, and order-sustaining men should unite for mutual protection, and for the salvation of the community. Being united, they must act in harmony, repress disorder, punish crime, and prevent outrage, or their organization would be a failure from the start, and society would collapse in the throes of anarchy. None but extreme penalties inflicted with promptitude are of any avail to quell the spirit of the desperadoes with whom they have to contend; considerable numbers are required to cope successfully with the gangs of murderers, desperadoes and robbers who infest mining countries, and who, though faithful to no other bond, yet all league willingly against the law. Secret they must be, in council and membership, or they will remain nearly useless for the detection of crime, in a country where equal facilities for the transmission of intelligence are at the command of the criminal and the judiciary; and an organization on this footing is a *Vigilance Committee.*

Such was the state of affairs, when five men in Virginia, and four in Bannack, initiated the movement which resulted in the formation of a tribunal, supported by an omnipresent executive, comprising within itself nearly every good man in the Territory, and pledged to render impartial justice to friend and foe, without regard to clime, creed, race or politics. In a few short weeks it was known that the voice of justice had spoken, in tones that might not be disregarded. The face of society was changed, as if by magic; for the Vigilantes, holding in one hand the invisible yet effectual shield of protection, and in the other, the swift descending and inevitable sword of retribution, struck from his nerveless grasp the weapon of the assassin; commanded the brawler to cease from strife; warned the thief to steal no more; bade the good citizen take courage; and compelled the ruffians and marauders who had so long maintained the "reign of terror" in Montana, to fly the Territory, or meet the just rewards of their crimes. Need we say that they were at once obeyed? Yet not before more than one hundred valuable lives had been pitilessly sacrificed and twenty-four miscreants had met a dog's doom as the reward of their crimes.

To this hour, the whispered words, "Virginia Vigilantes" would blanch the cheek of the wildest and most redoubtable desperado, and necessitate an instant election between flight and certain doom.

The administration of the *lex talionis* by self-constituted authority is, undoubtedly, in civilized and settled communities, an outrage on mankind. It is there wholly unnecessary; but the sight of a few of the mangled corpses of beloved friends and valued citizens, the whistle of the desperado's bullet, and the plunder of the fruits of the patient toil of years spent in weary exile from home, in places where civil law is as powerless as a palsied arm, from sheer lack of ability to enforce its decrees, alter the basis of the reasoning, and reverse the conclusion. In the case of the Vigilantes of Montana, it must be also remembered that the Sheriff himself was the leader of the Road Agents, and his deputies were the prominent members of the band.

The question of the propriety of establishing a Vigilance Committee depends upon the answers which ought to be given to the following queries: Is it lawful for citizens to slay robbers or murderers, when they catch them; or ought they to wait for policemen, where there are none, or put them in penitentiaries not yet erected?

Gladly, indeed, we feel sure, would the Vigilantes cease from their labor, and joyfully would they hail the advent of power, civil or military, to take their place; but till this is furnished by Government, society must be preserved from demoralization and anarchy; murder, arson and robbery must be prevented or punished, and road agents must die. Justice, and protection from wrong to person or property, are the birthright of every American citizen, and these must be furnished in the best and most effectual manner that circumstances render possible. Furnished, however, they must be by constitutional law, undoubtedly, wherever practical and efficient provision can be made for its enforcement. But where justice is powerless as well as blind, the strong arm of the mountaineer must wield her sword; for "self-preservation is the first law of nature."

The Arrest and Execution of Captain J.A. Slade

"Some write him hero, some a very knave;
Curses and tears are mingled at his grave."—Anon.

J.A. Slade, or, as he was often called, Captain Slade, was raised in Clinton County, Ill., and was a member of a highly respectable family. He bore a good character for several years in that place. The acts which have given so wide a celebrity to his name were performed especially on the Overland Line, of which he was for years an official. Reference to these matters will be made in a subsequent part of this chapter.

Captain J.A. Slade came to Virginia City in the spring of 1863. He was a man gifted with the power of making money, and when free from the influence of alcoholic stimulants, which seemed to reverse his nature, and to change a kind-hearted and intelligent gentleman into a reckless demon, no man in the Territory had a greater faculty of attracting the favorable notice of even strangers, and in spite of the wild lawlessness which characterized his frequent spells of intoxication, he had many, very many friends whom no commission of crime itself could detach from his personal companionship. Another and less desirable class of friends were attracted by his very recklessness. There are probably a thousand individuals in the West possessing a correct knowledge of the leading incidents of a career that terminated at the gallows, who still speak of Slade as a perfect gentleman, and who not only lament his death, but talk in the highest terms of his character, and pronounce his execution a murder. One way of accounting for the diversity of opinion regarding Slade is sufficiently obvious. Those who saw him in his natural state only would pronounce him to be a kind husband, a most hospitable host and a courteous gentleman. On the contrary, those who met him when maddened with liquor and surrounded by a gang of armed roughs, would pronounce him a fiend incarnate.

During the summer of 1863 he went to Milk River as a freighter. For this business he was eminently qualified, and he made a great deal of money. Unfortunately his habit of profuse expenditure was uncontrollable, and at the time of his execution he was deeply in debt almost everywhere.

After the execution of the five men on the 14th of January the Vigilantes considered that their work was nearly ended. They had freed the country from highwaymen and murderers to a great extent, and they determined that in the absence of the regular civil authority they would establish a People's Court, where all offenders should be tried by judge and jury. This was the nearest approach to social order that the circumstances permitted, and

though strict legal authority was wanting yet the people were firmly determined to maintain its efficiency and to enforce its decrees. It may here be mentioned that the overt act
which was the last round on the fatal ladder leading to the scaffold on which Slade perished,
was the tearing in pieces and stamping upon a writ of this court, followed by the arrest of
the judge, Alex. Davis, by authority of a presented derringer and with his own hands.

J.A. Slade was himself, we have been informed, a Vigilanter; he openly boasted of it,
and said he knew all that they knew. He was never accused or even suspected of either murder or robbery committed in this Territory (the latter crimes were never laid to his charge
in any place); but that he had killed several men in other localities was notorious, and his
bad reputation in this respect was a most powerful argument in determining his fate, when
he was finally arrested for the offence above mentioned. On returning from Milk River he
became more and more addicted to drinking; until at last it was a common feat for him and
his friends to "take the town." He and a couple of his dependents might often be seen on one
horse, galloping through the streets, shouting and yelling, firing revolvers, etc. On many
occasions he would ride his horse into stores, break up bars, toss the scales out of doors, and
use most insulting language to parties present. Just previous to the day of his arrest, he had
given a fearful beating to one of his followers; but such was his influence over them that the
man wept bitterly at the gallows and begged for his life with all his power. It had become
quite common when Slade was on a spree for the shopkeepers and citizens to close the
stores and put out all the lights; being fearful of some outrage at his hands. One store in
Nevada he never ventured to enter—that of the Lott Brothers—as they had taken care to let
him know that any attempt of the kind would be followed by his sudden death, and though
he often rode down there, threatening to break in and raise ____, yet he never attempted to
carry his threat into execution. For his wanton destruction of goods and furniture he was
always ready to pay when sober if he had money; but there were not a few who regarded
payment as small satisfaction for the outrage, and these men were his personal enemies.

From time to time, Slade received warnings from men that he well knew would not
deceive him, of the certain end of his conduct. There was not a moment, for weeks previous to his arrest, in which the public did not expect to hear of some bloody outrage. The
dread of his very name and the presence of the armed band of hangers-on who followed
him, alone prevented a resistance which must certainly have ended in the instant murder or
mutilation of the opposing party.

Slade was frequently arrested by order of the court whose organization we have
described, and had treated it with respect by paying one or two fines, and promising to pay
the rest when he had the money; but in the transaction, and goaded by passion and the
hatred of restraint, he sprang into the embrace of death.

Slade had been drunk and "cutting up" all night. He and his companions had made the
town a perfect hell. In the morning, J.M. Fox, the Sheriff, met him, arrested him, took him
into court, and commenced reading a warrant that he had for his arrest, by way of arraign-
ment. He became uncontrollably furious, and seizing the writ, he tore it up, threw it on the
ground, and stamped upon it. The clicking of the locks of his companions' revolvers was
instantly heard and a crisis was expected. The Sheriff did not attempt his capture; but

being at least as prudent as he was valiant, he succumbed, leaving Slade the master of the situation, and the conqueror and ruler of the courts, law and law-makers. This was a declaration of war, and was so accepted. The Vigilance Committee now felt that the question of social order and the preponderance of the law-abiding citizens had then and there to be decided. They knew the character of Slade, and they were well aware that they must submit to his rule without murmur, or else that he must be dealt with in such fashion as would prevent his being able to wreak his vengeance on the Committee, who could never have hoped to live in the Territory secure from outrage or death, and who could never leave it without encountering his friends, whom his victory would have emboldened and stimulated to a pitch that would have rendered them reckless of consequences. The day previous, he had ridden into Dorris's store, and on being requested to leave, he drew his revolver and threatened to kill the gentleman who spoke to him. Another saloon he had led his horse into, and buying a bottle of wine, he tried to make the animal drink it. This was not considered an uncommon performance, as he had often entered saloons, and commenced firing at the lamps, causing a wild stampede.

A leading member of the Committee met Slade, and informed him in the quiet, earnest manner of one who feels the importance of what he is saying, "Slade, get your horse at once, and go home, or there will be ___ to pay." Slade started and took a long look with his dark and piercing eyes, at the gentleman—"What do you mean?" said he. "You have no right to ask me what I mean," was the quiet reply, "get your horse at once, and remember what I tell you." After a short pause he promised to do so, and actually got into the saddle; but, being still intoxicated, he began calling aloud to one after another of his friends, and at last seemed to have forgotten the warning he had received and became again uproarious, shouting the name of a well-known prostitute in company with those of two men whom he considered heads of the Committee, as a sort of challenge; perhaps, however, as a single act of bravado. It seems probable that the intimation of personal danger he had received had not been forgotten entirely; though, fatally for him, he took a foolish way of showing his remembrance of it. He sought out Alexander Davis, the Judge of the Court, and drawing a cocked derringer, he presented it at his head, and told him that he should hold him as a hostage for his own safety. As the Judge stood perfectly quiet, and offered no resistance to his captor, no further outrage followed on this score. Previous to this, on account of the critical state of affairs, the Committee had met, and at last resolved to arrest him. His execution had not been agreed upon, and, at that time, would have been negatived, most assuredly. A messenger rode down to Nevada to inform the leading men of what was on hand, as it was desirable to show that there was a feeling of unanimity on the subject, all along the Gulch.

The miners turned out almost en masse, leaving their work and forming in solid column, about six hundred strong, armed to the teeth, they marched up to Virginia. The leader of the body well knew the temper of his men on the subject. He spurred on ahead of them, and hastily calling a meeting of the Executive, he told them plainly that the miners meant "business," and that, if they came up, they would not stand in the street to be shot down by Slade's friends and that they would take him and hang him. The meeting was small, as the

Virginia men were loath to act at all. This momentous announcement of the feeling of the Lower Town was made to a cluster of men, who were deliberating behind a wagon, at the rear of a store on Main street, where the Ohlinghouse stone building now stands.

The Committee was most unwilling to proceed to extremities. All the duty they had ever performed seemed as nothing to the task before them; but they had to decide, and that quickly. It was finally agreed that if the whole body of the miners were of the opinion that he should be hanged, the Committee left it in their hands to deal with him. Off, at hot speed, rode the leader of the Nevada men to join his command.

Slade had found out what was intended, and the news sobered him instantly. He went into P.S. Pfout's store, where Davis was, and apologized for his conduct, saying that he would take it all back.

The head of the column now wheeled into Wallace street and marched up at quick time. Halting in front of the store, the executive officer of the Committee stepped forward and arrested Slade, who was at once informed of his doom, and inquiry was made as to whether he had any business to settle. Several parties spoke to him on the subject; but to all such inquiries he turned a deaf ear, being entirely absorbed in the terrifying reflections on his own awful position. He never ceased his entreaties for life, and to see his dear wife. The unfortunate lady referred to, between whom and Slade there existed a warm affection, was at this time living at their ranch on the Madison. She was possessed of considerable personal attractions; tall, well-formed, of graceful carriage, pleasing manners, and was, withal, an accomplished horsewoman.

A messenger from Slade rode at full speed to inform her of her husband's arrest. In an instant she was in the saddle, and with all the energy that love and despair could lend to an ardent temperament and a strong physique, she urged her fleet charger over the twelve miles of rough and rocky ground that intervened between her and the object of her passionate devotion.

Meanwhile a party of volunteers had made the necessary preparations for the execution, in the valley traversed by the branch. Beneath the site of Pfout's and Russell's stone building there was a corral, the gate-posts of which were strong and high. Across the top was laid a beam, to which the rope was fastened, and a dry-goods box served for the platform. To this place Slade was marched, surrounded by a guard, composing the best-armed and most numerous force that has ever appeared in Montana Territory.

The doomed man had so exhausted himself by tears, prayers, and lamentations, that he had scarcely strength left to stand under the fatal beam. He repeatedly exclaimed, "My God! my God! must I die? Oh, my dear wife!"

On the return of the fatigue party, they encountered some friends of Slade, staunch and reliable citizens and members of the Committee, but who were personally attached to the condemned. On hearing of his sentence, one of them, a stout-hearted man, pulled out his handkerchief and walked away, weeping like a child. Slade still begged to see his wife most piteously, and it seemed hard to deny his request; but the bloody consequences that were sure to follow the inevitable attempt at a rescue, that her presence and entreaties would have certainly incited, forbade the granting of his request. Several gentlemen were sent for to see him in his last moments, one of whom (Judge Davis) made a short address to the people; but in such low tones as to be inaudible, save to a few in his immediate vicinity. One of his friends, after exhausting his powers of entreaty, threw off his coat and declared that the prisoner could not be hanged until he himself was killed. A hundred guns were instantly leveled at him; whereupon he turned and fled; but, being brought back, he was compelled to resume his coat, and to give a promise of future peaceable demeanor.

Scarcely a leading man in Virginia could be found, though numbers of the citizens joined the ranks of the guard when the arrest was made. All lamented the stern necessity which dictated the execution.

Everything being ready the command was given. "Men, do your duty," and the box being instantly slipped from beneath his feet, he died almost instantaneously.

The body was cut down and carried to the Virginia Hotel, where, in a darkened room, it was scarcely laid out, when the unfortunate and betrayed companion of the deceased arrived, at headlong speed, to find that all was over, and that she was a widow. Her grief and heart-piercing cries were terrible evidences of the depth of her attachment for her lost husband, and a considerable period elapsed before she could regain the command of her excited feelings.

J.A. Slade was, during his connection with the Overland Stage Company, frequently involved in quarrels which terminated fatally for his antagonists. The first and most memorable of these was his encounter with Jules, a station keeper at Julesburg, on the Platte River. Between the inhabitants, the emigrants and the stage people, there was a constant feud, arising from quarrels about missing stock, alleged to have been stolen by the settlers, which constantly resulted in personal difficulties such as beating, shooting, stabbing, etc., and it was from this cause that Slade became involved in a transaction which has become inseparably associated with his name, and which has given a coloring and tone to all descriptions of him, from the date of the occurrence to the present day.

There have been so many versions of the affair, all of them differing more or less in important particulars, that it has seemed impossible to get at the exact truth; but the following account may be relied on as substantially correct:

From overlanders and dwellers on the road we learn that Jules was himself a lawless aud tyrranical man, taking such liberties with the coach stock and carrying matters with so high a hand that the company determined on giving the agency of the division to J.A. Slade. In a business point of view, they were correct in their selection. The coach went through at all hazards. It is not to be supposed that Jules would submit to the authority of a newcomer, or, indeed, of any man that he could intimidate; and a very limited intercourse was sufficient to increase the mutual dislike of the parties, so far as to occasion an open rupture and bloodshed. Slade, it is said, had employed a man discharged by Jules, which irritated the latter considerably; but the overt act that brought matters to a crisis was the recovery by Slade of a team "sequestered" by Jules. Some state that there had been a previous altercation between the two; but, whether this be true or not, it appears certain that on the arrival of the coach, with Slade as a passenger, Jules determined to arrest the team, then and there; and that, finding Slade was equally determined on putting them through, a few expletives were exchanged, and Jules fired his gun, loaded with buckshot, at Slade, who was unarmed at the time, wounding him severely. At his death, Slade carried several of these shot in his body. Slade went down the road, till he recovered of his wound. Jules left the place, and in his travels never failed to let everybody know that he would kill Slade, who, on his part, was not backward in reciprocating such promises. At last, Slade got well, and shortly after was informed that his enemy had been "corralled by the boys," whereupon he went to the place designated, and, tying him fast, shot him to death by degrees. He also cut off his ears, and carried them in his vest pocket for a long time.

One man declares that Slade went up to the ranch where he had heard that Jules was and, "getting the drop on him," that is to say, covering him with his pistol before he was ready to defend himself, he said, "Jules, I am going to kill you"; to which the other replied, "Well, I suppose I am gone up; you've got me now"; and that Slade immediately opened fire and killed him with his revolver.

The first story is the one almost universally believed in the West, and the act is considered entirely justifiable by the wild Indian fighters of the frontier. Had he simply killed Jules, he would have been justified by the accepted Western law of retaliation. The prolonged agony and mutilation of his enemy, however, admit of no excuse.

While on the road Slade ruled supreme. He would ride down to the station, get into a quarrel, turn the house out of windows, and maltreat the occupants most cruelly. The unfortunates had no means of redress, and were compelled to recuperate as best they could. On one of these occasions, it is said, he killed the father of the fine little half-breed boy, Jemmy, whom he adopted, and who lived with his widow atter his execution. He was a gentle, well-behaved child, remarkable for his beautiful, soft black eyes, and for his polite address.

Sometimes Slade acted as a lyncher. On one occasion, some emigrants had their stock either lost or stolen, and told Slade, who happened to visit their camp. He rode with a single companion, to a ranch, the owners of which he suspected, and opening the door, commenced firing at them, killing three and wounding the fourth.

As for minor quarrels and shootings, it is absolutely certain that a minute history of Slade's life would be one long record of such practices. He was feared a great deal more, generally, than the Almighty, from Kearney, west. There was, it seems, something in his bold reckless, lavish generosity, and firm attachment to his friends, whose quarrel he would back, everywhere and at any time, that endeared him to the wild denizens of the prairie, and this personal attachment it is that has cast a veil over his faults, so dark that his friends could never see his real character, or believe their idol to be a blood-stained desperado.

Stories of his hanging men, and of innumerable assaults, shootings, stabbings and beatings, in which he was a principal actor, form part of the legends of the stage line; nevertheless, such is the veneration still cherished for him by many of the old stagers, that any insult offered to his memory would be fearfully and quickly avenged. Whatever he did to others, he was their friend, they say; and so they will say and feel till the tomb closes over the last of his old friends and comrades of the Overland.

It should be stated that Slade was, at the time of his coming West, a fugitive from justice in Illinois, where he killed a man with whom he had been quarreling. Finding his antagonist to be more than his match, he ran away from him, and, in his flight, picking up a stone, he threw it with such deadly aim and violence that it penetrated the skull of his pursuer, over the eye, and killed him. Johnson, the Sheriff, who pursued him for nearly four hundred miles, was in Virginia City not long since, as we have been informed by persons who knew him well.

Such was Captain J.A. Slade, the idol of his followers, the terror of his enemies and of all that were not within the charmed circle of his dependents. In him, generosity and destructiveness, brutal lawlessness and courteous kindness, firm friendship and volcanic outbreaks of fury, were so mingled that he seems like one born out of date. He should have lived in feudal times, and have been the comrade of the Front de Boeufs, De Lacys, and Rois Guilberts, of days almost forgotten. In modern times, he stands nearly alone.

The execution of Slade had a most wonderful effect upon society. Henceforth, all knew that no one man could domineer or rule over the community. Reason and civilization then drove brute force from Montana.

One of his principal friends wisely absconded, and so escaped sharing his fate, which would have been a thing almost certain had he remained.

It has often been asked why Slade's friends were permitted to go scot free, seeing that they accompanied him in all his "raids," and both shared and defended his wild and lawless exploits. The answer is very simple. The Vigilantes deplored the sad but imperative necessity for the making of one example. That, they knew, would be sufficient. They were right in their judgment, and immovable in their purpose. Could it but be made known how many lives were at their mercy, society would wonder at the moderation that ruled in their counsels. Necessity was the arbiter of these men's fate. When the stern Goddess spoke not, the doom was unpronounced, and the criminal remained at large. They acted for the public good, and when examples were made, it was because the safety of the community demanded a warning to the lawless and the desperate, that might neither be despised nor soon forgotten.

The execution of the road agents of Plummer's gang was the result of the popular verdict and judgment against robbers and murderers. The death of Slade was the protest of society on behalf of social order and the rights of man.

On the Sociology of Deviance*
Kai T. Erikson

In 1895 Emile Durkheim wrote a book called *The Rules of Sociological Method* which was intended as a working manual for persons interested in the systematic study of society. One of the most important themes of Durkheim's work was that sociologists should formulate a new set of criteria for distinguishing between "normal" and "pathological" elements in the life of a society. Behavior which looks abnormal to the psychiatrist or the judge, he suggested, does not always look abnormal when viewed through the special lens of the sociologist; and thus students of the new science should be careful to understand that even the most aberrant forms of individual behavior may still be considered normal from this broader point of view. To illustrate his argument, Durkheim made the surprising observation that crime was really a natural kind of social activity, "an integral part of all healthy societies."

Durkheim's interest in this subject had been expressed several years before when *The Division of Labor in Society* was first published. In that important book, he had suggested that crime (and by extension other forms of deviation) may actually perform a needed service to society by drawing people together in a common posture of anger and indignation. The deviant individual violates rules of conduct which the rest of the community holds in high respect; and when these people come together to express their outrage over the offense and to bear witness against the offender, they develop a tighter bond of solidarity than existed earlier. The excitement generated by the crime, in other words, quickens the tempo of interaction in the group and creates a climate in which the private sentiments of many separate persons are fused together into a common sense of morality.

> Crime brings together upright consciences and concentrates them. We have only to notice what happens, particularly in a small town, when some moral scandal has just been committed. They stop each other on the street, they visit each other, they seek to come together to talk of the event and to wax indignant in common. From all the similar impressions which are exchanged, for all the temper that gets itself expressed, there emerges a unique temper . . . which is everybody's without being anybody's in particular. That is the public temper.

The deviant act, then, creates a sense of mutuality among the people of a community by supplying a focus for group feeling. Like a war, a flood, or some other emergency, deviance makes people more alert to the interests they share in common and draws attention to those values which constitute the "collective conscience" of the community. Unless the rhythm of group life is punctuated by occasional moments of deviant behavior, presumably, social organization would be impossible.

This brief argument has been regarded a classic of sociological thinking ever since it was first presented, even though it has not inspired much in the way of empirical work. The purpose of the present chapter is to consider Durkheim's suggestion in terms more congenial to modern social theory and to see if these insights can be translated into useful research hypotheses. The pages to follow may range far afield from the starting point rec-

---

ommended by Durkheim, but they are addressed to the question he originally posed: does it make any sense to assert that deviant forms of behavior are a natural and even beneficial part of social life?

I

One of the earliest problems the sociologist encounters in his search for a meaningful approach to deviant behavior is that the subject itself does not seem to have any natural boundaries. Like people in any field, sociologists find it convenient to assume that the deviant person is somehow "different" from those of his fellows who manage to conform, but years of research into the problem have not yielded any important evidence as to what, if anything, this difference might be. Investigators have studied the character of the deviant's background, the content of his dreams, the shape of his skull, the substance of his thoughts—yet none of this information has enabled us to draw a clear line between the kind of person who commits deviant acts and the kind of person who does not. Nor can we gain a better perspective on the matter by shifting our attention away from the individual deviant and looking instead at the behavior he enacts. Definitions of deviance vary widely as we range over the various classes found in a single society or across the various cultures into which mankind is divided, and it soon becomes apparent that there are no objective properties which all deviant acts can be said to share in common—even within the confines of a given group. Behavior which qualifies one man for prison may qualify another for sainthood, since the quality of the act itself depends so much on the circumstances under which it was performed and the temper of the audience which witnessed it.

This being the case, many sociologists employ a far simpler tactic in their approach to the problem—namely, to let each social group in question provide its own definitions of deviant behavior. In this study, as in others dealing with the same general subject, the term "deviance" refers to conduct which the people of a group consider so dangerous or embarrassing or irritating that they bring special sanctions to bear against the persons who exhibit it. Deviance is not a property *inherent in* any particular kind of behavior; it is a property *conferred upon* that behavior by the people who come into direct or indirect contact with it. The only way an observer can tell whether or not a given style of behavior is deviant, then, is to learn something about the standards of the audience which responds to it.

This definition may seem a little awkward in practice, but it has the advantage of bringing a neglected issue into proper focus. When the people of a community decide that it is time to "do something" about the conduct of one of their number, they are involved in a highly intricate process. After all, even the worst miscreant in society conforms most of the time, if only in the sense that he uses the correct silver at dinner, stops obediently at traffic lights, or in a hundred other ways respects the ordinary conventions of his group. And if his fellows elect to bring sanctions against him for the occasions when he does misbehave, they are responding to a few deviant details scattered among a vast array of entirely acceptable conduct. The person who appears in a criminal court and is stamped a "thief" may have spent no more than a passing moment engaged in that activity, and the same can be said for many of the people who pass in review before some agency of control and return from the experience with a deviant label of one sort or another. When the community nominates someone to the deviant class, then, it is sifting a few important details out of the stream of behavior he has emitted and is in effect declaring that these details reflect the kind of person he "really" is. In law as well as in public opinion, the fact that someone has committed a felony or has been known to use narcotics can become the major identifying badge of his person: the very expression "he is a thief" or "he is an addict" seems to provide at once a description of his position in society and a profile of his character.

The manner in which a community sifts these telling details out of a person's overall performance, then, is an important part of its social control apparatus. And it is important to notice that the people of a community take a number of factors into account when they pass judgment on one another which are not immediately related to the deviant act itself: whether or not a person will be considered deviant, for instance, has something to do with his social class, his past record as an offender, the amount of remorse he manages to convey, and many similar concerns which take hold in the shifting mood of the community. Perhaps this is not so apparent in cases of serious crime or desperate illness, where the offending act looms so darkly that it obscures most of the other details of the person's life; but in the day-by-day sifting processes which take place throughout society this feature is always present. Some men who drink heavily are called alcoholics and others are not, some men who behave oddly are committed to hospitals and others are not, some men with no visible means of support are charged with vagrancy and others are not—and the difference between those who earn a deviant title in society and those who go their own way in peace is largely determined by the way in which the community filters out and codes the many details of behavior which come to its attention.

Once the problem is phrased in this manner we can ask: how does a community decide which of these behavioral details are important enough to merit special attention? And why, having made this decision, does it build institutions like prisons and asylums to detain the persons who perform them? The conventional answer to that question, of course, is that a society creates the machinery of control in order to protect itself against the "harmful" effects of deviation, in much the same way that an organism mobilizes its resources to combat an invasion of germs. Yet this simple view of the matter is apt to pose many more problems than it actually settles. As both Emile Durkheim and George Herbert Mead pointed out long ago, it is by no means evident that all acts considered deviant in society are in fact (or even in principle) harmful to group life. It is undoubtedly true that no culture would last long if its members engaged in murder or arson among themselves on any large scale, but there is no real evidence that many other of the activities considered deviant throughout the world (certain dietary prohibitions are a prominent example) have any relationship to the group's survival. In our own day, for instance, we might well ask why prostitution or marihuana smoking or homosexuality are thought to endanger the health of the social order. Perhaps these activities are dangerous, but to accept this conclusion without a thoughtful review of the situation is apt to blind us to the important fact that people in every corner of the world manage to survive handsomely while engaged in practices which their neighbors regard as extremely abhorrent. In the absence of any surer footing, then, it is quite reasonable for sociologists to return to the most innocent and yet the most basic question which can be asked about deviation: why does a community assign one form of behavior rather than another to the deviant class?

The following paragraphs will suggest one possible answer to that question.

II

Human actors are sorted into various kinds of collectivity, ranging from relatively small units such as the nuclear family to relatively large ones such as a nation or culture. One of the most stubborn difficulties in the study of deviation is that the problem is defined differently at each one of these levels: behavior that is considered unseemly within the context of a single family may be entirely acceptable to the community in general, while behavior that attracts severe censure from the members of the community may go altogether unnoticed elsewhere in the culture. People in society, then, must learn to deal separately with deviance at each one of these levels and to distinguish among them in his own daily activity. A man may disinherit his son for conduct that violates old family traditions or ostracize a neighbor for conduct that violates some local custom, but he is not expected to employ either of these standards when he serves as a juror in a court of law. In each of the three situations he is required to use a different set of criteria to decide whether or not the behavior in question exceeds tolerable limits.

In the next few pages we shall be talking about deviant behavior in social units called "communities," but the use of this term does not mean that the argument applies only at that level of organization. In theory, at least, the argument being made here should fit all kinds of human collectivity—families as well as whole cultures, small groups as well as nations— and the term "community" is only being used in this context because it seems particularly convenient.

The people of a community spend most of their lives in close contact with one another, sharing a common sphere of experience which makes them feel that they belong to a special "kind" and live in a special "place." In the formal language of sociology, this means that communities are boundary maintaining: each has a specific territory in the world as a whole, not only in the sense that it occupies a defined region of geographical space but also in the sense that it takes over a particular niche in what might be called cultural space and develops its own "ethos" or "way" within that compass. Both of these dimensions of group space, the geographical and the cultural, set the community apart as a special place and provide an important point of reference for its members.

When one describes any system as boundary maintaining, one is saying that it controls the fluctuation of its constituent parts so that the whole retains a limited range of activity, a given pattern of constancy and stability, within the larger environment. A human community can be said to maintain boundaries, then, in the sense that its members tend to confine themselves to a particular radius of activity and to regard any conduct which drifts outside that radius as somehow inappropriate or immoral. Thus the group retains a kind of cultural integrity, a voluntary restriction on its own potential for expansion, beyond that which is strictly required for accommodation to the environment. Human behavior can vary over an enormous range, but each community draws a symbolic set of parentheses around a certain segment of that range and limits its own activities within that narrower zone. These parentheses, so to speak, are the community's boundaries.

Now people who live together in communities cannot relate to one another in any coherent way or even acquire a sense of their own stature as group members unless they learn something about the boundaries of the territory they occupy in social space, if only because they need to sense what lies beyond the margins of the group before they can appreciate the special quality of the experience which takes place within it. Yet how do people learn about the boundaries of their community? And how do they convey this information to the generations which replace them?

To begin with, the only material found in a society for marking boundaries is the behavior of its members—or rather, the networks of interaction which link these members together in regular social relations. And the interactions which do the most effective job of locating and publicizing the group's outer edges would seem to be those which take place between deviant persons on the one side and official agents of the community on the other. The deviant is a person whose activities have moved outside the margins of the group, and when the community calls him to account for that vagrancy it is making a statement about the nature and placement of its boundaries. It is declaring how much variability and diversity can be tolerated within the group before it begins to lose its distinctive shape, its unique identity. Now there may be other moments in the life of the group which perform a similar service: wars, for instance, can publicize a group's boundaries by drawing attention to the line separating the group from an adversary, and certain kinds of religious ritual, dance ceremony, and other traditional pageantry can dramatize the difference between "we" and "they" by portraying a symbolic encounter between the two. But on the whole, members of a community inform one another about the placement of their boundaries by participating in the confrontations which occur when persons who venture out to the edges of the group are met by policing agents whose special business it is to guard the cultural integrity of the community. Whether these confrontations take the form of criminal trials, excommunication hearings, courts-martial, or even psychiatric case conferences, they act as boundary-maintaining devices in the sense that they demonstrate to whatever audience is concerned where the line is drawn between behavior that belongs in the special universe of the group and behavior that does not. In general, this kind of information is not easily relayed by the straightforward use of language. Most readers of this paragraph, for instance, have a fairly clear idea of the line separating theft from more legitimate forms of commerce, but few of them have ever seen a published statute describing these differences. More likely than not, our information on the subject has been drawn from publicized instances in which the relevant laws were applied—and for that matter, the law itself is largely a collection of past cases and decisions, a synthesis of the various confrontations which have occurred in the life of the legal order.

It may be important to note in this connection that confrontations between deviant offenders and the agents of control have always attracted a good deal of public attention. In our own past, the trial and punishment of offenders were staged in the market place and afforded the crowd a chance to participate in a direct, active way. Today, of course, we no longer parade deviants in the town square or expose them to the carnival atmosphere of a Tyburn, but it is interesting that the "reform" which brought about this change in penal practice coincided almost exactly with the development of newspapers as a medium of mass information. Perhaps this is no more than an accident of history, but it is nonetheless true that newspapers (and now radio and television) offer much the same kind of entertainment as public hangings or a Sunday visit to the local gaol. A considerable portion of what we call "news" is devoted to reports about deviant behavior and its consequences, and it is no simple matter to explain why these items should be considered newsworthy or why they should command the extraordinary attention they do. Perhaps they appeal to a number of psychological perversities among the mass audience, as commentators have suggested, but at the same time they constitute one of our main sources of information about the normative outlines of society. In a figurative sense, at least, morality and immorality meet at the public scaffold, and it is during this meeting that the line between them is drawn.

Boundaries are never a fixed property of any community. They are always shifting as the people of the group find new ways to define the outer limits of their universe, new ways to position themselves on the larger cultural map. Sometimes changes occur within the structure of the group which require its members to make a new survey of their territory—a change of leadership, a shift of mood. Sometimes changes occur in the surrounding environment, altering the background against which the people of the group have measured their own uniqueness. And always, new generations are moving in to take their turn guarding old institutions and need to be informed about the contours of the world they are inheriting. Thus single encounters between the deviant and his community are only fragments of an ongoing social process. Like an article of common law, boundaries remain a meaningful point of reference only so long as they are repeatedly tested by persons on the fringes of the group and repeatedly defended by persons chosen to represent the group's inner morality. Each time the community moves to censure some act of deviation, then, and convenes a formal ceremony to deal with the responsible offender, it sharpens the authority of the violated norm and restates where the boundaries of the group are located.

For these reasons, deviant behavior is not a simple kind of leakage which occurs when the machinery of society is in poor working order, but may be, in controlled quantities, an important condition for preserving the stability of social life. Deviant forms of behavior, by marking the outer edges of group life, give the inner structure its special character and thus supply the framework within which the people of the group develop an orderly sense of their own cultural identity. Perhaps this is what Aldous Huxley had in mind when he wrote:

> Now tidiness is undeniably good—but a good of which it is easily possible to have too much and at too high a price. . . . The good life can only be lived in a society in which tidiness is preached and practiced, but not too fanatically, and where efficiency is always haloed, as it were, by a tolerated margin of mess.

This raises a delicate theoretical issue. If we grant that human groups often derive benefit from deviant behavior, can we then assume that they are organized in such a way as to promote this resource? Can we assume, in other words, that forces operate in the social structure to recruit offenders and to commit them to long periods of service in the deviant ranks? This is not a question which can be answered with our present store of empirical data, but one observation can be made which gives the question an interesting perspective—namely, that deviant forms of conduct often seem to derive nourishment from the very agencies devised to inhibit them. Indeed, the agencies built by society for preventing deviance are often so poorly equipped for the task that we might well ask why this is regarded as their "real" function in the first place.

It is by now a thoroughly familiar argument that many of the institutions designed to discourage deviant behavior actually operate in such a way as to perpetuate it. For one thing, prisons, hospitals, and other similar agencies provide aid and shelter to large numbers of deviant persons, sometimes giving them a certain advantage in the competition for social resources. But beyond this, such institutions gather marginal people into tightly segregated groups, give them an opportunity to teach one another the skills and attitudes of a deviant career, and even provoke them into using these skills by reinforcing their sense of alienation from the rest of society. Nor is this observation a modern one:

> The misery suffered in gaols is not half their evil; they are filled with every sort of corruption that poverty and wickedness can generate; with all the shameless and profligate enormities that can be produced by the impudence of ignominy, the rage of want, and the malignity of dispair. In a prison the check of the public eye is removed; and the power of the law is spent. There are few fears, there are no blushes. The lewd inflame the more modest; the audacious harden the timid. Everyone fortifies himself as he can against his own remaining sensibility; endeavoring to practice on others the arts that are practiced on himself; and to gain the applause of his worst associates by imitating their manners.

These lines, written almost two centuries ago, are a harsh indictment of prisons, but many of the conditions they describe continue to be reported in even the most modern studies of prison life. Looking at the matter from a long-range historical perspective, it is fair to conclude that prisons have done a conspicuously poor job of reforming the convicts placed in their custody; but the very consistency of this failure may have a peculiar logic of its own. Perhaps we find it difficult to change the worst of our penal practices because we *expect* the prison to harden the inmate's commitment to deviant forms of behavior and draw him more deeply into the deviant ranks. On the whole, we are a people who do not really expect deviants to change very much as they are processed through the control agencies we provide for them, and we are often reluctant to devote much of the community's resources to the job of rehabilitation. In this sense, the prison which graduates long rows of accomplished criminals (or, for that matter, the state asylum which stores its most severe cases away in some back ward) may do serious violence to the aims of its founders, but it does very little violence to the expectations of the population it serves.

These expectations, moreover, are found in every corner of society and constitute an important part of the climate in which we deal with deviant forms of behavior.

To begin with, the community's decision to bring deviant sanctions against one of its members is not a simple act of censure. It is an intricate rite of transition, at once moving the individual out of his ordinary place in society and transferring him into a special deviant position. The ceremonies which mark this change of status, generally, have a number of related phases. They supply a formal stage on which the deviant and his community can confront one another (as in the criminal trial); they make an announcement about the nature of his deviancy (a verdict or diagnosis, for example); and they place him in a particular role which is thought to neutralize the harmful effects of his misconduct (like the role of prisoner or patient). These commitment ceremonies tend to be occasions of wide public interest and ordinarily take place in a highly dramatic setting. Perhaps the most obvious example of a commitment ceremony is the criminal trial, with its elaborate formality and exaggerated ritual, but more modest equivalents can be found wherever procedures are set up to judge whether or not someone is legitimately deviant.

Now an important feature of these ceremonies in our own culture is that they are almost irreversible. Most provisional roles conferred by society—those of the student or conscripted soldier, for example—include some kind of terminal ceremony to mark the individual's movement back out of the role once its temporary advantages have been exhausted. But the roles allotted the deviant seldom make allowance for this type of passage. He is ushered into the deviant position by a decisive and often dramatic ceremony, yet is retired from it with scarcely a word of public notice. And as a result, the deviant often returns home with no proper license to resume a normal life in the community. Nothing has happened to cancel out the stigmas imposed upon him by earlier commitment ceremonies; nothing has happened to revoke the verdict or diagnosis pronounced upon him at that time. It should not be surprising, then, that the people of the community are apt to greet the returning deviant with a considerable degree of apprehension and distrust, for in a very real sense they are not at all sure who he is.

A circularity is thus set into motion which has all the earmarks of a "self-fulfilling prophesy," to use Merton's fine phrase. On the one hand, it seems quite obvious that the community's apprehensions help reduce whatever chances the deviant might otherwise have had for a successful return home. Yet at the same time, everyday experience seems to show that these suspicions are wholly reasonable, for it is a well-known and highly publicized fact that many if not most ex-convicts return to crime after leaving prison and that large numbers of mental patients require further treatment after an initial hospitalization. The common feeling that deviant persons never really change, then, may derive from a faulty premise; but the feeling is expressed so frequently and with such conviction that it eventually creates the facts which later "prove" it to be correct. If the returning deviant encounters this circularity often enough, it is quite understandable that he, too, may begin to wonder whether he has fully graduated from the deviant role, and he may respond to the uncertainty by resuming some kind of deviant activity. In many respects, this may be the only way for the individual and his community to agree what kind of person he is.

Moreover this prophesy is found in the official policies of even the most responsible agencies of control. Police departments could not operate with any real effectiveness if they did not regard ex-convicts as a ready pool of suspects to be tapped in the event of trouble, and psychiatric clinics could not do a successful job in the community if they were not always alert to the possibility of former patients suffering relapses. Thus the prophesy gains currency at many levels within the social order, not only in the poorly informed attitudes of the community at large, but in the best informed theories of most control agencies as well.

In one form or another this problem has been recognized in the West for many hundreds of years, and this simple fact has a curious implication. For if our culture has supported a steady flow of deviation throughout long periods of historical change, the rules which apply to any kind of evolutionary thinking would suggest that strong forces must be at work to keep the flow intact—and this because it contributes in some important way to the survival of the culture as a whole. This does not furnish us with sufficient warrant to declare that deviance is "functional" (in any of the many senses of that term), but it should certainly make us wary of the assumption so often made in sociological circles that any well-structured society is somehow designed to prevent deviant behavior from occurring.

It might be then argued that we need new metaphors to carry our thinking about deviance onto a different plane. On the whole, American sociologists have devoted most of their attention to those forces in society which seem to assert a centralizing influence on human behavior, gathering people together into tight clusters called "groups" and bringing them under the jurisdiction of governing principles called "norms" or "standards." The questions which sociologists have traditionally asked of their data, then, are addressed to the uniformities rather than the divergencies of social life: how is it that people learn to think in similar ways, to accept the same group moralities, to move by the same rhythms of behavior, to see life with the same eyes? How is it, in short, that cultures accomplish the incredible alchemy of making unity out of diversity, harmony out of conflict, order out of confusion? Somehow we often act as if the differences between people can be taken for granted, being too natural to require comment, but that the symmetry which human groups manage to achieve must be explained by referring to the molding influence of the social structure.

But variety, too, is a product of the social structure. It is certainly remarkable that members of a culture come to look so much alike; but it is also remarkable that out of all this sameness a people can develop a complex division of labor, move off into diverging career lines, scatter across the surface of the territory they share in common, and create so many differences of temper, ideology, fashion, and mood. Perhaps we can conclude, then, that two separate yet often competing currents are found in any society: those forces which promote a high degree of conformity among the people of the community so that they know what to expect from one another, and those forces which encourage a certain degree of diversity so that people can be deployed across the range of group space to survey its potential, measure its capacity, and, in the case of those we call deviants, patrol its boundaries. In such a scheme, the deviant would appear as a natural product of group differentiation. He is not a bit of debris spun out by faulty social machinery, but a relevant figure in the community's overall division of labor.

III

The foregoing statement has introduced a number of different themes which lend themselves to one or another kind of historical analysis, and the object of the present section will be to draw attention to three of them. Each of these themes will become the underlying motif of a later chapter as we begin to apply the sociological argument to the historical example and see whether it helps explain what happened in seventeenth century New England.

The first and most important theme has to do with the relationship between a community's boundaries and the kinds of deviation experienced. Every human community has its own special set of boundaries, its own unique identity, and so we may presume that every community also has its own characteristic styles of deviant behavior. Societies which place a high premium on ownership of property, for example, are likely to experience a greater volume of theft than those which do not, while societies which emphasize political orthodoxy are apt to discover and punish more sedition than their less touchy neighbors. This obvious parallel occurs for at least two reasons. In the first place, any community which feels jeopardized by a particular form of behavior will impose more severe sanctions against it and devote more time and energy to the task of rooting it out. At the same time, however, the very fact that a group expresses its concern about a given set of values often seems to draw a deviant response from certain of its members. There are people in any society who appear to "choose" a deviant style exactly *because* it offends an important value of the group—some of them because they have an inner need to challenge this value in a direct test, and some of them, as Merton has pointed out, because they clumsily violate a norm in their very eagerness to abide by it. In either of these events, the deviant and his more conventional counterpart live in much the same world of symbol and meaning, sharing a similar set of interests in the universe around them. The thief and his victim share a common respect for the value of property; the heretic and the inquisitor speak much the same language and are keyed to the same religious mysteries; the traitor and the patriot act in reference to the same political institutions, often use the same methods, and for that matter are sometimes the same person. Nor is this a trivial observation, for these pairs of adversaries are so well attuned to one another that they can and often do reverse roles with minor shifts in the historical climate. Joseph Conrad put the case very well in one of his novels when he described the policeman and the criminal as individuals "making countermoves in the same game": "Products of the same machine," he pointed out, "one classified as useful and the other as noxious, they take the machine for granted in different ways but with a seriousness essentially the same."

The deviant and the conformist, then, are creatures of the same culture, inventions of the same imagination. And thus it can happen that the most feared and most respected styles of behavior known to a particular age often seem to mirror one another—so accurately, in fact, that observers looking in from another point in time cannot always tell them apart. A twentieth-century American, for example, is supposed to understand that larceny and other forms of commercial activity are wholly different, standing "on opposite sides of the law." A seventeenth-century American, on the other hand, if he lived in New England, was supposed to understand that Congregationalism and Antinomianism were as far apart as God and the Devil. Yet if we were to examine the contrasts of this sort which have been drawn in varying periods of the past or are currently drawn in other cultures than our own, we would find many of them rather obscure. It takes a keen theological eye to see where the Puritans drew the line between orthodoxy and some of the more serious forms of heresy, and it is quite conceivable that any Puritan who found himself transported to the middle of the present century would find it difficult to understand some of the distinctions we make, say, between proper and improper sexual conduct. Or to use a more current example, many Soviet commentators in our own day do not see any real difference between the forms of enterprise which put some Americans at the head of corporations and others in prison, while we, in our turn, cannot easily distinguish among the various shades of opinion which have meant the difference between life and death in the Soviet Union. Thus variations in action and attitude which mean "worlds of difference" at one time in history may seem like so many split hairs when exposed to the hard light of another.

At the height of the witchcraft hysteria in Massachusetts, the sociologist in Cotton Mather began to notice that the witches who terrorized the countryside were really very similar to the honest men who prosecuted them:

> 'Tis very remarkable to see what an impious and impudent imitation of divine things is apishly affected by the Devil, in several of those matters, whereof the confessions of our witches and the afflictions of our sufferers have informed us. . . . The witches do say, that they form themselves much after the manner of Congregational churches; and that they have a baptism and a supper, and officers among them, abominably resembling those of our Lord. . . . What is their striking down with a fierce look? What is their making of the afflicted rise, with a touch of their hand? What is their transportation thro' the air? What is their travelling in spirit, while their body is cast into a trance? What is their causing of cattle to run mad and perish? What is their entering their names in a book? What is their coming together from all parts, at the sound of a trumpet? What is their appearing sometimes clothed with light or fire upon them? What is their covering of themselves and their instruments with invisibility? But a blasphemous imitation of certain things recorded about our Savior or His Prophets, or the saints of the Kingdom of God.

If deviation and conformity are so alike, it is not surprising that deviant behavior should seem to appear in a community at exactly those points where it is most feared. Men who fear witches soon find themselves surrounded by them; men who become jealous of private property soon encounter eager thieves. And if it is not always easy to know whether fear creates the deviance or deviance the fear, the affinity of the two has been a continuing course of wonder in human affairs. Observers of a later age may look back and understand that the witches and the magistrates were using the same cultural vocabulary and moving to the same cultural rhythms, but on the whole this secret is not known to the people of the time. To them, deviant behavior seems to come out of nowhere, an uninvited, perverse thrust at the very heart of the community. This feeling was caught nicely by one historian writing about deviance in the Bay colony:

> Here we note a very natural relation between the spirit of persecution and the spirit which obstinately and even wantonly or perversely provoked it. The fathers

were anxiously, we say morbidly and timidly, dreading lest their bold venture in the wilderness should be prostrated before it could strike root. . . . *Their troublers came precisely in the form and shape in which they apprehended them.* . . . As will soon appear, there was something extraordinary in the odd variety, the grotesque characteristics, and the specially irritating and exasperating course of that strange succession of men and women, of all sorts of odd opinions and notions, who presented themselves during a period of thirty years, seeming to have in common no other object than to grieve and exasperate the Puritan magistrates.

The magistrates may well have been surprised by the form and shape in which their persistent troublers appeared, but these were only the forms and shapes of Puritan life itself—the reflected image of those values which stood at the core of the Puritan consciousness. Indeed, as we shall later see, it was during these meetings between the magistrates and their wayward countrymen that the forms of American Puritanism moved into focus, developed their own special character, and became the identifying landmarks of the larger community. In the process of defining the nature of deviation, the settlers were also defining the boundaries of their new universe . . . .

The second implication of the introductory essay which will be pursued in this study has to do with the *volume* of deviant behavior found in social life. It is one of the arguments of the present study that the amount of deviation a community encounters is apt to remain fairly constant over time. To start at the beginning, it is a simple logistic fact that the number of deviancies which come to a community's attention are limited by the kinds of equipment it uses to detect and handle them, and to that extent the rate of deviation found in a community is at least in part a function of the size and complexity of its social control apparatus. A community's capacity for handling deviance, let us say, can be roughly estimated by counting its prison cells and hospital beds, its policemen and psychiatrists, its courts and clinics—and while this total cannot tell us anything important about the underlying psychological motives involved, it does say something about the manner in which the community views the problem. Most communities, it would seem, operate with the expectation that a relatively constant number of control agents is necessary to cope with a relatively constant number of offenders. The amount of men, money, and material assigned by society to "do something" about deviant behavior does not vary appreciably over time, and the implicit logic which governs the community's efforts to man a police force or maintain suitable facilities for the mentally ill seems to be that there is a fairly stable quota of trouble which should be anticipated.

In this sense, the agencies of control often seem to define their job as that of keeping deviance *within bounds* rather than that of obliterating it altogether. Many judges, for example, assume that severe punishments are a greater deterrent to crime than moderate ones, and so it is important to note that many of them are apt to impose harder penalties when crime seems to be on the increase and more lenient ones when it does not, almost as if the power of the bench were being used to keep the crime rate from getting out of hand.

Generally speaking, we invoke emergency measures when the volume of deviance threatens to grow beyond some level we have learned to consider "normal," but we do not react with the same alarm when the volume of deviance stays within those limits. As George Bernard Shaw once pointed out, a society completely intent on suppressing crime would punish every offender with all the severity it could manage—for the present system, with its careful attention to the formula that punishment should vary with the circum- stances of the crime, only seems to suggest that society can afford certain kinds of crime more readily than others. From this point of view, every society acts on the assumption that it possesses the machinery for curbing crime—the power to impose inhibiting punish- ments—yet that power is ordinarily used in such a way as to stabilize rather than eliminate the amount of crime in the social order.

The same tendency toward stabilization can be seen in the field of mental health, where the number of available hospital beds and outpatient hours exercise a strict control over the number of people who are or can be regarded as sick. If the size of a hospital's waiting list grows too long, the only practical strategy is to discharge its present occupants more rapidly; and conversely, if the waiting list diminishes to the point where the hospital confronts a loss of revenue or a shortage of patients for teaching purposes, local practi- tioners are urged to send more referrals. In moments of severe pressure, perhaps, physicians may sometimes discharge a patient about whom they have private doubts, but the statistics of mental health do not record these reservations and the community is not ordinarily aware of them. When the community tries to assess the size of its deviant population, then, it is usually measuring the capacity of its own social control apparatus and not the inclina- tions toward deviance found among its members.

The reason for drawing attention to this logistic problem is not simply to point out that the community has poor measuring instruments for surveying the size of its deviant prob- lem, but rather to suggest that the community develops its definition of deviance so that it encompasses a range of behavior roughly equivalent to the available space in its control apparatus—a kind of inverted Parkinson's law. That is, when the community calibrates its control machinery to handle a certain volume of deviant behavior, it tends to adjust its legal and psychiatric definitions of the problem in such a way that this volume is in fact real- ized. After all, every control agent and every control facility is "needed" by society. If the police should somehow learn to contain most of the crimes it now contends with, and if at the same time medical science should discover a cure for most of the mental disorders it now treats, it is still improbable that the existing control machinery would go unused. More likely, the agencies of control would turn their attention to other forms of behavior, even to the point of defining as deviant certain styles of conduct which were not regarded so earlier.

At any given time, then, the "worst" people in the community are considered its criminals, the "sickest" its patients, no matter how serious these conditions may appear according to some universal standard. In that sense, deviance can be defined as behavior which falls on the outer edge of the group's experience, whether the range of that experi- ence is wide or narrow. In his earlier paper on the subject, Durkheim used an instructive example:

Imagine a society of saints, a perfect cloister of exemplary individuals. Crimes, properly so called, will there be unknown; but faults which appear venial to the layman will create there the same scandal that the ordinary offense does in ordinary consciousness. If, then, this society has the power to judge and punish, it will define these acts as criminal and will treat them as such.

And much the same thing can be said about changes in the community as it moves from one period to another. If a community were able simply to lop off its most marginal people—banishing them to another part of the world, for instance, or executing them by the carload—it is unlikely that the volume of deviation in the community would really be reduced. Either new ranks of offenders would move into the vacuum in place of their departed fellows (as England discovered when it tried a policy of wholesale transportation to the colonies) or the agencies of control would focus on a new target area and develop an interest in the behavior taking place there.

According to this argument, then, we should expect to find that the amount of deviation experienced by a community will remain fairly stable over time . . . .

The third implication of the introductory essay which will command further attention has to do with the way a society handles its deviant members. As has been suggested before, deviant persons can be said to supply needed services to society by marking the outer limits of group experience and providing a point of contrast which gives the norm some scope and dimension. Yet it is important to keep in mind that every society deals with this resource differently: each has its own method for naming people to deviant positions and its own method for deploying them across the range of group space. For the moment we may call these methods "deployment patterns" to indicate that they regulate the flow of deviant persons to and from the boundaries of the group and in this way govern the amount of deviation in the structure at any given time.

It cannot be the purpose of this study to make an inventory of the various deployment patterns known in different parts of the world, but we might note three which seem to reappear frequently in ethnological literature. First, there are societies which appoint special days or occasions as periods of general license, during which members of the group are permitted (if not expected) to violate rules they have observed during the preceding season and will observe again during the coming season. Second, there are societies in which deviance is regarded as a "natural" form of behavior for adolescents and young people generally, although individuals who take advantage of this exemption are expected to change their ways the moment they move through defined ceremonies into adulthood. Finally, there are societies which have special clubs or orders whose stated business it is to infringe the ordinary rules of the group in some prescribed manner.

Now it might be argued that in each of these cases the resulting behavior is entirely "expected" and therefore the product of normative structuring: after all, the tribesman who curses the gods and eats forbidden food during a festival is only responding to a new set of holiday rules, the youth who joins street riots or profanes a sacred ceremony has a kind of permit from his elders to behave in that fashion, and the "contrary" who obstinately refuses to follow the ordinary conventions of his group is only doing what everyone expects of him anyway. Clearly, the sanctions governing these departures from the norm suggest that we are speaking of "deviance" in a rather special sense. Yet it is one of the implications of this study that deviant behavior in our own culture may be more tightly patterned than we ordinarily think, and while it may seem absurd to argue that people who act deviantly in our courts and clinics are responding to "rules" in much the same sense as a participant in a festival, it is still instructive to note the many parallels between these deployment patterns and the mechanisms at work in our own social order. All of these patterns allow people of the group an intimate experience of the line separating morality from immorality; all of them exercise strict control over the volume of deviance found in the system at any given time—not because they prevent it from occurring, to be sure, but because they can schedule its appearance according to some cultural timetable. When a group can halt a general period of license by declaring the end of a festival, or transform rioting youths into responsible adults by the use of a single rite of passage, it is demonstrating a remarkable degree of control. And perhaps we can look for similar mechanisms in other cultures where the "rules" governing deviant behavior are not so apparent.

Notes and Questions

1. Assume you are the local prosecutor in the jurisdiction described in *The Lottery*. What crimes, if any, would you consider prosecuting?

2. Do the people in *The Lottery* seem like criminals? Should that matter?

3. Does it make sense to call something a "crime" if virtually everyone is committing it? Why might that be problematic?

4. Did the villagers in *The Lottery* think there were good reasons for what they did to Tessie? If so, what were those reasons? If you had been there, what would you have thought?

5. Tessie complains several times about the "fairness" of the procedures by which she was selected. Was the lottery fair?

6. Tessie also complains at the end that the lottery was not "right." Is that a different sort of claim?

7. What were the main factual and legal arguments against the "witches"? Could you make any of those arguments in a courtroom today? Why or why not?

8. What crimes did Captain Slade commit? Should they have been considered capital offenses? What would the vigilantes say?

9. What is the Mountain Code, and what are its main tenets?

10. Prof. Thomas J. Dimsdale, author of *The Vigilantes of Montana,* was

> an educated Englishman and one-time Oxonian who arrived in Virginia City via Canada during the summer of 1863. He suffered from consumption and had come to the mountains seeking health. During the winter of 1863-64 he taught a private school, tuition $2.00 a week for each pupil, and also conducted a singing school. A man of culture and refinement, he drew to himself all that was best of the society of that time in Virginia City.

E. DeGolyer, Introduction, *The Vigilantes of Montana* ix (new ed. 1953). The original edition of *The Vigilantes of Montana* appeared in 1866. It was the first book to be published in Montana.

Suggestions For Further Reading

Kai T. Erikson, Wayward Puritans: A Study in the Sociology of Deviance (1966)

Gilbert Geis & Ivan Bunn, A Trial of Witches: A Seventeenth-Century Witchcraft Prosecution (1997)

Will Kymlicka, Community, in A Companion to Contemporary Political Philosophy (Robert E. Goodin & Philip Pettit eds. 1993)

Sir Henry Maine, Ancient Law, ch. 5 (1861)

Ferdinand Tönnies, Community and Society (Charles P. Loomis trans. 1988)

Chapter 2
From Community to Society

The Tragedy of the Commons[*]
Garrett Hardin

At the end of a thoughtful article on the future of nuclear war, Wiesner and York concluded that: "Both sides in the arms race are . . . confronted by the dilemma of steadily increasing military power and steadily decreasing national security. *It is our considered professional judgment that this dilemma has no technical solution.* If the great powers continue to look for solutions in the area of science and technology only, the result will be to worsen the situation."

I would like to focus your attention not on the subject of the article (national security in a nuclear world) but on the kind of conclusion they reached, namely that there is no technical solution to the problem. An implicit and almost universal assumption of discussions published in professional and semipopular scientific journals is that the problem under discussion has a technical solution. A technical solution may be defined as one that requires a change only in the techniques of the natural sciences, demanding little or nothing in the way of change in human values or ideas of morality.

In our day (though not in earlier times) technical solutions are always welcome. Because of previous failures in prophecy, it takes courage to assert that a desired technical solution is not possible. Wiesner and York exhibited this courage; publishing in a science journal, they insisted that the solution to the problem was not to be found in the natural sciences. They cautiously qualified their statement with the phrase, "It is our considered professional judgment. . . ." Whether they were right or not is not the concern of the present article. Rather, the concern here is with the important concept of a class of human problems which can be called "no technical solution problems," and, more specifically, with the identification and discussion of one of these.

It is easy to show that the class is not a null class. Recall the game of tick-tack-toe. Consider the problem, "How can I win the game of tick-tack-toe?" It is well known that I cannot, if I assume (in keeping with the conventions of game theory) that my opponent understands the game perfectly. Put another way, there is no "technical solution" to the problem. I can win only by giving a radical meaning to the word "win." I can hit my opponent over the head; or I can drug him; or I can falsify the records. Every way in which I

---

[*] Reprinted with permission from Garrett Hardin, The Tragedy of the Commons, Science, Volume 162 (December 1968), pages 1243-1248. Copyright 1968 American Association for the Advancement of Science.

"win" involves, in some sense, an abandonment of the game, as we intuitively understand it. (I can also, of course, openly abandon the game—refuse to play it. This is what most adults do.)

The class of "No technical solution problems" has members. My thesis is that the "population problem," as conventionally conceived, is a member of this class. How it is conventionally conceived needs some comment. It is fair to say that most people who anguish over the population problem are trying to find a way to avoid the evils of overpopulation without relinquishing any of the privileges they now enjoy. They think that farming the seas or developing new strains of wheat will solve the problem—technologically. I try to show here that the solution they seek cannot be found. The population problem cannot be solved in a technical way, any more than can the problem of winning the game of tick-tack-toe.

What Shall We Maximize?

Population, as Malthus said, naturally tends to grow "geometrically," or, as we would now say, exponentially. In a finite world this means that the per capita share of the world's goods must steadily decrease. Is ours a finite world?

A fair defense can be put forward for the view that the world is infinite; or that we do not know that it is not. But, in terms of the practical problems that we must face in the next few generations with the foreseeable technology, it is clear that we will greatly increase human misery if we do not, during the immediate future, assume that the world available to the terrestrial human population is finite. "Space" is no escape.

A finite world can support only a finite population; therefore, population growth must eventually equal zero. (The case of perpetual wide fluctuations above and below zero is a trivial variant that need not be discussed.) When this condition is met, what will be the situation of mankind? Specifically, can Bentham's goal of "the greatest good for the greatest number" be realized?

No—for two reasons, each sufficient by itself. The first is a theoretical one. It is not mathematically possible to maximize for two (or more) variables at the same time. This was clearly stated by von Neumann and Morgenstern, but the principle is implicit in the theory of partial differential equations, dating back at least to D'Alembert (1717-1783).

The second reason springs directly from biological facts. To live, any organism must have a source of energy (for example, food). This energy is utilized for two purposes: mere maintenance and work. For man, maintenance of life requires about 1600 kilocalories a day ("maintenance calories"). Anything that he does over and above merely staying alive will be defined as work, and is supported by "work calories" which he takes in. Work calories are used not only for what we call work in common speech; they are also required for all forms of enjoyment, from swimming and automobile racing to playing music and writing poetry. If our goal is to maximize population it is obvious what we must do: We must make the work calories per person approach as close to zero as possible. No gourmet meals, no vacations, no sports, no music, no literature, no art. . . . I think that everyone will grant, without argument or proof, that maximizing population does not maximize goods. Bentham's goal is impossible.

In reaching this conclusion I have made the usual assumption that it is the acquisition of energy that is the problem. The appearance of atomic energy has led some to question this assumption. However, given an infinite source of energy, population growth still produces an inescapable problem. The problem of the acquisition of energy is replaced by the problem of its dissipation, as J.H. Fremlin has so wittily shown. The arithmetic signs in the analysis are, as it were, reversed; but Bentham's goal is still unobtainable.

The optimum population is, then, less than the maximum. The difficulty of defining the optimum is enormous; so far as I know, no one has seriously tackled this problem. Reaching an acceptable and stable solution will surely require more than one generation of hard analytical work—and much persuasion.

We want the maximum good per person; but what is good? To one person it is wilderness, to another it is ski lodges for thousands. To one it is estuaries to nourish ducks for hunters to shoot; to another it is factory land. Comparing one good with another is, we usually say, impossible because goods are incommensurable. Incommensurables cannot be compared.

Theoretically this may be true; but in real life incommensurables *are* commensurable. Only a criterion of judgment and a system of weighting are needed. In nature the criterion is survival. Is it better for a species to be small and hideable, or large and powerful? Natural selection commensurates the incommensurables. The compromise achieved depends on a natural weighting of the values of the variables.

Man must imitate this process. There is no doubt that in fact he already does, but unconsciously. It is when the hidden decisions are made explicit that the arguments begin. The problem for the years ahead is to work out an acceptable theory of weighting. Synergistic effects, nonlinear variation, and difficulties in discounting the future make the intellectual problem difficult, but not (in principle) insoluble.

Has any cultural group solved this practical problem at the present time, even on an intuitive level? One simple fact proves that none has: there is no prosperous population in the world today that has, and has had for some time, a growth rate of zero. Any people that has intuitively identified its optimum point will soon reach it, after which its growth rate becomes and remains zero.

Of course, a positive growth rate might be taken as evidence that a population is below its optimum. However, by any reasonable standards, the most rapidly growing populations on earth today are (in general) the most miserable. This association (which need not be invariable) casts doubt on the optimistic assumption that the positive growth rate of a population is evidence that it has yet to reach its optimum.

We can make little progress in working toward optimum population size until we explicitly exorcize the spirit of Adam Smith in the field of practical demography. In economic affairs, *The Wealth of Nations* (1776) popularized the "invisible hand," the idea that an individual who "intends only his own gain," is, as it were, "led by an invisible hand to promote . . . the public interest." Adam Smith did not assert that this was invariably true, and perhaps neither did any of his followers. But he contributed to a dominant tendency of thought that has ever since interfered with positive action based on rational analysis, namely, the tendency to assume that decisions reached individually will, in fact, be the best decisions for an entire society. If this assumption is correct it justifies the continuance of our present policy of laissez-faire in reproduction. If it is correct we can assume that men will control their individual fecundity so as to produce the optimum population. If the assumption is not correct, we need to reexamine our individual freedoms to see which ones are defensible.

Tragedy of Freedom in a Commons

The rebuttal to the invisible hand in population control is to be found in a scenario first sketched in a little-known pamphlet in 1833 by a mathematical amateur named William Forster Lloyd (1794-1852). We may well call it "the tragedy of the commons," using the word "tragedy" as the philosopher Whitehead used it: "The essence of dramatic tragedy is not unhappiness. It resides in the solemnity of the remorseless working of things." He then goes on to say, "This inevitableness of destiny can only be illustrated in terms of human life by incidents which in fact involve unhappiness. For it is only by them that the futility of escape can be made evident in the drama."

The tragedy of the commons develops in this way. Picture a pasture open to all. It is to be expected that each herdsman will try to keep as many cattle as possible on the commons. Such an arrangement may work reasonably satisfactorily for centuries because tribal wars, poaching, and disease keep the numbers of both man and beast well below the carrying capacity of the land. Finally, however, comes the day of reckoning, that is, the day when the long-desired goal of social stability becomes a reality. At this point, the inherent logic of the commons remorselessly generates tragedy.

As a rational being, each herdsman seeks to maximize his gain. Explicitly or implicitly, more or less consciously, he asks, "What is the utility *to me* of adding one more animal to my herd?" This utility has one negative and one positive component.

1) The positive component is a function of the increment of one animal. Since the herdsman receives all the proceeds from the sale of the additional animal, the positive utility is nearly +1.

2) The negative component is a function of the additional overgrazing created by one more animal. Since, however, the effects of overgrazing are shared by all the herdsmen, the negative utility for any particular decision-making herdsman is only a fraction of -1.

Adding together the component partial utilities, the rational herdsman concludes that the only sensible course for him to pursue is to add another animal to his herd. And another; and another. . . . But this is the conclusion reached by each and every rational herdsman sharing a commons. Therein is the tragedy. Each man is locked into a system that compels him to increase his herd without limit—in a world that is limited. Ruin is the destination toward which all men rush, each pursuing his own best interest in a society that believes in the freedom of the commons. Freedom in a commons brings ruin to all.

Some would say that this is a platitude. Would that it were! In a sense, it was learned thousands of years ago, but natural selection favors the forces of psychological denial. The individual benefits as an individual from his ability to deny the truth even though society as a whole, of which he is a part, suffers. Education can counteract the natural tendency to do the wrong thing, but the inexorable succession of generations requires that the basis for this knowledge be constantly refreshed.

A simple incident that occurred a few years ago in Leominster, Massachusetts, shows how perishable the knowledge is. During the Christmas shopping season the parking meters downtown were covered with plastic bags that bore tags reading: "Do not open until after Christmas. Free parking courtesy of the mayor and city council." In other words, facing the prospect of an increased demand for already scarce space, the city fathers reinstituted the system of the commons. (Cynically, we suspect that they gained more votes than they lost by this retrogressive act.)

In an approximate way, the logic of the commons has been understood for a long time, perhaps since the discovery of agriculture or the invention of private property in real estate. But it is understood mostly only in special cases which are not sufficiently generalized. Even at this late date, cattlemen leasing national land on the western ranges demonstrate no more than an ambivalent understanding, in constantly pressuring federal authorities to increase the head count to the point where overgrazing produces erosion and weed-dominance. Likewise, the oceans of the world continue to suffer from the survival of the philosophy of the commons. Maritime nations still respond automatically to the shibboleth of the "freedom of the seas." Professing to believe in the "inexhaustible resources of the oceans," they bring species after species of fish and whales closer to extinction.

The National Parks present another instance of the working out of the tragedy of the commons. At present, they are open to all, without limit. The parks themselves are limited in extent—there is only one Yosemite Valley—whereas population seems to grow without limit. The values that visitors seek in the parks are steadily eroded. Plainly, we must soon cease to treat the parks as commons or they will be of no value to anyone.

What shall we do? We have several options. We might sell them off as private property. We might keep them as public property, but allocate the right to enter them. The allocation might be on the basis of wealth, by the use of an auction system. It might be on the basis of merit, as defined by some agreed-upon standards. It might be by lottery. Or it might be on a first-come, first-served basis, administered to long queues. These, I think, are all the reasonable possibilities. They are all objectionable. But we must choose—or acquiesce in the destruction of the commons that we call our National Parks.

Pollution

In a reverse way, the tragedy of the commons reappears in problems of pollution. Here it is not a question of taking something out of the commons, but of putting something in—sewage, or chemical, radioactive, and heat wastes into water; noxious and dangerous fumes into the air; and distracting and unpleasant advertising signs into the line of sight. The calculations of utility are much the same as before. The rational man finds that his share of the cost of the wastes he discharges into the commons is less than the cost of purifying his wastes before releasing them. Since this is true for everyone, we are locked into a system of "fouling our own nest," so long as we behave only as independent, rational, free-enterprisers.

The tragedy of the commons as a food basket is averted by private property, or something formally like it. But the air and waters surrounding us cannot readily be fenced, and so the tragedy of the commons as a cesspool must be prevented by different means, by coercive laws or taxing devices that make it cheaper for the polluter to treat his pollutants than to discharge them untreated. We have not progressed as far with the solution of this problem as we have with the first. Indeed, our particular concept of private property, which deters us from exhausting the positive resources of the earth, favors pollution. The owner of a factory on the bank of a stream—whose property extends to the middle of the stream, often has difficulty seeing why it is not his natural right to muddy the waters flowing past his door. The law, always behind the times, requires elaborate stitching and fitting to adapt it to this newly perceived aspect of the commons.

The pollution problem is a consequence of population. It did not much matter how a lonely American frontiersman disposed of his waste. "Flowing water purifies itself every 10 miles," my grandfather used to say, and the myth was near enough to the truth when he was a boy, for there were not too many people. But as population became denser, the natural chemical and biological recycling processes became overloaded, calling for a redefinition of property rights.

How To Legislate Temperance?

Analysis of the pollution problem as a function of population density uncovers a not generally recognized principle of morality, namely: *the morality of an act is a function of the state of the system at the time it is performed.* Using the commons as a cesspool does not harm the general public under frontier conditions, because there is no public; the same behavior in a metropolis is unbearable. A hundred and fifty years ago a plainsman could kill an American bison, cut out only the tongue for his dinner, and discard the rest of the animal. He was not in any important sense being wasteful. Today, with only a few thousand bison left, we would be appalled at such behavior.

In passing, it is worth noting that the morality of an act cannot be determined from a photograph. One does not know whether a man killing an elephant or setting fire to the grassland is harming others until one knows the total system in which his act appears. "One picture is worth a thousand words," said an ancient Chinese; but it may take 10,000 words to validate it. It is as tempting to ecologists as it is to reformers in general to try to persuade others by way of the photographic shortcut. But the essense of an argument cannot be photographed: it must be presented rationally—in words.

That morality is system-sensitive escaped the attention of most codifiers of ethics in the past. "Thou shalt not . . ." is the form of traditional ethical directives which make no allowance for particular circumstances. The laws of our society follow the pattern of ancient ethics, and therefore are poorly suited to governing a complex, crowded, changeable world. Our epicyclic solution is to augment statutory law with administrative law. Since it is practically impossible to spell out all the conditions under which it is safe to burn trash in the back yard or to run an automobile without smog-control, by law we delegate the details to bureaus. The result is administrative law, which is rightly feared for an ancient reason—*Quis custodiet ipsos custodes?*—"Who shall watch the watchers themselves?" John Adams said that we must have "a government of laws and not men." Bureau administrators, trying to evaluate the morality of acts in the total system, are singularly liable to corruption, producing a government by men, not laws.

Prohibition is easy to legislate (though not necessarily to enforce); but how do we legislate temperance? Experience indicates that it can be accomplished best through the mediation of administrative law. We limit possibilities unnecessarily if we suppose that the sentiment of *Quis custodiet* denies us the use of administrative law. We should rather retain the phrase as a perpetual reminder of fearful dangers we cannot avoid. The great challenge facing us now is to invent the corrective feedbacks that are needed to keep custodians honest. We must find ways to legitimate the needed authority of both the custodians and the corrective feedbacks.

Freedom To Breed Is Intolerable

The tragedy of the commons is involved in population problems in another way. In a world governed solely by the principle of "dog eat dog"—if indeed there ever was such a world—how many children a family had would not be a matter of public concern. Parents who bred too exuberantly would leave fewer descendants, not more, because they would be unable to care adequately for their children. David Lack and others have found that such a negative feedback demonstrably controls the fecundity of birds. But men are not birds, and have not acted like them for millenniums, at least.

If each human family were dependent only on its own resources; *if* the children of improvident parents starved to death; *if,* thus, overbreeding brought its own "punishment" to the germ line—*then* there would be no public interest in controlling the breeding of families. But our society is deeply committed to the welfare state, and hence is confronted with another aspect of the tragedy of the commons.

In a welfare state, how shall we deal with the family, the religion, the race, or the class (or indeed any distinguishable and cohesive group) that adopts overbreeding as a policy to secure its own aggrandizement? To couple the concept of freedom to breed with the belief that everyone born has an equal right to the commons is to lock the world into a tragic course of action.

Unfortunately this is just the course of action that is being pursued by the United Nations. In late 1967, some 30 nations agreed to the following:

> The Universal Declaration of Human Rights describes the family as the natural and fundamental unit of society. It follows that any choice and decision with regard to the size of the family must irrevocably rest with the family itself, and cannot be made by anyone else.

It is painful to have to deny categorically the validity of this right; denying it, one feels as uncomfortable as a resident of Salem, Massachusetts, who denied the reality of witches in the 17th century. At the present time, in liberal quarters, something like a taboo acts to inhibit criticism of the United Nations. There is a feeling that the United Nations is "our last and best hope," that we shouldn't find fault with it; we shouldn't play into the hands of archconservatives. However, let us not forget what Robert Louis Stevenson said: "The truth that is suppressed by friends is the readiest weapon of the enemy." If we love the truth, we must openly deny the validity of the Universal Declaration of Human Rights, even though it is promoted by the United Nations. We should also join with Kingsley Davis in attempting to get Planned Parenthood-World Population to see the error of its ways in embracing the same tragic ideal.

Conscience Is Self-Eliminating

It is a mistake to think that we can control the breeding of mankind in the long run by an appeal to conscience. Charles Galton Darwin made this point when he spoke on the centennial of the publication of his grandfather's great book. The argument is straightforward and Darwinian.

People vary. Confronted with appeals to limit breeding, some people will undoubtedly respond to the plea more than others. Those who have more children will produce a larger fraction of the next generation than those with more susceptible consciences. The difference will be accentuated, generation by generation.

In C.G. Darwin's words: "It may well be that it would take hundreds of generations for the progenitive instinct to develop in this way, but if it should do so, nature would have taken her revenge, and the variety *Homo contracipiens* would become extinct and would be replaced by the variety *Homo progenitivus*."

The argument assumes that conscience or the desire for children (no matter which) is hereditary—but hereditary only in the most general formal sense. The result will be the same whether the attitude is transmitted through germ cells, or exosomatically, to use A.J. Lotka's term. (If one denies the latter possibility as well as the former, then what's the point of education?) The argument has here been stated in the context of the population problem, but it applies equally well to any instance in which society appeals to an individual exploiting a commons to restrain himself for the general good—by means of his conscience. To make such an appeal is to set up a selective system that works toward the elimination of conscience from the race.

Pathogenic Effects of Conscience

The long-term disadvantage of an appeal to conscience should be enough to condemn it; but has serious short-term disadvantages as well. If we ask a man who is exploiting a commons to desist "in the name of conscience," what are we saying to him? What does he hear?—not only at the moment but also in the wee small hours of the night when, half asleep, he remembers not merely the words we used but also the nonverbal communication cues we gave him unawares? Sooner or later, consciously or subconsciously, he senses that he has received two communications, and that they are contradictory: (i) (intended communication) "If you don't do as we ask, we will openly condemn you for not acting like a responsible citizen"; (ii) (the unintended communication) "If you *do* behave as we ask, we will secretly condemn you for a simpleton who can be shamed into standing aside while the rest of us exploit the commons."

Everyman then is caught in what Bateson has called a "double bind." Bateson and his co-workers have made a plausible case for viewing the double bind as an important causative factor in the genesis of schizophrenia. The double bind may not always be so damaging, but it always endangers the mental health of anyone to whom it is applied. "A bad conscience," said Nietzsche, "is a kind of illness."

To conjure up a conscience in others is tempting to anyone who wishes to extend his control beyond the legal limits. Leaders at the highest level succumb to this temptation. Has any President during the past generation failed to call on labor unions to moderate voluntarily their demands for higher wages, or to steel companies to honor voluntary guidelines on prices? I can recall none. The rhetoric used on such occasions is designed to produce feelings of guilt in noncooperators.

For centuries it was assumed without proof that guilt was a valuable, perhaps even an indispensable, ingredient of the civilized life. Now, in this post-Freudian world, we doubt it.

Paul Goodman speaks from the modern point of view when he says: "No good has ever come from feeling guilty, neither intelligence, policy, nor compassion. The guilty do not pay attention to the object but only to themselves, and not even to their own interests, which might make sense, but to their anxieties."

One does not have to be a professional psychiatrist to see the consequences of anxiety. We in the Western world are just emerging from a dreadful two-centuries-long Dark Ages of Eros that was sustained partly by prohibition laws, but perhaps more effectively by the anxiety-generating mechanism of education. Alex Comfort has told the story well in *The Anxiety Makers;* it is not a pretty one.

Since proof is difficult, we may even concede that the results of anxiety may sometimes, from certain points of view, be desirable. The larger question we should ask is whether, as a matter of policy, we should ever encourage the use of a technique the tendency (if not the intention) of which is psychologically pathogenic. We hear much talk these days of responsible parenthood; the coupled words are incorporated into the titles of some organizations devoted to birth control. Some people have proposed massive propaganda campaigns to instill responsibility into the nation's (or the world's) breeders. But what is the meaning of the word responsibility in this context? Is it not merely a synonym for the word conscience? When we use the word responsibility in the absence of substantial sanctions are we not trying to browbeat a free man in a commons into acting against his own interest? Responsibility is a verbal counterfeit for a substantial *quid pro quo*. It is an attempt to get something for nothing.

If the word responsibility is to be used at all, I suggest that it be in the sense Charles Frankel uses it. "Responsibility," says this philosopher, "is the product of definite social arrangements." Notice that Frankel calls for social arrangements—not propaganda.

Mutual Coercion, Mutually Agreed upon

The social arrangements that produce responsibility are arrangements that create coercion, of some sort. Consider bank-robbing. The man who takes money from a bank acts as if the bank were a commons. How do we prevent such action? Certainly not by trying to control his behavior solely by a verbal appeal to his sense of responsibility. Rather than rely on propaganda we follow Frankel's lead and insist that a bank is not a commons; we seek the definite social arrangements that will keep it from becoming a commons. That we thereby infringe on the freedom of would-be robbers we neither deny nor regret.

The morality of bank-robbing is particularly easy to understand because we accept complete prohibition of this activity. We are willing to say "Thou shalt not rob banks," without providing for exceptions. But temperance also can be created by coercion. Taxing is a good coercive device. To keep downtown shoppers temperate in their use of parking space we introduce parking meters for short periods, and traffic fines for longer ones. We need not actually forbid a citizen to park as long as he wants to; we need merely make it increasingly expensive for him to do so. Not prohibition, but carefully biased options are what we offer him. A Madison Avenue man might call this persuasion; I prefer the greater candor of the word coercion.

Coercion is a dirty word to most liberals now, but it need not forever be so. As with the four-letter words, its dirtiness can be cleansed away by exposure to the light, by saying it over and over without apology or embarrassment. To many, the word coercion implies arbitrary decisions of distant and irresponsible bureaucrats; but this is not a necessary part of its meaning. The only kind of coercion I recommend is mutual coercion, mutually agreed upon by the majority of the people affected.

To say that we mutually agree to coercion is not to say that we are required to enjoy it, or even to pretend we enjoy it. Who enjoys taxes? We all grumble about them. But we accept compulsory taxes because we recognize that voluntary taxes would favor the conscienceless. We institute and (grumblingly) support taxes and other coercive devices to escape the horror of the commons.

An alternative to the commons need not be perfectly just to be preferable. With real estate and other material goods, the alternative we have chosen is the institution of private property coupled with legal inheritance. Is this system perfectly just? As a genetically trained biologist I deny that it is. It seems to me that, if there are to be differences in individual inheritance, legal possession should be perfectly correlated with biological inheritance—that those who are biologically more fit to be the custodians of property and power should legally inherit more. But genetic recombination continually makes a mockery of the doctrine of "like father, like son" implicit in our laws of legal inheritance. An idiot can inherit millions, and a trust fund can keep his estate intact. We must admit that our legal system of private property plus inheritance is unjust—but we put up with it because we are not convinced, at the moment, that anyone has invented a better system. The alternative of the commons is too horrifying to contemplate. Injustice is preferable to total ruin.

It is one of the peculiarities of the warfare between reform and the status quo that it is thoughtlessly governed by a double standard. Whenever a reform measure is proposed it is often defeated when its opponents triumphantly discover a flaw in it. As Kingsley Davis has pointed out, worshippers of the status quo sometimes imply that no reform is possible without unanimous agreement, an implication contrary to historical fact. As nearly as I can make out, automatic rejection of proposed reforms is based on one of two unconscious assumptions: (i) that the status quo is perfect; or (ii) that the choice we face is between reform and no action; if the proposed reform is imperfect, we presumably should take no action at all, while we wait for a perfect proposal.

But we can never do nothing. That which we have done for thousands of years is also action. It also produces evils. Once we are aware that the status quo is action, we can then compare its discoverable advantages and disadvantages with the predicted advantages and disadvantages of the proposed reform, discounting as best we can for our lack of experience. On the basis of such a comparison, we can make a rational decision which will not involve the unworkable assumption that only perfect systems are tolerable.

Recognition of Necessity

Perhaps the simplest summary of this analysis of man's population problems is this: the commons, if justifiable at all, is justifiable only under conditions of low-population density. As the human population has increased, the commons has had to be abandoned in one aspect after another.

First we abandoned the commons in food gathering, enclosing farm land and restricting pastures and hunting and fishing areas. These restrictions are still not complete throughout the world.

Somewhat later we saw that the commons as a place for waste disposal would also have to be abandoned. Restrictions on the disposal of domestic sewage are widely accepted in the Western world; we are still struggling to close the commons to pollution by automobiles, factories, insecticide sprayers, fertilizing operations, and atomic energy installations.

In a still more embryonic state is our recognition of the evils of the commons in matters of pleasure. There is almost no restriction on the propagation of sound waves in the public medium. The shopping public is assaulted with mindless music, without its consent. Our government is paying out billions of dollars to create supersonic transport which will disturb 50,000 people for every one person who is whisked from coast to coast 3 hours faster. Advertisers muddy the airwaves of radio and television and pollute the view of travelers. We are a long way from outlawing the commons in matters of pleasure. Is this because our Puritan inheritance makes us view pleasure as something of a sin, and pain (that is, the pollution of advertising) as the sign of virtue?

Every new enclosure of the commons involves the infringement of somebody's personal liberty. Infringements made in the distant past are accepted because no contemporary complains of a loss. It is the newly proposed infringements that we vigorously oppose; cries of "rights" and "freedom" fill the air. But what does "freedom" mean? When men mutually agreed to pass laws against robbing, mankind became more free, not less so. Individuals locked into the logic of the commons are free only to bring on universal ruin; once they see the necessity of mutual coercion, they become free to pursue other goals. I believe it was Hegel who said, "Freedom is the recognition of necessity."

The most important aspect of necessity that we must now recognize, is the necessity of abandoning the commons in breeding. No technical solution can rescue us from the misery of overpopulation. Freedom to breed will bring ruin to all. At the moment, to avoid hard decisions many of us are tempted to propagandize for conscience and responsible parenthood. The temptation must be resisted, because an appeal to independently acting consciences selects for the disappearance of all conscience in the long run, and an increase in anxiety in the short.

The only way we can preserve and nurture other and more precious freedoms is by relinquishing the freedom to breed, and that very soon. "Freedom is the recognition of necessity"—and it is the role of education to reveal to all the necessity of abandoning the freedom to breed. Only so, can we put an end to this aspect of the tragedy of the commons.

The Federalist No. 10
(James Madison)

Among the numerous advantages promised by a well constructed Union, none deserves to be more accurately developed than its tendency to break and control the violence of faction. . . .

By a faction, I understand a number of citizens, whether amounting to a majority or a minority of the whole, who are united and actuated by some common impulse of passion, or of interest, adverse to the rights of other citizens, or to the permanent and aggregate interests of the community.

There are two methods of curing the mischiefs of faction: the one, by removing its causes; the other, by controlling its effects.

There are again two methods of removing the causes of faction: the one, by destroying the liberty which is essential to its existence; the other, by giving to every citizen the same opinions, the same passions, and the same interests.

It could never be more truly said than of the first remedy, that it was worse than the disease. Liberty is to faction what air is to fire, an aliment without which it instantly expires. But it could not be less folly to abolish liberty, which is essential to political life, because it nourishes faction, than it would be to wish the annihilation of air, which is essential to animal life, because it imparts to fire its destructive agency.

The second expedient is as impracticable as the first would be unwise. As long as the reason of man continues fallible, and he is at liberty to exercise it, different opinions will be formed. As long as the connection subsists between his reason and his self-love, his opinions and his passions will have a reciprocal influence on each other; and the former will be objects to which the latter will attach themselves. The diversity in the faculties of men, from which the rights of property originate, is not less an insuperable obstacle to a uniformity of interests. The protection of these faculties is the first object of government. From the protection of different and unequal faculties of acquiring property, the possession of different degrees and kinds of property immediately results; and from the influence of these on the sentiments and views of the respective proprietors, ensues a division of the society into different interests and parties.

The latent causes of faction are thus sown in the nature of man; and we see them everywhere brought into different degrees of activity, according to the different circumstances of civil society. A zeal for different opinions concerning religion, concerning government, and many other points, as well of speculation as of practice; an attachment to different leaders ambitiously contending for pre-eminence and power; or to persons of other descriptions whose fortunes have been interesting to the human passions, have, in turn, divided mankind into parties, inflamed them with mutual animosity, and rendered them much more disposed to vex and oppress each other than to co-operate for their common good. So strong is this propensity of mankind to fall into mutual animosities, that where no substantial occasion presents itself, the most frivolous and fanciful distinctions have been sufficient to kindle their unfriendly passions and excite their most violent conflicts. But the most common and durable source of factions has been the various and unequal distribution of property. Those who hold and those who are without property have ever formed distinct interests in society. Those who are creditors, and those who are debtors, fall under a like discrimination. A landed interest, a manufacturing interest, a mercantile interest, a moneyed interest, with many lesser interests, grow up of necessity in civilized nations, and divide them into different classes, actuated by different sentiments and views. The regulation of these various and interfering interests forms the principal task of modern legislation, and involves the spirit of party and faction in the necessary and ordinary operations of the government.

No man is allowed to be a judge in his own cause, because his interest would certainly bias his judgment, and, not improbably, corrupt his integrity. With equal, nay with greater reason, a body of men are unfit to be both judges and parties at the same time; yet what are many of the most important acts of legislation, but so many judicial determinations, not indeed concerning the rights of single persons, but concerning the rights of large bodies of citizens? And what are the different classes of legislators but advocates and parties to the causes which they determine? Is a law proposed concerning private debts? It is a question to which the creditors are parties on one side and the debtors on the other. Justice ought to hold the balance between them. Yet the parties are, and must be, themselves the judges; and the most numerous party, or, in other words, the most powerful faction must be expected to prevail. Shall domestic manufactures be encouraged, and in what degree, by restrictions on foreign manufactures? are questions which would be differently decided by the landed and the manufacturing classes, and probably by neither with a sole regard to justice and the public good. The apportionment of taxes on the various descriptions of property is an act which seems to require the most exact impartiality; yet there is, perhaps, no legislative act in which greater opportunity and temptation are given to a predominant party to trample on the rules of justice. Every shilling with which they overburden the inferior number, is a shilling saved to their own pockets.

It is in vain to say that enlightened statesmen will be able to adjust these clashing interests, and render them all subservient to the public good. Enlightened statesmen will not always be at the helm. Nor, in many cases, can such an adjustment be made at all without taking into view indirect and remote considerations, which will rarely prevail over the immediate interest which one party may find in disregarding the rights of another or the good of the whole.

The inference to which we are brought is, that the *CAUSES* of faction cannot be removed, and that relief is only to be sought in the means of controlling its *EFFECTS*.

If a faction consists of less than a majority, relief is supplied by the republican principle, which enables the majority to defeat its sinister views by regular vote. It may clog the administration, it may convulse the society; but it will be unable to execute and mask its violence under the forms of the Constitution. When a majority is included in a faction, the form of popular government, on the other hand, enables it to sacrifice to its ruling passion or interest both the public good and the rights of other citizens. To secure the public good and private rights against the danger of such a faction, and at the same time to preserve the spirit and the form of popular government, is then the great object to which our inquiries are directed. Let me add that it is the great desideratum by which this form of government can be rescued from the opprobrium under which it has so long labored, and be recommended to the esteem and adoption of mankind.

By what means is this object attainable? Evidently by one of two only. Either the existence of the same passion or interest in a majority at the same time must be prevented, or the majority, having such coexistent passion or interest, must be rendered, by their number and local situation, unable to concert and carry into effect schemes of oppression. If the impulse and the opportunity be suffered to coincide, we well know that neither moral nor religious motives can be relied on as an adequate control. They are not found to be such on the injustice and violence of individuals, and lose their efficacy in proportion to the number combined together, that is, in proportion as their efficacy becomes needful.

From this view of the subject it may be concluded that a pure democracy, by which I mean a society consisting of a small number of citizens, who assemble and administer the government in person, can admit of no cure for the mischiefs of faction. A common passion or interest will, in almost every case, be felt by a majority of the whole; a communication and concert result from the form of government itself; and there is nothing to check the inducements to sacrifice the weaker party or an obnoxious individual. Hence it is that such democracies have ever been spectacles of turbulence and contention; have ever been found incompatible with personal security or the rights of property; and have in general been as short in their lives as they have been violent in their deaths. Theoretic politicians, who have patronized this species of government, have erroneously supposed that by reducing mankind to a perfect equality in their political rights, they would, at the same time, be perfectly equalized and assimilated in their possessions, their opinions, and their passions.

A republic, by which I mean a government in which the scheme of representation takes place, opens a different prospect, and promises the cure for which we are seeking. Let us examine the points in which it varies from pure democracy, and we shall comprehend both the nature of the cure and the efficacy which it must derive from the Union.

The two great points of difference between a democracy and a republic are: first, the delegation of the government, in the latter, to a small number of citizens elected by the rest; secondly, the greater number of citizens, and greater sphere of country, over which the latter may be extended.

The effect of the first difference is, on the one hand, to refine and enlarge the public views, by passing them through the medium of a chosen body of citizens, whose wisdom may best discern the true interest of their country, and whose patriotism and love of justice will be least likely to sacrifice it to temporary or partial considerations. Under such a regulation, it may well happen that the public voice, pronounced by the representatives of the people, will be more consonant to the public good than if pronounced by the people themselves, convened for the purpose. On the other hand, the effect may be inverted. Men of factious tempers, of local prejudices, or of sinister designs, may, by intrigue, by corruption, or by other means, first obtain the suffrages, and then betray the interests, of the people. The question resulting is, whether small or extensive republics are more favorable to the election of proper guardians of the public weal; and it is clearly decided in favor of the latter by two obvious considerations:

In the first place, it is to be remarked that, however small the republic may be, the representatives must be raised to a certain number, in order to guard against the cabals of a few; and that, however large it may be, they must be limited to a certain number, in order to guard against the confusion of a multitude. Hence, the number of representatives in the two cases not being in proportion to that of the two constituents, and being proportionally greater in the small republic, it follows that, if the proportion of fit characters be not less in the large than in the small republic, the former will present a greater option, and consequently a greater probability of a fit choice.

In the next place, as each representative will be chosen by a greater number of citizens in the large than in the small republic, it will be more difficult for unworthy candidates to practice with success the vicious arts by which elections are too often carried; and the suffrages of the people being more free, will be more likely to centre in men who possess the most attractive merit and the most diffusive and established characters.

It must be confessed that in this, as in most other cases, there is a mean, on both sides of which inconveniences will be found to lie. By enlarging too much the number of electors, you render the representatives too little acquainted with all their local circumstances and lesser interests; as by reducing it too much, you render him unduly attached to these, and too little fit to comprehend and pursue great and national objects. The federal Constitution forms a happy combination in this respect; the great and aggregate interests being referred to the national, the local and particular to the State legislatures.

The other point of difference is, the greater number of citizens and extent of territory which may be brought within the compass of republican than of democratic government; and it is this circumstance principally which renders factious combinations less to be dreaded in the former than in the latter. The smaller the society, the fewer probably will be the distinct parties and interests composing it; the fewer the distinct parties and interests, the more frequently will a majority be found of the same party; and the smaller the number of individuals composing a majority, and the smaller the compass within which they are placed, the more easily will they concert and execute their plans of oppression. Extend the sphere, and you take in a greater variety of parties and interests; you make it less probable that a majority of the whole will have a common motive to invade the rights of other citizens; or if such a common motive exists, it will be more difficult for all who feel it to discover their own strength, and to act in unison with each other. Besides other impediments, it may be remarked that, where there is a consciousness of unjust or dishonorable purposes, communication is always checked by distrust in proportion to the number whose concurrence is necessary.

Hence, it clearly appears, that the same advantage which a republic has over a democracy, in controlling the effects of faction, is enjoyed by a large over a small republic—is enjoyed by the Union over the States composing it. Does the advantage consist in the substitution of representatives whose enlightened views and virtuous sentiments render them superior to local prejudices and schemes of injustice? It will not be denied that the representation of the Union will be most likely to possess these requisite endowments. Does it consist in the greater security afforded by a greater variety of parties, against the event of any one party being able to outnumber and oppress the rest? In an equal degree does the increased variety of parties comprised within the Union, increase this security. Does it, in fine, consist in the greater obstacles opposed to the concert and accomplishment of the secret wishes of an unjust and interested majority? Here, again, the extent of the Union gives it the most palpable advantage.

The influence of factious leaders may kindle a flame within their particular States, but will be unable to spread a general conflagration through the other States. A religious sect may degenerate into a political faction in a part of the Confederacy; but the variety of sects dispersed over the entire face of it must secure the national councils against any danger from that source. A rage for paper money, for an abolition of debts, for an equal division of property, or for any other improper or wicked project, will be less apt to pervade the whole body of the Union than a particular member of it; in the same proportion as such a malady is more likely to taint a particular county or district, than an entire State.

In the extent and proper structure of the Union, therefore, we behold a republican remedy for the diseases most incident to republican government. And according to the degree of pleasure and pride we feel in being republicans, ought to be our zeal in cherishing the spirit and supporting the character of Federalists.

PUBLIUS.

Papachristou v. City of Jacksonville
405 U.S. 156 (1972)

Mr. Justice Douglas delivered the opinion of the Court.

This case involves eight defendants who were convicted in a Florida municipal court of violating a Jacksonville, Florida, vagrancy ordinance. . . .[1] For reasons which will appear, we reverse. . . .

The facts are stipulated. Papachristou and Calloway are white females. Melton and Johnson are black males. Papachristou was enrolled in a job-training program sponsored by the State Employment Service at Florida Junior College in Jacksonville. Calloway was a typing and shorthand teacher at a state mental institution located near Jacksonville. She was the owner of the automobile in which the four defendants were arrested. Melton was a Vietnam war veteran who had been released from the Navy after nine months in a veterans' hospital. On the date of his arrest he was a part-time computer helper while attending college as a full-time student in Jacksonville. Johnson was a tow-motor operator in a grocery chain warehouse and was a lifelong resident of Jacksonville.

At the time of their arrest the four of them were riding in Calloway's car on the main thoroughfare in Jacksonville. They had left a restaurant owned by Johnson's uncle where they had eaten and were on their way to a nightclub. The arresting officers denied that the racial mixture in the car played any part in the decision to make the arrest. The arrest, they said, was made because the defendants had stopped near a used-car lot which had been broken into several times. There was, however, no evidence of any breaking and entering on the night in question.

Of these four charged with "prowling by auto" none had been previously arrested except Papachristou who had once been convicted of a municipal offense.

Jimmy Lee Smith and Milton Henry (who is not a petitioner) were arrested between 9 and 10 a.m. on a weekday in downtown Jacksonville, while waiting for a friend who was to lend them a car so they could apply for a job at a produce company. Smith was a part-time produce worker and part-time organizer for a Negro political group. He had a common-law wife and three children supported by him and his wife. He had been arrested several times but convicted only once. Smith's companion, Henry, was an 18-year-old high school student with no previous record of arrest.

---

[1]   Jacksonville Ordinance Code § 26—57 provided at the time of these arrests and convictions as follows: "Rogues and vagabonds, or dissolute persons who go about begging, common gamblers, persons who use juggling or unlawful games or plays, common drunkards, common night walkers, thieves, pilferers or pickpockets, traders in stolen property, lewd, wanton and lascivious persons, keepers of gambling places, common railers and brawlers, persons wandering or strolling around from place to place without any lawful purpose or object, habitual loafers, disorderly persons, persons neglecting all lawful business and habitually spending their time by frequenting houses of ill fame, gaming houses, or places where alcoholic beverages are sold or served, persons able to work but habitually living upon the earnings of their wives or minor children shall be deemed vagrants and, upon conviction in the Municipal Court shall be punished as provided for Class D offenses."

This morning it was cold, and Smith had no jacket, so they went briefly into a dry cleaning shop to wait, but left when requested to do so. They thereafter walked back and forth two or three times over a two-block stretch looking for their friend. The store owners, who apparently were wary of Smith and his companion, summoned two police officers who searched the men and found neither had a weapon. But they were arrested because the officers said they had no identification and because the officers did not believe their story.

Heath and a codefendant were arrested for "loitering" and for "common thief." Both were residents of Jacksonville, Heath having lived there all his life and being employed at an automobile body shop. Heath had previously been arrested but his codefendant had no arrest record. Heath and his companion were arrested when they drove up to a residence shared by Heath's girl friend and some other girls. Some police officers were already there in the process of arresting another man. When Heath and his companion started backing out of the driveway, the officers signaled to them to stop and asked them to get out of the car, which they did. Thereupon they and the automobile were searched. Although no contraband or incriminating evidence was found, they were both arrested, Heath being charged with being a "common thief" because he was reputed to be a thief. The codefendant was charged with "loitering" because he was standing in the driveway, an act which the officers admitted was done only at their command.

Campbell was arrested as he reached his home very early one morning and was charged with "common thief." He was stopped by officers because he was traveling at a high rate of speed, yet no speeding charge was placed against him.

Brown was arrested when he was observed leaving a downtown Jacksonville hotel by a police officer seated in a cruiser. The police testified he was reputed to be a thief, narcotics pusher, and generally opprobrious character. The officer called Brown over to the car, intending at that time to arrest him unless he had a good explanation for being on the street. Brown walked over to the police cruiser, as commanded, and the officer began to search him, apparently preparatory to placing him in the car. In the process of the search he came on two small packets which were later found to contain heroin. When the officer touched the pocket where the packets were, Brown began to resist. He was charged with "disorderly loitering on street" and "disorderly conduct—resisting arrest with violence." While he was also charged with a narcotics violation, that charge was *nolled*.

Jacksonville's ordinance and Florida's statute were "derived from early English law" and employ "archaic language" in their definitions of vagrants. The history is an often-told tale. The break-up of feudal estates in England led to labor shortages which in turn resulted in the Statutes of Laborers, designed to stabilize the labor force by prohibiting increases in wages and prohibiting the movement of workers from their home areas in search of improved conditions. Later vagrancy laws became criminal aspects of the poor laws. The series of laws passed in England on the subject became increasingly severe. But "the theory of the Elizabethan poor laws no longer fits the facts." The conditions which spawned these laws may be gone, but the archaic classifications remain.

This ordinance is void for vagueness, both in the sense that it "fails to give a person of ordinary intelligence fair notice that his contemplated conduct is forbidden by the statute," and because it encourages arbitrary and erratic arrests and convictions.

Living under a rule of law entails various suppositions, one of which is that "[all persons] are entitled to be informed as to what the State commands or forbids.". . .

The poor among us, the minorities, the average householder are not in business and not alerted to the regulatory schemes of vagrancy laws; and we assume they would have no understanding of their meaning and impact if they read them. Nor are they protected from being caught in the vagrancy net by the necessity of having a specific intent to commit an unlawful act.

The Jacksonville ordinance makes criminal activities which by modern standards are normally innocent. "Nightwalking" is one. Florida construes the ordinance not to make criminal one night's wandering, only the "habitual" wanderer or, as the ordinance describes it, "common night walkers." We know, however, from experience that sleepless people often walk at night, perhaps hopeful that sleep-inducing relaxation will result.

Luis Munoz-Marin, former Governor of Puerto Rico, commented once that "loafing" was a national virtue in his Commonwealth and that it should be encouraged. It is, however, a crime in Jacksonville.

"[P]ersons able to work but habitually living upon the earnings of their wives or minor children"—like habitually living "without visible means of support"—might implicate unemployed pillars of the community who have married rich wives.

"[P]ersons able to work but habitually living upon the earnings of their wives or minor children" may also embrace unemployed people out of the labor market, by reason of a recession or disemployed by reason of technological or so-called structural displacements.

Persons "wandering or strolling" from place to place have been extolled by Walt Whitman and Vachel Lindsay. The qualification "without any lawful purpose or object" may be a trap for innocent acts. Persons "neglecting all lawful business and habitually spending their time by frequenting . . . places where alcoholic beverages are sold or served" would literally embrace many members of golf clubs and city clubs.

Walkers and strollers and wanderers may be going to or coming from a burglary. Loafers or loiterers may be "casing" a place for a holdup. Letting one's wife support him is an intra-family matter, and normally of no concern to the police. Yet it may, of course, be the setting for numerous crimes.

The difficulty is that these activities are historically part of the amenities of life as we have known them. They are not mentioned in the Constitution or in the Bill of Rights. These unwritten amenities have been in part responsible for giving our people the feeling of independence and self-confidence, the feeling of creativity. These amenities have dignified the right of dissent and have honored the right to be nonconformists and the right to defy submissiveness. They have encouraged lives of high spirits rather than hushed, suffocating silence.

They are embedded in Walt Whitman's writings, especially in his "Song of the Open Road." They are reflected too, in the spirit of Vachel Lindsay's "I Want to Go Wandering," and by Henry D. Thoreau.[2]

---

[2]   "I have met with but one or two persons in the course of my life who understood the art of Walking, that is, of taking walks,—who had a genius, so to speak, for sauntering: which word is beautifully derived 'from

This aspect of the vagrancy ordinance before us is suggested by what this Court said in 1876 about a broad criminal statute enacted by Congress: "It would certainly be dangerous if the legislature could set a net large enough to catch all possible offenders, and leave it to the courts to step inside and say who could be rightfully detained, and who should be set at large."

While that was a federal case, the due process implications are equally applicable to the States and to this vagrancy ordinance. Here the net cast is large, not to give the courts the power to pick and choose but to increase the arsenal of the police. . . .

Where the list of crimes is so all-inclusive and generalized as the one in this ordinance, those convicted may be punished for no more than vindicating affronts to police authority:

> The common ground which brings such a motley assortment of human troubles before the magistrates in vagrancy-type proceedings is the procedural laxity which permits "conviction" for almost any kind of conduct and the existence of the House of Correction as an easy and convenient dumping-ground for problems that appear to have no other immediate solution.

Foote, Vagrancy-Type Law and Its Administration, 104 U. Pa. L. Rev. 603, 631.

Another aspect of the ordinance's vagueness appears when we focus, not on the lack of notice given a potential offender, but on the effect of the unfettered discretion it places in the hands of the Jacksonville police. Caleb Foote, an early student of this subject, has called the vagrancy-type law as offering "punishment by analogy." Such crimes, though long common in Russia, are not compatible with our constitutional system. We allow our police to make arrests only on "probable cause," a Fourth and Fourteenth Amendment standard applicable to the States as well as to the Federal Government. Arresting a person on suspicion, like arresting a person for investigation, is foreign to our system, even when the arrest is for past criminality. Future criminality, however, is the common justification for the presence of vagrancy statutes. Florida has, indeed, construed her vagrancy statute "as necessary regulations," inter alia, "to deter vagabondage and prevent crimes."

A direction by a legislature to the police to arrest all "suspicious" persons would not pass constitutional muster. A vagrancy prosecution may be merely the cloak for a convic-

---

idle people who roved about the country, in the Middle Ages, and asked charity, under pretence of going a la Sainte Terre,' to the Holy Land, till the children exclaimed, 'There goes a Sainte Terrer,' a Saunterer, a Holy-Lander. They who never go to the Holy Land in their walks, as they pretend, are indeed mere idlers and vagabonds; but they who do go there are saunterers in the good sense, such as I mean. Some, however, would derive the word from sans terre, without land or a home, which, therefore, in the good sense, will mean, having no particular home, but equally at home everywhere. For this is the secret of successful sauntering. He who sits still in a house all the time may be the greatest vagrant of all; but the saunterer, in the good sense, is no more vagrant than the meandering river, which is all the while sedulously seeking the shortest course to the sea. But I prefer the first, which, indeed, is the most probable derivation. For every walk is a sort of crusade, preached by some Peter the Hermit in us, to go forth and reconquer this Holy Land from the hands of the Infidels." Excursions 251-52 (1893).

tion which could not be obtained on the real but undisclosed grounds for the arrest. But as Chief Justice Hewart said in *Frederick Dean:*

> It would be in the highest degree unfortunate if in any part of the country those who are responsible for setting in motion the criminal law should entertain, connive at or coquette with the idea that in a case where there is not enough evidence to charge the prisoner with an attempt to commit a crime, the prosecution may, nevertheless, on such insufficient evidence, succeed in obtaining and upholding a conviction under the Vagrancy Act, 1824.

Those generally implicated by the imprecise terms of the ordinance—poor people, nonconformists, dissenters, idlers—may be required to comport themselves according to the life style deemed appropriate by the Jacksonville police and the courts. Where, as here, there are no standards governing the exercise of the discretion granted by the ordinance, the scheme permits and encourages an arbitrary and discriminatory enforcement of the law. It furnishes a convenient tool for "harsh and discriminatory enforcement by local prosecuting officials, against particular groups deemed to merit their displeasure." It results in a regime in which the poor and the unpopular are permitted to "stand on a public sidewalk . . . only at the whim of any police officer." Shuttlesworth v. Birmingham. Under this ordinance,

> if some carefree type of fellow is satisfied to work just so much, and no more, as will pay for one square meal, some wine, and a flophouse daily, but a court thinks this kind of living subhuman, the fellow can be forced to raise his sights or go to jail as a vagrant.

Amsterdam, Federal Constitutional Restrictions on the Punishment of Crimes of Status, Crimes of General Obnoxiousness, Crimes of Displeasing Police Officers, and the Like, 3 Crim. L. Bull. 205, 226 (1967).

A presumption that people who might walk or loaf or loiter or stroll or frequent houses where liquor is sold, or who are supported by their wives or who look suspicious to the police are to become future criminals is too precarious for a rule of law. The implicit presumption in these generalized vagrancy standards—that crime is being nipped in the bud—is too extravagant to deserve extended treatment. Of course, vagrancy statutes are useful to the police. Of course, they are nets making easy the roundup of so-called undesirables. But the rule of law implies equality and justice in its application. Vagrancy laws of the Jacksonville type teach that the scales of justice are so tipped that even-handed administration of the law is not possible. The rule of law, evenly applied to minorities as well as majorities, to the poor as well as the rich, is the great mucilage that holds society together.

The Jacksonville ordinance cannot be squared with our constitutional standards and is plainly unconstitutional.

City of Chicago v. Wilson
75 Ill. 2d 525 (1978)

Moran, Justice.

Following a bench trial in the circuit court of Cook County, the defendants, Wallace Wilson and Kim Kimberley, were convicted of having violated section 192-8 of the Municipal Code of the City of Chicago (Code), which prohibits a person from wearing clothing of the opposite sex with the intent to conceal his or her sex. Each defendant was fined $100. The appellate court affirmed, and this court granted leave to appeal.

Defendants were arrested on February 18, 1974, minutes after they emerged from a restaurant where they had had breakfast. Defendant Wilson was wearing a black knee-length dress, a fur coat, nylon stockings and a black wig. Defendant Kimberley had a bouffant hair style and was wearing a pants suit, high-heeled shoes and cosmetic makeup. Defendants were taken to the police station and were required to pose for pictures in various stages of undress. Both defendants were wearing brassieres and garter belts; both had male genitals.

Prior to trial, defendants moved to dismiss the complaint on the grounds that section 192-8 was unconstitutional in that it denied them equal protection of the law and infringed upon their freedom of expression and privacy. This motion was denied.

At trial, the defendants testified that they were transsexuals, and were, at the time of their arrests, undergoing psychiatric therapy in preparation for a sex reassignment operation. As part of this therapy, both defendants stated, they were required to wear female clothing and to adopt a female life-style. Kimberley stated that he had explained this to the police at the time of his arrest. Both defendants said they had been transsexuals all of their lives and thought of themselves as females. The question of arrest is not an issue.

Section 192-8 of the Code provides:

> Any person who shall appear in a public place . . . in a dress not belonging to his or her sex, with intent to conceal his or her sex . . . shall be fined not less than twenty dollars nor more than five hundred dollars for each offense. . . .

This court has long recognized restrictions on the State's power to regulate matters pertinent to one's choice of a life-style which has not been demonstrated to be harmful to society's health, safety or welfare. E.g., People v. Fries (1969) (statute requiring the wearing of a motorcycle helmet held invalid); City of Chicago v. Drake Hotel Co. (1916) (ordinance prohibiting public dancing in restaurants held invalid); Town of Cortland v. Larson (1916) (ordinance prohibiting the private possession of liquor held invalid); City of Zion v. Behrens (1914) (ordinance prohibiting smoking in public parks and on public streets held invalid).

In Haller Sign Works v. Physical Culture Training School (1911), a case which involved the regulation of billboards for aesthetic purposes, this court noted:

> The citizen has always been supposed to be free to determine the style of architecture of his house, the color of the paint that he puts thereon, the number and

character of trees he will plant, the style and quality of the clothes that he and his family will wear, and it has never been thought that the Legislature could invade private rights so far as to prescribe the course to be pursued in these and other like matters, although the highly cultured may find on every street in every town and city many things that are not only open to criticism but shocking to the aesthetic taste.

The notion that the State can regulate one's personal appearance, unconfined by any constitutional strictures whatsoever, is fundamentally inconsistent with "values of privacy, self-identity, autonomy, and personal integrity that . . . the Constitution was designed to protect." Kelley v. Johnson (1976) (Marshall, J., dissenting).

Finding that the Constitution provides an individual some measure of protection with regard to his choice of appearance answers only the initial issue. Resolution of the second issue is more difficult: to determine the circumstances under which the interest can be infringed. It is at this juncture that *Kelley,* and cases subsequent thereto, offer little guidance. With the exception of one Federal decision . . . all of the cases subsequent to *Kelley* have involved regulations set in the context of an organized governmental activity. Such circumstance is distinguished from that in which a regulation, as here, controls the dress of the citizens at large. This distinction, as noted in *Kelley,* is "highly significant."

Even though one's choice of appearance is not considered a "fundamental" right, the State is not relieved from showing some justification for its intrusion. As *Kelley* suggests, the degree of protection to be accorded an individual's choice of appearance is dependent upon the context in which the right is asserted. It is, therefore, incumbent upon the court to analyze both the circumstances under which the right is asserted and the reasons which the State offers for its intrusion.

In this court, the city has asserted four reasons for the total ban against cross-dressing in public: (1) to protect citizens from being misled or defrauded; (2) to aid in the description and detection of criminals; (3) to prevent crimes in washrooms; and (4) to prevent inherently antisocial conduct which is contrary to the accepted norms of our society. The record, however, contains no evidence to support these reasons.

If we assume that the ordinance is, in part, directed toward curbing criminal activity, the city has failed to demonstrate any justification for infringing upon the defendants' choice of public dress under the circumstances of this case.

Both defendants testified that they are transsexuals and were, at the time of their arrest, undergoing psychiatric therapy in preparation for a sex-reassignment operation. . . . Neither of the defendants was engaged in deviate sexual conduct or any other criminal activity. Absent evidence to the contrary, we cannot assume that individuals who cross-dress for purposes of therapy are prone to commit crimes.

The city's fourth reason (as noted above) for prohibiting the defendants' choice of public dress is apparently directed at protecting the public morals. In its brief, however, the city has not articulated the manner in which the ordinance is designed to protect the public morals. It is presumably believed that cross-dressing in public is offensive to the general public's aesthetic preference. There is no evidence, however, that cross-dressing, when done as a part of a preoperative therapy program or otherwise, is, in and of itself, harmful to society. In this case, the aesthetic preference of society must be balanced against the individual's well-being.

Through the enactment of section 17(1)(d) of the Vital Records Act, which authorizes the issuance of a new certificate of birth following sex-reassignment surgery, the legislature has implicitly recognized the necessity and validity of such surgery. It would be inconsistent to permit sex-reassignment surgery yet, at the same time, impede the necessary therapy in preparation for such surgery. Individuals contemplating such surgery should, in consultation with their doctors, be entitled to pursue the therapy necessary to insure the correctness of their decision.

Inasmuch as the city has offered no evidence to substantiate its reasons for infringing on the defendants' choice of dress under the circumstances of this case, we do not find the ordinance invalid on its face; however, we do find that section 192-8 as applied to the defendants is an unconstitutional infringement of their liberty interest. The judgments of the appellate court and the circuit court are reversed and the cause is remanded to the circuit court with directions to dismiss.

Walker v. Superior Court
47 Cal. 3d 112 (1988)

Mosk, Justice.

We consider in this case whether a prosecution for involuntary manslaughter (Pen. Code, § 192, subd. (b)) and felony child endangerment (id., § 273a, subd. (1)) can be maintained against the mother of a child who died of meningitis after receiving treatment by prayer in lieu of medical attention. We conclude that the prosecution is permitted by statute as well as the free exercise and due process clauses of the state and federal Constitutions.

Defendant Laurie Grouard Walker is a member of the Church of Christ, Scientist (hereafter the Church). Her four-year-old daughter, Shauntay, fell ill with flu-like symptoms on February 21, 1984, and four days later developed a stiff neck. Consistent with the tenets of her religion, defendant chose to treat the child's illness with prayer rather than medical care. Defendant contacted an accredited Christian Science prayer practitioner who thereafter prayed for Shauntay and visited the child on two occasions. Defendant also engaged a Christian Science nurse who attended Shauntay on February 27 and again on March 6 and 8. Shauntay nevertheless lost weight, grew disoriented and irritable during the last week of her illness, and died on March 9 of acute purulent meningitis after a period of heavy and irregular breathing. During the 17 days she lay ill, the child received no medical treatment.

The People charged defendant with involuntary manslaughter and felony child endangerment based on allegations that her criminal negligence proximately caused Shauntay's death. Defendant moved to dismiss the prosecution on the grounds that (1) her conduct was specifically protected by law, and (2) the statutes under which she had been charged failed to provide fair notice that her conduct was criminal. The court denied her motion. . . .

Defendant and amici curiae offer a variety of statutory and constitutional arguments in support of their claim that the prosecution of defendant . . . is barred as a matter of law. For the reasons set forth below, we reject their contentions and conclude that defendant can be prosecuted as charged.

Statutory Contentions

. . . On September 30, 1987, the Governor signed into law Senate Bill No. 243, 1987-1988 Regular Session, which revised Welfare and Institutions Code section 300 (hereafter W & I section 300) in its entirety. Although the legislation will not take effect until January 1, 1989, its provisions dealing with the relationship of prayer treatment to dependency proceedings are critically significant to our interpretive task insofar as they represent the Legislature's most recent and detailed articulation of the protection to be assured seriously ill children receiving such care.

Newly amended W & I section 300 provides in pertinent part:

> Any minor who comes within any of the following descriptions is within the jurisdiction of the juvenile court which may adjudge that person to be a dependent child of the court. . . .

[¶] (b) The minor has suffered, or there is substantial risk that the minor will suffer, serious physical harm or illness . . . by the willful or negligent failure of the parent . . . to provide the minor with adequate food, clothing, shelter, or medical treatment. . . . Whenever it is alleged that a minor comes within the jurisdiction of the court on the basis of the parent's . . . willful failure to provide adequate medical treatment or specific decision to provide spiritual treatment through prayer, the court shall give deference to the parent's . . . medical treatment, nontreatment, or spiritual treatment through prayer alone in accordance with the tenets and practices of a recognized church or religious denomination by an accredited practitioner thereof and shall not assume jurisdiction *unless necessary to protect the minor from suffering serious physical harm or illness.*

(Italics added.)

Thus in any circumstance involving the threat of "serious physical harm or illness," the Legislature has empowered the juvenile court to intercede and assume custody for the express purpose of assuring medical care for a child whose parent is furnishing spiritual treatment by prayer alone. The expression of legislative intent is clear: when a child's health is seriously jeopardized, the right of a parent to rely exclusively on prayer must yield. This intent is implicit in the enumeration of necessities a parent must furnish to avert a dependency proceeding under W & I section 300; conspicuously absent from the list is any substitute for adequate medical treatment. It follows that the only tenable construction of the related provisions defining the relationship of prayer treatment to child neglect or abuse is the analysis offered by the Attorney General.

While dependency proceedings are civil rather than criminal, their relevance to our inquiry is plain. Parents possess a profound interest in the custody of their children. "Custody embraces the sum of parental rights with respect to the rearing of a child, including its care. It includes . . . the right to direct his activities and make decisions regarding his care and control, education, health, and religion." The United States Supreme Court has termed this constellation of parental interests "essential" (Meyers v. Nebraska), among the "basic civil rights of man" (Skinner v. Oklahoma), and "[r]ights far more precious . . . than property rights" (May v. Anderson). Consistent with the gravity of the prerogative at stake, parents involved in W & I section 300 proceedings are assured notice and a due process hearing while those who are indigent receive appointed counsel. The Legislature's willingness to intrude on a parental interest of such magnitude to assure that children receiving prayer treatment are spared serious physical harm certainly evinces no contrary intent with respect to the application of the penal laws, which in significant respects constitute a less intrusive method of advancing the state's paramount interest in the protection of its children.

Defendant's argument by analogy to civil neglect and dependency provisions therefore corroborates rather than refutes our previous determination that the Legislature has created no exemption under sections 192(b) and 273a(1) for parents who are charged with having killed or endangered the lives of their seriously ill children by providing prayer alone in lieu of medical care. The legislative design appears consistent: prayer treatment will be accommodated as an acceptable means of attending to the needs of a child only insofar as serious physical harm or illness is not at risk. When a child's life is placed in danger, we discern no intent to shield parents from the chastening prospect of felony liability.

Taking a wholly different tack, defendant next contends that she cannot be convicted under either the manslaughter or felony child-endangerment statutes regardless of the availability of a religious exemption. She rests this contention on a claim that the People will be unable to prove the degree of culpability necessary to convict her under either provision, both of which require criminal negligence in the commission of an offending act. We have defined criminal negligence as

> aggravated, culpable, gross, or reckless, that is, the conduct of the accused must be such a departure from what would be the conduct of an ordinarily prudent or careful man under the same circumstances as to be incompatible with a proper regard for human life, or, in other words, a disregard of human life or an indifference to consequences. . . . [Such negligence] is ordinarily to be determined pursuant to the general principles of negligence, the fundamental of which is knowledge, actual or imputed, that the act of the slayer tended to endanger life.

Defendant makes two arguments for the claim that her conduct cannot, as a matter of law, constitute such negligence.

She first contends that the defenses recognized at English common law are available to her under Civil Code section 22.2, which reads: "The common law of England, so far as it is not repugnant to or inconsistent with the Constitution of the United States, or the Constitution or laws of this State, is the rule of decision in all the courts of this State." She cites two English cases from the 19th century in support of the proposition that the common law recognized treatment by prayer in lieu of medicine as legally insufficient to constitute criminal negligence. While we note that common law defenses, with limited exceptions, are unavailable in California (Keeler v. Superior Court), we need look no further than the cases themselves to dispose of defendant's contention.

The opinion of the court in Regina v. Wagstaffe (Cen. Crim. Ct. 1868), 10 Cox. Crim. Cas. 530, consists of a vaguely worded jury charge. The court instructed the jury that criminal negligence "was a very wide question. . . . At different times people had come to different conclusions as to what might be done with a sick person. . . . [A] man might be convicted of manslaughter because he lived in a place where all the community was of a contrary opinion, and in another he might be acquitted because they were all of his opinion. . . ." The court asked rhetorically whether it was "intended by God Almighty that persons should content themselves by praying for His assistance, without helping themselves, or resorting to such means as were within their reach for that purpose?", and concluded with the observation that the defendants appeared sincere and affectionate. Although the defendants were subsequently acquitted, the fact that the jury itself resolved the question of criminal negligence negates the claim that the court in *Wagstaffe* recognized a legal defense to the charge. Furthermore, its jury instructions merely restated the principle that criminal negligence is a question of fact to be determined in light of contemporary community standards, which at the time made the particular question a close one.

The second case cited by defendant makes this point quite clearly. In Regina v. Hines (1874), 80 Cent. Crim. Ct. 309, the court dismissed an indictment for manslaughter against a parent who had exclusively prayed for an ill child. Although the court ruled that the conduct was not criminally negligent as a matter of law, to state the holding is to refute its application 114 years later: the court considered and rejected the proposition that a parent who treated a child by spiritual care "instead of calling in a doctor to apply blisters, leeches, and calomel," was guilty of criminal negligence. Were blisters, leeches and calomel the medical alternative to prayer today, quite likely defendant's reliance on *Hines* would more fully resonate with this court. Medical science has advanced dramatically, however, and we may fairly presume that the community standard for criminal negligence has changed accordingly. Nineteenth-century English common law thus fails to establish a defense, as a matter of law, to charges arising today for criminal negligence in the death of a child treated by prayer alone.

Defendant next contends that her actions are legally insufficient to constitute criminal negligence under the definition of that conduct established in the decisions of this court. Emphasizing her sincere concern and good faith in treating Shauntay with prayer, she claims that her conduct is incompatible with the required degree of culpability. Defendant does not dispute, however, that criminal negligence must be evaluated objectively. The question is whether "a reasonable person in defendant's position would have been aware of the risk involved. . . ." If so, "defendant is presumed to have had such an awareness.". . .

In view of this standard, we must reject defendant's assertion that no reasonable jury could characterize her conduct as criminally negligent for purposes of sections 192(b) and 273a(1). As the court . . . observed in affirming the involuntary manslaughter and felony child-endangerment conviction of a parent whose child died for want of medical care, criminal negligence "could have been found to have consisted of the [mother's] failure to seek prompt medical attention for [her son], rather than waiting several days. There is evidence she knew, or should have known, that [her son] was seriously injured. . . . Viewing [the evidence] in the light most favorable to the prosecution, there is substantial evidence here of involuntary manslaughter based on the lack of due caution and circumspection in omitting to take the child to a doctor." When divorced of her subjective intent, the alleged conduct of defendant here is essentially indistinguishable.

Defendant's arguments to the contrary are not persuasive. She first asserts that the various statutory exemptions enacted for Christian Scientists demonstrate a legislative acceptance of the reasonableness of their spiritual care that is incompatible with a finding of "gross, culpable, or reckless" negligence. As discussed at length above, however, California's statutory scheme reflects not an endorsement of the efficacy or reasonableness of prayer treatment for children battling life-threatening diseases but rather a willingness to accommodate religious practice when children do not face serious physical harm. Indeed, the relevant statutes suggest that prayer treatment for gravely ill children is sufficiently unreasonable to justify the state in taking the draconian step of depriving parents of their rights of custody. . . .

In sum, we reject the proposition that the provision of prayer alone to a seriously ill child cannot constitute criminal negligence as a matter of law. Whether this defendant's particular conduct was sufficiently culpable to justify conviction of involuntary manslaughter and felony child endangerment remains a question in the exclusive province of the jury.

Constitutional Defenses

A. Free Exercise under the First Amendment

In the absence of a statutory basis to bar defendant's prosecution, we necessarily reach her constitutional claims. Defendant and the Church first contend that her conduct is absolutely protected from criminal liability by the First Amendment to the United States Constitution and article I, section 4, of the California Constitution. We do not agree.

The First Amendment bars government from "prohibiting the free exercise" of religion. Although the clause absolutely protects religious belief, religiously motivated conduct "remains subject to regulation for the protection of society." (Cantwell v. Connecticut.) To determine whether governmental regulation of religious conduct is violative of the First Amendment, the gravity of the state's interest must be balanced against the severity of the religious imposition. (Wisconsin v. Yoder.) If the regulation is justified in view of the balanced interests at stake, the free exercise clause requires that the policy additionally represent the least restrictive alternative available to adequately advance the state's objectives.

Defendant does not dispute the gravity of the governmental interest involved in this case, as well she should not. Imposition of felony liability for endangering or killing an ill child by failing to provide medical care furthers an interest of unparalleled significance: the protection of the very lives of California's children, upon whose "healthy, well-rounded growth . . . into full maturity as citizens" our "democratic society rests, for its continuance. . . ." (Prince v. Massachusetts.) Balanced against this interest is a religious infringement of significant dimensions. Defendant unquestionably relied on prayer treatment as an article of genuine faith, the restriction of which would seriously impinge on the practice of her religion. We note, however, that resort to medicine does not constitute "sin" for a Christian Scientist, does not subject a church member to stigmatization, does not result in divine retribution, and, according to the Church's amicus curiae brief, is not a matter of church compulsion.

Regardless of the severity of the religious imposition, the governmental interest is plainly adequate to justify its restrictive effect. As the United States Supreme Court stated in Prince v. Massachusetts (1944), "Parents may be free to become martyrs themselves. But it does not follow they are free, in identical circumstances, to make martyrs of their children before they have reached the age of full legal discretion when they can make that choice for themselves." The Court in *Prince* considered a free-exercise claim asserted by parents whose religious beliefs required that their children sell religious tracts in violation of child labor laws. If parents are not at liberty to "martyr" children by taking their labor, it follows a fortiori that they are not at liberty to martyr children by taking their very lives. As the Court explained, "The right to practice religion freely does not include liberty to expose the community or child to communicable disease or the latter to ill health or death."

In an attempt to avoid this inexorable conclusion, the Church argues at length over the purportedly pivotal distinction between the governmental compulsion of a religiously objectionable act and the governmental prohibition of a religiously motivated act. Accepting arguendo the force of the distinction, we find that it has no relevance in a case involving an interest of this magnitude. As the Court in *Prince* recognized, parents have *no* right to free exercise of religion at the price of a child's life, regardless of the prohibitive or compulsive nature of the governmental infringement. Furthermore, the United States Supreme Court has specifically sustained the compulsion of religiously prohibited conduct for interests no more compelling than here implicated. In Jacobson v. Massachusetts (1905), the Court upheld a law compelling the vaccination of children for communicable diseases in the face of parental religious objections. In United States v. Lee (1982), the Court upheld a law requiring that the Amish violate the tenets of their faith by participating in the Social Security system. And in Gillette v. United States (1971), the Court upheld the government's right to compel certain conscientious objectors to make war despite the religious character of their objections. We see no basis in these precedents for the conclusion that parents may constitutionally insulate themselves from state compulsion so long as their life-threatening religious conduct takes the form of an omission rather than an act.

The imposition of felony liability for failure to seek medical care for a seriously ill child is thus justified by a compelling state interest. To survive a First Amendment challenge, however, the policy must also represent the least restrictive alternative available to the state. Defendant and the Church argue that civil dependency proceedings advance the governmental interest in a far less intrusive manner. This is not evident. First, we have already observed the profoundly intrusive nature of such proceedings; it is not clear that parents would prefer to lose custody of their children pursuant to a disruptive and invasive judicial inquiry than to face privately the prospect of criminal liability. Second, child dependency proceedings advance the governmental interest only when the state learns of a child's illness in time to take protective measures, which quite likely will be the exception rather than the rule: "Under ordinary circumstances . . . the case of a true believer in faith healing will not even come to the attention of the authorities, unless and until someone dies." Finally, the imposition of criminal liability is reserved for the actual loss or endangerment of a child's life and thus is narrowly tailored to those instances when governmental intrusion is absolutely compelled.

We conclude that an adequately effective and less restrictive alternative is not available to further the state's compelling interest in assuring the provision of medical care to gravely ill children whose parents refuse such treatment on religious grounds. Accordingly, the First Amendment and its California equivalent do not bar defendant's criminal prosecution.

B. Due Process Right to Fair Notice of Illegal Conduct

Article I, section 7, of the California Constitution and the Fourteenth Amendment to the United States Constitution both assure that no person shall be deprived of "life, liberty, or property without due process of law." Among the implications of this constitutional command is that the state must give its citizenry fair notice of potentially criminal conduct. This requirement has two components: "due process requires a statute to be definite enough to provide (1) a standard of conduct for those whose activities are proscribed and (2) a standard for police enforcement and for ascertainment of guilt." Defendant contends that sections 192(b) and 273a(1), when read together with section 270, violate this constitutional dictate.

We initially observe that these statutes do not invite standardless law enforcement. Unlike typical due process challenges involving an ambiguously worded statute applied in an arbitrary and unforeseeable manner (see, e.g., Lanzetta v. New Jersey), we consider here three separate provisions that clearly identify their respective proscriptions. Even if we accept arguendo defendant's contention that the intersection of the statutes creates uncertainty on the part of law enforcement officials regarding the legality of prayer treatment when a child's life is endangered or lost, the officials are nevertheless required to make only one discretionary judgment: whether or not to prosecute conduct otherwise within the reach of the felony statutes in view of the provisions of section 270. This discretion certainly is not "of such a standardless sweep [that it] allows policemen, prosecutors, and juries to pursue their personal predilections." (Smith v. Goguen.)

With respect to the remaining component of the due process analysis, defendant makes two arguments why the statutory scheme fails to provide fair notice. She first contends that sections 192(b) and 273a(1) provide no notice of the point at which lawful prayer treatment becomes unlawful, thus requiring her "at peril of life, liberty or property to speculate as to the meaning of penal statutes." (Lanzetta v. New Jersey.) She frames her argument in the form of a rhetorical question: "Is it lawful for a parent to rely solely on treatment by spiritual means through prayer for the care of his/her ill child during the first few days of sickness but not for the fourth or fifth day?" Justice Holmes correctly answers: "[T]he law is full of instances where a man's fate depends on his estimating rightly, that is, as the jury subsequently estimates it, some matter of degree. . . . 'An act causing death may be murder, manslaughter, or misadventure, according to the degree of danger attending it' by common experience in the circumstances known to the actor." (Nash v. United States.) The "matter of degree" that persons relying on prayer treatment must estimate rightly is the point at which their course of conduct becomes criminally negligent. In terms of notice, due process requires no more.

Defendant contends in conclusion that the statutory scheme violates her right to fair notice by allowing punishment under sections 192(b) and 273a(1) for the same conduct that is assertedly accommodated under section 270. She argues in essence that the statutes issue "inexplicably contradictory commands" and thus violate due process by precluding "an ordinary person [from] intelligently choos[ing], in advance, what course it is lawful for him to pursue." (Connally v. General Construction Co.)

In considering whether a legislative proscription is sufficiently clear to satisfy the requirements of fair notice, "we look first to the language of the statute, then to its legislative history, and finally to California decisions construing the statutory language." We thus require citizens to apprise themselves not only of statutory language but also of legislative history, subsequent judicial construction, and underlying legislative purposes. (See generally Amsterdam, The Void-For-Vagueness Doctrine in the Supreme Court, 109 U. Pa. L. Rev. 67

(1960).) These principles express the strong presumption that legislative enactments "must be upheld unless their unconstitutionality clearly, positively, and unmistakably appears. A statute should be sufficiently certain so that a person may know what is prohibited thereby and what may be done without violating its provisions, but it cannot be held void for uncertainty if any reasonable and practical construction can be given to its language."

As we have discussed at length above, the purposes of the statutes here at issue are evidently distinguishable: sections 192(b) and 273a(1) protect against grievous and immediate physical harm while section 270 assures the routine provision of child support at parental expense. In light of these distinguishable objectives, it cannot be said that the legality of defendant's conduct under section 270 constitutes an "inexplicably contradictory command" with respect to the separate requirements of sections 192(b) and 273a(1). Indeed, the legislative history of section 270 specifically demonstrates the Legislature's unwillingness to extend the statute's religious exemption to the felony provisions. Sections 270, 192(b), and 273a(1) thus provided constitutionally sufficient notice to defendant that the provision of prayer alone to her daughter would be accommodated only insofar as the child was not threatened with serious physical harm or illness.

Disposition

We conclude that the prosecution of defendant for involuntary manslaughter and felony child endangerment violates neither statutory law nor the California or federal Constitution. The judgment of the Court of Appeal is affirmed.

Paris Adult Theatre I v. Slaton
413 U.S. 49 (1973)

Mr. Chief Justice Burger delivered the opinion of the Court.

Petitioners are two Atlanta, Georgia, movie theaters and their owners and managers, operating in the style of "adult" theaters. On December 28, 1970, respondents, the local state district attorney and the solicitor for the local state trial court, filed civil complaints in that court alleging that petitioners were exhibiting to the public for paid admission two allegedly obscene films, contrary to Georgia Code Ann. § 26—2101. The two films in question, "Magic Mirror" and "It All Comes Out in the End," depict sexual conduct characterized by the Georgia Supreme Court as "hard core pornography" leaving "little to the imagination.". . .

[T]he films were produced by petitioners at a jury-waived trial. Certain photographs, also produced at trial, were stipulated to portray the single entrance to both Paris Adult Theatre I and Paris Adult Theatre II as it appeared at the time of the complaints. These photographs show a conventional, inoffensive theater entrance, without any pictures, but with signs indicating that the theaters exhibit "Atlanta's Finest Mature Feature Films." On the door itself is a sign saying: "Adult Theatre—You must be 21 and able to prove it. If viewing the nude body offends you, Please Do Not Enter."

The two films were exhibited to the trial court. The only other state evidence was testimony by criminal investigators that they had paid admission to see the films and that nothing on the outside of the theater indicated the full nature of what was shown. In particular, nothing indicated that the films depicted—as they did—scenes of simulated fellatio, cunnilingus, and group sex intercourse. There was no evidence presented that minors had ever entered the theaters. Nor was there evidence presented that petitioners had a systematic policy of barring minors, apart from posting signs at the entrance. On April 12, 1971, the trial judge dismissed respondents' complaints. He assumed "that obscenity is established," but stated:

> It appears to the court that the display of these films in a commercial theatre, when surrounded by requisite notice to the public of their nature and by reasonable protection against the exposure of these films to minors, is constitutionally permissible. . . .

We categorically disapprove the theory, apparently adopted by the trial judge, that obscene, pornographic films acquire constitutional immunity from state regulation simply because they are exhibited for consenting adults only. This holding was properly rejected by the Georgia Supreme Court. Although we have often pointedly recognized the high importance of the state interest in regulating the exposure of obscene materials to juveniles and unconsenting adults, see Miller v. California; Stanley v. Georgia; Redrup v. New York, this Court has never declared these to be the only legitimate state interests permitting regulation of obscene material. . . .

In particular, we hold that there are legitimate state interests at stake in stemming the tide of commercialized obscenity, even assuming it is feasible to enforce effective safeguards against exposure to juveniles and to passersby. Rights and interests "other than those of the advocates are involved." These include the interest of the public in the quality of life and the total community environment, the tone of commerce in the great city centers, and, possibly, the public safety itself. The Hill-Link Minority Report of the Commission on Obscenity and Pornography indicates that there is at least an arguable correlation between obscene material and crime. Quite apart from sex crimes, however, there remains one problem of large proportions aptly described by Professor Bickel:

> It concerns the tone of the society, the mode, or to use terms that have perhaps greater currency, the style and quality of life, now and in the future. A man may be entitled to read an obscene book in his room, or expose himself indecently there . . . . We should protect his privacy. But if he demands a right to obtain the books and pictures he wants in the market, and to foregather in public places— discreet, if you will, but accessible to all—with others who share his tastes, *then to grant him his right is to affect the world about the rest of us, and to impinge on other privacies.* Even supposing that each of us can, if he wishes, effectively avert the eye and stop the ear (which, in truth, we cannot), what is commonly read and seen and heard and done intrudes upon us all, want it or not.

22 The Public Interest 25-26 (Winter 1971). (Emphasis added.) As Mr. Chief Justice Warren stated, there is a "right of the Nation and of the States to maintain a decent society . . . ."[1]

But, it is argued, there are no scientific data which conclusively demonstrate that exposure to obscene material adversely affects men and women or their society. It is urged on behalf of the petitioners that, absent such a demonstration, any kind of state regulation is "impermissible." We reject this argument. It is not for us to resolve empirical uncertainties underlying state legislation, save in the exceptional case where that legislation plainly impinges upon rights protected by the Constitution itself. Mr. Justice Brennan, speaking for the Court in Ginsberg v. New York, said: "We do not demand of legislatures 'scientifically certain criteria of legislation.'" Although there is no conclusive proof of a connection between antisocial behavior and obscene material, the legislature of Georgia could quite reasonably determine that such a connection does or might exist. In deciding *Roth,* this Court implicitly accepted that a legislature could legitimately act on such a conclusion to protect *"the social interest in order and morality."*. . .[2]

---

[1] "In this and other cases in this area of the law, which are coming to us in ever-increasing numbers, we are faced with the resolution of rights basic both to individuals and to society as a whole. Specifically, we are called upon to reconcile the right of the Nation and of the States to maintain a decent society and, on the other hand, the right of individuals to express themselves freely in accordance with the guarantees of the First and Fourteenth Amendments." Jacobellis v. Ohio (Warren, C.J., dissenting).

[2] "It has been well observed that such [lewd and obscene] utterances are no essential part of any exposition of ideas, and are of such slight social value as a step to truth that any benefit that may be derived from them is clearly outweighed by the social interest in order and morality." Chaplinsky v. New Hampshire.

If we accept the unprovable assumption that a complete education requires the reading of certain books, and the well nigh universal belief that good books, plays, and art lift the spirit, improve the mind, enrich the human personality, and develop character, can we then say that a state legislature may not act on the corollary assumption that commerce in obscene books, or public exhibitions focused on obscene conduct, have a tendency to exert a corrupting and debasing impact leading to antisocial behavior? The sum of experience, including that of the past two decades, affords an ample basis for legislatures to conclude that a sensitive, key relationship of human existence, central to family life, community welfare, and the development of human personality, can be debased and distorted by crass commercial exploitation of sex. Nothing in the Constitution prohibits a State from reaching such a conclusion and acting on it legislatively simply because there is no conclusive evidence or empirical data.

It is argued that individual "free will" must govern, even in activities beyond the protection of the First Amendment and other constitutional guarantees of privacy, and that government cannot legitimately impede an individual's desire to see or acquire obscene plays, movies, and books. We do indeed base our society on certain assumptions that people have the capacity for free choice. Most exercises of individual free choice—those in politics, religion, and expression of ideas—are explicitly protected by the Constitution. Totally unlimited play for free will, however, is not allowed in our or any other society. We have . . . noted, for example, that neither the First Amendment nor "free will" precludes States from having "blue sky" laws to regulate what sellers of securities may write or publish about their wares. Such laws are to protect the weak, the uninformed, the unsuspecting, and the gullible from the exercise of their own volition. Nor do modern societies leave disposal of garbage and sewage up to the individual "free will," but impose regulation to protect both public health and the appearance of public places. States are told by some that they must await a "laissez-faire" market solution to the obscenity-pornography problem, paradoxically "by people who have never otherwise had a kind word to say for laissez-faire," particularly in solving urban, commercial, and environmental pollution problems. . . .

It is asserted, however, that standards for evaluating state commercial regulations are inapposite in the present context, as state regulation of access by consenting adults to obscene material violates the constitutionally protected right to privacy enjoyed by petitioners' customers. . . .

Our prior decisions recognizing a right to privacy guaranteed by the Fourteenth Amendment included "only personal rights that can be deemed 'fundamental' or 'implicit in the concept of ordered liberty.'" Roe v. Wade. This privacy right encompasses and protects the personal intimacies of the home, the family, marriage, motherhood, procreation, and child rearing. . . . Nothing, however, in this Court's decisions intimates that there is any "fundamental" privacy right "implicit in the concept of ordered liberty" to watch obscene movies in places of public accommodation. . . .

It is also argued that the State has no legitimate interest in "control [of] the moral content of a person's thoughts," Stanley v. Georgia, and we need not quarrel with this. But we reject the claim that the State of Georgia is here attempting to control the minds or thoughts of those who patronize theaters. Preventing unlimited display or distribution of obscene material, which by definition lacks any serious literary, artistic, political, or scientific value as communication, Miller v. California, is distinct from a control of reason and the intellect. Where communication of ideas, protected by the First Amendment, is not involved, or the particular privacy of the home protected by *Stanley,* or any of the other "areas or zones" of constitutionally protected privacy, the mere fact that, as a consequence, some human "utterances" or "thoughts" may be incidentally affected does not bar the State from acting to protect legitimate state interests. The fantasies of a drug addict are his own and beyond the reach of government, but government regulation of drug sales is not prohibited by the Constitution.

Finally, petitioners argue that conduct which directly involves "consenting adults" only has, for that sole reason, a special claim to constitutional protection. Our Constitution establishes a broad range of conditions on the exercise of power by the States, but for us to say that our Constitution incorporates the proposition that conduct involving consenting adults only is always beyond state regulation, is a step we are unable to take. Commercial exploitation of depictions, descriptions, or exhibitions of obscene conduct on commercial premises open to the adult public falls within a State's broad power to regulate commerce and protect the public environment. The issue in this context goes beyond whether someone, or even the majority, considers the conduct depicted as "wrong" or "sinful." The States have the power to make a morally neutral judgment that public exhibition of obscene material, or commerce in such material, has a tendency to injure the community as a whole, to endanger the public safety, or to jeopardize in Mr. Chief Justice Warren's words, the States' "right . . . to maintain a decent society." . . .

Vacated and remanded.

Mr. Justice Brennan, with whom Mr. Justice Stewart and Mr. Justice Marshall join, dissenting.

This case requires the Court to confront once again the vexing problem of reconciling state efforts to suppress sexually oriented expression with the protections of the First Amendment, as applied to the States through the Fourteenth Amendment. No other aspect of the First Amendment has, in recent years, demanded so substantial a commitment of our time, generated such disharmony of views, and remained so resistant to the formulation of stable and manageable standards. I am convinced that the approach initiated 16 years ago in Roth v. United States, and culminating in the Court's decision today, cannot bring stability to this area of the law without jeopardizing fundamental First Amendment values, and I have concluded that the time has come to make a significant departure from that approach.
. . .

In Roth v. United States the Court held that obscenity, although expression, falls outside the area of speech or press constitutionally protected under the First and Fourteenth Amendments against state or federal infringement. But at the same time we emphasized in *Roth* that "sex and obscenity are not synonymous," and that matter which is sexually oriented but not obscene is fully protected by the Constitution. For we recognized that "[s]ex, a great and mysterious motive force in human life, has indisputably been a subject of absorbing interest to mankind through the ages; it is one of the vital problems of human interest and public concern." *Roth* rested, in other words, on what has been termed a two-level approach to the question of obscenity. While much criticized, that approach has been endorsed by all but two members of this Court who have addressed the question since *Roth*. Yet our efforts to implement that approach demonstrate that agreement on the existence of something called "obscenity" is still a long and painful step from agreement on a workable definition of the term.

Recognizing that "the freedoms of expression . . . are vulnerable to gravely damaging yet barely visible encroachments," we have demanded that "sensitive tools" be used to carry out the "separation of legitimate from illegitimate speech." The essence of our problem in the obscenity area is that we have been unable to provide "sensitive tools" to separate obscenity from other sexually oriented but constitutionally protected speech, so that efforts to suppress the former do not spill over into the suppression of the latter. The attempt, as the late Mr. Justice Harlan observed, has only "produced a variety of views among the members of the Court unmatched in any other course of constitutional adjudication."

To be sure, five members of the Court did agree in *Roth* that obscenity could be determined by asking "whether to the average person, applying contemporary community standards, the dominant theme of the material taken as a whole appeals to prurient interest." But agreement on that test—achieved in the abstract and without reference to the particular material before the Court—was, to say the least, short lived. . . .

Our experience with the *Roth* approach has certainly taught us that the outright suppression of obscenity cannot be reconciled with the fundamental principles of the First and Fourteenth Amendments. For we have failed to formulate a standard that sharply distinguishes protected from unprotected speech, and out of necessity, we have resorted to the *Redrup* approach, which resolves cases as between the parties, but offers only the most obscure guidance to legislation, adjudication by other courts, and primary conduct. By disposing of cases through summary reversal or denial of certiorari we have deliberately and effectively obscured the rationale underlying the decisions. It comes as no surprise that judicial attempts to follow our lead conscientiously have often ended in hopeless confusion.

Of course, the vagueness problem would be largely of our own creation if it stemmed primarily from our failure to reach a consensus on any one standard. But after 16 years of experimentation and debate I am reluctantly forced to the conclusion that none of the available formulas, including the one announced today, can reduce the vagueness to a tolerable level while at the same time striking an acceptable balance between the protections of the First and Fourteenth Amendments, on the one hand, and on the other the asserted state interest in regulating the dissemination of certain sexually oriented materials. Any effort to draw a constitutionally acceptable boundary on state power must resort to such indefinite concepts as "prurient interest," "patent offensiveness," "serious literary value," and the like. The meaning of these concepts necessarily varies with the experience, outlook, and even idiosyncrasies of the person defining them. Although we have assumed that obscenity does exist and that we "know it when [we] see it," Jacobellis v. Ohio (Stewart, J., concurring), we are manifestly unable to describe it in advance except by reference to concepts so elusive that they fail to distinguish clearly between protected and unprotected speech. . . .

In short, while I cannot say that the interests of the State—apart from the question of juveniles and unconsenting adults—are trivial or nonexistent, I am compelled to conclude that these interests cannot justify the substantial damage to constitutional rights and to this Nation's judicial machinery that inevitably results from state efforts to bar the distribution even of unprotected material to consenting adults. I would hold, therefore, that at least in the absence of distribution to juveniles or obtrusive exposure to unconsenting adults, the First and Fourteenth Amendments prohibit the State and Federal Governments from attempting wholly to suppress sexually oriented materials on the basis of their allegedly "obscene" contents. Nothing in this approach precludes those governments from taking action to serve what may be strong and legitimate interests through regulation of the manner of distribution of sexually oriented material. . . .

Notes and Questions

1. Suppose that *The Federalist No. 10* had been written in response to Garrett Hardin's *The Tragedy of the Commons.* How satisfactory a response would it be?

2. What is the difference between a "community" and a "society"? How should the legal system take account of this difference? How did it do so in the *Papachristou* and *Wilson* cases?

3. In Miller v. California, decided the same day as the *Paris Adult Theatre* case, the U.S. Supreme Court declared:

> Under a National Constitution, fundamental First Amendment limitations on the powers of the States do not vary from community to community, but this does not mean that there are, or should or can be, fixed, uniform national standards of precisely what appeals to the "prurient interest" or is "patently offensive.". . . It is neither realistic nor constitutionally sound to read the First Amendment as requiring that the people of Maine or Mississippi accept public depiction of conduct found tolerable in Las Vegas, or New York City.

What are the implications of this statement for obscenity law, and indeed for law in general?

Suggestions For Further Reading

Bruce A. Ackerman, Social Justice in the Liberal State, ch. 1 (1980)

Hannah Arendt, The Human Condition, pt. II (1958)

Charles E. Larmore, Patterns of Moral Complexity, ch. 3 (1987)

Stephen Macedo, Toleration and Fundamentalism, in A Companion to Contemporary Political Philosophy (Robert E. Goodin & Philip Pettit eds. 1993)

John Rawls, The Idea of Public Reason Revisited, 64 University of Chicago Law Review 765 (1997)

Mark D. Rosen, The Outer Limits of Community Self-Governance in Residential Associations, Municipalities, and Indian Country: A Liberal Theory, 84 Virginia Law Review 1053 (1998)

Part II
Freedom and Necessity

Law is addressed to us in our capacity as intelligent moral agents; its commands make no sense if we are not free to obey or disobey them. (Otherwise, the law would not bother to "command" us at all but would simply force us into compliance.)

The theme of *freedom and necessity* is basic to jurisprudential theory, because freedom is generally understood to be a prerequisite for legal responsibility. Conversely, the lack of freedom—i.e., "necessity"—will supply a defense to legal liability, such as a justification or excuse. Yet, it eventually becomes evident that the law does not understand necessity in the strict and absolute sense of mechanical causation or physical compulsion. Self-defense, for example, is still available as a legal defense even when some alternatives or choices were available to the defendant. In many circumstances, therefore, what seemed to be a definitional issue of freedom or necessity becomes a matter of degree and a relatively open question, to be answered in the light of social policy, legal doctrine, and the specific facts of particular cases.

The following chapters cover a wide range of important circumstances in which freedom and necessity are at issue; at the same time they present a correspondingly wide array of opinions as to the applicable legal concepts of freedom and necessity.

Chapter 3
Life or Death

Regina v. Dudley and Stephens
14 Q.B.D. 273 (1884)

Indictment for the murder of Richard Parker on the high seas within the jurisdiction of the Admiralty.

At the trial before Huddleston, B., at the Devon and Cornwall Winter Assizes, November 7, 1884, the jury, at the suggestion of the learned judge, found the facts of the case in a special verdict which stated "that on July 5, 1884, the prisoners, Thomas Dudley and Edward Stephens, with one Brooks, all able-bodied English seamen, and the deceased also an English boy, between seventeen and eighteen years of age, the crew of an English yacht, a registered English vessel, were cast away in a storm on the high seas 1600 miles from the Cape of Good Hope, and were compelled to put into an open boat belonging to the said yacht. That in this boat they had no supply of water and no supply of food, except two 1 lb. tins of turnips, and for three days they had nothing else to subsist upon. That on the fourth day they caught a small turtle, upon which they subsisted for a few days, and this was the only food they had up to the twentieth day when the act now in question was committed. That on the twelfth day the turtle were entirely consumed, and for the next eight days they had nothing to eat. That they had no fresh water, except such rain as they from time to time caught in their oilskin capes. That the boat was drifting on the ocean, and was probably more than 1000 miles away from land. That on the eighteenth day, when they had been seven days without food and five without water, the prisoners spoke to Brooks as to what should be done if no succour came, and suggested that some one should be sacrificed to save the rest, but Brooks dissented, and the boy, to whom they were understood to refer, was not consulted. That on the 24th of July, the day before the act now in question, the prisoner Dudley proposed to Stephens and Brooks that lots should be cast who should be put to death to save the rest, but Brooks refused consent, and it was not put to the boy, and in point of fact there was no drawing of lots. That on that day the prisoners spoke of their having families, and suggested it would be better to kill the boy that their lives should be saved, and Dudley proposed that if there was no vessel in sight by the morrow morning the boy should be killed. That next day, the 25th of July, no vessel appearing, Dudley told Brooks that he had better go and have a sleep, and made signs to Stephens and Brooks that the boy had better be killed. The prisoner Stephens agreed to the act, but Brooks dissented from it. That the boy was then lying at the bottom of the boat quite helpless, and extremely weakened by famine and by drinking sea water, and unable to make any resistance, nor did he ever assent to his being killed. The prisoner Dudley offered a prayer asking forgiveness for them all if either of them should be tempted to commit a rash act, and that their souls might be saved. That Dudley, with the assent of Stephens, went to the boy, and telling him that his time was come, put a knife into his throat and killed him then and there; that the three men fed upon the body and blood of the boy for four days; that on the fourth day after the act had been committed the boat was picked up by a passing vessel, and the prisoners were rescued, still alive, but in the lowest state of prostration. That they were carried to the port of Falmouth, and committed for trial at Exeter. That if the men had not fed upon the body of the boy they would probably not have survived to be so picked up and rescued, but would within the four days have died of famine. That the boy, being in a much weaker condition, was likely to have died before them. That at the time of the act in question there was no sail in sight, nor any reasonable prospect of relief. That under these circumstances there appeared to the prisoners every probability that unless they then fed or very soon fed upon the boy or one of themselves they would die of starvation. That there was no appreciable chance of saving life except by killing some one for the others to eat. That assuming any necessity to kill anybody, there was no greater necessity for killing the boy than any of the other three men. But whether upon the whole matter by the jurors found the killing of Richard Parker by Dudley and Stephens be felony and murder the jurors are ignorant, and pray the advice of the Court thereupon, and if upon the whole matter the Court shall be of opinion that the killing of Richard Parker be felony and murder, then the jurors say that Dudley and Stephens were each guilty of felony and murder as alleged in the indictment."

The judgment of the Court . . . was delivered by Lord Coleridge, C.J.

The two prisoners, Thomas Dudley and Edwin Stephens, were indicted for the murder of Richard Parker on the high seas on the 25th of July in the present year. They were tried before my Brother Huddleston at Exeter on the 6th of November, and under the direction of my learned Brother, the jury returned a special verdict, the legal effect of which has been argued before us, and on which we are now to pronounce judgment.

The special verdict as, after certain objections by Mr. Collins to which the Attorney General yielded, it is finally settled before us is as follows. [His Lordship read the special verdict as above set out.] From these facts, stated with the cold precision of a special verdict, it appears sufficiently that the prisoners were subject to terrible temptation, to sufferings which might break down the bodily power of the strongest man and try the conscience of the best. Other details yet more harrowing, facts still more loathsome and appalling, were presented to the jury, and are to be found recorded in my learned Brother's notes. But nevertheless this is clear, that the prisoners put to death a weak and unoffending boy upon the chance of preserving their own lives by feeding upon his flesh and blood after he was killed, and with the certainty of depriving *him* of any possible chance of survival. The verdict finds in terms that "if the men had not fed upon the body of the boy they would *probably* not have survived," and that, "the boy being in a much weaker condition was *likely* to have died before them." They might possibly have been picked up next day by a passing ship; they might possibly not have been picked up at all; in either case it is obvious that the killing of the boy would have been an unnecessary and profitless act. It is found by the verdict that the boy was incapable of resistance, and, in fact, made none; and it is not even suggested that his death was due to any violence on his part attempted against, or even so much as feared by, those who killed him. Under these circumstances the jury say that they are ignorant whether those who killed him were guilty of murder, and have referred it to this Court to determine what is the legal consequence which follows from the facts which they have found. . . .

There remains to be considered the real question in the case—whether killing under the circumstances set forth in the verdict be or be not murder. The contention that it could be anything else was, to the minds of us all, both new and strange, and we stopped the Attorney General in his negative argument in order that we might hear what could be said in support of a proposition which appeared to us to be at once dangerous, immoral, and opposed to all legal principle and analogy. All, no doubt, that can be said has been urged before us, and we are now to consider and determine what it amounts to. First it is said that it follows from various definitions of murder in books of authority, which definitions imply, if they do not state, the doctrine, that in order to save your own life you may lawfully take away the life of another, when that other is neither attempting nor threatening yours, nor is guilty of any illegal act whatever towards you or any one else. But if these definitions be looked at they will not be found to sustain this contention. The earliest in point of date is the passage cited to us from Bracton, who lived in the reign of Henry III. It was at one time the fashion to discredit Bracton, as Mr. Reeve tells us, because he was supposed to mingle too much of the canonist and civilian with the common lawyer. There is now no such feeling, but the passage upon homicide, on which reliance is placed, is a remarkable example of the kind of writing which may explain it. Sin and crime are spoken of as apparently equally illegal, and the crime of murder, it is expressly declared, may be committed "lingua vel facto"; so that a man, like Hero "done to death by slanderous tongues," would, it seems, in the opinion of Bracton, be a person in respect of whom might be grounded a legal indictment for murder. But in the very passage as to necessity, on which reliance has been placed, it is clear that Bracton is speaking of necessity in the ordinary sense—the repelling by violence, violence justified so far as it was necessary for the object, any illegal violence used towards oneself. If, says Bracton, the necessity be "evitabilis, et evadere posset absque occisione, tunc erit reus homicidii"—words which shew clearly that he is thinking of physical danger from which *escape* may be possible, and that the "inevitabilis necessitas" of which he speaks as justifying homicide is a necessity of the same nature.

It is, if possible, yet clearer that the doctrine contended for receives no support from the great authority of Lord Hale. It is plain that in his view the necessity which justified homicide is that only which has always been and is now considered a justification. "In all these cases of homicide by necessity," says he, "as in pursuit of a felon, in killing him that assaults to rob, or comes to burn or break a house, or the like, which are in themselves no felony." Again, he says that "the necessity which justifies homicide is of two kinds: (1) the necessity which is of a private nature; (2) the necessity which relates to the public justice and safety. The former is that necessity which obligeth a man to his own defence and safeguard, and this takes in these inquiries: (I.) What may be done for the safeguard of a man's own life;" and then follow three other heads not necessary to pursue. Then Lord Hale proceeds: "As touching the first of these—viz., homicide in defence of a man's own life, which is usually styled se defendendo." It is not possible to use words more clear to shew that Lord Hale regarded the private necessity which justified, and alone justified, the taking the life of another for the safeguard of one's own to be what is commonly called "self-defence."

But if this could be even doubtful upon Lord Hale's words, Lord Hale himself has made it clear. For in the chapter in which he deals with the exemption created by compulsion or necessity he thus expresses himself: "If a man be desperately assaulted and in peril of death, and cannot otherwise escape unless, to satisfy his assailant's fury, he will kill an innocent person then present, the fear and actual force will not acquit him of the crime and punishment of murder, if he commit the fact, for he ought rather to die himself than kill an innocent; but if he cannot otherwise save his own life the law permits him in his own defence to kill the assailant, for by the violence of the assault, and the offence committed upon him by the assailant himself, the law of nature and necessity, hath made him his own protector cum debito moderamine inculpatae tutelae."

But, further still, Lord Hale in the following chapter deals with the position asserted by the casuists and sanctioned, as he says, by Grotius and Puffendorf, that in a case of extreme necessity, either of hunger or clothing; "theft is no theft, or at least not punishable as theft, as some even of our own lawyers have asserted the same." "But," says Lord Hale, "I take it that here in England, that rule, at least by the laws of England, is false; and therefore, if a person, being under necessity for want of victuals or clothes, shall upon that account clandestinely and animo furandi steal another man's goods, it is felony, and a crime by the laws of England punishable with death." If therefore, Lord Hale is clear—as he is—that extreme necessity of hunger does not justify larceny, what would he have said to the doctrine that it justified murder?

It is satisfactory to find that another great authority, second, probably, only to Lord Hale, speaks with the same unhesitating clearness on this matter. Sir Michael Foster, in the 3rd chapter of his Discourse on Homicide, deals with the subject of "homicide founded in necessity"; and the whole chapter implies, and is insensible unless it does imply, that in the view of Sir Michael Foster "necessity and self-defence" (which he defines as "opposing force to force even to the death") are convertible terms. There is no hint, no trace, of the doctrine now contended for; the whole reasoning of the chapter is entirely inconsistent with it. In East's Pleas of the Crown the whole chapter on homicide by necessity is taken up with an elaborate discussion of the limits within which necessity in Sir Michael Foster's sense (given above) of self-defence is a justification of or excuse for homicide. There is a short section at the end very generally and very doubtfully expressed, in which the only instance discussed is the well-known one of two shipwrecked men on a plank able to sustain only one of them, and the conclusion is left by Sir Edward East entirely undetermined.

What is true of Sir Edward East is true also of Mr. Serjeant Hawkins. The whole of his chapter on justifiable homicide assumes that the only justifiable homicide of a private nature is the defence against force of a man's person, house, or goods. In the 26th section we find again the case of the two shipwrecked men and the single plank, with the significant expression from a careful writer, "*It is said* to be justifiable." So, too, Dalton clearly considers necessity and self-defence in Sir Michael Foster's sense of that expression, to be convertible terms, though he prints without comment Lord Bacon's instance of the two men on one plank as a quotation from Lord Bacon, adding nothing whatever to it of his own. And there is a remarkable passage . . . in which he says that even in the case of a murderous assault upon a man, yet before he may take the life of the man who assaults him even in self-defence, "cuncta prius tentanda."

The passage in Staundforde, on which almost the whole of the dicta we have been considering are built, when it comes to be examined, does not warrant the conclusion which has been derived from it. The necessity to justify homicide must be, he says, inevitable, and the example which he gives to illustrate his meaning is the very same which has just been cited from Dalton, shewing that the necessity he was speaking of was a physical necessity, and the self-defence a defence against physical violence. Russell merely repeats the language of the old text-books, and adds no new authority, nor any fresh considerations.

Is there, then, any authority for the proposition which has been presented to us? Decided cases there are none. The case of the seven English sailors referred to by the commentator on Grotius and by Puffendorf has been discovered by a gentleman of the Bar, who communicated with my Brother Huddleston, to convey the authority (if it conveys so much) of a single judge of the island of St. Kitts, when that island was possessed partly by France and partly by this country, somewhere about the year 1641. It is mentioned in a medical treatise published at Amsterdam, and is altogether, as authority in an English Court, as unsatisfactory as possible. The American case cited by my Brother Stephen in his Digest, from Wharton on Homicide, in which it was decided, correctly indeed, that sailors had no right to throw passengers overboard to save themselves, but on the somewhat strange ground that the proper mode of determining who was to be sacrificed was to vote upon the subject by ballot, can hardly, as my Brother Stephen says, be an authority satisfactory to a court in this country. The observations of Lord Mansfield in the case of Rex v. Stratton and Others, striking and excellent as they are, were delivered in a political trial, where the question was whether a political necessity had arisen for deposing a Governor of Madras. But they have little application to the case before us, which must be decided on very different considerations.

The one real authority of former time is Lord Bacon, who, in his commentary on the maxim, "necessitas inducit privilegium quoad jura privata" (necessity gives a privilege with respect to private rights), lays down the law as follows: "Necessity carrieth a privilege in itself. Necessity is of three sorts—necessity of conservation of life, necessity of obedience, and necessity of the act of God or of a stranger. First of conservation of life; if a man steal viands to satisfy his present hunger, this is no felony nor larceny. So if divers be in danger of drowning by the casting away of some boat or barge, and one of them get to some plank or on the boat's side to keep himself above water, and another to save his life thrust him from it, whereby he is drowned, this is neither se defendendo nor by misadventure, but justifiable." On this it is to be observed that Lord Bacon's proposition that stealing to satisfy hunger is no larceny is hardly supported by Staundforde, whom he cites for it, and is expressly contradicted by Lord Hale in the passage already cited. And for the proposition as to the plank or boat, it is said to be derived from the canonists. At any rate he cites no authority for it, and it must stand upon his own. Lord Bacon was great even as a lawyer; but it is permissible to much smaller men, relying upon principle and on the authority of others, the equals and even the superiors of Lord Bacon as lawyers, to question the soundness of his dictum. There are many conceivable states of things in which it might possibly be true, but if Lord Bacon meant to lay down the broad proposition that a man may save his life by killing, if necessary, an innocent and unoffending neighbour, it certainly is not law at the present day.

There remains the authority of my Brother Stephen, who, both in his Digest and in his History of the Criminal Law, uses language perhaps wide enough to cover this case. The language is somewhat vague in both places, but it does not in either place cover this case of necessity, and we have the best authority for saying that it was not meant to cover it. If it had been necessary, we must with true deference have differed from him, but it is satisfactory to know that we have, probably at least, arrived at no conclusion in which if he had been a member of the Court he would have been unable to agree. Neither are we in conflict with any opinion expressed upon the subject by the learned persons who formed the commission for preparing the Criminal Code. They say on this subject:

"We are certainly not prepared to suggest that necessity should in every case be a justification. We are equally unprepared to suggest that necessity should in no case be a defence; we judge it better to leave such questions to be dealt with when, if ever, they arise in practice by applying the principles of law to the circumstances of the particular case."

It would have been satisfactory to us if these eminent persons could have told us whether the received definitions of legal necessity were in their judgment correct and exhaustive, and if not, in what way they should be amended, but as it is we have, as they say, "to apply the principles of law to the circumstances of this particular case."

Now, except for the purpose of testing how far the conservation of a man's own life is in all cases and under all circumstances, an absolute, unqualified, and paramount duty, we exclude from our consideration all the incidents of war. We are dealing with a case of private homicide, not one imposed upon men in the service of their Sovereign and in the defence of their country. Now it is admitted that the deliberate killing of this unoffending and unresisting boy was clearly murder, unless the killing can be justified by some well-recognised excuse admitted by the law. It is further admitted that there was in this case no such excuse, unless the killing was justified by what has been called "necessity." But the temptation to the act which existed here was not what the law has ever called necessity. Nor is this to be regretted. Though law and morality are not the same, and many things may be immoral which are not necessarily illegal, yet the absolute divorce of law from morality would be of fatal consequence; and such divorce would follow if the temptation to murder in this case were to be held by law an absolute defence of it. It is not so. To preserve one's life is generally speaking a duty, but it may be the plainest and the highest duty to sacrifice it. War is full of instances in which it is a man's duty not to live, but to die. The duty, in case of shipwreck, of a captain to his crew, of the crew to the passengers, of soldiers to women and children, as in the noble case of the *Birkenhead;* these duties impose on men the moral necessity, not of the preservation but of the sacrifice of their lives for others, from which in no country, least of all, it is to be hoped, in England, will men ever shrink, as indeed, they have not shrunk. It is not correct, therefore, to say that there is any absolute or unqualified necessity to preserve one's life. "Necesse est ut eam, non ut vivam" ("It is necessary to go [to war], not to live"), is a saying of a Roman officer quoted by Lord Bacon himself with high eulogy in the very chapter on necessity to which so much reference has been made. It would be a very easy and cheap display of commonplace learning to quote from Greek and Latin authors, from Horace, from Juvenal, from Cicero, from Euripides, passage after passage, in which the duty of dying for others has been laid down in glowing and emphatic language as resulting from the principles of heathen ethics; it is enough in a Christian country to remind ourselves of the Great Example whom we profess to follow. It is not needful to point out the awful danger of admitting the principle which has been contended for. Who is to be the judge of this sort of necessity? By what measure is the comparative value of lives to be measured? Is it to be strength, or intellect, or what? It is plain that the principle leaves to him who is to profit by it to determine the necessity which will justify him in deliberately taking another's life to save his own. In this case the weakest, the youngest, the most unresisting, was chosen. Was it more necessary to kill him than one of the grown men? The answer must be "No"—

> So spake the Fiend, and with necessity,
> The tyrant's plea, excused his devilish deeds.

It is not suggested that in this particular case the deeds were "devilish," but it is quite plain that such a principle once admitted might be made the legal cloak for unbridled passion and atrocious crime. There is no safe path for judges to tread but to ascertain the law to the best of their ability and to declare it according to their judgment; and if in any case the law appears to be too severe on individuals, to leave it to the Sovereign to exercise that prerogative of mercy which the Constitution has intrusted to the hands fittest to dispense it.

It must not be supposed that in refusing to admit temptation to be an excuse for crime it is forgotten how terrible the temptation was; how awful the suffering; how hard in such trials to keep the judgment straight and the conduct pure. We are often compelled to set up standards we cannot reach ourselves, and to lay down rules which we could not ourselves satisfy. But a man has no right to declare temptation to be an excuse, though he might himself have yielded to it, nor allow compassion for the criminal to change or weaken in any manner the legal definition of the crime. It is therefore our duty to declare that the prisoners' act in this case was wilful murder, that the facts as stated in the verdict are no legal justification of the homicide; and to say that in our unanimous opinion the prisoners are upon this special verdict guilty of murder.

The Court then proceeded to pass sentence of death upon the prisoners.

[This sentence was afterwards commuted by the Crown to six months' imprisonment.]

United States v. Holmes
26 F. Cas. 360 (C.C.E.D. Pa. 1842)

The American ship William Brown, left Liverpool on the 13th of March, 1841, bound for Philadelphia, in the United States. She had on board (besides a heavy cargo) seventeen of a crew, and 65 passengers, Scotch and Irish emigrants. About ten o'clock on the night of the 19th of April, when distant 250 miles southeast of Cape Race, Newfoundland, the vessel struck an iceberg, and began to fill so rapidly that it was evident she must soon go down. The long-boat and jolly-boat were cleared away and lowered. The captain, the second mate, seven of the crew, and one passenger got into the jolly-boat. The first mate, eight seamen, of whom the prisoner was one (these nine being the entire remainder of the crew), and 32 passengers, in all 41 persons, got indiscriminately into the long-boat. The remainder of the passengers, 31 persons, were obliged to remain on board the ship. In an hour and a half from the time when the ship struck, she went down, carrying with her every person who had not escaped to one or the other of the small boats.

Thirty-one passengers thus perished.

On the following morning (Tuesday) the captain, being about to part company with the long-boat, gave its crew several directions, and, among other counsel, advised them to obey all the orders of the mate, as they would obey his, the captain's. This the crew promised that they would do.

The long-boat was believed to be in general good condition; but she had not been in the water since leaving Liverpool, now thirty-five days; and as soon as she was launched, began to leak. She continued to leak the whole time; but the passengers had buckets and tins, and, by bailing, were able to reduce the water, so as to make her hold her own. The plug was about an inch and a half in diameter. It came out more than once, and, finally, got lost; but its place was supplied by different expedients.

It appeared by the depositions of the captain, and of the second mate (the latter of whom had followed the sea twenty-one years; the former being, likewise, well-experienced), that on Tuesday morning when the two boats parted company, the long-boat and all on board were in great jeopardy. The gunwale was within from 5 to 12 inches of the water. "From the experience" which they had had, they thought "the long-boat was too unmanageable to be saved." If she had been what, in marine phrase, is called a "leaky boat," she must have gone down. Even without a leak she would not have supported one-half her company, had there been "a moderate blow." "She would have swamped very quickly." The people were half naked, and were "all crowded up together like sheep in a pen." "A very little irregularity in the stowage would have capsized the long-boat." "If she had struck any piece of ice she would inevitably have gone down. There was great peril of ice for any boat." (Captain's and second mate's depositions.) Without going into more detail, the evidence of both these officers went to show that, loaded as the long-boat was on Tuesday morning, the chances of living were much against her. But the captain thought, that even if lightened to the extent to which she afterwards was, "it would have been impossible to row her to land; and that the chances of her being picked up, were ninety-nine to one against her."

It appeared, further, that on Monday night, when the passengers on the ship (then set-tling towards her head and clearly going down) were shrieking, and calling on the captain to take them off on his boat, the mate on the long-boat said to them: "Poor souls! You're only going down a short time before we do." And, further, that on the following morning, before the boats parted company, the mate, in the long-boat, told the captain, in the jolly-boat, that the long-boat was unmanageable, and, that unless the captain would take some of the long-boat's passengers, it would be necessary to cast lots and throw some overboard. "I know what you mean," or, as stated by one witness, "I know what you'll have to do," said the captain. "Don't speak of that now. Let it be the last resort."

There was little or no wind at this time; but pieces of ice were floating about.

Notwithstanding all this, the long-boat, loaded as she is above described to have been, did survive throughout the night of Monday, the day of Tuesday, and till ten o'clock of Tuesday night; full twenty-four hours after the ship struck the iceberg. The crew rowed, turn about, at intervals, and the passengers bailed.

On Tuesday morning, after the long-boat and jolly-boat parted, it began to rain, and continued to rain throughout the day and night of Tuesday. At night the wind began to freshen, the sea grew heavier, and once, or oftener, the waves splashed over the boat's bow so as to wet, all over, the passengers who were seated there. Pieces of ice were still float-ing around, and, during the day, icebergs had been seen.

About ten o'clock of Tuesday night, the prisoner and the rest of the crew began to throw over some of the passengers, and did not cease until they had thrown over fourteen male passengers. These, with the exception of two married men and a small boy, constituted all the male passengers aboard.

Not one of the crew was cast over. One of them, the cook, was a negro.

It was among the facts of this case that, during these solemn and distressful hours, scarce a remark appeared to have been made in regard to what was going to be done, nor, while it was being done, as to the necessity for doing it. None of the crew of the long-boat were present at the trial, to testify; and, with the exception of one small boy, all the wit-nesses from the long-boat were women, mostly quite young. It is probable, that by Tuesday night (the weather being cold, the persons on the boat partially naked, and the rain falling heavily), the witnesses had become considerably overpowered by exhaustion and cold, hav-ing been twenty-four hours in the boat. None of them spoke in a manner entirely explicit and satisfactory in regard to the most important point, viz. the degree and imminence of the jeopardy at ten o'clock on Tuesday night, when the throwing over began.

As has been stated, few words were spoken. It appeared, only, that about ten o'clock of Tuesday night, it being then dark, the rain falling rather heavily, the sea somewhat fresh-ening, and the boat having considerable water in it, the mate, who had been bailing for some time, gave it up, exclaiming: "This work won't do. Help me, God! Men, go to work." Some of the passengers cried out, about the same time: "The boat is sinking. The plug's out. God have mercy on our poor souls!"

Holmes and the crew did not proceed upon this order; and after a little while, the mate exclaimed again: "Men, you *must* go to work, or we shall all perish." They then went to work; and, as has been already stated, threw out, before they ended, fourteen male passengers, and also two women.

The mate directed the crew "not to part man and wife, and not to throw over any women." There was no other principle of selection. There was no evidence of combination among the crew. No lots were cast, nor had the passengers, at any time, been either informed or consulted as to what was now done.

Holmes was one of the persons who assisted in throwing the passengers over. The first man thrown over was one Riley, whom Holmes and the others told to stand up, which he did. They then threw him over, and afterwards Duffy, who, in vain, besought them to spare him, for the sake of his wife and children, who were on shore. They then seized a third man, but, his wife being aboard, he was spared. Coming to Charles Conlin, the man exclaimed: "Holmes, dear, sure you won't put *me* out?" "Yes, Charley," said Holmes, "you must go, too." And so he was thrown over. Next was Francis Askin, for the "manslaughter" of whom the prisoner was indicted. When laid hold of, he offered Holmes five sovereigns to spare his life till morning, "when," said he, "if God don't send us some help, we'll draw lots, and if the lot falls on me, I'll go over like a man." Holmes said, "I don't want your money, Frank," and put him overboard.

When one McAvoy was seized, he asked for five minutes to say his prayers, and, at the interposition of a negro, the cook, was allowed time to say them before he was cast overboard. It appeared, also, that when Askin was put out, he had struggled violently, yet the boat had not sunk.

Two men, very stiff with cold, who had hidden themselves, were thrown over after daylight on Wednesday morning, when, clearly, there was no necessity for it.

On Wednesday morning, while yet in the boat, some of the witnesses had told the crew that they (i.e. the crew) should be made to die the death they had given to the others.

The boat had provisions for six or seven days, close allowance; that is to say, 75 pounds of bread, 6 gallons of water, 8 or 10 pounds of meat, and a small bag of oatmeal. The mate had a chart, quadrant and compass. The weather was cold, and the passengers, being half clothed, much benumbed.

On Wednesday morning the weather cleared, and early in the morning the long-boat was picked up by the ship "Crescent." All the persons who had not been thrown overboard were thus saved.

On the other hand the character of the prisoner stood forth, in many points, in manly and interesting relief. A Finn by birth, he had followed the sea from youth, and his frame and countenance would have made an artist's model for decision and strength. He had been the last man of the crew to leave the sinking ship. His efforts to save the passengers, at the time the ship struck, had been conspicuous; and, but that they were in discharge of duty, would have been called self-forgetful and most generous. As a sailor, his captain and the second mate testified, that he had ever been obedient to orders, faithful to his duty, and efficient in the performance of it; "remarkably so," said the second mate. "He was kind and obliging in every respect," said the captain; "to the passengers, to his shipmates, and to everybody. Never heard one speak against him. He was always obedient to officers. I never had a better man on board ship. He was a first-rate man." (Captain's deposition.) While on the long-boat, in order to protect the women, he had parted with all his clothes, except his shirt and pantaloons; and his conduct and language to the women were kind. After Askin had been thrown out, someone asked if any more were to be thrown over. "No," said Holmes, "no more shall be thrown over. If any more are lost, we will all be lost together." Of both passengers and crew, he finally became the only one whose energies and whose hopes did not sink into prostration. He was the first to descry the vessel which took them up, and by his exertions the ship was made to see, and finally, to save them.

The prisoner was indicted under the act of April 30, 1790, "for the punishment of certain crimes against the United States" (1 Story's Laws 83 [1 Stat. 115]), an act which ordains, § 12, "that if any Seaman &c. shall commit *manslaughter* upon the high seas" &c., on conviction, he shall be imprisoned not exceeding three years, and fined not exceeding one thousand dollars. The indictment charged that Holmes: First, with force, &c. "unlawfully and feloniously" did make an assault &c. and cast and throw Askin from a vessel, belonging &c. whose name was unknown, into the high seas, by means of which &c. Askin, in and with the waters thereof, then and there was suffocated and drowned; second, in the same way, on board the long-boat of the ship William Brown, belonging &c. did make an assault &c. and cast &c.

The trial of the prisoner came on upon the 13th of April, 1842, a few days before the anniversary of the calamitous events referred to. The case was replete with incidents of deep romance, and of pathetic interest. These, not being connected with the law of the case, of course do not appear in this report; but they had become known, in a general way, to the public, before the trial; and on the day assigned for the trial, at the opening of the court, several stenographers connected with the newspaper press appeared within the bar, ready to report the evidence for their expectant readers. . . .

The prosecution was conducted by Mr. Wm. M. Meredith, U.S. Dist. Atty., Mr. Dallas, and O. Hopkinson; the defence by David Paul Brown, Mr. Hazlehurst, and Mr. Armstrong.

Mr. Dallas. The prisoner is charged with "unlawful homicide," as distinguished from that sort which is malicious. His defence is that the homicide was necessary to self-preservation. First, then, we ask: Was the homicide thus necessary? That is to say, was the danger instant, overwhelming, leaving no choice of means, no moment for deliberation? For, unless the danger were of this sort, the prisoner, under any admission, has no right, without notice or consultation, or lot, to sacrifice the lives of sixteen fellow beings. Peril, even extreme peril, is not enough to justify a sacrifice such as this was. Nor would even the certainty of death be enough, if death were yet prospective. It must be *instant*. The law regards every man's life as of equal value. It regards it, likewise, as of sacred value. Nor may any man take away his brother's life, but where the sacrifice is indispensable to save his own. [Mr. Dallas then examined the evidence, and contended that the danger was not so extreme as is requisite to justify homicide.]

But it will be answered, that death being certain, there was no obligation to wait until the moment of death had arrived. Admitting, then, the fact that death was certain, and that the safety of some persons was to be promoted by an early sacrifice of the others, what law, we ask, gives a crew, in such a case, to be the arbiters of life and death, settling, for themselves, both the time and the extent of the necessity? No! We protest against giving to seamen the power thus to make jettison of human beings, as of so much cargo; of allowing sailors, for their own safety, to throw overboard, whenever they may like, whomsoever they may choose. If the mate and seamen believed that the ultimate safety of a portion was to be advanced by the sacrifice of another portion, it was the clear duty of that officer, and of the seamen, to give full notice to all on board. Common settlement would, then, have fixed the principle of sacrifice; and, the mode of selection involving all, a sacrifice of any would have been resorted to only in dire extremity.

Thus far, the argument admits that, at sea, sailor and passenger stand upon the same base, and in equal relations. But we take, third, stronger ground. The seaman, we hold, is bound, beyond the passenger, to encounter the perils of the sea. To the last extremity, to death itself, must he protect the passenger. *It is his duty.* It is on account of these risks that he is paid. It is because the sailor is expected to expose himself to every danger, that beyond all mankind, by every law, his wages are secured to him. It is for this exposure that the seamen's claims are a "sacred lien," and "that if only a single nail of the ship is left, they are entitled to it." (3 Kent, Comm. 197, and in note.) Exposure, risk, hardship, death, are the sailor's vocation; the seaman's daily bread. He must perform whatever belongs to his duty. To this effect speaks Lord Bacon, when he says "that the law imposeth it upon every subject that he prefer the urgent service of his prince and country before the safety of his life." His lordship goes on to say that, "if a man be commanded to bring ordnance or munition to relieve any of the king's towns that are distressed, then he cannot, for any danger of tempest, justify the throwing of them overboard; for there it holdeth which was spoken by the Roman when he alleged the same necessity of weather to hold him from embarking: 'Necesse est et ut eam; non ut vivam.'" No other doctrine than this one can be adopted. Promulgate as law that the prisoner is guiltless, and our marine will be disgraced in the eyes of civilized nations. The thousand ships which now traverse the ocean in safety will be consigned to the absolute power of their crews. And, worse than the dangers of the sea, will be added such as come from the violence of men more reckless than any upon earth.

Mr. Armstrong opened the defence, and was followed by Mr. Brown.

We protest against the prisoner being made a victim to the reputation of the marine law of the country. It cannot be, God forbid that it should ever be, that the sacrifice of innocence shall be the price at which the name and honour of American jurisprudence is to be preserved in this country, or in foreign lands. The malediction of an unrighteous sentence will rest more heavily on the law, than on the prisoner. This court (it would be indecent to think otherwise) will administer the law, "uncaring consequences."

But this case should be tried in a long-boat, sunk down to its very gunwale with forty-one half naked, starved, and shivering wretches; the boat leaking from below, filling from above, a hundred leagues from land, at midnight, surrounded by ice, unmanageable from its load, and subject to certain destruction from the change of the most changeful of the elements, the winds and the waves. To these superadd the horrours of famine and the recklessness of despair, madness, and all the prospects, past utterance, of this unutterable condition. Fairly to sit in judgment on the prisoner, we should, then, be actually translated to his situation. It was a conjuncture which no fancy can image. Terrour had assumed the throne of reason, and passion had become judgment. Are the United States to come here, now, a year after the events, when it is impossible to estimate the elements which combined to make the risk, or to say to what extent the jeopardy was imminent? Are they, with square, rule and compass, deliberately to measure this boat, in this room, to weigh these passengers, call in philosophers, discuss specific gravities, calculate by the tables of a life insurance company the chances of life; and because they, these judges, find that, by *their* calculation, this unfortunate boat's crew might have had the thousandth part of one poor chance of escape, to condemn this prisoner to chains and a dungeon, for what he did in the terrour and darkness of that dark and terrible night! Such a mode of testing men's acts and motives is monstrous.

We contend, therefore, that what is honestly and reasonably believed to be certain death will justify self-defence to the degree requisite for excuse. According to Dr. Rutherford: "This law," i. e. the law of nature, "cannot be supposed to oblige a man to expose his life to such dangers as may be guarded against, and to *wait till the danger is just coming upon him,* before it allows him to secure himself." In other words, he need not wait till the certainty of the danger has been proved, past doubt, by its result. Yet this is the doctrine of the prosecution. They ask us to wait until the boat has sunk. We may, then, make an effort to prevent her from sinking. They tell us to wait till all are drowned. We may, then, make endeavours to save a part. They command us to stand still till we are all lost past possibility of redemption. And then we may rescue as many as can be saved.

Where the danger is instantaneous, the mind is too much disturbed, says Rutherford, in a passage hereafter cited, to deliberate upon the method of providing for one's own safety, with the least hurt to an aggressor. The same author then proceeds: "I see not, therefore, any want of benevolence which can be reasonably charged upon a man in these circumstances, if he takes the most obvious way of preserving himself, *though perhaps some other method might have been found out, which would have preserved him as effectually, and have produced less hurt to the aggressor,* if he had been calm enough, and had been allowed time enough to deliberate about it."

Nor is this the language of approved text writers alone. The doctrine has the solemnity of judicial establishment. In Grainger v. State, the supreme court of Tennessee deliberately adjudge, that "if a man, though in no great danger of serious bodily harm, through fear, alarm, or cowardice, kill another under the impression that great bodily injury is about to be inflicted on him, it is neither manslaughter nor murder, but self-defence." "It is a different thing," say the Supreme Court of the United States, in The Mariana Flora, "to sit in judgment upon this case, after full legal investigations, aided by the regular evidence of all parties, and to draw conclusions at sea, with very imperfect means of ascertaining facts and principles which ought to direct the judgment." The decision in the case just cited, carried out this principle into practice, as the case of The Louis, decided by Sir William Scott, had done before.

But the prospect of sinking was not imaginary. It was well founded. It is not to be supposed that Holmes, who, from infancy, had been a child of the ocean, was causelessly alarmed; and, there being no pretence of animosity, but the contrary, we must infer that the peril was extreme. As regards the two men cast over on Wednesday, the presumption is that they were either frozen, or freezing to death. There being, at this time, no prospect of relief, the act is deprived of its barbarity. The evidence is that the two men were "very stiff with cold."

Besides, this indictment is in regard to Askin alone. There is no evidence of inhumanity on Tuesday night, when this throwing over began; though it is possible enough, that, having proceeded so far in the work of horrour, the feelings of the crew became, at last, so disordered as to become unnatural. [The learned counsel then examined the evidence, in order to shew the extremity of the danger.]

Counsel say that lots are the law of the ocean. Lots, in cases of famine, where means of subsistence are wanting for all the crew, is what the history of maritime disaster records; but who has ever told of casting lots at midnight, in a sinking boat, in the midst of darkness, of rain, of terrour, and of confusion? To cast lots when all are going down, to decide who shall be spared; to cast lots when the question is, whether any can be saved, is a plan easy to suggest; rather difficult to put in practice. The danger was instantaneous; a case, says Rutherford, when "the mind is too much disturbed to deliberate," and where, if it were "more calm," there is no time for deliberation. The sailors adopted the only principle of selection which was possible in an emergency like theirs; a principle more humane than lots. Man and wife were not torn asunder, and the women were all preserved. Lots would have rendered impossible this clear dictate of humanity.

But again: The crew either were in their ordinary and original state of subordination to their officers, or they were in a state of nature. If in the former state, they are excusable in law, for having obeyed the order of the mate; an order twice imperatively given. Independent of the mate's general authority in the captain's absence, the captain had pointedly directed the crew to obey all the mate's orders as they would his, the captain's; and the crew had promised to do so.

It imports not to declare that a crew is not bound to obey an unlawful order, for to say that this order was unlawful is to postulate what remains to be proved. Who is to judge of the unlawfulness? The circumstances were peculiar. The occasion was emergent, without precedent, or parallel. The lawfulness of the order is the very question which we are disputing; a question about which this whole community has been agitated, and is still divided; the discussion of which crowds this room with auditors past former example; a question which this court, with all its resources, is now engaged in considering—as such a question demands to be considered—*most deliberately, most anxiously, most cautiously*. It is no part of a sailor's duty to moralize and to speculate, in such a moment as this was, upon the orders of his superiour officers. The commander of a ship, like the commander of an army, "gives desperate commands. He requires instantaneous obedience." The sailor, like the soldier, obeys by instinct. In the memorable, immortal words of Carnot, when he surrendered Antwerp in obedience to a command which his pride, his patriotism, and his views of policy all combined to oppose: "The armed force is essentially obedient. It acts, but never deliberates." This greatest man of the French Revolution did here but define with the precision of the algebraist, what he conceived with the comprehension of a statesman; and his answer was justification with every soldier in Europe! How far the principle was felt by this crew, let witness the case of this very mate, and of some of these very sailors, who, by the captain's order, left the jolly-boat, which had but ten persons, for the long-boat, with more than four times that number. They all regarded this as going into the jaws of death. Yet not a murmur! It is a well-known fact that in no marine on the ocean is obedience to orders so habitual and so implicit as in our own. The prisoner had been always distinguished by obedience.

Whether the *mate,* if on trial here, would be found innocent, is a question which we need not decide. That question is a different one from the guilt or innocence of the *prisoner;* and one more difficult.

But if the whole company were reduced to a state of nature, then the sailors were bound to no duty, not mutual, to the passengers. The contract of the shipping articles had become dissolved by an unforeseen and overwhelming necessity. The sailor was no longer a sailor, but a drowning man. Having fairly done his duty to the last extremity, he was not to lose the rights of a human being, because he wore a roundabout instead of a frock-coat. We do not seek authorities for such doctrine. The instinct of these men's hearts is our authority—the best authority. Whoever opposes it must be wrong; for he opposes human nature. All the contemplated conditions, all the contemplated possibilities of the voyage, were ended. The parties, sailor and passenger, were in a new state. All persons on board the vessel became equal. All became their own lawgivers; for artificial distinctions cease to prevail when men are reduced to the equality of nature. Every man on board had a right to make law with his own right hand; and the law which did prevail on that awful night having been the law of necessity, and the law of nature too, it is the law which will be upheld by this court, to the liberation of this prisoner. . . .

Mr. Justice Baldwin proceeded, afterwards, to charge the jury.

He alluded to the touching character of the case; and, after stating to the jury what was the offence laid in the indictment, his honour explained, with particularity, the distinction between murder and manslaughter. He said that malice was of the essence of murder, while want of criminal intention was consistent with the nature of manslaughter. He impressed strongly upon the jury, that the mere absence of malice did not render homicide excusable; that the act might be unlawful, as well as the union of the act and intention, in which union consisted the crime of murder. After giving several familiar instances of manslaughter, to explain that, although homicide was committed, there was yet an absence of bad motive, his honour proceeded with his charge nearly as follows:

In such cases the law neither excuses the act nor permits it to be justified as innocent; but, although inflicting some punishment, she yet looks with a benignant eye, through the thing done, to the mind and to the heart; and when, on a view of all the circumstances connected with the act, no evil spirit is discerned, her humanity forbids the exaction of life for life.

But though, said the court, cases of this kind are viewed with tenderness, and punished in mercy, we must yet bear in mind that man, in taking away the life of a fellow being, assumes an awful responsibility to God, and to society; and that the administrators of public justice do themselves assume that responsibility if, when called on to pass judicially upon the act, they yield to the indulgence of misapplied humanity. It is one thing to give a favourable interpretation to evidence in order to mitigate an offence. It is a different thing, when we are asked, not to extenuate, but to justify, the act. In the former case, as I have said, our decision may in some degree be swayed by feelings of humanity; while, in the latter, it is *the law of necessity,* alone, which can disarm the vindicatory justice of the country. Where, indeed, a case does arise, embraced by this "law of necessity," the penal laws pass over such case in silence; for law is made to meet but the ordinary exigencies of life.

But the case does not become "a case of necessity," unless all ordinary means of self-preservation have been exhausted. The peril must be instant, overwhelming; leaving no alternative but to lose our own life, or to take the life of another person.

An illustration of this principle occurs in the ordinary case of self-defense against lawless violence aiming at the destruction of life, or designing to inflict grievous injury to the person; and within this range may fall the taking of life under other circumstances where the act is indispensably requisite to self-existence. For example, suppose that two persons who owe no duty to one another that is not mutual, should, by accident, not attributable to either, be placed in a situation where both cannot survive. Neither is bound to save the other's life by sacrificing his own; nor would either commit a crime in saving his own life in a struggle for the only means of safety. Of this description of cases are those which have been cited to you by counsel, from writers on natural law; cases which we rather leave to your imagination than attempt minutely to describe.

And I again state that when this great "law of necessity" does apply, and is not improperly exercised, the taking of life is divested of unlawfulness.

But in applying this law, we must look, not only to the jeopardy in which the parties are, but also to the relations in which they stand. The slayer must be under no obligation to make his own safety secondary to the safety of others.

A familiar application of this principle presents itself in the obligations which rest upon the owners of stages, steamboats, and other vehicles of transportation. In consideration of the payment of fare, the owners of the vehicle are bound to transport the passengers to the place of contemplated destination. Having, in all emergencies, the conduct of the journey, and the control of the passengers, the owners rest under every obligation for care, skill, and general capacity; and if, from defect of any of these requisites, grievous injury is done to the passenger, the persons employed are liable. The passenger owes no duty but submission. He is under no obligation to protect and keep the conductor in safety, nor is the passenger bound to labour, except in cases of emergency, where his services are required by unanticipated and uncommon danger.

Such, said the court, is the relation which exists on shipboard. The passenger stands in a position different from that of the officers and seamen. It is the sailor who must encounter the hardships and perils of the voyage.

Nor can this relation be changed when the ship is lost by tempest or other danger of the sea, and all on board have betaken themselves, for safety, to the small boats; for imminence of danger can not absolve from duty. The sailor is bound, as before, to undergo whatever hazard is necessary to preserve the boat and the passengers. Should the emergency become so extreme as to call for the sacrifice of life, there can be no reason why the law does not still remain the same. The passenger, not being bound either to labour or to incur the risk of life, cannot be bound to sacrifice his existence to preserve the sailor's. The captain, indeed, and a sufficient number of seamen to navigate the boat, must be preserved; for, *except these abide in the ship, all will perish.* But if there be more seamen than are necessary to manage the boat, the supernumerary sailors have no right, for *their* safety, to sacrifice the passengers. The sailors and passengers, in fact, cannot be regarded as in equal positions. The sailor (to use the language of a distinguished writer) *owes more benevolence to another than to himself.* He is bound to set a greater value on the life of others than on his own. And while we admit that sailor and sailor may lawfully struggle with each other for the plank which can save but one, we think that if the passenger is on the plank, even "the law of necessity" justifies not the sailor who takes it from him.

This rule may be deemed a harsh one towards the sailor, who may have thus far done his duty; but when the danger is so extreme, that the only hope is in sacrificing either a sailor or a passenger, any alternative is hard; and would it not be the hardest of any, to sacrifice a passenger in order to save a supernumerary sailor?

But, in addition, if the source of the danger have been obvious, and destruction ascertained to be certainly about to arrive, though at a future time, there should be consultation, and some mode of selection fixed, by which those in equal relations may have equal chance for their life. By what mode then should selection be made? The question is not without difficulty; nor do we know of any rule prescribed, either by statute or by common law, or even by speculative writers on the law of nature.

In fact, no rule of general application can be prescribed for contingencies which are wholly unforeseen. There is, however, one condition of extremity for which all writers have prescribed the same rule. When the ship is in no danger of sinking, but all sustenance is exhausted, and a sacrifice of one person is necessary to appease the hunger of others, the selection is by lot. This mode is resorted to as the fairest mode; and, in some sort, as an appeal to *God* for selection of the victim. This manner, obviously, was regarded by the mate, in parting with the captain, as the one which it was proper to adopt, in case the long-boat could not live with all who were on board on Tuesday morning. The same manner, as would appear from the response given to the mate, had already suggested itself to the captain.

For ourselves, we can conceive of no mode so consonant both to humanity and to justice; and the occasion, we think, must be peculiar, which will dispense with its exercise. If, indeed, the peril be instant and overwhelming, leaving no chance of means, and no moment for deliberation; then, of course, there is no power to consult, to cast lots, or in any such way to decide; but even where the final disaster is thus sudden, if it have been foreseen as certainly about to arrive; if no new cause of danger have arisen to bring on the closing catastrophe; if time have existed to cast lots, and to select the victims; then, as we have said, sortition should be adopted. In no other than this or some like way, are those having equal rights, put upon an equal footing; and in no other way is it possible to guard against partiality and oppression, violence and conflict. What scene, indeed, more horrible, can imagination draw, than a struggle between sailor and sailor, passenger and passenger, or it may be, a mixed affray, in which, promiscuously, all destroy one another? This, too, in circumstances which have allowed time to decide, with justice, whose life should be calmly surrendered.

When the selection has been made by lots, the victim yields of course to his fate; or, if he resist, force may be employed to coerce submission.

Whether or not "a case of necessity" has arisen, or whether the law under which death has been inflicted have been so exercised as to hold the executioner harmless, cannot depend on his own opinion; for no man may pass upon his own conduct when it concerns the rights, and especially, when it affects the lives of others. We have already stated to you that, by the law of the land, homicide is sometimes justifiable; and the law defines the occasions in which it is so. The transaction must, therefore, be justified to the law; and the person accused rests under obligation to satisfy those who judicially scrutinize his case, that it really transcended ordinary rules. In fact, any other principle would be followed by pernicious results; and, moreover, would not be practicable in application. Opinion or belief may be assumed, whether it exist or not; and if this mere opinion of the sailors will justify *them* in making a sacrifice of the passengers, of course, the mere opinion of the passengers would, in turn, justify *these* in making a sacrifice of the sailors. The passengers may have confidence in their own capacity to manage and preserve the boat; or the effort of either sailors or passengers to save the boat, may be clearly unavailing; and what, then, in a struggle against force and numbers, becomes of the safety of the seamen? Hard as is a seaman's life, would it not become yet more perilous, if the passengers, who may outnumber them tenfold, should be allowed to judge when the dangers of the sea will justify a sacrifice of life? We are, therefore, satisfied, that in requiring proof which shall be satisfactory to *you,* of the existence of the necessity, we are fixing the rule which is, not merely the only one which is practicable, but, moreover, the only one which will secure the safety of the sailors themselves.

The court said, briefly, that the principles which had been laid down by them, as applicable to the crew, applied to the mate likewise; and that his order (on which much stress had been laid), if an unlawful order, would be no justification to the seamen; for that even seamen are not justified, in law, by obedience to commands which are unlawful.

The court added, that the case was one which involved questions of gravest consideration; and as the facts, in some sort, were without precedent, that the court preferred to state the law, in the shape of such general principles as would comprehend the case, under any view which the jury might take of the evidence.

After a few remarks upon the evidence, the case was given to the jury; who, about sixteen hours afterwards, and after having once returned to the bar, unable to agree, with some difficulty found a verdict of *guilty.* The prisoner was, however, recommended to the mercy of the court.

On the same day, a rule was obtained to show cause why judgment should not be arrested and a new trial granted. The following ground was relied on for a new trial: Because the court, instead of telling the jury that in a state of imminent and deadly peril, all men are reduced to *a state of nature,* and that there is, then, no distinction between the rights of sailor and passenger, adopted a contrary doctrine, and charged the jury accordingly.

Mr. Brown subsequently showed cause. He insisted largely upon the existence of the state of nature, as distinguished from the social state; and contended that to this state of nature the persons in the long-boat had become reduced on Tuesday night, at ten o'clock, when Askin was thrown overboard. He iterated, illustrated, and enforced the argument contained in the closing part of the defence. . . .

The court held the application for some days under advisement; and, at a subsequent day, discharged the rule. They said that, during the trial (aware that no similar case was recorded in juridical annals), they had given to the subject studious and deliberate consideration; and they had paid like regard to what was now urged; but that notwithstanding all that had been said (and the arguments, it was admitted, were powerful), no error had been perceived by the court in its instructions to the jury.

It is true, said the court, as is known by every one, that we do find in the text writers, and sometimes in judicial opinions, the phrases, "the law of nature," "the principles of natural right," and other expressions of a like signification; but, as applied to civilized men, nothing more can be meant by those expressions than that there are certain great and fundamental principles of justice which, in the constitution of nature, lie at the foundation and make part of all civil law, independently of express adoption or enactment. And to give to the expressions any other signification; to claim them as shewing an independent code, and one contrariant to those settled principles, which, however modified, make a part of civil law in all Christian nations; would be, to make the writers who use the expressions, lay down, as rules of action, principles which, in their nature, admit of no practical ascertainment or application. The law of nature forms part of the municipal law; and in a proper case (as of self-defence), homicide is justifiable, not because the municipal law is subverted by the law of nature, but because no rule of the municipal law makes homicide, in such cases, criminal. It is, said the court, the municipal or civil law, as thus comprehensive; as founded in moral and social justice—the law of the land, in short, as existing and administered amongst us and all enlightened nations—that regulates the social duties of men, the duties of man towards his neighbour, everywhere. Everywhere are civilized men under its protection; everywhere subject to its authority. It is part of the universal law. We cannot escape it, in a case where it is applicable; and if for the decision of any question the proper rule is to be found in the municipal law, no code can be referred to as annulling its authority.

Varying however, or however modified, the laws of all civilized nations, and, indeed, the very nature of the social constitution, place sailors and passengers in different relations. And without stopping to speculate upon over-nice questions not before us, or to involve ourselves in the labyrinth of ethical subtleties, we may safely say that the sailor's duty is, the protection of the persons intrusted to his care, not their sacrifice; a duty—we must again declare our opinion—that rests on him in every emergency of his calling; and from which it would be senseless, indeed, to absolve him exactly at those times when the obligation is most needed. . . .

When the prisoner was brought up for sentence, the learned judge said to him, that many circumstances in the affair were of a character to commend him to regard; yet, that the case was one in which some punishment was demanded; that it was in the power of the court to inflict the penalty of an imprisonment for a term of three years, and a fine of $1,000; but, in view of all the circumstances, and especially as the prisoner had been already confined in gaol several months, that the court would make the punishment more lenient. The convict was then sentenced to undergo an imprisonment in the Eastern Penitentiary of Pennsylvania (solitary confinement) at hard labour, for the term of six months, and to pay a fine of $20.

[Note: Considerable sympathy having been excited in favour of Holmes, by the popular press, an effort was made by several persons, and particularly by the Seaman's Friend Society, to obtain a pardon from the executive. President Tyler refused, however, to grant any pardon, in consequence of the court's not uniting in the application. The penalty was subsequently remitted.]

Lon L. Fuller
The Case of the Speluncean Explorers
In the Supreme Court of Newgarth, 4300[*]

The defendants, having been indicted for the crime of murder, were convicted and sentenced to be hanged by the Court of General Instances of the County of Stowfield. They bring a petition of error before this Court. The facts sufficiently appear in the opinion of the Chief Justice.

Truepenny, C.J. The four defendants are members of the Speluncean Society, an organization of amateurs interested in the exploration of caves. Early in May of 4299 they, in the company of Roger Whetmore, then also a member of the Society, penetrated into the interior of a limestone cavern of the type found in the Central Plateau of this Commonwealth. While they were in a position remote from the entrance to the cave, a landslide occurred. Heavy boulders fell in such a manner as to block completely the only known opening to the cave. When the men discovered their predicament they settled themselves near the obstructed entrance to wait until a rescue party should remove the detritus that prevented them from leaving their underground prison. On the failure of Whetmore and the defendants to return to their homes, the Secretary of the Society was notified by their families. It appears that the explorers had left indications at the headquarters of the Society concerning the location of the cave they proposed to visit. A rescue party was promptly dispatched to the spot.

The task of rescue proved one of overwhelming difficulty. It was necessary to supplement the forces of the original party by repeated increments of men and machines, which had to be conveyed at great expense to the remote and isolated region in which the cave was located. A huge temporary camp of workmen, engineers, geologists, and other experts was established. The work of removing the obstruction was several times frustrated by fresh landslides. In one of these, ten of the workmen engaged in clearing the entrance were killed. The treasury of the Speluncean Society was soon exhausted in the rescue effort, and the sum of eight hundred thousand frelars, raised partly by popular subscription and partly by legislative grant, was expended before the imprisoned men were rescued. Success was finally achieved on the thirty-second day after the men entered the cave.

Since it was known that the explorers had carried with them only scant provisions, and since it was also known that there was no animal or vegetable matter within the cave on which they might subsist, anxiety was early felt that they might meet death by starvation before access to them could be obtained. On the twentieth day of their imprisonment it was learned for the first time that they had taken with them into the cave a portable wireless machine capable of both sending and receiving messages. A similar machine was promptly installed in the rescue camp and oral communication established with the unfortunate men within the mountain. They asked to be informed how long a time would be required to release them. The engineers in charge of the project answered that at least ten days would

---

[*] Lon L. Fuller, The Case of the Speluncean Explorers, Harvard Law Review, Volume 62 (1949), pages 616-645. Copyright © 1949 by the Harvard Law Review Association.

be required even if no new landslides occurred. The explorers then asked if any physicians were present, and were placed in communication with a committee of medical experts. The imprisoned men described their condition and the rations they had taken with them, and asked for a medical opinion whether they would be likely to live without food for ten days longer. The chairman of the committee of physicians told them that there was little possibility of this. The wireless machine within the cave then remained silent for eight hours. When communication was re-established the men asked to speak again with the physicians. The chairman of the physicians' committee was placed before the apparatus, and Whetmore, speaking on behalf of himself and the defendants, asked whether they would be able to survive for ten days longer if they consumed the flesh of one of their number. The physicians' chairman reluctantly answered this question in the affirmative. Whetmore asked whether it would be advisable for them to cast lots to determine which of them should be eaten. None of the physicians present was willing to answer the question. Whetmore then asked if there were among the party a judge or other official of the government who would answer this question. None of those attached to the rescue camp was willing to assume the role of advisor in this matter. He then asked if any minister or priest would answer their question, and none was found who would do so. Thereafter no further messages were received from within the cave, and it was assumed (erroneously, it later appeared) that the electric batteries of the explorers' wireless machine had become exhausted. When the imprisoned men were finally released it was learned that on the twenty-third day after their entrance into the cave Whetmore had been killed and eaten by his companions.

From the testimony of the defendants, which was accepted by the jury, it appears that it was Whetmore who first proposed that they might find the nutriment without which survival was impossible in the flesh of one of their own number. It was also Whetmore who first proposed the use of some method of casting lots, calling the attention of the defendants to a pair of dice he happened to have with him. The defendants were at first reluctant to adopt so desperate a procedure, but after the conversations by wireless related above, they finally agreed on the plan proposed by Whetmore. After much discussion of the mathematical problems involved, agreement was finally reached on a method of determining the issue by the use of the dice.

Before the dice were cast, however, Whetmore declared that he withdrew from the arrangement, as he had decided on reflection to wait for another week before embracing an expedient so frightful and odious. The others charged him with a breach of faith and proceeded to cast the dice. When it came Whetmore's turn, the dice were cast for him by one of the defendants, and he was asked to declare any objections he might have to the fairness of the throw. He stated that he had no such objections. The throw went against him, and he was then put to death and eaten by his companions.

After the rescue of the defendants, and after they had completed a stay in a hospital where they underwent a course of treatment for malnutrition and shock, they were indicted for the murder of Roger Whetmore. At the trial, after the testimony had been concluded, the foreman of the jury (a lawyer by profession) inquired of the court whether the jury might not find a special verdict, leaving it to the court to say whether on the facts as found the defendants were guilty. After some discussion, both the Prosecutor and counsel for the defendants indicated their acceptance of this procedure, and it was adopted by the court. In a lengthy special verdict the jury found the facts as I have related them above, and found further that if on these facts the defendants were guilty of the crime charged against them, then they found the defendants guilty. On the basis of this verdict, the trial judge ruled that the defendants were guilty of murdering Roger Whetmore. The judge then sentenced them to be hanged, the law of our Commonwealth permitting him no discretion with respect to the penalty to be imposed. After the release of the jury, its members joined in a communication to the Chief Executive asking that the sentence be commuted to an imprisonment of six months. The trial judge addressed a similar communication to the Chief Executive. As yet no action with respect to these pleas has been taken, as the Chief Executive is apparently awaiting our disposition of this petition of error.

It seems to me that in dealing with this extraordinary case the jury and the trial judge followed a course that was not only fair and wise, but the only course that was open to them under the law. The language of our statute is well known: "Whoever shall willfully take the life of another shall be punished by death." N.C.S.A. (n.s.) § 12-A. This statute permits of no exception applicable to this case, however our sympathies may incline us to make allowance for the tragic situation in which these men found themselves.

In a case like this the principle of executive clemency seems admirably suited to mitigate the rigors of the law, and I propose to my colleagues that we follow the example of the jury and the trial judge by joining in the communications they have addressed to the Chief Executive. There is every reason to believe that these requests for clemency will be heeded, coming as they do from those who have studied the case and had an opportunity to become thoroughly acquainted with all its circumstances. It is highly improbable that the Chief Executive would deny these requests unless he were himself to hold hearings at least as extensive as those involved in the trial below, which lasted for three months. The holding of such hearings (which would virtually amount to a retrial of the case) would scarcely be compatible with the function of the Executive as it is usually conceived. I think we may therefore assume that some form of clemency will be extended to these defendants. If this is done, then justice will be accomplished without impairing either the letter or spirit of our statutes and without offering any encouragement for the disregard of law.

Foster, J. I am shocked that the Chief Justice, in an effort to escape the embarrassments of this tragic case, should have adopted, and should have proposed to his colleagues, an expedient at once so sordid and so obvious. I believe something more is on trial in this case than the fate of these unfortunate explorers; that is the law of our Commonwealth. If this Court declares that under our law these men have committed a crime, then our law is itself convicted in the tribunal of common sense, no matter what happens to the individuals involved in this petition of error. For us to assert that the law we uphold and expound compels us to a conclusion we are ashamed of, and from which we can only escape by appealing to a dispensation resting within the personal whim of the Executive, seems to me to amount to an admission that the law of this Commonwealth no longer pretends to incorporate justice.

For myself, I do not believe that our law compels the monstrous conclusion that these men are murderers. I believe, on the contrary, that it declares them to be innocent of any crime. I rest this conclusion on two independent grounds, either of which is of itself sufficient to justify the acquittal of these defendants.

The first of these grounds rests on a premise that may arouse opposition until it has been examined candidly. I take the view that the enacted or positive law of this Commonwealth, including all of its statutes and precedents, is inapplicable to this case, and that the case is governed instead by what ancient writers in Europe and America called "the law of nature."

This conclusion rests on the proposition that our positive law is predicated on the possibility of men's coexistence in society. When a situation arises in which the coexistence of men becomes impossible, then a condition that underlies all of our precedents and statutes has ceased to exist. When that condition disappears, then it is my opinion that the force of our positive law disappears with it. We are not accustomed to applying the maxim *cessante ratione legis, cessat et ipsa lex* to the whole of our enacted law, but I believe that this is a case where the maxim should be so applied.

The proposition that all positive law is based on the possibility of men's coexistence has a strange sound, not because the truth it contains is strange, but simply because it is a truth so obvious and pervasive that we seldom have occasion to give words to it. Like the air we breathe, it so pervades our environment that we forget that it exists until we are suddenly deprived of it. Whatever particular objects may be sought by the various branches of our law, it is apparent on reflection that all of them are directed toward facilitating and improving men's coexistence and regulating with fairness and equity the relations of their life in common. When the assumption that men may live together loses its truth, as it obviously did in this extraordinary situation where life only became possible by the taking of life, then the basic premises underlying our whole legal order have lost their meaning and force.

Had the tragic events of this case taken place a mile beyond the territorial limits of our Commonwealth, no one would pretend that our law was applicable to them. We recognize that jurisdiction rests on a territorial basis. The grounds of this principle are by no means obvious and are seldom examined. I take it that this principle is supported by an assumption that it is feasible to impose a single legal order upon a group of men only if they live together within the confines of a given area of the earth's surface. The premise that men shall coexist in a group underlies, then, the territorial principle, as it does all of law. Now I contend that a case may be removed morally from the force of a legal order, as well as geographically. If we look to the purposes of law and government, and to the premises underlying our positive law, these men when they made their fateful decision were as remote from our legal order as if they had been a thousand miles beyond our boundaries. Even in a physical sense, their underground prison was separated from our courts and writ-servers by a solid curtain of rock that could be removed only after the most extraordinary expenditures of time and effort.

I conclude, therefore, that at the time Roger Whetmore's life was ended by these defendants, they were, to use the quaint language of nineteenth-century writers, not in a "state of civil society" but in a "state of nature." This has the consequence that the law applicable to them is not the enacted and established law of this Commonwealth, but the law derived from those principles that were appropriate to their condition. I have no hesitancy in saying that under those principles they were guiltless of any crime.

What these men did was done in pursuance of an agreement accepted by all of them and first proposed by Whetmore himself. Since it was apparent that their extraordinary predicament made inapplicable the usual principles that regulate men's relations with one another, it was necessary for them to draw, as it were, a new charter of government appropriate to the situation in which they found themselves.

It has from antiquity been recognized that the most basic principle of law or government is to be found in the notion of contract or agreement. Ancient thinkers, especially during the period from 1600 to 1900, used to base government itself on a supposed original social compact. Skeptics pointed out that this theory contradicted the known facts of history, and that there was no scientific evidence to support the notion that any government was ever founded in the manner supposed by the theory. Moralists replied that, if the compact was a fiction from a historical point of view, the notion of compact or agreement furnished the only ethical justification on which the powers of government, which include that of taking life, could be rested. The powers of government can only be justified morally on the ground that these are powers that reasonable men would agree upon and accept if they were faced with the necessity of constructing anew some order to make their life in common possible.

Fortunately, our Commonwealth is not bothered by the perplexities that beset the ancients. We know as a matter of historical truth that our government was founded upon a contract or free accord of men. The archeological proof is conclusive that in the first period following the Great Spiral the survivors of that holocaust voluntarily came together and drew up a charter of government. Sophistical writers have raised questions as to the power of those remote contractors to bind future generations, but the fact remains that our government traces itself back in an unbroken line to that original charter.

If, therefore, our hangmen have the power to end men's lives, if our sheriffs have the power to put delinquent tenants in the street, if our police have the power to incarcerate the inebriated reveler, these powers find their moral justification in that original compact of our forefathers. If we can find no higher source for our legal order, what higher source should we expect these starving unfortunates to find for the order they adopted for themselves?

I believe that the line of argument I have just expounded permits of no rational answer. I realize that it will probably be received with a certain discomfort by many who read this opinion, who will be inclined to suspect that some hidden sophistry must underlie a demonstration that leads to so many unfamiliar conclusions. The source of this discomfort is, however, easy to identify. The usual conditions of human existence incline us to think of human life as an absolute value, not to be sacrificed under any circumstances. There is much that is fictitious about this conception even when it is applied to the ordinary relations of society. We have an illustration of this truth in the very case before us. Ten workmen were killed in the process of removing the rocks from the opening to the cave. Did not the engineers and government officials who directed the rescue effort know that the operations they were undertaking were dangerous and involved a serious risk to the lives of the workmen executing them? If it was proper that these ten lives should be sacrificed to save the lives of five imprisoned explorers, why then are we told it was wrong for these explorers to carry out an arrangement which would save four lives at the cost of one?

Every highway, every tunnel, every building we project involves a risk to human life. Taking these projects in the aggregate, we can calculate with some precision how many deaths the construction of them will require; statisticians can tell you the average cost in human lives of a thousand miles of a four-lane concrete highway. Yet we deliberately and knowingly incur and pay this cost on the assumption that the values obtained for those who survive outweigh the loss. If these things can be said of a society functioning above ground in a normal and ordinary manner, what shall we say of the supposed absolute value of a human life in the desperate situation in which these defendants and their companion Whetmore found themselves?

This concludes the exposition of the first ground of my decision. My second ground proceeds by rejecting hypothetically all the premises on which I have so far proceeded. I concede for purposes of argument that I am wrong in saying that the situation of these men removed them from the effect of our positive law, and I assume that the Consolidated Statutes have the power to penetrate five hundred feet of rock and to impose themselves upon these starving men huddled in their underground prison.

Now it is, of course, perfectly clear that these men did an act that violates the literal wording of the statute which declares that he who "shall willfully take the life of another" is a murderer. But one of the most ancient bits of legal wisdom is the saying that a man may break the letter of the law without breaking the law itself. Every proposition of positive law, whether contained in a statute or a judicial precedent, is to be interpreted reasonably, in the light of its evident purpose. This is a truth so elementary that it is hardly necessary to expatiate on it. Illustrations of its application are numberless and are to be found in every branch of the law. In Commonwealth v. Staymore the defendant was convicted under a statute making it a crime to leave one's car parked in certain areas for a period longer than two hours. The defendant had attempted to remove his car, but was prevented from doing so because the streets were obstructed by a political demonstration in which he took no part and which he had no reason to anticipate. His conviction was set aside by this Court, although his case fell squarely within the wording of the statute. Again, in Fehler v. Neegas there was before this Court for construction a statute in which the word "not" had plainly been transposed from its intended position in the final and most crucial section of the act. This transposition was contained in all the successive drafts of the act, where it was apparently overlooked by the draftsmen and sponsors of the legislation. No one was able to prove how the error came about, yet it was apparent that, taking account of the contents of the statute as a whole, an error had been made, since a literal reading of the final clause rendered it inconsistent with everything that had gone before and with the object of the enactment as stated in its preamble. This Court refused to accept a literal interpretation of the statute, and in effect rectified its language by reading the word "not" into the place where it was evidently intended to go.

The statute before us for interpretation has never been applied literally. Centuries ago it was established that a killing in self-defense is excused. There is nothing in the wording of the statute that suggests this exception. Various attempts have been made to reconcile the legal treatment of self-defense with the words of the statute, but in my opinion these are all merely ingenious sophistries. The truth is that the exception in favor of self-defense cannot be reconciled with the *words* of the statute, but only with its *purpose*.

The true reconciliation of the excuse of self-defense with the statute making it a crime to kill another is to be found in the following line of reasoning. One of the principal objects underlying any criminal legislation is that of deterring men from crime. Now it is apparent that if it were declared to be the law that a killing in self-defense is murder such a rule could not operate in a deterrent manner. A man whose life is threatened will repel his aggressor, whatever the law may say. Looking therefore to the broad purposes of criminal legislation, we may safely declare that this statute was not intended to apply to cases of self-defense.

When the rationale of the excuse of self-defense is thus explained, it becomes apparent that precisely the same reasoning is applicable to the case at bar. If in the future any group of men ever find themselves in the tragic predicament of these defendants, we may be sure that their decision whether to live or die will not be controlled by the contents of our criminal code. Accordingly, if we read this statute intelligently it is apparent that it does not apply to this case. The withdrawal of this situation from the effect of the statute is justified by precisely the same considerations that were applied by our predecessors in office centuries ago to the case of self-defense.

There are those who raise the cry of judicial usurpation whenever a court, after analyzing the purpose of a statute, gives to its words a meaning that is not at once apparent to the casual reader who has not studied the statute closely or examined the objectives it seeks to attain. Let me say emphatically that I accept without reservation the proposition that this Court is bound by the statutes of our Commonwealth and that it exercises its powers in subservience to the duly expressed will of the Chamber of Representatives. The line of reasoning I have applied above raises no question of fidelity to enacted law, though it may possibly raise a question of the distinction between intelligent and unintelligent fidelity. No superior wants a servant who lacks the capacity to read between the lines. The stupidest housemaid knows that when she is told "to peel the soup and skim the potatoes" her mistress does not mean what she says. She also knows that when her master tells her to "drop everything and come running" he has overlooked the possibility that she is at the moment in the act of rescuing the baby from the rain barrel. Surely we have a right to expect the same modicum of intelligence from the judiciary. The correction of obvious legislative errors or oversights is not to supplant the legislative will, but to make that will effective.

I therefore conclude that on any aspect under which this case may be viewed these defendants are innocent of the crime of murdering Roger Whetmore, and that the conviction should be set aside.

Tatting, J. In the discharge of my duties as a justice of this Court, I am usually able to dissociate the emotional and intellectual sides of my reactions, and to decide the case before me entirely on the basis of the latter. In passing on this tragic case I find that my usual resources fail me. On the emotional side I find myself torn between sympathy for these men and a feeling of abhorrence and disgust at the monstrous act they committed. I had hoped that I would be able to put these contradictory emotions to one side as irrelevant, and to decide the case on the basis of a convincing and logical demonstration of the result demanded by our law. Unfortunately, this deliverance has not been vouchsafed me.

As I analyze the opinion just rendered by my brother Foster, I find that it is shot through with contradictions and fallacies. Let us begin with his first proposition: these men were not subject to our law because they were not in a "state of civil society" but in a "state of nature." I am not clear why this is so, whether it is because of the thickness of the rock that imprisoned them, or because they were hungry, or because they had set up a "new charter of government" by which the usual rules of law were to be supplanted by a throw of the dice. Other difficulties intrude themselves. If these men passed from the jurisdiction of our law to that of "the law of nature," at what moment did this occur? Was it when the entrance to the cave was blocked, or when the threat of starvation reached a certain undefined degree of intensity, or when the agreement for the throwing of the dice was made? These uncertainties in the doctrine proposed by my brother are capable of producing real difficulties. Suppose, for example, one of these men had had his twenty-first birthday while he was imprisoned within the mountain. On what date would we have to consider that he had attained his majority—when he reached the age of twenty-one, at which time he was, by hypothesis, removed from the effects of our law, or only when he was released from the cave and became again subject to what my brother calls our "positive law"? These difficulties may seem fanciful, yet they only serve to reveal the fanciful nature of the doctrine that is capable of giving rise to them.

But it is not necessary to explore these niceties further to demonstrate the absurdity of my brother's position. Mr. Justice Foster and I are the appointed judges of a court of the Commonwealth of Newgarth, sworn and empowered to administer the laws of that Commonwealth. By what authority do we resolve ourselves into a Court of Nature? If these men were indeed under the law of nature, whence comes our authority to expound and apply that law? Certainly *we* are not in a state of nature.

Let us look at the contents of this code of nature that my brother proposes we adopt as our own and apply to this case. What a topsy-turvy and odious code it is! It is a code in which the law of contracts is more fundamental than the law of murder. It is a code under which a man may make a valid agreement empowering his fellows to eat his own body. Under the provisions of this code, furthermore, such an agreement once made is irrevocable, and if one of the parties attempts to withdraw, the others may take the law into their own hands and enforce the contract by violence—for though my brother passes over in convenient silence the effect of Whetmore's withdrawal, this is the necessary implication of his argument.

The principles my brother expounds contain other implications that cannot be tolerated. He argues that when the defendants set upon Whetmore and killed him (we know not how, perhaps by pounding him with stones) they were only exercising the rights conferred upon them by their bargain. Suppose, however, that Whetmore had had concealed upon his person a revolver, and that when he saw the defendants about to slaughter him he had shot them to death in order to save his own life. My brother's reasoning applied to these facts would make Whetmore out to be a murderer, since the excuse of self-defense would have to be denied to him. If his assailants were acting rightfully in seeking to bring about his death, then of course he could no more plead the excuse that he was defending his own life than could a condemned prisoner who struck down the executioner lawfully attempting to place the noose about his neck.

All of these considerations make it impossible for me to accept the first part of my brother's argument. I can neither accept his notion that these men were under a code of nature which this Court was bound to apply to them, nor can I accept the odious and perverted rules that he would read into that code. I come now to the second part of my brother's opinion, in which he seeks to show that the defendants did not violate the provisions of N.C.S.A. (n.s.) § 12-A. Here the way, instead of being clear, becomes for me misty and ambiguous, though my brother seems unaware of the difficulties that inhere in his demonstrations.

The gist of my brother's argument may be stated in the following terms: No statute, whatever its language, should be applied in a way that contradicts its purpose. One of the purposes of any criminal statute is to deter. The application of the statute making it a crime to kill another to the peculiar facts of this case would contradict this purpose, for it is impossible to believe that the contents of the criminal code could operate in a deterrent manner on men faced with the alternative of life or death. The reasoning by which this exception is read into the statute is, my brother observes, the same as that which is applied in order to provide the excuse of self-defense.

On the face of things this demonstration seems very convincing indeed. My brother's interpretation of the rationale of the excuse of self-defense is in fact supported by a decision of this court, Commonwealth v. Parry, a precedent I happened to encounter in my research on this case. Though Commonwealth v. Parry seems generally to have been overlooked in the texts and subsequent decisions, it supports unambiguously the interpretation my brother has put upon the excuse of self-defense.

Now let me outline briefly, however, the perplexities that assail me when I examine my brother's demonstration more closely. It is true that a statute should be applied in the light of its purpose, and that *one* of the purposes of criminal legislation is recognized to be deterrence. The difficulty is that other purposes are also ascribed to the law of crimes. It has been said that one of its objects is to provide an orderly outlet for the instinctive human demand for retribution. Commonwealth v. Scape. It has also been said that its object is the rehabilitation of the wrongdoer. Commonwealth v. Makeover. Other theories have been propounded. Assuming that we must interpret a statute in the light of its purpose, what are we to do when it has many purposes or when its purposes are disputed?

A similar difficulty is presented by the fact that although there is authority for my brother's interpretation of the excuse of self-defense, there is other authority which assigns to that excuse a different rationale. Indeed, until I happened on Commonwealth v. Parry I had never heard of the explanation given by my brother. The taught doctrine of our law schools, memorized by generations of law students, runs in the following terms: The statute concerning murder requires a "willful" act. The man who acts to repel an aggressive threat to his own life does not act "willfully," but in response to an impulse deeply ingrained in human nature. I suspect that there is hardly a lawyer in this Commonwealth who is not familiar with this line of reasoning, especially since the point is a great favorite of the bar examiners.

Now the familiar explanation for the excuse of self-defense just expounded obviously cannot be applied by analogy to the facts of this case. These men acted not only "willfully" but with great deliberation and after hours of discussing what they should do. Again we encounter a forked path, with one line of reasoning leading us in one direction and another in a direction that is exactly the opposite. This perplexity is in this case compounded, as it were, for we have to set off one explanation, incorporated in a virtually unknown precedent of this Court, against another explanation, which forms a part of the taught legal tradition of our law schools, but which, so far as I know, has never been adopted in any judicial decision.

I recognize the relevance of the precedents cited by my brother concerning the displaced "not" and the defendant who parked overtime. But what are we to do with one of the landmarks of our jurisprudence, which again my brother passes over in silence? This is Commonwealth v. Valjean. Though the case is somewhat obscurely reported, it appears that the defendant was indicted for the larceny of a loaf of bread, and offered as a defense that he was in a condition approaching starvation. The court refused to accept this defense. If hunger cannot justify the theft of wholesome and natural food, how can it justify the killing and eating of a man? Again, if we look at the thing in terms of deterrence, is it likely that a man will starve to death to avoid a jail sentence for the theft of a loaf of bread? My brother's demonstrations would compel us to overrule Commonwealth v. Valjean, and many other precedents that have been built on that case.

Again, I have difficulty in saying that no deterrent effect whatever could be attributed to a decision that these men were guilty of murder. The stigma of the word "murderer" is such that it is quite likely, I believe, that if these men had known that their act was deemed by the law to be murder they would have waited for a few days at least before carrying out their plan. During that time some unexpected relief might have come. I realize that this observation only reduces the distinction to a matter of degree, and does not destroy it altogether. It is certainly true that the element of deterrence would be less in this case than is normally involved in the application of the criminal law.

There is still a further difficulty in my brother Foster's proposal to read an exception into the statute to favor this case, though again a difficulty not even intimated in his opinion. What shall be the scope of this exception? Here the men cast lots and the victim was himself originally a party to the agreement. What would we have to decide if Whetmore had refused from the beginning to participate in the plan? Would a majority be permitted to overrule him? Or, suppose that no plan were adopted at all and the others simply conspired to bring about Whetmore's death, justifying their act by saying that he was in the weakest condition. Or again, that a plan of selection was followed but one based on a different justification than the one adopted here, as if the others were atheists and insisted that Whetmore should die because he was the only one who believed in an afterlife. These illustrations could be multiplied, but enough have been suggested to reveal what a quagmire of hidden difficulties my brother's reasoning contains.

Of course I realize on reflection that I may be concerning myself with a problem that will never arise, since it is unlikely that any group of men will ever again be brought to commit the dread act that was involved here. Yet, on still further reflection, even if we are certain that no similar case will arise again, do not the illustrations I have given show the lack of any coherent and rational principle in the rule my brother proposes? Should not the soundness of a principle be tested by the conclusions it entails, without reference to the accidents of later litigational history? Still, if this is so, why is it that we of this Court so often discuss the question whether we are likely to have later occasion to apply a principle urged for the solution of the case before us? Is this a situation where a line of reasoning not originally proper has become sanctioned by precedent, so that we are permitted to apply it and may even be under an obligation to do so?

The more I examine this case and think about it, the more deeply I become involved. My mind becomes entangled in the meshes of the very nets I throw out for my own rescue. I find that almost every consideration that bears on the decision of the case is counterbalanced by an opposing consideration leading in the opposite direction. My brother Foster has not furnished to me, nor can I discover for myself, any formula capable of resolving the equivocations that beset me on all sides.

I have given this case the best thought of which I am capable. I have scarcely slept since it was argued before us. When I feel myself inclined to accept the view of my brother Foster, I am repelled by a feeling that his arguments are intellectually unsound and approach mere rationalization. On the other hand, when I incline toward upholding the conviction, I am struck by the absurdity of directing that these men be put to death when their lives have been saved at the cost of the lives of ten heroic workmen. It is to me a matter of regret that the Prosecutor saw fit to ask for an indictment for murder. If we had a provision in our statutes making it a crime to eat human flesh, that would have been a more appropriate charge. If no other charge suited to the facts of this case could be brought against the defendants, it would have been wiser, I think, not to have indicted them at all. Unfortunately, however, the men have been indicted and tried, and we have therefore been drawn into this unfortunate affair.

Since I have been wholly unable to resolve the doubts that beset me about the law of this case, I am with regret announcing a step that is, I believe, unprecedented in the history of this tribunal. I declare my withdrawal from the decision of this case.

Keen, J. I should like to begin by setting to one side two questions which are not before this Court.

The first of these is whether executive clemency should be extended to these defendants if the conviction is affirmed. Under our system of government, that is a question for the Chief Executive, not for us. I therefore disapprove of that passage in the opinion of the Chief Justice in which he in effect gives instructions to the Chief Executive as to what he should do in this case and suggests that some impropriety will attach if these instructions are not heeded. This is a confusion of governmental functions—a confusion of which the judiciary should be the last to be guilty. I wish to state that if I were the Chief Executive I would go farther in the direction of clemency than the pleas addressed to him propose. I would pardon these men altogether, since I believe that they have already suffered enough to pay for any offense they may have committed. I want it to be understood that this remark is made in my capacity as a private citizen who by the accident of his office happens to have acquired an intimate acquaintance with the facts of this case. In the discharge of my duties as judge, it is neither my function to address directions to the Chief Executive, nor to take into account what he may or may not do, in reaching my own decision, which must be controlled entirely by the law of this Commonwealth.

The second question that I wish to put to one side is that of deciding whether what these men did was "right" or "wrong," "wicked" or "good." That is also a question that is irrelevant to the discharge of my office as a judge sworn to apply, not my conceptions of morality, but the law of the land. In putting this question to one side I think I can also safely dismiss without comment the first and more poetic portion of my brother Foster's opinion. The element of fantasy contained in the arguments developed there has been sufficiently revealed in my brother Tatting's somewhat solemn attempt to take those arguments seriously.

The sole question before us for decision is whether these defendants did, within the meaning of N.C.S.A. (n.s.) § 12-A, willfully take the life of Roger Whetmore. The exact language of the statute is as follows: "Whoever shall willfully take the life of another shall be punished by death." Now I should suppose that any candid observer, content to extract from these words their natural meaning, would concede at once that these defendants did "willfully take the life" of Roger Whetmore.

Whence arise all the difficulties of the case, then, and the necessity for so many pages of discussion about what ought to be so obvious? The difficulties, in whatever tortured form they may present themselves, all trace back to a single source, and that is a failure to distinguish the legal from the moral aspects of this case. To put it bluntly, my brothers do not like the fact that the written law requires the conviction of these defendants. Neither do I, but unlike my brothers I respect the obligations of an office that requires me to put my personal predilections out of my mind when I come to interpret and apply the law of this Commonwealth.

Now, of course, my brother Foster does not admit that he is actuated by a personal dislike of the written law. Instead he develops a familiar line of argument according to which the court may disregard the express language of a statute when something not contained in the statute itself, called its "purpose," can be employed to justify the result the court considers proper. Because this is an old issue between myself and my colleague, I should like, before discussing his particular application of the argument to the facts of this case, to say something about the historical background of this issue and its implications for law and government generally.

There was a time in this Commonwealth when judges did in fact legislate very freely, and all of us know that during that period some of our statutes were rather thoroughly made over by the judiciary. That was a time when the accepted principles of political science did not designate with any certainty the rank and function of the various arms of the state. We all know the tragic issue of that uncertainty in the brief civil war that arose out of the conflict between the judiciary, on the one hand, and the executive and the legislature, on the other. There is no need to recount here the factors that contributed to that unseemly struggle for power, though they included the unrepresentative character of the Chamber, resulting from a division of the country into election districts that no longer accorded with the actual distribution of the population, and the forceful personality and wide popular following of the then Chief Justice. It is enough to observe that those days are behind us, and that in place of the uncertainty that then reigned we now have a clear-cut principle, which is the supremacy of the legislative branch of our government. From that principle flows the obligation of the judiciary to enforce faithfully the written law, and to interpret that law in accordance with its plain meaning without reference to our personal desires or our individual conceptions of justice. I am not concerned with the question whether the principle that forbids the judicial revision of statutes is right or wrong, desirable or undesirable; I observe merely that this principle has become a tacit premise underlying the whole of the legal and governmental order I am sworn to administer.

Yet though the principle of the supremacy of the legislature has been accepted in theory for centuries, such is the tenacity of professional tradition and the force of fixed habits of thought that many of the judiciary have still not accommodated themselves to the restricted role which the new order imposes on them. My brother Foster is one of that group; his way of dealing with statutes is exactly that of a judge living in the 3900's.

We are all familiar with the process by which the judicial reform of disfavored legislative enactments is accomplished. Anyone who has followed the written opinions of Mr. Justice Foster will have had an opportunity to see it at work in every branch of the law. I am personally so familiar with the process that in the event of my brother's incapacity I am sure I could write a satisfactory opinion for him without any prompting whatever, beyond being informed whether he liked the effect of the terms of the statute as applied to the case before him.

The process of judicial reform requires three steps. The first of these is to divine some single "purpose" which the statute serves. This is done although not one statute in a hundred has any such single purpose, and although the objectives of nearly every statute are differently interpreted by the different classes of its sponsors. The second step is to discover that a mythical being called "the legislator," in the pursuit of this imagined "purpose," overlooked something or left some gap or imperfection in his work. Then comes the final and most refreshing part of the task, which is, of course, to fill in the blank thus created. *Quod erat faciendum.*

My brother Foster's penchant for finding holes in statutes reminds one of the story told by an ancient author about the man who ate a pair of shoes. Asked how he liked them, he replied that the part he liked best was the holes. That is the way my brother feels about statutes; the more holes they have in them the better he likes them. In short, he doesn't like statutes.

One could not wish for a better case to illustrate the specious nature of this gap-filling process than the one before us. My brother thinks he knows exactly what was sought when men made murder a crime, and that was something he calls "deterrence." My brother Tatting has already shown how much is passed over in that interpretation. But I think the trouble goes deeper. I doubt very much whether our statute making murder a crime really has a "purpose" in any ordinary sense of the term. Primarily, such a statute reflects a deeply-felt human conviction that murder is wrong and that something should be done to the man who commits it. If we were forced to be more articulate about the matter, we would probably take refuge in the more sophisticated theories of the criminologists, which, of course, were certainly not in the minds of those who drafted our statute. We might also observe that men will do their own work more effectively and live happier lives if they are protected against the threat of violent assault. Bearing in mind that the victims of murders are often unpleasant people, we might add some suggestion that the matter of disposing of undesirables is not a function suited to private enterprise, but should be a state monopoly. All of which reminds me of the attorney who once argued before us that a statute licensing physicians was a good thing because it would lead to lower life insurance rates by lifting the level of general health. There is such a thing as overexplaining the obvious.

If we do not know the purpose of § 12-A, how can we possibly say there is a "gap" in it? How can we know what its draftsmen thought about the question of killing men in order to eat them? My brother Tatting has revealed an understandable, though perhaps slightly exaggerated revulsion to cannibalism. How do we know that his remote ancestors did not feel the same revulsion to an even higher degree? Anthropologists say that the dread felt for a forbidden act may be increased by the fact that the conditions of a tribe's life create special temptations toward it, as incest is most severely condemned among those whose village relations make it most likely to occur. Certainly the period following the Great Spiral was one that had implicit in it temptations to anthropophagy. Perhaps it was for that very reason that our ancestors expressed their prohibition in so broad and unqualified a form. All of this is conjecture, of course, but it remains abundantly clear that neither I nor my brother Foster knows what the "purpose" of § 12-A is.

Considerations similar to those I have just outlined are also applicable to the exception in favor of self-defense, which plays so large a role in the reasoning of my brothers Foster and Tatting. It is of course true that in Commonwealth v. Parry an obiter dictum justified this exception on the assumption that the purpose of criminal legislation is to deter. It may well also be true that generations of law students have been taught that the true explanation of the exception lies in the fact that a man who acts in self-defense does not act "willfully," and that the same students have passed their bar examinations by repeating what their professors told them. These last observations I could dismiss, of course, as irrelevant for the simple reason that professors and bar examiners have not as yet any commission to make our laws for us. But again the real trouble lies deeper. As in dealing with the statute, so in dealing with the exception, the question is not the conjectural *purpose* of the rule, but its *scope*. Now the scope of the exception in favor of self-defense as it has been applied by this Court is plain: it applies to cases of resisting an aggressive threat to the party's own life. It is therefore too clear for argument that this case does not fall within the scope of the exception, since it is plain that Whetmore made no threat against the lives of these defendants.

The essential shabbiness of my brother Foster's attempt to cloak his remaking of the written law with an air of legitimacy comes tragically to the surface in my brother Tatting's opinion. In that opinion Justice Tatting struggles manfully to combine his colleague's loose moralisms with his own sense of fidelity to the written law. The issue of this struggle could only be that which occurred, a complete default in the discharge of the judicial function. You simply cannot apply a statute as it is written and remake it to meet your own wishes at the same time.

Now I know that the line of reasoning I have developed in this opinion will not be acceptable to those who look only to the immediate effects of a decision and ignore the long-run implications of an assumption by the judiciary of a power of dispensation. A hard decision is never a popular decision. Judges have been celebrated in literature for their sly prowess in devising some quibble by which a litigant could be deprived of his rights where the public thought it was wrong for him to assert those rights. But I believe that judicial dispensation does more harm in the long run than hard decisions. Hard cases may even have a certain moral value by bringing home to the people their own responsibilities toward the law that is ultimately their creation, and by reminding them that there is no principle of personal grace that can relieve the mistakes of their representatives.

Indeed, I will go farther and say that not only are the principles I have been expounding those which are soundest for our present conditions, but that we would have inherited a better legal system from our forefathers if those principles had been observed from the beginning. For example, with respect to the excuse of self-defense, if our courts had stood steadfast on the language of the statute the result would undoubtedly have been a legislative revision of it. Such a revision would have drawn on the assistance of natural philosophers and psychologists, and the resulting regulation of the matter would have had an understandable and rational basis, instead of the hodgepodge of verbalisms and metaphysical distinctions that have emerged from the judicial and professorial treatment.

These concluding remarks are, of course, beyond any duties that I have to discharge with relation to this case, but I include them here because I feel deeply that my colleagues are insufficiently aware of the dangers implicit in the conceptions of the judicial office advocated by my brother Foster.

I conclude that the conviction should be affirmed.

Handy, J. I have listened with amazement to the tortured ratiocinations to which this simple case has given rise. I never cease to wonder at my colleagues' ability to throw an obscuring curtain of legalisms about every issue presented to them for decision. We have heard this afternoon learned disquisitions on the distinction between positive law and the law of nature, the language of the statute and the purpose of the statute, judicial functions and executive functions, judicial legislation and legislative legislation. My only disappointment was that someone did not raise the question of the legal nature of the bargain struck in the cave—whether it was unilateral or bilateral, and whether Whetmore could not be considered as having revoked an offer prior to action taken thereunder.

What have all these things to do with the case? The problem before us is what we, as officers of the government, ought to do with these defendants. That is a question of practical wisdom, to be exercised in a context, not of abstract theory, but of human realities. When the case is approached in this light, it becomes, I think, one of the easiest to decide that has ever been argued before this Court.

Before stating my own conclusions about the merits of the case, I should like to discuss briefly some of the more fundamental issues involved—issues on which my colleagues and I have been divided ever since I have been on the bench.

I have never been able to make my brothers see that government is a human affair, and that men are ruled, not by words on paper or by abstract theories, but by other men. They are ruled well when their rulers understand the feelings and conceptions of the masses. They are ruled badly when that understanding is lacking.

Of all branches of the government, the judiciary is the most likely to lose its contact with the common man. The reasons for this are, of course, fairly obvious. Where the masses react to a situation in terms of a few salient features, we pick into little pieces every situation presented to us. Lawyers are hired by both sides to analyze and dissect. Judges and attorneys vie with one another to see who can discover the greatest number of difficulties and distinctions in a single set of facts. Each side tries to find cases, real or imagined, that will embarrass the demonstrations of the other side. To escape this embarrassment, still further distinctions are invented and imported into the situation. When a set of facts has been subjected to this kind of treatment for a sufficient time, all the life and juice have gone out of it and we have left a handful of dust.

Now I realize that wherever you have rules and abstract principles lawyers are going to be able to make distinctions. To some extent the sort of thing I have been describing is a necessary evil attaching to any formal regulation of human affairs. But I think that the area which really stands in need of such regulation is greatly overestimated. There are, of course, a few fundamental rules of the game that must be accepted if the game is to go on at all. I would include among these the rules relating to the conduct of elections, the appointment of public officials, and the term during which an office is held. Here some restraint on discretion and dispensation, some adherence to form, some scruple for what does and what does not fall within the rule, is, I concede, essential. Perhaps the area of basic principle should be expanded to include certain other rules, such as those designed to preserve the free civilmoign system.

But outside of these fields I believe that all government officials, including judges, will do their jobs best if they treat forms and abstract concepts as instruments. We should take as our model, I think, the good administrator, who accommodates procedures and principles to the case at hand, selecting from among the available forms those most suited to reach the proper result.

The most obvious advantage of this method of government is that it permits us to go about our daily tasks with efficiency and common sense. My adherence to this philosophy has, however, deeper roots. I believe that it is only with the insight this philosophy gives that we can preserve the flexibility essential if we are to keep our actions in reasonable accord with the sentiments of those subject to our rule. More governments have been wrecked, and more human misery caused, by the lack of this accord between ruler and ruled than by any other factor that can be discerned in history. Once drive a sufficient wedge between the mass of people and those who direct their legal, political, and economic life, and our society is ruined. Then neither Foster's law of nature nor Keen's fidelity to written law will avail us anything.

Now when these conceptions are applied to the case before us, its decision becomes, as I have said, perfectly easy. In order to demonstrate this I shall have to introduce certain realities that my brothers in their coy decorum have seen fit to pass over in silence, although they are just as acutely aware of them as I am.

The first of these is that this case has aroused an enormous public interest, both here and abroad. Almost every newspaper and magazine has carried articles about it; columnists have shared with their readers confidential information as to the next governmental move; hundreds of letters-to-the-editor have been printed. One of the great newspaper chains made a poll of public opinion on the question, "What do you think the Supreme Court should do with the Speluncean explorers?" About ninety per cent expressed a belief that the defendants should be pardoned or let off with a kind of token punishment. It is perfectly clear, then, how the public feels about the case. We could have known this without the poll, of course, on the basis of common sense, or even by observing that on this Court there are apparently four-and-a-half men, or ninety per cent, who share the common opinion.

This makes it obvious, not only what we should do, but what we must do if we are to preserve between ourselves and public opinion a reasonable and decent accord. Declaring these men innocent need not involve us in any undignified quibble or trick. No principle of statutory construction is required that is not consistent with the past practices of this Court. Certainly no layman would think that in letting these men off we had stretched the statute any more than our ancestors did when they created the excuse of self-defense. If a more detailed demonstration of the method of reconciling our decision with the statute is required, I should be content to rest on the arguments developed in the second and less visionary part of my brother Foster's opinion.

Now I know that my brothers will be horrified by my suggestion that this Court should take account of public opinion. They will tell you that public opinion is emotional and capricious, that it is based on half-truths and listens to witnesses who are not subject to cross-examination. They will tell you that the law surrounds the trial of a case like this with elaborate safeguards, designed to insure that the truth will be known and that every rational consideration bearing on the issues of the case has been taken into account. They will warn you that all of these safeguards go for naught if a mass opinion formed outside this framework is allowed to have any influence on our decision.

But let us look candidly at some of the realities of the administration of our criminal law. When a man is accused of crime, there are, speaking generally, four ways in which he may escape punishment. One of these is a determination by a judge that under the applicable law he has committed no crime. This is, of course, a determination that takes place in a rather formal and abstract atmosphere. But look at the other three ways in which he may escape punishment. These are: (1) a decision by the Prosecutor not to ask for an indictment; (2) an acquittal by the jury; (3) a pardon or commutation of sentence by the executive. Can anyone pretend that these decisions are held within a rigid and formal framework of rules that prevents factual error, excludes emotional and personal factors, and guarantees that all the forms of the law will be observed?

In the case of the jury we do, to be sure, attempt to cabin their deliberations within the area of the legally relevant, but there is no need to deceive ourselves into believing that this attempt is really successful. In the normal course of events the case now before us would have gone on all of its issues directly to the jury. Had this occurred we can be confident that there would have been an acquittal or at least a division that would have prevented a conviction. If the jury had been instructed that the men's hunger and their agreement were no defense to the charge of murder, their verdict would in all likelihood have ignored this instruction and would have involved a good deal more twisting of the letter of the law than any that is likely to tempt us. Of course the only reason that didn't occur in this case was the fortuitous circumstance that the foreman of the jury happened to be a lawyer. His learning enabled him to devise a form of words that would allow the jury to dodge its usual responsibilities.

My brother Tatting expresses annoyance that the Prosecutor did not, in effect, decide the case for him by not asking for an indictment. Strict as he is himself in complying with the demands of legal theory, he is quite content to have the fate of these men decided out of court by the Prosecutor on the basis of common sense. The Chief Justice, on the other hand, wants the application of common sense postponed to the very end, though like Tatting, he wants no personal part in it.

This brings me to the concluding portion of my remarks, which has to do with executive clemency. Before discussing that topic directly, I want to make a related observation about the poll of public opinion. As I have said, ninety per cent of the people wanted the Supreme Court to let the men off entirely or with a more or less nominal punishment. The ten per cent constituted a very oddly assorted group, with the most curious and divergent opinions. One of our university experts has made a study of this group and has found that its members fall into certain patterns. A substantial portion of them are subscribers to "crank" newspapers of limited circulation that gave their readers a distorted version of the facts of the case. Some thought that "Speluncean" means "cannibal" and that anthropophagy is a tenet of the Society. But the point I want to make, however, is this: although almost every conceivable variety and shade of opinion was represented in this group, there was, so far as I know, not one of them, nor a single member of the majority of ninety per cent, who said, "I think it would be a fine thing to have the courts sentence these men to be hanged, and then to have another branch of the government come along and pardon them." Yet this is a solution that has more or less dominated our discussions and which our Chief Justice proposes as a way by which we can avoid doing an injustice and at the same time preserve respect for law. He can be assured that if he is preserving anybody's morale, it is his own, and not the public's, which knows nothing of his distinctions. I mention this matter because I wish to emphasize once more the danger that we may get lost in the patterns of our own thought and forget that these patterns often cast not the slightest shadow on the outside world.

I come now to the most crucial fact in this case, a fact known to all of us on this Court, though one that my brothers have seen fit to keep under the cover of their judicial robes. This is the frightening likelihood that if the issue is left to him, the Chief Executive will refuse to pardon these men or commute their sentence. As we all know, our Chief Executive is a man now well advanced in years, of very stiff notions. Public clamor usually operates on him with the reverse of the effect intended. As I have told my brothers, it happens that my wife's niece is an intimate friend of his secretary. I have learned in this indirect, but, I think, wholly reliable way, that he is firmly determined not to commute the sentence if these men are found to have violated the law.

No one regrets more than I the necessity for relying in so important a matter on information that could be characterized as gossip. If I had my way this would not happen, for I would adopt the sensible course of sitting down with the Executive, going over the case with him, finding out what his views are, and perhaps working out with him a common program for handling the situation. But of course my brothers would never hear of such a thing.

Their scruple about acquiring accurate information directly does not prevent them from being very perturbed about what they have learned indirectly. Their acquaintance with the facts I have just related explains why the Chief Justice, ordinarily a model of decorum, saw fit in his opinion to flap his judicial robes in the face of the Executive and threaten him with excommunication if he failed to commute the sentence. It explains, I suspect, my brother Foster's feat of levitation by which a whole library of law books was lifted from the shoulders of these defendants. It explains also why even my legalistic brother Keen emulated Pooh-Bah in the ancient comedy by stepping to the other side of the stage to address a few remarks to the Executive "in my capacity as a private citizen." (I may remark, incidentally, that the advice of Private Citizen Keen will appear in the reports of this court printed at taxpayers' expense.)

I must confess that as I grow older I become more and more perplexed at men's refusal to apply their common sense to problems of law and government, and this truly tragic case has deepened my sense of discouragement and dismay. I only wish that I could convince my brothers of the wisdom of the principles I have applied to the judicial office since I first assumed it. As a matter of fact, by a kind of sad rounding of the circle, I encountered issues like those involved here in the very first case I tried as Judge of the Court of General Instances in Fanleigh County.

A religious sect had unfrocked a minister who, they said, had gone over to the views and practices of a rival sect. The minister circulated a handbill making charges against the authorities who had expelled him. Certain lay members of the church announced a public meeting at which they proposed to explain the position of the church. The minister attended this meeting. Some said he slipped in unobserved in a disguise; his own testimony was that he had walked in openly as a member of the public. At any rate, when the speeches began he interrupted with certain questions about the affairs of the church and made some statements in defense of his own views. He was set upon by members of the audience and given a pretty thorough pommeling, receiving among other injuries a broken jaw. He brought a suit for damages against the association that sponsored the meeting and against ten named individuals who he alleged were his assailants.

When we came to the trial, the case at first seemed very complicated to me. The attorneys raised a host of legal issues. There were nice questions on the admissibility of evidence, and, in connection with the suit against the association, some difficult problems turning on the question whether the minister was a trespasser or a licensee. As a novice on the bench I was eager to apply my law school learning and I began studying these question closely, reading all the authorities and preparing well-documented rulings. As I studied the case I became more and more involved in its legal intricacies and I began to get into a state approaching that of my brother Tatting in this case. Suddenly, however, it dawned on me that all these perplexing issues really had nothing to do with the case, and I began examining it in the light of common sense. The case at once gained a new perspective, and I saw that the only thing for me to do was to direct a verdict for the defendants for lack of evidence.

I was led to this conclusion by the following considerations. The melee in which the plaintiff was injured had been a very confused affair, with some people trying to get to the center of the disturbance, while others were trying to get away from it; some striking at the plaintiff, while others were apparently trying to protect him. It would have taken weeks to find out the truth of the matter. I decided that nobody's broken jaw was worth that much to the Commonwealth. (The minister's injuries, incidentally, had meanwhile healed without disfigurement and without any impairment of normal faculties.) Furthermore, I felt very strongly that the plaintiff had to a large extent brought the thing on himself. He knew how inflamed passions were about the affair, and could easily have found another forum for the expression of his views. My decision was widely approved by the press and public opinion, neither of which could tolerate the views and practices that the expelled minister was attempting to defend.

Now, thirty years later, thanks to an ambitious Prosecutor and a legalistic jury foreman, I am faced with a case that raises issues which are at bottom much like those involved in that case. The world does not seem to change much, except that this time it is not a question of a judgment for five or six hundred frelars, but of the life or death of four men who have already suffered more torment and humiliation than most of us would endure in a thousand years. I conclude that the defendants are innocent of the crime charged, and that the conviction and sentence should be set aside.

Tatting, J. I have been asked by the Chief Justice whether, after listening to the two opinions just rendered, I desire to reexamine the position previously taken by me. I wish to state that after hearing these opinions I am greatly strengthened in my conviction that I ought not to participate in the decision of this case.

The Supreme Court being evenly divided, the conviction and sentence of the Court of General Instances is *affirmed.* It is ordered that the execution of the sentence shall occur at

6 a.m., Friday, April 2, 4300, at which time the Public Executioner is directed to proceed with all convenient dispatch to hang each of the defendants by the neck until he is dead.

Postscript

Now that the court has spoken its judgment, the reader puzzled by the choice of date may wish to be reminded that the centuries which separate us from the year 4300 are roughly equal to those that have passed since the Age of Pericles. There is probably no need to observe that the *Speluncean Case* itself is intended neither as a work of satire nor as a prediction in any ordinary sense of the term. As for the judges who make up Chief Justice Truepenny's court, they are, of course, as mythical as the facts and precedents with which they deal. The reader who refuses to accept this view, and who seeks to trace out contemporary resemblances where none is intended or contemplated, should be warned that he is engaged in a frolic of his own, which may possibly lead him to miss whatever modest truths are contained in the opinions delivered by the Supreme Court of Newgarth. The case was constructed for the sole purpose of bringing into a common focus certain divergent philosophies of law and government. These philosophies presented men with live questions of choice in the days of Plato and Aristotle. Perhaps they will continue to do so when our era has had its say about them. If there is any element of prediction in the case, it does not go beyond a suggestion that the questions involved are among the permanent problems of the human race.

Notes and Questions

1. Consider the probabilistic assumptions made by the *Dudley and Stephens* jury toward the end of its special verdict. Do you disagree with any of those assumptions?

2. Given those probabilistic assumptions, were the actions of the *Dudley and Stephens* defendants unreasonable? Were there any better solutions?

3. Why is Lord Coleridge unwilling to consider probabilistic reasoning on the part of the defendants? What is he so worried about?

4. Is the *Dudley and Stephens* case like the example of two drowning men struggling over a plank that will support only one of them? What is Lord Coleridge saying about the plank example?

5. At the end of his opinion Lord Coleridge writes:

We are often compelled to set up standards we cannot reach ourselves, and to lay down rules which we could not ourselves satisfy.

How might that statement be criticized?

6. The defense attorney in the *Holmes* case argues that "this case should be tried in a long-boat." What does he mean by that?

7. The *Holmes* defense attorney also argues that "every man on board had a right to make law with his own right hand." What would "law" mean then?

8. Is it possible to argue for any constraints on individual freedom in a "state of nature"? What does the *Holmes* court suggest? What does Justice Foster in the *Speluncean Explorers* case suggest?

9. Would you rather be in the situation of the *Dudley and Stephens* defendants, that of Holmes, or that of the Speluncean Explorers? How did their situations differ, and what different threats did they face?

10. Is the absolute sanctity of innocent human life an inviolable principle of our own legal system? Can you think of exceptions to the principle?

11. Justice Handy writes:

Men are ruled, not by words on paper or by abstract theories, but by other men. They are ruled well when their rulers understand the feelings and conceptions of the masses. They are ruled badly when that understanding is lacking.

Why might that view be problematic?

12. What is probably going to happen in Newgarth after the Speluncean Explorers are executed?

Suggestions For Further Reading

The Case of the Speluncean Explorers: A Fiftieth Anniversary Symposium, 112 Harvard Law Review 1834 (1999)

George C. Christie, The Defense of Necessity Considered from the Legal and Moral Points of View, 48 Duke Law Journal 975 (1999)

William N. Eskridge, Jr., The Case of the Speluncean Explorers: Twentieth-Century Statutory Interpretation in a Nutshell, 61 George Washington Law Review 1731 (1993)

Leo Katz, Bad Acts and Guilty Minds, ch. 1 (1987)

A.W. Brian Simpson, Cannibalism and the Common Law (1984)

Glanville Williams, A Commentary on R. v. Dudley and Stephens, 8 Cambrian Law Review 94 (1977)

Chapter 4
Self-Defense and Its Limits

Bill Bell v. State
17 Tex. Crim. 538 (1885)

[Defendant, who drove a horse-drawn carriage in Waco, Texas, stabbed to death a customer who became belligerent during an argument over his change. The defendant was found guilty of second-degree murder and sentenced to seven years in the penitentiary.

[According to the state's first witness, the deceased became seemingly very angry and excited, and the witness took hold of him. Other parties also interfered and tried to get the defendant to give the deceased the quarter. The defendant stood perfectly still, and said several times: "He will get his change directly." Finally the deceased said: "Turn me loose, boys, and you will see some fun." The witness did not, at that time, release the deceased. Some further talk between the parties ensued, and after a time the deceased remarked that he did not intend to allow the defendant to steal that quarter. Thereupon defendant stepped towards but not up to the deceased, and said: "Don't you accuse me of trying to steal a quarter of a dollar."

[About the time that the defendant made the remark last quoted, the witness released the deceased, and the deceased and defendant ran together. The witness did not know and could not state which of the two was the aggressor, or which struck the first blow. The collision was over in a moment, not more than two or three blows passing between the parties.

[The defendant appeared very cool throughout the difficulty. The witness did not see him advance upon or strike the deceased. It was impossible for the witness to say who struck the first blow.

[Defendant made no effort to press the difficulty or to strike the deceased after the latter was pulled back. No one held the defendant.]

Wilson, Judge.

It cannot be questioned but that the evidence is sufficient to sustain the conviction. It is not so clear and conclusive of the defendant's guilt, however, as to exclude a lower grade of homicide than murder in the second degree, or justifiable homicide in self-defense. As we view the evidence, it demanded of the trial court to instruct the jury, 1st. Upon the law of murder in the second degree; 2nd. Upon the law of manslaughter; and, 3d. Upon the law of self-defense. In the main charge the court sufficiently, and with substantial correctness, explained to the jury the law of murder in the second degree and of manslaughter.

It omitted entirely to submit the issue of self-defense. To supply this omission, defendant's counsel requested a special instruction in the following language, viz.: "If the jury believe, from all the facts and circumstances in evidence, that, at the time of the difficulty between the deceased Moreland and the defendant Bell, and at the time Bell inflicted the injury which proved fatal (if the jury find that Bell did inflict the injury), that Bell did not intend to kill Moreland, and only intended by his acts to defend himself from an unlawful and violent attack made upon him by Moreland, and used no means in such resistance disproportioned to such attack, considering the relative disproportion in size of the combatants (if there was such disproportion), and Bell had reason to believe and did believe that such attack was likely to endanger his own life, or result in serious bodily injury to himself, then the homicide would be justifiable, and the jury will acquit." This special charge was given, and it constitutes the only charge given to the jury upon the issue of self-defense—nor did the defendant request any additional charge upon the subject.

At the time of the trial no exceptions were taken by the defendant to the charge of the court or any portion of it, but in his motion for a new trial several objections to it are urged, which are insisted upon in this court, and among them, that "the court erred in failing to define justifiable homicide, and in failing to submit to the jury proper issues arising upon the evidence as to the law of self-defense and justifiable homicide." This objection is, we think, well taken. As far as it goes the special charge we have quoted is correct and applicable to the evidence. It does not, however, go far enough. It does not give *all* the law of self-defense demanded by the evidence. It should have stated that the defendant, if unlawfully attacked by the deceased, was not bound to retreat in order to avoid the necessity of killing him. . . . This is a very material part of the law of self-defense, and is a statutory innovation upon the common law, and upon the common view of what constitutes self-defense. The common law required the assailed party to "retreat to the wall," and this requirement, while it no longer exists as the law of this State, is still believed by many who are unlearned in the law to be in force. In all cases, therefore, where the issue of self-defense arises from the evidence, the jury should be instructed that the assailed party is not bound to retreat in order to make perfect his right of self-defense. And when the evidence presents the issue of self-defense, the law, and *all* the law, applicable to that issue, as made by the evidence, should be given in charge to the jury, whether requested or not. . . .

When the court omits to do this it is error, and, if excepted to at the time of the trial, the conviction would necessarily be set aside. But if the error be not excepted to, but be called to the attention of the trial court for the first time in a motion for new trial, it will not be cause for reversal unless it should appear to this court that the defendant's rights have probably been injured thereby. . . .

In the case before us, the inquiry therefore arises, did the error of the court, in failing to instruct the jury that the defendant was not bound to retreat, probably weaken his plea of self-defense, and prejudice his legal rights in respect thereto? In view of the evidence in the case, we must say that in our opinion it was calculated to have that effect. It was within the power of the defendant to have retreated, and by this means to have avoided the necessity of killing the deceased. It may have been the opinion of the jury that he should have retreated, and that, as he did not in this way avoid his assailant, he was not justified in slaying him. They should have been told by the court that the law of this State does not require retreat under any circumstances. By giving the special charge requested, the trial judge conceded, and we think correctly, that the issue of self-defense was presented by the evidence, and this special charge called his attention to that issue, and, being imperfect, it was the duty of the court to supply its defects by additional instructions. Because the charge as requested was not as full as the law required, should not, we think, be regarded as a waiver by the defendant of his right to a full and correct charge, and should not be held to relieve the court of the duty of giving such charge. Considering the evidence of this case, we think the failure of the court to give in charge article 573 of the Penal Code was material error calculated to injure the rights of the defendant, and is therefore reversible error although not excepted to at the time of the trial. . . .

But we are not prepared to say that the special charge was even abstractly correct, especially in view of the evidence in the case. It was not shown clearly that the wounds inflicted upon deceased were inflicted with a knife, and, if with a knife, that it was such a one as was calculated ordinarily to produce death or serious bodily injury, when used in the manner and under the circumstances here shown. There were but two wounds upon deceased, one in the arm, which was slight, and the other in the temple above the eye, which proved fatal. These wounds were made with some sharp pointed instrument and were small. It is quite reasonable to infer that the wounds were made with a knife, but still the testimony does not place this conclusion beyond doubt. If made with a knife, evidently it was a small one, as demonstrated by the small size of the wounds. The fatal wound was fatal because perhaps of its locality. The instrument used penetrated at the suture or lap in the skull bone, fracturing the bone to some extent, and wounding the brain, producing meningitis which caused death. Had the blow fallen on almost any other portion of the body it might not have been serious, much less mortal. Therefore, the fact that the wound produced death does not of itself warrant the deduction that the instrument used was of a character calculated ordinarily, when so used, to produce death or serious bodily injury.

It is not every *knife* that is a deadly or even a dangerous weapon, and yet with any kind of a knife it is possible, no doubt, to produce death or serious bodily injury. A small sewing needle is not an instrument that could be considered deadly or dangerous, and yet one skilled in human anatomy might, under favorable circumstances, use it with fatal effect, or it might be so used accidentally, or without any intention to kill or seriously injure. Considering the absence of any evidence, except the fatal result of the wound, to show the deadly or dangerous character of the weapon used, we are of the opinion that the special charge is not even abstractly correct when viewed with reference to the facts of this case, and that under the circumstances it was erroneous, and prejudicial to the defendant's rights. It was furthermore not in harmony with the main charge, which submitted to the jury, as a question to be determined from the evidence, whether or not, in inflicting the blows, it was the intention of the defendant to kill or inflict serious bodily injury. The special charge, in a great measure, supplied this question of fact with a presumption of the law, and that, too, without explaining that this presumption of the law was not a conclusive one, but that it might be removed by other evidence showing an absence of such criminal intent. The *intent* with which the wounds were inflicted was a most vital issue to the defendant. Upon this pivot hung his fate. In the main charge this issue was properly submitted to the jury to be determined by them from the evidence, without the aid of any presumption of law, except that the defendant should be presumed innocent until his guilt was established by competent evidence. Here, we think, upon this issue, the charge should have rested. . . .

We are of the opinion that the facts of this case are of a character which demanded of the trial court a full and correct charge upon justifiable homicide in self-defense, and also a full and correct charge upon the issue of the defendant's intent in inflicting the wounds, leaving the jury to determine that intent from the evidence in the case, without incumbering such determination with any arbitrary presumption of the law, adverse to the presumption of innocence. Believing that he has not had the benefit of such a charge, and that thereby his rights have probably been prejudiced, the judgment is reversed and the cause is remanded.

People v. Goetz
68 N.Y.2d 96 (1986)

Opinion of the Court

Chief Judge Wachtler.

A Grand Jury has indicted defendant on attempted murder, assault, and other charges for having shot and wounded four youths on a New York City subway train after one or two of the youths approached him and asked for $5. The lower courts, concluding that the prosecutor's charge to the Grand Jury on the defense of justification was erroneous, have dismissed the attempted murder, assault and weapons possession charges. We now reverse and reinstate all counts of the indictment.

The precise circumstances of the incident giving rise to the charges against defendant are disputed, and ultimately it will be for a trial jury to determine what occurred. We feel it necessary, however, to provide some factual background to properly frame the legal issues before us. Accordingly, we have summarized the facts as they appear from the evidence before the Grand Jury. We stress, however, that we do not purport to reach any conclusions or holding as to exactly what transpired or whether defendant is blameworthy. The credibility of witnesses and the reasonableness of defendant's conduct are to be resolved by the trial jury.

On Saturday afternoon, December 22, 1984, Troy Canty, Darryl Cabey, James Ramseur, and Barry Allen boarded an IRT express subway train in The Bronx and headed south toward lower Manhattan. The four youths rode together in the rear portion of the seventh car of the train. Two of the four, Ramseur and Cabey, had screwdrivers inside their coats, which they said were to be used to break into the coin boxes of video machines.

Defendant Bernhard Goetz boarded this subway train at 14th Street in Manhattan and sat down on a bench towards the rear section of the same car occupied by the four youths. Goetz was carrying an unlicensed .38 caliber pistol loaded with five rounds of ammunition in a waistband holster. The train left the 14th Street station and headed towards Chambers Street.

It appears from the evidence before the Grand Jury that Canty approached Goetz, possibly with Allen beside him, and stated "give me five dollars." Neither Canty nor any of the other youths displayed a weapon. Goetz responded by standing up, pulling out his handgun and firing four shots in rapid succession. The first shot hit Canty in the chest; the second struck Allen in the back; the third went through Ramseur's arm and into his left side; the fourth was fired at Cabey, who apparently was then standing in the corner of the car, but missed, deflecting instead off of a wall of the conductor's cab. After Goetz briefly surveyed the scene around him, he fired another shot at Cabey, who then was sitting on the end bench of the car. The bullet entered the rear of Cabey's side and severed his spinal cord.

All but two of the other passengers fled the car when, or immediately after, the shots were fired. The conductor, who had been in the next car, heard the shots and instructed the motorman to radio for emergency assistance. The conductor then went into the car where the shooting occurred and saw Goetz sitting on a bench, the injured youths lying on the floor or slumped against a seat, and two women who had apparently taken cover, also lying on the floor. Goetz told the conductor that the four youths had tried to rob him.

While the conductor was aiding the youths, Goetz headed towards the front of the car. The train had stopped just before the Chambers Street station and Goetz went between two of the cars, jumped onto the tracks and fled. Police and ambulance crews arrived at the scene shortly thereafter. Ramseur and Canty, initially listed in critical condition, have fully recovered. Cabey remains paralyzed, and has suffered some degree of brain damage.

On December 31, 1984, Goetz surrendered to police in Concord, New Hampshire, identifying himself as the gunman being sought for the subway shootings in New York nine days earlier. Later that day, after receiving *Miranda* warnings, he made two lengthy statements, both of which were tape recorded with his permission. In the statements, which are substantially similar, Goetz admitted that he had been illegally carrying a handgun in New York City for three years. He stated that he had first purchased a gun in 1981 after he had been injured in a mugging. Goetz also revealed that twice between 1981 and 1984 he had successfully warded off assailants simply by displaying the pistol.

According to Goetz's statement, the first contact he had with the four youths came when Canty, sitting or lying on the bench across from him, asked "how are you," to which he replied "fine." Shortly thereafter, Canty, followed by one of the other youths, walked over to the defendant and stood to his left, while the other two youths remained to his right, in the corner of the subway car. Canty then said "give me five dollars." Goetz stated that he knew from the smile on Canty's face that they wanted to "play with me." Although he was certain that none of the youths had a gun, he had a fear, based on prior experiences, of being "maimed."

Goetz then established "a pattern of fire," deciding specifically to fire from left to right. His stated intention at that point was to "murder [the four youths], to hurt them, to make them suffer as much as possible." When Canty again requested money, Goetz stood up, drew his weapon, and began firing, aiming for the center of the body of each of the four. Goetz recalled that the first two he shot "tried to run through the crowd [but] they had nowhere to run." Goetz then turned to his right to "go after the other two." One of these two "tried to run through the wall of the train, but . . . he had nowhere to go." The other youth (Cabey) "tried pretending that he wasn't with [the others]" by standing still, holding on to one of the subway hand straps, and not looking at Goetz. Goetz nonetheless fired his fourth shot at him. He then ran back to the first two youths to make sure they had been "taken care of." Seeing that they had both been shot, he spun back to check on the latter two. Goetz noticed that the youth who had been standing still was now sitting on a bench and seemed unhurt. As Goetz told the police, "I said '[y]ou seem to be all right, here's another'," and he then fired the shot which severed Cabey's spinal cord. Goetz added that "if I was a little more under self-control . . . I would have put the barrel against his forehead and fired." He also admitted that "if I had had more [bullets], I would have shot them again, and again, and again."

After waiving extradition, Goetz was brought back to New York and arraigned on a felony complaint charging him with attempted murder and criminal possession of a weapon.

The matter was presented to a Grand Jury in January 1985, with the prosecutor seeking an indictment for attempted murder, assault, reckless endangerment, and criminal possession of a weapon. Neither the defendant nor any of the wounded youths testified before this Grand Jury. On January 25, 1985, the Grand Jury indicted defendant on one count of criminal possession of a weapon in the third degree, for possessing the gun used in the subway shootings, and two counts of criminal possession of a weapon in the fourth degree, for possessing two other guns in his apartment building. It dismissed, however, the attempted murder and other charges stemming from the shootings themselves.

Several weeks after the Grand Jury's action, the People, asserting that they had newly available evidence, moved for an order authorizing them to resubmit the dismissed charges to a second Grand Jury. Supreme Court, Criminal Term, after conducting an in camera inquiry, granted the motion. Presentation of the case to the second Grand Jury began on March 14, 1985. Two of the four youths, Canty and Ramseur, testified. Among the other witnesses were four passengers from the seventh car of the subway who had seen some portions of the incident. Goetz again chose not to testify, though the tapes of his two statements were played for the grand jurors, as had been done with the first Grand Jury.

On March 27, 1985, the second Grand Jury filed a 10-count indictment, containing four charges of attempted murder, four charges of assault in the first degree, one charge of reckless endangerment in the first degree, and one charge of criminal possession of a weapon in the second degree. Goetz was arraigned on this indictment on March 28, 1985, and it was consolidated with the earlier three-count indictment.

On October 14, 1985, Goetz moved to dismiss the charges contained in the second indictment alleging, among other things, that the evidence before the second Grand Jury was not legally sufficient to establish the offenses charged and that the prosecutor's instructions to that Grand Jury on the defense of justification were erroneous and prejudicial to the defendant so as to render its proceedings defective.

On November 25, 1985, while the motion to dismiss was pending before Criminal Term, a column appeared in the *New York Daily News* containing an interview which the columnist had conducted with Darryl Cabey the previous day in Cabey's hospital room. The columnist claimed that Cabey had told him in this interview that the other three youths had all approached Goetz with the intention of robbing him. The day after the column was published, a New York City police officer informed the prosecutor that he had been one of the first police officers to enter the subway car after the shootings, and that Canty had said to him "we were going to rob [Goetz]." The prosecutor immediately disclosed this information to the court and to defense counsel, adding that this was the first time his office had been told of this alleged statement and that none of the police reports filed on the incident contained any such information. Goetz then orally expanded his motion to dismiss, asserting that resubmission of the charges voted by the second Grand Jury was required . . . because it appeared, from this new information, that Ramseur and Canty had committed perjury. . . .

Penal Law article 35 recognizes the defense of justification, which "permits the use of force under certain circumstances." One such set of circumstances pertains to the use of force in defense of a person, encompassing both self-defense and defense of a third person. Penal Law § 35.15(1) sets forth the general principles governing all such uses of force: "[a] person may . . . use physical force upon another person when and to the extent he *reasonably believes* such to be necessary to defend himself or a third person from what he *reasonably believes* to be the use or imminent use of unlawful physical force by such other person" (emphasis added).

Section 35.15(2) sets forth further limitations on these general principles with respect to the use of "deadly physical force": "A person may not use deadly physical force upon another person under circumstances specified in subdivision one unless (a) He *reasonably believes* that such other person is using or about to use deadly physical force . . . or (b) He *reasonably believes* that such other person is committing or attempting to commit a kidnapping, forcible rape, forcible sodomy or robbery" (emphasis added).

Thus, consistent with most justification provisions, Penal Law § 35.15 permits the use of deadly physical force only where requirements as to triggering conditions and the necessity of a particular response are met. As to the triggering conditions, the statute requires that the actor "reasonably believes" that another person either is using or about to use deadly physical force or is committing or attempting to commit one of certain enumerated felonies, including robbery. As to the need for the use of deadly physical force as a response, the statute requires that the actor "reasonably believes" that such force is necessary to avert the perceived threat.

Because the evidence before the second Grand Jury included statements by Goetz that he acted to protect himself from being maimed or to avert a robbery, the prosecutor correctly chose to charge the justification defense in section 35.15 to the Grand Jury. The prosecutor properly instructed the grand jurors to consider whether the use of deadly physical force was justified to prevent either serious physical injury or a robbery, and, in doing so, to separately analyze the defense with respect to each of the charges. He elaborated upon the prerequisites for the use of deadly physical force essentially by reading or paraphrasing the language in Penal Law § 35.15. The defense does not contend that he committed any error in this portion of the charge.

When the prosecutor had completed his charge, one of the grand jurors asked for clarification of the term "reasonably believes." The prosecutor responded by instructing the grand jurors that they were to consider the circumstances of the incident and determine "whether the defendant's conduct was that of a reasonable man in the defendant's situation." It is this response by the prosecutor—and specifically his use of "a reasonable man"— which is the basis for the dismissal of the charges by the lower courts. As expressed repeatedly in the Appellate Division's plurality opinion, because section 35.15 uses the term "*he* reasonably believes," the appropriate test, according to that court, is whether a defendant's beliefs and reactions were "reasonable *to him.*" Under that reading of the statute, a jury which believed a defendant's testimony that he felt that his own actions were warranted and were reasonable would have to acquit him, regardless of what anyone else in defendant's situation might have concluded. Such an interpretation defies the ordinary meaning and significance of the term "reasonably" in a statute, and misconstrues the clear intent of the

Legislature, in enacting section 35.15, to retain an objective element as part of any provision authorizing the use of deadly physical force.

Penal statutes in New York have long codified the right recognized at common law to use deadly physical force, under appropriate circumstances, in self-defense. These provisions have never required that an actor's belief as to the intention of another person to inflict serious injury be correct in order for the use of deadly force to be justified, but they have uniformly required that the belief comport with an objective notion of reasonableness. The 1829 statute, using language which was followed almost in its entirety until the 1965 recodification of the Penal Law, provided that the use of deadly force was justified in self-defense or in the defense of specified third persons "when there shall be a reasonable ground to apprehend a design to commit a felony, or to do some great personal injury, and there shall be imminent danger of such design being accomplished.". . .

We cannot lightly impute to the Legislature an intent to fundamentally alter the principles of justification to allow the perpetrator of a serious crime to go free simply because that person believed his actions were reasonable and necessary to prevent some perceived harm. To completely exonerate such an individual, no matter how aberrational or bizarre his thought patterns, would allow citizens to set their own standards for the permissible use of force. It would also allow a legally competent defendant suffering from delusions to kill or perform acts of violence with impunity, contrary to fundamental principles of justice and criminal law.

We can only conclude that the Legislature retained a reasonableness requirement to avoid giving a license for such actions. The plurality's interpretation, as the dissenters below recognized, excises the impact of the word "reasonably.". . .

Goetz also argues that the introduction of an objective element will preclude a jury from considering factors such as the prior experiences of a given actor and thus, require it to make a determination of "reasonableness" without regard to the actual circumstances of a particular incident. This argument, however, falsely presupposes that an objective standard means that the background and other relevant characteristics of a particular actor must be ignored. To the contrary, we have frequently noted that a determination of reasonableness must be based on the "circumstances" facing a defendant or his "situation." Such terms encompass more than the physical movements of the potential assailant. [T]hese terms include any relevant knowledge the defendant had about that person. They also necessarily bring in the physical attributes of all persons involved, including the defendant. Furthermore, the defendant's circumstances encompass any prior experiences he had which could provide a reasonable basis for a belief that another person's intentions were to injure or rob him or that the use of deadly force was necessary under the circumstances.

Accordingly, a jury should be instructed to consider this type of evidence in weighing the defendant's actions. The jury must first determine whether the defendant had the requisite beliefs under section 35.15, that is, whether he believed deadly force was necessary to avert the imminent use of deadly force or the commission of one of the felonies enumerated therein. If the People do not prove beyond a reasonable doubt that he did not have such beliefs, then the jury must also consider whether these beliefs were reasonable. The jury would have to determine, in light of all the "circumstances," as explicated above, if a reasonable person could have had these beliefs.

The prosecutor's instruction to the second Grand Jury that it had to determine whether, under the circumstances, Goetz's conduct was that of a reasonable man in his situation was thus essentially an accurate charge. It is true that the prosecutor did not elaborate on the meaning of "circumstances" or "situation" and inform the grand jurors that they could consider, for example, the prior experiences Goetz related in his statement to the police. We have held, however, that a Grand Jury need not be instructed on the law with the same degree of precision as the petit jury. This lesser standard is premised upon the different functions of the Grand Jury and the petit jury: the former determines whether sufficient evidence exists to accuse a person of a crime and thereby subject him to criminal prosecution; the latter ultimately determines the guilt or innocence of the accused, and may convict only where the People have proven his guilt beyond a reasonable doubt. . . .

Of course, as noted above, where the evidence suggests that a complete defense such as justification may be present, the prosecutor must charge the grand jurors on that defense, providing enough information to enable them to determine whether the defense, in light of the evidence, should preclude the criminal prosecution. The prosecutor more than adequately fulfilled this obligation here. His instructions were not as complete as the court's charge on justification should be, but they sufficiently apprised the Grand Jury of the existence and requirements of that defense to allow it to intelligently decide that there is sufficient evidence tending to disprove justification and necessitating a trial. The Grand Jury has indicted Goetz. It will now be for the petit jury to decide whether the prosecutor can prove beyond a reasonable doubt that Goetz's reactions were unreasonable and therefore excessive. . . .

Accordingly, the order of the Appellate Division should be reversed, and the dismissed counts of the indictment reinstated.

Notes and Questions

1. Under English common law, a threatened person had a "duty to retreat" as far as possible before using lethal force in self-defense. Should the English rule apply on the American frontier? In a New York City subway car?

2. According to one commentator,

> The struggle between passion and reason in the law of self-defense is played out against a background of shared, albeit vague, assumptions about the contours of the defense. First, in order to be properly resisted, an attack must be *imminent*. Further, the defender's response must be both *necessary* and *proportional* to the feared attack. And finally, the defender must act with the *intention* not of hurting the victim per se, but of thwarting the attack. There is no statute or authoritative legal source that expresses this consensus, but lawyers all over the world would readily concur that these are the basic, structural elements of a valid claim of self-defense.

George P. Fletcher, A Crime of Self-Defense 19 (1988). Assess the facts of the *Bill Bell* and *Goetz* cases in terms of these elements.

3. Should the standard for self-defense be:

(a) whether the defendant's conduct was that of a reasonable man in the defendant's situation; or

(b) whether the defendant sincerely believed his actions were reasonable and necessary, regardless of what anyone else in the defendant's situation might have thought?

What are some problems with either view?

Suggestions For Further Reading

Richard Maxwell Brown, No Duty to Retreat (1991)

George P. Fletcher, A Crime of Self-Defense: Bernhard Goetz and the Law on Trial (1988)

Cynthia K.Y. Lee, The Act-Belief Distinction in Self-Defense Doctrine, 2 Buffalo Criminal Law Review 191 (1998)

Chapter 5
Other Forms of Necessity

Bird v. Jones
7 Q.B. 742 (1845)

Coleridge, J.

. . . This point is, whether certain facts, which may be taken as clear upon the evidence, amount to an imprisonment. These facts, stated shortly, and as I understand them, are in effect as follows.

A part of a public highway was inclosed, and appropriated for spectators of a boat race, paying a price for their seats. The plaintiff was desirous of entering this part, and was opposed by the defendant: but, after a struggle, during which no momentary detention of his person took place, he succeeded in climbing over the inclosure. Two policemen were then stationed by the defendant to prevent, and they did prevent, him from passing onwards in the direction in which he declared his wish to go: but he was allowed to remain unmolested where he was, and was at liberty to go, and was told that he was so, in the only other direction by which he could pass. This he refused for some time, and, during that time, remained where he had thus placed himself.

These are the facts: and, setting aside those which do not properly bear on the question now at issue, there will remain these: that the plaintiff, being in a public highway and desirous of passing along it, in a particular direction, is prevented from doing so by the orders of the defendant, and that the defendant's agents for the purpose are policemen, from whom, indeed, no unnecessary violence was to be anticipated, or such as they believed unlawful, yet who might be expected to execute such commands as they deemed lawful with all necessary force, however resisted. But, although thus obstructed, the plaintiff was at liberty to move his person and go in any other direction, at his free will and pleasure: and no actual force or restraint on his person was used, unless the obstruction before mentioned amounts to so much.

I lay out of consideration the question of right or wrong between these parties. The acts will amount to imprisonment neither more nor less from their being wrongful or capable of justification.

And I am of opinion that there was no imprisonment. To call it so appears to me to confound partial obstruction and disturbance with total obstruction and detention. A prison may have its boundary large or narrow, visible and tangible, or, though real, still in the conception only; it may itself be moveable or fixed: but a boundary it must have; and that boundary the party imprisoned must be prevented from passing; he must be prevented from leaving that place, within the ambit of which the party imprisoning would confine him, except by prison-breach. Some confusion seems to me to arise from confounding imprisonment of the body with mere loss of freedom: it is one part of the definition of freedom to be able to go whithersoever one pleases; but imprisonment is something more than the mere loss of this power; it includes the notion of restraint within some limits defined by a will or power exterior to our own.

In Com. Dig. Imprisonment (G), it is said: "Every restraint of the liberty of a free man will be an imprisonment." For this the authorities cited are 2 Inst. 482, Cro. Car. 210. But, when these are referred to, it will be seen that nothing was intended at all inconsistent with what I have ventured to lay down above. In both books, the object was to point out that a prison was not necessarily what is commonly so called, a place locally defined and appointed for the reception of prisoners. Lord Coke is commenting on the Statute of Westminster 2d, "in personâ," and says, "Every restraint of the liberty of a freeman is an imprisonment, although he be not within the walls of any common prison." The passage in Cro. Car. is from a curious case of an information against Sir Miles Hobart and Mr. Stroud for escaping out of the Gate House prison, to which they had been committed by the King. The question was, whether, under the circumstances, they had ever been there imprisoned. Owing to the sickness in London, and through the favour of the keeper, these gentlemen had not, except on one occasion, ever been within the walls of the Gate House: the occasion is somewhat singularly expressed in the decision of the Court, which was "that their voluntary retirement to the close stool" in the Gate House "made them to be prisoners." The resolution, however, in question is this: "That the prison of the King's Bench is not any local prison confined only to one place, and that every place where any person is restrained of his liberty is a prison; as if one take sanctuary and depart thence, he shall be said to break prison."

On a case of this sort, which, if there be difficulty in it, is at least purely elementary, it is not easy nor necessary to enlarge: and I am unwilling to put any extreme case hypothetically: but I wish to meet one suggestion, which has been put as avoiding one of the difficulties which cases of this sort might seem to suggest. If it be said that to hold the present case to amount to an imprisonment would turn every obstruction of the exercise of a right of way into an imprisonment, the answer is, that there must be something like personal menace or force accompanying the act of obstruction, and that, with this, it will amount to imprisonment. I apprehend that is not so. If, in the course of a night, both ends of a street were walled up, and there was no egress from the house but into the street, I should have no difficulty in saying that the inhabitants were thereby imprisoned; but, if only one end were walled up, and an armed force stationed outside to prevent any scaling of the wall or passage that way, I should feel equally clear that there was no imprisonment. If there were, the street would obviously be the prison; and yet, as obviously, none would be confined to it.

Knowing that my Lord has entertained strongly an opinion directly contrary to this, I am under serious apprehension that I overlook some difficulty in forming my own: but, if it exists, I have not been able to discover it, and am therefore bound to state that, according to my view of the case, the rule should be absolute for a new trial.

Williams, J.

. . . A part of Hammersmith Bridge, which is generally used as a public footway, was appropriated for seats to view a regatta on the river, and separated for that purpose from the carriage way by a temporary fence. The plaintiff insisted upon passing along the part so appropriated, and attempted to climb over the fence. The defendant (clerk of the Bridge Company) pulled him back; but the plaintiff succeeded in climbing over the fence. The defendant then stationed two policemen to prevent, and they did prevent, the plaintiff from proceeding forwards along the footway in the direction he wished to go. The plaintiff, however, was at the same time told that he might go back into the carriage way and proceed to the other side of the bridge, if he pleased. The plaintiff refused to do so, and remained where he was so obstructed, about half an hour.

And, if a partial restraint of the will be sufficient to constitute an imprisonment, such undoubtedly took place. He wished to go in a particular direction, and was prevented; but, at the same time, another course was open to him. About the meaning of the word imprisonment, and the definitions of it usually given, there is so little doubt that any difference of opinion is scarcely possible. Certainly, so far as I am aware, none such exists upon the present occasion. The difficulty, whatever it may be, arises when the general rule is applied to the facts of a particular case.

"Every confinement of the person" (according to Blackstone), "is an imprisonment, whether it be in a common prison, or in a private house, or in the stocks, or even by forcibly detaining one in the public street," which, perhaps, may seem to imply the application of force more than is really necessary to make an imprisonment. Lord Coke, in his Second Institute, speaks of "a prison in law" and "a prison in deed": so that there may be a constructive, as well as an actual, imprisonment: and, therefore, it may be admitted that personal violence need not be used in order to amount to it. "If the bailiff who has a process against one, says to him, 'You are my prisoner, I have a writ against you,' upon which he submits, turns back or goes with him, though the bailiff never touched him, yet it is an arrest, because he submitted to the process." So, if a person should direct a constable to take another in custody, and that person should be told by the constable to go with him, and the orders are obeyed, and they walk together in the direction pointed out by the constable, that is, constructively, an imprisonment, though no actual violence be used. In such cases, however, though little may be said, much is meant and perfectly understood. The party addressed in the manner above supposed feels that he has no option, no more power of going in any but the one direction prescribed to him than if the constable or bailiff had actually hold of him: no return or deviation from the course prescribed is open to him. And it is that entire restraint upon the will which, I apprehend, constitutes the imprisonment. In the passage cited from Buller's Nisi Prius it is remarked that, if the party addressed by the bailiff, instead of complying, had run away, it could be no arrest, unless the bailiff actually laid hold of him, and for obvious reasons. Suppose (and the supposition is perhaps objectionable, as only putting the case before us over again) any person to erect an obstruction across a public passage in a town, and another, who had a right of passage, to be refused permission by the party obstructing, and, after some delay, to be compelled to return and take another and circuitous route to his place of destination: I do not think that, during such detention, such person was under imprisonment, or could maintain an action for false imprisonment, whatever other remedy might be open to him.

I am desirous only to illustrate my meaning and explain the reason why I consider the imprisonment in this case not to be complete. The reason shortly is, that I am aware of no case, nor of any definition, which warrants the supposition of a man being imprisoned during the time that an escape is open to him if he chooses to avail himself of it.

Lord Denman, C.J. I have not drawn up a formal judgment in this case, because I hoped to the last that the arguments which my learned brothers would produce in support of their opinion might alter mine. We have freely discussed the matter both orally and in written communications; but, after hearing what they have advanced, I am compelled to say that my first impression remains. If, as I must believe, it is a wrong one, it may be in some measure accounted for by the circumstances attending the case. A company unlawfully obstructed a public way for their own profit, extorting money from passengers, and hiring policemen to effect this purpose. The plaintiff, wishing to exercise his right of way, is stopped by force, and ordered to move in a direction which he wished not to take. He is told at the same time that a force is at hand ready to compel his submission. That proceeding appears to me equivalent to being pulled by the collar out of the one line and into the other.

There is some difficulty perhaps in defining imprisonment in the abstract without reference to its illegality; nor is it necessary for me to do so, because I consider these acts as amounting to imprisonment. That word I understand to mean any restraint of the person by force. In Buller's Nisi Prius it is said: "Every restraint of a man's liberty under the custody of another, either in a gaol, house, stocks or in the street, is in law an imprisonment; and whenever it is done without a proper authority, is false imprisonment, for which the law gives an action; and this is commonly joined to assault and battery; for every imprisonment includes a battery, and every battery an assault." It appears, therefore, that the technical language has received a very large construction, and that there need not be any touching of the person: a locking up would constitute an imprisonment, without touching. From the language of Thorpe, C.J., which Mr. Selwyn cites from the Book of Assizes, it appears that, even in very early times, restraint of liberty by force was understood to be the reasonable definition of imprisonment.

I had no idea that any person in these times supposed any particular boundary to be necessary to constitute imprisonment, or that the restraint of a man's person from doing what he desires ceases to be an imprisonment because he may find some means of escape.

It is said that the party here was at liberty to go in another direction. I am not sure that in fact he was, because the same unlawful power which prevented him from taking one course might, in case of acquiescence, have refused him any other. But this liberty to do something else does not appear to me to affect the question of imprisonment. As long as I am prevented from doing what I have a right to do, of what importance is it that I am permitted to do something else? How does the imposition of an unlawful condition shew that I am not restrained? If I am locked in a room, am I not imprisoned because I might effect my escape through a window, or because I might find an exit dangerous or inconvenient to myself, as by wading through water or by taking a route so circuitous that my necessary affairs would suffer by delay?

It appears to me that this is a total deprivation of liberty with reference to the purpose for which he lawfully wished to employ his liberty: and, being effected by force, it is not the mere obstruction of a way, but a restraint of the person. The case cited as occurring before Lord Chief Justice Tindal, as I understand it, is much in point. He held it an imprisonment where the defendant stopped the plaintiff on his road till he had read a libel to him. Yet he did not prevent his escaping in another direction.

United States v. Moore
486 F.2d 1139 (D.C. Cir. 1973)

Wilkey, Circuit Judge, with whom Circuit Judges MacKinnon and Robb join.

This is an appeal from a conviction under two federal statutes for possession of heroin. Appellant contends that his conviction was improper because he is a heroin addict with an overpowering need to use heroin and should not, therefore, be held responsible for being in possession of the drug. After careful consideration, we must reject appellant's contention and affirm the conviction by the trial court. . . .

Appellant's Common Law Defense

. . . According to appellant this case has one central issue:

> Is the proffered evidence of Appellant's long and intensive dependence on (addiction to) injected heroin, resulting in substantial impairment of his behavior controls and a loss of self-control over the use of heroin, relevant to his criminal responsibility for unlawful possession. . . .

In other words, is appellant's addiction a defense to the crimes, involving only possession, with which he is charged? Arguing that he has lost the power of self-control with regard to his addiction, appellant maintains that by applying "the broad principles of common law criminal responsibility" we must decide that he is entitled to dismissal of the indictment or a jury trial on this issue. The gist of appellant's argument here is that "the common law has long held that the capacity to control behavior is a prerequisite for criminal responsibility."

It is inescapable that the logic of appellant's argument, if valid, would carry over to all other illegal acts of any type whose purpose was to obtain narcotics for his own use, a fact which is admitted by Judge Wright in his opinion. Appellant attempts to justify only the acts of possession and purchase of narcotics, both illegal, and both prohibited because if successfully prohibited they would eliminate drug addiction. The justification is on the basis that the addict has lost the power of control over his choice of acts. Appellant argues that the same rationale, justifying a tolerance of these two illegal acts by this court, or a strained construction of the statute that Congress really did not intend to prohibit such acts, or that it is constitutionally impermissible to prohibit such acts, would not carry over to other actions for the same purpose of obtaining narcotics for his own use.

In the case of any addict there are two factors that go to make up the "self-control" (or absence thereof) which governs his activities, and which determines whether or not he will perform certain acts, such as crimes, to obtain drugs. One factor is the physical craving to have the drug. The other is what might be called the addict's "character," or his moral standards. In any case where the addict's moral standards are overcome by his physical craving for the drug, he may be said to lose "self-control," and it is at this point, and not until this point, that an addict will commit acts that violate his moral standards. For our purposes here, we may think of such acts as crimes to obtain drugs.

The legally determinative matter under appellant's theory must be the sum or result of the two factors. Putting it in mathematical terms, if the addict's craving is 4 on a scale of 10, and his strength of character is only 3, he will have a resulting loss of self-control and commit some illegal act to acquire drugs, perhaps only an illegal purchase and possession. For a different example, let us assume a medically induced addict, whose craving is 6, but whose strength of character is 8; with him there will be no resulting loss of self-control, and presumably no illegal acts of any kind. A third example, an addict with a craving of 8, and a strength of character of 3, may result in a loss of self-control to a degree that the addict robs a bank at gunpoint to obtain money to buy drugs.

In all these examples the legally important factor is the resulting loss of self-control. Drug addiction of varying degrees may or may not result in loss of self-control, depending on the strength of character opposed to the drug craving. Under appellant's theory, adopted by the dissenters, only if there is a resulting loss of self-control can there be an absence of *free will* which, under the extension of the common law theory, would provide a valid defense to the addict. If there is a demonstrable absence of free will (loss of self-control), the illegal acts of possession and acquisition cannot be charged to the user of the drugs.

But if it is absence of free will which excuses the mere possessor-acquirer, the more desperate bank robber for drug money has an even more demonstrable lack of free will and derived from precisely the same factors as appellant argues should excuse the mere possessor.

In oral argument appellant maintained that there are different kinds of addicts, that is, some who are able to confine their law violation to possession and acquisition for their own use and some who will commit crimes other than possession or acquisition to feed their habits; and that it is only the latter whom we should punish for their addiction. This position of appellant is, unfortunately, logically untenable, if one accepts appellant's own rationale that we must not punish addicts for possession because of the compulsion under which they act to acquire the drugs.

By definition we have assumed crimes of two classes—first, simple possession and acquisition, or second, greater crimes such as robbery—both motivated by the compulsive need to obtain drugs resulting in loss of self-control. If we punish the second, we can do so only because we find *free will*. If *free will* can exist for the second, it likewise must exist for the first class. If, like appellant, one takes the position that any addict who commits crimes (i.e. robbery) to feed his habit may be punished, one is making a judgment that this addict possesses *free will*, that he is somehow guilty in a way that the addict who does not commit such crimes to feed his habit (other than the crimes of acquisition and possession) is not. In other words, it follows necessarily that the quality that makes this addict commit such crimes to obtain the drugs is not the compulsion of addiction and the loss of "self-control," but is something apart from his addiction—but if we are dealing with a motivating factor other than drugs, this is another case, it is not the example called for by appellant's rationale. What the analysis just made demonstrates, even in the case of the addict-robber, is that his crime is caused by the same compulsion, his loss of self-control, due to his addiction.

Although attempted by appellant here, there can be no successful differentiation between the source of the drive, the compulsion and resulting loss of control which, appellant argues, vitiates legal accountability, hence the same compulsion would necessarily serve as the basis of the defense for each of the posited illegal acts. It is only a matter of degree. In fact, it seems clear that the addict who restrains himself from committing any other crimes except acquisition and possession, assuming he obtains his funds by lawful means, has demonstrated a greater degree of self-control than the addict who in desperation robs a bank to buy at retail. If the addict can restrain himself from committing any other illegal act except purchase and possession, then he is demonstrating a degree of self-control greater than that of the one who robs a pharmacy or a bank, and thus his defense of loss of control and accountability is even less valid than that of the addict who robs the pharmacy or the bank.

From the dissenting opinions it is not clear whether they ignore the logical inconsistency of this position, or whether the dissenters vaguely recognize the inconsistency and arbitrarily draw a line beyond which, to crimes other than acquisition and possession by a proven addict, the defense of lack of *free will* may not be deployed. . . .

The obvious danger is that this defense *will be* extended to all other crimes—bank robberies, street muggings, burglaries—which can be shown to be the product of the same drug-craving compulsion. Not only would the extension of the defense be on the same logical basis as the defense urged here, and as made indubitably certain in Judge Bazelon's separate opinion, but the words of Judge Wright indicate that the door would be open to another possible extension of the newly created defense not hitherto envisaged:

> [We limit] the availability of the addiction defense to only those acts which, like *mere purchase,* receipt or possession of narcotics for personal use, are inseparable from the disease itself and, at the same time, *inflict no direct harm upon other members of society.*

(emphasis supplied). We find cold comfort in Judge Wright's words.

If "mere purchase" *by* the addict is protected, what about "mere sale" *to* the same addict? Could not the sale of narcotics to a poor drug-crazed addict, driven by the compulsion of his unsatisfied needs, be defended as a humane act "inflict[ing] no direct harm upon other members of society"? Why would the supplying of narcotics by an illicit trafficker to a certified addict be any less humane, or inflict any more harm on other members of society, than the supplying of narcotics to the same addict by a licensed member of the medical profession?

1. All of this points up the wisdom of Justice Black's observations in Powell v. Texas, where he reached the conclusion that questions of "voluntariness" or "compulsion" should not be "controlling on the question [of] whether a specific instance of human behavior should be immune from punishment as a constitutional matter"; his arguments also show how the so-called "common-law defense" of compulsion may be unwisely applied here:

> When we say that appellant's [act] is caused not by "his own" volition but rather by some other force, we are clearly thinking of a force that is nevertheless "his" except in some special sense. The accused undoubtedly commits the proscribed act and the only question is whether the act can be attributed to a part of "his"

personality that should not be regarded as criminally responsible. Almost all of the traditional purposes of the criminal law can be significantly served by punishing the person who in fact committed the proscribed act, without regard to whether his action was "compelled" by some elusive "irresponsible" aspect of his personality. As I have already indicated, punishment of such a defendant can clearly be justified in terms of deterrence, isolation, and treatment. On the other hand, medical decisions concerning the use of a term such as "disease" or "volition," based as they are on the clinical problems of diagnosis and treatment, bear no necessary correspondence to the legal decision whether the overall objectives of the criminal law can be furthered by imposing punishment.

Just as Justice Black turned away from the proposed constitutional rule, we spurn the proposed "common law" rule, not only because the recently created statutory scheme of dealing with narcotics addicts stands a reasonable chance of reaching the objectives of "deterrence, isolation, and treatment," but also because the particular nature of the problem of the heroin traffic makes certain policies necessary that should not be weakened by the creation of this defense. There is no compelling policy requiring us to intervene here.

2. Furthermore, if such a judgment weighing and balancing conflicting public interests and policies is to be made, it should be made by Congress, which . . . has by its activity in this area demonstrated both that it possesses more adequate facilities to deal with the problems of narcotic addiction, and that we in the judiciary are somewhat circumscribed in our activity in this area. . . .

Wright, Circuit Judge, with whom Bazelon, Chief Judge, and Tamm and Robinson, Circuit Judges, join, dissenting:

In Robinson v. California, the Supreme Court recognized that narcotic addiction, like mental illness, leprosy and venereal disease, is an illness and not a crime. The Court therefore held that a California statute making the "status" of addiction a criminal offense inflicted cruel and unusual punishment in violation of the Eighth and Fourteenth Amendments. Some eight years later, in Watson v. United States, this court noted that as a practical matter an addict's purchase, receipt, possession and use of narcotics are acts inseparable from the disease itself. As a result we suggested, without deciding, that "if *Robinson*'s deployment of the Eighth Amendment as a barrier to California's making addiction a crime means anything, it must also mean in all logic that (1) Congress either did not intend to expose the non-trafficking addict possessor to criminal punishment, or (2) its effort to do so is as unavailing constitutionally as that of the California legislature."

Today this court rejects the *Watson* rationale and holds that a non-trafficking addict is a criminal because he possesses drugs to satisfy his addiction. In my judgment stigmatization of such persons as criminals, rather than treatment of them for their disease, raises serious questions of constitutionality, is contrary to established common law notions of criminal responsibility, and is not mandated by Congress' intent in adopting the relevant legislation. Moreover, this insensitive approach to drug addiction is tragically counter-productive. Twenty years of rigid criminal enforcement of drug laws against addicts has brought this country, not only a dramatic increase in organized crime, but a harvest of street crime unknown in our history. Yet the court presses on, still hoping that some day, somehow, the criminal sanction will bring relief. With due respect, I suggest that the law can do better. I suggest that the development of the common law of *mens rea* has reached the point where it should embrace a new principle: a drug addict who, by reason of his use of drugs, lacks substantial capacity to conform his conduct to the requirements of the law may not be held criminally responsible for mere possession of drugs for his own use. The trial judge refused appellant's request to give the jury an instruction based on this principle. I would, therefore, reverse this conviction and remand the case for a new trial. . . .

The concept of criminal responsibility is, by its very nature, "an expression of the moral sense of the community." In western society, the concept has been shaped by two dominant value judgments—that punishment must be morally legitimate, and that it must not unduly threaten the liberties and dignity of the individual in his relationship to society. As a result, there has historically been a strong conviction in our jurisprudence that to hold a man criminally responsible his actions must have been the product of a "free will." See, e.g., 4 W. Blackstone, Commentaries 20-21, 27 (1854); 2 J. Stephen, History of the Criminal Law of England 99, 183 (1883). And this conviction "is no provincial or transient notion. It is as universal and persistent in mature systems of law as belief in freedom of the human will and a consequent ability and duty of the normal individual to choose between good and evil." Morissette v. United States. Thus criminal responsibility is assessed only when through "free will" a man elects to do evil, and if he is not a free agent, or is unable to choose or to act voluntarily, or to avoid the conduct which constitutes the crime, he is outside the postulate of the law of punishment.

Despite this general principle, however, it is clear that our legal system does not exculpate all persons whose capacity for control is impaired, for whatever cause or reason. Rather, in determining responsibility for crime, the law assumes "free will" and then recognizes known deviations "where there is a broad consensus that free will does not exist" with respect to the particular condition at issue. The evolving nature of this process is amply demonstrated in the gradual development of such defenses as infancy, duress, insanity, somnambulism and other forms of automatism, epilepsy and unconsciousness, involuntary intoxication, delirim tremens, and chronic alcoholism.

A similar consensus exists today in the area of narcotics addiction. In Easter v. District of Columbia, this court held that a "chronic alcoholic cannot have the *mens rea* necessary to be held responsible criminally for being drunk in public" since such an individual "is in fact a sick person who has *lost control* over his use of alcoholic beverages." (Emphasis added.) The World Health Organization has ranked heroin addiction as the most intensive form of drug dependence, far more severe than alcoholism. Indeed, the primary element of the most widely accepted definition of opiate addiction is "an *overpowering* desire or need to continue taking the drug," and Congress has repeatedly defined as an addict any individual who is "so far addicted to the use of narcotic drugs as to have *lost the power of self-control* with reference to his addiction." Thus it can no longer seriously be questioned that for at least some addicts the "overpowering" psychological and physiological need to possess and inject narcotics cannot be overcome by mere exercise of "free will."

Moreover, recognition of a defense of "addiction" for crimes such as possession of narcotics is consistent not only with our historic common law notions of criminal responsibility and moral accountability, but also with the traditional goals of penology—retribution, deterrence, isolation and rehabilitation.

Unlike other goals of penology, the retributive theory of criminal justice looks solely to the past for justification, without regard to considerations of prevention or reformation. Although the primordial desire for vengeance is an understandable emotion, it is a testament to the constantly evolving nature of our social and moral consciousness that the law has, in recent decades, come to regard this "eye-for-an-eye" philosophy as an improper basis for punishment. But even if this barbaric notion of justice retained its validity, it clearly would be inapplicable to those persons who act under a compulsion. Revenge, if it is ever to be legitimate, must be premised on moral blameworthiness, and what segment of our society would feel its need for retribution satisfied when it wreaks vengeance upon those who are diseased because of their disease?

It is of course true that there may have been a time in the past before the addict lost control when he made a conscious decision to use drugs. But imposition of punishment on this basis would violate the long-standing rule that "[t]he law looks to the immediate, and not to the remote cause; to the actual state of the party, and not to the causes, which remotely produced it.". . . I would adhere to that view today, for no matter how the addict came to be addicted, once he has reached that stage he clearly is sick, and a bare desire for vengeance cannot justify his treatment as a criminal. Indeed, the need for retribution "can never be permitted in a civilized society to degenerate into a sadistic form of revenge."

The most widely employed argument in favor of punishing addicts for crimes such as possession of narcotics is that such punishment or threat of punishment has a substantial deterrent effect. Given our present knowledge, however, the merits of this argument appear doubtful. Deterrence presupposes rationality—it proceeds on the assumption that the detriments which would inure to the prospective criminal upon apprehension can be made so severe that he will be dissuaded from undertaking the criminal act. In the case of the narcotic addict, however, the normal sense of reason, which is so essential to effective functioning of deterrence, is overcome by the psychological and physiological compulsions of the disease. As a result, it is widely agreed that the threat of even harsh prison sentences cannot deter the addict from using and possessing the drug.

A similar situation prevails insofar as deterrence of *potential* addicts is concerned. At the outset, it must be noted that nothing in this opinion would in any way affect the criminal responsibility of non-addict users for crimes they may commit—including illegal possession of narcotics. Such persons are not compelled by the disease of addiction to use and possess the drug, and they are therefore proper subjects for punishment. Thus the concept of deterrence in this context is relevant only insofar as punishment of addict possessors might inhibit non-addicts, who are themselves subject to punishment, from using narcotics. Simply to state the problem is, of course, to answer it. Since the nonaddict may still be punished for his possession of narcotics, the only consolation he might find in exculpation of addict possessors is that if he eventually attains the status of "addict" he must be treated rather than punished. But given what we now know about the pitiable life of an addict, this somewhat dubious consolation is hardly likely to "encourage" persons to use narcotics.

There is another side to the question of deterrence, however, which should not be ignored. The criminal law may serve as a deterrent not only through the fear of apprehension and prosecution, but also through the more general educative or moralizing effect the law may have upon society. Viewed in this manner, punishment as a concrete expression of society's disapproval of particular conduct helps to instill a desired moral code in the citizenry against commission of the proscribed acts. Indeed, the history of public attitudes in this nation toward addiction exemplifies the potential impact this moralizing effect can achieve. But in an effort to shape these attitudes, the architects of our policies swept too broadly, perpetrating such myths as the "dope-crazed sex fiend" and condemning not only the volitional drug abuser but the confirmed addict as well. And although society may and indeed should voice its disapproval of non-medical use of narcotics, it is highly questionable whether it should also condemn as "moral degenerates" those pathetic individuals who, because of the disease of addiction, can no longer control their use of the drug.

Moreover, in any discussion of deterrence we must recognize that when an individual is punished, not for his own good, but to set an example for others, he "suffers not for what he has done but on account of other people's tendency to do likewise." In such situations, the offender serves simply as a tool in the hands of society, and if punishment premised on considerations of deterrence is to be morally legitimate, the punishment meted out must be justifiable in light of the gravity of the offense and the culpability of the offender. Since the addict's possession of narcotics is simply a symptom of his disease and not an act of "free will," however, this conduct cannot properly be deemed "culpable," and it would therefore seem inappropriate for society to utilize him as a mere vehicle through which to deter others.

This is not to suggest, of course, that society has no legitimate interest in deterring drug abuse. Narcotic addiction presents a danger to both the addict and society generally, and society therefore has a right and indeed a duty to institute those measures which are reasonably necessary to curtail its incidence. But punishment of addict possessors is neither a reasonable nor a necessary means to achieve this goal. Indeed, in enacting the Narcotic Addict Rehabilitation Act of 1966, Congress itself recognized that the need to rehabilitate addicts generally outweighs any deterrent impact their imprisonment might achieve. Moreover, it should be noted that in some sense the entire question of deterrence in this context may in reality be meaningless. For after nearly two decades of experience with the harsh penalty provisions adopted in the 1950's, Congress concluded that "the severity of penalties . . . does not affect the extent of drug abuse." And acting upon this conclusion, Congress enacted the Comprehensive Drug Abuse Prevention and Control Act of 1970, in which the penalties for crimes of possession were decreased dramatically.

Shifting our focus now to the goal of isolating the offender, we arrive here at not only a justifiable basis for action but one which, in some cases at least, may be vital to the interests of society. Under our system of law, it must be remembered, criminal sanctions are withheld in cases of incompetence out of a moral sense of compassion and understanding. It would be obviously intolerable, however, if those suffering from a disease of such a nature as to relieve them of criminal responsibility were to be set free to continue to pose a danger to society. Thus, as with any individual who is afflicted with a dangerous or contagious disease, when the addict's freedom may seriously jeopardize the safety and security of the community, society has a legitimate interest in restraining him in order to protect its citizens.

This does not mean, however, that the goal of isolation justifies infliction of criminal punishment upon the addict. On the contrary, this interest may be fully vindicated through a program of civil commitment with treatment as well as by criminal incarceration. And since the addict is not a culpable offender, treatment is clearly a preferable alternative to mere imprisonment. Moreover, the community's security may be even better protected under civil commitment for, as we shall see, although incarceration may restrain the addict for the period of his sentence, it does nothing to reduce the likelihood that upon his return to the streets he will again resort to the use of drugs. Finally, we should make certain that, in the words of the President's Commission on Law Enforcement and Administration of Justice, when civil commitment is utilized as a means to isolate the addict, it "must not become the civil equivalent of imprisonment. The programs must offer the best possible treatment, including new techniques as they become available, and the duration of the commitment, either within or outside an institution, must be no longer than is reasonably necessary."

This, then, brings us to the final and most important goal of modern penology—to rehabilitate the offender. In this age of enlightened correctional philosophy, we now recognize that society has a responsibility to both the individual and the community to treat the offender so that upon his release he may function as a productive, law-abiding citizen. And this is all the more true where, as with the non-trafficking addict possessor, the offender has acted under the compulsion of a disease. The task of rehabilitating the narcotic addict is not, as once was thought, a hopeless task. Great strides have been made in recent years toward development of effective and humane treatment techniques at both community-based and institutional levels, and the cure rate for addiction is now far higher than that of many other illnesses. Thus, with the possible exception of those addicts who remain incurable, society clearly cannot meet its responsibilities simply by confining the addict without treatment. Such an approach does nothing to cure the chronic relapsing aspects of the disease, and where confinement takes the form of imprisonment the addict is thrust inevitably into a "revolving door" of arrest, conviction, imprisonment, release and arrest, with the period of incarceration serving as but a temporary and futile stopping point in an otherwise interminable cycle.

Under existing law, of course, at least some addicts may escape this cycle through the involuntary civil commitment procedures of Title II of the Narcotic Addict Rehabilitation Act, 18 U.S.C. § 4251 et seq. In enacting this legislation, however, Congress specifically limited its applicability to only those addicts who have been charged, prosecuted and convicted of a criminal offense. Thus, with the recognition of the defense of addiction, these procedures presumably would no longer be available to non-trafficking addict possessors. But this does not mean, as some may fear, that these addicts would be deprived of treatment or released without care or confinement to "prey on society."

For the addict who may affirmatively desire treatment, there are, of course, many options available, including the possibility of voluntary civil commitment. Moreover, there exist in the District of Columbia established procedures for involuntary commitment of known addicts even though they have not been charged, prosecuted or convicted of a criminal offense. See Hospital Treatment for Drug Addicts Act for the District of Columbia, 24 D.C. Code § 601 et seq. (1967). Under this Act, the Commissioner of the District of Columbia must conduct a preliminary examination whenever he has probable cause to believe that any person within the District is an addict. If evidence of addiction is found at the preliminary examination, the patient is committed to a hospital for examination by two physicians, at least one of whom must be a psychiatrist. Within five days these physicians must report their conclusions to the United States Attorney, who may, in his discretion, present a commitment petition to the Superior Court of the District of Columbia. If, after a hearing, the court finds the patient to be an addict, he is committed to a hospital until confinement for treatment is no longer necessary or until he has received "maximum benefits." After his release, the patient is supervised in the community for a period of two years to insure that he does not return to the use of drugs. Finally, the patient in these proceedings "shall not be deemed a criminal and the commitment of any such patient shall not be deemed a conviction."

Despite the existence of these provisions, however, the Government contends that, since the Act has rarely been utilized, the facilities presently available are inadequate to make the statute effective. Confronted with a similar argument in *Easter,* supra, this court held unequivocally that "[o]ne who has committed no crime cannot be validly sentenced as a criminal because of a lack of rehabilitative and caretaking facilities." Like the chronic alcoholic who is drunk in public, the non-trafficking addict possessor has committed no crime. The absence of treatment facilities is the responsibility, not of the addict, but of society generally, and the addict should not be treated as a criminal simply because society has failed to meet its responsibility. Had Congress acted to implement this statute with the necessary appropriations and facilities, this problem would not exist today. The statute is already on the books, and indeed has been for almost 20 years. Only the implementation is missing.

The genius of the common law has long been its responsiveness to changing times, its ability to reflect new knowledge and developing social and moral values. What the law cannot do, if it is to remain true to its tradition, is to stand still while the world is in flux. See, e.g., O.W. Holmes, The Path of the Law, 10 Harv. L. Rev. 457, 469 (1897). Drawing upon the past, the law must serve—as it always has served—the needs of the present. Thus on the basis of the considerations discussed above, I conclude that imposition of criminal liability on the non-trafficking addict possessor is contrary to our historic common law traditions of criminal responsibility. This being so, it is clear that a defense of "addiction" must exist for these individuals unless Congress has expressly and unequivocally manifested its intent to preclude such a defense. . . .

Bazelon, Chief Judge (concurring in part and dissenting in part):

. . . On the issue of guilt or innocence, Judge Wright's views are closest to my own. I cannot, however, accept his view that the addiction/responsibility defense should be limited to the offense of possession. I would also permit a jury to consider addiction as a defense to a charge of, for example, armed robbery or trafficking in drugs, to determine whether the defendant was under such duress or compulsion, because of his addiction, that he was unable to conform his conduct to the requirements of the law. . . .

Bailey v. Alabama
219 U.S. 219 (1911)

Mr. Justice Hughes delivered the opinion of the Court:

This is a writ of error to review a judgment of the supreme court of the state of Alabama, affirming a judgment of conviction in the Montgomery city court. The statute upon which the conviction was based is assailed as in violation of the . . . 13th Amendment, and of the act of Congress providing for the enforcement of that Amendment, in that the effect of the statute is to enforce involuntary servitude by compelling personal service in liquidation of a debt.

The statute in question . . . provided that any person who, with intent to injure or defraud his employer, entered into a written contract for service, and thereby obtained from his employer money or other personal property, and with like intent and without just cause, and without refunding the money or paying for the property, refused to perform the service, should be punished as if he had stolen it. In 1903 the section was amended so as to make the refusal or failure to perform the service, or to refund the money, or pay for the property, without just cause, *prima facie* evidence of the intent to injure or defraud. . . .

There is also a rule of evidence enforced by the courts of Alabama which must be regarded as having the same effect as if read into the statute itself, that the accused, for the purpose of rebutting the statutory presumption, shall not be allowed to testify "as to his uncommunicated motives, purpose, or intention." . . .

Upon the trial the following facts appeared: On December 26, 1907, Bailey entered into a written contract with the Riverside Company, which provided:

> That I, Lonzo Bailey, for and in consideration of the sum of $15 in money, this day in hand paid to me by said The Riverside Company, the receipt whereof I do hereby acknowledge, I, the said Lonzo Bailey, do hereby consent, contract, and agree to work and labor for the said Riverside Company as a farm hand on their Scott's Bend place in Montgomery county, Alabama, from the 30 day of December, 1907, to the 30 day of December, 1908, at and for the sum of $12 per month. . . .

The manager of the employing company testified that at the time of entering into this contract there were present only the witness and Bailey, and that the latter then obtained from the company the sum of $15; that Bailey worked under the contract throughout the month of January and for three or four days in February, 1908, and then, "without just cause, and without refunding the money, ceased to work for said Riverside Company, and has not since that time performed any service for said company in accordance with or under said contract, and has refused and failed to perform any further service thereunder, and has, without just cause, refused and failed to refund said $15." He also testified, in response to a question from the attorney for the defendant, and against the objection of the state, that Bailey was a negro. No other evidence was introduced.

The court, after defining the crime in the language of the statute, charged the jury, in accordance with its terms, as follows:

> And the refusal of any person who enters into such contract to perform such act or service, or refund such money, or pay for such property, without just cause, shall be *prima facie* evidence of the intent to injure his employer, or to defraud him. . . .

The jury found the accused guilty, fixed the damages sustained by the injured party at $15, and assessed a fine of $30. Thereupon Bailey was sentenced by the court to pay the fine of $30 and the costs, and in default thereof to hard labor "for twenty days in lieu of said fine, and one hundred and sixteen days on account of said costs.". . .

We at once dismiss from consideration the fact that the plaintiff in error is a black man. While the action of a state, through its officers charged with the administration of a law fair in appearance, may be of such a character as to constitute a denial of the equal protection of the laws (Yick Wo v. Hopkins), such a conclusion is here neither required nor justified. The statute, on its face, makes no racial discrimination, and the record fails to show its existence in fact. No question of a sectional character is presented, and we may view the legislation in the same manner as if it had been enacted in New York or in Idaho. Opportunities for coercion and oppression, in varying circumstances, exist in all parts of the Union, and the citizens of all the states are interested in the maintenance of the constitutional guaranties, the consideration of which is here involved.

Prior to the amendment of the year 1903, enlarged in 1907, the statute did not make the mere breach of the contract, under which the employee had obtained from his employer money which was not refunded or property which was not paid for, a crime. The essential ingredient of the offense was the intent of the accused to injure or defraud. To justify conviction, it was necessary that this intent should be established by competent evidence, aided only by such inferences as might logically be derived from the facts proved, and should not be the subject of mere surmise or arbitrary assumption. . . .

We pass, then, to the consideration of the amendment, through the operation of which under the charge of the trial court this conviction was obtained. No longer was it necessary for the prosecution . . . to establish the intent to injure or defraud which . . . constituted the gist of the offense. It was "the difficulty in proving the intent," . . . which "suggested the amendment of 1903." By this amendment it was provided, in substance, that the refusal or failure to perform the service contracted for, or to refund the money obtained, without just cause, should be *prima facie* evidence of the intent to injure or defraud.

But the refusal or failure to perform the service, without just cause, constitutes the breach of the contract. The justice of the grounds of refusal or failure must, of course, be determined by the contractual obligation assumed. Whatever the reason for leaving the service, if, judged by the terms of the contract, it is insufficient in law, it is not "just cause." The money received and repayable, nothing more being shown, constitutes a mere debt. The asserted difficulty of proving the intent to injure or defraud is thus made the occasion for dispensing with such proof, so far as the *prima facie* case is concerned. And the mere breach of a contract for personal service, coupled with the mere failure to pay a debt which was to be liquidated in the course of such service, is made sufficient to warrant a conviction.

It is no answer to say that the jury must find, and here found, that a fraudulent intent existed. The jury by their verdict cannot add to the facts before them. If nothing be shown but a mere breach of a contract of service and a mere failure to pay a debt, the jury have nothing else to go upon, and the evidence becomes nothing more because of their finding. Had it not been for this statutory presumption, supplied by the amendment, no one would be heard to say that Bailey could have been convicted. . . .

While, in considering the natural operation and effect of the statute, as amended, we are not limited to the particular facts of the case at the bar, they present an illuminating illustration. We may briefly restate them. Bailey made a contract to work for a year at $12 a month. He received $15, and he was to work this out, being entitled monthly only to $10.75 of his wages. No one was present when he made the contract but himself and the manager of the employing company. There is not a particle of evidence of any circumstance indicating that he made the contract or received the money with any intent to injure or defraud his employer. On the contrary, he actually worked for upwards of a month. His motive in leaving does not appear, the only showing being that it was without legal excuse and that he did not repay the money received. For this he is sentenced to a fine of $30 and to imprisonment at hard labor, in default of the payment of the fine and costs, for 136 days. Was not the case the same in effect as if the statute had made it a criminal act to leave the service without just cause and without liquidating the debt? To say that he has been found guilty of an intent to injure or defraud his employer, and not merely for breaking his contract and not paying his debt, is a distinction without a difference to Bailey.

Consider the situation of the accused under this statutory presumption. If, at the outset, nothing took place but the making of the contract and the receipt of the money, he could show nothing else. If there was no legal justification for his leaving his employment, he could show none. If he had not paid the debt, there was nothing to be said as to that. The law of the state did not permit him to testify that he did not intend to injure or defraud. Unless he were fortunate enough to be able to command evidence of circumstances affirmatively showing good faith, he was helpless. He stood, stripped by the statute of the presumption of innocence, and exposed to conviction for fraud upon evidence only of breach of contract and failure to pay. . . .

We cannot escape the conclusion that, although the statute in terms is to punish fraud, still its natural and inevitable effect is to expose to conviction for crime those who simply fail or refuse to perform contracts for personal service in liquidation of a debt; and judging its purpose by its effect, that it seeks in this way to provide the means of compulsion through which performance of such service may be secured. The question is whether such a statute is constitutional. . . .

In the present case it is urged that the statute as amended, through the operation of the presumption for which it provides, violates the 13th Amendment of the Constitution of the United States and the act of Congress passed for its enforcement.

The 13th Amendment provides:

Section 1. Neither slavery nor involuntary servitude, except as a punishment for crime whereof the party shall have been duly convicted, shall exist within the United States, or any place subject to their jurisdiction.

Section 2. Congress shall have power to enforce this article by appropriate legislation.

Pursuant to the authority thus conferred, Congress passed the act of March 2, 1867, as follows:

The holding of any person to service or labor under the system known as peonage is abolished and forever prohibited in the territory of New Mexico, or in any other territory or state of the United States; and all acts, laws, resolutions, orders, regulations, or usages of the territory of New Mexico, or of any other territory or state, which have heretofore established, maintained, or enforced, or by virtue of which any attempt shall hereafter be made to establish, maintain, or enforce, directly or indirectly, the voluntary or involuntary service or labor of any persons as peons, in liquidation of any debt or obligation, or otherwise, are declared null and void. . . .

The words involuntary servitude have a "larger meaning than slavery."

"It was very well understood that, in the form of apprenticeship for long terms, as it had been practised in the West India Islands, on the abolition of slavery by the English government, or by reducing the slaves to the condition of serfs attached to the plantation, the purpose of the article might have been evaded, if only the word 'slavery' had been used." Slaughter-House Cases. The plain intention was to abolish slavery of whatever name and form and all its badges and incidents; to render impossible any state of bondage; to make labor free, by prohibiting that control by which the personal service of one man is disposed of or coerced for another's benefit, which is the essence of involuntary servitude. . . .

Peonage is a term descriptive of a condition which has existed in Spanish America, and especially in Mexico. The essence of the thing is compulsory service in payment of a debt. A peon is one who is compelled to work for his creditor until his debt is paid. And in this explicit and comprehensive enactment, Congress was not concerned with mere names or manner of description, or with a particular place or section of the country. It was concerned with a fact, wherever it might exist; with a condition, however named and wherever it might be established, maintained, or enforced.

The fact that the debtor contracted to perform the labor which is sought to be compelled does not withdraw the attempted enforcement from the condemnation of the statute. The full intent of the constitutional provision could be defeated with obvious facility if, through the guise of contracts under which advances had been made, debtors could be held to compulsory service. It is the compulsion of the service that the statute inhibits, for when that occurs, the condition of servitude is created, which would be not less involuntary because of the original agreement to work out the indebtedness. The contract exposes the debtor to liability for the loss due to the breach, but not to enforced labor. . . .

The act of Congress, nullifying all state laws by which it should be attempted to enforce the "service or labor of any persons as peons, in liquidation of any debt or obligation, or otherwise," necessarily embraces all legislation which seeks to compel the service or labor by making it a crime to refuse or fail to perform it. Such laws would furnish the readiest means of compulsion. The 13th Amendment prohibits involuntary servitude except as punishment for crime. But the exception, allowing full latitude for the enforcement of penal laws, does not destroy the prohibition. It does not permit slavery or involuntary servitude to be established or maintained through the operation of the criminal law by making it a crime to refuse to submit to the one or to render the service which would constitute the other. The state may impose involuntary servitude as a punishment for crime, but it may not compel one man to labor for another in payment of a debt, by punishing him as a criminal if he does not perform the service or pay the debt.

If the statute in this case had authorized the employing company to seize the debtor, and hold him to the service until he paid the $15, or had furnished the equivalent in labor, its invalidity would not be questioned. It would be equally clear that the state could not authorize its constabulary to prevent the servant from escaping, and to force him to work out his debt. But the state could not avail itself of the sanction of the criminal law to supply the compulsion any more than it could use or authorize the use of physical force. . . .

What the state may not do directly it may not do indirectly. If it cannot punish the servant as a criminal for the mere failure or refusal to serve without paying his debt, it is not permitted to accomplish the same result by creating a statutory presumption which, upon proof of no other fact, exposes him to conviction and punishment. Without imputing any actual motive to oppress, we must consider the natural operation of the statute here in question, and it is apparent that it furnishes a convenient instrument for the coercion which the Constitution and the act of Congress forbid; an instrument of compulsion peculiarly effective as against the poor and the ignorant, its most likely victims. There is no more important concern than to safeguard the freedom of labor upon which alone can enduring prosperity be based. The provision designed to secure it would soon become a barren form if it were possible to establish a statutory presumption of this sort, and to hold over the heads of laborers the threat of punishment for crime, under the name of fraud, but merely upon evidence of failure to work out their debts. The act of Congress deprives of effect all legislative measures of any state through which, directly or indirectly, the prohibited thing, to wit, compulsory service to secure the payment of a debt, may be established or maintained; and we conclude that § 4730, as amended, of the Code of Alabama, in so far as it makes the refusal or failure to perform the act or service, without refunding the money or paying for the property received, *prima facie* evidence of the commission of the crime which the section defines, is in conflict with the 13th Amendment, and the legislation authorized by that Amendment, and is therefore invalid. . . .

Mr. Justice Holmes, dissenting:

We all agree that this case is to be considered and decided in the same way as if it arose in Idaho or New York. Neither public document nor evidence discloses a law which, by its administration, is made something different from what it appears on its face, and therefore the fact that in Alabama it mainly concerns the blacks does not matter. Yick Wo v. Hopkins does not apply. I shall begin, then, by assuming for the moment what I think is not true, and shall try to show not to be true, that this statute punishes the mere refusal to labor according to contract as a crime, and shall inquire whether there would be anything contrary to the 13th Amendment or the statute if it did, supposing it to have been enacted in the state of New York. I cannot believe it. The 13th Amendment does not outlaw contracts for labor. That would be at least as great a misfortune for the laborer as for the man that employed him. For it certainly would affect the terms of the bargain unfavorably for the laboring man if it were understood that the employer could do nothing in case the laborer saw fit to break his word. But any legal liability for breach of a contract is a disagreeable consequence which tends to make the contractor do as he said he would. Liability to an action for damages has that tendency as well a fine. If the mere imposition of such consequences as tend to make a man keep to his promise is the creation of peonage when the contract happens to be for labor, I do not see why the allowance of a civil action is not, as well as an indictment ending in fine. Peonage is service to a private master at which a man is kept by bodily compulsion against his will. But the creation of the ordinary legal motives for right conduct does not produce it. Breach of a legal contract without excuse is wrong conduct, even if the contract is for labor; and if a state adds to civil liability a criminal liability to fine, it simply intensifies the legal motive for doing right; it does not make the laborer a slave.

But if a fine may be imposed, imprisonment may be imposed in case of a failure to pay it. Nor does it matter if labor is added to the imprisonment. Imprisonment with hard labor is not stricken from the statute books. On the contrary, involuntary servitude as a punishment for crime is excepted from the prohibition of the 13th Amendment in so many words. Also the power of the states to make breach of contract a crime is not done away with by the abolition of slavery. But if breach of contract may be made a crime at all, it may be made a crime with all the consequences usually attached to crime. There is produced a sort of illusion if a contract to labor ends in compulsory labor in a prison. But compulsory work for no private master in a jail is not peonage. If work in a jail is not condemned in itself, without regard to what the conduct is it punishes, it may be made a consequence of any conduct that the state has power to punish at all. I do not blink the fact that the liability to imprisonment may work as a motive when a fine without it would not, and that it may induce the laborer to keep on when he would like to leave. But it does not strike me as an objection to a law that it is effective. If the contract is one that ought not to be made, prohibit it. But if it is a perfectly fair and proper contract, I can see no reason why the state should not throw its weight on the side of performance. There is no relation between its doing so in the manner supposed, and allowing a private master to use private force upon a laborer who wishes to leave.

But all that I have said so far goes beyond the needs of the case as I understand it. I think it a mistake to say that this statute attaches its punishment to the mere breach of a contract to labor. It does not purport to do so; what it purports to punish is fraudulently obtaining money by a false pretense of an intent to keep the written contract in consideration of which the money is advanced. . . .

To sum up, I think that obtaining money by fraud may be made a crime as well as murder or theft; that a false representation, expressed or implied, at the time of making a contract of labor, that one intends to perform it, and thereby obtaining an advance, may be declared a case of fraudulently obtaining money as well as any other; that if made a crime it may be punished like any other crime; and that an unjustified departure from the promised service without repayment may be declared a sufficient case to go to the jury for their judgment; all without in any way infringing the 13th Amendment or the statutes of the United States.

Coercion and Distribution in a Supposedly Non-Coercive State[*]
Robert L. Hale

> And while the House of Peers withholds its legislative hand,
> And noble statesman do not itch
> To interfere with matters which
> They cannot understand,
> As bright will shine Great Britain's rays
> As in King George's glorious days.
> —From W.S. Gilbert's *Iolanthe*

The so-called individualist would expand this philosophy to include all statesmen, whether noble or not, and to include all economic matters as among those which they cannot understand. The practical function of economic theory is merely to prove to statesmen the wisdom of leaving such matters alone, not to aid them in the process of interfering. And in foreign as well as in domestic affairs, they should make no effort to control the natural working of economic events. This would seem to be the general view of Professor Thomas Nixon Carver,[1] although he likewise speaks frequently as a nationalist. But a careful scrutiny will, it is thought, reveal a fallacy in this view, and will demonstrate that the systems advocated by professed upholders of *laissez-faire* are in reality permeated with coercive restrictions of individual freedom, and with restrictions, moreover, out of conformity with any formula of "equal opportunity" or of "preserving the equal rights of others." Some sort of coercive restriction of individuals, it is believed, is absolutely unavoidable, and cannot be made to conform to any Spencerian formula. Since coercive restrictions are bound to affect the distribution of income and the direction of economic activities, and are bound to affect the economic interests of persons living in foreign parts, statesmen cannot avoid interfering with economic matters, both in domestic and in foreign affairs. There is accordingly a need for the development of economic and legal theory to guide them in the process.

. . .

What is the government doing when it "protects a property right"? Passively, it is abstaining from interference with the owner when he deals with the thing owned; actively, it is forcing the non-owner to desist from handling it, unless the owner consents. Yet Mr. Carver would have it that the government is merely preventing the non-owner from using force against the owner. This explanation is obviously at variance with the facts—for the non-owner is forbidden to handle the owner's property even where his handling of it involves no violence or force whatever. Any lawyer could have told him that the right of property is much more extensive than the mere right to protection against forcible dispossession. In protecting property the government is doing something quite apart from merely keeping the peace. It is exerting coercion wherever that is necessary to protect each owner,

---

[*]   Robert L. Hale, Coercion and Distribution in a Supposedly Non-Coercive State, Political Science Quarterly, Volume 38 (1923), pages 470-478.

[1]   Thomas Nixon Carver, Principles of National Economy (1921).

not merely from violence, but also from peaceful infringement of his sole right to enjoy the thing owned.

That, however, is not the most significant aspect of present-day coercion in connection with property. The owner can remove the legal duty under which the non-owner labors with respect to the owner's property. He can remove it, or keep it in force, at his discretion. To keep it in force may or may not have unpleasant consequences to the non-owner—consequences which spring from the law's creation of legal duty. To avoid these consequences, the non-owner may be willing to obey the will of the owner, provided that the obedience is not in itself more unpleasant than the consequences to be avoided. Such obedience may take the trivial form of paying five cents for legal permission to eat a particular bag of peanuts, or it may take the more significant form of working for the owner at disagreeable toil for a slight wage. In either case the conduct is motivated, not by any desire to do the act in question, but by a desire to escape a more disagreeable alternative. In the peanut case, the consequence of abstaining from a particular bag of peanuts would be, either to go without such nutriment altogether for the time being, or to conform to the terms of some other owner. Presumably at least one of these consequences would be as bad as the loss of the five cents, or the purchaser would not buy; but one of them, at least, would be no worse, or the owner would be able to compel payment of more. In the case of the labor, what would be the consequence of refusal to comply with the owner's terms? It would be either absence of wages, or obedience to the terms of some other employer. If the worker has no money of his own, the threat of any particular employer to withhold any particular amount of money would be effective in securing the worker's obedience in proportion to the difficulty with which other employers can be induced to furnish a "job." If the non-owner works for anyone, it is for the purpose of warding off the threat of at least one owner of money to withhold that money from him (with the help of the law). Suppose, now, the worker were to refuse to yield to the coercion of any employer, but were to choose instead to remain under the legal duty to abstain from the use of any of the money which anyone owns. He must eat. While there is no law against eating in the abstract, there is a law which forbids him to eat any of the food which actually exists in the community—and that law is the law of property. It can be lifted as to any specific food at the discretion of its owner, but if the owners unanimously refuse to lift the prohibition, the non-owner will starve unless he can himself produce food. And there is every likelihood that the owners will be unanimous in refusing, if he has no money. There is no law to compel them to part with their food for nothing. Unless, then, the non-owner can produce his own food, the law compels him to starve if he has no wages, and compels him to go without wages unless he obeys the behests of some employer. It is the law that coerces him into wage-work under penalty of starvation— unless he can produce food. Can he? Here again there is no law to prevent the production of food in the abstract; but in every settled country there is a law which forbids him to cultivate any particular piece of ground unless he happens to be an owner. This again is the law of property. And this again will not be likely to be lifted unless he already has money. That way of escape from the law-made dilemma of starvation or obedience is closed to him. It may seem that one way of escape has been overlooked—the acquisition of money in other ways than by wage-work. Can he not "make money" by selling goods? But here again, things cannot be produced in quantities sufficient to keep him alive, except with the use of elaborate mechanical equipment. To use any such equipment is unlawful, except on the owner's terms. Those terms usually include an implied abandonment of any claim of title to the products. In short, if he be not a property owner, the law which forbids him to produce with any of the existing equipment, and the law which forbids him to eat any of the existing food, will be lifted *only* in case he works for an employer. It is the law of property which coerces people into working for factory owners—though, as we shall see shortly, the workers can as a rule exert sufficient counter-coercion to limit materially the governing power of the owners.

Not only does the law of property secure for the owners of factories their labor; it also secures for them the revenue derived from the customers. The law compels people to desist from consuming the products of the owner's plant, except with his consent; and he will not consent unless they pay him money. They can escape, of course, by going without the product. But that does not prevent the payment being compulsory, any more than it prevents the payment of the government tax on tobacco from being compulsory. The penalty for failure to pay, in each case, may be light, but it is sufficient to compel obedience in all those cases where the consumer buys rather than go without. . . . Mr. Carver attempts to distinguish on the ground that in the case of the tax the government "did not produce the tobacco but only charges the manufacturer or the dealer for the privilege of manufacturing or selling." But this is equally true of the owner of the factory, if he is an absentee owner. Whether the owner has rendered a service or not bears only on the question of the justification of the income which he collects, not on whether the process of collecting it was coercive.

As already intimated, however, the owner's coercive power is weakened by the fact that both his customers and his laborers have the power to make matters more or less unpleasant for him—the customers through their law-given power to withhold access to their cash, the laborers through their *actual* power (neither created nor destroyed by the law) to withhold their services. Even without this power, it is true, he would have to give his laborers enough to sustain them, just as it is to his own interest to feed his horses enough to make them efficient. But whatever they get beyond this minimum is obtained either by reason of the employer's generosity and sense of moral obligation, or by his fear that they will exercise the threat to work elsewhere or not at all. If obtained through this fear, it is a case where he submits by so much to their wills. It is not a "voluntary" payment, but a payment as the price of escape from damaging behavior of others. Furnishing food to one's slaves is essentially different; the owner may do it reluctantly, but if there is any "coercion" it is the impersonal coercion by the facts of nature which account for the slaves' labor being less efficient without the food; he is not influenced by the will of any human being. In paying high wages to wage-earners, on the other hand, he is. But for their will to obtain the high wages, and their power of backing up that will, he has no reason for paying them. Yet he does. What else is "coercion"?

There is, however, a natural reluctance so to term it. This can be explained, I think, by the fact that some of the grosser forms of private coercion are illegal, and the undoubtedly coercive character of the pressure exerted by the property-owner is disguised. Hence the natural reaction to any recognized form of private coercion is, "forbid it." One who would not wish to take from the laboring man his power to quit the employer, or to deny him the wages that he gets for *not* quitting, is apt to resent the suggestion that those wages are in fact coercive. But were it once recognized that nearly all incomes are the result of private coercion, some with the help of the state, some without it, it would then be plain that to admit the coercive nature of the process would not be to condemn it. Yet popular thought undoubtedly does require special justification for any conduct, private or governmental, which is labeled "coercive," while it does not require such special justification for conduct to which it does not apply that term. Popular judgment of social problems, therefore, is apt to be distorted by the popular recognition or non-recognition of "coercion." Hence it may be worth while to run down into more detail the distinctions popularly made between coercion and other forms of influence over people's conduct.

"Threats" are often distinguished from "promises." If I tell a man I will do some positive act whose results will be unpleasant to him, unless he pays me money, and if as a result he pays it, I would usually be said to be collecting it by means of a "threat." If, on the other hand, I tell him I will do some positive act, whose results will be pleasant to him, *if* he pays me money, and he does, it would be said more commonly that I collected it by means of a "promise." Partly as a result of the moral connotation generally given to these terms, partly as its cause, the law more frequently interferes to prevent the doing of harmful acts than it does to compel the doing of helpful ones. Many (but not all) positive acts which are disadvantageous to others are forbidden; not so many positive acts that are advantageous to others are compelled. In other words, most torts and crimes consist of positive acts. Failure to help does not as a rule give rise to legal punishment or a right of action. Yet there are exceptions. Certain acts not in themselves actionable at law, may give rise to legal duties to perform positive acts. If I start an automobile in motion, I have committed no legal wrong; but if subsequently I fail to perform the act of stopping it when "reasonable care" would require me to do so, the victim of my failure to act can recover damages for my nonperformance. Again, and more significant, if I have promised to do certain things (with certain formalities or "consideration"), my act of promising was not a legal wrong. But if I subsequently fail to perform at the time specified, the promisee has a right of action for my failure to act. It is significant of the reluctance to admit the existence of positive legal duties, that in both cases language is used which makes my wrong conduct seem to consist of wrongful acts instead of wrongful *failure* to act. It is said, in the one case, that I "ran over" the victim, in the other that I "*committed* a breach of contract." Yet in neither was the wrong an act, but a failure to act: in the first case, my failure to make the requisite motions for stopping the car; in the second, my failure to perform the act promised.

Now suppose that instead of actually refraining from doing the acts which the law requires, I say to a man, "Pay me a thousand dollars, and when I meet you on the road walking I will use sufficient care to stop my car or to steer it so that it will not hit you; otherwise I will do nothing about it." Is that a "threat" or a "promise"? Or if I say, "Pay me a thousand dollars and I will perform the acts I have already contracted to perform"? I believe most people would call these statements threats rather than promises. Why? It may be partly due to the misleading language which speaks of the *act* of running over and the *act* of breaking a contract. But even were the fact recognized that payment were demanded as the price of *not abstaining*, I believe the demands would still be called threats. The reason, I believe, is partly because to abstain is contrary to legal duty, partly because it is adjudged to be contrary to moral duty. Popular speech in this case seems to apply the term coercion to demands made as a price of not violating a legal or moral duty, whether the duty consists of acting or of letting alone. But this criterion will not do, either.

If an act is called "coercion" when, and only when, one submits to demands in order to prevent another from violating a legal duty, then every legal system by very definition forbids the private exercise of coercion—it is not coercion unless the law does forbid it. And no action which the law forbids, and which could be used as a means of influencing another, can fail to be coercion—again by definition. Hence it would be idle to discuss whether any particular legal system forbids private coercion. And if an act is called "coercion" when, and only when, one submits to demands in order to prevent another from violating a *moral* duty, we get right back to the use of the term to express our conclusion as to the justifiability of the use of the pressure in question; with the ensuing circular reasoning of condemning an act because we have already designated it "coercive." One is likely, that is, to have a vague feeling against the use of a particular form of economic pressure, then to discover that this pressure is "coercive"—forgetting that coerciveness is not a ground for condemnation except when used in the sense of influence under pain of doing a morally unjustified act. And obviously to pronounce the pressure unjustified because it is an unjustified pressure is to reason in a circle. Hence, it seems better, in using the word "coercion," to use it in a sense which involves no moral judgment.

But popular feeling sometimes makes another distinction. If I plan to do an act or to leave something undone for no other purpose than to induce payment, that might be conceded to be a "threat." But if I plan to do a perfectly lawful act for my own good, or to abstain from working for another because I prefer to do something else with my time, then I take payment for changing my course of conduct in either respect, it would not be called a threat. If a man pays me to keep out of a particular business, or if he pays me to work for him (when I am not legally bound by contract to do so), then it seems absurd to many to say that he paid me under threat of coercion—unless, in the first case, my sole motive in entering the business was to bring him to terms, and unless in the second I preferred working for him to any other occupation of my time, and my sole motive in abstaining was again to bring him to terms. For purposes of ordinary conversation, some other word than coercion may be preferred to describe payments made to a man who makes a sacrifice to "earn" them. But can a line be drawn? I believe the popular distinction along these lines is based on moral judgment. If a man gives up a job he likes, or if he works for another man, why shouldn't he be paid for it?—it will be asked. Perhaps he should. But unless the term "coercion" is applied only to conduct adjudged immoral, does the justifiability of the receipt of payment prevent it from being coercive?

If those distinctions are all invalid, then, which seek to remove the term "coercive" from some of the influences exerted to induce another to act against his will, it seems to follow that the income of each person in the community depends on the relative strength of his power of coercion, offensive and defensive. In fact it appears that what Mr. Carver calls the "productivity" of each factor means no more nor less than this coercive power. It is measured not by what one actually *is* producing, which could not be determined in the case of joint production, but by the extent to which production would fall off if one left and if the marginal laborer were put in his place—by the extent, that is, to which the execution of his threat of withdrawal would damage the employer. Not only does the distribution of income depend on this mutual coercion; so also does the distribution of that power to exert further compulsion which accompanies the management of an industry. . . . This power is frequently highly centralized, with the result that the worker is frequently deprived, during working hours and even beyond, of all choice over his own activities.

To take this control by law from the owner of the plant and to vest it in public officials or in a guild or in a union organization elected by the workers would neither add to nor subtract from the constraint which is exercised with the aid of the government. It would merely transfer the constraining power to a different set of persons. It might result in greater or in less actual power of free initiative all round, but this sort of freedom is not to be confused with the "freedom" which means absence of governmental constraint. Mr. Carver himself points out that the governmental constraint involved in the maintenance of traffic police results in giving the average individual *greater* "freedom of movement." But "freedom of movement" does not mean freedom from governmental constraint, or even from constraint by private individuals. It means freedom from physical obstruction—in other words, greater physical *power* to move. Whether in other cases, too, physical power to exercise one's will is enhanced by a certain amount of legal restriction depends upon the particular facts of each case. Whether Mr. Carver's scheme of things would be more or less "free" (in the sense of giving people greater power to express their wills) than would a state of communism, depends largely on the economic results of communism respecting the character of factory work. Neither can be said to be any "freer" than the other in the sense that it involves less coercion on the part of other human beings, official or unofficial.

The distribution of income, to repeat, depends on the relative power of coercion which the different members of the community can exert against one another. Income is the price paid for not using one's coercive weapons. One of these weapons consists of the power to withhold one's labor. Another is the power to consume all that can be bought with one's lawful income instead of investing part of it. Another is the power to call on the government to lock up certain pieces of land or productive equipment. Still another is the power to decline to undertake an enterprise which may be attended with risk. By threatening to use these various weapons, one gets (with or without sacrifice) an income in the form of wages, interest, rent or profits. The resulting distribution is very far from being equal, and the inequalities are very far from corresponding to needs or to sacrifice.

Notes and Questions

1. What would the Texas court that decided the *Bill Bell* case have thought about the English case of Bird v. Jones?

2. Assume that the plaintiff in the *Bird* case is your client and that you want to advance a theory of false imprisonment based on the necessity doctrine. Formulate an argument.

3. Justice Holmes, dissenting in the *Bailey* case, says that "obtaining money by fraud may be made a crime as well as murder or theft." Did Bailey obtain money by fraud? Why do you suppose Bailey's employer advanced him the fifteen dollars?

Suggestions For Further Reading

Isaiah Berlin, Two Concepts of Liberty, in The Proper Study of Mankind 191 (Henry Hardy & Roger Hausheer eds. 1997)

Richard C. Boldt, The Construction of Responsibility in the Criminal Law, 140 University of Pennsylvania Law Review 2245 (1992)

Barbara H. Fried, The Progressive Assault on Laissez Faire: Robert Hale and the First Law and Economics Movement, chs. 1-2 (1998)

Part III
The Reach of the Law

[I]t is feasible to impose a single legal order upon a group of men only if they live together within the confines of a given area of the earth's surface. The premise that men shall coexist in a group underlies, then, the territorial principle, as it does all of law. Now I contend that a case may be removed morally from the force of a legal order, as well as geographically.[1]

Not all problems that raise legal issues admit of a satisfactory solution within the existing legal system. Such cases suggest the need to articulate principled limits on *"the reach of the law."*

It sometimes becomes questionable whether the law can serve its traditional functions (e.g., deterrence) when extended beyond its normal limits, either spatial (territorial, jurisdictional) or moral (cases of extreme necessity, the "state of nature"). In the previous part, for example, the defense attorney in the *Holmes* case argued that "this case should be tried in a long-boat"—implying that the usual legal standards should not be extended to cover the extreme circumstances of that case.

The reach of the law is invoked in a somewhat different sense when the same defense attorney in *Holmes* continues: "Fairly to sit in judgment on the prisoner, we should . . . be actually translated to his situation." The materials in this part probe the reach of the law in this second sense, beginning with a few classic scientific experiments that document the truly remarkable social and psychological influences to which ordinary people are subject.

Should the purview of the law be extended to include consideration of a defendant's background, history, environment, and development—all with an eye toward allowing defenses to legal liability for actions taken in the immediate past? In effect, such defendants are asking that the time-frame of the relevant "facts of the case" be extended broadly into the more or less remote past.

The reach of the law in this sense is an issue of great and increasing concern today, when defendants are successfully fashioning ever more elaborate and creative defenses based on past forces and distant influences to which they may have been exposed. The logical limit of this tendency is expressed well by the French proverb "tout comprendre c'est tout pardonner" (to understand everything is to forgive everything). When we have finally succeeded in putting ourselves—completely and literally—"in the defendant's shoes," then we shall have arrived at the point where we, too, could ultimately have done nothing different.

---

[1]   The Case of the Speluncean Explorers (Foster, J.).

Chapter 6
Some Findings of Social Science

Opinions and Social Pressure[*]
Solomon E. Asch

Exactly what is the effect of the opinions of others on our own? In other words, how strong is the urge toward social conformity? The question is approached by means of some unusual experiments.

That social influences shape every person's practices, judgments and beliefs is a truism to which anyone will readily assent. A child masters his "native" dialect down to the finest nuances; a member of a tribe of cannibals accepts cannibalism as altogether fitting and proper. All the social sciences take their departure from the observation of the profound effects that groups exert on their members. For psychologists, group pressure upon the minds of individuals raises a host of questions they would like to investigate in detail.

How, and to what extent, do social forces constrain people's opinions and attitudes? This question is especially pertinent in our day. The same epoch that has witnessed the unprecedented technical extension of communication has also brought into existence the deliberate manipulation of opinion and the "engineering of consent." There are many good reasons why, as citizens and as scientists, we should be concerned with studying the ways in which human beings form their opinions and the role that social conditions play.

Studies of these questions began with the interest in hypnosis aroused by the French physician Jean Martin Charcot (a teacher of Sigmund Freud) toward the end of the nineteenth century. Charcot believed that only hysterical patients could be fully hypnotized, but this view was soon challenged by two other physicians, Hyppolyte Bernheim and A.A. Liébault, who demonstrated that they could put most people under the hypnotic spell. Bernheim proposed that hypnosis was but an extreme form of a normal psychological process which became known as "suggestibility." It was shown that monotonous reiteration of instructions could induce in normal persons in the waking state involuntary bodily changes such as swaying or rigidity of the arms, and sensations such as warmth and odor.

It was not long before social thinkers seized upon these discoveries as a basis for explaining numerous social phenomena, from the spread of opinion to the formation of

---

[*] From Solomon E. Asch, Opinions and Social Pressure, Scientific American, Volume 193, No. 5 (November 1955), pages 31-34. Copyright © 1955 by Scientific American, Inc. All rights reserved.

crowds and the following of leaders. The sociologist Gabriel Tarde summed it all up in the aphorism: "Social man is a somnambulist."

When the new discipline of social psychology was born at the beginning of this century, its first experiments were essentially adaptations of the suggestion demonstration. The technique generally followed a simple plan. The subjects, usually college students, were asked to give their opinions or preferences concerning various matters; some time later they were again asked to state their choices, but now they were also informed of the opinions held by authorities or large groups of their peers on the same matters. (Often the alleged consensus was fictitious.) Most of these studies had substantially the same result: confronted with opinions contrary to their own, many subjects apparently shifted their judgments in the direction of the views of the majorities or the experts. The late psychologist Edward L. Thorndike reported that he had succeeded in modifying the esthetic preferences of adults by this procedure. Other psychologists reported that people's evaluations of the merit of a literary passage could be raised or lowered by ascribing the passage to different authors. Apparently the sheer weight of numbers or authority sufficed to change opinions, even when no arguments for the opinions themselves were provided.

Now the very ease of success in these experiments arouses suspicion. Did the subjects actually change their opinions, or were the experimental victories scored only on paper? On grounds of common sense, one must question whether opinions are generally as watery as these studies indicate. There is some reason to wonder whether it was not the investigators who, in their enthusiasm for a theory, were suggestible, and whether the ostensibly gullible subjects were not providing answers which they thought good subjects were expected to give.

The investigations were guided by certain underlying assumptions, which today are common currency and account for much that is thought and said about the operations of propaganda and public opinion. The assumptions are that people submit uncritically and painlessly to external manipulation by suggestion or prestige, and that any given idea or value can be "sold" or "unsold" without reference to its merits. We should be skeptical, however, of the supposition that the power of social pressure necessarily implies uncritical submission to it: independence and the capacity to rise above group passion are also open to human beings. Further, one may question on psychological grounds whether it is possible as a rule to change a person's judgment of a situation or an object without first changing his knowledge or assumptions about it.

In what follows I shall describe some experiments in an investigation of the effects of group pressure which was carried out recently with the help of a number of my associates. The tests not only demonstrate the operations of group pressure upon individuals but also illustrate a new kind of attack on the problem and some of the more subtle questions that it raises.

A group of seven to nine young men, all college students, are assembled in a classroom for a "psychological experiment" in visual judgment. The experimenter informs them that they will be comparing the lengths of lines. He shows two large white cards. On one is a single vertical black line—the standard whose length is to be matched. On the other card are three vertical lines of various lengths. The subjects are to choose the one that is of the same length as the line on the other card. One of the three actually is of the same length; the other two are substantially different, the difference ranging from three quarters of an inch to an inch and three quarters.

The experiment opens uneventfully. The subjects announce their answers in the order in which they have been seated in the room, and on the first round every person chooses the same matching line. Then a second set of cards is exposed; again the group is unanimous. The members appear ready to endure politely another boring experiment. On the third trial there is an unexpected disturbance. One person near the end of the group disagrees with all the others in his selection of the matching line. He looks surprised, indeed incredulous, about the disagreement. On the following trial he disagrees again, while the others remain unanimous in their choice. The dissenter becomes more and more worried and hesitant as the disagreement continues in succeeding trials; he may pause before announcing his answer and speak in a low voice, or he may smile in an embarrassed way.

What the dissenter does not know is that all the other members of the group were instructed by the experimenter beforehand to give incorrect answers in unanimity at certain points. The single individual who is not a party to this prearrangement is the focal subject of our experiment. He is placed in a position in which, while he is actually giving the correct answers, he finds himself unexpectedly in a minority of one, opposed by a unanimous and arbitrary majority with respect to a clear and simple fact. Upon him we have brought to bear two opposed forces: the evidence of his senses and the unanimous opinion of a group of his peers. Also, he must declare his judgments in public, before a majority which has also stated its position publicly.

The instructed majority occasionally reports correctly in order to reduce the possibility that the naive subject will suspect collusion against him. (In only a few cases did the subject actually show suspicion; when this happened, the experiment was stopped and the results were not counted.) There are 18 trials in each series, and on 12 of these the majority responds erroneously. How do people respond to group pressure in this situation? I shall report first the statistical results of a series in which a total of 123 subjects from three institutions of higher learning (not including my own, Swarthmore College) were placed in the minority situation described above.

Two alternatives were open to the subject: he could act independently, repudiating the majority, or he could go along with the majority, repudiating the evidence of his senses. Of the 123 put to the test, a considerable percentage yielded to the majority. Whereas in ordinary circumstances individuals matching the lines will make mistakes less than 1 percent of the time, under group pressure the minority subjects swung to acceptance of the misleading majority's wrong judgments in 36.8 percent of the selections.

Of course individuals differed in response. At one extreme, about one quarter of the subjects were completely independent and never agreed with the erroneous judgments of the majority. At the other extreme, some individuals went with the majority nearly all the time. The performances of individuals in this experiment tend to be highly consistent. Those who strike out on the path of independence do not, as a rule, succumb to the majority even over an extended series of trials, while those who choose the path of compliance are unable to free themselves as the ordeal is prolonged.

The reasons for the startling individual differences have not yet been investigated in detail. At this point we can only report some tentative generalizations from talks with the subjects, each of whom was interviewed at the end of the experiment. Among the independent individuals were many who held fast because of staunch confidence in their own judgment. The most significant fact about them was not absence of responsiveness to the majority but a capacity to recover from doubt and to reestablish their equilibrium. Others who acted independently came to believe that the majority was correct in its answers, but they continued their dissent on the simple ground that it was their obligation to call the play as they saw it.

Among the extremely yielding persons we found a group who quickly reached the conclusion: "I am wrong, they are right." Others yielded in order "not to spoil your results." Many of the individuals who went along suspected that the majority were "sheep" following the first responder, or that the majority were victims of an optical illusion; nevertheless, these suspicions failed to free them at the moment of decision. More disquieting were the reactions of subjects who construed their difference from the majority as a sign of some general deficiency in themselves, which at all costs they must hide. On this basis they desperately tried to merge with the majority, not realizing the longer-range consequences to themselves. All the yielding subjects underestimated the frequency with which they conformed.

Which aspect of the influence of a majority is more important—the size of the majority or its unanimity? The experiment was modified to examine this question. In one series the size of the opposition was varied from one to fifteen persons. The results showed a clear trend. When a subject was confronted with only a single individual who contradicted his answers, he was swayed little: he continued to answer independently and correctly in nearly all trials. When the opposition was increased to two, the pressure became substantial: minority subjects now accepted the wrong answer 13.6 percent of the time. Under the pressure of a majority of three, the subjects' errors jumped to 31.8 percent. But further increases in the size of the majority apparently did not increase the weight of the pressure substantially. Clearly the size of the opposition is important only up to a point.

Disturbance of the majority's unanimity had a striking effect. In this experiment the subject was given the support of a truthful partner—either another individual who did not know of the prearranged agreement among the rest of the group, or a person who was instructed to give correct answers throughout.

The presence of a supporting partner depleted the majority of much of its power. Its pressure on the dissenting individual was reduced to one-fourth: that is, subjects answered incorrectly only one-fourth as often as under the pressure of a unanimous majority. The weakest persons did not yield as readily. Most interesting were the reactions to the partner. Generally the feeling toward him was one of warmth and closeness; he was credited with inspiring confidence. However, the subjects repudiated the suggestion that the partner decided them to be independent.

Was the partner's effect a consequence of his dissent, or was it related to his accuracy? We now introduced into the experimental group a person who was instructed to dissent from the majority but also to disagree with the subject. In some experiments the majority was always to choose the worst of the comparison lines and the instructed dissenter to pick the line that was closer to the length of the standard one; in others the majority was consistently intermediate and the dissenter most in error. In this manner we were able to study the relative influence of "compromising" and "extremist" dissenters.

Again the results are clear. When a moderate dissenter is present, the effect of the majority on the subject decreases by approximately one-third, and extremes of yielding disappear. Moreover, most of the errors the subjects do make are moderate, rather than flagrant. In short, the dissenter largely controls the choice of errors. To this extent the subjects broke away from the majority even while bending to it.

On the other hand, when the dissenter always chose the line that was more flagrantly different from the standard, the results were of quite a different kind. The extremist dissenter produced a remarkable freeing of the subjects; their errors dropped to only 9 percent. Furthermore, all the errors were of the moderate variety. We were able to conclude that dissent *per se* increased independence and moderated the errors that occurred, and that the direction of dissent exerted consistent effects.

In all the foregoing experiments each subject was observed only in a single setting. We now turned to studying the effects upon a given individual of a change in the situation to which he was exposed. The first experiment examined the consequences of losing or gaining a partner. The instructed partner began by answering correctly on the first six trials. With his support the subject usually resisted pressure from the majority: eighteen of twenty-seven subjects were completely independent. But after six trials the partner joined the majority. As soon as he did so, there was an abrupt rise in the subjects' errors. Their submission to the majority was just about as frequent as when the minority subject was opposed by a unanimous majority throughout.

It was surprising to find that the experience of having had a partner and of having braved the majority opposition with him had failed to strengthen the individuals' independence. Questioning at the conclusion of the experiment suggested that we had overlooked an important circumstance; namely, the strong specific effect of "desertion" by the partner to the other side. We therefore changed the conditions so that the partner would simply leave the group at the proper point. (To allay suspicion it was announced in advance that he had an appointment with the dean.) In this form of the experiment, the partner's effect outlasted his presence. The errors increased after his departure, but less markedly than after a partner switched to the majority.

In a variant of this procedure the trials began with the majority unanimously giving correct answers. Then they gradually broke away until on the sixth trial the naive subject was alone and the group unanimously against him. As long as the subject had anyone on his side, he was almost invariably independent, but as soon as he found himself alone, the tendency to conform to the majority rose abruptly.

As might be expected, an individual's resistance to group pressure in these experiments depends to a considerable degree on how wrong the majority is. We varied the discrepancy between the standard line and the other lines systematically, with the hope of reaching a point where the error of the majority would be so glaring that every subject would repudiate it and choose independently. In this we regretfully did not succeed. Even when the difference between the lines was seven inches, there were still some who yielded to the error of the majority.

The study provides clear answers to a few relatively simple questions, and it raises many others that await investigation. We would like to know the degree of consistency of persons in situations which differ in content and structure. If consistency of independence or conformity in behavior is shown to be a fact, how is it functionally related to qualities of character and personality? In what ways is independence related to sociological or cultural conditions? Are leaders more independent than other people, or are they adept at following their followers? These and many other questions may perhaps be answerable by investigations of the type described here.

Life in society requires consensus as an indispensable condition. But consensus, to be productive, requires that each individual contribute independently out of his experience and insight. When consensus comes under the dominance of conformity, the social process is polluted and the individual at the same time surrenders the powers on which his functioning as a feeling and thinking being depends. That we have found the tendency to conformity in our society so strong that reasonably intelligent and well-meaning young people are willing to call white black is a matter of concern. It raises questions about our ways of education and about the values that guide our conduct.

Yet anyone inclined to draw too pessimistic conclusions from this report would do well to remind himself that the capacities for independence are not to be underestimated. He may also draw some consolation from a further observation: those who participated in this challenging experiment agreed nearly without exception that independence was preferable to conformity.

References

Asch, S.E. Effects of group pressure upon the modification and distortion of judgments, in Groups, leadership, and men, Harold Guetzdow (ed.). Carnegie Press, 1951.

Asch, S.E. Social psychology. Prentice-Hall, Inc., 1952.

Miller, N.E. and Dollard, J. Social learning and imitation. Yale University Press, 1941.

Behavioral Study of Obedience[*]
Stanley Milgram

This chapter describes a procedure for the study of destructive obedience in the laboratory. It consists of ordering a naive subject to administer increasingly more severe punishment to a victim in the context of a learning experiment. Punishment is administered by means of a shock generator with thirty graded switches ranging from Slight Shock to Danger: Severe Shock. The victim is a confederate of the experimenter. The primary dependent variable is the maximum shock the subject is willing to administer before he refuses to continue further. Twenty-six subjects obeyed the experimental commands fully, and administered the highest shock on the generator. Fourteen subjects broke off the experiment at some point after the victim protested and refused to provide further answers. The procedure created extreme levels of nervous tension in some subjects. Profuse sweating, trembling and stuttering were typical expressions of this emotional disturbance. One unexpected sign of tension—yet to be explained—was the regular occurrence of nervous laughter, which in some subjects developed into uncontrollable seizures. The variety of interesting behavioral dynamics observed in the experiment, the reality of the situation for the subject, and the possibility of parametric variation within the framework of the procedure, point to the fruitfulness of further study.

Obedience is as basic an element in the structure of social life as one can point to. Some system of authority is a requirement of all communal living, and it is only the man dwelling in isolation who is not forced to respond, through defiance or submission, to the commands of others. Obedience, as a determinant of behavior, is of particular relevance to our time. It has been reliably established that from 1933–1945 millions of innocent persons were systematically slaughtered on command. Gas chambers were built, death camps were guarded, daily quotas of corpses were produced with the same efficiency as the manufacture of appliances. These inhumane policies may have originated in the mind of a single person, but they could only be carried out on a massive scale if a very large number of persons obeyed orders.

Obedience is the psychological mechanism that links individual action to political purpose. It is the dispositional cement that binds men to systems of authority. Facts of recent history and observation in daily life suggest that for many persons obedience may be a deeply ingrained behavior tendency, indeed, a prepotent impulse overriding training in ethics, sympathy, and moral conduct. C.P. Snow (1961) points to its importance when he writes:

When you think of the long and gloomy history of man, you will find more hideous crimes have been committed in the name of obedience than have ever

---

[*] Stanley Milgram, Behavioral Study of Obedience, Journal of Abnormal and Social Psychology, Volume 67, No. 4 (1963), pages 371-378.

been committed in the name of rebellion. If you doubt that, read William Shirer's "Rise and Fall of the Third Reich." The German Officer Corps were brought up in the most rigorous code of obedience . . . in the name of obedience they were party to, and assisted in, the most wicked large scale actions in the history of the world.

While the particular form of obedience dealt with in the present study has its antecedents in these episodes, it must not be thought all obedience entails acts of aggression against others. Obedience serves numerous productive functions. Indeed, the very life of society is predicated on its existence. Obedience may be ennobling and educative and refer to acts of charity and kindness, as well as to destruction.

General Procedure

A procedure was devised which seems useful as a tool for studying obedience (Milgram, 1961). It consists of ordering a naive subject to administer electric shock to a victim. A simulated shock generator is used, with 30 clearly marked voltage levels that range from 15 to 450 volts. The instrument bears verbal designations that range from Slight Shock to Danger: Severe Shock. The responses of the victim, who is a trained confederate of the experimenter, are standardized. The orders to administer shocks are given to the naive subject in the context of a "learning experiment" ostensibly set up to study the effects of punishment on memory. As the experiment proceeds the naive subject is commanded to administer increasingly more intense shocks to the victim, even to the point of reaching the level marked Danger: Severe Shock. Internal resistances become stronger, and at a certain point the subject refuses to go on with the experiment. Behavior prior to this rupture is considered "obedience," in that the subject complies with the commands of the experimenter. The point of rupture is the act of disobedience. A quantitative value is assigned to the subject's performance based on the maximum intensity shock he is willing to administer before he refuses to participate further. Thus for any particular subject and for any particular experimental condition the degree of obedience may be specified with a numerical value. The crux of the study is to systematically vary the factors believed to alter the degree of obedience to the experimental commands.

The technique allows important variables to be manipulated at several points in the experiment. One may vary aspects of the source of command, content and form of command, instrumentalities for its execution, target object, general social setting, etc. The problem, therefore, is not one of designing increasingly more numerous experimental conditions, but of selecting those that best illuminate the *process* of obedience from the sociopsychological standpoint.

Related Studies

The inquiry bears an important relation to philosophic analyses of obedience and authority (Arendt, 1958; Friedrich, 1958; Weber, 1947), an early experimental study of obedience by Frank (1944), studies in "authoritarianism" (Adorno, Frenkel-Brunswik, Levinson, and Sanford, 1950; Rokeach, 1961), and a recent series of analytic and empirical studies in social power (Cartwright, 1959). It owes much to the long concern with *suggestion* in social psychology, both in its normal forms (e.g., Binet, 1900) and in its clinical manifestations (Charcot, 1881). But it derives, in the first instance, from direct observation of a social fact; the individual who is commanded by a legitimate authority ordinarily obeys. Obedience comes easily and often. It is a ubiquitous and indispensable feature of social life.

Method

Subjects

The subjects were 40 males between the ages of 20 and 50, drawn from New Haven and the surrounding communities. Subjects were obtained by a newspaper advertisement and direct mail solicitation. Those who responded to the appeal believed they were to participate in a study of memory and learning at Yale University. A wide range of occupations is represented in the sample. Typical subjects were postal clerks, high school teachers, salesmen, engineers, and laborers. Subjects ranged in educational level from one who had not finished elementary school, to those who had doctorate and other professional degrees. They were paid $4.50 for their participation in the experiment. However, subjects were told that payment was simply for coming to the laboratory, and that the money was theirs no matter what happened after they arrived.

Personnel and Locale

The experiment was conducted on the grounds of Yale University in the elegant interaction laboratory. (This detail is relevant to the perceived legitimacy of the experiment. In further variations, the experiment was dissociated from the university, with consequences for performance.) The role of experimenter was played by a 31-year-old high school teacher of biology. His manner was impassive, and his appearance somewhat stern throughout the experiment. He was dressed in a gray technician's coat. The victim was played by a 47-year-old accountant, trained for the role; he was of Irish-American stock, whom most observers found mild-mannered and likable.

Procedure

One naive subject and one victim (an accomplice) performed in each experiment. A pretext had to be devised that would justify the administration of electric shock by the naive subject. This was effectively accomplished by the cover story. After a general introduction on the presumed relation between punishment and learning, subjects were told:

> But actually, we know very *little* about the effect of punishment on learning, because almost no truly scientific studies have been made of it in human beings.
>
> For instance, we don't know how *much* punishment is best for learning—and we don't know how much difference it makes as to who is giving the punishment, whether an adult learns best from a younger or an older person than himself—or many things of that sort.

So in this study we are bringing together a number of adults of different occupations and ages. And we're asking some of them to be teachers and some of them to be learners.

We want to find out just what effect different people have on each other as teachers and learners, and also what effect *punishment* will have on learning in this situation.

Therefore, I'm going to ask one of you to be the teacher here tonight and the other one to be the learner.

Does either of you have a preference?

Subjects then drew slips of paper from a hat to determine who would be the teacher and who would be the learner in the experiment. The drawing was rigged so that the naive subject was always the teacher and the accomplice always the learner. (Both slips contained the word "Teacher.") Immediately after the drawing the teacher and learner were taken to an adjacent room and the learner was strapped into an "electric chair" apparatus.

The experimenter explained that the straps were to prevent excessive movement while the learner was being shocked. The effect was to make it impossible for him to escape from the situation. An electrode was attached to the learner's wrist, and electrode paste was applied "to avoid blisters and burns." Subjects were told that the electrode was attached to the shock generator in the adjoining room.

In order to improve credibility the experimenter declared, in response to a question by the learner: "Although the shocks can be extremely painful, they cause no permanent tissue damage."

Learning task. The lesson administered by the subject was a paired-associate learning task. The subject read a series of word pairs to the learner, and then read the first word of the pair along with four terms. The learner was to indicate which of the four terms had originally been paired with the first word. He communicated his answer by pressing one of four switches in front of him, which in turn lit up one of four numbered quadrants in an answer-box located atop the shock generator.

Shock generator. The instrument panel consists of 30 lever switches set in a horizontal line. Each switch is clearly labeled with a voltage designation that ranges from 15 to 450 volts. There is a 15-volt increment from one switch to the next going from left to right. In addition, the following verbal designations are clearly indicated for groups of four switches going from left to right: Slight Shock, Moderate Shock, Strong Shock, Very Strong Shock, Intense Shock, Extreme Intensity Shock, Danger: Severe Shock. (Two switches after this last designation are simply marked XXX.)

Upon depressing a switch: a pilot light corresponding to each switch is illuminated in bright red; an electric buzzing is heard; an electric blue light, labeled "voltage energizer," flashes; the dial on the voltage meter swings to the right; various relay clicks are sounded.

The upper left-hand corner of the generator is labeled Shock Generator, Type ZLB, Dyson Instrument Company, Waltham, Mass. Output 15 Volts—450 Volts.

Details of the instrument were carefully handled to insure an appearance of authenticity. The panel was engraved by precision industrial engravers, and all components were of high quality. No subject in the experiment suspected that the instrument was merely a simulated shock generator.

Sample shock. Each naive subject is given a sample shock on the shock generator, prior to beginning his run as teacher. This shock is always 45 volts, and is applied by pressing the third switch of the generator. The shock is applied to the wrist of the naive subject, and has its source in a 45-volt battery wired into the generator. This further convinces the subject of the authenticity of the generator.

Shock instructions. The subject is told to administer a shock to the learner each time he gives a wrong response. Moreover—and this is the key command—the subject is instructed to "move one lever higher on the shock generator each time the learner flashes a wrong answer." He is also instructed to announce the voltage level before administering a shock. This serves to continually remind subjects of the increasing intensity of shocks administered to the learner.

Preliminary and regular run. Pretests revealed that the procedure of reading words and administering shocks requires some practice before it can be handled smoothly. Therefore, immediately preceding the regular run, the teacher is given a preliminary series of 10 words to read to the learner. There are 3 neutral words in the practice series (i.e., words that the learner answers correctly), so that shocks are administered for 7 of the words, with the maximum shock at 105 volts (moderate shock). Almost all subjects master the procedure by the time the preliminary run is over.

Subjects are then presented with a second list, and are told that the procedure is the same as for the first list; the experimenter adds, however:

> When you get to the bottom of the list, repeat it over again, and continue giving shocks, until the learner has learned all the pairs correctly.

The experimenter instructs the subject to

> start from 15 volts and increase the shock level one step each time the learner gives a wrong answer.

Feedback from the victim. In all conditions the learner gives a predetermined set of responses to the word pair test, based on a schedule of approximately three wrong answers to one correct answer. In the present experimental condition no vocal response or other sign of protest is heard from the learner until Shock Level 300 is reached. When the 300-volt shock is administered, the learner pounds on the wall of the room in which he is bound to the electric chair. The pounding can be heard by the subject. From this point on, the learner's answers no longer appear on the four-way panel.

At this juncture, subjects ordinarily turn to the experimenter for guidance. The experimenter instructs the subject to treat the absence of a response as a wrong answer, and to shock the subject according to the usual schedule. He advises the subjects to allow 5—10 seconds before considering no response as a wrong answer, and to increase the shock level one step each time the learner fails to respond correctly. The learner's pounding is repeated after the 315-volt shock is administered; afterwards he is not heard from, nor do his answers reappear on the four-way signal box.

Experimenter feedback. At various points in the experiment the subject may turn to the experimenter for advice on whether he should continue to administer shocks. Or he may indicate that he does not wish to go on. It was important to standardize the experimenter's responses to these inquiries and reactions.

If the subject indicated his unwillingness to go on, the experimenter responded with a sequence of "prods," using as many as necessary to bring the subject into line.

Prod 1: Please continue. *or* Please go on.
Prod 2: The experiment requires that you continue.
Prod 3: It is absolutely essential that you continue.
Prod 4: You have no other choice, you *must* go on.

The prods were always made in sequence: Only if Prod 1 had been unsuccessful, could Prod 2 be used. If the subject refused to obey the experimenter after Prod 4, the experiment was terminated. The experimenter's tone of voice was at all times firm, but not impolite. The sequence was begun anew on each occasion that the subject balked or showed reluctance to follow orders.

Special prods. If the subject asked if the learner was liable to suffer permanent physical injury, the experimenter said:

Although the shocks may be painful, there is no permanent tissue damage, so please go on. [Followed by Prods 2, 3, and 4 if necessary.]

If the subject said that the learner did not want to go on, the experimenter replied:

Whether the learner likes it or not, you must go on until he has learned all the word pairs correctly. So please go on. [Followed by Prods 2, 3, and 4 if necessary.]

Dependent Measures

The primary dependent measure for any subject is the maximum shock he administers before he refuses to go any further. In principle this may vary from 0 (for a subject who refuses to administer even the first shock) to 30 (for a subject who administers the highest shock on the generator). A subject who breaks off the experiment at any point prior to administering the thirtieth shock level is termed a *defiant* subject. One who complies with experimental commands fully, and proceeds to administer all shock levels commanded, is termed an *obedient* subject.

Further records. With few exceptions, experimental sessions were recorded on magnetic tape. Occasional photographs were taken through one-way mirrors. Notes were kept on any unusual behavior occurring during the course of the experiments. On occasion, additional observers were directed to write objective descriptions of the subjects' behavior. The latency and duration of shocks were measured by accurate timing devices.

Interview and dehoax. Following the experiment, subjects were interviewed; open-ended questions, projective measures, and attitude scales were employed. After the interview, procedures were undertaken to assure that the subject would leave the laboratory in a state of well being. A friendly reconciliation was arranged between the subject and the victim, and an effort was made to reduce any tensions that arose as a result of the experiment.

Results

Preliminary Notions

Before giving an account of the experimental results, it is instructive to consider how persons predict others will perform when commanded to administer powerful shocks to another person. Fourteen Yale seniors, all psychology majors, were provided with a detailed description of the experimental situation. They were asked to reflect carefully on it, and to predict the behavior of 100 hypothetical subjects. More specifically, they were instructed to plot the distribution of obedience of "100 Americans of diverse occupations, and ranging in age from 20 to 50 years," who were placed in the experimental situation.

There was considerable agreement among the respondents on the expected behavior of hypothetical subjects. All respondents predicted that only an insignificant minority would go through to the end of the shock series. (The estimates ranged from 0 to 3 percent; i.e., the most "pessimistic" member of the class predicted that of 100 persons, 3 would continue through to the most potent shock available on the shock generator—450 volts.) The class mean was 1.2 percent. The question was also posed informally to colleagues of the author, and the most general feeling was that few if any subjects would go beyond the designation Very Strong Shock.

Result of Experiment I

Subjects accept situation. With few exceptions subjects were convinced of the reality of the experimental situation, that they were administering shocks to another person, and the most potent shocks were extremely painful. In the post-experimental interview subjects were asked: "How painful to the learner were the last few shocks that you administered to him?" Subjects were instructed to indicate their answers on a printed 14-point scale ranging from "Not at all painful" to "Extremely painful." The modal response was 14 (Extremely painful) with the mean at 13.42.

Signs of extreme tension. Many subjects showed signs of nervousness in the experimental situation, and especially upon administering the more powerful shocks. In a large number of cases the degree of tension reached extremes that are rarely seen in sociopsychological laboratory studies. Subjects were observed to sweat, tremble, stutter, bite their lips, groan, and dig their fingernails into their flesh. These were characteristic rather than exceptional responses to the experiment.

One sign of tension was the regular occurrence of nervous laughing fits. Fourteen of the 40 subjects showed definite signs of nervous laughter and smiling. The laughter seemed entirely out of place, even bizarre. Full-blown, uncontrollable seizures were observed for 3 subjects. On one occasion we observed a seizure so violently convulsive that it was necessary to call a halt to the experiment. The subject, a 46-year-old encyclopedia salesman, was seriously embarrassed by his untoward and uncontrollable behavior. In the post-experimental interviews subjects took pains to point out that they were not sadistic types, and that the laughter did not mean they enjoyed shocking the victim.

Distribution of scores. It had been conjectured that persons would not, in general, agree to administer shocks beyond the level designated as Very Strong Shock. The obtained distribution of scores deviates radically from the prediction.

Upon command of the experimenter, each of the 40 subjects went beyond the expected breakoff point. No subject stopped prior to administering Shock Level 20. (At this level—300 volts—the victim kicks on the wall and no longer provides answers to the teacher's multiple-choice questions.)

Of the 40 subjects, 5 refused to obey the experimental commands beyond the 300-volt level. Four more subjects administered one further shock, and then refused to go on. Two broke off at the 330-volt level, and 1 each at 345, 360, and 375 volts. Thus a total of 14 subjects defied the experimenter. It is instructive to reprint their remarks at the point of defiance, as transcribed from the tape recordings:

[0124] I think he's trying to communicate, he's knocking. . . . Well it's not fair to shock the guy . . . these are terrific volts. I don't think this is very humane. . . . Oh, I can't go on with this; no, this isn't right. It's a hell of an experiment. The guy is suffering in there. No, I don't want to go on. This is crazy. [Subject refused to administer more shocks.]

[0123] He's banging in there. I'm gonna chicken out. I'd like to continue, but I can't do that to a man. . . . I'm sorry I can't do that to a man. I'll hurt his heart. You take your check. . . . No really, I couldn't do it.

These subjects were frequently in a highly agitated and even angered state. Sometimes, verbal protest was at a minimum, and the subject simply got up from his chair in front of the shock generator, and indicated that he wished to leave the laboratory.

Of the 40 subjects, 26 obeyed the orders of the experimenter to the end, proceeding to punish the victim until they reached the most potent shock available on the shock generator. At that point, the experimenter called a halt to the session. (The maximum shock is labeled 450 volts, and is two steps beyond the designation: Danger: Severe Shock.) Although obedient subjects continued to administer shocks, they often did so under extreme stress. Some expressed reluctance to administer shocks beyond the 300-volt level, and displayed fears similar to those who defied the experimenter; yet they obeyed.

After the maximum shocks had been delivered, and the experimenter called a halt to the proceedings, many obedient subjects heaved sighs of relief, mopped their brows, rubbed their fingers over their eyes, or nervously fumbled cigarettes. Some shook their heads, apparently in regret. Some subjects had remained calm throughout the experiment, and displayed only minimal signs of tension from beginning to end.

Discussion

The experiment yielded two findings that were surprising. The first finding concerns the sheer strength of obedient tendencies manifested in this situation. Subjects have learned from childhood that it is a fundamental breach of moral conduct to hurt another person against his will. Yet, 26 subjects abandon this tenet in following the instructions of an authority who has no special powers to enforce his commands. To disobey would bring no material loss to the subject; no punishment would ensue. It is clear from the remarks and outward behavior of many participants that in punishing the victim they are often acting against their own values. Subjects often expressed deep disapproval of shocking a man in the face of his objections, and others denounced it as stupid and senseless. Yet the majority complied with the experimental commands. This outcome was surprising from two perspectives: first, from the standpoint of predictions made in the questionnaire described earlier. (Here, however, it is possible that the remoteness of the respondents from the actual situation, and the difficulty of conveying to them the concrete details of the experiment, could account for the serious underestimation of obedience.)

But the results were also unexpected to persons who observed the experiment in progress, through one-way mirrors. Observers often uttered expressions of disbelief upon seeing a subject administer more powerful shocks to the victim. These persons had a full acquaintance with the details of the situation, and yet systematically underestimated the amount of obedience that subjects would display.

The second unanticipated effect was the extraordinary tension generated by the procedures. One might suppose that a subject would simply break off or continue as his conscience dictated. Yet, this is very far from what happened. There were striking reactions of tension and emotional strain. One observer related:

> I observed a mature and initially poised businessman enter the laboratory smiling and confident. Within 20 minutes he was reduced to a twitching, stuttering wreck, who was rapidly approaching a point of nervous collapse. He constantly pulled on his earlobe, and twisted his hands. At one point he pushed his fist into his forehead and muttered: "Oh God, let's stop it." And yet he continued to respond to every word of the experimenter, and obeyed to the end.

Any understanding of the phenomenon of obedience must rest on an analysis of the particular conditions in which it occurs. The following features of the experiment go some distance in explaining the high amount of obedience observed in the situation.

1. The experiment is sponsored by and takes place on the grounds of an institution of unimpeachable reputation, Yale University. It may be reasonably presumed that the personnel are competent and reputable. The importance of this background authority is now being studied by conducting a series of experiments outside of New Haven, and without any visible ties to the university.

2. The experiment is, on the face of it, designed to attain a worthy purpose—advancement of knowledge about learning and memory. Obedience occurs not as an end in itself, but as an instrumental element in a situation that the subject construes as significant, and meaningful. He may not be able to see its full significance, but he may properly assume that the experimenter does.

3. The subject perceives that the victim has voluntarily submitted to the authority system of the experimenter. He is not (at first) an unwilling captive impressed for involuntary service. He has taken the trouble to come to the laboratory presumably to aid the experi-

mental research. That he later becomes an involuntary subject does not alter the fact that, initially, he consented to participate without qualification. Thus he has in some degree incurred an obligation toward the experimenter.

4. The subject, too, has entered the experiment voluntarily, and perceives himself under obligation to aid the experimenter. He has made a commitment, and to disrupt the experiment is a repudiation of this initial promise of aid.

5. Certain features of the procedure strengthen the subject's sense of obligation to the experimenter. For one, he has been paid for coming to the laboratory. In part this is canceled out by the experimenter's statement that:

> Of course, as in all experiments, the money is yours simply for coming to the laboratory. From this point on, no matter what happens, the money is yours.

6. From the subject's standpoint, the fact that he is the teacher and the other man the learner is purely a chance consequence (it is determined by drawing lots) and he, the subject, ran the same risk as the other man in being assigned the role of learner. Since the assignment of positions in the experiment was achieved by fair means, the learner is deprived of any basis of complaint on this count. (A similar situation obtains in Army units, in which—in the absence of volunteers—a particularly dangerous mission may be assigned by drawing lots, and the unlucky soldier is expected to bear his misfortune with sportsmanship.)

7. There is, at best, ambiguity with regard to the prerogatives of a psychologist and the corresponding rights of his subject. There is a vagueness of expectation concerning what a psychologist may require of his subject, and when he is overstepping acceptable limits. Moreover, the experiment occurs in a closed setting, and thus provides no opportunity for the subject to remove these ambiguities by discussion with others. There are few standards that seem directly applicable to the situation, which is a novel one for most subjects.

8. The subjects are assured that the shocks administered to the subject are "painful but not dangerous." Thus they assume that the discomfort caused the victim is momentary, while the scientific gains resulting from the experiment are enduring.

9. Through Shock Level 20 the victim continues to provide answers on the signal box. The subject may construe this as a sign that the victim is still willing to "play the game." It is only after Shock Level 20 that the victim repudiates the rules completely, refusing to answer further.

These features help to explain the high amount of obedience obtained in this experiment. Many of the arguments raised need not remain matters of speculation, but can be reduced to testable propositions to be confirmed or disproved by further experiments.

The following features of the experiment concern the nature of the conflict which the subject faces.

10. The subject is placed in a position in which he must respond to the competing demands of two persons: the experimenter and the victim. The conflict must be resolved by meeting the demands of one or the other; satisfaction of the victim and the experimenter are mutually exclusive. Moreover, the resolution must take the form of a highly visible action,

that of continuing to shock the victim or breaking off the experiment. Thus the subject is forced into a public conflict that does not permit any completely satisfactory solution.

11. While the demands of the experimenter carry the weight of scientific authority, the demands of the victim spring from his personal experience of pain and suffering. The two claims need not be regarded as equally pressing and legitimate. The experimenter seeks an abstract scientific datum; the victim cries out for relief from physical suffering caused by the subject's actions.

12. The experiment gives the subject little time for reflection. The conflict comes on rapidly. It is only minutes after the subject has been seated before the shock generator that the victim begins his protests. Moreover, the subject perceives that he has gone through but two-thirds of the shock levels at the time the subject's first protests are heard. Thus he understands that the conflict will have a persistent aspect to it, and may well become more intense as increasingly more powerful shocks are required. The rapidity with which the conflict descends on the subject, and his realization that it is predictably recurrent may well be sources of tension to him.

13. At a more general level, the conflict stems from the opposition of two deeply ingrained behavior dispositions: first, the disposition not to harm other people, and second, the tendency to obey those whom we perceive to be legitimate authorities.

References

Adorno, T., Frenkel-Brunswik, Else, Levinson, D.J., and Sanford, R.N. The authoritarian personality. New York: Harper, 1950.

Arendt, H. What was authority?, in C.J. Friedrich (ed.), Authority. Cambridge: Harvard Univer. Press, 1958. Pp. 81–112.

Binet, A. La suggestibilité. Paris: Schleicher, 1900.

Buss, A.H. The psychology of aggression. New York: Wiley, 1961.

Cartwright, S. (ed.) Studies in social power. Ann Arbor: University of Michigan Institute for Social Research, 1959.

Charcot, J.M. Oeuvres complètes. Paris: Bureaux du progrès Médical, 1881.

Frank, J.D. Experimental studies of personal pressure and resistance. J. gen. Psychol., 1944, 30, 23–64.

Friedrich, C.J. (ed.) Authority. Cambridge: Harvard Univer. Press, 1958.

Milgram, S. Dynamics of obedience. Washington: National Science Foundation, 25 January 1961. (Mimeo)

Milgram, S. Some conditions of obedience and disobedience to authority. Hum. Relat., 1965, 18, 57–76.

Rokeach, M. Authority, authoritarianism, and conformity, in I.A. Berg and B.M. Bass (eds.), Conformity and deviation. New York: Harper, 1961. Pp. 230–257.

Snow, C.P. Either-or. Progressive, 1961 (Feb.), 24.

Weber, M. The theory of social and economic organization. Oxford: Oxford Univer. Press, 1947.

A Study of Prisoners and Guards in a Simulated Prison[*]
Craig Haney, Curtis Banks, and Philip Zimbardo

In this study, Dr. Zimbardo fabricated a simulation of the essential characteristics of a prison environment. From a highly selected group of college students, Dr. Zimbardo randomly assigned half as "guards" (with all attendant powers) and half as "prisoners" (under the complete subjugation of the "guards"). Essentially then, a group of intelligent, "normal" young men were put into a situation which demanded close contact over a period of several days. There was a well-defined authority/subordinate relationship between "guards" and "prisoners." The "prison" environment was further manipulated to promote anonymity, depersonalization, and dehumanization among the subjects. The study demonstrates how these variables combine to increase the incidence of aggressive behavior on the part of the "guards" and submissive and docile conformity on the part of the "prisoners."

Introduction

After he had spent four years in a Siberian prison the great Russian novelist Dostoevsky commented surprisingly that his time in prison had created in him a deep optimism about the ultimate future of mankind because, as he put it, if man could survive the horrors of prison life he must surely be a "creature who could withstand anything." The cruel irony which Dostoevsky overlooked is that the reality of prison bears witness not only to the resiliency and adaptiveness of the men who tolerate life within its walls, but as well to the "ingenuity" and tenacity of those who devised and still maintain our correctional and reformatory systems.

Nevertheless, in the century which has passed since Dostoevsky's imprisonment, little has changed to render the main thrust of his statement less relevant. Although we have passed through periods of enlightened humanitarian reform, in which physical conditions within prison have improved somewhat, and the rhetoric of rehabilitation has replaced the language of punitive incarceration, the social institution of prison has continued to fail. On purely pragmatic grounds, there is substantial evidence that prisons really neither "rehabilitate" nor act as a deterrent to future crime—in America, recidivism rates upwards of 75 percent speak quite decisively to these criteria. And, to perpetuate what is also an economic failure, American taxpayers alone must provide an expenditure for "corrections" of 1.5 billion dollars annually. On humanitarian grounds as well, prisons have failed: our mass media are increasingly filled with accounts of atrocities committed daily, man against man, in reaction to the penal system or in the name of it. The experience of prison creates undeniably, almost to the point of cliche, an intense hatred and disrespect in most inmates for the authority and the established order of society into which they will eventually return. And

[*] Craig Haney, Curtis Banks and Philip Zimbardo, A Study of Prisoners and Guards in a Simulated Prison, Naval Research Reviews, Volume XXVI, No. 9 (September 1973), pages 1-17.

the toll it takes in the deterioration of human spirit for those who must administer it, as well as for those upon whom it is inflicted, is incalculable.

Attempts to provide an explanation of the deplorable condition of our penal system and its dehumanizing effects upon prisoners and guards, often focus upon what might be called the *dispositional hypothesis*. While this explanation is rarely expressed explicitly, it is central to a prevalent nonconscious ideology: that the state of the social institution of prison is due to the "nature" of the people who administrate it, or the "nature" of the people who populate it, or both. That is, a major contributing cause to despicable conditions, violence, brutality, dehumanization and degradation existing within any prison can be traced to some innate or acquired characteristic of the correctional and inmate population. Thus on the one hand, there is the contention that violence and brutality exist within prison because guards are sadistic, uneducated, and insensitive people. It is the "guard mentality," a unique syndrome of negative traits which they bring into the situation, that engenders the inhumane treatment of prisoners. On the other hand, there is the argument that prison violence and brutality are the logical and predictable results of the involuntary confinement of a collective of individuals whose life histories are, by definition, characterized by disregard for law, order and social convention and a concurrent propensity for impulsivity and aggression. In seeming logic, it follows that these individuals, having proven themselves incapable of functioning satisfactorily within the "normal" structure of society, cannot do so either inside the structure provided by prisons. To control such men, the argument continues, whose basic orientation to any conflict situation is to react with physical power or deception, force must be met with force, and a certain number of violent encounters must be expected and tolerated by the public.

The dispositional hypothesis has been embraced by the proponents of the prison *status quo* (blaming conditions on the evil in the prisoners), as well as by its critics (attributing the evil to guards and staff with their evil motives and deficient personality structures). The appealing simplicity of this proposition localizes the source of prison riots, recidivism and corruption in these "bad seeds" and not in the conditions of the "prison soil." Such an analysis directs attention away from the complex matrix of social, economic and political forces that combine to make prisons what they are—and what would require complex, expensive, revolutionary actions to bring about any meaningful change. Instead, rioting prisoners are identified, punished, transferred to maximum security institutions or shot, outside agitators sought, and corrupt officials suspended—while the system itself goes on essentially unchanged, its basic structure unexamined and unchallenged.

However, the dispositional hypothesis cannot be critically evaluated directly through observation in existing prison settings, because such naturalistic observation necessarily confounds the acute effects of the environment with the chronic characteristics of the inmate and guard populations. To separate the effects of the prison environment *per se* from those attributable to *a priori* dispositions of its inhabitants requires a research strategy in which a "new" prison is constructed, comparable in its fundamental social psychological milieu to existing prison systems, but entirely populated by individuals who are undifferentiated in all essential dimensions from the rest of society.

Such was the approach taken in the present empirical study, namely, to create a prison-like situation in which the guards and inmates were initially comparable and characterized as being "normal-average," and then to observe the patterns of behavior which resulted, as well as the cognitive, emotional and attitudinal reactions which emerged. Thus, we began our experiment with a sample of individuals who were in the normal range of the general population on a variety of dimensions we were able to measure. Half were randomly assigned to the role of "prisoner," the others to that of "guard," neither group having any history of crime, emotional disability, physical handicap or even intellectual or social disadvantage.

The environment created was that of a "mock" prison which physically constrained the prisoners in barred cells and psychologically conveyed the sense of imprisonment to all participants. Our intention was not to create a *literal* simulation of an American prison, but rather a functional representation of one. For ethical, moral and pragmatic reasons we could not exercise the threat and promise of severe physical punishment, we could not allow homosexual or racist practices to flourish, nor could we duplicate certain other specific aspects of prison life. Nevertheless, we believed that we could create a situation with sufficient mundane realism to allow the role-playing participants to go beyond the superficial demands of their assignment into the deep structure of the characters they represented. To do so, we established functional equivalents for the activities and experiences of actual prison life which were expected to produce qualitatively similar psychological reactions in our subjects—feelings of power and powerlessness, of control and oppression, of satisfaction and frustration, of arbitrary rule and resistance to authority, of status and anonymity, of machismo and emasculation. In the conventional terminology of experimental social psychology, we first identified a number of relevant conceptual variables through analysis of existing prison situations, then designed a setting in which these variables were operationalized. No specific hypotheses were advanced other than the general one that assignment to the treatment of "guard" or "prisoner" would result in significantly different reactions on behavioral measures of interaction, emotional measures of mood state and pathology, attitudes toward self, as well as other indices of coping and adaptation to this novel situation. What follows is a discussion of how we created and peopled our prison, what we observed, what our subjects reported, and finally, what we can conclude about the nature of the prison environment and the psychology of imprisonment which can account for the failure of our prisons.

Method

Overview

The effects of playing the role of "guard" or "prisoner" were studied in the context of an experimental simulation of a prison environment. The research design was a relatively simple one, involving as it did only a single treatment variable, the random assignment to either a "guard" or "prisoner" condition. These roles were enacted over an extended period of time (nearly one week) within an environment that was physically constructed to resemble a prison. Central to the methodology of creating and maintaining a psychological state of imprisonment was the functional simulation of significant properties of "real prison life" (established through information from former inmates, correctional personnel and texts).

The "guards" were free within certain limits to implement the procedures of induction into the prison setting and maintenance of custodial retention of the "prisoners." These inmates, having voluntarily submitted to the conditions of this total institution in which they now lived, coped in various ways with its stresses and its challenges. The behavior of both groups of subjects was observed, recorded, and analyzed. The dependent measures were of two general types: (1) transactions between and within each group of subjects, recorded on video and audio tape as well as directly observed; (2) individual reactions on questionnaires, mood inventories, personality tests, daily guard shift reports, and post-experimental interviews.

Subjects

The 22 subjects who participated in the experiment were selected from an initial pool of 75 respondents, who answered a newspaper ad asking for male volunteers to participate in a psychological study of "prison life" in return for payment of $15 per day. Each respondent completed an extensive questionnaire concerning his family background, physical and mental health history, prior experience and attitudinal propensities with respect to sources of psychopathology (including their involvements in crime). Each respondent also was interviewed by one of two experimenters. Finally, the 24 subjects who were judged to be most stable (physically and mentally), most mature, and least involved in anti-social behaviors were selected to participate in the study. On a random basis, half of the subjects were assigned the role of "guard," half were assigned the role of "prisoner."

The subjects were normal, healthy, male college students who were in the Stanford area during the summer. They were largely of middle class socioeconomic status and Caucasians (with the exception of one Oriental subject). Initially they were strangers to each other, a selection precaution taken to avoid the disruption of any pre-existing friendship patterns and to mitigate any transfer into the experimental situation of previously established relationships or patterns of behavior.

This final sample of subjects was administered a battery of psychological tests on the day prior to the start of the simulation, but to avoid any selective bias on the part of the experimenter-observers, scores were not tabulated until the study was completed.

Two subjects who were assigned to be a "stand-by" in case an additional "prisoner" was needed were not called, and one assigned to be a "stand-by" guard decided against participating just before the simulation phase began—thus, our data analysis is based upon ten prisoners and eleven guards in our experimental conditions.

Procedure

Physical Aspects of the Prison

The prison was built in a 35-foot section of a basement corridor in the psychology building at Stanford University. It was partitioned by two fabricated walls; one was fitted with the only entrance door to the cell block and the other contained a small observation screen. Three small cells (6 x 9 ft.) were made from converted laboratory rooms by replacing the usual doors with steel barred, black painted ones, and removing all furniture.

A cot (with mattress, sheet and pillow) for each prisoner was the only furniture in the cells. A small closet across from the cells served as a solitary confinement facility; its dimensions were extremely small (2 x 2 x 7 ft.), and it was unlighted.

In addition, several rooms in an adjacent wing of the building were used as guards' quarters (to change in and out of uniform or for rest and relaxation), a bedroom for the "warden" and "superintendent," and an interview-testing room. Behind the observation screen at one end of the "yard" (small enclosed room representing the fenced prison grounds) was video recording equipment and sufficient space for several observers.

Operational Details

The "prisoner" subjects remained in the mock-prison 24 hours per day for the duration of the study. Three were arbitrarily assigned to each of the three cells; the others were on stand-by call at their homes. The "guard" subjects worked on three-man, eight-hour shifts; remaining in the prison environment only during their work shift and going about their usual lives at other times.

Role Instructions

All subjects had been told that they would be assigned either the guard or the prisoner role on a completely random basis and all had voluntarily agreed to play either role for $15.00 per day for up to two weeks. They signed a contract guaranteeing a minimally adequate diet, clothing, housing and medical care as well as the financial remuneration in return for their stated "intention" of serving in the assigned role for the duration of the study.

It was made explicit in the contract that those assigned to be prisoners should expect to be under surveillance (have little or no privacy) and to have some of their basic civil rights suspended during their imprisonment, excluding physical abuse. They were given no other information about what to expect nor instructions about behavior appropriate for a prisoner role. Those actually assigned to this treatment were informed by phone to be available at their place of residence on a given Sunday when we would start the experiment.

The subjects assigned to be guards attended an orientation meeting on the day prior to the induction of the prisoners. At this time they were introduced to the principal investigators, the "Superintendent" of the prison (the author) and an undergraduate research assistant who assumed the administrative role of "Warden." They were told that we wanted to try to simulate a prison environment within the limits imposed by pragmatic and ethical considerations. Their assigned task was to "maintain the reasonable degree of order within the prison necessary for its effective functioning," although the specifics of how this duty might be implemented were not explicitly detailed. They were made aware of the fact that, while many of the contingencies with which they might be confronted were essentially unpredictable (e.g., prisoner escape attempts), part of their task was to be prepared for such eventualities and to be able to deal appropriately with the variety of situations that might arise. The "Warden" instructed the guards in the administrative details, including: the work-shifts, the mandatory daily completion of "critical incident" reports which detailed unusual occurrences, and the administration of meals, work and recreation programs for the prisoners. In order to begin to involve these subjects in their roles even before the first prisoner was incarcerated, the guards assisted in the final phases of completing the prison complex—putting the cots in the cells, signs on the walls, setting up the guards' quarters, moving furniture, water coolers, refrigerators, etc.

The guards generally believed that we were primarily interested in studying the behavior of the prisoners. Of course, we were as interested in the effects which enacting the role of guard in this environment would have on their behavior and subjective states.

To optimize the extent to which their behavior would reflect their genuine reactions to the experimental prison situation and not simply their ability to follow instructions, they were intentionally given only minimal guidelines for what it meant to be a guard. An explicit and categorical prohibition against the use of physical punishment or physical aggression was, however, emphasized by the experimenters. Thus, with this single notable exception, their roles were relatively unstructured initially, requiring each "guard" to carry out activities necessary for interacting with a group of "prisoners" as well as with other "guards" and the "correctional staff."

Uniforms

In order to promote feelings of anonymity in the subjects each group was issued identical uniforms. For the guards, the uniform consisted of plain khaki shirts and trousers, a whistle, a police night-stick (wooden baton), and reflecting sunglasses which made eye contact impossible. The prisoners' uniform consisted of a loose fitting muslin smock with an identification number on front and back, no underclothes, a light chain and lock around one ankle, rubber sandals and a cap made from a nylon stocking. Each prisoner also was issued a toothbrush, soap, soapdish, towel and bed linen. No personal belongings were allowed in the cells.

The outfitting of both prisoners and guards in this manner served to enhance group identity and reduce individual uniqueness within the two groups. The khaki uniforms were intended to convey a military attitude, while the whistle and nightstick were carried as symbols of control and power. The prisoners' uniforms were designed not only to deindividuate the prisoners but to be humiliating and serve as symbols of their dependence and subservience. The ankle chain was a constant reminder (even during their sleep when it hit the other ankle) of the oppressiveness of the environment. The stocking cap removed any distinctiveness associated with hair length, color or style (as does shaving of heads in some "real" prisons and the military). The ill-fitting uniforms made the prisoners feel awkward in their movements; since these "dresses" were worn without undergarments, the uniforms forced them to assume unfamiliar postures, more like those of a woman than a man— another part of the emasculating process of becoming a prisoner.

Induction Procedure

With the cooperation of the Palo Alto City Police Department all of the subjects assigned to the prisoner treatment were unexpectedly "arrested" at their residences. A police officer charged them with suspicion of burglary or armed robbery, advised them of their legal rights, handcuffed them, thoroughly searched them (often as curious neighbors looked on) and carried them off to the police station in the rear of the police car. At the station they went through the standard routines of being fingerprinted, having an identification file prepared and then being placed in a detention cell. Each prisoner was blindfolded and subsequently driven by one of the experimenters and a subject-guard to our mock prison. Throughout the entire arrest procedure, the police officers involved maintained a formal, serious attitude, avoiding answering any questions of clarification as to the relation of this "arrest" to the mock prison study.

Upon arrival at our experimental prison, each prisoner was stripped, sprayed with a delousing preparation (a deodorant spray) and made to stand alone naked for a while in the cell yard. After being given the uniform described previously and having an I.D. picture taken ("mug shot"), the prisoner was put in his cell and ordered to remain silent.

Administrative Routine

When all the cells were occupied, the warden greeted the prisoners and read them the rules of the institution (developed by the guards and the warden). They were to be memorized and to be followed. Prisoners were to be referred to only by the number on their uniforms, also in an effort to depersonalize them.

The prisoners were to be served three bland meals per day, were allowed three supervised toilet visits, and given two hours daily for the privilege of reading or letterwriting. Work assignments were issued for which the prisoners were to receive an hourly wage to constitute their $15 daily payment. Two visiting periods per week were scheduled, as were movie rights and exercise periods. Three times a day prisoners were lined up for a "count" (one on each guard work-shift). The initial purpose of the "count" was to ascertain that all prisoners were present, and to test them on their knowledge of the rules and their I.D. numbers. The first perfunctory counts lasted only about ten minutes, but on each successive day (or night) they were spontaneously increased in duration until some lasted several hours. Many of the preestablished features of administrative routine were modified or abandoned by the guards, and some privileges were forgotten by the staff over the course of the study.

Results

Overview

Although it is difficult to anticipate exactly what the influence of incarceration will be upon the individuals who are subjected to it and those charged with its maintenance, especially in a simulated reproduction, the results of the present experiment support many commonly held conceptions of prison life and validate anecdotal evidence supplied by articulate ex-convicts. The environment of arbitrary custody had great impact upon the affective states of both guards and prisoners as well as upon the interpersonal processes taking place between and within those role-groups.

In general, guards and prisoners showed a marked tendency toward increased negativity of affect, and their overall outlook became increasingly negative. As the experiment progressed, prisoners expressed intentions to do harm to others more frequently. For both prisoners and guards, self-evaluations were more deprecating as the experience of the prison environment became internalized.

Overt behavior was generally consistent with the subjective self-reports and affective expressions of the subjects. Despite the fact that guards and prisoners were essentially free to engage in any form of interaction (positive or negative, supportive or affrontive, etc.), the characteristic nature of their encounters tended to be negative, hostile, affrontive and dehumanizing. Prisoners immediately adopted a generally passive response mode while guards assumed a very active initiative role in all interactions. Throughout the experiment, commands were the most frequent form of verbal behavior and, generally, verbal exchanges were strikingly impersonal, with few references to individual identity. Although it was clear to all subjects that the experimenters would not permit physical violence to take place, varieties of less direct aggressive behavior were observed frequently (especially on the part of guards). In lieu of physical violence, verbal affronts were used as one of the most frequent forms of interpersonal contact between guards and prisoners.

The most dramatic evidence of the impact of this situation upon the participants was seen in the gross reactions of five prisoners who had to be released because of extreme emotional depression, crying, rage and acute anxiety. The pattern of symptoms was quite similar in four of the subjects and began as early as the second day of imprisonment. The fifth subject was released after being treated for a psychosomatic rash which covered portions of his body. Of the remaining prisoners, only two said they were not willing to forfeit the money they had earned in return for being "paroled." When the experiment was terminated prematurely after only six days, all the remaining prisoners were delighted by their unexpected good fortune. In contrast, most of the guards seemed to be distressed by the decision to stop the experiment and it appeared to us that they had become sufficiently involved in their roles that they now enjoyed the extreme control and power which they exercised and were reluctant to give it up. One guard did report being personally upset at the suffering of the prisoners, and claimed to have considered asking to change his role to become one of them—but never did so. None of the guards ever failed to come to work on time for their shift, and indeed, on several occasions guards remained on duty voluntarily and uncomplaining for extra hours—without additional pay.

The extremely pathological reactions which emerged in both groups of subjects testify to the power of the social forces operating, but still there were individual differences seen in styles of coping with this novel experience and in degrees of successful adaptation to it. Half the prisoners did endure the oppressive atmosphere, and not all the guards resorted to hostility. Some guards were tough but fair ("played by the rules"), some went far beyond their roles to engage in creative cruelty and harassment, while a few were passive and rarely instigated any coercive control over the prisoners.

Reality of the Simulation

At this point it seems necessary to confront the critical question of "reality" in the simulated prison environment: were the behaviors observed more than the mere acting out of assigned roles convincingly? To be sure, ethical, legal and practical considerations set limits upon the degree to which this situation could approach the conditions existing in actual prisons and penitentiaries. Necessarily absent were some of the most salient aspects of prison life reported by criminologists and documented in the writing of prisoners. There was no involuntary homosexuality, no racism, no physical beatings, no threat to life by prisoners against each other or the guards. Moreover, the maximum anticipated "sentence" was only two weeks and, unlike some prison systems, could not be extended indefinitely for infractions of the internal operating rules of the prison.

In one sense, the profound psychological effects we observed under the relatively minimal prison-like conditions which existed in our mock prison made the results even more significant, and force us to wonder about the devastating impact of chronic incarceration in real prisons. Nevertheless, we must contend with the criticism that our conditions were too minimal to provide a meaningful analogue to existing prisons. It is necessary to demonstrate that the participants in this experiment transcended the conscious limits of their preconceived stereotyped roles and their awareness of the artificiality and limited duration of imprisonment. We feel there is abundant evidence that virtually all of the subjects at one time or another experienced reactions which went well beyond the surface demands of role-playing and penetrated the deep structure of the psychology of imprisonment.

Although instructions about how to behave in the roles of guard or prisoner were not explicitly defined, demand characteristics in the experiment obviously exerted some directing influence. Therefore, it is enlightening to look to circumstances where role demands were minimal, where the subjects believed they were not being observed, or where they should not have been behaving under the constraints imposed by their roles (as in "private" situations), in order to assess whether the role behaviors reflected anything more than public conformity or good acting.

When the private conversations of the prisoners were monitored, we learned that almost all (a full 90 percent) of what they talked about was directly related to immediate prison conditions, that is, food, privileges, punishment, guard harassment, etc. Only one-tenth of the time did their conversations deal with their life outside the prison. Consequently, although they had lived together under such intense conditions, the prisoners knew surprisingly little about each other's past history or future plans. This excessive concentration on the vicissitudes of their current situation helped to make the prison experience more oppressive for the prisoners because, instead of escaping from it when they had a chance to do so in the privacy of their cells, the prisoners continued to allow it to dominate their thoughts and social relations. The guards too, rarely exchanged personal information during their relaxation breaks. They either talked about "problem prisoners," other prison topics, or did not talk at all. There were few instances of any personal communication across the two role groups. Moreover, when prisoners referred to other prisoners during interviews, they typically deprecated each other, seemingly adopting the guards' negative attitude.

From post-experimental data, we discovered that when individual guards were alone with solitary prisoners and out of range of any recording equipment, as on the way to or in the toilet, harassment often was greater than it was on the "Yard." Similarly, video-taped analyses of total guard aggression showed a daily escalation even after most prisoners had ceased resisting and prisoner deterioration had become visibly obvious to them. Thus, guard aggression was no longer elicited as it was initially in response to perceived threats, but was emitted simply as a "natural" consequence of being in the uniform of a "guard" and asserting the power inherent in that role. In specific instances we noted cases of a guard (who did not know he was being observed) in the early morning hours pacing the Yard as the prisoners slept—vigorously pounding his night stick into his hand while he "kept watch" over his captives. Or another guard who detained an "incorrigible" prisoner in solitary confinement beyond the duration set by the guards' own rules and then conspired to keep him in the hole all night while attempting to conceal this information from the experimenters who were thought to be too soft on the prisoners.

In passing we may note an additional point about the nature of role-playing and the extent to which actual behavior is "explained away" by reference to it. It will be recalled that many guards continued to intensify their harassment and aggressive behavior even after the second day of the study, when prisoner deterioration became marked and visible and emotional breakdowns began to occur (in the presence of the guards). When questioned after the study about their persistent affrontive and harassing behavior in the face of prisoner emotional trauma, most guards replied that they were "just playing the role" of a tough guard, although none ever doubted the magnitude or validity of the prisoners' emotional response. The reader may wish to consider to what extremes an individual may go, how great must be the consequences of his behavior for others, before he can no longer rightfully attribute his actions to "playing a role" and thereby abdicate responsibility.

When introduced to a Catholic priest, many of the role-playing prisoners referred to themselves by their prison numbers rather than their Christian names. Some even asked him to get a lawyer to help them get out. When a public defender was summoned to interview those prisoners who had not yet been released, almost all of them strenuously demanded that he "bail" them out immediately.

One of the most remarkable incidents of the study occurred during a parole board hearing when each of five prisoners eligible for parole was asked by the senior author whether he would be willing to forfeit all the money earned as a prisoner if he were to be paroled (released from the study). Three of the five prisoners said, "yes," they would be willing to do this. Notice that the original incentive for participating in the study had been the promise of money, and they were, after only four days, prepared to give this up completely. And, more suprisingly, when told that this possibility would have to be discussed with the members of the staff before a decision could be made, each prisoner got up quietly and was escorted by a guard back to his cell. If they regarded themselves simply as "subjects" participating in an experiment for money, there was no longer any incentive to remain in the study and they could have easily escaped this situation which had so clearly become aversive for them by quitting. Yet, so powerful was the control which the situation had come to have over them, so much a reality had this simulated environment become, that they were unable to see that their original and singular motive for remaining no longer obtained, and they returned to their cells to await a "parole" decision by their captors.

The reality of the prison was also attested to by our prison consultant who had spent over 16 years in prison, as well as the priest who had been a prison chaplain and the public defender, all of whom were brought into direct contact with our simulated prison environment. Further, the depressed affect of the prisoners, the guards' willingness to work overtime for no additional pay, the spontaneous use of prison titles and I.D. numbers in non-role-related situations all point to a level of reality as real as any other in the lives of all those who shared this experience.

To understand how an illusion of imprisonment could have become so real, we need now to consider the uses of power by the guards as well as the effects of such power in shaping the prisoner mentality.

Pathology of Power

Being a guard carried with it social status within the prison, a group identity (when wearing the uniform), and above all, the freedom to exercise an unprecedented degree of control over the lives of other human beings. This control was invariably expressed in terms of sanctions, punishment, demands, and with the threat of manifest physical power. There was no need for the guards to rationally justify a request as they did in their ordinary life, and merely to make a demand was sufficient to have it carried out. Many of the guards showed in their behavior and revealed in post-experimental statements that this sense of power was exhilarating.

The use of power was self-aggrandizing and self-perpetuating. The guard power, derived initially from an arbitrary and randomly assigned label, was intensified whenever there was any perceived threat by the prisoners and this new level subsequently became the baseline from which further hostility and harassment would begin. The most hostile guards on each shift moved spontaneously into the leadership roles of giving orders and deciding on punishments. They became role models whose behavior was emulated by other members of the shift. Despite minimal contact between the three separate guard shifts and nearly 16 hours a day spent away from the prison, the absolute level of aggression, as well as more subtle and "creative" forms of aggression manifested, increased in a spiralling function. Not to be tough and arrogant was to be seen as a sign of weakness by the guards, and even those "good" guards who did not get as drawn into the power syndrome as the others respected the implicit norm of *never* contradicting or even interfering with an action of a more hostile guard on their shift.

After the first day of study, practically all prisoner rights (even such things as the time and conditions of sleeping and eating) came to be redefined by the guards as "privileges" which were to be earned by obedient behavior. Constructive activities such as watching movies or reading (previously planned and suggested by the experimenters) were arbitrarily cancelled until further notice by the guards—and were subsequently never allowed. "Reward" then became granting approval for prisoners to eat, sleep, go to the toilet, talk, smoke a cigarette, wear eyeglasses, or the temporary diminution of harassment. One wonders about the conceptual nature of "positive" reinforcement when subjects are in such conditions of deprivation, and the extent to which even minimally acceptable conditions become rewarding when experienced in the context of such an impoverished environment.

We might also question whether there are meaningful non-violent alternatives as models for behavior modification in real prisons. In a world where men are either powerful or powerless, everyone learns to despise the lack of power in others and in oneself. It seems to us, that prisoners learn to admire power for its own sake—power becoming the ultimate reward. Real prisoners soon learn the means to gain power whether through ingratiation, informing, sexual control of other prisoners or development of powerful cliques. When they are released from prison, it is likely they will never want to feel so powerless again and will take action to establish and assert a sense of power.

The Pathological Prisoner Syndrome

Various coping strategies were employed by our prisoners as they began to react to their perceived loss of personal identity and the arbitrary control of their lives. At first they exhibited disbelief at the total invasion of their privacy, constant surveillance, and atmosphere of oppression in which they were living. Their next response was rebellion, first by the use of direct force, and later by subtle divisive tactics designed to foster distrust among the prisoners. They then tried to work within the system by setting up an elected grievance committee. When that collective action failed to produce meaningful changes in their existence, individual self-interests emerged. The breakdown in prisoner cohesion was the start of social disintegration which gave rise not only to feelings of isolation, but deprecation of other prisoners as well. As noted before, half the prisoners coped with the prison situation by becoming "sick"—extremely disturbed emotionally—as a passive way of demanding attention and help. Others became excessively obedient in trying to be "good" prisoners. They sided with the guards against a solitary fellow prisoner who coped with his situation by refusing to eat. Instead of supporting this final and major act of rebellion, the prisoners treated him as a troublemaker who deserved to be punished for his disobedience. It is likely that the negative self-regard among the prisoners noted by the end of the study was the product of their coming to believe that the continued hostility toward all of them was justified because they "deserved it" (following Walster, 1966). As the days wore on, the model prisoner reaction was one of passivity, dependence, and flattened affect.

Let us briefly consider some of the relevant processes involved in bringing about these reactions.

Loss of personal identity. For most people identity is conferred by social recognition of one's uniqueness and established through one's name, dress, appearance, behavior style, and history. Living among strangers who do not know your name or history (who refer to you only by number), dressed in a uniform exactly like all other prisoners, not wanting to call attention to oneself because of the unpredictable consequences it might provoke—all led to a weakening of self-identity among the prisoners. As they began to lose initiative and emotional responsivity, while acting ever more compliantly, indeed, the prisoners became deindividuated not only to the guards and the observers, but also to themselves.

Arbitrary control. In post-experimental questionnaires, the most frequently mentioned aversive aspect of the prison experience was that of being subjugated to the patently arbitrary, capricious decisions and rules of the guards. A question by a prisoner as often elicited derogation and aggression as it did a rational answer. Smiling at a joke could be punished in the same way that failing to smile might be. An individual acting in defiance of the rules could bring punishment to innocent cell partners (who became, in effect, "mutually yoked controls"), to himself, or to all.

As the environment became more unpredictable, and previously learned assumptions about a just and orderly world were no longer functional, prisoners ceased to initiate any action. They moved about on orders and when in their cells rarely engaged in any purposeful activity. Their zombie-like reaction was the functional equivalent of the learned helplessness phenomenon reported by Seligman & Groves (1970). Since their behavior did not seem to have any contingent relationship to environmental consequences, the prisoners essentially gave up and stopped behaving. Thus the subjective magnitude of aversiveness was manipulated by the guards not in terms of physical punishment but rather by controlling the psychological dimension of environmental predictability (Glass & Singer, 1972).

Dependency and emasculation. The network of dependency relations established by the guards not only promoted helplessness in the prisoners but served to emasculate them as well. The arbitrary control by the guards put the prisoners at their mercy for even the daily, commonplace functions like going to the toilet. To do so, required publicly obtained permission (not always granted) and then a personal escort to the toilet while blindfolded and handcuffed. The same was true for many other activities ordinarily practiced spontaneously without thought, such as lighting a cigarette, reading a novel, writing a letter, drinking a glass of water, or brushing one's teeth. These were all privileged activities requiring permission and necessitating a prior show of good behavior. These low level dependencies engendered a regressive orientation in the prisoners. Their dependency was defined in terms of the extent of the domain of control over all aspects of their lives which they allowed other individuals (the guards and prison staff) to exercise.

As in real prisons, the assertive, independent, aggressive nature of male prisoners posed a threat which was overcome by a variety of tactics. The prisoner uniforms resembled smocks or dresses, which made them look silly and enabled the guards to refer to them as "sissies" or "girls." Wearing these uniforms without any underclothes forced the prisoners to move and sit in unfamiliar, feminine postures. Any sign of individual rebellion was labelled as indicative of "incorrigibility" and resulted in loss of privileges, solitary confinement, humiliation, or punishment of cell mates. Physically smaller guards were able to induce stronger prisoners to act foolishly and obediently. Prisoners were encouraged to belittle each other publicly during the counts. These and other tactics all served to engender in the prisoners a lessened sense of their masculinity (as defined by their external culture). It followed then, that although the prisoners usually outnumbered the guards during line-ups and counts (nine vs. three) there never was an attempt to directly overpower them. (Interestingly, after the study was terminated, the prisoners expressed the belief that the basis for assignment to guard and prisoner groups was physical size. They perceived the guards were "bigger," when, in fact, there was no difference in average height or weight between these randomly determined groups.)

In conclusion, we believe this demonstration reveals new dimensions in the social psychology of imprisonment worth pursuing in future research. In addition, this research provides a paradigm and information base for studying alternatives to existing guard training, as well as for questioning the basic operating principles on which penal institutions rest. If our mock prison could generate the extent of pathology it did in such a short time, then the punishment of being imprisoned in a real prison does not "fit the crime" for most prisoners—indeed, it far exceeds it! Moreover, since both prisoners and guards are locked into a dynamic, symbiotic relationship which is destructive to their human nature, guards are also society's prisoners.

References

Adorno, T.W., Frenkel-Brunswik, E., Levinson, D.J., and Sanford, R.N. The authoritarian personality. New York: Harper, 1950.

Charriere, H. Papillon. Robert Laffont, 1969.

Cristie, R., and Geis, F.L. (Eds.) Studies in machiavellianism. New York: Academic Press, 1970.

Comrey, A.L. Comrey personality scales. San Diego: Educational and Industrial Testing Service, 1970.

Glass, D.C., and Singer, J.E. Behavioral after-effects of unpredictable and uncontrollable aversive events. American Scientist, 1972, 6, No. 4, 457–465.

Jackson, G. Soledad brother: The prison letters of George Jackson. New York: Bantam Books, 1970.

Milgram, S. Some conditions of obedience and disobedience to authority. Human Relations, 1965, 18, No. 1, 57–76.

Mischel, W. Personality and assessment. New York: Wiley, 1968.

Schein, E. Coercive persuasion. New York: Norton, 1961.

Seligman, M.E. and Groves, D.P. Nontransient learned helplessness. Psychonomic Science, 1970, 19, No. 3, 191–192.

Walster, E. Assignment of responsibility for an accident. Journal of Personality and Social Psychology, 1966, 3, No. 1, 73–79.

Katz v. Superior Court
73 Cal. App. 3d 952 (1977)

Sims, Acting P.J.

The proceedings reviewed below were instituted in this court on March 25, 1977, by a petition for extraordinary relief in the nature of prohibition and mandamus filed on behalf of five adults who were each the subject of a substantially identical order appointing a parent or both parents as temporary conservator of the petitioner. They sought an alternative writ which, after hearing, would lead to a peremptory writ that would prohibit continuing the orders in force, or which, in the alternative, would prohibit the respective temporary conservators from subjecting their respective temporary conservatees to the process of "deprogramming." In response to a further prayer in the petition, and after reviewing opposition filed by the conservators, on March 28, 1977, we issued a stay, pending determination of the petition, which substantially modified the powers of the temporary conservators.
. . .

In examining the contentions made in support of the petition we find that the former provisions of section 1751 of the Probate Code, which the temporary conservators relied upon in these proceedings, were too vague to justify the appointment of temporary conservators of the persons as granted herein; that the former statutes did not authorize the appointments, as made by the court, under the most favorable interpretation of the evidence; and that under the circumstances of this case it was a violation of the petitioners' rights to religious freedom to appoint temporary conservators of their persons under the provisions of the Probate Code. . . .

The record reflects that the petitions for appointment were entitled "Application For Appointment Of A Guardian (Conservator) Of The Person." Each alleged in pertinent part: "The appointment request for the proposed ward is required because of mental illness or weakness and unsound mind. The proposed ward is unable to properly care for the person or the property of the proposed ward and is likely to be deceived by artful and designing persons."

Simultaneously the parents each filed an "Application For Appointment Of Temporary Guardianship (Conservatorship) Of The Person And For The Powers To Remove Said Person From Custody Of A Certain Group And Place With Petitioner." Each application alleged in pertinent part, "[T]he proposed ward is 21 years old. The appointment for a temporary guardian of the person until a permanent guardian is appointed is necessary because Petitioner is informed and believes and thereon alleges, that said proposed ward is deprived of the ability to manage his person, is likely to be deceived by persons of artful and cunning design, and is in grave need of immediate psychiatric or other counseling"; and "The temporary Guardian of the person should be given powers to take said proposed ward into personal custody, and then examined by a physician of the temporary guardian's choice, including, but not limited to, psychiatrists, psychologist social workers, lay persons, etc., and to resist any attempts by the proposed ward or others to remove said proposed ward from proposed Guardian's care." The petitions all alleged and the record reflects that the petitioners in this matter were all adults over the age of 21 years.

We therefore are concerned only with those former provisions of section 1751 which provided that the court "shall appoint a conservator of the . . . person . . . [first] of any adult person who by reason of advanced age, *illness,* injury, *mental weakness,* intemperance, addiction to drugs or other disability, *or other cause* is unable properly to care for himself or for his property, or [second] who *for said causes or for any other cause is likely to be deceived or imposed upon by artful or designing persons."* (Italics added.)

The court's orders following the hearing contain no findings of fact which would disclose the ground or grounds on which the orders were based. In announcing its decisions the trial court gave no clue to what facts he considered were established by the evidence. The petitioners point out that there is nothing to show that the petitioners were unable to care for themselves, and that there was only limited evidence to show that care of property was involved, and that issue was not directly raised. They conclude that the appointments must stand, if at all, on the second ground, and that it is unconstitutionally vague as applied in the circumstances of this case. . . .

As applied in the present case an individual seeking salvation through religion or associating in a social or political cause cannot tell whether or not he will be placed in the custody of another on charges that he has been deceived by artful and designing persons. When such charges are laid, the court or jury in examining the precepts and associates selected by the proposed conservatee has no better standards under which to evaluate the latter's conduct. Finally, there may be severe inroads on the individual's freedom to practice his religion, and to associate with whom he pleases because of the threat of proceedings such as this.

Although the words "likely to be deceived or imposed upon by artful or designing persons" may have some meaning when applied to the loss of property which can be measured, they are too vague to be applied in the world of ideas. In an age of subliminal advertising, television exposure, and psychological salesmanships, everyone is exposed to artful and designing persons at every turn. It is impossible to measure the degree of likelihood that some will succumb. In the field of beliefs, and particularly religious tenets, it is difficult, if not impossible, to establish a universal truth against which deceit and imposition can be measured. . . .

In view of the values involved we conclude that the provisions of section 1751 as it read prior to July 1, 1977, were too vague to be applied in proceedings to deprive an adult of his freedom of action as proposed by the parents in this case. If there was mental deterioration, proceedings under the Welfare and Institutions Code were available. If there was duress or physical restraint criminal sanctions should have been sought. . . .

The case was heard for over two weeks and resulted in a reporter's transcript of almost 1,700 pages. The parents offered the testimony of the mother and father of one of the proposed conservatees who later recanted. It was stipulated that the declarations of the other parents would be received in evidence. They also produced two former members of the Unification Church, and a psychiatrist and a psychologist. Each of the proposed conservatees, the original petitioners here, testified in opposition to the petitions, and a psychiatrist, a psychologist, and two persons who had been subjected to deprogramming testified on their behalf.

[T]he court, on a motion of local counsel for the parents, there being no objection, permitted two Arizona attorneys to join in presenting the case. The framework of the case was announced in the opening statement as follows: "Our goal here is, of course, to obtain temporary conservatorships of five young adults for a period of thirty days. . . . [¶] I think each of them are in the courtroom here today, sitting near their parents. [¶] Our contention, our allegation and our proof will demonstrate that these young adults, individuals, are the victims of artful and designing persons, that is to say, specifically of the leadership of the New Educational Development which is a front organization for the Unification Church. [¶] The factors which will be demonstrated through this proceeding are that the following items have been utilized on these young individuals to one extent or another, at one time or another during this programming: Food deprivation; sleep deprivation; isolation; the use of fear tactics; the use of guilt feelings, and indoctrination, the same tactics used on our prisoners of war during the Korean War crises. [¶] As a loose definition of what these items constitute, it is oftentimes referred to as 'coercive conversion' or 'thought reform,' or commonly referred to as 'brainwashing,' which of course is a very elusive term in our society today because of the quantitative and qualitative nature of brainwashing. . . . [¶] It is our position that the proof will demonstrate that these people are victims of artful and designing persons due to coercive conversion which is oftentimes referred to as thought control, thought reform, or brainwashing. [¶] As a loose definition of what I referred to by the word 'brainwashing' or 'coercive conversion' I mean generally, and it will be more specifically explained by the medical personnel which we will present, as being basically behavior of an individual, determined not by his own internal decision, but rather by coercion from outside forces, and specifically in this case, through the use of fear and guilt tactics. [¶] The facts we will prove are that these five young adult individuals are victims of artful and designing persons. . . . [¶] In terms of solution our evidence, specifically through our medical personnel, will indicate that the solution to this problem lies in reality-inducing therapy which consists of adequate food, sleep, books to read on coercive persuasion, and the ability to have opportunities to speak with former cult members. . . . [¶] Additionally our evidence will show these young people are victims of psychological kidnaping, and that basically for the most part they are young, idealistic and naive individuals. [¶] There is no crime against brainwashing, and this [is] why we have turned to this Court. And our evidence will show even the initial recruitment of these individuals was through deceit."

The father of petitioner Underwood, who has recanted, testified to personality changes in his 25-year-old daughter during the four years she had been a member of the Unification Church. He stated: "Her demeanor was quite different than it had been before. [¶] Whereas before she was open and curious and very interested in all kinds of ideas, political and social, she was no longer, after she was in the movement, interested in all those things. [¶] She became somewhat child-like in her belief and acceptance of this unitary system of beliefs, and her interests were almost totally devoted to that system of beliefs, to the exclusion of virtually all else, and she had had very broad interests before. [¶] So her demeanor was, I would say, child-like, broad, somewhat artificially cheerful I felt at times in making the best of everything, whereas before she felt free to be somewhat critical of things that impinged on her life adversely." He also noted a change in her cultural interests, hobbies, in her vocational goals and objectives, in her participation in civic activities, and in her voice which became high-pitched rather than hoarse. He opined that she was being imposed upon because she was devoting all her time, many hours a day, to raising funds for the movement without receiving any compensation personally other than minimal food and a place to put down a sleeping bag.

On cross-examination he acknowledged that his daughter looked healthy at the hearing, and had always appeared to be when they had visited in the previous year. He further stated: "I think she has her own mind, but I think it is controlled like someone under hypnosis; and in certain areas, she cannot function as an independent human being."

Mrs. Underwood testified in similar vein regarding the changes in her daughter's personality. She opined that her daughter was incapable of freely arriving at a decision.

A former member of the Unification Church testified that he joined while a student at the University of California in Berkeley; that he was at times a director of the church seminar and training camp in Booneville, manager of its coffee restaurant in Oakland, and a staff member of the Bay Area Unification Church and its affiliated New Ideal Development; and that he had been a leader of fund raising teams in Berkeley and around the country. He stated that he left the church in December 1976, following a temporary conservatorship in which he experienced therapy counseling which enabled him to see certain deceptive practices of the Unification Church. He explained the treatment he received. He opined that previously he would not freely have chosen to leave because when he had any doubts about the group, he was taught to and did attribute it to his inability to do or appreciate what was right.

He stated he became interested in the group in response to representatives of what purported to be "International Ideal City Project," and only later found out it was a religious organization and was known as the Unification Church. Among the other practices of which he complained were peer pressure; negating the value of the individual so that identity existed only in relationship to the group; a tremendous polarization of thinking to see the world in terms of good and evil, with goodness existing only within the confines and actions of the group itself, and everything outside evil and Satanic. He referred to tactics of "mind control" which he defined as "a situation where a set of beliefs or doctrines are imposed upon a person through a process of either isolation or force, or using tactics of fear and guilt to impose these ideas on a person so they become unquestionable or unimpeachable." The witness testified that the daily objectives of the group were to make money and bring in new members. He acknowledged that the overall objectives of the Unification Church were to establish a heavenly kingdom on earth, to obtain all the worldly material so Reverend Moon has all the power and wealth of the world in his hands.

He explained the arduous routine followed by fund raising teams—from 7 a.m. to 1 a.m., six days a week. The court refused to permit inquiry regarding what the church did with its collection. He testified that "New Educational Development" was another offshoot of the church and that such names were used to overcome the reluctance of some prospects to at first attend dinners or seminars held by the church. According to him he worked long hours to raise money to pay for various facilities the Unification Church was purchasing throughout the country, large training centers, large estates, beautiful homes, and personal jewelry, fur coats and cars for the leaders; and that he was under emotional and psychological pressure to fulfill a responsibility to make money for the Reverend Moon and the Unification Church in order to establish a heavenly kingdom on earth. He felt compelled to follow the religious and political teachings of Reverend Moon.

A second former member of the church from 1972 to 1976 testified that he directed church operations in the State of Pennsylvania in 1973, was lecturer on the staff of the Tarrytown, New York Center in 1974-1975, and assistant director of planning and development for the Unification Church Seminary in 1975, where he had been a student and teaching assistant responsible for recruiting faculty and teaching them some of the ideas of the movement. In 1976 he worked as editor of a propaganda magazine known as "New World." He was among the hierarchy on the East Coast. He left the church because after a court proceeding he learned facts about the church and the techniques of mental subversion that had been practiced on him. At the time of the hearing he was the director of the Freedom Ranch Rehabilitation Center of the Freedom of Thought Foundation at Tucson, Arizona.

He explained these techniques as follows: A very strong isolation of the individual from his home, from his friends, and even from his own mind; a completely structured program from 7 a.m. to 12:30 or 1 a.m. at night; every single activity a person engaged in— including washing, exercising, eating, going to lectures, participating in sports—was done by a group, and a person was given no free time whatsoever; an intense schedule and a deluge of religious concepts which left the participant confused and too fatigued at the end of the day to reflect on the day's activities and lectures; a limited amount of sleep and food which left the participants sluggish; and the inculcation of a feeling of personal guilt if the participant doubted or failed to follow the teachings.

He explained the deprogramming routine and acknowledged that those subjected to it were told that they could not leave and should stay and listen to the deprogrammers.

The psychiatrist, who jointly with a psychologist examined the proposed conservatees on behalf of the petitioning parents, testified that he took a history from the parents and from the individual examined, and based his findings on those histories and his observations in the course of an hour and a quarter or so interview and confrontation with the subject. His findings, to which he also testified, were incorporated in a written statement prepared at the request of the attorney for the parents to determine in his opinion if five members of the Unification Church were under the influence of coercive persuasion which would render them vulnerable to artful and designing persons. It reads:

> It is my opinion that all five of these well-meaning, well-intentioned young people—Jan Kaplan, Leslie Brown, John Hovard, Jacqueline Katz and Barbara Underwood—have several symptoms which are not present in the average individual of their ages and background.

During my interviews with them, it was as though these individuals responded to a pre-set (i.e., there was an effort made to answer all questions out of a limited set of answers). This limited set of answers appeared to be alien or inconsistent with those of their non-cult peers.

They all suffered from gross lack of information regarding current events; they all seemed to be preoccupied with a concern about their selfishness, but all reported that they worked as much as twenty hours a day.

They all showed a moderate degree of memory impairment, especially about their childhoods; their functional vocabulary in terms of the words that they used during the interview was limited and constricted.

Their affects were blunted, emotionality frozen in a child-like inappropriate smile to all input, whether it be hostile or otherwise.

They were all wide-eyed, had short attention spans and a decreased ability to concentrate.

They were all vague, with limited ability towards abstractions; they were full of inconsistencies, contradictions and confabulations when pressured.

They uniformly held that the Unification Church was not responsible for anything unless it was positive.

They had very little concern for previous and future personal goals; they were paranoid about previous relationships, and had defensive attitudes toward id urges.

Their inner sense of authority was lost, and all responded as if they were influenced by an outside authority.

They all showed various degrees of regression and child-like attitudes, especially when stressed.

In general, they did not respond as one would expect from their background and personality types.

He further stated that the symptoms he found were the result of "coercive persuasion." He explained that by "coercive persuasion" he meant a series of techniques principally introduced to this country by the prisoners of war who returned from the Korean War and the Vietnamese conflicts; and that is a term used by professionals to explain what the laymen call "brainwashing." He stated that it is the result of a systematic ritualistic procedure that people undergo who usually are in captivity, until they basically take on the identity of the individuals that they are around; that the captor or dominant individual reinforces this by either withholding food or withholding sleep, by initiating anxiety and fear, by essentially controlling the individual until that person loses his own identity and takes up the identity of the individuals that they are involved with; that many times the individuals are hypnotized and are objects of hypnosis and autohypnosis where certain key phrases and certain words will trigger a certain kind of thought pattern within the individual.

He testified that Miss Underwood was not psychotic, that she did not have any symptoms of a standard medical diagnosis of mental disturbance, and that she was not hypnotized. He did conclude that her symptoms were consistent with those of an individual who had been subjected to coercive persuasion, and that she was likely to be deceived by artful and designing persons. He also opined that she required immediate psychiatric treatment because she was in an abnormal situation and she should not be further exposed to it. He stated that it was difficult to predict for lack of data what the outcome would be but he believed that from long exposure Miss Underwood's symptoms were more stationary and severe than the others. He acknowledged, however, that he could not tell from his examination whether there would be an abrupt change in her mental status over the ensuing 30 days, and that there was no indication that there would be a rapid deterioration in her mental state during that period.

The doctor stated that Hovard was the most disturbed of the five individuals he examined, and that he had some concerns about his mental health. He opined that whether Hovard's mental health would deteriorate in the ensuing 30 to 60 days would depend on the stress he was subjected to. With respect to Miss Brown, the doctor testified that her mental, emotional state would not substantially deteriorate within the ensuing 30 to 60 days if she remained with the organization. With respect to Miss Kaplan, the doctor stated that he was doubtful, and it was possible her mental or emotional state could deteriorate if she were left in her former environment. He generally stated that it would not be in the best interests of the health of any of the five to continue whatever it was they were doing for the next six months, and that he felt this most strongly with respect to Hovard.

A qualified clinical psychologist who had done research in the field of repatriated prisoners of war and interned civilians from the Korean War, also testified for the parents on the results of the joint examination. She testified that pictures drawn by the young adults at her request at the conclusion of the interview displayed the characteristics of pictures drawn by prisoners of war who had been subjected to coercive persuasion. On the basis of the drawings, the history received from the parents and their offspring, her interviews of from 40 to 50 former young adults who had been members of the Unification Church, and her examination of proposed conservatees, she stated that each was the victim of artful and designing persons as a result of the coercive persuasion to which he or she had been subjected during the time they were in the Unification Church; that there was an emergency situation and they all were in need of treatment; and that only reality therapy as was provided by the staff of Freedom Ranch was appropriate. In each case the psychologist found a generally impaired level of functioning, and an unwillingness to make evaluative statements or comparisons, which reflected an impairment of judgment.

She acknowledged that what she observed and found did not fit into any class under headings offered in a standard psychiatric and psychological diagnostic and statistical manual; and that the constraint attendant to the treatment program did not involve a psychiatric problem. She at first studiously avoided testifying that the Unification Church practiced coercive persuasion, but consistently referred to the personal experiences of persons whom she had studied and of the conservatees while with members of the church as consistent with those used for coercive persuasion. She did finally opine on the basis of that data that the Unification Church practiced coercive persuasion on its members. She concluded that in a broad sense that church was a religion, but in a limited sense it was not.

The proposed conservatees each testified in opposition to the parent's petitions. Each sought to follow the beliefs and mode of living he or she had elected to follow. Each denied any coercive persuasion, and pointed out that there was no physical restraint exercised. In fact Miss Brown had left the group and returned after four days of reflection. Each explained the manner in which he or she was invited to join and become a member of the group, and the experiences that resulted thereafter. From their testimony it appeared that proselyting was done in the name of an organization other than the church, and that the Unification Church itself or Reverend Moon were not mentioned until the prospect had been with the group for a period of time; that the converts led Spartan lives with respect to food, accommodations and hours of fund raising activities; and that on occasion evasive answers were given while soliciting funds. They also explained their reaction to the examination and confrontation with the parents' psychiatrist and psychologist, and insisted on their competency.

A psychiatrist and a psychologist, who actually tested the proposed conservatees, also testified on their behalf. The former pointed out that "coercive persuasion" in the absence of drugs, hypnosis, physical captivity or some greater fear was no more than speculative theory, and that the experiences relied upon by the parents' experts were no more than usually accompany devotion to a religious belief. He also confirmed that the proposed conservatees did not suffer from any mental pathological condition, and disagreed with the existence of the symptoms found by the parents' experts, and their conclusions as to the exposure of the prospective conservatees to "coercive persuasion" as used by those experts, and their conclusions as to the young adults' susceptibility to being deceived or imposed upon by artful and designing persons. This psychiatrist had a law degree, as well as a medical degree, and admittedly had testified against legislation which would permit guardianship proceedings to be applied to persons who become members of a nonconforming organization, or in other than gravely serious situations. He questioned the propriety of the artful and designing person test because of the difficulty of distinguishing between what could be considered proper or improper art and design.

The conservatees' clinical psychologist gave each a clean bill of health on the basis of three tests he conducted. He testified that these tests would reveal symptoms similar to those experienced by prisoners of war who were subjected to similar tests but that they did not with the conservatees. He expressly repudiated the findings of the parents' experts with regard to some of the symptoms they relied upon, and he made it clear that there was no emergency.

The conservatees also presented the testimony of two persons who had undergone deprogramming under the auspices of those with whom it was proposed to place the conservatees. One was a member of the Unification Church. . . .

Reasonable minds could differ over the validity of the concept advanced by the parents' experts, and the validity of their findings concerning the psychological state of the proposed conservatees. It must, however, be conceded that there was testimony, which if believed, sustained the implied conclusion from the court's order that each of the conservatees was a person, who because of having been subjected to coercive persuasion (popularly "brainwashing"), was likely to be deceived or imposed upon by artful or designing persons, and that it was necessary to reverse that process. We feel that the evidence was insufficient to sustain a finding that there was any emergency authorizing good cause for appointment of a temporary conservator, but since there was a full hearing in this case and other reasons compel a setting aside of the order, we do not dwell on that point.

Here it is not the conservatee's estate that is to be protected, but his mind. The statutory authorization has been analyzed as follows: "An individual who is not otherwise in need of a conservator and who is willing to accept, and able to carry out, the decisions made for him by relatives or friends about personal matters—where to live, what to do, and what to eat—does not require a conservator of the person, regardless of his physical or mental condition. Conversely, an individual who is unwilling or unable to accept reasonable directions in the conduct of his personal life requires a conservator of the person. So does one who is physically or mentally unable to consent to medical or dental services." As we have noted, the law now provides that a conservatorship of the person shall be appointed if an individual "is unable properly to provide for his personal needs for physical health, food, clothing or shelter." (§ 1751, as amended.) We take that as declaratory of the former first ground—"unable properly to care for himself." There is no real showing here that the conservatees are physically unhealthy, or actually deprived of, or unable to secure food, clothing and shelter. Justification for the appointment under the second ground can only be attributed to a necessity to secure treatment medical or otherwise, which it cannot be gainsayed, is to affect the conservatee's mental health. . . .

If an adult person is less than gravely disabled we find no warrant for depriving him or her of liberty and freedom of action under either the former provisions of the Probate Code, or the Welfare and Institutions Code. If there is coercive persuasion or brainwashing which requires treatment, the existence of such a mental disability and the necessity of legal control over the mentally disabled person for the purpose of treatment should be ascertained after compliance with the protection of civil liberties provided by the Welfare and Institutions Code. To do less is to license kidnaping for the purpose of thought control. We conclude that the provisions of the Probate Code could not be applied to justify the appointment of a conservator of the person on the evidence presented in this case. . . .

Notes and Questions

1. Asch's experimental results indicate that 74% of his subjects (37 out of 50) contradicted the evidence of their senses at least once. In the control group, only two out of 37 subjects did so.

2. Have you ever had an experience comparable to that of the subjects in Asch's experiment? Try to think of a situation that would require such an uncomfortable, public disagreement over something so basic as visual perception.

3. If you had been an unsuspecting subject in Milgram's experiment, what would you have done?

4. The main version of Milgram's experiment was one in which the teacher could hear the learner's verbal protests from an adjoining room. The learner's protests began at 120 volts with complaints, followed by demands to be released from the experiment (150 volts), agonized shouts (270 volts), refusal to answer further questions (300 volts), violent, vehement, and prolonged screams (315 volts), followed by dead silence thereafter (330 volts).

Under these conditions, the average level of highest shock administered was 368 volts, and 25 out of 40 subjects proceeded all the way up to the maximum level of 450 volts. Some continued to administer shocks on the assumption that the "learner" was by then dead.

5. "With numbing regularity," writes Milgram, "good people . . . who are in everyday life responsible and decent were seduced by the trappings of authority, by the control of their perceptions, and by the uncritical acceptance of the experimenter's definition of the situation" into performing harsh and punitive acts they otherwise would never have performed. What were some of the "trappings of authority" that contributed to Milgram's results, and how did the control of the subjects' perceptions add to that authority?

6. Suppose a close friend or relative of yours suddenly underwent a radical conversion and abandoned all of his or her previous interests, beliefs, and values to join up full-time with the Unification Church. Under what circumstances, if any, would you consider partipating in the (illegal) kidnapping and "deprogramming" of that person?

Suggestions For Further Reading

Elliot Aronson, The Social Animal (8th ed. 1999)

Elliot Aronson, Readings About the Social Animal (8th ed. 1999)

Roger Brown, Social Psychology, ch. 1 (2d ed. 1986)

Robert B. Cialdini, Influence: Science and Practice (2d ed. 1988)

Charles W. Collier, Intellectual Authority and Institutional Authority, 42 Journal of Legal Education 151 (1992)

Stanley Milgram, Obedience to Authority: An Experimental View (1974)

Chapter 7

Warfare and the Reach of the Law

The Nuremberg Trials:
Justice Jackson's Report to the President
June 7, 1945

My Dear Mr. President:

I have the honor to report accomplishments during the month since you named me as Chief of Counsel for the United States in prosecuting the principal Axis War Criminals. In brief, I have selected staffs from the several services, departments and agencies concerned; worked out a plan for preparation, briefing, and trial of the cases; allocated the work among the several agencies; instructed those engaged in collecting or processing evidence; visited the European Theater to expedite the examination of captured documents, and the interrogation of witnesses and prisoners; coordinated our preparation of the main case with preparation by Judge Advocates of many cases not included in my responsibilities; and arranged cooperation and mutual assistance with the United Nations War Crimes Commission and with Counsel appointed to represent the United Kingdom in the joint prosecution. . . .

III

The time, I think, has come when it is appropriate to outline the basic features of the plan of prosecution on which we are tentatively proceeding in preparing the case of the United States.

1. The American case is being prepared on the assumption that an inescapable responsibility rests upon this country to conduct an inquiry, preferably in association with others, but alone if necessary, into the culpability of those whom there is probable cause to accuse of atrocities and other crimes. We have many such men in our possession. What shall we do with them? We could, of course, set them at large without a hearing. But it has cost unmeasured thousands of American lives to beat and bind these men. To free them without a trial would mock the dead and make cynics of the living. On the other hand, we could execute or otherwise punish them without a hearing. But undiscriminating executions or punishments without definite findings of guilt, fairly arrived at, would violate pledges repeatedly given, and would not set easily on the American conscience or be remembered by our children with pride. The only other course is to determine the innocence or guilt of the accused after a hearing as dispassionate as the times and the horrors we deal with will permit, and upon a record that will leave our reasons and motives clear.

2. These hearings, however, must not be regarded in the same light as a trial under our system, where defense is a matter of constitutional right. Fair hearings for the accused are, of course, required to make sure that we punish only the right men and for the right reasons. But the procedure of these hearings may properly bar obstructive and dilatory tactics resorted to by defendants in our ordinary criminal trials.

Nor should such a defense be recognized as the obsolete doctrine that a head of state is immune from legal liability. There is more than a suspicion that this idea is a relic of the doctrine of the divine right of kings. It is, in any event, inconsistent with the position we take toward our own officials, who are frequently brought to court at the suit of citizens who allege their rights to have been invaded. We do not accept the paradox that legal responsibility should be the least where power is the greatest. We stand on the principle of responsible government declared some three centuries ago to King James by Lord Chief Justice Coke, who proclaimed that even a King is still "under God and the law."

With the doctrine of immunity of a head of state usually is coupled another, that orders from an official superior protect one who obeys them. It will be noticed that the combination of these two doctrines means that nobody is responsible. Society as modernly organized cannot tolerate so broad an area of official irresponsibility. There is doubtless a sphere in which the defense of obedience to superior orders should prevail. If a conscripted or enlisted soldier is put on a firing squad, he should not be held responsible for the validity of the sentence he carries out. But the case may be greatly altered where one has discretion because of rank or the latitude of his orders. And of course, the defense of superior orders cannot apply in the case of voluntary participation in a criminal or conspiratorial organization, such as the Gestapo or the S.S. An accused should be allowed to show the facts about superior orders. The Tribunal can then determine whether they constitute a defense or merely extenuating circumstances, or perhaps carry no weight at all.

3. Whom will we accuse and put to their defense? We will accuse a large number of individuals and officials who were in authority in the government, in the military establishment, including the General Staff, and in the financial, industrial, and economic life of Germany who by all civilized standards are provable to be common criminals. We also propose to establish the criminal character of several voluntary organizations which have played a cruel and controlling part in subjugating first the German people and then their neighbors. It is not, of course, suggested that a person should be judged a criminal merely because he voted for certain candidates or maintained political affiliations in the sense that we in America support political parties. The organizations which we will accuse have no resemblance to our political parties. Organizations such as the Gestapo and the S.S. were direct action units, and were recruited from volunteers accepted only because of aptitude for, and fanatical devotion to, their violent purposes.

In examining the accused organizations in the trial, it is our proposal to demonstrate their declared and covert objectives, methods of recruitment, structure, lines of responsibility, and methods of effectuating their programs. In this trial, important representative members will be allowed to defend their organizations as well as themselves. The best practicable notice will be given, that named organizations stand accused and that any member is privileged to appear and join in their defense. If in the main trial an organization is found to be criminal, the second stage will be to identify and try before regular military tribunals individual members not already personally convicted in the principal case. Findings in the main trial that an organization is criminal in nature will be conclusive in any subsequent proceedings against individual members. The individual member will thereafter be allowed to plead only personal defenses or extenuating circumstances, such as that he joined under duress, and as to those defenses he should have the burden of proof. There is nothing novel in the idea that one may lose a part of or all his defense if he fails to assert it in an appointed forum at an earlier time. In United States wartime legislation, this principle has been utilized and sustained as consistent with our concept of due process of law.

4. Our case against the major defendants is concerned with the Nazi master plan, not with individual barbarities and perversions which occurred independently of any central plan. The groundwork of our case must be factually authentic and constitute a well-documented history of what we are convinced was a grand, concerted pattern to incite and commit the aggressions and barbarities which have shocked the world. We must not forget that when the Nazi plans were boldly proclaimed they were so extravagant that the world refused to take them seriously. Unless we write the record of this movement with clarity and precision, we cannot blame the future if in days of peace it finds incredible the accusatory generalities uttered during the war. We must establish incredible events by credible evidence.

5. What specifically are the crimes with which these individuals and organizations should be charged, and what marks their conduct as criminal?

There is, of course, real danger that trials of this character will become enmeshed in voluminous particulars of wrongs committed by individual Germans throughout the course of the war, and in the multitude of doctrinal disputes which are part of a lawyer's paraphernalia. We can save ourselves from those pitfalls if our test of what legally is crime gives recognition to those things which fundamentally outraged the conscience of the American people and brought them finally to the conviction that their own liberty and civilization could not persist in the same world with the Nazi power.

Those acts which offended the conscience of our people were criminal by standards generally accepted in all civilized countries, and I believe that we may proceed to punish those responsible in full accord with both our own traditions of fairness and with standards of just conduct which have been internationally accepted. I think also that through these trials we should be able to establish that a process of retribution by law awaits those who in the future similarly attack civilization. Before stating these offenses in legal terms and concepts, let me recall what it was that affronted the sense of justice of our people.

Early in the Nazi regime, people of this country came to look upon the Nazi Government as not constituting a legitimate state pursuing the legitimate objective of a member of the international community. They came to view the Nazis as a band of brigands, set on subverting within Germany every vestige of a rule of law which would entitle an aggregation of people to be looked upon collectively as a member of the family of nations. Our people were outraged by the oppressions, the cruelest forms of torture, the large-scale murder, and the wholesale confiscation of property which initiated the Nazi regime within

Germany. They witnessed persecution of the greatest enormity on religious, political and racial grounds, the breakdown of trade unions, and the liquidation of all religious and moral influences. This was not the legitimate activity of a state within its own boundaries, but was preparatory to the launching of an international course of aggression and was with the evil intention, openly expressed by the Nazis, of capturing the form of the German state as an instrumentality for spreading their rule to other countries. Our people felt that these were the deepest offenses against that International Law described in the Fourth Hague Convention of 1907 as including the "laws of humanity and the dictates of the public conscience."

Once these international brigands, the top leaders of the Nazi party, the S.S. and the Gestapo, had firmly established themselves within Germany by terrorism and crime, they immediately set out on a course of international pillage. They bribed, debased, and incited to treason the citizens and subjects of other nations for the purpose of establishing their fifth columns of corruption and sabotage within those nations. They ignored the commonest obligations of one state respecting the internal affairs of another. They lightly made and promptly broke international engagements as a part of their settled policy to deceive, corrupt, and overwhelm. They made, and made only to violate, pledges respecting the demilitarized Rhineland, and Czechoslovakia, and Poland, and Russia. They did not hesitate to instigate the Japanese to treacherous attack on the United States. Our people saw in this succession of events the destruction of the minimum elements of trust which can hold the community of nations together in peace and progress. Then, in consummation of their plan, the Nazis swooped down upon the nations they had deceived and ruthlessly conquered them. They flagrantly violated the obligations which states, including their own, have undertaken by convention or tradition as a part of the rules of land warfare, and of the law of the sea. They wantonly destroyed cities like Rotterdam for no military purpose. They wiped out whole populations, as at Lidice, where no military purposes were to be served. They confiscated property of the Poles and gave it to party members. They transported in labor battalions great sectors of the civilian populations of the conquered countries. They refused the ordinary protections of law to the populations which they enslaved. The feeling of outrage grew in this country, and it became more and more felt that these were crimes committed against us and against the whole society of civilized nations by a band of brigands who had seized the instrumentality of a state.

I believe that those instincts of our people were right and that they should guide us as the fundamental tests of criminality. We propose to punish acts which have been regarded as criminal since the time of Cain and have been so written in every civilized code.

In arranging these trials we must also bear in mind the aspirations with which our people have faced the sacrifices of war. After we entered the war, and as we expended our men and our wealth to stamp out these wrongs, it was the universal feeling of our people that out of this war should come unmistakable rules and workable machinery from which any who might contemplate another era of brigandage would know that they would be held personally responsible and would be personally punished. Our people have been waiting for these trials in the spirit of Woodrow Wilson, who hoped to "give to international law the kind of vitality which it can only have if it is a real expression of our moral judgment."

Against this background it may be useful to restate in more technical lawyer's terms the legal charges against the top Nazi leaders and those voluntary associations such as the S.S. and Gestapo which clustered about them and were ever the prime instrumentalities, first, in capturing the German state, and then, in directing the German state to its spoliations against the rest of the world.

(a) Atrocities and offenses against persons or property constituting violations of International Law, including the laws, rules, and customs of land and naval warfare. The rules of warfare are well established and generally accepted by the nations. They make offenses of such conduct as killing of the wounded, refusal of quarter, ill treatment of prisoners of war, firing on undefended localities, poisoning of wells and streams, pillage and wanton destruction, and ill treatment of inhabitants in occupied territory.

(b) Atrocities and offenses, including atrocities and persecutions on racial or religious grounds, committed since 1933. This is only to recognize the principles of criminal law as they are generally observed in civilized states. These principles have been assimilated as a part of International Law at least since 1907. The Fourth Hague Convention provided that inhabitants and belligerents shall remain under the protection and the rule of "the principles of the law of nations, as they result from the usages established among civilized peoples, from the laws of humanity and the dictates of the public conscience."

(c) invasions of other countries and initiation of wars of aggression in violation of International Law or treaties.

The persons to be reached by these charges will be determined by the rule of liability, common to all legal systems, that all who participate in the formulation or execution of a criminal plan involving multiple crimes are liable for each of the offenses committed and responsible for the acts of each other. All are liable who have incited, ordered, procured, or counseled the commission of such acts, or who have taken what the Moscow Declaration describes as "a consenting part" therein. . . .

Respectfully yours,
Robert H. Jackson

The Nuremberg Trials:
Proceedings[*]

Defense Arguments

Dr. Hans Laternser: My Lord, Gentlemen of the Tribunal:

It has happened more than once in the history of nations that after a war the military leaders of the defeated party were brought to trial. If the defeated war leaders or generals could not be reproached with ineptitude or negligence of their military duties, they were suspected of treason, of pursuing political aims, or they were accused of infringing the rules of warfare or the limitations of their military powers.

There is one feature, however, which must be noted: as a rule, trials were conducted and verdicts rendered by their own state, and not by the enemy victors. To find examples for the latter case, one must go back into history by more than 2,000 years. The Romans strangled their enemy Jugurtha in jail, and persecuted Hannibal with their vengeance until they were able to force the cup of poison into his hands at the court of his host. In more recent history, there is the sole example of Napoleon I, who was banished by the victorious powers to St. Helena, where he died; but he was not taken to account by the victors because he had served his country as a French general, but because he was the Emperor of the French, and consequently the political head of his country.

Hitler, who was the head of the German Reich, and the Supreme Commander of the Armed Forces, has eluded judicial responsibility by his death. Since he can no longer be dealt with, the Prosecution have taken the highest military commanders instead of the Supreme Commander and head of the State, made them summarily also political leaders, and are attempting in this way to render them responsible.

This method is indeed unique and without precedent in the history of nations, and may well be contemplated with peculiar feelings by all soldiers of the world.

If one thing stands out clearly from the collection of evidence—and I shall have to deal with this in detail later on—it is the fact that the German military leaders did not dominate their country and did not drive it into the war, that they were not politicians, but exclusively, and perhaps even too exclusively, soldiers—which is the tragic part. Had they been politicians, Germany would not have fallen into this abyss. If we keep this clearly in our minds, it is obvious that these men are in fact facing trial before this Court only because they served their country as soldiers.

If the Prosecutor, Colonel Taylor, argues that Hitler could not have waged his wars without the assistance of the Armed Forces, that argument cannot be invalidated. Nobody has ever been able to wage a war without soldiers. However, what Carlyle says is true for the German military leaders as for all soldiers:

*   Reprinted with the generous assistance of, and by special arrangement with, the Avalon Project at the Yale Law School and its Co-Director, William C. Fray.

If a man becomes a soldier, his soul and his body thereby become the property of his commanding officer. He is not allowed to decide for himself whether the cause for which he fights is good or bad. His enemies are selected for him, and not by him. It is his duty to obey and to ask no questions.

If the German military leaders are today indicted before this Court as an alleged "criminal organization," this indictment does not only apply to them, but is in fact directed—however strongly it may be desired to deny this publicly—at the soldiers in general, or at least at the military leaders as a class.

By indicting the military leader—who, obeying the orders of his government, has fulfilled his military duties—because the Prosecution declares the action of his government to be illegal and represents him as a partner to such action of the government, the Prosecution places upon him the obligation to examine the legality of his country's policy, and raises him to the position of a judge called upon to give a verdict on the policy of his state.

It cannot be my task to present the consequences of such a mental revolution for the soldiers of the world. . . .

Since Hitler is dead, the Prosecution leaves him in the background, and looks for other responsible parties. Yet no one can deny that Hitler alone wielded the power of the Reich in his hands, and consequently also had the sole and total responsibility. The essence of every dictatorship ultimately lies in the fact that one man's will is almighty, that his will is decisive in all matters. In no other dictatorship was this principle developed so exclusively as in Hitler's dictatorship. If all military men and all politicians emphasize this repeatedly, it is impossible to suspect every one of them of lack of courage to stand by his conviction; it must have been a fact. The dictator exercised the power given to him with an almost demonic strength of will. Other than his, there was no will, no plan, no conspiracy. As regards the soldiers, it was particularly significant for them that Hitler had been called upon to assume power by Reich President Von Hindenburg, and had then been made absolute head of State by Reich law and public plebiscite. The perfectly legal and formally correct transfer of legislative power, and of the power to give orders, resulted in the fact that the soldiers, too, submitted to Hitler's personality. Furthermore, he knew how to play off one party against the other, but in his decisive resolutions he had neither advisers nor did he allow independent planning.

Hitler's character is truly comparable with that of Lucifer; just as Lucifer starts out on his radiant course of light with tremendous speed and immense momentum, gaining the highest pinnacle before falling into utter darkness, so Hitler followed a similar course. Who ever heard that Lucifer needed assistance, advisers, helpers in his lightning ascent? Does he not rather by the force of his personality carry with him to the dizzy heights all the others, and then pull them down into the depths with the same force? Is it imaginable that a man of this kind should have engaged in a long-term preparation of a plan, surrounded himself with a circle of conspirators, and sought their advice and assistance for his ascent?

This picture should not be interpreted as an attempt to elude responsibility: every German general is enough of a man to stand up for his actions; but if justice is to be done, the actual circumstances, as they really were, must be recognized and serve as a basis for the final judgment. The best proof, however, against the participation of the generals in Hitler's plans is given by Hitler himself when he says: "I do not expect my generals to understand my orders; I only expect them to obey them.". . .

The last count of the Indictment, that the military leaders had rendered themselves guilty because they tolerated in practice Hitler's criminal plans and deeds, instead of revolting against them, returns us again to the central problem of these proceedings against the soldiers: the problem of the duty to obey. It has been repeatedly stated that the Führer order was not only a military order, but that it had, over and above this, a legislative effect.

Thus were not the military leaders simply bound to obey the law? If the duty to obey does not exist in the case of an order which aims at a civil crime, it is because the order demands an action directed against the authority of the State. But can there be any question of a crime if the order requires action which is not directed against the authority of the State, but on the contrary is demanded by that authority? And even if we reply to this question in the affirmative, what citizen of any country in the world is in a position to recognize the criminal nature of his action?

It is not sufficient, in order to ascertain guilt, that the Prosecution explain what the defendants should not have done—at the same time, they should tell us what they might, ought, and should have done, for any legal prohibition must also include a positive directive. If I suppose that, in spite of the sovereignty of the individual states, a legal obligation existed for the generals to act in accordance with international law and moral requirements even against the law of their own State, such a legal obligation could only be affirmed if the corresponding action offered a chance of success. After all, to allow oneself to be hanged merely to evade one's duties, to betray one's country without any prospect of being able to change matters—these things cannot be demanded by virtue of any morality. After all, there is no obligation for anybody to become a martyr.

And what were the possibilities of negative or positive action against orders and law on the part of the indicted generals? What were the chances of success? The simple rejection of unlawful plans or orders, be it by contradiction, warning, representations, objections, or the like, would have been in theory possible, but utterly unsuccessful in practice. To a certain extent this remained ineffective for the simple reason that the generals received no knowledge of many of the objectionable things. In the political and ideological struggle, these methods were so carefully kept secret from the generals, that they did not even hear about mass executions, to say nothing of being able to prevent them.

In the military sphere Hitler's closest assistants may perhaps have been heard on the question as to how a resolution was to be carried out militarily, but their opinions were never asked for as to the resolution itself.

In the majority of cases the military leaders indicted before this Court only learned of these decisions at the moment when they were called upon to carry them out as soldiers. As far as possible they made objections. Before the Rhineland was occupied the Commander-in-Chief of the Army, Baron von Fritsch, advised against a policy which might produce a war on two fronts, as well as against rearmament, and was dismissed. The Chief of the General Staff, Beck, raised political warnings, and was relieved of his functions. General

Adam also opposed the intended policies, and was discharged. The OKH opposed the offensive in the West and the infringements of neutrality, and was eliminated. The Commander-in-Chief of the Army remonstrated in connection with outrages in Poland; the result was that the military agencies were excluded from the administration of the occupied territories. Warnings, objections, factual representations were never successful, and in the majority of cases only produced the effect that Hitler maintained his own opinions more stubbornly than ever, and insisted on his order being carried out. If even the steps taken by the highest commanders thus remained without success, what could the other indicted commanders of lower rank have achieved in this respect?

A democratic politician might say that they could have resigned. That is a practical possibility for a parliamentary minister in a democratic country—a German officer could not resign. He was bound by his military oath, which was a supreme obligation for the veteran officer, more than for anyone else. A German general could only ask for approval of his resignation. Whether that request was successful or not was beyond his influence. Moreover, during the war, Hitler prohibited any such request, and placed resignation on the same footing as desertion. A collective request for resignation, not feasible anyway in practice, would have amounted to mutiny, and would merely have served to bring compliant elements into the leadership, but would never have had enough influence on Hitler as to cause him to change his policy, his orders, or his methods. The attempts at resignation which were actually made by some Field Marshals, and in particular by the Commander-in-Chief of the Army in November 1939, were flatly rejected. The subsequent dismissal was the result of Hitler's decision. The resignation of the field commanders would nevertheless have been their obvious duty and would have to be effected at all costs if these leaders had been faced with tasks in which, according to their conception, the honor of the German nation had been at stake. But precisely these tasks, among which I count the mass exterminations and the atrocities in the concentration camps, were outside the sphere of the generals and were even carefully kept secret from them.

Now, would open disobedience have been more readily possible, and would it have offered greater chances of success? The American Chief Prosecutor, in his report to the President of the United States, expresses himself as follows on this point:

> If a soldier drafted into the Army is detailed to an execution squad, he cannot be held responsible for the legality of the sentence he carries out. But the case may be different with a man who by virtue of his rank or the elasticity of the orders given him could act as he saw fit.

This view was not shared by the generals. On the contrary, a simple soldier's disobedience is easily offset in its effect by punishment, but the disobedience of a high military leader is liable to shatter the structure of the Army, and even of the State itself.

If there is anything in the world that is indivisible, it is military obedience. No one has defined the meaning and the character of a soldier's duty of obedience more correctly than the British Field Marshal, Lord Montgomery. In a speech which he made at Portsmouth on 2 July 1946, he declared that as the servant of the nation the Army is above politics, and so it must remain. Its devotion is given to the State, and it does not behoove the soldier to change his devotion on account of his political views. It must be made clear that the Army is not an assembly of individuals, but a fighting arm molded by discipline and controlled by the leader. The essence of democracy is freedom, the essence of the Army is discipline. It does not matter how intelligent the soldier is—the Army would let the Nation down if it were not accustomed to obey orders instantaneously. The difficult problem of achieving strict obedience to orders can only be mastered in a democratic age by the inculcation of three principles:

1. the Nation is something that is worthwhile;

2. the Army is the necessary arm of the Nation;

3. it is the duty of the soldier unquestioningly to obey all orders which the Army, that is, the Nation, gives him.

And the German generals—according to the opinion expressed by the Prosecution—should not only have asked questions when they obeyed the Supreme Commander and the Nation, but they should even have rebelled openly!

Whoever wishes to render a just decision on this question ought himself once to have been an army commander during a war, in the front lines and in particularly serious circumstances, because there is a great difference between the commander on a heavily contested front line, who bears the responsibility for the life and death of hundreds of thousands of soldiers, and an officer who has no responsibility at the front line, or who is engaged only in a quiet sector. If the military leaders nevertheless unceasingly defended their soldierly conceptions and acted in accordance with them to the limit of their possibilities, this attitude ultimately produced no other effect than their complete elimination towards the end of the war. This is proved by a short survey of the fate of the military leaders:

Out of 17 Field Marshals who were serving in the Army, 10 were relieved of their functions in the course of the war. Three lost their lives in connection with the events of 20 July 1944. Two were killed in action, one was taken prisoner, and only a single general remained in service until the end of the war without being subjected to any disciplinary action. Of 36 generals (Generalobersten), 26 were removed from their posts, from among whom three were executed in connection with the events of 20 July 1944, and two were dishonorably discharged. Seven were killed in action, and only three remained in service until the end of the war without being subjected to disciplinary action. Those who were subjected to disciplinary action were highly qualified officers who had given a good account of themselves in combat.

Let me recapitulate:

(1) Military disobedience is and remains a violation of duty, in times of war a crime punishable with the death penalty.

(2) There exists no duty to disobey for any soldier in the world, as long as states with a sovereignty of their own continue to exist.

(3) Under Hitler's dictatorship, open disobedience would only have led to the destruction of the subordinate, but never to a repeal of orders given.

(4) No class has made, through its highest representatives, such great sacrifices for its conceptions as opposed to Hitler's methods, as the circle of officers who are indicted before this Tribunal.

In view of the impossibility and the ineffectiveness of any passive resistance, there would have remained only the method of violence, rebellion, and *coup d'état*. Whoever contemplated this method had to be aware of the fact that it would have to involve the removal of Hitler and of the leading men of the Party in such a way that these men would be put to death. There was, therefore, at the beginning of each *coup d'état* the inexorable compulsion to liquidate Hitler and the leading men of the Party.

To the soldier this meant murder and disloyalty to his oath. Even if it is demanded that the generals, for reasons of a higher world morality, ought to have sacrificed their personal and military honor, how could they have been justified in taking such action against the will of the Nation, and when could such action have been effected with good chances of success and for the benefit of the people? After the incorporation of the Protectorate, Hitler was at the crest of his successes and was considered by a great many Germans as the greatest of all Germans. If Churchill said of him, on 4 October 1938, that

> . . . Our leadership must have at least a fraction of the spirit of that German corporal who, when everything around him had fallen in ruins, when Germany seemed to have sunk into chaos for all times, did not hesitate to march against the formidable phalanx of victorious nations . . .

is that not proof enough that the wrath of the German nation would have annihilated the generals who would have laid hands on Hitler? Were the generals to remove Hitler at a time when a peaceful settlement with Poland was still a practical possibility, when it was impossible for the German people to foresee that the war would actually come, and what consequences it would have—as they are today openly visible to all our eyes?

Then war did come, and it brought another and very decisive obligation for the military leaders. Any rebellion in war would have amounted to a catastrophe for the Reich. Even then, as long as there were victories, no rebellion would have had any chance of success. But when it became clear after Stalingrad that the fight now had to be continued for the very existence of the German people, the military leaders had even less of a moral right to bring about a collapse of the front lines and the whole country by a *coup d'état*. In those days, large sections of the German people still believed in Hitler. Would the military leaders not have been made responsible for everything that the German nation is feeling so heavily today as a consequence of the capitulation? Can one really consider a *coup d'état*, disloyalty to the given oath, and murder, as a legal obligation of the soldier in the midst of a war for the very life and death of the Nation? As Field Marshal Von Rundstedt said in the witness stand:

> Nothing would have been changed for the German people, but my name would have gone down in history as that of the greatest traitor.

To what extent any such attempt was condemned to failure is proved by the unsuccessful attempt on Hitler's life on 20 July 1944. Even the preparation of this attempt over a number of years and the participation of men from all walks of life were not able to assure its success. How, therefore, could the 129 indicted officers have successfully carried out a *coup d'état*?

Certainly, if they had been the united association which the Prosecution would so very much like to regard them, they might perhaps also have contemplated a commonly-planned violent revolt; but since they were not a closed organization, since they were not politicians but "only" soldiers, they could do nothing on their part to bring about a change of conditions. They could only obey to the last, in spite of the fact that they knew how desperate the military situation was. The German military leaders found themselves hemmed in between their rights as men and their duties as soldiers.

As citizens of the State they might have claimed for themselves the right to refuse service to a Führer and a system which, the longer the war lasted, proved to be more and more harmful. They might thus have evaded their personal responsibility, they might have—as the prosecutor puts it—"saved their skins." Perhaps they would not now be before this Tribunal. But by taking such a decision they would at the same time have let down their soldiers who trusted them and for whom they felt responsible. Therefore there remained for them as soldiers only the duty to fight. This "duty" might, in a wider sense of the word, have consisted in overthrowing the system. In war, however, this would practically have amounted to nothing less than inviting defeat. No soldier could take that upon himself. No military leader can for years demand of his soldiers that they should give their lives, and then abandon his post himself and go down in history as a traitor to his nation.

Thus there remained for the German military leaders only the duty to fight the enemy to the last. Confronted with the tragic decision between personal rights and soldierly duties, they decided in favor of their duties, and thus acted in the spirit of soldierly morale.

Prosecution Arguments

Sir David Maxwell-Fyfe:

Let me conclude by reminding you of the opinion of the Supreme Court, the supreme guardian of National Socialist honor and discipline, to whose august authority and jurisdiction the members of all these organizations were subject. Of the murders committed during the 1938 demonstrations by Hoheitsträger and members of the SA and SS, the investigation of which had been entrusted to the Secret State Police and Party jurisdiction of Gauleiter and other Political Leaders, it was pleaded that, I quote, "in such cases as when Jews were killed without an order or contrary to orders, ignoble motives could not be determined." The purpose of those proceedings in the Party Court were, I quote again, "to protect those Party comrades who, motivated by decent National Socialist attitude and initiative, had overshot their mark."

In those few lines you have the secret of all the death and suffering, the horror and tragedy, that these defendants and the members of these organizations have brought upon the world. You see to what depths of evil they corrupted the human conscience. No ignoble motive—the murder of women and children through "decent National Socialist attitude and initiative." Such was the National Socialist creed which the members of these organizations fanatically accepted, the creed which—can one doubt—they still cherish and, given the opportunity to do so, would revive. . . .

The men involved have joined in wars which they knew were unjust wars of aggression. They have borne essential parts in the deeds which in the hands of their immediate perpetrators are undeniably war crimes and crimes against humanity. Yet they protest their innocence.

Our case against them has as clear a basis on the facts of this case as in the lessons of history.

They carried out orders which on the admission of many of them bit deep into the remnants of their consciences. They knew that they were doing what was wrong, but they now say "Befehl ist Befehl"—an order is an order.

All decent men find it difficult to blame others for absence of moral courage—they are only too conscious of their own failings in that direction. But there comes a point when, faced with crimes which are obvious murder or barbarity, there is a higher duty. Even Dr. Laternser admitted this was so. His suggestion to the witness Schreiber that he ought to have protested at the Army Staff's proposals for bacteriological warfare came strangely on behalf of these men whose very defense has been to declare the impossibility and uselessness of protest. What nonsense—what utter nonsense—is this which you have been asked to listen to by these defendants and their generals when their own counsel, to discredit a witness, must ask the very question which the Prosecution have been asking of themselves since the day this Trial began. In fairness to all military tradition it should not go forth that soldiers have sheltered behind the letter of a command from facing moral problems—and deciding them, rightly or wrongly, as moral problems. Great captains are not automata to be weighed against a rubber stamp. I need not traverse the history of our military figures—the philosophy of Montrose, the brooding thoughts of Marshal Ney, the troubled heart of Robert E. Lee in 1861—to find examples. Two of the greatest names in German military history spring to one's mind: Von Clausewitz leaving the Prussian Army to serve in that of Russia; Yorck von Wartenburg making his decision of neutrality—both put what they deemed the needs of Europe and humanity above the orders of the moment. How much more clear and obvious was the duty when the work of drafting, issuing, and carrying out the Nacht und Nebel Decree, the Commando Order, the Commissar Order, Hitler's order to murder our 50 Air Force officers, meant the defiling of every idea which every soldier cherishes and holds dear; when—as all of them who ever served upon the Eastern Front could see with their own eyes—they were asked to support and co-operate in a calculated system of mass-extermination and utter brutality.

These men, of all men, knew their leader to be a callous murderer, yet for years they had met in conference after conference to sit at his feet and listen to his words. They fed his lust for power and enslavement with the best of their professional skill. While the defenseless peoples of the East, the men, women and children of Poland, of the Soviet Union, and of the Baltic states, were being deliberately slaughtered and deported into slavery to allow for German "Lebensraum," these men talked of the necessities of war. When their own cities were bombed and Germans killed, they called it murder. Only in July 1944, when

Hitler's star was dimmed, did three Field Marshals and five Colonel Generals recognize that he was murdering also their own country and took action. When that star was rising in victory they had hailed it and ignored the blood-red colour of the clouds from which it rose.

Brigadier General Telford Taylor:

The Defense appears to contend that membership in this group was not voluntary. I say "appears to," because in one breath we are told that the generals could not withdraw from the positions they occupied, and in the next, that many of them resigned because of disagreements with Hitler.

The question is, I think, a simple one. We are not concerned here with the ordinary German conscript who made up the bulk of the Wehrmacht. We are concerned entirely with professional soldiers, and with the most zealous, ambitious, and able German officers in the business. Most of them chose a military career because it was in their blood; as Manstein put it, "they considered the glory of war as something great." They slaved at it and were devoted to their profession, and if they reached the status of commander-in-chief, they were, like Manstein, proud that an army had been entrusted to them. No one became a German commander-in-chief unless he wanted to.

It is true that in time of war a professional soldier cannot resign his commission or his post at his own free will. But this does not turn the professional officer into a conscript or make his status an involuntary one. No one becomes a professional officer without knowing in advance the obligations that will bind him in time of war. The fanatical Nazis who rushed to volunteer for the early Waffen-SS divisions or who voluntarily joined other paramilitary sections of the Party could not thereafter resign at will, but I have not heard it urged that they were conscripts or involuntary members. The members of the General Staff and High Command Group were keen professional warriors, who competed with others like themselves for the responsibilities and honors of being commanders-in-chief. They rose within the Wehrmacht just as an ambitious Party member might rise to be a Kreisleiter or Gauleiter.

In fact, retirement was easier for the commander-in-chief than anyone else in the Wehrmacht. The junior officer who protested against what was going on around him, might lose advancement or be moved to a less desirable assignment, or be court-martialed and disgraced. He was not given the option of retiring, and he was usually too young to plead illness plausibly. The commanders-in-chief were in a far better position. No War Office or War Department wants a field commander-in-chief who is in constant and fundamental disagreement with his instructions. Such a commander-in-chief must be removed. Yet often he has sufficient seniority, prestige, and acknowledged ability so that his demotion or disgrace would be embarrassing, and retirement or acceptance of resignation is the best solution for all concerned.

And this is just what happened with some of the commanders-in-chief. The record is replete with testimony by or about commanders-in-chief who openly disagreed with Hitler on tactical matters and as a result of such disagreements were retired or allowed to resign. I note in passing that the record is notably barren of evidence that any commander-in-chief openly disagreed with Hitler decisively on the issuance of orders which violated the laws of war, or who forced his retirement on account of these orders. At all events, it is quite clear that a commander-in-chief who wanted to retire could contrive to do so, whether by pleading illness or by honest blunt behavior. If he had the will, there was a way out. And it is worth noting that the three Field Marshals who testified before this Tribunal had all found or fallen into the way out, and the record shows that many others were equally successful and that few of them thereafter suffered serious harm on this account. . . .

Let us look once more at these military leaders whose actions we have just examined. They are a group in more ways than one. They are more than a group; they are a class, almost a caste. They have a course of thought and a way of life. They have distinctive qualities of mind, which have been noted and commented on by the rest of the world for many decades, and which have their roots in centuries. They have been a historical force, and are still to be reckoned with. They are proud of it.

To escape the consequences of their actions, these men now deny all this. But in their very denial, the truth is apparent. Their group spirit and unity of outlook and purpose is so deep that it drops from their lips willy-nilly. Read their testimony; always they refer to themselves as "we" or "we old soldiers," and they are forever stating "our" attitude on this or that subject. Rundstedt's testimony is full of such expressions of the attitude of the German military leaders as a group on a great variety of questions. Manstein told us that "we soldiers mistrusted all parties"; "we all considered ourselves the trustees of the unity of Germany"; and "the National Socialist aim of unification was according to our attitude, though not the National Socialist methods."

What are the characteristics of the German military leaders? They have been familiar to students of history for a long time; books have been written by them and about them. They are manifest in the documents and testimony before the Tribunal.

They are careful observers of Germany's internal politics, but their tradition and policy is not to identify themselves with parties or internal political movements. This is the only true note in the refrain, which has been sung so often at this Trial, that "we were soldiers and not politicians." They regard themselves as above politics and politicians. They are concerned only with what they consider to be the deeper, unchanging interests of Germany as a nation. As Manstein put it:

> We soldiers mistrusted all parties, because every party in Germany placed its own interests above the interests of Germany. We all considered ourselves the trustees of the unity of Germany in this respect. . . .

The German military leaders are deeply interested in foreign politics and diplomacy. Any intelligent professional officer must be. Training is conducted, equipment is built, and plans are evolved in the light of what is known about the military potential and intentions of other countries. No officers in the world were more aware of this than the Germans; none studied the international scene as closely or with such cold calculation. It was their mentor, Clausewitz, who described war as an instrument of politics.

The German military leaders want Germany to be free from political fluctuations, and a government which will mobilize German resources behind the Wehrmacht and inculcate in the German public the spirit and purposes of militarism. This is what Rundstedt meant when he said that: "The National Socialist ideas which were good were usually ideas which were carried over from old Prussian times and which we had known already without the National Socialists." That is what Manstein meant by the "unity" of Germany.

The German military leaders believe in war. They regard it as part of a normal, well-rounded life. Manstein told us from the witness box that they "naturally considered the glory of war as something great." The "considered opinion" of OKW in 1938 recited that:

> Despite all attempts to outlaw it, war is still a law of nature which may be challenged but not eliminated. It serves the survival of the race and state or the assurance of its historical future.

> This high moral purpose gives war its total character and its ethical justification.

These characteristics of the German military leaders are deep and permanent. They have been bad for the world, and bad for Germany too. Their philosophy is so perverse that they regard a lost war, and a defeated and prostrate Germany, as a glorious opportunity to start again on the same terrible cycle. Their attitude of mind is nowhere better set forth than in a speech delivered by General Beck before the German War Academy in 1935. The audience of young officers was told that "the hour of death of our old magnificent Army" in 1919 "led to the new life of the young Reichswehr," and that the German Army returned from the first World War "crowned with the laurels of immortality." Later on they were told that if the military leaders have displayed intelligence and courage, then losing a war "is ennobled by the pride of a glorious fall." In conclusion, they are reminded that Germany is a "military-minded nation" and are exhorted to remember "the duty which they owe to the man who recreated and made strong again the German Wehrmacht."

In 1935, that man was Hitler. In previous years it was other men. The German militarist will join forces with any man or government that offers fair prospect of effective support for military exploits. Men who believe in war as a way of life learn nothing from the experience of losing one.

I have painted this picture of the German military leaders not because it is an unfamiliar one, but because it is so familiar that it may be in danger of being overlooked. We must not become preoccupied with the niceties of a chart or details of military organization at the expense of far more important things which are matters of common knowledge. The whole world has long known about and suffered at the hands of the German military leadership. Its qualities and conduct are open and notorious. Is the world now to be told that there is no such group? Is it to hear that the German war lords cannot be judged because they were a bunch of conscripts? We have had to deal seriously with such arguments only because there are no others.

That the case against the German militarists is clear does not make it the less important. We are at grips here with something big and evil and durable; something that was not born in 1933, or even 1921; something much older than anyone here; something far more important than any individual in the dock; something that is not yet dead and that cannot be killed by a rifle or a hangman's noose.

For nine months this courtroom has been a world of gas chambers, mountains of corpses, human-skin lampshades, shrunken skulls, freezing experiments, and bank vaults filled with gold teeth. It is vital to the conscience of the world that all the participants in these enormities shall be brought to justice. But these exhibits, gruesome as they are, do not lie at the heart of this case. Little will be accomplished by shaking the poisoned fruit from the tree. It is much harder to dig the tree up by the roots, but only this will in the long run do much good.

The tree which bore this fruit is German militarism. Militarism is as much the core of the Nazi Party as of the Wehrmacht itself. Militarism is not the profession of arms. Militarism is embodied in the "military-minded nation" whose leaders preach and practice conquest by force of arms, and relish war as something desirable in itself. Militarism inevitably leads to cynical and wicked disregard of the rights of others and of the very elements of civilization. Militarism destroys the moral character of the nation that practises it and, because it can be overthrown only by its own weapons, undermines the character of nations that are forced to combat it.

The wellspring of German militarism through the years had been the group of professional military leaders who have become known to the world as the "German General Staff." That is why the exposure and discrediting of this group through the declaration of criminality is far more important than the fate of the uniformed individuals in the box, or of other members of this group as individuals. Keitel and Raeder and Rundstedt and Kesselring and Manstein have shot their bolt. They will not lead the legions of the Wehrmacht again.

What is really at stake now is not the lives of these particular men, but the future influence of the German General Staff within Germany, and, consequently, on the lives of people in all countries. That is why it was declared at Yalta:

> It is our inflexible purpose to destroy German militarism and Nazism, and to ensure that Germany will never again be able to disturb the peace of the world. We are determined to disarm and disband all German armed forces; break up for all time the German General Staff that has repeatedly contrived the resurgence of German militarism.

The first steps toward the revival of German militarism have been taken right here in this courtroom. The German General Staff has had plenty of time to think since the spring of 1945, and it well knows what is at stake here. The German militarists know that their future strength depends on re-establishing the faith of the German people in their military powers and in disassociating themselves from the atrocities which they committed in the service of the Third Reich. Why did the Wehrmacht meet with defeat? Hitler interfered too much in military affairs, says Manstein. What about the atrocities? The Wehrmacht committed none. Hitler's criminal orders were discarded and disregarded by the generals. Any atrocities which did occur were committed by other men, such as Himmler, and other agencies, such as the SS. Could not the generals have taken any steps to prevent Germany's engulfment in war and eventual destruction? No; the generals were bound by their oath of obedience to the Chief of State. Did not an SS general say that the Field Marshals could have prevented many of the excesses and atrocities? The reaction is one of superiority and scorn: "I think it is impertinent for an SS man to make such statements about a Field Marshal," says Rundstedt. The documents and testimony show that these are transparent fabrications. But here, in embryo, are the myths and legends which the German militarists will seek to propagate in the German mind. These lies must be stamped and labeled for what they are now while the proof is fresh.

This is as important within our own countries as it is here in Germany. Militarism has flourished far more widely and obstinately in Germany than elsewhere, but it is a plant which knows no national boundaries; it grows everywhere. It lifts its voice to say that war between East and West, or Left and Right, or White and Yellow, is inevitable. It whispers that newly devised weapons are so terrible that they should be hurled now lest some other country use them first. It makes the whole world walk under the shadow of death.

German militarism, if it comes again, will not necessarily reappear under the aegis of Nazism. The German militarists will tie themselves to any man or party that offers expectation of a revival of German armed might. They will calculate deliberately and coldly. They will not be deterred by fanatical ideologies or hideous practices; they will take crime in their stride to reach the goal of German power and terror. We have seen them do it before.

The truth is spread on the record before us, and all we have to do is state the truth plainly. The German militarists joined forces with Hitler and with him created the Third Reich; with him they deliberately made a world in which might was all that mattered; with him they plunged the world into war, and spread terror and devastation over the continent of Europe. They dealt a blow at all mankind; a blow so savage and foul that the conscience of the world will reel for years to come. This was not war; it was crime. This was not soldiering; it was savagery. These things need to be said. We cannot here make history over again, but we can see that it is written true.

The Nuremberg Trials:
Judgment of the International Military Tribunal
Nuremberg, 30th September and 1st October, 1946

The Charter Provisions

The individual defendants are indicted under Article 6 of the Charter, which is as follows:

> Article 6. The Tribunal established by the Agreement referred to in Article 1 hereof for the trial and punishment of the major war criminals of the European Axis countries shall have the power to try and punish persons who, acting in the interests of the European Axis countries, whether as individuals or as members of organisations, committed any of the following crimes:
>
> The following acts, or any of them, are crimes, coming within the jurisdiction of the Tribunal for which there shall be individual responsibility:
>
> (a) Crimes against Peace: namely, planning, preparation, initiation, or waging of a war of aggression, or a war in violation of international treaties, agreements, or assurances, or participation in a common plan or conspiracy for the accomplishment of any of the foregoing.
>
> (b) War Crimes: namely, violations of the laws or customs of war. Such violations shall include, but not be limited to, murder, ill-treatment, or deportation to slave labour or for any other purpose of civilian population of or in occupied territory, murder or ill-treatment of prisoners of war or persons on the seas, killing of hostages, plunder of public or private property, wanton destruction of cities, towns, or villages, or devastation not justified by military necessity.
>
> (c) Crimes against Humanity: namely, murder, extermination, enslavement, deportation, and other inhumane acts committed against any civilian population, before or during the war, or persecutions on political, racial or religious grounds in execution of or in connection with any crime within the jurisdiction of the Tribunal, whether or not in violation of the domestic law of the country where perpetrated.
>
> Leaders, organisers, instigators, and accomplices participating in the formulation or execution of a common plan or conspiracy to commit any of the foregoing crimes are responsible for all acts performed by any persons in execution of such plan.

These provisions are binding upon the Tribunal as the law to be applied to the case. . . .

The Law of the Charter

The jurisdiction of the Tribunal is defined in the Agreement and Charter, and the crimes coming within the jurisdiction of the Tribunal, for which there shall be individual responsibility, are set out in Article 6. The law of the Charter is decisive, and binding upon the Tribunal.

The making of the Charter was the exercise of the sovereign legislative power by the countries to which the German Reich unconditionally surrendered; and the undoubted right of these countries to legislate for the occupied territories has been recognised by the civilised world. The Charter is not an arbitrary exercise of power on the part of the victorious nations, but in the view of the Tribunal, as will be shown, it is the expression of international law existing at the time of its creation; and to that extent is itself a contribution to international law.

The Signatory Powers created this Tribunal, defined the law it was to administer, and made regulations for the proper conduct of the Trial. In doing so, they have done together what any one of them might have done singly; for it is not to be doubted that any nation has the right thus to set up special courts to administer law. With regard to the constitution of the Court, all that the defendants are entitled to ask is to receive a fair trial on the facts and law. . . .

It was submitted that international law is concerned with the action of sovereign states and provides no punishment for individuals; and further, that where the act in question is an act of state, those who carry it out are not personally responsible, but are protected by the doctrine of the sovereignty of the state. In the opinion of the Tribunal, both these submissions must be rejected. That international law imposes duties and liabilities upon individuals as well as upon states has long been recognised. In the recent case of *ex parte* Quirin before the Supreme Court of the United States, persons were charged during the war with landing in the United States for purposes of spying and sabotage. The late Chief Justice Stone, speaking for the Court, said:

> From the very beginning of its history this Court has applied the law of war as including that part of the law of nations which prescribes for the conduct of war, the status, rights, and duties of enemy nations as well as enemy individuals.

He went on to give a list of cases tried by the courts, where individual offenders were charged with offences against the laws of nations, and particularly the laws of war. Many other authorities could be cited, but enough has been said to show that individuals can be punished for violations of international law. Crimes against international law are committed by men, not by abstract entities, and only by punishing individuals who commit such crimes can the provisions of international law be enforced.

The provisions of Article 228 of the Treaty of Versailles, already referred to, illustrate and enforce this view of individual responsibility.

The principle of international law which, under certain circumstances, protects the representatives of a state, cannot be applied to acts which are condemned as criminal by international law. The authors of these acts cannot shelter themselves behind their official position in order to be freed from punishment in appropriate proceedings. Article 7 of the Charter expressly declares:

> The official position of defendants, whether as heads of state, or responsible officials in government departments, shall not be considered as freeing them from responsibility, or mitigating punishment.

On the other hand the very essence of the Charter is that individuals have international duties which transcend the national obligations of obedience imposed by the individual state. He who violates the laws of war cannot obtain immunity while acting in pursuance of the authority of the state, if the state in authorising action moves outside its competence under international law.

It was also submitted on behalf of most of these defendants that in doing what they did they were acting under the orders of Hitler, and therefore cannot be held responsible for the acts committed by them in carrying out these orders. The Charter specifically provides in Article 8:

> The fact that the defendant acted pursuant to order of his Government or of a superior shall not free him from responsibility, but may be considered in mitigation of punishment.

The provisions of this article are in conformity with the law of all nations. That a soldier was ordered to kill or torture in violation of the international law of war has never been recognised as a defence to such acts of brutality, though, as the Charter here provides, the order may be urged in mitigation of the punishment. The true test, which is found in varying degrees in the criminal law of most nations, is not the existence of the order, but whether moral choice was in fact possible.

United States v. Calley
22 C.M.A. 534 (1973)

Quinn, Judge:

First Lieutenant Calley stands convicted of the premeditated murder of 22 infants, children, women, and old men, and of assault with intent to murder a child of about 2 years of age. All the killings and the assault took place on March 16, 1968 in the area of the village of My Lai in the Republic of South Vietnam. The Army Court of Military Review affirmed the findings of guilty and the sentence, which, as reduced by the convening authority, includes dismissal and confinement at hard labor for 20 years. The accused petitioned this Court for further review, alleging 30 assignments of error. We granted three of these assignments. . . .

In his second assignment of error the accused contends that the evidence is insufficient to establish his guilt beyond a reasonable doubt. Summarized, the pertinent evidence is as follows:

Lieutenant Calley was a platoon leader in C Company, a unit that was part of an organization known as Task Force Barker, whose mission was to subdue and drive out the enemy in an area in the Republic of Vietnam known popularly as Pinkville. Before March 16, 1968, this area, which included the village of My Lai 4, was a Viet Cong stronghold. C Company had operated in the area several times. Each time the unit had entered the area it suffered casualties by sniper fire, machine gun fire, mines, and other forms of attack. Lieutenant Calley had accompanied his platoon on some of the incursions.

On March 15, 1968, a memorial service for members of the company killed in the area during the preceding weeks was held. After the service Captain Ernest L. Medina, the commanding officer of C Company, briefed the company on a mission in the Pinkville area set for the next day. C Company was to serve as the main attack formation for Task Force Barker. In that role it would assault and neutralize My Lai 4, 5, and 6 and then mass for an assault on My Lai 1. Intelligence reports indicated that the unit would be opposed by a veteran enemy battalion, and that all civilians would be absent from the area. The objective was to destroy the enemy. Disagreement exists as to the instructions on the specifics of destruction.

Captain Medina testified that he instructed his troops that they were to destroy My Lai 4 by "burning the hootches, to kill the livestock, to close the wells and to destroy the food crops." Asked if women and children were to be killed, Medina said he replied in the negative, adding that, "You must use common sense. If they have a weapon and are trying to engage you, then you can shoot back, but you must use common sense." However, Lieutenant Calley testified that Captain Medina informed the troops they were to kill every living thing—men, women, children, and animals—and under no circumstances were they to leave any Vietnamese behind them as they passed through the villages enroute to their final objective. Other witnesses gave more or less support to both versions of the briefing.

On March 16, 1968, the operation began with interdicting fire. C Company was then brought to the area by helicopters. Lieutenant Calley's platoon was on the first lift. This platoon formed a defense perimeter until the remainder of the force was landed. The unit received no hostile fire from the village.

Calley's platoon passed the approaches to the village with his men firing heavily. Entering the village, the platoon encountered only unarmed, unresisting men, women, and children. The villagers, including infants held in their mothers' arms, were assembled and moved in separate groups to collection points. Calley testified that during this time he was radioed twice by Captain Medina, who demanded to know what was delaying the platoon. On being told that a large number of villagers had been detained, Calley said Medina ordered him to "waste them." Calley further testified that he obeyed the orders because he had been taught the doctrine of obedience throughout his military career. Medina denied that he gave any such order.

One of the collection points for the villagers was in the southern part of the village. There, Private First Class Paul D. Meadlo guarded a group of between 30 to 40 old men, women, and children. Lieutenant Calley approached Meadlo and told him, "You know what to do," and left. He returned shortly and asked Meadlo why the people were not yet dead. Meadlo replied he did not know that Calley had meant that they should be killed. Calley declared that he wanted them dead. He and Meadlo then opened fire on the group, until all but a few children fell. Calley then personally shot these children. He expended 4 or 5 magazines from his M-16 rifle in the incident.

Lieutenant Calley and Meadlo moved from this point to an irrigation ditch on the east side of My Lai 4. There, they encountered another group of civilians being held by several soldiers. Meadlo estimated that this group contained from 75 to 100 persons. Calley stated, "We got another job to do, Meadlo," and he ordered the group into the ditch. When all were in the ditch, Calley and Meadlo opened fire on them. Although ordered by Calley to shoot, Private First Class James J. Dursi refused to join in the killings, and Specialist Four Robert E. Maples refused to give his machine gun to Calley for use in the killings. Lieutenant Calley admitted that he fired into the ditch, with the muzzle of his weapon within 5 feet of people in it. He expended between 10 to 15 magazines of ammunition on this occasion.

With his radio operator, Private Charles Sledge, Calley moved to the north end of the ditch. There, he found an elderly Vietnamese monk, whom he interrogated. Calley struck the man with his rifle butt and then shot him in the head. Other testimony indicates that immediately afterwards a young child was observed running toward the village. Calley seized him by the arm, threw him into the ditch, and fired at him. Calley admitted interrogating and striking the monk, but denied shooting him. He also denied the incident involving the child.

Appellate defense counsel contend that the evidence is insufficient to establish the accused's guilt. They do not dispute Calley's participation in the homicides, but they argue that he did not act with the malice or *mens rea* essential to a conviction of murder; that the orders he received to kill everyone in the village were not palpably illegal; that he was acting in ignorance of the laws of war; that since he was told that only "the enemy" would be in the village, his honest belief that there were no innocent civilians in the village exonerates him of criminal responsibility for their deaths; and, finally, that his actions were in the heat of passion caused by reasonable provocation.

In assessing the sufficiency of the evidence to support findings of guilty, we cannot reevaluate the credibility of the witnesses or resolve conflicts in their testimony and thus decide anew whether the accused's guilt was established beyond a reasonable doubt. Our function is more limited; it is to determine whether the record contains enough evidence for the triers of the facts to find beyond a reasonable doubt each element of the offenses involved.

The testimony of Meadlo and others provided the court members with ample evidence from which to find that Lieutenant Calley directed and personally participated in the intentional killing of men, women, and children, who were unarmed and in the custody of armed soldiers of C Company. If the prosecution's witnesses are believed, there is also ample evidence to support a finding that the accused deliberately shot the Vietnamese monk whom he interrogated, and that he seized, threw into a ditch, and fired on a child with the intent to kill.

Enemy prisoners are not subject to summary execution by their captors. Military law has long held that the killing of an unresisting prisoner is murder.

> While it is lawful to kill an enemy "in the heat and exercise of war," yet "to kill such an enemy after he has laid down his arms . . . is murder."

Conceding for the purposes of this assignment of error that Calley believed the villagers were part of "the enemy," the uncontradicted evidence is that they were under the control of armed soldiers and were offering no resistance. In his testimony, Calley admitted he was aware of the requirement that prisoners be treated with respect. He also admitted he knew that the normal practice was to interrogate villagers, release those who could satisfactorily account for themselves, and evacuate the suspect among them for further examination. Instead of proceeding in the usual way, Calley executed all, without regard to age, condition, or possibility of suspicion. On the evidence, the court-martial could reasonably find Calley guilty of the offenses before us.

At trial, Calley's principal defense was that he acted in execution of Captain Medina's order to kill everyone in My Lai 4. Appellate defense counsel urge this defense as the most important factor in assessment of the legal sufficiency of the evidence. The argument, however, is inapplicable to whether the evidence is *legally* sufficient. Captain Medina denied that he issued any such order, either during the previous day's briefing or on the date the killings were carried out. Resolution of the conflict between his testimony and that of the accused was for the triers of the facts. The general findings of guilty, with exceptions as to the number of persons killed, does not indicate whether the court members found that Captain Medina did not issue the alleged order to kill, or whether, if he did, the court members believed that the accused knew the order was illegal. For the purpose of the legal sufficiency of the evidence, the record supports the findings of guilty. . . .

We turn to the contention that the judge erred in his submission of the defense of superior orders to the court. After fairly summarizing the evidence, the judge gave the following instructions pertinent to the issue:

The killing of resisting or fleeing enemy forces is generally recognized as a justifiable act of war, and you may consider any such killings justifiable in this case. The law attempts to protect those persons not actually engaged in warfare, however; and limits the circumstances under which their lives may be taken.

Both combatants captured by and noncombatants detained by the opposing force, regardless of their loyalties, political views, or prior acts, have the right to be treated as prisoners until released, confined, or executed, in accordance with law and established procedures, by competent authority sitting in judgment of such detained or captured individuals. Summary execution of detainees or prisoners is forbidden by law. Further, it's clear under the evidence presented in this case, that hostile acts or support of the enemy North Vietnamese or Viet Cong forces by inhabitants of My Lai (4) at some time prior to 16 March 1968, would not justify the summary execution of all or a part of the occupants of My Lai (4) on 16 March, nor would hostile acts committed that day, if, following the hostility, the belligerents surrendered or were captured by our forces. I therefore instruct you, as a matter of law, that if unresisting human beings were killed at My Lai (4) while within the effective custody and control of our military forces, their deaths cannot be considered justified, and any order to kill such people would be, as a matter of law, an illegal order. Thus, if you find that Lieutenant Calley received an order directing him to kill unresisting Vietnamese within his control or within the control of his troops, *that order would be an illegal order.*

A determination that an order is illegal does not, of itself, assign criminal responsibility to the person following the order for acts done in compliance with it. Soldiers are taught to follow orders, and special attention is given to obedience of orders on the battlefield. Military effectiveness depends upon obedience to orders. On the other hand, the obedience of a soldier is not the obedience of an automaton. A soldier is a reasoning agent, obliged to respond, not as a machine, but as a person. The law takes these factors into account in assessing criminal responsibility for acts done in compliance with illegal orders.

The acts of a subordinate done in compliance with an unlawful order given him by his superior are excused and impose no criminal liability upon him unless the superior's order is one which a man of *ordinary sense and understanding* would, under the circumstances, know to be unlawful, or if the order in question is actually known to the accused to be unlawful. . . .

In determining what orders, if any, Lieutenant Calley acted under, if you find him to have acted, you should consider all of the matters which he has testified reached him and which you can infer from other evidence that he saw and heard. Then, unless you find beyond a reasonable doubt that he was not acting under orders directing him in substance and effect to kill unresisting occupants of My Lai (4), you must determine whether Lieutenant Calley actually knew those orders to be unlawful. . . .

In determining whether or not Lieutenant Calley had knowledge of the unlawfulness of any order found by you to have been given, you may consider all relevant facts and circumstances, including Lieutenant Calley's rank; educational background; OCS schooling; other training while in the Army, including basic training, and his training in Hawaii and Vietnam; his experience on prior operations involving contact with hostile and friendly Vietnamese; his age; and any other evidence tending to prove or disprove that on 16 March 1968, Lieutenant Calley knew the order was unlawful. If you find beyond a reasonable doubt, on the basis of all the evidence, that *Lieutenant Calley actually knew* the order under which he asserts he operated was unlawful, the fact that the order was given operates as no defense.

Unless you find beyond reasonable doubt that the accused acted with actual knowledge that the order was unlawful, you must proceed to determine whether, under the circumstances, *a man of ordinary sense and understanding would have known the order was unlawful. Your deliberations on this question do not focus on Lieutenant Calley and the manner in which he perceived the legality of the order found to have been given him. The standard is that of a man of ordinary sense and understanding under the circumstances.*

Think back to the events of 15 and 16 March 1968. . . . Then determine, in light of all the surrounding circumstances, whether the order, which to reach this point you will have found him to be operating in accordance with, is one which a man of ordinary sense and understanding would know to be unlawful. Apply this to each charged act which you have found Lieutenant Calley to have committed. Unless you are satisfied from the evidence, beyond a reasonable doubt, that a man of ordinary sense and understanding would have known the order to be unlawful, you must acquit Lieutenant Calley for committing acts done in accordance with the order. (Emphasis added.)

Appellate defense counsel contend that these instructions are prejudicially erroneous in that they require the court members to determine that Lieutenant Calley knew that an order to kill human beings in the circumstances under which he killed was illegal by the standard of whether "a man of ordinary sense and understanding" would know the order was illegal. They urge us to adopt as the governing test whether the order is so palpably or manifestly illegal that a person of "the commonest understanding" would be aware of its illegality. They maintain the standard stated by the judge is too strict and unjust; that it confronts members of the armed forces who are not persons of ordinary sense and understanding with the dilemma of choosing between the penalty of death for disobedience of an order in time of war on the one hand and the equally serious punishment for obedience on the other. Some thoughtful commentators on military law have presented much the same argument.[1]

---

[1]   In the words of one author: "If the standard of reasonableness continues to be applied, we run the unacceptable risk of applying serious punishment to one whose only crime is the slowness of his wit or his stu-

The "ordinary sense and understanding" standard is set forth in the present Manual for Courts-Martial, United States (1969 Rev.). It appeared as early as 1917. Apparently, it originated in a quotation from F. Wharton, Homicide § 485 (3d ed. 1907). Wharton's authority is Riggs v. State (Tenn. 1866), in which the court approved a charge to the jury as follows:

> [I]n its substance being clearly illegal, so that a man of ordinary sense and understanding would know as soon as he heard the order read or given that such order was illegal, would afford a private no protection for a crime committed under such order.

Other courts have used other language to define the substance of the defense. Typical is McCall v. McDowell (C.C.D. Cal. 1867), in which the court said:

> But I am not satisfied that Douglas ought to be held liable to the plaintiff at all. He acted not as a volunteer, but as a subordinate in obedience to the order of his superior. Except in a plain case of excess of authority, where at first blush it is apparent and palpable to the commonest understanding that the order is illegal, I cannot but think that the law should excuse the military subordinate when acting in obedience to the orders of his commander. Otherwise he is placed in the dangerous dilemma of being liable in damages to third persons for obedience to an order, or to the loss of his commission and disgrace for disobedience thereto. . . . The first duty of a soldier is obedience, and without this there can be neither discipline nor efficiency in an army. If every subordinate officer and soldier were at liberty to question the legality of the orders of the commander, and obey them or not as they may consider them valid or invalid, the camp would be turned into a debating school, where the precious moment for action would be wasted in wordy conflicts between the advocates of conflicting opinions.

Colonel William Winthrop, the leading American commentator on military law, notes:

> But for the inferior to assume to determine the question of the lawfulness of an order given him by a superior would of itself, as a general rule, amount to insubordination, and such an assumption carried into practice would subvert military discipline. Where the order is apparently regular and *lawful on its face,* he is not to go behind it to satisfy himself that his superior has proceeded with authority, but is to obey it according to its terms, *the only exceptions recognized to the rule of obedience being cases of orders so manifestly beyond the legal power or discretion of the commander as to admit of no rational doubt of their unlawfulness. . . .*

---

pidity. The soldier, who honestly believes that he must obey an order to kill and is punished for it, is convicted not of murder but of simple negligence." Finkelstein, Duty to Obey as a Defense, March 9, 1970 (unpublished essay, Army War College).

Except in such instances of palpable illegality, which must be of rare occurrence, the inferior should presume that the order was lawful and authorized and obey it accordingly, and in obeying it can scarcely fail to be held justified by a military court.

(emphasis added).

In the stress of combat, a member of the armed forces cannot reasonably be expected to make a refined legal judgment and be held criminally responsible if he guesses wrong on a question as to which there may be considerable disagreement. But there is no disagreement as to the illegality of the order to kill in this case. For 100 years, it has been a settled rule of American law that even in war the summary killing of an enemy, who has submitted to, and is under, effective physical control, is murder. Appellate defense counsel acknowledge that rule of law and its continued viability, but they say that Lieutenant Calley should not be held accountable for the men, women and children he killed because the court-martial could have found that he was a person of "commonest understanding" and such a person might not know what our law provides; that his captain had ordered him to kill these unarmed and submissive people and he only carried out that order as a good disciplined soldier should.

Whether Lieutenant Calley was the most ignorant person in the United States Army in Vietnam, or the most intelligent, he must be presumed to know that he could not kill the people involved here. The United States Supreme Court has pointed out that "[t]he rule that 'ignorance of the law will not excuse' [a positive act that constitutes a crime] . . . is deep in our law." Lambert v. California. An order to kill infants and unarmed civilians who were so demonstrably incapable of resistance to the armed might of a military force as were those killed by Lieutenant Calley is, in my opinion, so palpably illegal that whatever conceptional difference there may be between a person of "commonest understanding" and a person of "common understanding," that difference could not have had any "impact on a court of lay members receiving the respective wordings in instructions," as appellate defense counsel contend. In my judgment, there is no possibility of prejudice to Lieutenant Calley in the trial judge's reliance upon the established standard of excuse of criminal conduct, rather than the standard of "commonest understanding" presented by the defense, or by the new variable test postulated in the dissent, which, with the inclusion of such factors for consideration as grade and experience, would appear to exact a higher standard of understanding from Lieutenant Calley than that of the person of ordinary understanding.

In summary, as reflected in the record, the judge was capable and fair, and dedicated to assuring the accused a trial on the merits as provided by law; his instructions on all issues were comprehensive and correct. Lieutenant Calley was given every consideration to which he was entitled, and perhaps more. We are impressed with the absence of bias or prejudice on the part of the court members. They were instructed to determine the *truth* according to the law and this they did with due deliberation and full consideration of the evidence. Their findings of guilty represent the truth of the facts as they determined them to be and there is substantial evidence to support those findings. No mistakes of procedure cast doubt upon them.

Consequently, the decision of the Court of Military Review is affirmed.

Duncan, Judge (concurring in the result):

My difference of opinion from Judge Quinn's view of the defense of obedience to orders is narrow. The issue of obedience to orders was raised in defense by the evidence. Contrary to Judge Quinn, I do not consider that a presumption arose that the appellant knew he could not kill the people involved. The Government, as I see it, is not entitled to a presumption of what the appellant knew of the illegality of an order. It is a matter for the factfinders under proper instructions.

Paragraph 216, Manual for Courts-Martial, United States (1969 Rev.), provides for special defenses: excuse because of accident or misadventure; self-defense; entrapment; coercion or duress; physical or financial inability; and obedience to apparently lawful orders. Subparagraph *d* of paragraph 216 is as follows:

> An order requiring the performance of a military duty may be inferred to be legal. An act performed manifestly beyond the scope of authority, or pursuant to an order that a man of ordinary sense and understanding would know to be illegal, or in a wanton manner in the discharge of a lawful duty, is not excusable.

The military judge clearly instructed the members pursuant to this provision of the Manual. The heart of the issue is whether, under the circumstances of this case, he should have abandoned the Manual standard and fashioned another. The defense urges a purely subjective standard; the dissent herein yet another. I suggest that there are important general as well as certain specific considerations which convince me that the standard should not be abandoned. The process of promulgating Manual provisions is geared to produce requirements for the system only after most serious reflection by knowledgeable and concerned personnel. These persons have full regard for the needs of the armed forces and genuine concern for the plight of one accused. Those who prepared the Manual provision and the President of the United States, the Commander-in-Chief, who approved and made the provision a part of our law, were aware that disobedience to orders is the anathema to an efficient military force. Judge Quinn points out that this Court has established as precedent the applicability of the special defense upon proof adduced pursuant to the Manual standard. These are important general reasons for not aborting a standard that has been long in existence and often used.

It is urged that in using the Manual test of "a man of ordinary sense and understanding" those persons at the lowest end of the scale of intelligence and experience in the services may suffer conviction while those more intelligent and experienced would possess faculties which would cause them to abjure the order with impunity. Such an argument has some attraction but in my view falls short of that which should impel a court to replace that which is provided to us as law.

It appears to me that all tests which measure an accused's conduct by an objective standard—whether it is the test of "palpable illegality to the commonest understanding" or whether the test establishes a set of profile considerations by which to measure the accused's ability to assess the legality of the order—are less than perfect, and they have a certain potential for injustice to the member having the slowest wit and quickest obedience. Obviously the higher the standard, the likelihood is that fewer persons will be able to measure up to it. Knowledge of the fact that there are other standards that are arguably more fair does not convince me that the standard used herein is unfair, on its face, or as applied to Lieutenant Calley.

Perhaps a new standard, such as the dissent suggests, has merit; however, I would leave that for the legislative authority or for the cause where the record demonstrates harm from the instructions given. I perceive none in this case. The general verdict in this case implies that the jury believed a man of ordinary sense and understanding would have known the order in question to be illegal. Even conceding arguendo that this issue should have been resolved under instructions requiring a finding that almost every member of the armed forces would have immediately recognized that the order was unlawful, as well as a finding that as a consequence of his age, grade, intelligence, experience, and training, Lieutenant Calley should have recognized the order's illegality, I do not believe the result in this case would have been different. . . .

Darden, Chief Judge (dissenting):

Although the charge the military judge gave on the defense of superior orders was not inconsistent with the Manual treatment of this subject, I believe the Manual provision is too strict in a combat environment. Among other things, this standard permits serious punishment of persons whose training and attitude incline them either to be enthusiastic about compliance with orders or not to challenge the authority of their superiors. The standard also permits conviction of members who are not persons of ordinary sense and understanding.

The principal opinion has accurately traced the history of the current standard. Since this Manual provision is one of substantive law rather than one relating to procedure or modes of proof, the Manual rule is not binding on this Court, which has the responsibility for determining the principles that govern justification in the law of homicide. My impression is that the weight of authority, including the commentators whose articles are mentioned in the principal opinion, supports a more liberal approach to the defense of superior orders. Under this approach, superior orders should constitute a defense except "in a plain case of excess of authority, where at first blush it is apparent and palpable to the commonest understanding that the order is illegal."

While this test is phrased in language that now seems "somewhat archaic and ungrammatical," the test recognizes that the essential ingredient of discipline in any armed force is obedience to orders and that this obedience is so important it should not be penalized unless the order would be recognized as illegal, not by what some hypothetical reasonable soldier would have known, but also by "those persons at the lowest end of the scale of intelligence and experience in the services." This is the real purpose in permitting superior orders to be a defense, and it ought not to be restricted by the concept of a fictional reasonable man so that, regardless of his personal characteristics, an accused judged after the fact may find himself punished for either obedience or disobedience, depending on whether the evidence will support the finding of simple negligence on his part.

It is true that the standard of a "reasonable man" is used in other areas of military criminal law, e.g., in connection with the provocation necessary to reduce murder to voluntary manslaughter; what constitutes an honest and reasonable mistake; and, indirectly, in connection with involuntary manslaughter. But in none of these instances do we have the countervailing consideration of avoiding the subversion of obedience to discipline in combat by encouraging a member to weigh the legality of an order or whether the superior had the authority to issue it.

The preservation of human life is, of course, of surpassing importance. To accomplish such preservation, members of the armed forces must be held to standards of conduct that will permit punishment of atrocities and enable this nation to follow civilized concepts of warfare. In defending the current standard, the Army Court of Military Review expressed the view that:

> Heed must be given not only to the subjective innocence-through-ignorance in the soldier, but to the consequences for his victims. Also, barbarism tends to invite reprisal to the detriment of our own force or disrepute which interferes with the achievement of war aims, even though the barbaric acts were preceded by orders for their commission. Casting the defense of obedience to orders solely in subjective terms of *mens rea* would operate practically to abrogate those objective restraints which are essential to functioning rules of war.

I do not disagree with these comments. But while humanitarian considerations compel us to consider the impact of actions by members of our armed forces on citizens of other nations, I am also convinced that the phrasing of the defense of superior orders should have as its principal objective fairness to the unsophisticated soldier and those of somewhat limited intellect who nonetheless are doing their best to perform their duty.

The test of palpable illegality to the commonest understanding properly balances punishment for the obedience of an obviously illegal order against protection to an accused for following his elementary duty of obeying his superiors. Such a test reinforces the need for obedience as an essential element of military discipline by broadly protecting the soldier who has been effectively trained to look to his superiors for direction. It also promotes fairness by permitting the military jury to consider the particular accused's intelligence, grade, training, and other elements directly related to the issue of whether he should have known an order was illegal. Finally, that test imputes such knowledge to an accused not as a result of simple negligence but on the much stronger circumstantial concept that almost anyone in the armed forces would have immediately recognized that the order was palpably illegal.

I would adopt this standard as the correct instruction for the jury when the defense of superior orders is in issue. Because the original case language is archaic and somewhat ungrammatical, I would rephrase it to require that the military jury be instructed that, despite his asserted defense of superior orders, an accused may be held criminally accountable for his acts, allegedly committed pursuant to such orders, if the court members are convinced beyond a reasonable doubt (1) that almost every member of the armed forces would have immediately recognized that the order was unlawful, and (2) that the accused should have recognized the order's illegality as a consequence of his age, grade, intelligence, experience, and training. . . .

In the instant case, Lieutenant Calley's testimony placed the defense of superior orders in issue, even though he conceded that he knew prisoners were normally to be treated with respect and that the unit's normal practice was to interrogate Vietnamese villagers, release those who could account for themselves, and evacuate those suspected of being a part of the enemy forces. Although crucial parts of his testimony were sharply contested, according to Lieutenant Calley, (1) he had received a briefing before the assault in which he was instructed that every living thing in the village was to be killed, including women and children; (2) he was informed that speed was important in securing the village and moving forward; (3) he was ordered that under no circumstances were any Vietnamese to be allowed to stay behind the lines of his forces; (4) the residents of the village who were taken into custody were hindering the progress of his platoon in taking up the position it was to occupy; and (5) when he informed Captain Medina of this hindrance, he was ordered to kill the villagers and to move his platoon to a proper position.

In addition to the briefing, Lieutenant Calley's experience in the Pinkville area caused him to know that, in the past, when villagers had been left behind his unit, the unit had immediately received sniper fire from the rear as it pressed forward. Faulty intelligence apparently led him also to believe that those persons in the village were not innocent civilians but were either enemies or enemy sympathizers. For a participant in the My Lai operation, the circumstances that could have obtained there may have caused the illegality of alleged orders to kill civilians to be much less clear than they are in a hindsight review.[2]

Since the defense of superior orders was not submitted to the military jury under what I consider to be the proper standard, I would grant Lieutenant Calley a rehearing.

---

[2]   A New York Times Book Reviewer has noted, "One cannot locate the exact moment in his [Calley's] narrative when one can be absolutely certain that one would have acted differently given the same circumstances."

Notes and Questions

1. Is the law of the Nuremberg Tribunal anything more than the "justice of the victors"? Why should the winning side in a war get to impose its version of law on the losers? Is this merely a case of "might makes right"? Or is there a higher standard?

2. The Nuremberg court states that "the true test . . . is not the existence of the order, but whether moral choice was in fact possible." Given Lieutenant Calley's situation, and assuming he had been ordered to kill the villagers, did he have any other (realistic) choice? What other options, if any, did he have?

3. Assume you are prosecuting former East German border guards who had been ordered to fire on civilians attempting to flee from East Berlin. Did the border guards have "the possibility of moral choice"?

4. Chief Judge Darden, dissenting in the *Calley* case, argues that to convict in the face of a superior orders defense, the jury must be convinced beyond a reasonable doubt that:

(1) almost every member of the armed forces would have immediately recognized that the order was unlawful; and
(2) the accused should have recognized the order's illegality as a consequence of his age, grade, intelligence, experience, and training.

How does this standard differ from that adopted by the majority, and what implications would it have?

Suggestions For Further Reading

Herbert C. Kelman & V. Lee Hamilton, Crimes of Obedience: Toward a Social Psychology of Authority and Responsibility (1989)

Mark Kelman, Interpretive Construction in the Substantive Criminal Law, 33 Stanford Law Review 591 (1981)

Mark J. Osiel, Obeying Orders: Atrocity, Military Discipline, and the Law of War, 86 California Law Review 939 (1998)

Chapter 8
The Abuse Excuse

United States v. Alexander and Murdock
471 F.2d 923 (D.C. Cir. 1972)

Per Curiam:

The Evidence Presented at Trial

Five United States Marine Lieutenants—Ellsworth Kramer, Thaddeus Lesnick, William King, Frank Marasco, and Daniel LeGear—attended a dinner at the Marine Corps Base in Quantico, Virginia, on the evening of June 4, 1968, in celebration of their near-completion of basic officers' training. After dinner, they drove to Washington, arriving about midnight, still wearing their formal dress white uniforms. They stopped for about an hour-and-a-half at a nightclub, where they each had a drink. They were well-behaved and "conducted themselves like gentlemen." At the nightclub they met Barbara Kelly, a good friend of Lieutenant Kramer. They accompanied her to her apartment, which she shared with another young woman, and visited there with the two women until about 2:40 a.m. When the five Marines departed, Miss Kelly accompanied them, intending to return to the nightclub to meet another friend. Along the way, they decided to stop at a hamburger shop to get some coffee and sandwiches before the trip back to Quantico. The six of them entered the shop, stood by the take-out counter, and ordered their food. They noticed three Negro males sitting at the other end of the counter. As described by Lieutenant Kramer, "[T]heir hair was in Afro-bush cut, wearing medallions, jersey knit shirts, sport jackets. . . . [T]hey were what I consider in eccentric dress." The three men were Alexander, Murdock, and Cornelius Frazier. The critical events which subsequently took place in the restaurant were described by the four survivors of the Marine group and by Murdock and Frazier. Alexander chose not to take the stand.

According to the prosecution witnesses, Lieutenant Kramer realized that appellant Alexander was staring at him, and he returned the stare. "[I]t was on the order of a Mexican stand-off type thing where you just keep staring at one another for an indefinite period of time." No words were exchanged between the two men, and Lieutenant Kramer soon turned and faced the counter. Shortly thereafter Frazier, Murdock, and Alexander got up from where they were sitting and walked to the door behind the Marines. Murdock and Frazier left the shop, but Alexander stopped in the doorway. He tapped Lieutenant Kramer on the shoulder. When the Marine turned around, Alexander poked his uniform name tag and said, "You want to talk about it more? You want to come outside and talk about it more?" When Lieutenant Kramer replied, "Yes, I am ready to come out" or "Yes, I guess so," Alexander added, "I am going to make you a Little Red Ridinghood." At this point, Lieutenant King stepped up beside Lieutenant Kramer and made a remark variously reported by the prosecution witnesses as "What you God-damn niggers want?", "What do you want, you nigger?", "What do you want, dirty nigger bastard?", and "Get out of here nigger." Thereupon Alexander abruptly drew a long-barrelled .38 caliber revolver, cocked it, and pointed it at the group or directly into Lieutenant King's chest, saying, "I will show you what I want," or "This is what I want."

The Marines possessed no weapons whatsoever and, according to their testimony, were not advancing toward Alexander. As they stood there, shocked at the sight of the gun, Murdock reentered the shop at Alexander's left and rear, and drew a short-barrelled .38 caliber revolver. A series of shots suddenly rang out, and the Marines and Miss Kelly fell or dived to the floor. None attempted to retaliate because they all were taking cover and trying to get out of the line of fire. Alexander and Murdock withdrew from the shop, but one of them stuck his arm back into the shop and attempted—unsuccessfully—to fire his weapon several times more. Only Lieutenant Kramer attempted to identify this man, and he said it was Murdock.

Lieutenants King and Lesnick were mortally wounded in the fusillade; they died within minutes. Lieutenant Kramer was wounded in the head, but he remained conscious, as did Miss Kelly, who had been shot in the hip. Only Lieutenants LeGear and Marasco were not hit.

Alexander, Murdock, and Frazier fled to Alexander's automobile and drove off rapidly in the wrong direction on a one-way street. Alexander was driving, and as the car drove off, Murdock fired three more shots from the window of the car, at the door of the hamburger shop, and at people in the street. A nearby scout car raced after the fleeing car and stopped them within a few blocks. Two revolvers were recovered from the front floorboard of Alexander's automobile.

For the defense, Frazier and appellant Murdock testified that the Marines in the restaurant had been drunk and loud. Frazier testified that they had obstructed his exit as he left. He walked around them and left the restaurant just ahead of Murdock, but when he looked back, Murdock had gone back inside. He then heard shots and ran to Alexander's car.

Murdock testified that when he realized that Alexander had not followed him out of the restaurant, he returned, and as he entered he heard someone say, "Get out, you black bastards." He then saw the Marine advancing towards him. Murdock called to Alexander to leave with him, and Alexander turned as if to go. Murdock then heard a "sound like all the feet in the place were moving," turned around himself, and saw Alexander's drawn gun. Murdock pulled his own gun, as a reflex, and testified that he "commenced firing about the time one of them was actually right up on me. . . . [M]aybe a foot away." He testified that the other Marines were advancing toward him fast, and he felt they were going to kill him. On cross-examination he admitted that he emptied his fully-loaded revolver at the Marine group in the restaurant, testified that he didn't know if Alexander had fired, and admitted that he fired three shots from Alexander's gun from the window of the car as it was driven off.

Who fired the bullets inside the restaurant was an issue of some importance during the trial, but because of the testimony of the Government's firearms expert, both sides seem now to agree that Alexander did not fire his revolver inside the restaurant, and that Murdock—as he testified himself—emptied his gun at the Marines and Miss Kelly, picked up Alexander's gun in the automobile, and fired three shots with it from the window.

Bazelon, Chief Judge, dissenting:

. . . I turn finally to what I regard as a serious error in the jury charge on the issue of criminal responsibility. In order to put the problem in perspective, it will be necessary to review the testimony in some detail.

1. Murdock relied primarily on the testimony of Dr. Williams, a board-certified psychiatrist, and professor at Howard University Medical School. Dr. Williams had examined Murdock on two occasions during his confinement in St. Elizabeths Hospital. According to the testimony of Dr. Williams, Murdock was strongly delusional, though not hallucinating or psychotic; he was greatly preoccupied with the unfair treatment of Negroes in this country, and the idea that racial war was inevitable. He showed compulsiveness in his behavior, emotional immaturity, and some psychopathic traits. Since his emotional difficulties were closely tied to his sense of racial oppression, it is probable that when the Marine in the Little Tavern called him a "black bastard" Murdock had an irresistible impulse to shoot. His emotional disorder had its roots in his childhood, in the Watts section of Los Angeles; particularly important was the fact that his father had deserted his mother, and he grew up in a large family with little money and little love or attention.

Dr. Williams stated firmly that in his view Murdock was suffering from an abnormal mental condition that substantially impaired his behavior controls. But he stated just as firmly that the condition did not amount to a mental illness:

> My idea of mental illness is that an individual is out of touch with reality. He has auditory hallucinations, he has delusions, he has mannerisms that set him off as a different individual. He withdraws from society. And his behavior as such is tremendously bizarre. This is what I call, what they would call at Johns Hopkins, a major psychosis and a form of mental illness. . . .
> I look on [Murdock's condition] as psychoneurosis, but not, as such, a form of mental illness. It is not a psychotic reaction, which I consider a mental illness. It is an emotional response, an emotional illness. Not a mental illness in that it is psychotic.

This court has made it perfectly plain that for purposes of the insanity defense, "mental illness" is a legal term of art. A criminal defendant's responsibility cannot turn on the label attached to his condition. The insanity defense is neither expanded nor contracted by changing fashions in psychiatric terminology. In particular, mental illness for our purposes is not limited to psychosis; it includes any "abnormal condition of the mind that substantially affects mental or emotional processes and substantially impairs behavior controls."

Defense counsel was thus confronted with a serious dilemma, arising from the fact that "mental illness" meant one thing to his witness, and another to the law. It was clear that the law would permit a jury to find mental illness on the basis of Dr. Williams's testimony about Murdock's "abnormal condition." In practice, however, a jury might well be reluctant to look beyond the doctor's statement that the condition did not amount to mental illness as he understood the term.

Counsel's strategy was to bypass the troublesome term "mental illness," and invite the jury to focus directly on the legal definition of that term. He conceded to the jury that Murdock "did not have a mental disease in the classic sense," i.e., he did not have a psychosis. But, counsel argued, the expert testimony showed that at the critical moment Murdock did not have control of his conduct, and the reason for that lack of control was a deepseated emotional disorder that was rooted in his "rotten social background." Accordingly, he asked the trial court to omit the term "mental disease or defect" from the jury instructions. I think his proposal was ingenious; the trial court might well have framed a suitable instruction asking the jury to consider whether Murdock's act was the product, not of "mental illness," but of an "abnormal condition of the mind that substantially affects mental or emotional processes and substantially impairs behavior controls."

While the trial court denied the requested instruction, we cannot say that ruling was error. The judge carefully instructed the jury to resolve the question of mental illness in accordance with its legal definition; he told them they were not bound by medical conclusions as to what is or is not a mental disease, and he told them to ignore defense counsel's concession that Murdock was without mental disease. In this respect the instructions conform to the requirements set forth in our cases.

But the judge injected into the instructions a special note of caution, in response to the testimony and argument presented in this case. He told the jury:

> We are not concerned with a question of whether or not a man had a rotten social background. We are concerned with the question of his criminal responsibility. That is to say, whether he had an abnormal condition of the mind that affected his emotional and behavioral processes at the time of the offense.

Defense counsel had objected to that instruction before it was given, because his theory of the case was that Murdock had an abnormal mental condition caused in part by his "rotten social background." The trial court overruled his objection, deeming the instruction necessary to counteract what he saw as an attempt by defense counsel to appeal to the jurors on the basis of sympathy, or passion, or prejudice.

It may well be that the trial judge was motivated by a reasonable fear that the jury would reach its decision on the basis not of the law but of sympathy for the victims of a racist society. Nevertheless, I think that the quoted instruction was reversible error. It had the effect of telling the jury to disregard the testimony relating to Murdock's social and economic background and to consider only the testimony framed in terms of "illness." Such an instruction is contrary to law, and it clearly undermined Murdock's approach to the insanity defense in this case. For Murdock's strategy had two parts: first, he sought to convince the jury to disregard Dr. Williams' finding of no "mental illness," and then he sought to persuade them to find mental illness in the legal sense of the term. The jury could hardly consider the issue of mental illness without considering Murdock's background, in view of the fact that all the witnesses traced such disabilities as they found at least in part to his background.

2. No matter what the trial judge intended, his instruction may have deprived Murdock of a fair trial on the issue of responsibility. But even if that instruction had not been offered, Murdock could argue that he was denied a fair opportunity to present his particular responsibility defense—a defense not clearly grounded on any medically recognized "mental disease or defect." While the language of our responsibility test theoretically leaves room for such a defense, our experience reveals that in practice it imposes illogical constraints on the flow of information to the jury and also on the breadth of the jury's inquiry. Our test demands an "abnormal condition of the mind," and that term carries implications that may mislead counsel, the court, and the jury.

McDonald defined mental illness for purposes of the responsibility defense as an abnormal condition of the mind that "substantially affects mental or emotional processes and substantially impairs behavior controls." The thrust of Murdock's defense was that the environment in which he was raised—his "rotten social background"—conditioned him to respond to certain stimuli in a manner most of us would consider flagrantly inappropriate. Because of his early conditioning, he argued, he was denied any meaningful choice when the racial insult triggered the explosion in the restaurant. He asked the jury to conclude that his "rotten social background," and the resulting impairment of mental or emotional processes and behavior controls, ruled his violent reaction in the same manner that the behavior of a paranoid schizophrenic may be ruled by his "mental condition." Whether this impairment amounted to an "abnormal condition of the mind" is, in my opinion, at best an academic question. But the consequences we predicate on the answer may be very meaningful indeed.

We have never said that an exculpatory mental illness must be reflected in some organic or pathological condition. Nor have we enshrined psychosis as a prerequisite of the defense. But our experience has made it clear that the terms we use—"mental disease or defect" and "abnormal condition of the mind"—carry a distinct flavor of pathology. And they deflect attention from the crucial, functional question—did the defendant lack the ability to make any meaningful choice of action—to an artificial and misleading excursion into the thicket of psychiatric diagnosis and nomenclature.

It does not necessarily follow, however, that we should push the responsibility defense to its logical limits and abandon all of the trappings of the medical or disease model. However illogical and disingenuous, that model arguably serves important interests. Primarily, by offering a rationale for detention of persons who are found not guilty by reason of "insanity," it offers us shelter from a downpour of troublesome questions. If we were to facilitate Murdock's defense, as logic and morality would seem to command, so that a jury might acquit him because of his "rotten social background" rather than any treatable mental illness, the community would have to decide what to do with him.

If acquitted because he lacked responsibility, Murdock would automatically have been committed to St. Elizabeths Hospital for further examination. He could then obtain an unconditional release only upon the certification of the hospital superintendent "(1) that such person has recovered his sanity, (2) that, in the opinion of the superintendent, such person will not in the reasonable future be dangerous to himself or others . . . ." Plainly, the Hospital would find it difficult to justify holding Murdock on the grounds that he was insane in any conventional sense. None of the psychiatrists who testified at trial, including those from St. Elizabeths, suggested that his "sanity" had ever been lost.

Nevertheless, Murdock may well be dangerous. We have no carefully-crafted technique for resolving the complex of legal, moral, and political questions concealed in the determination of dangerousness. Regrettably, those questions are now decided, at least in the first instance, by psychiatrists. We can only speculate on the outcome of their inquiry.

They might conclude that Murdock's rage and resentment were burned off by the explosion in the restaurant; the cathartic effect of his violent outburst may have made its repetition unlikely. On the other hand, the crime Murdock committed is a prototype of the crimes that arouse the greatest public anxiety. He seems to be a man whose bitterness and racial hostility have turned into blasting powder which can be touched off by a spark. Since there is no obvious way to insulate him from further sparks, and since the powder is not being deactivated, further explosions may be unavoidable. It would not be surprising if the psychiatrists took the view that Murdock is now, and is likely to remain, extremely dangerous.

However accurate the prediction of dangerousness, it is not at all clear that the statute would permit Murdock's confinement. Read literally, the statute seems to establish a return to sanity and an absence of dangerousness as independent pre-conditions of unconditional release. That reading would require the hospitalization of a dangerous person who lacked any mental illness whatsoever. Our cases have made it clear, however, that "dangerousness" refers to "dangerousness by reason of mental illness." Thus, a defendant who was dangerous but no longer insane could not be involuntarily hospitalized. If Murdock cannot be considered insane, the hospital would have to release him.

We are left, therefore, with an obligation to choose among four unattractive alternatives:

A. We can impose narrow and admittedly illogical limitations on the responsibility defense to insure that a defendant like Murdock will not be acquitted on the theory that he lacked responsibility. By confining such a defendant in a penitentiary, we can avoid the difficult questions presented by the effort to hold him in confinement following a successful use of the responsibility defense.

B. If we remove the practical impediments to Murdock's defense and he is, in fact, acquitted for lack of responsibility, he could be released from custody in spite of his apparent dangerousness. That result would conform with the principle that civil commitment is ordinarily barred where a defendant is dangerous but not mentally ill. And there are even precedents for the acquittal and release of dangerous defendants who have been brought to trial on a criminal charge. The fourth amendment exclusionary rule, for example, effectively precludes conviction of some defendants who appear to be dangerous. But that rule has been subjected to heavy assault even though it serves important, extrinsic interests—the redress and deterrence of unconstitutional action and the preservation of judicial integrity. Acquitting a defendant like Murdock and returning him to the street might also protect our integrity. But it would probably be more difficult to obtain public support for, or even unfriendly acquiescence in, Murdock's release than to defend the operation of the exclusionary rule. It could be said, after all, that acquittal would result not in spite of Murdock's dangerousness, but precisely because of it. Thus, while there may be no reason in logic why Murdock could not be returned to the street, as a practical matter that is probably an unfeasible result.

C. If the community will not tolerate Murdock's release we can strive to find a vaguely therapeutic purpose for hospitalization. Skinnerian-like techniques may be available to re-program his behavior. We might conclude that they should be used and that their use justifies his confinement. But that will require us to stretch the medical model substantially so that new techniques can be applied to many persons not conventionally considered "sick."

I do not mean to suggest the existence of a bold line which segregates the orthodox, universally-admired techniques, from the techniques which are unconventional, morally and legally troublesome, and as yet unaccepted. Some commentators have insisted that the most traditional techniques, including psychotherapy, should never be imposed on an unwilling subject. And some of the techniques which raise the most profound moral and legal questions are already being put to use. Still, there does seem to be a continuum running from the less controversial to the more controversial techniques. Without suggesting that we can blink at the techniques that are now widely used, it seems clear to me that we must, at the very least, scrutinize with care the implications of advancing further along the continuum.

D. Finally, if there are no known or foreseeable techniques for "curing" someone like Murdock (or if we are unwilling to utilize the techniques that may be available), and if the incapacitation of the defendant is a practical imperative, we will have to confine him in exclusive reliance on a prediction of dangerousness. That confinement would be nothing more or less than unadorned preventive detention.

The options that would permit us to acquit Murdock but hold him in custody nonetheless—preventive detention and a stretching of the medical model to permit the use of new techniques—raise profound moral and legal questions. Resolution of those questions would require a prolonged and thorough public debate. But however they are resolved, it is at least clear that each of these options requires an expansion of the boundaries of the civil commitment doctrine. We could strive to limit the expansion by applying the new rationale only to persons who have undergone a criminal trial and been acquitted for lack of responsibility. But as a practical matter it seems very unlikely that the expansion could be so confined. The new rationale would permit—perhaps demand—that all persons who are rendered dangerous by a "rotten social background" should be preventively detained. Or that all persons who exhibit antisocial behavior patterns should have their behavior re-conditioned. We cannot escape the probability, if not absolute certainty, that every effort to diminish the class of persons who can be found criminally responsible will produce a concomitant expansion in the class of persons who can be subjected to involuntary civil commitment. The implications in this context are staggering. The price of permitting Murdock to claim the benefit of a logical aspect of the responsibility doctrine may be the unleashing of a detention device that operates, by hypothesis, at the exclusive expense of the lowest social and economic class.

That result can certainly be avoided—even if we are unwilling to return the defendant to the street—by reading the responsibility doctrine so narrowly that the issue of post-acquittal custody rarely arises. We could, for example, redefine the concept of responsibility so that it would approximate the concept of self-defense. All civil and criminal sanctions on the nonresponsible defendant would be barred, and the test would be reformulated to ask explicitly, which defendants should escape all state-imposed sanctions. Alternatively, we could retain the medical model and acknowledge its illogic as a significant virtue. Psychosis may be an irrational test of criminal responsibility, but it does have a recognizable symptomatology. In the civil commitment context it may provide the only manageable stopping point short of a fullfledged scheme of preventive detention. These limitations on the responsibility defense permit an avoidance—perhaps to the good—of a confrontation with the difficult questions posed by preventive detention and the various forms of behavior control.

On the other hand, we sacrifice a great deal by discouraging Murdock's responsibility defense. If we could remove the practical impediments to the free flow of information we might begin to learn something about the causes of crime. We might discover, for example, that there is a significant causal relationship between violent criminal behavior and a "rotten social background." That realization would require us to consider, for example, whether income redistribution and social reconstruction are indispensable first steps toward solving the problem of violent crime.

Each of these approaches to the responsibility doctrine has significant advantages and disadvantages. No one can fault us for choosing the wrong approach. We can be faulted, however, for refusing to make any choice at all—or at least for refusing to confront the implications and shortcomings of our de facto choice. It is a critical responsibility of courts, legislatures and commentators to undertake a purposive analysis of the responsibility defense, instead of merely paying it lip-service in deference to its historical significance and our "liberal" consciences. Under each of the prevailing tests of criminal responsibility, the operation of the defense has been haphazard, perfunctory, and virtually inexplicable. If we cannot overcome the irrational operation of the defense, we may have no honest choice but to abandon it and hold all persons criminally responsible for their action.

McGowan, Circuit Judge:

The tragic and senseless events giving rise to these appeals are a recurring byproduct of a society which, unable as yet to eliminate explosive racial tensions, appears equally paralyzed to deny easy access to guns. Cultural infantilism of this kind inevitably exacts a high price, which in this instance was paid by the two young officers who were killed. The ultimate responsibility for their deaths reaches far beyond these appellants.

As courts, however, we administer a system of justice which is limited in its reach. We deal only with those formally accused under laws which define criminal accountability narrowly. Our function on these appeals is to determine whether appellants had a fair opportunity to defend themselves, and were tried and sentenced according to law. . . .

Judge Bazelon . . . finds reversal to be compelled by reason of a statement made to the jury by the court in the course of its instructions. The bare words used are not a faulty statement of the law. They remind the jury that the issue before them for decision is not one of the shortcomings of society generally, but rather that of appellant Murdock's criminal responsibility for the illegal acts of which he had earlier been found guilty; and, the court added in the next breath, that issue turns on "whether [appellant] had an abnormal condition of the mind that affected his emotional and behavioral processes at the time of the offense." This last is, of course, an unexceptionable statement of what we have declared to be the law in this jurisdiction. . . .

In this context, the court's statement cannot be regarded as either being intended to do more, or as having the effect of doing more, than to focus the attention of the jury more precisely upon the exact legal formulation within which, and by reference to which, it was required to consider the evidence. . . .

Jahnke v. State
682 P.2d 991 (Wyo. 1984)

Thomas, Justice.

The essential questions presented in this case arise out of a notion that a victim of abuse has some special justification for patricide. . . .

The appellant's father, Richard Chester Jahnke, died on November 16, 1982, as a result of gunshot wounds. Those gunshot wounds were inflicted by the appellant, and that fact has never been an issue in this case. . . .

The material facts relating to the death of the appellant's father can be briefly stated. On the night of his death the father took the mother out to dinner, apparently to celebrate the anniversary of their meeting. Earlier the appellant had been involved in a violent altercation with his father, and he had been warned not to be at the home when the father and mother returned. During the absence of his parents the appellant made elaborate preparation for the final confrontation with his father. He changed into dark clothing and prepared a number of weapons which he positioned at various places throughout the family home that he selected to serve as "backup" positions in case he was not successful in his first effort to kill his father. These weapons included two shotguns, three rifles, a .38 caliber pistol and a Marine knife. In addition, he armed his sister, Deborah, with a .30 caliber M-1 carbine which he taught her how to operate so that she could protect herself in the event that he failed in his efforts. The appellant removed the family pets from the garage to the basement to protect them from injury in a potential exchange of gunfire between him and his father, and he closed the garage door. He then waited inside the darkened garage in a position where he could not be seen but which permitted him to view the lighted driveway on the other side of the garage door. Shortly before 6:30 p.m. the parents returned, and the appellant's father got out of the vehicle and came to the garage door. The appellant was armed with a 12-gauge shotgun loaded with slugs, and when he could see the head and shoulders of his father through the spacing of the slats of the shade covering the windows of the garage door, he blew his R.O.T.C. command-sergeant-major's whistle for courage, and he opened fire. All six cartridges in the shotgun were expended, and four of them in one way or another struck the father. . . .

After the shooting, and while the mother still was screaming in the driveway, the appellant and his sister exited the family home through a window in the mother's bedroom, which was at the far end of the house from the garage. The appellant and his sister then went separate ways, and the appellant was arrested at the home of his girl friend. Prior to the arrival of authorities the appellant told his girl friend's father that he had shot his dad for revenge. Subsequently, after being advised of his constitutional rights, the appellant made a statement in which he explained he had shot his father "for past things.". . .

It is clear that self-defense is circumscribed by circumstances involving a confrontation, usually encompassing some overt act or acts by the deceased, which would induce a reasonable person to fear that his life was in danger or that at least he was threatened with great bodily harm. . . .

Although many people, and the public media, seem to be prepared to espouse the notion that a victim of abuse is entitled to kill the abuser that special justification defense is antithetical to the mores of modern civilized society. It is difficult enough to justify capital punishment as an appropriate response of society to criminal acts even after the circumstances have been carefully evaluated by a number of people. To permit capital punishment to be imposed upon the subjective conclusion of the individual that prior acts and conduct of the deceased justified the killing would amount to a leap into the abyss of anarchy. . . .

This record contained no evidence that the appellant was under either actual or threatened assault by his father at the time of the shooting. Reliance upon the justification of self-defense requires a showing of an actual or threatened imminent attack by the deceased. . . .

Absent a showing of the circumstances involving an actual or threatened assault by the deceased upon the appellant, the reasonableness of appellant's conduct at the time was not an issue in the case, and the trial court, at the time it made its ruling, properly excluded the hearsay testimony sought to be elicited from the forensic psychiatrist. . . .

Rose, Justice, dissenting, with whom Cardine, Justice, joins. . . .

This case concerns itself with what happens—or can happen—and did happen when a cruel, ill-tempered, insensitive man roams, gun in hand, through his years of family life as a battering bully—a bully who, since his two children were babies, beat both of them and his wife regularly and unmercifully. Particularly, this appeal has to do with a 16-year-old boy who could stand his father's abuse no longer—who could not find solace or friendship in the public services which had been established for the purpose of providing aid, comfort and advice to abused family members—and who had no place to go or friends to help either him or his sister for whose protection he felt responsible and so—in fear and fright, and with fragmented emotion, Richard Jahnke shot and killed his father one night in November of 1982. . . .

The Reasonableness of Self-Defense

. . . In contemplating the overall problem which brings on my dissent, it is initially necessary to be aware of at least these following facts:

Richard Jahnke, a sensitive boy who had never been in any sort of trouble in his life, had been beaten regularly and unmercifully by his father since he was two years old. On the night of the homicide he had received a severe beating, and when his father and mother left the house to go to dinner that night, his father said: "I'm disgusted with the shit you turned out to be. I don't want you to be here when I get back." The father also said: "I don't care what I have to do, I'm going to get rid of you. I don't know how but I'm going to get rid of you, you bastard."

The boy felt he had to protect his sister who was hysterical when the mother and father left for dinner. He did not believe that there was any place or anyone where or to whom they could go for safety. The mother testified that the elder Jahnke always carried a gun, and Richard believed he had one with him that night. Mrs. Jahnke said that when the father said to Richard, "I'm going to get rid of you"—"He was trying to frighten him and maybe do something else besides just throwing him out of the house."

When Richard was in the garage after having stationed his father's guns around the house for "backup," he reflected upon past confrontations with his father and he was afraid the father would kill him when he returned and found what Richard had done with the guns. Even as he contemplated these things, the father drove the car into the driveway. Richard said he wanted to go and hug him and tell him he loved him, but he remembered when he had done this before, he had received a beating for his efforts. He knew from past experience that when his father "stomped" after him that he was in for a beating. He testified about how his father approached the garage door that night:

> I remember he was stomping. When he stomped down the hall when he was really mad and really prepared to beat someone up, beat on one of us. I remember being a little kid, just sitting in my room. My dad stomping after me to hit me, that I could never stop him. This time I stopped him.

[I]n the *ordinary* self-defense situation where there are no psychiatric implications and where the jury is permitted to know what the accused knew about the violent character of his victim, there need be no expert testimony touching upon the reasonableness of the defendant's behavior. In normal circumstances, these are things that jurors can fathom for themselves. However, when the beatings of 14 years have—or may have—caused the accused to harbor types of fear, anxiety and apprehension with which the nonbrutalized juror is unfamiliar and which result in the taking of unusual defensive measures which, in the ordinary circumstances, might be thought about as premature, excessive or lacking in escape efforts by those who are uninformed about the fear and anxiety that permeate the world of the brutalized—then expert testimony is necessary to explain the battered-person syndrome and the way these people respond to what they understand to be the imminence of danger and to explain their propensity to employ deadly force in their self-defensive conduct. Given this information, the jury is then qualified to decide the reasonableness of a self-defense defendant's acts at the time and place in question. . . .

The Proffered Testimony of the Forensic Psychiatrist

Dr. McDonald, a forensic psychiatrist, was offered by the defendant for the purpose of testifying about the behavior of battered children—that Richard was a battered child—all as an aid to the triers of fact with respect to their obligation to decide whether or not this defendant—as a battered person—behaved reasonably on the night of November 16, 1982, but the court would not permit the jury to hear the testimony.

The defendant suggests that his offer of proof represented that Dr. McDonald would testify that:

1. The doctor had diagnosed Richard Jahnke as a battered child, based on interviews with him and upon other information.
2. Battered children behave differently from other children, and perceive things differently from other children.

3. Because he was a battered child, Jahnke reasonably believed himself to be in immediate danger on the night he shot his father, and perceived himself as acting in self-defense. . . .

The doctor described an extensive background of Richard receiving physical abuse from his father. His earliest memory was of his father beating him, his mother and his sister. Between the ages of four and 12, there was seldom a day without some sort of punishment by his father. The punishment became less frequent between 12 and 15—more like every other day, but there were more beatings when his father used his fists on him. He was beaten with his father's fists every couple of weeks between 15 and 16. He would be beaten for such things as not cleaning the basement the right way—for walking along with his mouth open—for spending too much time polishing his ROTC uniform. At one juncture, the doctor testified that the children were forced to eat with plastic spoons and forks because their father did not like the noise they made while eating with ordinary utensils. Dr. McDonald testified that Richard related that he would be beaten for things like defending his sister. If Richard would react to verbal abuse by changing facial expression, the father would physically abuse him. When Richard and his mother had an argument, she would call him a "bastard" and report him to his father who would beat him.

On May 2, 1982, after a severe beating by his father, he ran out of the house in his bare feet, then put his sneakers on and ran five miles to his ROTC instructor's home. He sat outside the instructor's house, afraid to go in, and was finally discovered there by the instructor. The doctor explained that children who are victims of abuse are often reluctant to report their problems to others. In Richard's case, he believed for many years that child beatings were the normal behavior for a father. He was humiliated by the abuse and even had trouble reporting it to the ROTC instructor with whom he had a close relationship. On this occasion, however, the instructor and Richard went to the sheriff to report the abuse. The family was then interviewed together, and Richard chose to return home rather than go to a foster home, principally because he saw himself as the protector of his mother and sister.

Richard believed the May visit to the sheriff's office was useless even though his father did not beat him for a week or more. When he returned from reporting his beating to the sheriff, he put a chair against his door every night so his father could not get in. A week and a half after the sheriff's incident, the father exclaimed, "That bastard reported me to the Sheriff," and would say things like "I'll give him something that he can really complain about, that is if he can talk," the implication being that he would be in a condition that would prevent him from talking about anything. . . .

In his transfer hearing, the doctor took other factors into account to reach his evaluation conclusion. For example, the beatings and verbal abuse had an adverse effect on Richard's psychological development. He testified that the boy does not have the ability to handle stress that other young people of his age have and any ability he does have in this regard has come about as a developed defensive mechanism against the brutality of his father. That was the problem on November 16, 1982—that is, when his mother turned on him, blaming him for all the trouble with her marriage and in the home generally, and when she kept calling him a bastard and throwing things at him it was too much for him to stand. He felt victimized when his mother reported him to his father that night because she reported things that he had never said about her. This series of events and its repercussions, together with his father's beating him that night and the father's threat that he should leave home, was more than Richard Jahnke could handle. In addition, according to Dr. McDonald, he was afraid of another beating when his father and mother returned from dinner. Therefore, taking all of these things into account, he was under unusual and, for him, unbearable pressure on the evening of November 16, 1982. . . .

The Insanity Misconception

Both the State and the trial court believed the defendant was urging an insanity or diminished-capacity defense and thus were of the opinion that the proffered testimony was irrelevant. . . .

The theory of Richard Jahnke's defense was misunderstood by the prosecuting attorney, the trial court and now, I submit, this court. This was indeed a proper case for self-defense, and the offer of proof was made on the recognized grounds that battered children behave differently than other children—their brutalized conditioning mandates that they perceive danger differently—and that this defendant believed, as an abused 16-year-old boy would be expected to believe in these and similar circumstances, that he was in imminent danger when he shot his father and that he perceived himself to be acting in self-defense. . . .

Richard Jahnke did not offer Dr. McDonald's testimony to establish *insanity* or any form of a diminished capacity; his defense was *sanity*, i.e., the reasonableness of the behavior of a brutalized human being where the plea is self-defense. Furthermore, the proof of the defendant's intent at the time and place in question was not the purpose of the offer, nor was the defendant's intent ever in issue in this case. It was conceded throughout the trial and appellate court proceedings that the defendant *intended* to use deadly force against his father because he believed he was in imminent danger. Whether that belief was the reasonable belief of a battered 16-year-old, sane human being was the issue—not his intent. . . .

In these proceedings, the mental state of Richard Jahnke was not offered as a defense as would be the case with an insanity plea. Neither his mental capacity nor his intent to commit the crime was in issue. Rather, the specific defense is self-defense, which requires a showing that Jahnke reasonably believed it was necessary to use deadly force to prevent imminent death or great bodily harm to himself. In this situation, the expert testimony is offered, when the battered defendant pleads self-defense, as an aid to the jury in interpreting the surrounding circumstances as they affected the reasonableness of his belief. The expert testimony offered was secondary to the defense asserted. Given the opportunity, the defendant would not seek to show through the expert testimony that the mental and physical mistreatment which he suffered affected his mental state so that he *could not be responsible* for his actions; rather, the testimony was offered to show that, because he suffered from 14 years of brutalizing, *it was reasonable* for him to have remained in the home—to have prepared to respond to the beating that he had been promised would surely come and to have believed at that time and place that he was in imminent danger. . . .

It is because a jury would not understand and would not be expected to understand why Richard Jahnke would remain in that environment and believe that he was in imminent danger that the expert testimony is critical to aid and assist them in evaluating these conditions, circumstances and behavior patterns. . . .

In this case, it was necessary to explain to the jury that, because Richard Jahnke had been the recipient of the battering and brutalizing that this record reveals this young boy had experienced at the hands of his father, his behavior was—from a psychiatric point of view—the expectable concomitant of that kind of treatment. Therefore, scientific explanation was necessary to assist the trier of fact to understand the evidence and determine the essential fact in issue—namely, whether there was a cause-and-effect relationship between the boy's abuse and his behavior and, if there was, whether his conduct was that of a reasonable person behaving in the same or similar circumstances. . . .

I turn to that section of the majority opinion which treats with and upholds the trial court's rejection of the proffered expert testimony on the ground that there was no self-defense testimony before the court when the offer was rejected. The majority reason that this is so because there was no "actual or threatened assault" evidence in the record and therefore the reasonableness of Richard Jahnke's behavior was not in issue.

The majority puts the proposition this way:

> This record contained no evidence that the appellant was under either *actual or threatened assault* by his father at the time of the shooting. *Reliance upon the justification of self-defense requires a showing of an actual or threatened imminent attack by the deceased.*

(Emphasis added.) The opinion goes on to say:

> Absent a showing of the circumstances involving *an actual or threatened assault* by the deceased upon the appellant, the reasonableness of appellant's conduct at the time was not an issue in the case, and the trial court, at the time it made its ruling, properly excluded the hearsay testimony sought to be elicited from the forensic psychiatrist.

(Emphasis added.) These assumptions and conclusions . . . either overlook the fact that the transfer-hearing testimony was made a part of the defendant's offer of proof or they do not conceive that the testimony of Dr. McDonald in the transfer hearing contains such evidence of threat or assault as would call into question the reasonableness of the defendant's behavior. Certainly the transfer testimony contains evidence of what Richard Jahnke as a battered person *could have reasonably believed* was an actual or threatened imminent assault thus calling into issue the reasonableness of his conduct—and, as the offer of proof would have shown, *he did believe* himself to be threatened and in the process of being assaulted when the shots were fired. . . .

As I have noted, it seems clear to me that the majority misstate the Wyoming law of self-defense and the law of this case on self-defense when the opinion assumes that, for self-defense to be a viable protection in a criminal prosecution in this state, the defendant must be under "an actual or threatened assault" before the reasonableness of his conduct will raise a self-defense issue. As has been mentioned . . . the assault, the threat and the imminence of danger must only be of such a character as to create, in the mind of the defendant, a reasonable belief that the danger is imminent and that it is necessary to use deadly force against his assailant in order to protect himself from death or great bodily harm. . . .

Perhaps this concept is best exemplified in our opinion which reverses the trial court in State v. Radon. In that case, [the court said]:

> *Some act, of course, had to take place to give the appearance of danger,* and to give the defendant reasonable ground therefor. *But an actual assault or attack on the defendant was not necessary, if the circumstances gave reasonable ground for apprehension of imminent danger.* In the case at bar the deceased walked toward the defendant. He had a package in his hands, wrapped in paper. That, apparently, turned out to be a pair of gloves. Still, while there is no specific evidence of the size of the gloves, how the deceased held the package, and whether it gave the appearance that it contained a gun or other dangerous weapon, *the defendant says that the attitude of deceased put him in fear,* evidently intending to convey the idea, in his broken accent, *that he thought that the deceased was carrying a deadly weapon, and we are not prepared to hold that, as a matter of law, in view of previous difficulties and threats, he might not have had reasonable ground to believe that he was in imminent danger, even though the deceased was not guilty of any actual assault.* . . .

[T]he rule . . . for which I contend [is that] the defendant must have had "a bona-fide belief that he was in imminent danger." This is different than saying that there must be an "actual or threatened assault" before the fact-finder may consider the reasonableness of the accused's purported self-defensive behavior. . . .

State v. Norman
324 N.C. 253 (1989)

Mitchell, Justice.

The defendant was tried at the 16 February 1987 Criminal Session of Superior Court for Rutherford County upon a proper indictment charging her with the first degree murder of her husband. The jury found the defendant guilty of voluntary manslaughter. The defendant appealed from the trial court's judgment sentencing her to six years imprisonment.

The Court of Appeals granted a new trial, citing as error the trial court's refusal to submit a possible verdict of acquittal by reason of perfect self-defense. Notwithstanding the uncontroverted evidence that the defendant shot her husband three times in the back of the head as he lay sleeping in his bed, the Court of Appeals held that the defendant's evidence that she exhibited what has come to be called "the battered wife syndrome" entitled her to have the jury consider whether the homicide was an act of perfect self-defense and, thus, not a legal wrong.

We conclude that the evidence introduced in this case would not support a finding that the defendant killed her husband due to a reasonable fear of imminent death or great bodily harm, as is required before a defendant is entitled to jury instructions concerning either perfect or imperfect self-defense. Therefore, the trial court properly declined to instruct the jury on the law relating to self-defense. Accordingly, we reverse the Court of Appeals.

At trial, the State presented the testimony of Deputy Sheriff R.H. Epley of the Rutherford County Sheriff's Department, who was called to the Norman residence on the night of 12 June 1985. Inside the home, Epley found the defendant's husband, John Thomas Norman, lying on a bed in a rear bedroom with his face toward the wall and his back toward the middle of the room. He was dead, but blood was still coming from wounds to the back of his head. A later autopsy revealed three gunshot wounds to the head, two of which caused fatal brain injury. The autopsy also revealed a .12 percent blood alcohol level in the victim's body.

Later that night, the defendant related an account of the events leading to the killing, after Epley had advised her of her constitutional rights and she had waived her right to remain silent. The defendant told Epley that her husband had been beating her all day and had made her lie down on the floor while he slept on the bed. After her husband fell asleep, the defendant carried her grandchild to the defendant's mother's house. The defendant took a pistol from her mother's purse and walked the short distance back to her home. She pointed the pistol at the back of her sleeping husband's head, but it jammed the first time she tried to shoot him. She fixed the gun and then shot her husband in the back of the head as he lay sleeping. After one shot, she felt her husband's chest and determined that he was still breathing and making sounds. She then shot him twice more in the back of the head. The defendant told Epley that she killed her husband because "she took all she was going to take from him so she shot him."

The defendant presented evidence tending to show a long history of physical and mental abuse by her husband due to his alcoholism. At the time of the killing, the thirty-nine-year-old defendant and her husband had been married almost twenty-five years and had several children. The defendant testified that her husband had started drinking and abusing her about five years after they were married. His physical abuse of her consisted of frequent assaults that included slapping, punching and kicking her, striking her with various objects, and throwing glasses, beer bottles and other objects at her. The defendant described other specific incidents of abuse, such as her husband putting her cigarettes out on her, throwing hot coffee on her, breaking glass against her face and crushing food on her face. Although the defendant did not present evidence of ever having received medical treatment for any physical injuries inflicted by her husband, she displayed several scars about her face which she attributed to her husband's assaults.

The defendant's evidence also tended to show other indignities inflicted upon her by her husband. Her evidence tended to show that her husband did not work and forced her to make money by prostitution, and that he made humor of that fact to family and friends. He would beat her if she resisted going out to prostitute herself or if he was unsatisfied with the amounts of money she made. He routinely called the defendant "dog," "bitch" and "whore," and on a few occasions made her eat pet food out of the pets' bowls and bark like a dog. He often made her sleep on the floor. At times, he deprived her of food and refused to let her get food for the family. During those years of abuse, the defendant's husband threatened numerous times to kill her and to maim her in various ways.

The defendant said her husband's abuse occurred only when he was intoxicated, but that he would not give up drinking. She said she and her husband "got along very well when he was sober," and that he was "a good guy" when he was not drunk. She had accompanied her husband to the local mental health center for sporadic counseling sessions for his problem, but he continued to drink.

In the early morning hours on the day before his death, the defendant's husband, who was intoxicated, went to a rest area off I-85 near Kings Mountain where the defendant was engaging in prostitution and assaulted her. While driving home, he was stopped by a patrolman and jailed on a charge of driving while impaired. After the defendant's mother got him out of jail at the defendant's request later that morning, he resumed his drinking and abuse of the defendant.

The defendant's evidence also tended to show that her husband seemed angrier than ever after he was released from jail and that his abuse of the defendant was more frequent. That evening, sheriff's deputies were called to the Norman residence, and the defendant complained that her husband had been beating her all day and she could not take it anymore. The defendant was advised to file a complaint, but she said she was afraid her husband would kill her if she had him arrested. The deputies told her they needed a warrant before they could arrest her husband, and they left the scene.

The deputies were called back less than an hour later after the defendant had taken a bottle of pills. The defendant's husband cursed her and called her names as she was attended by paramedics, and he told them to let her die. A sheriff's deputy finally chased him back into his house as the defendant was put into an ambulance. The defendant's stomach was pumped at the local hospital, and she was sent home with her mother.

While in the hospital, the defendant was visited by a therapist with whom she discussed filing charges against her husband and having him committed for treatment. Before the therapist left, the defendant agreed to go to the mental health center the next day to discuss those possibilities. The therapist testified at trial that the defendant seemed depressed in the hospital, and that she expressed considerable anger toward her husband. He testified that the defendant threatened a number of times that night to kill her husband and that she said she should kill him "because of the things he had done to her."

The next day, the day she shot her husband, the defendant went to the mental health center to talk about charges and possible commitment, and she confronted her husband with that possibility. She testified that she told her husband later that day: "J.T., straighten up. Quit drinking. I'm going to have you committed to help you." She said her husband then told her he would "see them coming" and would cut her throat before they got to him.

The defendant also went to the social services office that day to seek welfare benefits, but her husband followed her there, interrupted her interview and made her go home with him. He continued his abuse of her, threatening to kill and to maim her, slapping her, kicking her, and throwing objects at her. At one point, he took her cigarette and put it out on her, causing a small burn on her upper torso. He would not let her eat or bring food into the house for their children.

That evening, the defendant and her husband went into their bedroom to lie down, and he called her a "dog" and made her lie on the floor when he lay down on the bed. Their daughter brought in her baby to leave with the defendant, and the defendant's husband agreed to let her baby-sit. After the defendant's husband fell asleep, the baby started crying and the defendant took it to her mother's house so it would not wake up her husband. She returned shortly with the pistol and killed her husband.

The defendant testified at trial that she was too afraid of her husband to press charges against him or to leave him. She said that she had temporarily left their home on several previous occasions, but he had always found her, brought her home and beaten her. Asked why she killed her husband, the defendant replied: "Because I was scared of him and I knowed when he woke up, it was going to be the same thing, and I was scared when he took me to the truck stop that night it was going to be worse than he had ever been. I just couldn't take it no more. There ain't no way, even if it means going to prison. It's better than living in that. That's worse hell than anything."

The defendant and other witnesses testified that for years her husband had frequently threatened to kill her and to maim her. When asked if she believed those threats, the defendant replied: "Yes. I believed him; he would, he would kill me if he got a chance. If he thought he wouldn't a had to went to jail, he would a done it."

Two expert witnesses in forensic psychology and psychiatry who examined the defendant after the shooting, Dr. William Tyson and Dr. Robert Rollins, testified that the defendant fit the profile of battered wife syndrome. This condition, they testified, is characterized by such abuse and degradation that the battered wife comes to believe she is unable to help herself and cannot expect help from anyone else. She believes that she cannot escape the complete control of her husband and that he is invulnerable to law enforcement and other sources of help.

Dr. Tyson, a psychologist, was asked his opinion as to whether, on 12 June 1985, "it appeared reasonably necessary for Judy Norman to shoot J.T. Norman?" He replied: "I believe that . . . Mrs. Norman believed herself to be doomed . . . to a life of the worst kind of torture and abuse, degradation that she had experienced over the years in a progressive way; that it would only get worse, and that death was inevitable. . . ." Dr. Tyson later added: "I think Judy Norman felt that she had no choice, both in the protection of herself and her family, but to engage, exhibit deadly force against Mr. Norman, and that in so doing, she was sacrificing herself, both for herself and for her family."

Dr. Rollins, who was the defendant's attending physician at Dorothea Dix Hospital when she was sent there for evaluation, testified that in his opinion the defendant was a typical abused spouse and that "[s]he saw herself as powerless to deal with the situation, that there was no alternative, no way she could escape it." Dr. Rollins was asked his opinion as to whether "on June 12th, 1985, it appeared reasonably necessary that Judy Norman would take the life of J.T. Norman?" Dr. Rollins replied that in his opinion, "that course of action did appear necessary to Mrs. Norman."

Based on the evidence that the defendant exhibited battered wife syndrome, that she believed she could not escape her husband nor expect help from others, that her husband had threatened her, and that her husband's abuse of her had worsened in the two days preceding his death, the Court of Appeals concluded that a jury reasonably could have found that her killing of her husband was justified as an act of perfect self-defense. The Court of Appeals reasoned that the nature of battered wife syndrome is such that a jury could not be precluded from finding the defendant killed her husband lawfully in perfect self-defense, even though he was asleep when she killed him. We disagree.

The right to kill in self-defense is based on the necessity, real or reasonably apparent, of killing an unlawful aggressor to save oneself from *imminent* death or great bodily harm at his hands. Our law has recognized that self-preservation under such circumstances springs from a primal impulse and is an inherent right of natural law.

In North Carolina, a defendant is entitled to have the jury consider acquittal by reason of *perfect* self-defense when the evidence, viewed in the light most favorable to the defendant, tends to show that at the time of the killing it appeared to the defendant and she believed it to be necessary to kill the decedent to save herself from imminent death or great bodily harm. That belief must be reasonable, however, in that the circumstances as they appeared to the defendant would create such a belief in the mind of a person of ordinary firmness. Further, the defendant must not have been the initial aggressor provoking the fatal confrontation. A killing in the proper exercise of the right of *perfect* self-defense is always completely justified in law and constitutes no legal wrong.

Our law also recognizes an *imperfect* right of self-defense in certain circumstances, including, for example, when the defendant is the initial aggressor, but without intent to kill or to seriously injure the decedent, and the decedent escalates the confrontation to a point where it reasonably appears to the defendant to be necessary to kill the decedent to save herself from imminent death or great bodily harm. Although the culpability of a defendant who kills in the exercise of *imperfect* self-defense is reduced, such a defendant is *not justified* in the killing so as to be entitled to acquittal, but is guilty at least of voluntary manslaughter.

The defendant in the present case was not entitled to a jury instruction on either perfect or imperfect self-defense. The trial court was not required to instruct on *either* form of self-defense unless evidence was introduced tending to show that at the time of the killing the defendant reasonably believed herself to be confronted by circumstances which necessitated her killing her husband to save herself from *imminent* death or great bodily harm. No such evidence was introduced in this case, and it would have been error for the trial court to instruct the jury on *either* perfect or imperfect self-defense.

The jury found the defendant guilty only of voluntary manslaughter in the present case. As we have indicated, an instruction on imperfect self-defense would have entitled the defendant to nothing more, since one who kills in the exercise of imperfect self-defense is guilty at least of voluntary manslaughter. Therefore, even if it is assumed arguendo that the defendant was entitled to an instruction on imperfect self-defense—a notion we have specifically rejected—the failure to give such an instruction was harmless in this case. Accordingly, although we recognize that the imminence requirement applies to both types of self-defense for almost identical reasons, we limit our consideration in the remainder of this opinion to the issue of whether the trial court erred in failing to instruct the jury to consider acquittal on the ground that the killing was justified and, thus, lawful as an act of *perfect* self-defense.

The killing of another human being is the most extreme recourse to our inherent right of self-preservation and can be justified in law only by the utmost real or apparent necessity brought about by the decedent. For that reason, our law of self-defense has required that a defendant claiming that a homicide was justified and, as a result, inherently lawful by reason of perfect self-defense must establish that she reasonably believed at the time of the killing she otherwise would have immediately suffered death or great bodily harm. Only if defendants are required to show that they killed due to a reasonable belief that death or great bodily harm was imminent can the justification for homicide remain clearly and firmly rooted in necessity. The imminence requirement ensures that deadly force will be used only where it is necessary as a last resort in the exercise of the inherent right of self-preservation. It also ensures that before a homicide is justified and, as a result, not a legal wrong, it will be reliably determined that the defendant reasonably believed that absent the use of deadly force, not only would an unlawful attack have occurred, but also that the attack would have caused death or great bodily harm. The law does not sanction the use of deadly force to repel simple assaults.

The term "imminent," as used to describe such perceived threats of death or great bodily harm as will justify a homicide by reason of perfect self-defense, has been defined as "immediate danger, such as must be instantly met, such as cannot be guarded against by calling for the assistance of others or the protection of the law." Black's Law Dictionary 676 (5th ed. 1979). Our cases have sometimes used the phrase "about to suffer" interchangeably with "imminent" to describe the immediacy of threat that is required to justify killing in self-defense.

The evidence in this case did not tend to show that the defendant reasonably believed that she was confronted by a threat of imminent death or great bodily harm. The evidence tended to show that no harm was "imminent" or about to happen to the defendant when she shot her husband. The uncontroverted evidence was that her husband had been asleep for some time when she walked to her mother's house, returned with the pistol, fixed the pistol after it jammed and then shot her husband three times in the back of the head. The defendant was not faced with an instantaneous choice between killing her husband or being killed or seriously injured. Instead, *all* of the evidence tended to show that the defendant had ample time and opportunity to resort to other means of preventing further abuse by her husband. There was no action underway by the decedent from which the jury could have found that the defendant had reasonable grounds to believe either that a felonious assault was imminent or that it might result in her death or great bodily injury. Additionally, no such action by the decedent had been underway immediately prior to his falling asleep. . . .

Additionally, the lack of any belief by the defendant—reasonable or otherwise—that she faced a threat of imminent death or great bodily harm from the drunk and sleeping victim in the present case was illustrated by the defendant and her own expert witnesses when testifying about her subjective assessment of her situation at the time of the killing. The psychologist and psychiatrist replied affirmatively when asked their opinions of whether killing her husband "appeared reasonably necessary" to the defendant at the time of the homicide. That testimony spoke of no *imminent* threat nor of any fear by the defendant of death or great bodily harm, imminent or otherwise. Testimony in the form of a conclusion that a killing "appeared reasonably necessary" to a defendant does not tend to show all that must be shown to establish self-defense. More specifically, for a killing to be in self-defense, the perceived necessity must arise from a reasonable fear of imminent death or great bodily harm.

Dr. Tyson additionally testified that the defendant "believed herself to be doomed . . . to a life of the worst kind of torture and abuse, degradation that she had experienced over the years in a progressive way; that it would only get worse, and that death was inevitable." Such evidence of the defendant's speculative beliefs concerning her remote and indefinite future, while indicating she had felt generally threatened, did not tend to show that she killed in the belief—reasonable or otherwise—that her husband presented a threat of *imminent* death or great bodily harm. Under our law of self-defense, a defendant's subjective belief of what might be "inevitable" at some indefinite point in the future does not equate to what she believes to be "imminent." Dr. Tyson's opinion that the defendant believed it was necessary to kill her husband for "the protection of herself and her family" was similarly indefinite and devoid of time frame and did not tend to show a threat or fear of *imminent* harm.

The defendant testified that, "I knowed when he woke up, it was going to be the same thing, and I was scared when he took me to the truck stop that night it was going to be worse than he had ever been." She also testified, when asked if she believed her husband's threats: "Yes. . . . [H]e would kill me if he got a chance. If he thought he wouldn't a had to went to jail, he would a done it." Testimony about such indefinite fears concerning what her sleeping husband might do at some time in the future did not tend to establish a fear—reasonable or otherwise—of *imminent death or great bodily harm* at the time of the killing.

We are not persuaded by the reasoning of our Court of Appeals in this case that when there is evidence of battered wife syndrome, neither an actual attack nor threat of attack by the husband at the moment the wife uses deadly force is required to justify the wife's killing of him in perfect self-defense. The Court of Appeals concluded that to impose such requirements would ignore the "learned helplessness," meekness and other realities of battered wife syndrome and would effectively preclude such women from exercising their right of self-defense. Other jurisdictions which have addressed this question under similar facts are divided in their views, and we can discern no clear majority position on facts closely similar to those of this case.

The reasoning of our Court of Appeals in this case proposes to change the established law of self-defense by giving the term "imminent" a meaning substantially more indefinite and all-encompassing than its present meaning. This would result in a substantial relaxation of the requirement of real or apparent necessity to justify homicide. Such reasoning proposes justifying the taking of human life not upon the reasonable belief it is necessary to prevent death or great bodily harm—which the imminence requirement ensures—but upon purely subjective speculation that the decedent probably would present a threat to life at a future time and that the defendant would not be able to avoid the predicted threat.

The Court of Appeals suggests that such speculation would have been particularly reliable in the present case because the jury, based on the evidence of the decedent's intensified abuse during the thirty-six hours preceding his death, could have found that the decedent's passive state at the time of his death was "but a momentary hiatus in a continuous reign of terror by the decedent [and] the defendant merely took advantage of her first opportunity to protect herself." Requiring jury instructions on perfect self-defense in such situations, however, would still tend to make opportune homicide lawful as a result of mere subjective predictions of indefinite future assaults and circumstances. Such predictions of future assaults to justify the defendant's use of deadly force in this case would be entirely speculative, because there was no evidence that her husband had ever inflicted any harm upon her that approached life-threatening injury, even during the "reign of terror." It is far from clear in the defendant's poignant evidence that any abuse by the decedent had ever involved the degree of physical threat required to justify the defendant in using deadly force, even when those threats were imminent. The use of deadly force in self-defense to prevent harm other than death or great bodily harm is excessive as a matter of law.

As we have stated, stretching the law of self-defense to fit the facts of this case would require changing the "imminent death or great bodily harm" requirement to something substantially more indefinite than previously required and would weaken our assurances that justification for the taking of human life remains firmly rooted in real or apparent necessity. That result in principle could not be limited to a few cases decided on evidence as poignant as this. The relaxed requirements for perfect self-defense proposed by our Court of Appeals would tend to categorically legalize the opportune killing of abusive husbands by their wives solely on the basis of the wives' testimony concerning their subjective speculation as to the probability of future felonious assaults by their husbands. Homicidal self-help would then become a lawful solution, and perhaps the easiest and most effective solution, to this problem. It has even been suggested that the relaxed requirements of self-defense found in what is often called the "battered woman's defense" could be extended in principle to *any type of case* in which a defendant testified that he or she subjectively believed that killing was necessary and proportionate to any perceived threat.

In conclusion, we decline to expand our law of self-defense beyond the limits of immediacy and necessity which have heretofore provided an appropriately narrow but firm basis upon which homicide may be justified and, thus, lawful by reason of perfect self-defense or upon which a defendant's culpability may be reduced by reason of imperfect self-defense. As we have shown, the evidence in this case did not entitle the defendant to jury instructions on either perfect or imperfect self-defense. . . .

Martin, Justice, dissenting.

. . . At the heart of the majority's reasoning is its unsubstantiated concern that to find that the evidence presented by defendant would support an instruction on self-defense would "expand our law of self-defense beyond the limits of immediacy and necessity." Defendant does not seek to expand or relax the requirements of self-defense and thereby "legalize the opportune killing of allegedly abusive husbands by their wives," as the majority overstates. Rather, defendant contends that the evidence as gauged by the existing laws of self-defense is sufficient to require the submission of a self-defense instruction to the jury. The proper issue for this Court is to determine whether the evidence, viewed in the light most favorable to the defendant, was sufficient to require the trial court to instruct on the law of self-defense. I conclude that it was. . . .

A defendant is entitled to an instruction on self-defense when there is evidence, viewed in the light most favorable to the defendant, that these four elements existed at the time of the killing:

(1) it appeared to defendant and he believed it to be necessary to kill the deceased in order to save himself from death or great bodily harm; and

(2) defendant's belief was reasonable in that the circumstances as they appeared to him at the time were sufficient to create such a belief in the mind of a person of ordinary firmness; and

(3) defendant was not the aggressor in bringing on the affray, i.e., he did not aggressively and willingly enter into the fight without legal excuse or provocation; and

(4) defendant did not use excessive force, i.e., did not use more force than was necessary or reasonably appeared to him to be necessary under the circumstances to protect himself from death or great bodily harm.

The first element requires that there be evidence that the defendant believed it was necessary to kill in order to protect herself from serious bodily harm or death; the second requires that the circumstances as defendant perceived them were sufficient to create such a belief in the mind of a person of ordinary firmness. Both elements were supported by evidence at defendant's trial.

Evidence presented by defendant described a twenty-year history of beatings and other dehumanizing and degrading treatment by her husband. In his expert testimony a clinical psychologist concluded that defendant fit "and exceed[ed]" the profile of an abused or battered spouse, analogizing this treatment to the dehumanization process suffered by prisoners of war under the Nazis during the Second World War and the brainwashing techniques of the Korean War. The psychologist described the defendant as a woman incarcerated by abuse, by fear, and by her conviction that her husband was invincible and inescapable:

> Mrs. Norman didn't leave because she believed, fully believed that escape was totally impossible. There was no place to go. He, she had left before; he had come and gotten her. She had gone to the Department of Social Services. He had come and gotten her. The law, she believed the law could not protect her; no one could protect her, and I must admit, looking over the records, that there was nothing done that would contradict that belief. She fully believed that he was invulnerable to the law and to all social agencies that were available; that nobody could withstand his power. As a result, there was no such thing as escape.

When asked if he had an opinion whether it appeared reasonably necessary for Judy Norman to shoot her husband, this witness responded:

> Yes. . . . I believe that in examining the facts of this case and examining the psychological data, that Mrs. Norman believed herself to be doomed . . . to a life of the worst kind of torture and abuse, degradation that she had experienced over the years in a progressive way; that it would only get worse, and that death was inevitable; death of herself, which was not such, I don't think was such an issue for her, as she had attempted to commit suicide, and in her continuing conviction of J.T. Norman's power over her, and even failed at that form of escape. I believe she also came to the point of beginning to fear for family members and her children, that were she to commit suicide that the abuse and the treatment that was heaped on her would be transferred onto them.

This testimony describes defendant's perception of circumstances in which she was held hostage to her husband's abuse for two decades and which ultimately compelled her to kill him. This testimony alone is evidence amply indicating the first two elements required for entitlement to an instruction on self-defense.

In addition to the testimony of the clinical psychologist, defendant presented the testimony of witnesses who had actually seen defendant's husband abuse her. These witnesses described circumstances that caused not only defendant to believe escape was impossible, but that also convinced *them* of its impossibility. Defendant's isolation and helplessness were evident in testimony that her family was intimidated by her husband into acquiescing in his torture of her. Witnesses also described defendant's experience with social service agencies and the law, which had contributed to her sense of futility and abandonment through the inefficacy of their protection and the strength of her husband's wrath when they failed. Where torture appears interminable and escape impossible, the belief that only the death of the oppressor can provide relief is reasonable in the mind of a person of ordinary firmness, let alone in the mind of the defendant, who, like a prisoner of war of some years, has been deprived of her humanity and is held hostage by fear. . . .

In the context of the doctrine of self-defense, the definition of "imminent" must be informed by the defendant's perceptions. It is not bounded merely by measurable time, but by all of the facts and circumstances. Its meaning depends upon the assessment of the facts by one of "ordinary firmness" with regard to whether the defendant's perception of impending death or injury was so pressing as to render reasonable her belief that it was necessary to kill.

Evidence presented in the case sub judice revealed no letup of tension or fear, no moment in which the defendant felt released from impending serious harm, even while the decedent slept. This, in fact, is a state of mind common to the battered spouse . . . . Psychologists have observed and commentators have described a "constant state of fear" brought on by the cyclical nature of battering as well as the battered spouse's perception that her abuser is both "omnipotent and unstoppable." Constant fear means a perpetual anticipation of the next blow, a perpetual expectation that the next blow will kill. "[T]he battered wife is constantly in a heightened state of terror because she is certain that one day her husband will kill her during the course of a beating. . . . Thus from the perspective of the battered wife, the danger is constantly 'immediate.'" For the battered wife, if there is no escape, if there is no window of relief or momentary sense of safety, then the next attack, which could be the fatal one, is imminent. In the context of the doctrine of self-defense, "imminent" is a term the meaning of which must be grasped from the defendant's point of view. Properly stated, the second prong of the question is not whether the threat was *in fact* imminent, but whether defendant's belief in the impending nature of the threat, given the circumstances as she saw them, was reasonable in the mind of a person of ordinary firmness.

Defendant's intense fear, based on her belief that her husband intended not only to maim or deface her, as he had in the past, but to kill her, was evident in the testimony of witnesses who recounted events of the last three days of the decedent's life. This testimony could have led a juror to conclude that defendant reasonably perceived a threat to her life as "imminent," even while her husband slept. Over these three days, her husband's anger was exhibited in an unprecedented crescendo of violence. The evidence showed defendant's fear and sense of hopelessness similarly intensifying, leading to an unsuccessful attempt to escape through suicide and culminating in her belief that escape would be possible only through her husband's death. . . .

From this evidence of the exacerbated nature of the last three days of twenty years of provocation, a juror could conclude that defendant believed that her husband's threats to her life were viable, that serious bodily harm was imminent, and that it was necessary to kill her husband to escape that harm. And from this evidence a juror could find defendant's belief in the necessity to kill her husband not merely reasonable but compelling.

The third element for entitlement to an instruction on self-defense requires that there be evidence that the defendant was not the aggressor in bringing on the affray. If the defendant was the aggressor and killed with murderous intent, that is, the intent to kill or inflict serious bodily harm, then she is not entitled to an instruction on self-defense. . . .

Where the defendant is a battered wife, the affray out of which the killing arises can be a continuing assault. There was evidence before the jury that it had not been defendant but her husband who had initiated "the affray," which the jury could have regarded as lasting twenty years, three days, or any number of hours preceding his death. And there was evidence from which the jury could infer that in defendant's mind the affray reached beyond the moment at which her husband fell asleep. Like the ongoing threats of death or great bodily harm, which she might reasonably have perceived as imminent, her husband continued to be the aggressor and she the victim.

Finally, the fourth element of self-defense poses the question of whether there was any evidence tending to show that the force used by defendant to repel her husband was not excessive, that is, more than reasonably appeared to be necessary under the circumstances. This question is answered in part by abundant testimony describing defendant's immobilization by fear caused by abuse by her husband. Three witnesses, including the decedent's best friend, all recounted incidents in which defendant passively accepted beating, kicks, commands, or humiliating affronts without striking back. From such evidence that she was paralyzed by her husband's presence, a jury could infer that it reasonably appeared to defendant to be necessary to kill her husband in order ultimately to protect herself from the death he had threatened and from severe bodily injury, a foretaste of which she had already experienced. . . .

Notes and Questions

1. Under the oldest legal test for insanity, the so-called "M'Naghten test" (1843), the defendant must have been:

> laboring under such a defect of reason, from disease of the mind, as not to know the nature and quality of the act he was doing; or, if he did know it, that he did not know he was doing what was wrong.

In the *Durham* case (1954), the U.S. Court of Appeals for the District of Columbia Circuit required only that the defendant's unlawful act be "the product of mental disease or defect." That test was later clarified by the same court in the *McDonald* case (1962) as follows:

> [T]he jury should be told that a mental disease or defect includes any abnormal condition of the mind which substantially affects mental or emotional processes and substantially impairs behavior controls.

Did the defendants' actions in U.S. v. Alexander and Murdock fall within any of these definitions of insanity?

2. In his closing argument, Murdock's defense attorney stated:

> The question is whether the rotten social background was a causative factor and prevented his keeping controls at that critical moment. . . . Now you have got to take the trip back through his lifetime with him and look at the effect that his lifetime had on him at that moment and determine whether he could control himself or not.

What are some strengths, and some weaknesses, of this approach?

3. The trial judge in the *Alexander and Murdock* case instructed the jury:

> We are not concerned with a question of whether or not a man had a rotten social background. We are concerned with the question of his criminal responsibility. That is to say, whether he had an abnormal condition of the mind that affected his emotional and behavioral processes at the time of the offense.

In response to the defense attorney's objection to this instruction, the judge declared:

> You were appealing in the most direct way to something that I am going to keep out of the courtroom, if I stay a Judge. I am not going to permit it to come in here.

What was the judge so concerned about?

4. On the night that he killed his father, were any of Richard Jahnke's preparations or actions irrational? If not, does Jahnke have any legal basis for appealing his conviction?

5. Is Jahnke's case like the case of State v. Radon, discussed at the end of Justice Rose's dissent?

6. Do Jahnke's and Norman's defenses come down to the claim that they are "reasonable battered persons"? Is that a valid defense?

Suggestions For Further Reading

Anne M. Coughlin, Excusing Women, 82 California Law Review 1 (1994)

Stephen J. Morse, Culpability and Control, 142 University of Pennsylvania Law Review 1587 (1994)

Stephen J. Morse, Neither Desert Nor Disease, 5 Legal Theory 265 (1999)

Ralph Reisner, Christopher Slobogin & Arti Rai, Law and the Mental Health System, ch. 7 (3d ed. 1998)

James J. Sing, Culture as Sameness: Toward a Synthetic View of Provocation and Culture in the Criminal Law, 108 Yale Law Journal 1845 (1999)

Part IV
The Legal and the Non-Legal

One way of getting at the nature of law is to compare it to other forms or systems of rule-governed behavior. What is distinctive about a "legal" system? Is it the nature of its rules? Or of its sanctions? What is it that distinguishes *the legal from the non-legal*?

The legal anthropologist Bronislaw Malinowski once described his methodology as follows:

> We shall approach our facts with a very elastic and wide conception of the problem before us. In looking for "law" and legal forces, we shall try merely to discover and analyse all the rules conceived and acted upon as binding obligations, to find out the nature of the binding forces, and to classify the rules according to the manner in which they are made valid. We shall see that by an inductive examination of facts, carried out without any preconceived idea or ready-made definition, we shall be enabled to arrive at a satisfactory classification of the norms and rules of a primitive community, at a clear distinction of primitive law from other forms of custom . . . .[1]

The following chapters utilize Malinowski's methodology by focusing on a variety of rule-governed systems that we would intuitively classify as "non-legal," as well as some where the question is much closer. The issue for discussion is always: "Is this a system of law (and why or why not)?"

The linguist Ferdinand de Saussure pondered the meaning of "laws" in language and came up with a useful definition: "[A]ny social law has two fundamental characteristics: it is *imperative* and it is *general*. It demands compliance, and it covers all cases, within certain limits of time and place, of course."[2]

Laws or rules may be of at least two kinds, descriptive and normative, and some are both. A descriptive or merely conventional rule is an observable regularity that "just happens" to prevail in a given social setting. A rule in the stronger, normative sense is something we "should" or even "must" obey, usually as dictated by some authoritative person or institution that enforces the rule through sanctions.

---

[1]   Crime and Custom in Savage Society 15 (1932).

[2]   Course in General Linguistics 90 (Roy Harris trans. 1986).

291

Similarly, sanctions may be either internal or external. Internal sanctions are self-enforcing in the sense that they are based upon our own self-interest. Wanting to play "tennis," for example, means wanting to play a game defined and governed by the rules of tennis, to which we therefore freely submit. And the psychological embarrassment or shame we feel upon violating a rule of etiquette may be the only real sanction for violating such a rule. By contrast, the sanctions characteristic of a true legal system may be said to be external, in the sense of opposing our own self-interest, narrowly conceived.

The following comparisons may prove useful:

Legal	Non-Legal
1. Overt, intentional behavior (conduct)	Expression of inner personality
2. External sanctions	Internal sanctions
3. Negative prohibitions	Affirmative duties
4. Minimal requirements	Aspirational goals
5. Universal application (society)	For a select group (community)

Obviously, even essentially "private" forms of association cannot insulate themselves entirely from, for example, the reach of the criminal law. But as the following materials illustrate, making such determinations may be difficult, complicated, and fact-specific.

Chapter 9
Rule-Governed Institutions

Invariability and Variability of the Sign[*]
Ferdinand de Saussure

§1. Invariability

The signal, in relation to the idea it represents, may seem to be freely chosen. However, from the point of view of the linguistic community, the signal is imposed rather than freely chosen. Speakers are not consulted about its choice. Once the language has selected a signal, it cannot be freely replaced by any other. There appears to be something rather contradictory about this. It is a kind of linguistic Hobson's choice. What can be chosen is already determined in advance. No individual is able, even if he wished, to modify in any way a choice already established in the language. Nor can the linguistic community exercise its authority to change even a single word.[1] The community, as much as the individual, is bound to its language.

A language cannot therefore be treated simply as a form of contract, and the linguistic sign is a particularly interesting phenomenon to study for this reason. For if we wish to demonstrate that the rules a community accepts are imposed upon it, and not freely agreed to, it is a language which offers the most striking proof.

Let us now examine how the linguistic sign eludes the control of our will. We shall then be able to see the important consequences which follow from this fact.

At any given period, however far back in time we go, a language is always an inheritance from the past. The initial assignment of names to things, establishing a contract between concepts and sound patterns, is an act we can conceive in the imagination, but no one has ever observed it taking place. The idea that it might have happened is suggested to us by our keen awareness of the arbitrary nature of the linguistic sign.

In fact, no society has ever known its language to be anything other than something inherited from previous generations, which it has no choice but to accept. That is why the

---

[*]   Reprinted by permission of Open Court Publishing Company, a division of Carus Publishing Company, Peru, IL, from Course in General Linguistics by Ferdinand de Saussure, translated and annotated by Roy Harris, copyright © 1986 by Open Court Publishing Company.

[1]   This is not a denial of the possibility of linguistic legislation, nor even of its potential effectiveness. What Saussure denies is that the collective ratification required is a matter for collective decision. It may be illegal for trade purposes to call Spanish sparkling wine 'champagne': but that will be merely one external factor bearing on speech, which may or may not ultimately affect the word *champagne* as a linguistic sign. (Translator's note.)

question of the origins of language does not have the importance generally attributed to it. It is not even a relevant question as far as linguistics is concerned. The sole object of study in linguistics is the normal, regular existence of a language already established. Any given linguistic state is always the product of historical factors, and these are the factors which explain why the linguistic sign is invariable, that is to say why it is immune from arbitrary alteration.

But to say that a language is an inheritance from the past explains nothing unless we take the question further. Is it not possible from time to time to change established laws which have been handed down from the past?

This question leads us to consider a language in its social context and to pursue our enquiry in the same terms as for any other social institution. How are social institutions handed down from generation to generation? This is the more general question which subsumes the question of invariability. It is first necessary to realise the different degrees of freedom enjoyed by other institutions. Each of them, it will be seen, achieves a different balance between the tradition handed down and society's freedom of action. The next question will be to discover why, in any given case, factors of one kind are more powerful or less powerful than factors of the other kind. Finally, reverting to linguistic matters in particular, it may then be asked why historical transmission is the overriding factor, to the point of excluding the possibility of any general or sudden linguistic change.

The answer to this question must take many considerations into account. It is relevant to point out, for example, that linguistic changes do not correspond to generations of speakers. There is no vertical structure of layers one above the other like drawers in a piece of furniture; people of all ages intermingle and communicate with one another. The continuous efforts required in order to learn one's native language point to the impossibility of any radical change. In addition, people use their language without conscious reflexion, being largely unaware of the laws which govern it. If they are not aware of these laws, how can they act to change them? In any case, linguistic facts are rarely the object of criticism, every society being usually content with the language it has inherited.

These considerations are important, but they are not directly to the point. Priority must be given to the following, which are more essential, more immediately relevant, and underlie all the rest.

1. *The arbitrary nature of the linguistic sign.* The arbitrary nature of the linguistic sign was adduced above as a reason for conceding the theoretical possibility of linguistic change. But more detailed consideration reveals that this very same factor tends to protect a language against any attempt to change it. It means that there is no issue for the community of language users to discuss, even were they sufficiently aware to do so. For in order to discuss an issue, there must be some reasonable basis for discussion. One can, for example, argue about whether monogamy is better than polygamy, and adduce reasons for and against. One could likewise discuss the pros and cons of a system of symbols, because a symbol has a rational connexion with what it symbolizes. But for a language, as a system of arbitrary signs, any such basis is lacking, and consequently there is no firm ground for discussion. No reason can be given for preferring *soeur* to *sister*, *Ochs* to *boeuf*, etc.[2]

---

[2]   Saussure's general point here is confirmed by the fact that current debates about, for instance, whether 'sexist' terms (such as *chairman*) should be replaced by unbiassed terms (e.g. *chairperson*) arise only when a

2. *The great number of signs necessary to constitute a language.* The implications of this fact are considerable. A system of writing, comprising between 20 and 40 letters, might conceivably be replaced in its entirety by an alternative system. The same would be true of a language if it comprised only a limited number of elements. But the inventory of signs in any language is countless.

3. *The complex character of the system.* A language constitutes a system. In this respect, it is not entirely arbitrary, for the system has a certain rationality. But precisely for this reason, the community is unable to change it at will. For the linguistic system is a complex mechanism. Its workings cannot be grasped without reflexion. Even speakers who use it daily may be quite ignorant in this regard. Any such change would require the intervention of specialists, grammarians, logicians, and others. But history shows that interference by experts is of no avail in linguistic matters.

4. *Collective inertia resists all linguistic innovations.* We come now to a consideration which takes precedence over all others. At any time a language belongs to all its users. It is a facility unrestrictedly available throughout a whole community. It is something all make use of every day. In this respect it is quite unlike other social institutions. Legal procedures, religious rites, ships' flags, etc. are systems used only by a certain number of individuals acting together and for a limited time. A language, on the contrary, is something in which everyone participates all the time, and that is why it is constantly open to the influence of all. This key fact is by itself sufficient to explain why a linguistic revolution is impossible. Of all social institutions, a language affords the least scope for such enterprise. It is part and parcel of the life of the whole community, and the community's natural inertia exercises a conservative influence upon it.

None the less, to say that a language is a product of social forces does not automatically explain why it comes to be constrained in the way it is. Bearing in mind that a language is always an inheritance from the past, one must add that the social forces in question act over a period of time. If stability is a characteristic of languages, it is not only because languages are anchored in the community. They are also anchored in time. The two facts are inseparable. Continuity with the past constantly restricts freedom of choice. If the Frenchman of today uses words like *homme* ('man') and *chien* ('dog'), it is because these words were used by his forefathers. Ultimately there is a connexion between these two opposing factors: the arbitrary convention which allows free choice, and the passage of time, which fixes that choice. It is because the linguistic sign is arbitrary that it knows no other law than that of tradition, and because it is founded upon tradition that it can be arbitrary.

§2. Variability

The passage of time, which ensures the continuity of a language, also has another effect, which appears to work in the opposite direction. It allows linguistic signs to be

---

reason can be given for preferring one to the other. But in such cases the reason given is usually social or political, rather than linguistic. (Translator's note.)

changed with some rapidity. Hence variability and invariability are both, in a certain sense, characteristic of the linguistic sign.[3]

In the final analysis, these two characteristics are intimately connected. The sign is subject to change because it continues through time. But what predominates in any change is the survival of earlier material. Infidelity to the past is only relative. That is how it comes about that the principle of change is based upon the principle of continuity.

Change through time takes various forms, each of which would supply the subject matter for an important chapter of linguistics. Without going into detail here, it is important to bring out the following points.

First of all, let there be no misunderstanding about the sense in which we are speaking of change. It must not be thought that we are referring particularly to phonetic changes affecting the signal, or to changes of meaning affecting the concept signified. Either view would be inadequate. Whatever the factors involved in change, whether they act in isolation or in combination, they always result in *a shift in the relationship between signal and signification.*

As examples, one might cite the following. The Latin word *necāre* meaning 'to kill' became in French *noyer* meaning 'to drown'. Here the sound pattern and the concept have both changed. It is pointless to separate one aspect of the change from the other. It suffices to note as a single fact that the connexion between sound and idea has changed. The original relationship no longer holds. If instead of comparing Latin *necāre* with French *noyer*, one contrasts it with Vulgar Latin *necare* of the fourth or fifth century, meaning 'to drown', the case is somewhat different. But even here, although the signal has undergone no appreciable change, there is a shift in the relationship between the idea and the signal.

The Old German word *dritteil* meaning 'a third' became in modern German *Drittel*. In this case, although the concept has remained the same, the relationship has changed in two ways. The signal has altered not only phonetically but also grammatically. We no longer recognise it as a combination including the unit *Teil* meaning 'part': instead, it has become a single unanalysable word. That counts too as a change in relationship.

In Anglo-Saxon, the preliterary form *fōt* meaning 'foot' remained as *fōt* (modern English *foot*), while its plural **fōti,* meaning 'feet', became *fēt* (modern English *feet*). Whatever changes may have been involved here, one thing is certain: a shift in the relationship occurred. New correlations between phonic substance and idea emerged.

A language is a system which is intrinsically defenceless against the factors which constantly tend to shift relationships between signal and signification. This is one of the consequences of the arbitrary nature of the linguistic sign.

Other human institutions—customs, laws, etc.—are all based in varying degrees on natural connexions between things. They exhibit a necessary conformity between ends and means. Even the fashion which determines the way we dress is not entirely arbitrary.

---

[3]   The striking contrast between these terms is intended simply to emphasise the fact that a language changes even though its speakers are incapable of changing it. One might also say that it is impervious to interference although open to development. (Editorial note.)

It cannot depart beyond a certain point from requirements dictated by the human body. A language, on the contrary, is in no way limited in its choice of means. For there is nothing at all to prevent the association of any idea whatsoever with any sequence of sounds whatsoever.

In order to emphasise that a language is nothing other than a social institution, Whitney quite rightly insisted upon the arbitrary character of linguistic signs. In so doing, he pointed linguistics in the right direction. But he did not go far enough. For he failed to see that this arbitrary character fundamentally distinguishes languages from all other institutions. This can be seen in the way in which a language evolves. The process is highly complex. A language is situated socially and chronologically by reference to a certain community and a certain period of time. No one can alter it in any particular. On the other hand, the fact that its signs are arbitrary implies theoretically a freedom to establish any connexion whatsoever between sounds and ideas. The result is that each of the two elements joined together in the linguistic sign retains its own independence to an unparalleled extent. Consequently a language alters, or rather evolves, under the influence of all factors which may affect either sounds or meanings. Evolution is inevitable: there is no known example of a language immune from it. After a certain time, changes can always be seen to have taken place.

This principle must even apply to artificial languages. Anyone who invents an artificial language retains control of it only as long as it is not in use. But as soon as it fulfils its purpose and becomes the property of the community, it is no longer under control. Esperanto is a case in point. If it succeeds as a language, can it possibly escape the same fate? Once launched, the language will in all probability begin to lead a semiological life of its own. Its transmission will follow laws which have nothing in common with those of deliberate creation, and it will then be impossible to turn the clock back. Anyone who thinks he can construct a language not subject to change, which posterity must accept as it is, would be like a hen hatching a duck's egg. The language he created would be subject to the same forces of change as any other language, regardless of its creator's wishes.

The continuity of signs through time, involving as it does their alteration in time, is a principle of general semiology. This principle is confirmed by systems of writing, by deaf-and-dumb languages, and so on.

But on what is the necessity for change based? We may perhaps be criticised for not being as explicit upon this point as upon the principle of invariability. The reason is that we have not gone into the different factors involved in change. A great variety of such factors must be taken into account in order to determine to what extent change is a necessity.

The causes of linguistic continuity are in principle available to observation. The same is not true of the causes of change through time. That is why in the first instance it would be misleading to attempt to identify them precisely. It is more prudent to speak in general terms of shifts in relations. For time changes everything. There is no reason why languages should be exempt from this universal law.

Law No. 94-665 of 4 August 1994
Relative to the Use of the French Language

Be it enacted, by the President of the Republic of France, by and with the advice and consent of the Constitutional Council through its decision No. 94-345 DC dated 29 July 1994, and the authority of the National Assembly and the Senate as follows:

Article 1.

Established by the Constitution as the language of the French Republic, the French language is a key element in the personality and the heritage of France.

French shall be the language of instruction, work, trade and exchanges and of the public services.

It shall be the chosen bond between the States comprising the community of French-speaking countries.

Article 2.

The use of French shall be mandatory for the designation, offer, presentation, instructions for use, and description of the scope and conditions of a warranty of goods, products and services, as well as bills and receipts.

The same provisions apply to any written, spoken, radio and television advertisement.

The provisions of the present article shall not apply to the names of typical products and specialities of foreign origin known by the general public. . . .

Article 3.

Any inscription or announcement posted or made on a public highway, in a place open to the public or in a public transport system and designed to inform the public must be expressed in French.

If the inscription drafted in breach of the foregoing provisions is posted by a third user on a good belonging to a public corporate body, the latter must serve a formal notice on the user demanding him to cease the observed irregularity at his own expense and within the deadline set by the public corporate body. If the formal notice is not complied with, depending on the seriousness of the breach, the use of the good may be withdrawn from the offending party, irrespective of the stipulations of the contract or the terms of authorisation granted the said offending party.

Article 4.

Where inscriptions and announcements referred to in Article 3 hereabove and posted or made by public corporate bodies or private persons on a public service assignment are the subject of translations, the translations must be at least two in number.

In all cases where the remarks, announcements and inscriptions referred to in articles 2 and 3 of the present law are completed by one or more translations, the presentation in French must be as legible, audible and intelligible as the presentation in the foreign languages. . . .

Article 5.

Whatever the substance and form, contracts signed by a public corporate body or a private person on a public service assignment must be drafted in French. Such contracts may neither contain expressions nor terms in a foreign language where a French term or expression with the same meaning exists and is approved under the conditions provided for by the rules relative to the enhancement of the French language. . . .

Article 6.

Any participant in an event, seminar or convention organised in France by natural persons or corporate bodies of French nationality has the right to express himself in French. Documents distributed to participants before and during the meeting for the presentation of the programme must be drafted in French and may include translations in one or more foreign languages.

Where an event, seminar or convention involves the distribution of preparatory documents or work documents to participants, or the publication of proceedings or minutes of work sessions, the texts or papers presented in the foreign language must be accompanied by at least a summary in French. . . .

Article 7.

Publications, reviews and papers distributed in France and drafted in a foreign language, shall include at least a summary in French when the said publications, reviews and papers are issued by a public corporate body, a private person on a public service assignment or a private person subsidised by public funds.

Article 8.

The last three paragraphs of Article L. 121-1 of the labour code are replaced by four paragraphs drafted as follows:

"The employment agreement expressed in writing must be drafted in French.

"Where the position covered by the agreement can only be designated by a foreign term without an equivalent in French, the employment agreement must include an explanation in French of the foreign term.

"Where the employee is a foreigner and the agreement is put in writing, the said contract must be translated, at the employee's request, into his native tongue. Both documents shall be considered as authentic and receivable in court. Should any inconsistency be observed between the two texts, only the agreement drafted in the native tongue of the foreign employee may be used against the latter.

"The employer cannot invoke the provisions of an employment agreement concluded in breach of the present article against an employee prejudiced thereby."

Article 9.

Article L. 122-35 of the labour code is completed by the paragraph below:

"The company rules shall be drafted in French. Translations in one or more foreign languages may be attached to them."

Article L. 122-39-1 herebelow is inserted after Article L. 122-39 of the labour code:

"Any document containing obligations for the employee or provisions which the employee needs to know for the proper execution of his work shall be drafted in French. Translations in one or more foreign languages may be attached to it. . . ."

Article L. 132-2-1 herebelow is inserted after Article L. 132-2 of the labour code:

"Labour agreements, union contracts and corporate or institution agreements must be drafted in French. Any provision drafted in a foreign language shall be non-invocable against the employee at which the grievance is directed."

Article 10.

The third paragraph of Article L. 311-4 of the labour code is as follows:

"Where the employment or position offered can only be designated by a foreign term without an equivalent in French, the French text must include a sufficiently detailed description to avoid any misleading interpretation . . . ."

Article 11.

The language of instruction, examinations and competitive examinations, as well as theses and dissertations in State and private educational institutions shall be French, except for cases justified by the need to teach foreign and regional languages and cultures or where the teachers are associate teachers or guest teachers.

Foreign schools or schools specially set up to teach foreign nationals as well as institutions providing instruction of an international nature are not bound by this obligation.

Article 12.

Article 20-1 herebelow has been inserted before Chapter 1 of Section II of Law No. 86-1067 of 30 September 1986 relative to the freedom of communication:

"The use of French is compulsory in all the programmes and advertising messages of radio and television broadcasting organisations and services, whatever their mode of dissemination or distribution, with the exception of motion picture and radio and television productions in their original language version.

"[T]he foregoing paragraph shall not apply to musical works which contain text written wholly or partly in a foreign language.

"The obligation laid down in the first paragraph applies neither to programmes, parts of programmes or advertisements included in the latter which are designed to be fully broadcast in a foreign language or which aim at the teaching of a language, nor to broadcasts of religious ceremonies.

"Where the broadcasts or advertising messages referred to in the first paragraph of the present Article are accompanied by translations in a foreign language, the presentation in French must be as legible, audible and intelligible as the presentation in the foreign language."

Article 14.

It is strictly forbidden for public corporate bodies to use a trademark, trade name or service brand made up of a foreign expression or term when an equivalent French term or expression with the same meaning exists and is approved under the conditions defined by the provisions of the rules relative to the enhancement of the French language.

This proscription also applies to private corporate bodies on a public service assignment during the performance of this assignment.

Article 15.

Beneficiaries of all types of grants and subsidies from public authorities and institutions are required to comply with the provisions of the present law.

Non-compliance with the foregoing may lead to the total or partial refunding of the subsidy or grant, after the concerned party has been summoned to provide explanations.

Article 16.

In addition to the officers and agents of the criminal investigation department acting in compliance with the rules of criminal procedure, the agents listed in . . . Article L. 215-1 of the consumer code are empowered to seek out and report breaches of the provisions of texts drafted for the application of Article 2 of the present law.

To this end, agents are authorised to enter, during the day, the premises and vehicles listed in the first paragraph of Article L. 213-4 of the same code, and other places where the activities mentioned in Article L. 216-1 are carried out, with the exception of places which are also used for residential purposes. They may ask to consult documents necessary for carrying out their task, make copies of them and collect the information and proof required for fulfilling their task either directly on the suspected party's premises or by summons to the agents' premises.

They may also take a sample of the goods or products implicated under the conditions provided for by decree of the Council of State.

Article 17.

Whosoever shall directly or indirectly impede the work of the agents mentioned in the first paragraph of Article 16 and consequently prevent them from carrying out their task, or refuse to place at their disposal all the means required for this purpose, shall be liable to the penalties provided for in the second paragraph of Article 433-5 of the criminal code. . . .

Etiquette
Emily Post

Chapter I
What Is Best Society?

"Society" is an ambiguous term; it may mean much or nothing. Every human being—unless dwelling alone in a cave—is a member of society of one sort or another, and therefore it is well to define what is to be understood by the term "Best Society" and why its authority is recognized. Best Society abroad is always the oldest aristocracy; composed not so much of persons of title, which may be new, as of those families and communities which have for the longest period of time known highest cultivation. Our own Best Society is represented by social groups which have had, since this is America, widest rather than longest association with old world cultivation. Cultivation is always the basic attribute of Best Society, much as we hear in this country of an "Aristocracy of wealth."

To the general public a long purse is synonymous with high position—a theory dear to the heart of the "yellow" press and eagerly fostered in the preposterous social functions of screen drama. It is true that Best Society is comparatively rich; it is true that the hostess of great wealth, who constantly and lavishly entertains, will shine, at least to the readers of the press, more brilliantly than her less affluent sister. Yet the latter, through her quality of birth, her poise, her inimitable distinction, is often the jewel of deeper water in the social crown of her time.

The most advertised commodity is not always intrinsically the best, but is sometimes merely the product of a company with plenty of money to spend on advertising. In the same way, money brings certain people before the public—sometimes they are persons of "quality," quite as often the so-called "society leaders" featured in the public press do not belong to good society at all, in spite of their many published photographs and the energies of their press-agents. Or possibly they do belong to "smart" society; but if too much advertised, instead of being the "queens" they seem, they might more accurately be classified as the court jesters of to-day.

The Imitation and the Genuine

New York, more than any city in the world, unless it be Paris, loves to be amused, thrilled and surprised all at the same time; and will accept with outstretched hand any one who can perform this astounding feat. Do not underestimate the ability that can achieve it: a scintillating wit, an arresting originality, a talent for entertaining that amounts to genius, and gold poured literally like rain, are the least requirements.

Puritan America on the other hand demanding, as a ticket of admission to her Best Society, the qualifications of birth, manners and cultivation, clasps her hands tight across her slim trim waist and announces severely that New York's "Best" is, in her opinion, very "bad" indeed. But this is because Puritan America, as well as the general public, mistakes the jester for the queen.

As a matter of fact, Best Society is not at all like a court with an especial queen or king, nor is it confined to any one place or group, but might better be described as an unlimited brotherhood which spreads over the entire surface of the globe, the members of which are invariably people of cultivation and worldly knowledge, who have not only perfect manners but a perfect manner. Manners are made up of trivialities of deportment which can be easily learned if one does not happen to know them; manner is personality—the outward manifestation of one's innate character and attitude toward life. A gentleman, for instance, will never be ostentatious or overbearing any more than he will ever be servile, because these attributes never animate the impulses of a well-bred person. A man whose manners suggest the grotesque is invariably a person of imitation rather than of real position.

Etiquette must, if it is to be of more than trifling use, include ethics as well as manners. Certainly what one is, is of far greater importance than what one appears to be. A knowledge of etiquette is of course essential to one's decent behavior, just as clothing is essential to one's decent appearance; and precisely as one wears the latter without being self-conscious of having on shoes and perhaps gloves, one who has good manners is equally unself-conscious in the observance of etiquette, the precepts of which must be so thoroughly absorbed as to make their observance a matter of instinct rather than of conscious obedience.

Thus Best Society is not a fellowship of the wealthy, nor does it seek to exclude those who are not of exalted birth; but it *is* an association of gentle-folk, of which good form in speech, charm of manner, knowledge of the social amenities, and instinctive consideration for the feelings of others, are the credentials by which society the world over recognizes its chosen members.

Chapter VII
Conversation

Ideal conversation should be a matter of equal give and take, but too often it is all "take." The voluble talker—or chatterer—rides his own hobby straight through the hours without giving anyone else, who might also like to say something, a chance to do other than exhaustedly await the turn that never comes. Once in a while—a very long while—one meets a brilliant person whose talk is a delight; or still more rarely a wit who manipulates every ordinary topic with the agility of a sleight-of-hand performer, to the ever increasing rapture of his listeners.

But as a rule the man who has been led to believe that he is a brilliant and interesting talker has been led to make himself a rapacious pest. No conversation is possible between others whose ears are within reach of his ponderous voice; anecdotes, long-winded stories, dramatic and pathetic, stock his repertoire; but worst of all are his humorous yarns at which he laughs uproariously though every one else grows solemn and more solemn.

There is a simple rule, by which if one is a voluble chatterer (to be a good talker necessitates a good mind) one can at least refrain from being a pest or a bore. And the rule is merely, to stop and think.

"Think Before You Speak"

Nearly all the faults or mistakes in conversation are caused by not thinking. For instance, a first rule for behavior in society is: "Try to do and say those things only which will be agreeable to others." Yet how many people, who really know better, people who are perfectly capable of intelligent understanding if they didn't let their brains remain asleep or locked tight, go night after night to dinner parties, day after day to other social gatherings, and absent-mindedly prate about this or that without ever taking the trouble to *think* what they are saying and to whom they are saying it! Would a young mother describe twenty or thirty cunning tricks and sayings of the baby to a bachelor who has been helplessly put beside her at dinner if she *thought*? She would know very well, alas! that not even a very dear friend would really care for more than a *hors d'oeuvre* of the subject, at the board of general conversation.

The older woman is even worse, unless something occurs (often when it is too late) to make her wake up and realize that she not only bores her hearers but prejudices everyone against her children by the unrestraint of her own praise. The daughter who is continually lauded as the most captivating and beautiful girl in the world, seems to the wearied perceptions of enforced listeners annoying and plain. In the same way the "magnificent" son is handicapped by his mother's—or his father's—overweening pride and love in exact proportion to its displayed intensity. On the other hand, the neglected wife, the unappreciated husband, the misunderstood child, takes on a glamor in the eyes of others equally out of proportion. That great love has seldom perfect wisdom is one of the great tragedies in the drama of life. In the case of the overloving wife or mother, some one should love *her* enough to make her *stop and think* that her loving praise is not merely a question of boring her hearers but of handicapping unfairly those for whom she would gladly lay down her life—and yet few would have the courage to point out to her that she would far better lay down her tongue.

The cynics say that those who take part in social conversation are bound to be either the bores or the bored; and that which you choose to be, is a mere matter of selection. And there must be occasions in the life of everyone when the cynics seem to be right; the man of affairs who, sitting next to an attractive looking young woman, is regaled throughout dinner with the detailed accomplishments of the young woman's husband; the woman of intellect who must listen with interest to the droolings of an especially prosy man who holds forth on the super-everything of his own possessions, can not very well consider that the evening was worth dressing, sitting up, and going out for.

People who talk too easily are apt to talk too much, and at times imprudently, and those with vivid imagination are often unreliable in their statements. On the other hand the "man of silence" who never speaks except when he has something "worth while" to say, is apt to wear well among his intimates, but is not likely to add much to the gaiety of a party.

Try not to repeat yourself; either by telling the same story again and again or by going back over details of your narrative that seemed especially to interest or amuse your hearer. Many things are of interest when briefly told and for the first time; *nothing* interests when too long dwelt upon; little interests that is told a second time. The exception is something very pleasant that you have heard about A. or more especially A.'s child, which having already told A. you can then tell B., and later C. in A.'s presence. Never do this as a habit, however, and never drag the incident into the conversation merely to flatter A., since if A. is a person of taste he will be far more apt to resent than be pleased by flattery that borders on the fulsome.

Be careful not to let amiable discussion turn into contradiction and argument. The tactful person keeps his prejudices to himself and even when involved in a discussion says quietly "No. I don't think I agree with you" or "It seems to me thus and so." One who is well-bred never says "You are wrong!" or "Nothing of the kind!" If he finds another's opinion utterly opposed to his own, he switches to another subject for a pleasanter channel of conversation. . . .

The Gift of Humor

The joy of joys is the person of light but unmalicious humor. If you know any one who is gay, beguiling and amusing, you will, if you are wise, do everything you can to make him prefer your house and your table to any other; for where he is, the successful party is also. What he says is of no matter, it is the twist he gives to it, the intonation, the personality he puts into his quip or retort or observation that delights his hearers, and in his case the ordinary rules do not apply.

Eugene Field could tell a group of people that it had rained to-day and would probably rain tomorrow, and make everyone burst into laughter—or tears if he chose—according to the way it was said. But the ordinary rest of us must, if we would be thought sympathetic, intelligent or agreeable, "go fishing."

Going Fishing for Topics

The charming talker is neither more nor less than a fisherman. (Fisherwoman rather, since in America women make more effort to be agreeable than men do.) Sitting next to a stranger she wonders which "fly" she had better choose to interest him. She offers one topic; not much of a nibble. So she tries another or perhaps a third before he "rises" to the bait.

The Door Slammers

There are people whose idea of conversation is contradiction and flat statement. Finding yourself next to one of these, you venture:

"Have you seen any good plays lately?"

"No, hate the theater."

"Which team are you for in the series?"

"Neither. Only an idiot could be interested in baseball."

"Country must have a good many idiots!" mockingly.

"Obviously it has." Full stop. In desperation you veer to the personal.

"I've never seen Mrs. Bobo Gilding as beautiful as she is to-night."

"Nothing beautiful about her. As for the name 'Bobo,' it's asinine."

"Oh, it's just one of those children's names that stick sometimes for life."

"Perfect rot. Ought to be called by his name," etc.

Another, not very different in type though different in method, is the self-appointed instructor whose proper place is on the lecture platform, not at a dinner table.

"The earliest coins struck in the Peloponnesus were stamped on one side only; their alloy—" etc.

Another is the expounder of the obvious: "Have you ever noticed," says he, deeply thinking, "how people's tastes differ?"

Then there is the vulgarian of fulsome compliment: "Why are you so beautiful? It is not fair to the others—" and so on.

Chapter XXIX
The Fundamentals of Good Behavior

Far more important than any mere dictum of etiquette is the fundamental code of honor, without strict observance of which no man, no matter how "polished," can be considered a gentleman. The honor of a gentleman demands the inviolability of his word, and the incorruptibility of his principles; he is the descendant of the knight, the crusader; he is the defender of the defenseless, and the champion of justice—or he is not a gentleman.

Decencies of Behavior

A gentleman does not, and a man who aspires to be one must not, ever borrow money from a woman, nor should he, except in unexpected circumstances, borrow money from a man. Money borrowed without security is a debt of honor which must be paid without fail and promptly as possible. The debts incurred by a deceased parent, brother, sister, or grown child, are assumed by honorable men and women, as debts of honor.

A gentleman never takes advantage of a woman in a business dealing, nor of the poor or the helpless.

One who is not well off does not "sponge," but pays his own way to the utmost of his ability.

One who is rich does not make a display of his money or his possessions. Only a vulgarian talks ceaselessly about how much this or that cost him.

A very well-bred man intensely dislikes the mention of money, and never speaks of it (out of business hours) if he can avoid it.

A gentleman never discusses his family affairs either in public or with acquaintances, nor does he speak more than casually about his wife. A man is a cad who tells anyone, no matter who, what his wife told him in confidence, or describes what she looks like in her bedroom. To impart details of her beauty is scarcely better than to publish her blemishes; to do either is unspeakable.

Nor does a gentleman ever criticise the behavior of a wife whose conduct is scandalous. What he says to her in the privacy of their own apartments is no one's affair but his own, but he must never treat her with disrespect before their children, or a servant, or any one.

A man of honor never seeks publicly to divorce his wife, no matter what he believes her conduct to have been; but for the protection of his own name, and that of the children, he allows her to get her freedom on other than criminal grounds. No matter who he may be, whether rich or poor, in high life or low, the man who publicly besmirches his wife's name, besmirches still more his own, and proves that he is not, was not, and never will be, a gentleman.

No gentleman goes to a lady's house if he is affected by alcohol. A gentleman seeing a young man who is not entirely himself in the presence of ladies, quietly induces the youth to depart. An older man addicted to the use of too much alcohol, need not be discussed, since he ceases to be asked to the houses of ladies.

A gentleman does not lose control of his temper. In fact, in his own self-control under difficult or dangerous circumstances, lies his chief ascendancy over others who impulsively betray every emotion which animates them. Exhibitions of anger, fear, hatred, embarrassment, ardor or hilarity, are all bad form in public. And bad form is merely an action which "jars" the sensibilities of others. A gentleman does not show a letter written by a lady, unless perhaps to a very intimate friend if the letter is entirely impersonal and written by some one who is equally the friend of the one to whom it is shown. But the occasions when the letter of a woman may be shown properly by a man are so few that it is safest to make it a rule never to mention a woman's letter.

A gentleman does not bow to a lady from a club window; nor according to good form should ladies ever be discussed in a man's club!

A man whose social position is self-made is apt to be detected by his continual cataloguing of prominent names. Mr. Parvenu invariably interlards his conversation with, "When I was dining at the Bobo Gildings'"; or even "at Lucy Gilding's," and quite often accentuates, in his ignorance, those of rather second-rate, though conspicuous position. "I was spending last week-end with the Richan Vulgars," or "My great friends, the Gotta Crusts." When a so-called gentleman insists on imparting information, interesting only to the Social Register, *shun him!*

The born gentleman avoids the mention of names exactly as he avoids the mention of what things cost; both are an abomination to his soul.

A gentleman's manners are an integral part of him and are the same whether in his dressing-room or in a ballroom, whether in talking to Mrs. Worldly or to the laundress bringing in his clothes. He whose manners are only put on in company is a veneered gentleman, not a real one.

A man of breeding does not slap strangers on the back nor so much as lay his fingertips on a lady. Nor does he punctuate his conversation by pushing or nudging or patting people, nor take his conversation out of the drawing-room! Notwithstanding the advertisements in the most dignified magazines, a discussion of underwear and toilet articles and their merit or their use, is unpleasant in polite conversation.

All thoroughbred people are considerate of the feelings of others no matter what the station of the others may be. Thackeray's climber who "licks the boots of those above him and kicks the faces of those below him on the social ladder," is a very good illustration of what a gentleman is *not*.

A gentleman never takes advantage of another's helplessness or ignorance, and assumes that no gentleman will take advantage of him.

Simplicity and Unconsciousness of Self

These words have been literally sprinkled through the pages of this book, yet it is doubtful if they convey a clear idea of the attributes meant.

Unconsciousness of self is not so much unselfishness as it is the mental ability to extinguish all thought of one's self—exactly as one turns out the light.

Simplicity is like it, in that it also has a quality of self-effacement, but it really means a love of the essential and of directness. Simple people put no trimmings on their phrases, nor on their manners; but remember, simplicity is not crudeness nor anything like it. On the contrary, simplicity of speech and manners means language in its purest, most limpid form, and manners of such perfection that they do not suggest "manner" at all.

The Instincts of a Lady

The instincts of a lady are much the same as those of a gentleman. She is equally punctilious about her debts, equally averse to pressing her advantage; especially if her adversary is helpless or poor.

As an unhappy wife, her dignity demands that she never show her disapproval of her husband, no matter how publicly he slights or outrages her. If she has been so unfortunate as to have married a man not a gentleman, to draw attention to his behavior would put herself on his level. If it comes actually to the point where she divorces him, she discusses her situation, naturally, with her parents or her brother or whoever are her nearest and wisest relatives, but she shuns publicity and avoids discussing her affairs with any one outside of her immediate family. One can not too strongly censure the unspeakable vulgarity of the woman so unfortunate as to be obliged to go through divorce proceedings, who confides the private details of her life to reporters.

The True Meaning of Etiquette[*]
Emily Post

It would be careless to think of etiquette as being of importance to none but brides, or diplomats, or perhaps persons lately elected to political office. There is truly not a single thing that we do, or say, or choose, or use, or even think, that does not follow—or break—one of the exactions of taste, tact, ethics, good manners, etiquette—call it what you will.

Considering manners even in their superficial aspect, no one—unless he be a hermit—can fail to gain from a proper, courteous, likable approach, or fail to be handicapped by an improper, offensive, resentful one. Certainly the greatest asset that a man or woman or even a child can have is charm. And charm cannot exist without the good manners that come to those who make a continuous practice of kind impulses.

It is hard to say why the word "etiquette" is so inevitably considered merely a synonym of the word "correct," as though it were no more than the fixed answer to a sum in arithmetic. In fact, it might be well to pull the word "correct" out by the roots and substitute "common sense." In short, I wish that those whose minds are focused on precise obedience to every precept would instead ask themselves, "What is the purpose of this rule? Does it help to make life pleasanter? Does it make the social machinery run more smoothly? Does it add to beauty? Is it essential to the code of good taste or to ethics?" If it serves any of these purposes, it is a rule to be cherished; but if it serves no helpful purpose, it is certainly not worth taking very seriously.

On the subject of the thousands of detailed rules essential to all ceremonial procedures, the importance of knowing the unending details, such as when to sit and when to stand, what to say and what to do upon this or that occasion, is most practically illustrated by a church service. It would be shocking to have people trotting in and out of the pews, talking out loud, or otherwise upsetting devotional tranquillity. For this reason we have set rules for all ceremonial functions, so that marriages, christenings, funerals, as well as Sunday services, shall be conducted with ease and smoothness. It is also essential to ease of living that certain mechanical conventions be observed. One of the simplest is that of extending our right hand when shaking hands, but think how confusing it would be if we did not all follow it.

The real point to be made is that rules of etiquette have not been contrived in order to make those who know them seem important and to publicly shame those who happen not to know them. Actually the so-called rules are nothing but the results of long experience handed down for reasons of practicality. This does not mean that the principles of good taste, or of beauty, or of consideration for the rights or feelings of others can ever be discarded. As a matter of fact, good taste is necessarily helpful. It must be the suitable thing, the comfortable thing, the useful thing for the occasion, the place, and the time, or it is not in good taste.

---

[*] Emily Post, Etiquette: The Blue Book of Social Usage (New York: Funk & Wagnalls Company, Inc., 10th edition 1960), pages 1-2. Copyright © 1965 by Funk & Wagnalls Company Inc. and HarperCollins Publishers Inc.

In the same way the code of ethics—which is also known as the code of a gentleman—is an immutable law of etiquette. Too many of us are likely to assume a rich man is of necessity a gentleman. Nothing could be further from the truth, since the quality of a gentleman is necessarily measured only by what he is and what he does—never by what he has. We've all heard the term "nature's nobleman," meaning a man of innately beautiful character who, though never having even heard of the code, follows it instinctively. In other words, the code of ethics is the code of instinctive decency, ethical integrity, self-respect, and loyalty. Decency means not merely propriety of speech and conduct, but honesty and trustworthiness in every obligation. Integrity includes not only honesty but a delicacy of motive and fairness in appraising the motives of others. Self-respect, among many other things, means refusal to accept obligations that one is unwilling to return. This word *unwilling* is of importance, since there is no more contemptible person than one who takes all he can get and gives as little as he can. Loyalty means faithfulness not only to friends, but also to principles.

Etiquette, if it is to be of more than trifling use, must go far beyond the mere mechanical rules of procedure or the equally automatic precepts of conventional behavior. Actually etiquette is most deeply concerned with every phase of ethical impulse or judgment and with every choice or expression of taste, since what one is, is of far greater importance than what one appears to be. A knowledge of etiquette is of course essential to one's decent behavior, just as clothing is essential to one's decent appearance; and precisely as one wears the latter without being self-conscious of having on shoes and perhaps gloves, one who has good manners is equally unself-conscious in the observance of etiquette, the precepts of which must be so thoroughly ingrained that their observance is a matter of instinct rather than of conscious obedience.

New York Rules of Court
Supreme Court, Appellate Division, All Departments
Standards of Civility

Preamble

The New York State Standards of Civility for the legal profession set forth principles of behavior to which the bar, the bench and court employees should aspire. They are not intended as rules to be enforced by sanction or disciplinary action, nor are they intended to supplement or modify the Rules Governing Judicial Conduct, the Code of Professional Responsibility and its Disciplinary Rules, or any other applicable rule or requirement governing conduct. Instead they are a set of guidelines intended to encourage lawyers, judges and court personnel to observe principles of civility and decorum, and to confirm the legal profession's rightful status as an honorable and respected profession where courtesy and civility are observed as a matter of course. The Standards are divided into four parts: lawyers' duties to other other lawyers, litigants and witnesses; lawyers' duties to the court and court personnel; judges' duties to lawyers, parties and witnesses; and court personnel's duties to lawyers and litigants.

As lawyers, judges and court employees, we are all essential participants in the judicial process. That process cannot work effectively to serve the public unless we first treat each other with courtesy, respect and civility.

Lawyers' Duties to Other Lawyers, Litigants and Witnesses

I. Lawyers should be courteous and civil in all professional dealings with other persons.

A. Lawyers should act in a civil manner regardless of the ill feelings that their clients may have toward others.

B. Lawyers can disagree without being disagreeable. Effective representation does not require antagonistic or acrimonious behavior. Whether orally or in writing, lawyers should avoid vulgar language, disparaging personal remarks or acrimony toward other counsel, parties or witnesses.

C. Lawyers should require that persons under their supervision conduct themselves with courtesy and civility.

II. When consistent with their clients' interests, lawyers should cooperate with opposing counsel in an effort to avoid litigation and to resolve litigation that has already commenced.

A. Lawyers should avoid unnecessary motion practice or other judicial intervention by negotiating and agreeing with other counsel whenever it is practicable to do so.

B. Lawyers should allow themselves sufficient time to resolve any dispute or disagreement by communicating with one another and imposing reasonable and meaningful deadlines in light of the nature and status of the case.

III. A lawyer should respect the schedule and commitments of opposing counsel, consistent with protection of their clients' interests.

A. In the absence of a court order, a lawyer should agree to reasonable requests for extensions of time or for waiver of procedural formalities when the legitimate interests of the client will not be adversely affected.

B. Upon request coupled with the simple representation by counsel that more time is required, the first request for an extension to respond to pleadings ordinarily should be granted as a matter of courtesy.

C. A lawyer should not attach unfair or extraneous conditions to extensions of time. A lawyer is entitled to impose conditions appropriate to preserve rights that an extension might otherwise jeopardize, and may request, but should not unreasonably insist on, reciprocal scheduling concessions.

D. A lawyer should endeavor to consult with other counsel regarding scheduling matters in a good faith effort to avoid scheduling conflicts. A lawyer should likewise cooperate with opposing counsel when scheduling changes are requested, provided the interests of his or her client will not be jeopardized.

E. A lawyer should notify other counsel and, if appropriate, the court or other persons at the earliest possible time when hearings, depositions, meetings or conferences are to be canceled or postponed.

IV. A lawyer should promptly return telephone calls and answer correspondence reasonably requiring a response.

V. The timing and manner of service of papers should not be designed to cause disadvantage to the party receiving the papers.

A. Papers should not be served in a manner designed to take advantage of an opponent's known absence from the office.

B. Papers should not be served at a time or in a manner designed to inconvenience an adversary.

C. Unless specifically authorized by law or rule, a lawyer should not submit papers to the court without serving copies of all such papers upon opposing counsel in such a manner that opposing counsel will receive them before or contemporaneously with the submission to the court.

VI. A lawyer should not use any aspect of the litigation process, including discovery and motion practice, as a means of harassment or for the purpose of unnecessarily prolonging litigation or increasing litigation expenses.

A. A lawyer should avoid discovery that is not necessary to obtain facts or perpetuate testimony or that is designed to place an undue burden or expense on a party.

B. A lawyer should respond to discovery requests reasonably and not strain to interpret the request so as to avoid disclosure of relevant and non-privileged information.

VII. In depositions and other proceedings, and in negotiations, lawyers should conduct themselves with dignity and refrain from engaging in acts of rudeness and disrespect.

A. Lawyers should not engage in any conduct during a deposition that would not be appropriate in the presence of a judge.

B. Lawyers should advise their clients and witnesses of the proper conduct expected of them in court, at depositions and at conferences, and, to the best of their ability, prevent clients and witnesses from causing disorder or disruption.

C. A lawyer should not obstruct questioning during a deposition or object to deposition questions unless necessary.

D. Lawyers should ask only those questions they reasonably believe are necessary for the prosecution or defense of an action. Lawyers should refrain from asking repetitive or argumentative questions and from making self-serving statements.

VIII. A lawyer should adhere to all express promises and agreements with other counsel, whether oral or in writing, and to agreements implied by the circumstances or by local customs.

IX. Lawyers should not mislead other persons involved in the litigation process.

A. A lawyer should not falsely hold out the possibility of settlement as a means for adjourning discovery or delaying trial.

B. A lawyer should not ascribe a position to another counsel that counsel has not taken or otherwise seek to create an unjustified inference based on counsel's statements or conduct.

C. In preparing written versions of agreements and court orders, a lawyer should attempt to correctly reflect the agreement of the parties or the direction of the court.

X. Lawyers should be mindful of the need to protect the standing of the legal profession in the eyes of the public. Accordingly, lawyers should bring the New York State Standards of Civility to the attention of other lawyers when appropriate.

Lawyers' Duties to the Court and Court Personnel

I. A lawyer is both an officer of the court and an advocate. As such, the lawyer should always strive to uphold the honor and dignity of the profession, avoid disorder and disruption in the courtroom, and maintain a respectful attitude toward the court.

A. Lawyers should speak and write civilly and respectfully in all communications with the court and court personnel.

B. Lawyers should use their best efforts to dissuade clients and witnesses from causing disorder or disruption in the courtroom.

C. Lawyers should not engage in conduct intended primarily to harass or humiliate witnesses.

D. Lawyers should be punctual and prepared for all court appearances; if delayed, the lawyer should notify the court and counsel whenever possible.

II. Court personnel are an integral part of the justice system and should be treated with courtesy and respect at all times.

Judges' Duties to Lawyers, Parties and Witnesses

A judge should be patient, courteous and civil to lawyers, parties and witnesses.

A. A judge should maintain control over the proceedings and insure that they are conducted in a civil manner.

B. Judges should not employ hostile, demeaning or humiliating words in opinions or in written or oral communications with lawyers, parties or witnesses.

C. Judges should, to the extent consistent with the efficient conduct of litigation and other demands on the court, be considerate of the schedules of lawyers, parties and witnesses when scheduling hearings, meetings or conferences.

D. Judges should be punctual in convening all trials, hearings, meetings and conferences; if delayed, they should notify counsel when possible.

E. Judges should make all reasonable efforts to decide promptly all matters presented to them for decision.

F. Judges should use their best efforts to insure that court personnel under their direction act civilly toward lawyers, parties and witnesses.

Duties of Court Personnel to the Court, Lawyers and Litigants

Court personnel should be courteous, patient and respectful while providing prompt, efficient and helpful service to all persons having business with the courts.

A. Court employees should respond promptly and helpfully to requests for assistance or information.

B. Court employees should respect the judge's directions concerning the procedures and atmosphere that the judge wishes to maintain in his or her courtroom.

Restatement of Love
(Tentative Draft)*

Reporters:
Gretchen Craft Rubin
Jamie G. Heller

Introduction

Custom has long been the authority in matters of love. Men and women have turned almost unthinkingly to tradition and prevailing social norms for guidance in the tender passion. Yet the Bar of late has come to acknowledge that the lack of codification in this realm has left a rent in the otherwise seamless web of the law. To address this gap, the Reporters have set forth the Restatement of Love.

No doubt some will question the departure from tradition that the Restatement of Love represents. Although the legal rules pertaining to marriage, divorce, and estates have been well established, the law's application to a relationship's early stages has hitherto been largely unexplored. Romantic relationships have been presumed unsusceptible to a structure of rules, perhaps because of the widespread belief that love is the most intimate and idiosyncratic of human emotions. The Restatement of Love, however, is premised on the view that love, like all other aspects of human interaction, can be subjected profitably to legal analysis.

Scope of this Restatement. Currently, matters of the heart are governed by a complicated network of unwritten norms that specify the parties' rights and obligations. These mores, though subject to extensive discussion in almost every field of human endeavor, ranging from art to literature to the social sciences, have yet to be put to the rigor of legal scrutiny. The Restatement undertakes this task. It codifies the underlying principles of love and, where appropriate, draws on established legal doctrines from other fields. The claim has been made that "[t]he heart has its reasons, of which reason knows nothing."[1] By distilling a universal, reasoned framework for relations of love, the Restatement will refute this widespread, but mistaken, view.

This Tentative Draft is not exhaustive. It merely begins the process of identifying and cataloging the law of love. Readers should not expect to find all applicable areas of the law treated fully and completely. The Reporters anticipate that the project will culminate in the compilation of a complete and authoritative code.

Organization. This Restatement consists of four Chapters. Chapter 1, *Meaning of Terms,* sets forth the basic definitions that this Draft employs. Chapter 2, *Courtship,* surveys the three principal models under which relationships begin: the blind date model, the informal acquaintance model, and the aggravating circumstances model. Chapter 3, *The Course of the Relationship,* examines four major legal areas in which developed doctrines

---

* Gretchen Craft Rubin and Jamie G. Heller, Restatement of Love. Reprinted by permission of the Yale Law Journal Company and Fred B. Rothman & Company from The Yale Law Journal, Vol. 104, pages 707-730.

[1] Blaise Pascal, Pensées 154 (A.J. Krailsheimer trans., Penguin Books 1966) (1670).

shed light on the law of relationships: jurisdiction, procedure, property, and torts. Chapter 4, *Dissolution,* governs the various aspects involved in the act of dissolving a relationship.

Chapter One

Meaning of Terms

This Chapter defines the terms used in this Tentative Draft. Many commentators resist established definitions in the context of love and argue that these "ancient" categories are "crude and unworkable."[2] Some contend that such categories are mere constructs, designed to push people toward conventional relationships.[3] But law, by its very nature, relies upon a common understanding of the terms that define it.[4] This Restatement will employ the following neutral and modern terms in order to encompass the greatest number of possible situations.[5]

§ 1.1. Interest

An interest is the object of any human desire.

Comment:

Although this definition mirrors that found in the Restatement of Torts, Second,[6] readers are cautioned that the term has somewhat different connotations in this field.

§ 1.2. Party

A party is any natural person engaged, or potentially engaged, in a relationship.

---

[2]   For leading criticism of "outworn" distinctions, see Rowland v. Christian, 443 P.2d 561, 567 (Cal. 1968):

> Whatever may have been the historical justifications for the common law distinctions [among trespasser, licensee, and invitee], it is clear that those distinctions are not justified in the light of our modern society and that the complexity and confusion which has arisen is not due to difficulty in applying the original common law rules . . . but is due to the attempts to apply just rules in our modern society within the ancient terminology.

[3]   Cf. Felix S. Cohen. Transcendental Nonsense and the Functional Approach, 35 Colum. L. Rev. 809, 812, 816 (1935) (criticizing "vivid fictions and metaphors of traditional jurisprudence").

[4]   See Wesley N. Hohfeld, Some Fundamental Legal Conceptions as Applied in Judicial Reasoning, 23 Yale L.J. 16, 20 (1913) (defining and discussing "the basic conceptions of the law,—the legal elements that enter into all types of jural interests" in order to clarify legal reasoning).

[5]   The Restatement does not discuss parties in gendered terms, nor does it address concerns peculiar to one sex or the other. To be sure, scholars have noted that men and women may have different perspectives on many subjects. See, e.g., Carol Gilligan, In a Different Voice 1 (1982) (noting "distinction in these [male and female] voices, two . . . modes of describing the relationship between other and self"). The Reporters have rejected this model, however, out of a commitment to the vision of ordered law that has shaped the work of the Restatements since the time of Christopher Columbus Langdell. As Grant Gilmore characterized it, the "Langdellian revolution" was founded on the belief, still powerful today, that "there really is such a thing as the one true rule of law, universal and unchanging, always and everywhere the same—a sort of mystical absolute." Grant Gilmore, The Death Of Contract 97-98 (1974) (footnote omitted).

For the same reason, the Restatement does not explore the doctrinal nuances that may distinguish heterosexual and homosexual relationships.

[6]   Restatement (Second) of Torts § 1 (1965) ("The word 'interest' is used throughout the Restatement of this Subject to denote the object of any human desire.").

Comment:

Alternate and colloquial terms to describe the parties within the relationship include, but are not limited to: boyfriend, girlfriend, significant other, partner, lover, sweetheart. Note that "ladyfriend" and "manfriend" are considered vulgar terms that are now in disrepute among all circuits.

§ 1.3. Relationship

A relationship is that status enjoyed by individuals who consider or comport themselves in a manner that indicates an ongoing romantic involvement.

Comment:

Alternate and colloquial terms for a relationship include, *inter alia:* going steady, dating, an item, seeing each other, involved.

§ 1.4. Love

Parties in "love" are those parties to a relationship who consider themselves engaged in the highest level of emotional intimacy attainable and who generally presume that such state will continue indefinitely.

Comment:

The English language contains no precise alternate term for "love." This fact is often decried as a constraint on the expression of emotional subtlety. For the purposes of this Restatement, however, one term is sufficient.

§ 1.5. Dissolution; breakup

A dissolution or breakup is any act by which a relationship is terminated.

Comment:

Dissolution may be accomplished by either unilateral or bilateral action.

Chapter Two

Courtship

Chapter Two reviews the three principal models of commencing a relationship: the blind date model, the informal acquaintance model, and the aggravating circumstances model. In recent history, the blind date model was paramount, and in fact it still remains strong in homogeneous urban and suburban communities.[7] Because the model is so prevalent, and because the parties necessarily bargain at arm's length, certain practices have become standard for blind dates. Blind dates are highly structured, formal transactions.

In contrast to the blind date model, parties to the informal acquaintance model—who already know each other—are not bound by standard terms. The informal acquaintance model prevails in school and work settings,[8] and its popularity has increased with the growth of coeducation and women in the workplace.

---

[7] Such communities include, e.g., Jewish Westchester, WASPy Main Line Philadelphia.

[8] The work-based variant of the informal acquaintance model is high risk. If it goes awry, a party can be left without romance and without a job. Cf. Burton G. Malkiel, A Random Walk Down Wall Street 310 (1990) ("Whatever the . . . objectives, the investor who's wise diversifies.").

The aggravating circumstances model transcends any particular geographic or contextual identification. It is acknowledged to be the most unstable and hazardous of the three methods of meeting.

§ 2.1. The Blind Date Model; Boilerplate Terms

Parties entering into a relationship through the blind date model are bound by the standard terms of the relevant jurisdiction. Standard terms applicable in all jurisdictions include the following:

(1) For a Saturday night date, the invitor extends an invitation on the immediately preceding Wednesday.

(2) The invitor calls the invitee at 3:30 p.m. or 9:30 p.m, or as near thereto as possible.

(3) In the course of the date, the parties eat a meal together.

(4) The invitor pays for meals and other date activities.

(5) Hopeless projects should be abandoned after three dates.

(6) Invitees and invitors should be screened in advance.

Comment:

a. Scope of boilerplate. The boilerplate terms and practices codified in this section have become standard after years of individual experimentation in blind dates. Parties may generally rely on boilerplate without further inquiry. Though individuals retain the option to contract around these default terms, attempts to depart from boilerplate may be regarded with suspicion. Due to the changing role of women in society, however, some boilerplate provisions are now being called into question.

b. Arranging the blind date. Wednesday has long been considered the proper day to call to arrange a Saturday night blind date. Calling on Tuesday is too eager; Thursday is arrogant; and Friday implies a belief that the invitee is available on demand. The Wednesday night caller acts reasonably, promoting the twin virtues of social efficiency and flexibility. Nine-thirty p.m., after dinner but before bedtime, is the most appropriate time to call an invitee at home. Three-thirty p.m. is preferable for a call to the office, because people generally doze at their desks or take a break at that time.[9]

c. Date activities; meals strongly recommended. The practice of eating a meal together on a blind date is overwhelmingly favored in all jurisdictions.[10] An invitor chooses

---

[9]   The advent of answering machines and voice mail complicates the traditional bright-line rules governing the most appropriate times to call. The question necessarily arises: If the person is unavailable, is it strategically wise to leave a message? Some of the legal issues raised by the intersection of courtship and technology are reported in Peter H. Lewis, Persistent E-Mail: Electronic Stalking or Innocent Courtship?, N.Y. Times, Sept. 16, 1994, at B18. The vast changes wrought by modern technology in this area warrant further examination. For a related discussion about how actors make strategic decisions when faced with a combination of choices and goals, see Robert Axelrod, The Evolution of Cooperation (1984); Eric Rasmusen, Games and Information: An Introduction to Game Theory (1989).

[10]   Nonmeal activities, such as sporting events or visits to museums, are not uncommon blind date activities, but they are inherently more risky because the parties' preferences are unknown to one another. Parties are advised to determine their own risk preferences, i.e., whether they prefer a high-risk, high-yield strategy, or whether they are more risk averse. For a discussion of risk/yield strategy, see generally William A. Klein & John C. Coffee, Jr., Business Organization and Finance: Legal and Economic Principles 227-35 (1993).

the date meal according to a multi-tiered structure that parallels equal protection analysis.[11] Dinner is the highest tier, signaling the most serious intent, because it entails significant expense, the investment of an evening's leisure time, and increased effort in primping. Just as a court, faced with an equal protection claim, employs strict scrutiny only in the most compelling situations, an invitor extends a dinner invitation only when the invitee is worthy of close scrutiny. Lunch, the lowest tier, is a casual part of the working day and is inherently less costly in time, energy, and expense. A lunch invitee is not subject to heightened scrutiny. If the first date is lunch, the invitor risks the appearance of ambivalence if he or she does not elevate the level of the second date to dinner.

In recent years, brunch has emerged as an intermediate tier.[12] This meal resembles lunch in time and expense, but connotes more familiarity than the workaday lunch. With its overtones of unmade beds, unshowered bodies, and lazy bliss, brunch promotes an atmosphere of intimacy. Combined, these elements warrant greater scrutiny than that necessitated by lunch, although somewhat less than that required for dinner.[13]

d. Invitor pays. Historically, the boilerplate rule has been that the man pays for dates. Most jurisdictions, however, now follow the rule that the invitor pays, regardless of sex. This shift demonstrates the evolution of the common law, which had presumed that the man and the invitor were always one and the same. It is no violation, but a fulfillment of the spirit of the common law, that dictates that the invitor pays.[14]

e. Three-date rule. Parties often query how many dates it is reasonable to go on in order to assess the possibilities of a relationship. The three-date rule is now standard.[15] Going on more than three dates, without the promise of a relationship, poses the risk of abusive practices, especially when one party insists on paying.[16] Even in the absence of bad-

---

[11]   See, e.g., Frontiero v. Richardson, 411 U.S. 677 (1973).

[12]   Note that breakfast, although formally a meal, is generally discouraged for a date, because it is frequently either wholly personal or taken in a business setting. If people do not have to work over breakfast, they resent a disruption of their morning routine.

[13]   Just as the contours of brunch are uncertain, as compared with the well-established dates of lunch and dinner, the new tier of intermediate scrutiny has been criticized for its failure to afford clear guidance to actors. See Craig v. Boren, 429 U.S. 190, 220-21 (1976) ("[The] Court's [standard of review] apparently comes out of thin air. . . . How is this Court to divine what objectives are important?") (Rehnquist, J., dissenting).

[14]   See Oliver W. Holmes, The Common Law 32 (Mark DeWolfe Howe ed., Little, Brown & Co. 1963) (1881) ("The truth is, that the law is always approaching, and never reaching, consistency. It is forever adopting new principles from life at one end, and it always retains old ones from history at the other, which have not yet been absorbed or sloughed off.").

[15]   It is unclear whether a similar cut-off point applied with equal rigor in previous times. For example, mothers claim that in "the Fifties," parties dated more than three times, and dated more than one person at a time, before "going steady."

[16]   There are reported cases of "churning" in dating, i.e., of continuous dating where the nonpaying party is simply seeking to tour the New York restaurant circuit. For related doctrine in the securities context, see Armstrong v. McAlpin, 699 F.2d 79, 90 (2d Cir.1983) (defining churning as "overtrading," i.e., "excessive rate of turnover in a controlled account for the purpose of increasing the amount of commissions") (citations omitted).

faith dealings, however, the three-date rule is a viable period of limitation that allows both parties to a "nonstarter" to proceed with their life business. Any shorter period may pose potential risks as well. A party may foreclose otherwise promising opportunities before discovery is complete.[17] It is the exceptional, albeit possible, case, where parties know they can settle the matter after the first date.

f. Screen before the blind date. It is reasonable, indeed advisable, for parties to engage in pre-date screening. Parties generally speak by telephone before the first date, but telephone evidence is often of limited reliability.[18] Though parties should refrain from operating in reliance, such discussions do provide ample fodder for a more thorough background check.

Independent investigation of the facts may entail interviews with classmates, work associates, and family members.[19] Due diligence often includes an attempt to secure the party's picture. With the advent of facebooks in law offices, investment banks, and other large firms, photographs of most professionals are readily available for immediate faxing.

Jurisdictions are split as to whether due diligence should extend to allow the inclusion of all available information, or whether the hearsay principles of reliability and relevance should govern.[20] Some circuits lean toward an importation of the "fresh start" policy of the

---

[17]   See, e.g., Hickman v. Taylor, 329 U.S. 495, 507 (1947) ("No longer can the time-honored cry of 'fishing expedition' serve to preclude a party from inquiring into the facts underlying his opponent's case. Mutual knowledge of all the relevant facts gathered by both parties is essential to proper litigation.") (footnote omitted).

[18]   The information is not fully reliable, because a certain amount of "puffing," by both the daters and intermediaries, is considered acceptable. The standard of reasonableness in puffing is derived from securities law. See Carl W. Schneider, Nits, Grits, and Soft Information in SEC Filings, 121 U. Pa. L. Rev. 254, 269 (1972) ("While blatant puffing is not considered proper under the . . . law, investors realize that, within a permissible range, managements may tend to be fairly optimistic, and management opinion can be evaluated in that light."). For an alternate perspective on puffing, see Carlill v. Carbolic Smoke Ball Co., [1893] 1 Q.B. 256, 261 (C.A. 1892) (distinguishing between "distinct promise" and "a mere puff" in advertising context).

[19]   Rule 11 requires that parties engage in a "reasonable inquiry" so that beliefs are "well-grounded in fact." Fed. R. Civ. P. 11. Parties occasionally resort to drastic measures, such as hiring private detectives to conduct background checks. See Dirk Johnson, Boy Meets Girl, '89, Can Be a Detective Story, N.Y. Times, Dec. 10, 1989, at 1. Overzealous investigations, however, may discourage potential partners.

Broker-dealers, intermediaries who set up the parties, must exercise caution in supplying them with background information. See Hanly v. SEC, 415 F.2d 589, 596 (2d Cir.1969) (holding that broker-dealers must have adequate basis for recommendations made to clients). Parties should be aware that a broker-dealer may not be a disinterested provider of information but may be an advocate for one party. Ideally, however, a broker-dealer acts as what the Model Rules term a "lawyer for the situation," who serves neither party individually but instead serves both their interests simultaneously. Model Rules of Professional Conduct, Rule 2.2 cmt. (1983) (suggesting role in "seeking to establish or adjust a relationship between clients on an amicable and mutually advantageous basis"); see also Geoffrey C. Hazard, Jr., Ethics in the Practice of Law 58-68 (1978) (describing Brandeis in role of "lawyer for the situation"). If the date is successful and the pair, later as a couple, spar, it is advisable at that point that the matchmaker interplead. See 28 U.S.C. § 1335 (1988) ("statutory" interpleader); Fed. R. Civ. P. 22 ("rule" interpleader).

[20]   Fed. R. Evid. 401-12 (governing relevancy and its limits); id. 601- 15 (governing, *inter alia,* reliability of witnesses).

Bankruptcy Code[21] and discourage consideration of past evidence that might unfairly tarnish an otherwise promising candidate. The majority view, however, is consistent with the liberal leanings of the Federal Rules of Evidence.[22]

§ 2.2. The Informal Acquaintance Model

In considering whether to enter into a relationship, informal acquaintances should:

(1) avoid any tendency toward willful blindness;

(2) establish a claim of right through possession; and

(3) refrain from stealing corporate opportunities.

Comment:

a. *Abusive practices; willful blindness.* A common injurious pattern seen in the informal acquaintance model is conspicuous flirting toward a friend or acquaintance by a party who lacks any romantic intentions. In such a situation, either or both parties may convince themselves that the other lacks or possesses romantic interest. Such fraudulent behavior encourages reliance and may foreclose the innocent party from pursuing other deals. Willful blindness on the part of the flirt is also inefficient, in that it causes a misallocation of resources. Parties may eventually face sanctions for their willful blindness.[23]

Illustration:

B is in a relationship with C but spends an inordinate amount of time with D. It is obvious to all that D is pining for B. When asked by others, B insists that B and D are "just good friends," and acts mystified or outraged at any suggestion to the contrary. B can persist in this belief only by deliberately avoiding discussion with D, because if asked, D would gladly reveal D's feelings.

b. *Pursuit of the object: possession establishes a claim of right.* The very informality of the informal acquaintance model gives rise to complications when friends and acquaintances develop overlapping affections. The ancient doctrine governing ownership of *ferae naturae* applies. The first person to establish a "claim" on an unattached newcomer has superior rights. Yet just as courts wrestle with the question of what action constitutes possession of a wild animal, interested parties may disagree about what constitutes a superior claim on a newcomer. Physical possession, or capture, is widely conceded to be proof of superior rights. More difficult is the claim of the person who has unsuccessfully attempted to establish a relationship, and who therefore feels a strong, though unrequited, attach-

---

[21] See 11 U.S.C. § 727 (1988) (providing for discharge of indebtedness).

[22] Parties who wish to conduct relationships armed with abundant information are advised to pursue the informal acquaintance model, which permits greater low-level discovery.

[23] For a more general discussion of willful blindness (also called conscious avoidance), see Glanville Williams, Criminal Law, The General Part § 57, at 157 (2d ed. 1961) (defining willful blindness as circumstance in which "party has his suspicion aroused but then deliberately omits to make further enquiries, because he wishes to remain in ignorance").

ment.[24] Ill will can be particularly strong when one party has long attempted to establish a relationship but has failed, only to see another succeed.[25]

c. *Corporate opportunity doctrine; exploitation by friends and acquaintances.* Related doctrine on this subject draws from the notion of stealing corporate opportunity.[26] In principle, if a person does not or cannot avail himself or herself of a relationship, then others may pursue the opportunity with impunity. In practice, however, such doctrines rarely apply neatly or painlessly. Those aggrieved by another's success, but who lack a legal right to relief, often seek other avenues of redress.[27]

Illustration:

A and C are roommates. A has had a longstanding crush on X, but has never successfully developed a romantic relationship. C meets X through A, and when C and X begin dating, A accuses C of exploiting corporate opportunity. Legally C is not liable, because A could not use this opportunity. Yet despite legal rules, informal relations within the household are sure to suffer.

§ 2.3. Aggravating Circumstances Model

Parties who enter into a relationship under aggravating circumstances must be careful to ensure that it will survive the dissipation of the forces that brought them together. Parties should be alert to undue influences, and proceed with extreme caution into rebound relationships.

Comment:

a. *Circumstances conducive to undue influence.* It is not uncommon for parties to meet at social gatherings at which the atmosphere is ripe for flirtation and sexual tension. Spontaneous passion may be induced by the consumption of alcohol, or other intoxicants, or by the arousal of intense emotion, such as that present at a wedding, reunion, or office

---

[24] The classic case of Pierson v. Post, 3 Cai. R. 175 (N.Y. Sup. Ct. 1805), established that "mere pursuit" does not confer possession. In love, however, pursuit may in certain situations grant a temporary right, albeit one that is not clearly defined. This right is subject to a reasonable statute of limitations. The impossibility of constructing a bright-line rule determining the length of the limitations period requires the exercise of discretion by all parties, so that no one is unfairly denied the chance to pursue a relationship for an unreasonably long period of time.

[25] Justice Livingston's dissent in Pierson v. Post rings true when it asks:

But who would . . . pursue the windings of this wily [bi]ped, if, just as night came on, and his stratagems and strength were nearly exhausted, a saucy intruder, who had not shared in the honours or labours of the chase, were permitted to come in . . . and bear away in triumph the object of pursuit?

Id. at 180 (Livingston, J., dissenting).

[26] See Guth v. Loft, Inc., 5 A.2d 503, 511 (Del. 1939) ("[I]f there is presented to a corporate officer or director a business opportunity which the corporation is financially able to undertake . . . and, by embracing the opportunity, the self-interest of the officer or director will be brought into conflict with that of his corporation, the law will not permit him to seize the opportunity for himself.").

[27] See generally Robert C. Ellickson, Order Without Law: How Neighbors Settle Disputes (1991).

Christmas party. While such a beginning may lead to a successful relationship, parties should be aware of the role played by these undue influences. The so-called "morning after" is not too soon to contemplate the wisdom and authenticity of the previous night's events.

b. Factors indicating rebound. The most prevalent aggravating circumstance is the rebound. A person on the rebound is almost always unable to evaluate a new relationship with judgment unclouded by the events of the previous relationship. While quick turn-around into a new, successful relationship is possible, a true rebound relationship is one that a party joins merely to be positioned in a relationship.

Rebound relationships occur with great frequency, and parties should look to the following multifactor test to determine whether a relationship is a rebound relationship: (1) amount of time elapsed from preceding relationship; (2) gravity of previous relationship; (3) degree to which party is inclined to be in a relationship "at any price"; and (4) extent to which party rationalizes drawbacks in the new party. If application of these factors to the totality of the circumstances indicates that the relationship is a rebound, parties should employ strict scrutiny to determine the sincerity of their emotions. . . .

Call for Comment:

The Reporters invite comment on the foregoing material. Given the gravity of the project, timely evaluation and modification are imperative. In the words of one of our predecessors, Herbert Wechsler, "Nowhere in the entire legal field is more at stake for the community or for the individual."[28] Address comments to the American Law Institute members' consultative group on the "Restatement of Love."

---

[28] Herbert Wechsler, The Challenge of a Model Penal Code, 65 Harv. L. Rev. 1097, 1098 (1952).

324 PART IV: THE LEGAL AND THE NON-LEGAL

Cornell University Sexual Harassment Procedures

Preamble

One of the distinguishing features of sexual harassment is that it is thought to be particularly heinous, but is rarely punished. Its perceived seriousness comes from its sexual aspect, which typically results in worry about potential damage to the reputations of those involved and the desire to handle sexual harassment cases in ways different from procedures governing other abuses occurring in the academic environment. The silence surrounding punishment of offenders and the excessive worry about lawsuits resulting from harassment cases are two products of the peculiar status of sexual harassment. In a world of complete equality, sexual harassment would be handled no differently from other sorts of misbehavior, like plagiarism or academic malfeasance, of which it is only a form, since its effect is to disrupt or harm the academic atmosphere of the University. Equal handling would rob sexual harassment of its peculiar cachet, break the silence which lets it thrive, and ensure regular and predictable sanctions. Unfortunately, public opinion at the University seems to demand special handling of such cases, if they are to be handled at all. Therefore, the College faculty have adopted the following guidelines.[*]

I. Senior Sexual Harassment Counselors

1. The Dean will appoint two Senior Counselors (a man and a woman) who will be tenured faculty members in the College to serve staggered three-year terms.
2. Training: all counselors will undergo training to familiarize them with typical patterns of harassment and difficulties in handling such cases.
3. Duties:
   a. To receive complaints of sexual harassment referred by Arts College and other sexual harassment counselors or from any member of the University community against Arts College faculty members;
   b. To keep locked records of such complaints (see III. 1 & 2);
   c. In cases where the complainant wishes to press formal charges, to decide if the case should be presented before the Professional Ethics Committee;
   d. If the case does proceed formally, to present it on behalf of the community before the Professional Ethics Committee;
   e. To search the locked file for previous written complaints against a faculty member who has currently been charged with sexual harassment (see III. 1 & 2);
   f. To recommend mediation where appropriate.

---

[*] The category of Faculty Member is to include all those, other than students registered at Cornell, holding an appointment in the College of Arts and Sciences with an academic title.

These procedures were approved by the College faculty on April 15, 1991.

II. Arts College Committee on Professional Ethics

1. Membership:
   a. An elected group of 8 tenured faculty members and 2 tenured faculty members who will act as alternates. All members will serve staggered 4-year terms;
   b. The committee should be constituted to include ample representation of women and minorities;
   c. The committee shall elect a Chairperson yearly, who will preside over hearings.
2. Training: the senior sexual harassment counselors and the members of the Professional Ethics Committee will undergo training by staff from the Office of Equal Opportunity to familiarize them with the typical patterns of harassment and difficulties in handling such cases.
3. Duties:
   a. To conduct hearings in those case where the complainant and a Senior Counselor have agreed to bring a formal complaint;
   b. To render a determination in writing that includes an opinion setting forth its reasoning;
   c. To recommend to the Dean appropriate sanctions against faculty members found guilty of harassment;
   d. To provide annual statistics to the Office of Equal Opportunity and to give an annual statistical report to be made public through appropriate channels (such as the Cornell Sun and/or Cornell Chronicle).

III. Procedures

1. Complainants may choose to file a signed, written complaint with a Senior Counselor, without proceeding (immediately) to a formal hearing. Such complaint will then be secured in a locked file to which only the current Senior Counselors will have access. If the Counselor judges the complaint to be without merit, the Counselor will clearly mark it as such, stating the reason and date. Persons filing such complaints may be contacted later by a Senior Counselor to determine if they want to proceed with a formal hearing in cases where another person has made a similar complaint against the same faculty member.
2. Complainants may file a written complaint with a Senior Counselor and request a formal hearing before the Professional Ethics Committee. The Senior Counselor will determine whether the case has merit and should be presented to the Professional Ethics Committee. If the Counselor judges the complaint to be without merit, the Counselor will clearly mark it as such, stating the reason and date. In the event the Senior Counselor's decision is negative, the complainant has recourse to other University grievance procedures.
   a. No case will be pursued or continued without the consent of the complainant. No complaint filed as in III.1 above will be used as evidence in a current case being heard before the Professional Ethics Committee without the consent of the complainant who filed it and who would then be considered a co-complainant in that case.

b. The accused faculty member shall be informed promptly of the complaint when the Senior Counselor has determined that the case has merit and will proceed to a formal hearing. The Chair of the Professional Ethics Committee will ensure that the proceedings are handled expeditiously, while allowing the accused reasonable time to prepare a response before a hearing is scheduled.

IV. The Hearing

1. The Senior Counselor will keep the complainant(s) and the accused informed of the status and substance of the case as long as it is pending.
2. The hearing shall be closed to the public.
3. Five (5) Professional Ethics Committee members shall constitute a quorum for a hearing.
4. The Professional Ethics Committee may question all those who appear before it and may be advised by legal counsel.
5. Rights of the complainant and accused:
   a. To call witnesses and to question witnesses called by the other party.
   b. To make written statements to the Professional Ethics Committee.
   c. To be represented by a friendly advisor and/or advised by legal counsel, if they desire.
   d. To avoid direct, face-to-face confrontation with each other. For this purpose, they may give their testimony without the other being present, but the Senior Counselor and the friendly advisor may ask questions of the person testifying.
6. All portions of the hearings must be tape recorded. Tape recordings and written records will be kept permanently by the Professional Ethics Committee. Audio recordings and other relevant materials will be available to both parties during the proceedings.
7. The Dean, the Chairperson of the accused person's department, the Office of Equal Opportunity, the accused person and the complainant(s) shall all receive a written report detailing the vote, determination, and recommendation of the Professional Ethics Committee.
8. The Professional Ethics Committee shall establish more detailed procedures, as necessary, to ensure that hearings are conducted fairly and that both parties have ample opportunity to present their cases and to respond.

V. Sanctions

1. In case of a determination against the accused, the Professional Ethics Committee will recommend to the Dean appropriate sanctions.
2. Demonstration of a repeated pattern of harassment, or a particularly egregious single incident, may be ground for denial of perquisites, merit raises, tenure, promotion, and, in the most serious cases, *may cause the Professional Ethics Committee to recommend that the Dean initiate procedures leading to dismissal from the University.*
3. Since abuse of power is one of the major characteristics of harassment, the Professional Ethics Committee may recommend to the Dean, or other appropriate person, that a guilty faculty member be asked to resign from, or be prevented from serving in, posi-

tions of power such as Graduate Faculty Representative, Director of Undergraduate Studies, Department Chair, Chair of Special Committees, member of Search, Fellowship, Admissions, or similar committees, Faculty-in-Residence, or Faculty Fellow, etc. Because such normal faculty duties are central to the functioning of the University, and because other faculty members will have to assume these responsibilities for the faculty member guilty of harassment, it is expected *that in nearly all cases the Committee will recommend to the Dean that the salary of the guilty party be reduced by an amount* appropriate to the service *she or he* will not be performing for the University. Otherwise, relieving convicted harassers of their normal duties will seem a reward.

VI. Appeal

1. In case of a determination of guilt by the Professional Ethics Committee, the accused person has the right to submit a timely, written appeal to the Dean. Grounds for appeal are limited to new evidence, procedural error, and unsuitability of sanction.
2. The accused person may submit to the Provost a timely, written appeal of the Dean's decision.

VII. Additional Measures to Reduce Sexual Harassment

1. To prevent retaliation by other faculty members, the Senior Counselor may choose, with the consent of the complainant, a faculty member preferably within the complainant's department, who could serve as a protector and confident, should that become necessary.
2. Sexual harassment seriously undermines a faculty member's responsibilities in the three categories of teaching, service, and scholarship by which the University decides whether he or she merits hiring, reappointment, tenure, promotion, and/or salary raises. Therefore, departments, ad hoc committees, and the Dean should, as a matter of course, address the issue of sexual harassment when a faculty member is being considered at these times in his/her career. Any official determination of sexual harassment should weigh in the decision.
3. All incoming faculty members should receive a booklet defining sexual harassment and making clear the serious consequences stemming from it.
4. These procedures for handling sexual harassment cases should be made public and distributed to all students, faculty, and staff in the Arts College.
5. Teaching assistants and their supervisors should receive instruction about sexual harassment at the beginning of each Fall semester to make clear the spectrum of misbehavior that is contained by that phrase. Various teaching aids, such as videotapes, are available to assist the instructional program.

VIII. Review

Four years following adoption of this document, the Chair of the Professional Ethics Committee and the Senior Harassment Counselors shall report to the Arts College faculty on these procedures and recommend any appropriate changes.

Wildey v. Springs
47 F.3d 1475 (7th Cir. 1995)

Cudahy, Circuit Judge.

This case involves an appeal from a jury's determination that a woman was entitled to recover various elements of damage because her fiance broke off their engagement. The plaintiff, Sharon Wildey, brought suit under Illinois's Breach of Promise Act (1993). She alleged that the broken engagement harmed her in several ways, and consequently sought recovery for medical expenses, lost business profits and pain and suffering. The jury returned a $178,000 verdict in her favor. The district judge remitted that amount by $60,000, concluding that the lost business profits were not fairly attributable to the broken engagement. The district judge left the remainder of the verdict intact, however. The parties now appeal, alleging various points of error. We agree with the suggestion that the case should have been dismissed because Sharon failed to provide her fiance with notice of each element specified by the statute. We therefore reverse.

I.

Sharon Wildey and Richard Springs enjoyed a relationship early in 1992. When Richard broke off the engagement at the end of April, Sharon became quite distressed. She eventually decided to sue under Illinois's Breach of Promise Act.

Sharon is an attorney in Chicago, and Richard is an Oregon cattle rancher. Introduced by a mutual friend, the two began their long-distance relationship over the telephone. After a number of telephone calls, Richard decided to visit Sharon in Chicago in January of 1992. The relationship apparently went well because Richard visited Chicago on two more occasions during January and February. The parties decided that a Florida vacation was in order.

At the end of the five-day Florida trip, the parties agreed to be married. While waiting for a plane in the Orlando airport, Sharon suggested that she and Richard consider marriage. Although Richard agreed to her suggestion, he expressed doubts about the couple's ability to overcome the practical difficulties of a long-distance relationship. Sharon wanted to stay in Chicago until her children got out of school; Richard did not intend to leave his Oregon ranch. The parties eventually decided on a "commuter-type" marriage for a five-year time period, leading to an eventual relocation for both in Florida or the Caribbean. They then flew back to Chicago, and Richard returned to Oregon.

Richard again visited Sharon later in March. Once in Chicago, he began shopping for engagement rings and eventually purchased one. When the ring was ready, Richard got down on one knee and formally proposed. The couple set a wedding date and planned a Chicago ceremony. All of these activities occurred in Chicago.

The couple spent more time together during April. Early in the month, Sharon visited Richard's ranch in Oregon. She and Richard later attended her son's wedding in Los Angeles. Afterwards, Sharon and her daughters flew to Oregon to spend several days on Richard's ranch. In another week or so, everyone flew to Chicago to spend time there.

After the last weekend in Chicago, however, Richard began having second thoughts about the marriage. On a flight to Florida on April 27, 1992, Richard decided to break the engagement. He composed a letter to Sharon explaining his doubts about the marriage. He also suggested that she keep the engagement ring and some money he had placed in a Chicago bank account.

Sharon responded with a letter. She stated that the broken engagement had caused her to become "extremely depressed and anxious," and she asked for financial help. Richard wrote back, defending himself and writing that he felt that he had fulfilled any obligations he may have had. Sharon drafted a second letter in which she apprised Richard of her intent to sue.

Sharon's second letter contains the date that the parties had planned to be married. It also references several elements of damage, such as medical bills from counseling and lost income, that Sharon believed she suffered as a result of the broken engagement. Sharon further wrote that she had spoken with an attorney and intended to file suit. She also stated that she had been willing to marry Richard and gave him the option of discussing the matter with her. Sharon did not, however, include any of the dates upon which the parties had exchanged marital promises.[1]

Sharon filed suit soon afterwards. She contended, among other things, that the broken engagement had occasioned large expenditures on medical care and had also caused her to

---

[1]   The full text of the notice letter reads:

I have just received your letter and am taken back by not only the tone of it but also by the perceptions you articulated of the circumstances of our engagement. It seems the man I fell in love with and waited to marry on September 5, 1992 was a person who never existed.

I do not understand how you could write such a hateful and angry letter to a woman you intended to marry just a month ago.

I have had to seek medical care and counseling for the depression and and anxiety caused by your unilateral actions and I anticipate that the girls will need it also. According to the doctors this treatment may take a while.

I also have no cash flow in my practice and while I read your letter as viewing yourself a "cash cow", you were never that and never perceived as that. I do not know where this attitude comes from nor where you get the facts you recite in your letter. Do you think that I didn't love you? If so, how could you possibly think that, given that I was willing to change my whole life for you.

In any event you cannot come into my life and the lives of my children and dump on us, emotionally and financially. We were doing just fine.

Although I would greatly have preferred to talk over any problems you perceived in our relationship (I was ready to marry you on September 5, 1992 at the Columbia Yacht Club not knowing you felt there were problems), and work on them as reasonable people, or to have a respectful conversation regarding the termination of our engagement, or to discuss rationally the impact of your decision on our lives, it is clear from your letter that you will not do that.

Therefore I have hired an attorney to bring suit against you for breach of promise in Illinois. I wish only to recover what is fair and what you have actually caused me to lose and that includes the medical bills and the cash flow in my practice.

The attorney, Mary Paulsen, has advised me to give you 30 days notice before we file suit, in the unlikely event that you wish to discuss the matter with me.

I cannot tell you how disappointed I am that I have to write a letter like this.

lose business income. She additionally sought recovery for pain and suffering. The jury returned a verdict totaling $178,000 in Sharon's favor. Of this amount, $25,000 was awarded for past and future medical costs; $60,000 was awarded for lost business profits; and $93,000 was awarded for pain and suffering.

At Richard's request, the district court remitted the award to $118,000, concluding that lost business profits were not attributable to the broken engagement. The court affirmed the verdict as to the other elements of damage, however. The district court also refused to reverse the verdict on various other grounds that Richard suggested. It concluded that Illinois law, rather than Florida law, had properly governed the issues at trial. It also determined that the notice Sharon provided in her second letter had been adequate; "substantial compliance" with the notice provision, in the district court's view, was all that Illinois law required.

II.

Richard now appeals. We agree with the district court that Illinois law properly governs this case. We do not agree, however, with that court's notice analysis. We believe instead that the omission of the date that the parties became engaged is fatal to Sharon's claim. The plain language of the Breach of Promise Act requires that a potential plaintiff include several items in the notice that must be sent to a defendant. The date that the parties became engaged is clearly one of these items. Although the strict construction that we rely on may seem unwarranted, several factors render it appropriate in this case. First, the history behind actions for the breach of a promise to marry argues in favor of a strict construction; the strictures of the Promise Act exist because these actions were unpopular and subject to abuse. Further, the date of the engagement, though plausibly insignificant when the fact of the engagement is not disputed, was potentially dispositive here. An admission concerning the date the parties became engaged determined the place of that engagement; for reasons that will become clear in the choice-of-law analysis, this fact threatened Sharon's ability to maintain her suit. In addition, we note that Sharon is a seasoned attorney. She had consulted with counsel when she drafted the second letter. In light of these considerations, and of the clarity of the Statute's requirements, we reverse.

Breach of a Promise to Marry: An Historical Perspective

The action for the breach of a promise to marry is of antique vintage. First conceived as a creature of the English ecclesiastical courts, the action was originally used to pressure a reluctant lover into fulfilling a marital promise. The common law eventually adopted the action, however, and permitted the recovery of monetary damages. Although developed by English courts, the action found its way into the American colonies and was later used by post-revolutionary American lawyers.

The action served dual ideals in colonial America. On the one hand, a breach of promise action continued to appeal to vestiges of the older notion that marriage was a property transaction completed after complex family negotiations. But on the other hand, the action began to pay tribute to the emerging ideal that marriage was a sacred contract premised upon affection and emotional commitment. The suits soon became utilized almost universally by women, and were justified by lawmakers largely on these grounds. Marriage was considered necessary to secure both a woman's social and financial security. But more importantly, the actions, and the judges who were willing to enforce them, recognized that promises to marry sometimes occasioned a loss of virginity. Because of the importance the society of that day placed on premarital chastity, the economic and social harm suffered by a jilted woman were often reflected in large damage awards.

The actions were characterized by a lack of legal formality peculiar for the law of that time. Foreign observers noted that, unlike wills or commercial contracts, little was needed to support an allegation that the parties had become engaged. Consequently, appellate courts deferred widely to jury determinations in credibility contests. Traditional rules relating to damages, too, were relaxed. Despite the originally contractual nature of the action, judges refused to confine the damage measure to immediate loss. Instead, they permitted recovery for elements such as mental anguish and a loss of social position.

Largely because of the perceived vagaries of the suits, the actions had fallen into disrepute by the early twentieth century. Three principal reasons are given for their decline in popularity. The first is the unfounded use of the suit, given the lax standards of proof, to extort out-of-court settlements. Second, the excessive damages awarded prompted disdain for the actions. Finally, the ideals that the action served came to be viewed as anachronistic. The greater social and economic freedom incident to women's entry into the workforce meant that the loss of an initial suitor posed a lower threat to future prospects than it might have in the nineteenth century.

As concerns grew, legislatures began to act. Florida and Illinois were among these. Florida abrogated the cause of action by enacting a statute providing that agreements to marry made in Florida could not be enforced "within or without this state." Illinois, too, outlawed the common law cause of action. In 1935, the Illinois legislature passed the "Heart Balm Act," making it "unlawful" to file an action based on the breach of a promise to marry. Although the Florida statute eliminating the cause of action remains in force, the Illinois statute soon encountered troubles.

In Heck v. Schupp (1946), the Illinois Supreme Court held the statute unconstitutional under provisions of the Illinois Constitution providing a legal remedy for all injuries. The Illinois legislature soon responded in kind. Faced with the court's determination that the State was required to leave plaintiffs a remedy for the breach of a promise to marry, the legislature enacted Illinois's Breach of Promise Act in 1947. This second attempt at circumscribing the perceived abuses of the common law action leaves the plaintiff's ability to recover intact. The statute does, however, suggest that actions for breach of promise were subject to both abuse and the danger of an excessive damage award. The legislature clearly states its misgivings in the Act's Preamble, determining that "the remedy heretofore provided by law for the enforcement of actions based upon breaches of promises or agreements to marry has been subject to grave abuses and has been used as an instrument for blackmail by unscrupulous persons for their own unjust enrichment. . . ." It therefore uses an elaborate notice provision and limits the types of damages that a plaintiff may recover. This constricted version of the original breach of promise action passed muster under the Illinois Constitution, Smith v. Hill (1958), and has survived until the present.

The Insufficiency of Notice

[H]ere . . . we are concerned with the sufficiency of the notice that Sharon mailed to Richard. . . . Richard complains that the notice was substantively insufficient; Sharon suggests that it was not. Unfortunately, the parties have pointed to no further authority construing the sufficiency of notice under Illinois's Promise Act. Instead, Sharon suggests that the Act's requirements should be relaxed for several reasons. First, she asserts that statutes in derogation of the common law should be liberally construed in favor of the plaintiff. This, she suggests, renders the notice valid in light of its purported substantial compliance with the statutory mandate. Finally, she claims that the date of the engagement was not important given the fact that the existence of the engagement was uncontested. Although we are sympathetic to Sharon's plight under an adverse ruling on this issue, we do not find any of these arguments persuasive.

Liberally construing the statute *in favor of a plaintiff* runs contrary to express legislative intent. The Promise Act was instituted to eliminate the perceived common law abuses of the actions. The Preamble to the Promise Act states that:

> . . . the remedy heretofore provided by law for the enforcement of actions based upon breaches of promises or agreements to marry has been subject to grave abuses and has been used as an instrument for blackmail by unscrupulous persons for their unjust enrichment, due to the indefiniteness of the damages recoverable in such actions and the consequent fear of persons threatened with such actions that exorbitant damages might be assessed against them. . . . Consequently, in the public interest, the necessity for the enactment of this chapter is hereby declared as a matter of legislative determination.

In light of this concern, the legislature engrafted various limitations, such as the notice provision, onto the common law cause of action. In interpreting these provisions, the legislature instructed that the "act shall be liberally construed to effectuate *the objects and the purposes thereof* and the public policy as herein declared." (emphasis added). Those objects and purposes were the avoidance of exorbitant damage awards and the winnowing of the multitude of claims. The Illinois legislature's wisdom in choosing these objects is none of our business. As a federal court sitting in diversity, we certainly have no mandate to assert any policy preferences we might have with respect to either the breach of promise lawsuits or the purported efforts to restrict them. We are bound by Illinois' statement of intent—a statement only recently endorsed by that state's courts. The legislature intended to make it *more* difficult for plaintiffs to bring these suits, not less. A liberal construction favoring plaintiffs is not, therefore, in order—despite the fact that the statute may place limitations on the common law. . . .

The legislature, in recognizing the indefinite nature of affairs of the heart, undoubtedly wished potential plaintiffs to spell out all facts relevant to the cause of action at an early point in time. By admitting certain facts in the required notice, a plaintiff would later be prevented from changing postures as litigation needs arose.

Here, the letter notifying Richard of the impending suit did not include an admission as to when (and consequently, where) the engagement occurred. Yet the express language of the Promise Act requires a plaintiff to put this item in the prescribed notice. Sharon's failure to do so therefore bars her cause of action. Sharon is a seasoned attorney. She consulted with an attorney before sending the required notice. Under these circumstances, we simply cannot ascribe the omission to ignorance. The history of Illinois's Promise Act, its pointed Preamble, and the controversy that has surrounded it, practically dictate this strict construction of the Act's provisions. In any event, the doctrine of substantial compliance is of no avail as Illinois courts have interpreted it; it does not apply to save notices that completely omit an item required by statute. Even if the doctrine applied, however, the fact that the agreement to marry was quite important to the resolution of this case would preclude relief.

We agree with the district court's conclusion that the parties' dispute was governed by Illinois law. But under the circumstances of this case, we cannot conclude that the notice provided was adequate.

For this reason, the judgment of the district court is REVERSED.

Notes and Questions

1. What is the sanction for violating a rule of language?

2. With its language law, is France attempting to legislate in a area that is essentially impervious to legal regulation? What would the linguist Saussure say?

3. Are the rules of etiquette arbitrary? Why is it customary for a man to remove his hat upon entering a church?

4. In what sense is it "arbitrary" which side of the road you drive on? In what sense is it not arbitrary at all?

5. What is the sanction for committing a breach of etiquette?

6. Emily Post's *Etiquette* was first published in 1922, and quickly became the #1 non-fiction bestseller in the United States. The tenth edition of 1960 was the last edition published in Emily Post's lifetime.

7. Would the New York "Standards of Civility" for the legal profession be an example of what Garrett Hardin (*The Tragedy of the Commons*) termed an appeal to conscience that "attempts to get something for nothing"?

8. If you were a defendant under Cornell University's sexual harassment procedures, what criticisms of the procedures might you have?

Suggestions For Further Reading

P.S. Atiyah & Robert S. Summers, Form and Substance in Anglo-American Law, chs. 1-5 (1987)

Sarah Buss, Appearing Respectful: The Moral Significance of Manners, 109 Ethics 795 (1999)

H.L.A. Hart, The Concept of Law, chs. 5-6 (2d ed. 1994)

E. Adamson Hoebel, The Law of Primitive Man, pt. I (1954)

Rebecca Tushnet, Rules of Engagement, 107 Yale Law Journal 2583 (1998)

Chapter 10
Smaller Groups and Associations

Boy Scouts of America
The Scout Law*

The Scout Law is the foundation on which the whole Scout movement is built. In the Scout Law are expressed the ideals a Scout puts before himself.

There have always been written and unwritten laws by which men have tried to live.

In the world of today, when you are a Scout, the Scout Law becomes *your* code of action by which you try to live.

There is something about the Scout Law that makes it different from other laws. Most other laws start with a "Do" or a "Don't." Not the Scout Law. The Scout Law is a statement of facts: "A Scout *is* trustworthy . . . loyal . . . helpful . . . friendly . . . courteous . . . kind . . . obedient . . . cheerful . . . thrifty . . . brave . . . clean . . . reverent." By doing your best to live up to the Scout Law, you are a Scout. If you should *willfully* break the Scout Law, you are not a Scout. It is as simple as that.

The ideals of the Scout Law are high—they are meant to be! It is only by striving toward high ideals and keeping faith with them that you can hope to become the MAN you want to be.

A Scout Is Trustworthy

A Scout's honor is to be trusted. If he were to violate his honor by telling a lie or by cheating or by not doing exactly a given task, when trusted on his honor, he may be directed to hand over his Scout badge.

A Scout Is Loyal

He is loyal to all to whom loyalty is due, his Scout leader, his home and parents and country.

A Scout Is Helpful

He must be prepared at any time to save life, help injured persons, and share the home duties. He must do at least one Good Turn to somebody every day.

A Scout Is Friendly

He is a friend to all and a brother to every other Scout.

---

* Boy Scout Handbook (New Brunswick, New Jersey: Boy Scouts of America, 7th edition 1965), pages 38-39, 404.

A Scout is Courteous

He is polite to all, especially to women, children, old people, and the weak and help-less. He must not take pay for being helpful or courteous.

A Scout Is Kind

He is a friend to animals. He will not kill nor hurt any living creature needlessly, but will strive to save and protect all harmless life.

A Scout Is Obedient

He obeys his parents, Scoutmaster, patrol leader, and all other duly constituted author-ities.

A Scout Is Cheerful

He smiles whenever he can. His obedience to orders is prompt and cheery. He never shirks nor grumbles at hardships.

A Scout Is Thrifty

He does not wantonly destroy property. He works faithfully, wastes nothing, and makes the best use of his opportunities. He saves his money so that he may pay his own way, be generous to those in need, and helpful to worthy objects. He may work for pay, but must not receive tips for courtesies or Good Turns.

A Scout Is Brave

He has the courage to face danger in spite of fear and to stand up for the right against the coaxings of friends or the jeers or threats of enemies, and defeat does not down him.

A Scout Is Clean

He keeps clean in body and thought; stands for clean speech, clean sport, clean habits; and travels with a clean crowd.

A Scout Is Reverent

He is reverent toward God. He is faithful in his religious duties and respects the con-victions of others in matters of custom and religion.

Obeying the Scout Law

What Others See. Several points of the Scout Law have to do with your behavior toward people with whom you come in contact. These people have a chance to judge whether you are trustworthy, loyal, helpful, friendly, courteous, kind, obedient, and cheer-ful. You prove these things in your everyday actions.

The most important of these people are the members of your own family. They must be able to depend on you. The way you act in your own home shows better than anything else what kind of boy you are.

Other people you deal with soon discover that you can be trusted by the way you keep your promises. They see your loyalty in the way you act at home and in school. They notice your willingness to be of help. They feel your friendliness and courtesy. They observe your kindness to animals and your obedience to your parents, your teachers, your leaders. They respond to your cheerfulness.

You will know from the way they act toward you how well you are obeying these points of the Scout Law.

What You Know Within Yourself. The way you live up to the remaining points of the Scout Law—thrifty, brave, clean, and reverent—is hidden to other people. Some of these traits have certain outward signs—but it is what happens within your heart that makes you know to what extent you have obeyed them.

Thrift, for instance, is more than going to the bank teller's window and passing over money—it is the way you make use of your earnings, your time, your abilities. Bravery is not often shown in heroic deeds—it is more often a matter of overcoming your fear, a decision within yourself to do what is right regardless of the consequences. Cleanliness is more than having a clean face and clean hands—only you know whether your thoughts are clean. Reverence is more than going to church or synagogue—it is the way your faith makes you act when only God is your witness.

Randall v. Orange County Council, Boy Scouts of America
17 Cal. 4th 736 (1998)

George, Chief Justice.

Plaintiffs were prohibited from continuing their membership and advancing in the Cub Scouts by defendant, a regional council of the Boy Scouts of America, because of plaintiffs' failure or refusal to participate in religion-related elements of the scout program and because of plaintiffs' refusal to affirm a belief in God. Plaintiffs successfully sought an injunction barring defendant from excluding them from scout activities on religious grounds.

[T]his case presents two issues: First, does defendant, in admitting or excluding members, come within the definition of those entities covered by California's public accommodation statute (Civ.Code, § 51, commonly known as the Unruh Civil Rights Act)? Second, if defendant's membership decisions are subject to the Unruh Civil Rights Act, would application of the Act to prohibit defendant from excluding plaintiffs from membership or advancement in the scout organization violate defendant's (or its members') right of intimate or expressive association under the First and Fourteenth Amendments of the federal Constitution? . . .

Plaintiffs Michael and William Randall, twin brothers, joined the Cub Scouts when they were seven years of age. They participated in a Cub Scout pack in Culver City for two years, advancing from "Tiger Cub" to "Bobcat" to "Wolf" rank. They testified at the trial below that on the rare occasions when they repeated the Cub Scout Promise, they did not say the word "God," and that when they explained their lack of belief in God to their den leader in Culver City, he permitted them to omit any reference to God. The den leader, on the other hand, testified that the boys had recited the entire promise in his den and never had raised any question regarding their belief in God.

When the family moved to Anaheim Hills in Orange County, the boys joined Cub Scout Den 4, which was affiliated with Pack 519, a part of defendant Orange County Council. While the boys were working on the requirements for advancement to the "Bear" rank in 1990, a problem arose. One of these requirements has a religious component, which was stated in the following terms in the materials provided to boys seeking advancement: "We are lucky the people who wrote and signed our constitution were very wise. They understood the need of Americans to worship God as they choose. A member of your family will be able to talk with you about your duty to God. Remember, this achievement is part of your Cub Scout Promise. 'I, ____, promise to do my best to do my duty to God and my country.'" Further, the Cub Scout seeking advancement to the "Bear" rank is instructed to: "Practice your religion as you are taught in your home, church, synagogue, mosque or other religious community." Religious emblems provided by the scout's own religious institution also may be earned at this point.

At a den meeting, the Randall boys stated they would have a problem with the religion requirement, and stated that they did not believe in God. The den leader observed that she thought belief in God was necessary to complete the religion requirement. After consulting with officials in defendant Orange County Council, the pack leader confirmed to the boys' mother that this was the policy.

Initially, defendant's position was that the boys could remain in the den, but that they could not advance in the Cub Scout ranks until they promised to do their duty to God. At trial, officials of defendant council stated that the boys may not participate at all as Cub Scouts if they do not believe in God, because such a state of disbelief is inconsistent with the Cub Scout Promise to perform a duty to God. Officials of the national scouting organization, Boy Scouts of America, made similar statements.

Plaintiffs, through their mother as guardian ad litem, filed a complaint for injunctive relief, naming the Orange County Council as defendant. The complaint alleged that defendant and its agents informed plaintiffs that they no longer were permitted to participate in or advance in scouting activities or be active members of the Boy Scouts of America, because plaintiffs refused to take part in religious requirements or activities, use the word "God" in the Boy Scout Pledge, worship God in song, prayer, or study, or earn religious medals or emblems as provided in the Big Bear Cub Scout Book. The complaint alleged a violation of the Unruh Civil Rights Act, in that plaintiffs claimed they were denied equal access to an organization covered by the Act because they had no religious beliefs. . . .

At trial, plaintiffs presented evidence intended to establish that the Orange County Council operated as a business establishment within the meaning of the Unruh Civil Rights Act because of its substantial holdings in real estate, its large-scale revenue-raising and revenue-earning activities (a portion of which are directed at the general public), its operation of commercial establishments open to the public, and its employment of 55 full-time and 12 part-time employees.

With respect to the constitutional questions, plaintiffs introduced evidence of the recreational and social quality of Cub Scout activities, and sought to establish that religion plays a minimal role in the Cub Scout program. In addition, plaintiffs introduced evidence of the nonsectarian, nonexclusive policies of the Boy Scouts of America and pointed to elements of the program materials provided by the Boy Scouts of America indicating that Cub Scouts are expected to learn about religion at home and through their religious organizations, rather than through their den leaders.

Plaintiffs also pointed out that defendant had accepted funds from the United Way charitable organization on the condition that any program so funded would not be limited to individuals of any particular religious belief, that such programs would be open to any individual regardless of religious belief, and that no individual served by any United Way program would be required to participate in any religious activity as a condition of receiving such service.

In responding to plaintiffs' evidence, defendant first presented evidence relevant to the issue of its status as a business establishment, demonstrating that most of its programs are carried out by volunteers rather than by its paid employees, who are employed to serve the volunteers; that its board of governors consists of volunteers; that much of its income is derived from charitable contributions; that its stores exist to serve the members and do not produce a profit; and that rental of camp facilities to nonmembers is for a nominal fee.

Defendant also stressed that it has a noncommercial, exclusively charitable purpose, namely to promote certain skills and moral values in its youth membership.

Defendant also produced extensive evidence regarding the nature and extent of its expressive function. It produced evidence intended to demonstrate that it does, in fact, have a religious message, as well as evidence intended to show how that message is meant to be conveyed to Cub Scouts.

It was stipulated by the parties that the Boy Scouts of America, which regulates the regional council's membership activities, requires as a condition of Cub Scout membership that all applicants for membership state that they recognize a duty to God. The Cub Scout application form contains the following affirmation: "I have read the Cub Scout Promise and the Law of the Pack and promise to try to live up to them." The Cub Scout Promise consists of the following: "I, _____, promise to do my best to do my duty to God and my country, to help other people, and to obey the law of the pack." The Cub Scout application form also informs parents that the "Boy Scouts of America recognizes the importance of religious faith and duty." It asks parents to affirm that they have read the Cub Scout Promise and will assist their son in observing the policies of the Boy Scouts. Not only Cub Scouts, but also Boy Scouts, are taught to do their duty to God. The Scout Law provides that the scout must be reverent and faithful in his religious duties. The director of the Orange County regional council testified that the plaintiffs are ineligible to participate in the council's program because they do not agree with the Cub Scout Promise, and that in order to participate, boys should not only say the promise, but believe it.

Defendant also introduced numerous formal declarations by the Boy Scouts of America to demonstrate the importance of religion, and the scout's duty to God, in its training of youth.

Evidence was presented regarding the process by which values of the Boy Scouts of America are instilled in youth membership. The organization conveys its precepts to scouts through education. With respect to the religious element of its teaching, although the Boy Scouts of America does not define what constitutes belief in God or membership in a religious organization, it strongly encourages boys to join and participate in the religious programs and activities of a church, synagogue, or other religious association. Adult leaders are trained to instill the values of the organization in their charges, including the value of reverence for God. Adult Cub Scout leaders are expected to convey to their scouts the fundamental belief that they cannot develop into the best kind of citizen without recognizing an obligation to God. Leaders specifically are instructed to introduce the idea and meaning of God to scouts, and to teach nonsectarian religious ideals by way of explaining the child's duty to God.

The evidence also showed that some of the moral teaching undertaken by the Boy Scouts of America is accomplished through requirements imposed upon boys wishing to advance through the ranks.

Several witnesses testified that the religious affirmation contained in the Cub Scout Promise is reinforced through regular repetition of the promise at den and pack meetings. In the view of one council leader, a purpose of the Cub Scout program is to create a protective environment for instruction in religious principles. This witness also testified that other scouting values, such as trustworthiness, depend upon a belief in God.

Parents of Cub Scouts in plaintiffs' den and pack testified that they hoped certain values, including religious ones, would be instilled through the Cub Scout program, as promised by the parent handbook for new Cub Scouts. Defendant also presented evidence that 50 percent of the dens within the regional council's territory are sponsored by religious organizations, and several leaders of religious organizations testified that they encourage their youth to participate in scouting because it reinforces the importance of religion in a boy's life.

Finally, defendant produced evidence intended to establish that requiring the inclusion of nonbelievers within the Cub Scouts would interfere with the organization's efforts to convey its religious message.

After considering the evidence presented by both parties, the trial court ruled in favor of plaintiffs. The trial court first determined that defendant is a business establishment within the meaning of the Unruh Civil Rights Act, relying upon the organization's nonexclusive membership policy and large membership, its commercial transactions with the public, its businesslike organizational structure, its large income and investments, its employment of a large professional staff, its fund-raising activities, and its opening of certain of its facilities to nonmembers.

With regard to the constitutional issues, the trial court found that the evidence did not support defendant's claim that the intimate associational rights of den leaders and Cub Scouts in the den would be seriously impaired if members who do not promise to fulfill a duty to God are permitted to join. As for the Orange County Council, the court determined that it was too large an organization to have intimate associational rights.

The trial court also concluded that the constitutional right of expressive associational freedom does not entitle defendant to exclude plaintiffs from membership. . . .

Defendant appealed, and the Court of Appeal affirmed the judgment in part and reversed it in part.

[W]e conclude that defendant's attributes and activities render the Unruh Civil Rights Act inapplicable to its membership decisions. Defendant not only is a charitable organization with a predominantly expressive social purpose unrelated to the promotion of the economic interests of its members, but offers to its members a program that is not the equivalent of a traditional place of public accommodation or amusement. Despite the organization's limited business transactions with the public, defendant does not sell the right to participate in the activities it offers to its members. For these reasons, with regard to its membership decisions, defendant is not operating as a business establishment within the purview of California's public accommodation statute.

Because we have concluded that the Unruh Civil Rights Act does not apply to defendant's membership decisions, we need not consider defendant's contention that application of the Unruh Civil Rights Act to its membership decisions under the circumstances of this case would violate its right of intimate or expressive association under the First and Fourteenth Amendments to the federal Constitution.

The judgment of the Court of Appeal is reversed to the extent it affirms the judgment of the trial court.

Mosk, Justice, concurring.

I concur in the result.

Through its Orange County Council, the Boy Scouts of America refused to permit Michael and William Randall, who were then Cub Scouts, to advance as members of the organization because of their religion—or, more precisely, because of their lack of religion.

Thereupon, the Randalls brought an action in the superior court against the Boy Scouts, specifically, the Orange County Council, claiming in substance that, by refusing to permit them to advance as members, it violated section 51 of the Civil Code (hereafter section 51), the so-called Unruh Civil Rights Act, which prohibits discrimination on bases including religion. . . .

I agree with my colleagues that, in pertinent part, we must reverse. I am of the view that section 51 does not cover the Boy Scouts in the formulating or implementing of membership policies as to members or potential members.

[S]ection 51 expresses a policy against discrimination, on certain bases, in the general area of relationships between private persons and entities: "All persons within the jurisdiction of this state are free and equal, and no matter what their sex, race, color, religion, ancestry, national origin, or disability are entitled to the full and equal accommodations, advantages, facilities, privileges, or services in all business establishments of every kind whatsoever." The phrase "business establishments" means areas of activity encompassing proprietor-patron relationships, which involve the providing of goods or services, nongratuitously, for a price or fee, in the course of relatively noncontinuous, nonpersonal, and nonsocial dealings.

It follows that section 51 does not cover the Boy Scouts, at any level of the organization, in the formulating or implementing of membership policies as to members or potential members. That is because at no level does it operate in that regard as a "business establishment"—that is to say, at no level does it occupy in that regard an area of activity encompassing proprietor-patron relationships. The record on appeal is unequivocal. For the relationship between the Boy Scouts and the member or potential member in the formulating and implementing of membership policies, at whatever level of the organization, does not, in actuality, involve the providing of goods or services, nongratuitously, for a price or fee, notwithstanding the payment of dues; moreover, the dealings in question are not relatively noncontinuous, nonpersonal, and nonsocial dealings, but quite the opposite.

For the reasons stated above, I join with my colleagues in reversing the judgment of the Court of Appeal to the extent that it affirms the judgment of the superior court in favor of the Randalls and against the Orange County Council.

Dale v. Boy Scouts of America
160 N.J. 562 (1999)

The opinion of the Court was delivered by Poritz, C.J.

In 1991, the New Jersey Legislature amended the Law Against Discrimination (LAD), N.J.S.A. 10:5-1 to -49, to include protections based on "affectional or sexual orientation." This case requires us to decide whether that law prohibits Boy Scouts of America (BSA) from expelling a member solely because he is an avowed homosexual.

Defendants BSA and Monmouth Council (collectively Boy Scouts) seek review of a decision of the Appellate Division holding that: (1) Boy Scouts is a place of public accommodation as defined by the LAD; (2) Boy Scouts' expulsion of plaintiff James Dale, an assistant scoutmaster, based solely on the club's policy of excluding avowed homosexuals from membership is prohibited by the LAD; and (3) the LAD prohibition does not violate Boy Scouts' First Amendment rights. . . . [We affirm.]

Boy Scouts of America

The Scout Oath and Scout Law set forth the guiding principles of BSA:

Scout Oath

On my honor I will do my best to do my duty to God and my country and to obey the Scout Law; to help other people at all times; to keep myself physically strong, mentally awake, and morally straight.

Scout Law

A Scout is TRUSTWORTHY. A Scout tells the truth. He keeps his promises. Honesty is a part of his code of conduct. People can always depend on him.

A Scout is LOYAL. A Scout is true to his family, friends, Scout leaders, school, nation, and world community.

A Scout is HELPFUL. A Scout is concerned about other people. He willingly volunteers to help others without expecting payment or reward.

A Scout is FRIENDLY. A Scout is a friend to all. He is a brother to other Scouts. He seeks to understand others. He respects those with ideas and customs that are different from his own.

A Scout is COURTEOUS. A Scout is polite to everyone regardless of age or position. He knows that good manners make it easier for people to get along together.

A Scout is KIND. A Scout understands there is strength in being gentle. He treats others as he wants to be treated. He does not harm or kill anything without reason.

A Scout is OBEDIENT. A Scout follows the rules of his family, school, and troop. He obeys the laws of his community and country. If he thinks these rules and laws are unfair, he tries to have them changed in an orderly manner rather than disobey them.

A Scout is CHEERFUL. A Scout looks for the bright side of life. He cheerfully does tasks that come his way. He tries to make others happy.

A Scout is THRIFTY. A Scout works to pay his way and to help others. He saves for the future. He protects and conserves natural resources. He carefully uses time and property.

A Scout is BRAVE. A Scout can face danger even if he is afraid. He has the courage to stand for what he thinks is right even if others laugh at him or threaten him.

A Scout is CLEAN. A Scout keeps his body and mind fit and clean. He goes around with those who believe in living by these same ideals. He helps keep his home and community clean.

A Scout is REVERENT. A Scout is reverent toward God. He is faithful in his religious duties. He respects the beliefs of others.

In its briefs below and to this Court, Boy Scouts claims that the language "morally straight" and "clean" in the Oath and Law, respectively, constitutes a rejection of homosexuality. . . .

Although one of BSA's stated purposes is to encourage members' ethical development, BSA does not endorse any specific set of moral beliefs. Instead, "moral fitness" is deemed an individual choice . . . .

BSA also does not espouse any one religion, explaining in the *Scoutmaster Handbook* that "[t]here is a close association between the Boy Scouts of America and virtually all religious bodies and denominations in the United States." Consistent with its nonsectarian nature, BSA Bylaws require "respect [for] the convictions of others in matters of custom and religion." Boy Scouts "encourages no particular affiliation, [and does not] assume [the] functions of religious bodies"; indeed, in a training manual entitled *Scoutmaster Fundamentals* prepared "for Scoutmasters, Assistant Scoutmasters, Troop Committee members, and parents," BSA categorically states: "Religious instruction is the responsibility of the home and church."

A large and diverse group of religions that subscribe to many different and sometimes contradictory beliefs sponsor BSA units throughout the United States. Some of those sponsors have participated in this case as amici curiae, taking a variety of positions in respect of homosexuality, i.e., that homosexuality is "immoral"; that "discrimination based upon sexual orientation" is to be "strongly condemn[ed]." BSA, however, encourages its leaders to refrain from talking about sexual topics. Although the *Boy Scout Handbook* contains a subchapter entitled "Sexual Responsibility" which states that "[f]or the followers of most religions, sex should take place only between married couples," sexual topics are not formally discussed during Boy Scout activities. Rather, BSA "believes that boys should learn about sex and family life from their parents, consistent with their spiritual beliefs."

Public Accommodation

We first consider whether Boy Scouts is subject to the LAD, which provides that "[a]ll persons shall have the opportunity . . . to obtain all the accommodations, advantages, facilities, and privileges of any place of public accommodation, . . . without discrimination because of . . . affectional or sexual orientation." Boy Scouts must therefore abide by the LAD if Boy Scouts is a place of public accommodation and does not meet any of the LAD exceptions. See, e.g., N.J.S.A. 10:5-51 (exempting "distinctly private" entities, religious educational facilities, and parents or individuals acting "in loco parentis" in respect of "the education and upbringing of a child"). . . .

Our case law identifies various factors that are helpful in determining whether Boy Scouts is a "public accommodation." We ask, generally, whether the entity before us engages in broad public solicitation, whether it maintains close relationships with the government or other public accommodations, or whether it is similar to enumerated or other previously recognized public accommodations. . . .

BSA engages in broad public solicitation through various media. In 1989, for example, BSA spent more than $1 million on a national television advertising campaign. A *New York Times* article describes one of Boy Scouts' "hip" television ads, quoting a BSA spokesman as stating, "scouting [is] a product and we've got to get the product into the hands of as many consumers as we can." BSA has also advertised in widely distributed magazines, such as *Sports Afield* and *Redbook*. Local Boy Scout councils engage in substantial public solicitation. BSA frequently supplies the councils with recruiting materials, such as television and radio public service announcements, advertisements, and other promotional products. Monmouth Council, in particular, has expressly invited the public by conducting recruiting drives and by providing local troops with BSA-produced posters and promotions aimed at attracting new members.

Boy Scout troops also take part in perhaps the most powerful invitation of all, albeit an implied one: the symbolic invitation extended by a Boy Scout each time he wears his uniform in public. A boy in a uniform may well be Boy Scouts' strongest recruiting tool. By encouraging scouts to wear their uniforms to school, and when participating in "School Nights" and public demonstrations, Boy Scouts invites the curiosity and awareness of others in the community. Boy Scouts admits that it encourages these displays in the hope of attracting new members.

On the facts before us, it cannot be controverted that Boy Scouts reaches out to the public in a myriad of ways designed to increase and sustain a broad membership base. Whether by advertising or active recruitment, or through the symbolism of a Boy Scout uniform, the intent is to send the invitation to as many members of the general public as possible. Once Boy Scouts has extended this invitation, the LAD requires that all members of the public must "have equal rights . . . and not be subjected to the embarrassment and humiliation of being invited[,] . . . only to find [the] doors barred to them."

Boy Scouts is a "public accommodation," not simply because of its solicitation activities, but also because it maintains close relationships with federal and state governmental bodies and with other recognized public accommodations. Our cases have held that certain

organizations that benefit from relationships with the government and other public accommodations are themselves places of public accommodation within the meaning of the LAD.
. . .

It is clear that Boy Scouts benefits from a close relationship with the federal government. Indeed, BSA was chartered by Congress in 1916, 36 U.S.C.A. § 30901, and has been the recipient of equipment, supplies, and services from the federal government, also by act of Congress, 10 U.S.C.A. § 2544. . . .

Since its inception, BSA has maintained a special association with each successive President of the United States. According to a BSA public relations fact sheet:

> One of the causes contributing to the success of the Boy Scouts of America has been the thoughtful, wholehearted way in which each President of the United States since William Howard Taft in 1910 has taken an active part in the work of the movement. Each served as Honorary President during his term in office.

Another fact sheet states that seventy-eight percent of the members of the 100th Congress participated in scouting.

Boy Scouts also maintains a close relationship with the military. According to a BSA pamphlet entitled *Organizations That Use Scouting,* "military personnel serve Scouting in many capacities." "At many [Army, Navy, Air Force, and National Coast Guard] installations, facilities are available for Scouting shows, meetings, training activities," and other "similar Scouting events." Monmouth Council, in particular, has used the New Jersey military installation known as Fort Monmouth.

Likewise, state and local governments have contributed to Boy Scouts' success. In New Jersey, the Legislature has authorized the Division of Fish, Game and Wildlife in the Department of Environmental Protection to "stock with fish any body of water in this state that is under the control of and for the use of . . . Boy Scouts," and has exempted Boy Scouts from having to pay motor vehicle registration fees. Local governmental agencies, such as fire departments and law enforcement agencies, serve Boy Scouts by sponsoring scouting units. Nationally, over 50,000 youth members belong to units sponsored by fire departments, whereas in New Jersey alone over 130 units are sponsored by fire departments and over 100 units are sponsored by law enforcement agencies.

Perhaps Boy Scouts' connection to public schools and school-affiliated groups constitutes its single most beneficial governmental relationship. *Organizations That Use Scouting* advises that "the education field holds our greatest potential." Boy Scouts currently recruits many of its members through its presence in and use of school facilities. A large percentage of scouting units nationally, as well as in New Jersey, are chartered by public schools and affiliated organizations.

Moreover, public schools and community colleges often host scouting meetings, activities, and recruiting events such as "School Nights." "School Night for Scouting [is a] recruiting plan operated by many councils in connection with the schools." Under this plan, an open scout meeting is held at a school in order to encourage students to join scouting. Public schools not only aid Boy Scouts by allowing the organization to use their facilities after school, but also during the school day. . . .

Boy Scouts accepts boys who come from diverse cultures and who belong to different religions. It teaches tolerance and understanding of differences in others. It presents itself to its members and to the public generally as a nonsectarian organization "available to all boys who meet the entrance age requirements." Its Charter and its Bylaws do not permit the exclusion of any boy. Boy Scouts is not "distinctly private" because it is not selective in its membership. . . .

The First Amendment

Our holding that New Jersey's Law Against Discrimination applies to Boy Scouts requires that we reach Boy Scouts' claim that its First Amendment rights are thereby violated. See U.S. Const. amend. I. Boy Scouts asserts the rights of its members "to enter into and maintain . . . intimate or private relationships . . . [and] to associate for the purpose of engaging in protected speech." . . .

Freedom of Expressive Association

When the government attempts "to interfere with the internal organization or affairs of the group," the members' freedom of expressive association may be curtailed. In this regard, the Supreme Court has said that "[t]here can be no clearer example of an intrusion into the internal structure or affairs of an association than a regulation that forces the group to accept members it does not desire." This does not mean, however, "that in every setting in which individuals exercise some discrimination in choosing associates, their selective process of inclusion and exclusion is protected by the Constitution." Rather, the Court has found that a group member infringes upon an organization's freedom of expressive association only if he or she "affect[s] 'in any significant way' the [other members'] ability . . . to . . . advocate public or private viewpoints." . . .

Moreover, "[t]he right to associate for expressive purposes is not . . . absolute." The Supreme Court has held that "[i]nfringements on that right may be justified by regulations adopted to serve compelling state interests, unrelated to the suppression of ideas, that cannot be achieved through means significantly less restrictive of associational freedom." State laws against discrimination may take precedence over the right of expressive association because "acts of invidious discrimination in the distribution of publicly available goods, services, and other advantages cause unique evils that government has a compelling interest to prevent—wholly apart from the point of view such conduct may transmit." The right of expressive association must, therefore, be weighed against this compelling interest in each case.

We find that the LAD does not violate Boy Scouts' freedom of expressive association because the statute does not have a significant impact on Boy Scout members' ability to associate with one another in pursuit of shared views. The organization's ability to disseminate its message is not significantly affected by Dale's inclusion because: Boy Scout members do not associate for the purpose of disseminating the belief that homosexuality is immoral; Boy Scouts discourages its leaders from disseminating *any* views on sexual issues; and Boy Scouts includes sponsors and members who subscribe to different views in respect of homosexuality.

Boy Scouts claims that its members' views regarding homosexuality are evident from its Scout Law and Oath, which embody general moral principles. The Scout Law requires Boy Scout members to be "trustworthy, loyal, helpful, friendly, courteous, kind, obedient, cheerful, thrifty, brave, clean, and reverent," whereas the Oath requires each scout to promise: "I will do my best to do my duty to God and my country and to obey the Scout Law; to help other people at all times; to keep myself physically strong, mentally awake, and morally straight." Boy Scouts asserts that it teaches those moral principles to its members through scouting activities. BSA Bylaws require that "in all activities, emphasis [is to] be placed upon practice in daily life of the principles of the Scout Oath.". . .

We agree that Boy Scouts expresses a belief in moral values and uses its activities to encourage the moral development of its members. We are not persuaded, however, that a "shared goal" of Boy Scout members is to associate in order to preserve the view that homosexuality is immoral.

Boy Scouts argues that the words "morally straight" and "clean" in the Scout Oath and Law explicitly or implicitly stand for the proposition that homosexuality is immoral. In support of its position, Boy Scouts relies on the *Boy Scout Handbook* definition of "morally straight" and "clean":

Morally Straight

To be a person of strong character, guide your life with honesty, purity, and justice. Respect and defend the rights of all people. Your relationships with others should be honest and open. Be clean in your speech and actions, and faithful in your religious beliefs. The values you follow as a Scout will help you become virtuous and self-reliant.

Clean

A Scout is CLEAN. A Scout keeps his body and mind fit and clean. He chooses the company of those who live by these same ideals. He helps keep his home and community clean.

You never need to be ashamed of dirt that will wash off. . . . There's another kind of dirt that won't come off by washing. It is the kind that shows up in foul language and harmful thoughts. Swear words, profanity, and dirty stories are weapons that ridicule other people and hurt their feelings. The same is true of racial slurs and jokes making fun of ethnic groups or people with physical or mental limitations. A Scout knows there is no kindness or honor in such mean-spirited behavior. He avoids it in his own words and deeds. He defends those who are the targets of insults.

The words "morally straight" and "clean" do not, on their face, express anything about sexuality, much less that homosexuality, in particular, is immoral. We doubt that young boys would ascribe any meaning to these terms other than a commitment to be good.

Boy Scouts also argues that the immorality of homosexuality can be implied from the moral principles expressed by the Scout Oath and Law. Yet, Boy Scouts teaches that "moral fitness" is an individual choice and defers the ultimate definition to its members:

> Morality . . . concerns the "principles of right and wrong" in our behavior, and "what is sanctioned by *our* conscience or ethical judgment.". . . In any consideration of moral fitness, a key word has to be "courage." A boy's courage to do what *his* head and *his* heart tell him is right. And the courage to refuse to do what *his* heart and *his* head say is wrong.

(emphasis added).

The *Boy Scout Handbook* also acknowledges that a member's concept of morality is intertwined with his "religious beliefs." The record in this case reveals that Boy Scouts' religious sponsors differ in their views about homosexuality. . . . On the record before us, it appears that no single view on this subject functions as a unifying associational goal of the organization.

We hold, therefore, that Dale's membership does not violate Boy Scouts' right of expressive association because his inclusion would not "affect in any significant way [Boy Scouts] existing members' ability to carry out their various purposes.". . . .

Boy Scouts is an American institution committed to bringing a diverse group of young boys and men together—wealthy and underprivileged, urban and rural, from different cultures and from different religions—to play and to learn. Boy Scouts' activities are designed to build character and instill moral principles. Nothing before us, however, suggests that one of Boy Scouts' purposes is to promote the view that homosexuality is immoral. Accordingly, application of the LAD does not infringe upon Boy Scouts' right of expressive association.

Unwritten Constitutions, Unwritten Law[*]
Walter O. Weyrauch

The power of state law to regulate society is not exclusive. A large body of unwritten law, based on oral legal traditions, coexists autonomously within any setting. It is supported by informal but effective sanctions. The rules of unwritten law may be layered in fundamental principles, constitutional in character, and provisions of lesser significance dealing with matters of daily concern. Jurisprudential questions may be asked as to how multitudes of autonomous legal systems, many of them of ephemeral nature, compete with and often support the law of the state. Empirical information is provided describing highly disparate communities: an experimental group on the Berkeley campus, the isolated population on the British island of Tristan da Cunha, and the Romani people (Gypsies) who reside in groups throughout the world but share a largely unknown legal culture. All these societies are subject to oral legal traditions and to the written laws of the respective nations and states in one form or another. In spite of their differences they have common features that can also be observed within American society. Autonomous unwritten law is only accessible to external controls within limits, but knowledge of its characteristics is critical for legal theory and practice. Awareness of unwritten law, as illustrated by individual cases, can offer strategic advantages and defenses.

I. Preface

By unwritten constitutions I mean the fundamental principles by which the people in any form of organization govern themselves.[1] Unwritten law is layered, just as written law, and can be found any place where a group gathers to pursue common objectives. The layers may extend from unwritten constitutional principles to lesser laws dealing with ordinary social discourse. Threat of informal but effective sanctions assures compliance. Most recently Michael Reisman has asserted that fundamental aspects of law can be also traced in short-term encounters. Even on this level one can probably distinguish between basic norms protecting physical integrity and survival and lesser provisions regulating daily occurrences. This essay submits empirical evidence in support of these propositions inviting further discussion.

Mostly unwritten constitutional law, as I will demonstrate, exists in any social unit, whether formal or informal, more or less permanent or of transitory existence. Marriage

---

[*]   Walter O. Weyrauch, Unwritten Constitutions, Unwritten Law, Washington and Lee Law Review, Volume 56, No. 4 (1999).

[1]   See, e.g., Thomas C. Grey, Do We Have an Unwritten Constitution?, 27 Stan. L. Rev. 703 (1975); id., Origins of the Unwritten Constitution: Fundamental Law in American Revolutionary Thought, 30 Stan. L. Rev. 843 (1978); id., The Constitution as Scripture, 37 Stan. L. Rev. 1, 23 (1984) (maintaining that judges should supplement the written constitution with an unwritten one, "in terms of the homely ethnography of the common law tradition"); Anthony Chase, Unwritten Constitution, Invisible Government, 18 Nova L. Rev. 1703 (1994). An early source is Karl N. Llewellyn, The Constitution as an Institution, 34 Colum. L. Rev. 1, 2 n. 5 (1934) (stating that the United States has an unwritten constitution, "whether anyone likes that fact or not").

and any form of business or governmental unit, including the United States as a whole, are mere illustrations. My definition is tied to a more general conception of law as being an inevitable and necessary consequence of any purposeful human association. In other words, law as perceived this way is not necessarily dependent on any formal lawgiving body of the state. The conception of law as emanating exclusively from the state is misleading and too limited. It has its historical base in the last centuries and the transformation of absolute monarchy into contemporary forms of powerful states.

Throughout my professional life I have been involved in experimentation, observation and analysis of informal, not necessarily legally recognized, social units and their law creating activities. I will discuss three examples of such units and whether it is appropriate to talk in this context of constitutional law. I will refrain from going into further detail of the three associations that are submitted here as empirical support for my hypotheses because, at this point, it is essential to set forth their rudimentary common features. The units involved are highly disparate and are merely given as illustrations of basic characteristics that they share with other forms of human associations. I will present them in the following order: in Part II, an experimental group of nine young men living in the spring of 1965 for three months under highly controlled conditions in a penthouse on the Berkeley campus; in Part III, the population of about three hundred persons living on the isolated island of Tristan da Cunha in the South Atlantic; and in Part IV, the Romani people, commonly referred to as "Gypsies"; in Part V, I submit some illustrations and hypotheses on layers of autonomous lawmaking in American law. I conclude in Part VI with general thoughts on fundamental notions of unwritten law.

One may ask, why rely on highly exceptional and unconventional social units to demonstrate what can be observed in more familiar settings? Yet, once the commonality of private lawmaking is demonstrated in wholly unrelated and anomalous groups, the reader can easily verify the hypotheses in any setting that is close at hand, for example, at home, in a university faculty, a law firm, or a governmental agency. Beginning with the familiar could be distracting because daily routines are not likely to be perceived as discrete forms of informal lawmaking. One practical implication of these oral legal traditions, as I will discuss in Part V dealing with American law, is in an unexpected area. It relates to the role of strategy in legal analyses, planning and litigation. Strategy, I suggest, gains whatever persuasive power it may possess from invocation of fundamental principles, based on the unwritten legal traditions of the people concerned.

I begin my observations with an account of an experiment in which I participated more than thirty years ago.

II. The Berkeley Penthouse Group[2]

The experiment, financed by the National Aeronautics and Space Administration (NASA), lasted three months in 1965. It tested a diet for purposes of space exploration. The

---

2   An abundance of factual detail is given throughout this article, because without facts empirical studies lack foundation. Elizabeth Warren & Jay Lawrence Westbrook, Searching for Reorganization Realities, 72 Wash. U.L.Q. 1257, 1260 passim (1994) (criticizing in legal scholarship "speculation without reference to

experimental rules were nutritional in design and required far-reaching isolation from external influences that could have disturbed minute scientific measurements. Nine male volunteers, all in their twenties, developed their own rules. They reacted in part to the compulsory scientific regime, but their rules were also significant beyond the scope of the experiment. The nutritionists believed, based on the peculiar orientation of their discipline, that digestive factors, social behavior and lawmaking might be interrelated. NASA's interest was not merely focused on the physical well-being of future astronauts, but also on maintaining its legal authority during their prolonged separation from ground control. There had been past incidents during space flight in which wives of astronauts had been asked to communicate with their husbands in critical situations because their authority proved to be more durable than the commands of ground control—in other words, of the state.

NASA was concerned about the potential growth of competing legal systems in case of prolonged space flights and eventual space exploration. I was brought into the experiment as a law professor. I met regularly with the volunteers, interviewed them and conducted joint sessions with them that are reported in a detailed log as part of my general report. I am not concerned here with discussing the purposes of NASA in conducting the experiment and with the nutritional or legal design of its execution, merely with reporting some of my more significant observations. The laws that were developed within the group under conditions of strict confinement were sufficiently specific that I could restate them in a published document having the appearance of a basic law or constitution.[3] What emerged was an elaborate and extremely complex set of rules, some being more fundamental than others, and all of them enforceable by sanctions.

The participants, who included one African-American, one Asian (native Chinese), and people of various religious and ideological persuasion, were mostly part of the general American culture. They brought American values with them to the penthouse. Many rules

---

reality" and calling for empirical research as an essential element of any policy debate). Extensively presented hypothetical facts have sometimes served as a substitute for reality in jurisprudential discussion. See Lon L. Fuller, The Case of the Speluncean Explorers, 62 Harv. L. Rev. 616 (1949) (discussing an imaginary criminal case for murder, brought against explorers who, after having been trapped in a cavern by a landslide, survived by killing and eating one member of their group). The facts that are submitted in the present article, although unusual, are real.

The specific Berkeley Penthouse Experiment in the text is described in Walter O. Weyrauch, The Law of a Small Group: A Report on the Berkeley Penthouse Experiments with Emphasis on Penthouse V (Space Sciences Laboratory, University of California, Berkeley, Internal Working Paper No. 54, 1967) (on file with University of California, Berkeley, Law Library and Columbia University Law Library). For a published shorter version, see Walter O. Weyrauch, Law in Isolation: The Penthouse Astronauts—An Experimental Group Cut Off From the World Makes Its Own Rules, Trans-Action, June 1968, at 39.

[3]   Walter O. Weyrauch, The "Basic Law" or "Constitution" of a Small Group, 25 J. Soc. Issues 49, 59-62 (1971), reprinted in Law, Justice, and the Individual in Society 41 (June L. Tapp & Felice J. Levine eds. 1977). The restatement of basic laws of this particular group involved 28 rules of considerable specificity, many of them having an impact on the conduct and outcome of the experiment. None of this had been considered in the design of the experiment.

that they generated reflected the ambivalence that can also be found on the outside. The rules were contradictory and often disturbingly hypocritical. One should realize though that this unwritten constitution was behavioral rather than aspirational in nature. Any unwritten constitution, although influenced by ideals, is largely a reflection of behavior. It is likely to contain common beliefs and even prejudices, side by side with ideals, that would not likely be expressed in a formal constitutional document. Rule 9 maintained, for example, that "[a]ll persons are born equal. If discrimination because of race or religion occurs, the fact of discrimination is to be denied."

Often the ambivalence expressed itself in the form of a basic rule and in exceptions. Rule 7 related to experimenters and staff members who were female. It dealt with the phenomenon that today might be referred to as sexism. "Women, if present, are to be treated with chivalry. Derogatory or obscene remarks can be made about them if they are absent. Obscene language is excusable if used as some form of relief in a stressful situation." Rule 10 could be restated as follows: "In matters considered as crucial, each member of the group has an absolute veto. However, a lone dissenter or a dissenting minority may be harassed to reach a desired unanimity."

Of particular interest was the main rule 1, making the efficacy of rules dependent on their level of articulation. This rule has also been discussed in the literature. It has been observed in families, law firms and law faculties. Because of its importance, I restate it in full, adding the related rule 2:

> 1. Rules are not to be articulated. In case of articulation they are to be discarded, regardless of whether such articulation was accidental or deliberate. If a substantial segment of the group has in fact talked about the rule, the level of articulation is reached and its existence acknowledged.
>
> A rule that has become spurious by articulation and acknowledgment can be discarded by any form of behavior designed to destroy its effectiveness, for instance by deliberate disregard in a demonstrative fashion without the normal group sanctions which otherwise would have been imposed.
>
> 2. The closer a rule comes to a taboo area, the less articulate it should be. Minor administrative matters may be articulated.
>
> The stringency of a rule is determined by the level of its articulation. The more articulate it is, the less it has to be followed.

In spite of common characteristics of age and gender, the subjects were not homogeneous. Subgroupings developed soon during the experiment. The opposing viewpoints caused a wide range of discussions on the experimental regime and almost any aspect of life. Although these discussions were often chaotic, they had positive aspects. They made the implicitly created rule structure visible which otherwise, because of the basic rule against articulation, would have been more difficult to detect. Race and violation of civil rights played important roles in these respects.

The ethnic factor caused problems almost from the beginning. The native Chinese and African-American members of the experimental group were subjected to ill treatment. The participants, possibly even the victims, were wholly unaware of any racism being involved. They were of above average educational level, some of them being graduate students, and considered themselves strongly supportive of civil rights, condemning racism in any form. Yet their behavior, perhaps due to the stresses of the experiment, belied their expressed beliefs. Their conduct, under contemporary standards and even in 1965, was highly offensive.

The Chinese man, born outside of the United States, was persistently treated badly and called "stupid" to his face. The most liberal member of the group, in crude language although supposedly in jest, compared the African-American member to a primate. The targets of these insults reacted in different fashion. The Chinese member became depressed and sullen. Probably as a release from tension he started to drink water excessively, thereupon being derided as an "aquaholic" by the other participants. Ultimately the experimenters intervened and removed him from the experiment because he had violated dietary rules. The African-American, a powerful individual, sustained himself successfully throughout the experiment. He reacted to insults by becoming noisy, an effective sanction within the crowded environment.

Toward the conclusion of the experiment certain irregularities occurred, including the smuggling of a "mood-altering agent," as the matter was referred to in the experimental reports. Interestingly, only the most conservative white member of the group and the African-American were wholly uninvolved in the violations. A form of quasi-judicial procedure followed, conducted by the nutritionists, resulting in docking of compensation in various degrees, depending on the seriousness of the individual offence and its impact on the scientific data. A plot was uncovered by a nurse to send the uninvolved black member to "Coventry," subjecting him to ostracism, to make him react foolishly and commit some violation to reduce his compensation too. In an independent incident, the African-American received a deep gash on his hand, a sharp-edged can being thrown at him with the shout "catch." Throughout these events the subjects, including the victim, denied that racism was involved. The insults were referred to as mere joking or teasing, and even the injury was characterized as an accident, caused by horseplay.

One may view these events as detrimental to the whole experimental undertaking, but they can be viewed as instructive. The experiment was not purely nutritional; it included my task of observing the law that emerged among the confined subjects. From that perspective the infractions were most valuable. They exposed the very core of the norms that had been generated to a stress test. In addition, even the value of the nutritional data may have been enhanced. Infractions are bound to occur in any setting. In a congenial group they are more likely to be covered up successfully, while in a mixed group they tend to become visible. There is some evidence that this happened also in the Penthouse Experiment.

The African-American member of the group established a relation of confidence to a nurse, who was of the same ethnic background. This ethnically determined subgroup, its membership cutting across the division between volunteers and experimenters, probably helped in exposing the irregularities that, otherwise, would have remained undetected. Thus what appeared to have a been a flaw in design may actually have improved the experimental rigor and the reliability of the nutritional data. Similarly, the presence of a law professor may have brought matters out in the open that in a homogeneous group of nutritional scientists may never have been noticed, and, if noticed, may have been suppressed.

My second illustration deals with empirical data, collected from an island population.

III. Tristan da Cunha

Tristan da Cunha is an isolated island in the South Atlantic, thousands of miles distant from Cape Town, Rio de Janeiro, and Buenos Aires.[4] The closest inhabited place is Saint Helena, another isolated island, some 1,500 miles to the north. Tristan is a British Colony and a dependency of Saint Helena. It is of about seven miles in diameter and has a volcanic mountain of 6,760 feet above sea level, snow covered in winter and last active in 1961. There is only very limited livable space for the population of about 300. The inhabitants originated from three settlers of Scottish and English descent, later joined in the earlier parts of the nineteenth century by a few men from whaling fleets and shipwrecked sailors. In 1827 the settlers, now five in number, asked the captain of a passing sailboat to bring them five women from Saint Helena who were in search of husbands. These women were of mixed African, Malayan and European origin.

Before 1816 the island, except for a few temporary occupants, was essentially uninhabited, but a small garrison of British soldiers was stationed there during the first year of Napoleon's exile in Saint Helena. The concern was that he might try to escape with French assistance. One member of this detachment, William Glass, asked for permission to stay when his unit returned to England. He was joined by two of his compatriots. Glass had married a young woman in South Africa, at that time a mere thirteen years old, with whom he later had sixteen children. His wife had been described as Cape Coloured or Cape Creole. In the later part of the nineteenth century the island was becoming increasingly isolated. Steamers replaced sailboats, and there was no longer a need to stop at Tristan for provisions and fresh water.

The isolation seems to have increased the need for autonomy and probably has aided in bringing about the distinct Tristan character traits that prevail today. At this point only seven family names exist, Glass, Green, Hagan, Lavarello, Repetto, Rogers, and Swain, all members of these families being more or less closely related through intermarriage. A fairly large percentage of marriages, possibly up to thirty percent, appear to have been entered between cousins. Yet marriages between persons of the same family name, although not prohibited, are in a jocular vein disparaged ("a Green upon a Green," "a Swain upon a Swain").

---

[4]   My discussion of Tristan da Cunha is based on Peter A. Munch, Sociology of Tristan da Cunha (Results of the Norwegian Scientific Expedition to Tristan da Cunha 1937-1938, No. 13, De Norske Videnskap-Akademi I Oslo, 1945); and id., Crisis in Utopia: The Ordeal of Tristan da Cunha (1971) (relating to the volcanic eruption of 1961 and its aftermath, evacuation to England and eventual return to Tristan).

Munch's description of Tristan da Cunha as Utopia refers in classical Greek to a "nowhere place." In its literary sense it connotes an imaginary island with ideal legal and political conditions of life. The term was coined by Sir Thomas More in his Libellus Vere Aureus, nec minus Salutaris, quam Festivus, de Optimo Reipublicae Statu desque Nova Insula Utopia ("On the Highest State of a Republic and on the New Island Utopia") (1516). Tristan da Cunha, however, is real.

In spite of possible genetic problems that may have existed, the population is of extra-ordinary health and longevity. Unless men die accidentally by drowning, reaching ages in the nineties is not uncommon. The people retain their original teeth fully intact until old age. Their diet is monotonous, consisting mainly of cooked fish and potatoes three times a day. On the other side of the island and difficult to reach is an apple orchard. The apples are consumed rapidly, preferably when still green, and no effort is made to store them. There are cows and sheep, providing milk, wool, and occasional meat.

The people of Tristan are intelligent and resourceful, have a well-developed sense of humor and are quick-witted. They are fundamentally trusting, hospitable and honest. In their communications with visiting foreigners they are polite, but have developed a reticence to reveal their innermost thoughts and feelings. Their frankness has been abused by reports that have depicted them as simpleminded and backward. One visiting author, after being initially denied admission to stay overnight, was told, "Mr. Winchester—you'll be careful with us now, won't you? We'll have to live with what you write for years to come. We'll read your words a thousand times. So be careful, for our own sakes." To some extent the Trista-nians are protected by the extreme difficulty of access. Actually, getting to Tristan might be easier than arranging for how and when to leave, transportation being only sporadically available.

The Tristan population has one basic law of absolute equality that, significantly, orig-inated from the written articles of a business partnership between the initial three settlers, William Glass, Samuel Burnell and John Nankevel, and witnessed by the commander of the British garrison and an officer of the Royal Navy. The document is dated November 17, 1817, and the original is preserved in the British Museum in London. It reads as follows:

> We, the Undersigned, having entered into Co-Partnership on the Island of Tristan da Cunha, have voluntarily entered into the following agreement—Viz.
>
> 1st That the stock and stores of every description in possession of the Firm shall be considered as belonging equally to each—
>
> 2nd That whatever profit may arise from the concern shall be equally divided—
>
> 3rd All Purchases to be paid equally by each—
>
> 4th That in order to assure the harmony of the Firm, No member shall assume any superiority whatever, but all to be considered as equal in every respect, each performing his proportion of labour, if not prevented by sick-ness—
>
> 5th In case any of the members wish to leave the Island, a valuation of the property to be made by persons fixed upon, whose valuation is to be considered as final—
>
> 6th William Glass is not to incur any additional expence on account of his wife and children.

This partnership agreement was later amended by a written document of December 10, 1821, a copy being in possession of the British Museum, providing in part:

7th No person subscribing to these articles are [*sic*] to continue reminding particular persons of their Duty in point of Work, or otherwise, as in such Case nothing but *Disunion* will be the consequence; Wm. Glass being at the head of the firm, will allot each individual every evening, his work for the following Day, not by way of task but merely for the purpose of causing all to do their best for the general good, which will be the means of insureing [*sic*] peace, and good will among the people as well as benefitting the Establishment, in which all are concerned.

These unusual documents, which can be called the constitution of Tristan da Cunha, although the actual wording is no longer available on the island and has been forgotten by later generations, have been transformed in the collective memory of the population into an understanding of fundamental equality. Numerous derivative rules have been generated over time that can be viewed as a highly effective body of unwritten law. In almost two hundred years of its existence this island community has experienced virtually no crime, no divorce or other social disruption. Occasional irregularities, such as what might be called petty theft in our society, are not treated as crimes under Tristan law. The only communal demand would be for return of the property to the owner, not even for damages in any form if a return is not possible.

There is really no need for police or any other form of authority, although a policeman has been appointed in recent years. The Colonial Office, through the Governor of Saint Helena and the Tristan Administrator, has tried to establish some formal procedures, elections and popular representation, also some rudimentary forms of civil service. The main effect of the latter seems to have been to enhance the position of women, the men being unavailable because of farming and fishing.[5] In other respects, these efforts, as is true of English common law that applies in theory, have stayed on the surface and do not actually govern the life of the community. Even the British Administrator, although treated with deference, has remained an outsider.

Commercial enterprise, especially since 1963 when the islanders returned to Tristan after being temporarily evacuated to England because of a volcanic eruption, may have had

---

[5]   A comparison of Tristan da Cunha with Pitcairn provides a striking contrast. Pitcairn, an island located in the Pacific halfway between Australia and South America, is another British Crown Colony. It is even smaller and more isolated than Tristan, with a population of less than one hundred. These people, of mixed English and Tahitian ancestry, are the descendants of the mutineers of the Bounty. The early history of Pitcairn was characterized by anarchy, betrayal, murder and mayhem, decimating the mutineers to a sole survivor, John Adams, his nine Tahitian consorts and the children of the men who had met a violent death. In spite of this history, and perhaps because of it, for a period of two hundred years and starting under the leadership of John Adams, the population has developed a detailed written legal system with penalties for infractions, culminating in an elaborate criminal code. They have an annually elected magistrate who must be born on the island and an inspector of police, a courthouse and a prison. For details, including a reproduction of the Pitcairn Criminal Code, see Ian M. Ball, Pitcairn: Children of Mutiny 317-28 (1973). Since Nov. 30, 1838, Pitcairn had a written constitution granting equal voting rights for men and women above 18 and mandating compulsory school attendance for children, drafted upon request of the islanders by the captain of a passing English ship. Trevor Lummis, Pitcairn Island: Life and Death in Eden 153-54 (1997); Ball, supra, at 308-09.

some impact. An emerging fishing industry introduced electricity to the island. Free school-ing and medical services are now available. By 1985, movies were shown, radio and even taped television programs were available in individual households. Reportedly, at least two automobiles cruised on the road of seven miles. According to an ordinance, relayed by the Governor of Saint Helena, they had to drive on the left side, following English custom. None of these innovations, some of which are of quixotical character, seem to have changed the traditional rules that govern the island.

Anglican ministers, sent by an English religious organization since 1851, have occa-sionally attempted to impose their authority on the islanders, in one instance even assum-ing the right of censorship of outgoing mail. The islanders who are deeply religious and regular churchgoers have treated these attempts with amused tolerance. When in one instance the clerical power was felt to be oppressive, a number of the islanders declared themselves to be Catholics, to avoid the jurisdiction of the Church of England. Assertion of leadership in any form by a Tristanian is perceived as a major violation of the basic rule of equality, to be sanctioned by teasing or possible shunning. Since there is no place to go, these sanctions appear to be formidable and effective.

Although the mixed ethnic origin of the population continues to be visible, some islanders being fair, some dark in complexion, there is no racial discrimination, because this would violate the basic tenet of equality. Perhaps a qualification should be added. Being fair skinned is perceived to be desirable and results, for instance, in improved marital chances for young women. This form of differentiation did not exist in the early years of the settle-ment. It appears that the awareness of skin color was imposed on the islanders from the out-side, and one source states that English missionaries were responsible for importing this distinction.

Yet skin color has no relation to achieving respect in the community through personal conduct and work. Indeed, merit achieved through personal effort is the main exception to equality, and repeated disregard of oral tradition may result in decline of status and com-munal respect. One may view the great dignity in personal conduct and in going about daily tasks, common to the islanders, as a means through which violation of their unwritten laws are avoided. If such dignity were not a common trait, the threat of its loss would become meaningless.

My third illustration deals with the unwritten basic laws of the people commonly referred to as Gypsies.

IV. The Romani People

The Romani people (Gypsies) are a nation without a territory. As any nation, unless one considers territory an essential element of sovereignty, they may assert autonomy and have their own laws.[6] The Roma originated from India which they left about one thousand

---

[6]   My presentation of Romani law (*Romaniya*) is based on Walter O. Weyrauch & Maureen A. Bell, Autonomous Lawmaking: The Case of the "Gypsies," 103 Yale L.J. 323 (1993). For further details, see Gypsy Law Symposium, 45 Am. J. Comp. L. 225 (1997).

years ago, being driven out by an invasion of Islamic forces. They have retained their language which is related to Sanskrit. Their legal system, *Romaniya*, depending on oral tradition, is based on behavior that is pure (*vujo*) or impure (*marime*). *Romaniya* is meant to help in achieving a state of spiritual equilibrium that contains religious elements and is similar to Western concepts of grace.

The Roma arrived in central Europe in the fifteenth century. They were enslaved in Romania for about five hundred years and ferociously persecuted elsewhere, culminating in the Nazi holocaust. An undetermined number of Roma, possibly more than one million, were murdered in concentration camps or summarily shot or hanged as alleged partisans, often without any other reason than being "Gypsies." The first Roma appeared on this continent with Columbus on his third voyage in 1498. Later they were deported from England and Sweden or fled from the persecution in Germany. Many came to the United States with the waves of immigration in the late nineteenth century. Their actual number is purely speculative because the United States Census has no appropriate category for them. Because of past persecution and as a nonwhite minority they are disinclined to characterize themselves as Gypsies. The majority of the Roma in the United States belong to the Vlach group originating from the Wallachian region in Romania. This group has courts, called *kris*, a term deriving from the Greek word *krisis* (judgment), the judges being elected by their peers for individual cases.

One may ask whether the oral legal traditions of the Roma are all basic, thereby eliminating any distinction between constitutional law and ordinary laws. Yet some fundamental notions exist also here. All the laws of *Romaniya* can be traced to zones of the human body, which acquire symbolic significance, the upper parts being pure and the lower parts impure. Metaphorically these zones of purity and impurity are extended to other areas of human conduct and interaction. The borderlines between the immediate and metaphorical applications of law are hazy. Hands have to be constantly washed because they may have touched polluted matters, for example, parts of the lower body. Food has to be prepared and served in specific ways. Male-female contact, especially of a sexual nature, can be severely contaminating. Childbirth takes place under extreme restriction. Contact with members of the dominant cultures, although permissible for earning a livelihood, is potentially contaminating because they do not adhere to the taboos.

Metaphorical expansion of the physical taboos may affect any phase of human conduct. Theft from another Rom is severely contaminating. According to orthodox views of some groups, apartments cannot be rented because the presence of women on the higher floors may contaminate the inhabitants of lower floors through the ceiling. If a house is purchased, kitchen sinks may have to be replaced by new ones, because of assumed improper use made of them by earlier occupants. Toilet facilities are problematical and should be segregated by gender, even in private living quarters. Women in general have the power to pollute because of menstruation. They may have, for example, the power to break up fights among men by the threat of symbolically tossing their skirts. Many of the rules are self-executory and prevent certain forms of infractions that are common in the non-Gypsy world. Crimes of violence are highly unusual among the Roma. Rape, in particular, would be such a serious offense that, if it were to occur, the culprit would be automatically expelled from the community of Roma, even in his own mind, thereby eliminating the need for a specific sentence.

Whether these rules of *Romaniya* make any sense under Western notions, is irrelevant as far as the Roma are concerned. They probably consider many of the dominant societies' laws absurd. Rationality is really little more than consistency within any system of beliefs. Few truly universal standards of rationality exist. Moreover, the efficacy of a legal rule may be enhanced by its being irrational, even within any given culture. Irrationality may imply that a rule of law has its source in divine forces, rather than in human reasoning. In addition, that the rules of *Romaniya* appear to make no sense to Western thinking, protects the integrity of the culture from being corrupted. It makes it less likely that intermarriage with outsiders will eventually lead to assimilation. Romani men are not inclined to enter prolonged intimate relations with non-Gypsy women and, in the reverse, it would be difficult for a woman from the dominant culture to put up with the demands of a Romani mother-in-law and with the orthodoxy of the rules to which she is expected to submit. Romani women, on the other hand, may become *marime* when living with or marrying an outsider and be banished from their culture.

A comparison with the previously discussed groups offers some striking parallels. For example, shared communal values, as in Tristan da Cunha, prevent major infractions and crime among the Romani people, although the de facto isolation of the Roma from the dominant environment does not quite match the extreme territorial isolation of Tristan. Even in the Berkeley Penthouse Experiment, involving an artificially and temporarily isolated group, one member expressed after its termination that the internal pressures to conform to shared values were enormous, a surprising observation because the group was more or less haphazardly thrown together. By way of illustration the subject explained that, soon after the start of the experiment, the group labeled each participant in a specific way, for example, in regard to personality and intelligence. Thereafter little could be done by the so characterized person to change this perception. The denial of recognition according to some preconceived "image," as the subject called it, thus became a powerful tool to sanction individuals and to keep them in line with group expectations.

Conceptions of shaming that were the basis of the rule making and application in the Berkeley Penthouse could be noticed in modified form in Tristan da Cunha and among the Romani people. They also apply to our society and legal system. A heavy price appears to be paid for recognized status within any institutional setting or community, consisting in a decrease or loss of individuality. One has to be cautious, though, in using the term individuality which is based on Western notions that are not universally shared and were not always present in Western history.

V. Fundamental Informal Lawmaking in American Law

The three illustrations of private lawmaking—the participants in the Berkeley Penthouse Experiment, the islanders of Tristan da Cunha, and the Romani people (Gypsies)—may seem to be entirely unrelated to each other. Yet they show some common characteristics that, because of their universality, may also affect American law. This impact is not readily apparent, but may gain in clarity as I outline the issues. Autonomous private lawmaking, for example, may be closely related to practical considerations, in particular the role of strategy in legal processes. Adjustments in legal theory may be needed to include these aspects of legal practice. The phenomenon of informal lawmaking appears to be fairly obvious at this stage, but what could it mean in actual application?

In all groups discussed unwritten law is layered in prescriptions of a fundamental nature and those of lesser significance. Some basic principles can be observed that take the place of what traditionally is referred to as a constitution. These basic legal notions are meant to be inviolate and not subject to change, except under extreme conditions. For example, tenets of equality in Tristan da Cunha could be temporarily suspended during the volcanic eruption, which occurred in 1961, or in an emergency on the ocean. Prohibitions against intimate body contact among the Roma may be sufficiently relaxed to permit procreation, although some orthodox Romani groups, such as the Kaale in Finland, perceive even marriage as a contaminating concept.

One could view the distinction between fundamental constitutional notions and ordinary law as imaginary and merely theoretical in the contexts of the Berkeley experiment, Tristan da Cunha, and the Romani people, but I disagree. The distinction has profound significance. The presence of deeply held basic legal notions within groups, regardless of their nature and whether one agrees with them, is probably the source of their vitality and gives internal strength and persuasive power to the more derivative autonomous law that they generate. Without these fundamental notions, groups are likely to lack internal cohesion and are bound to disintegrate.

Since the three groups are mere illustrations of what may happen or be present in any group, even within our culture, some lessons can be suggested. To disregard the oral legal traditions that are generated within groups and human associations could have serious consequences. While a judge's decision may be facilitated by a belief that the letter of written law governs, to adhere to this kind of limited view could hurt other participants in the legal process. Lacking awareness of unwritten law could jeopardize the cause of an attorney in any phase of his activities, in counseling, in planning, in negotiating, and in arguing before the court. . . .

Autonomous private law that grows spontaneously within groups and the law of the state are in a symbiotic relationship to each other. Even if at first impression the answer appears to be clear under the law of the state, room for argument nearly always exists to cast doubt on outcomes. . . . To rely on one's interpretation of the law of the state can then be severely damaging. It could narrow the lawyer's perspective and interfere with and limit the choices of legitimate strategies. It could diminish the capacity to appraise the strategies available to the opponent. These choices and appraisals can be made only if unwritten law is also considered.

Quite generally, the significance of strategy in legal analysis has not been fully realized. Private lawmaking has a crucial role in these respects. Strategy is a means to invoke, often in veiled form, the power of oral legal traditions as embodied in autonomous law. It suggests to the judge or jury that rules exist that are not adequately expressed in the law of the state as written. The persuasive power of strategy is due to this factor, but it also raises the question of how a possible conflict between clashing legal traditions is resolved. Issues of due process are of concern because autonomous private law does not necessarily adhere to standards of procedural fairness that are meant to govern the law of the state. Unwritten constitutions have no due process.

I have maintained that in clashes between the law of the state and unwritten legal tradition the latter often tends to prevail. This position is hard to accept by participants in the legal process who have been reared in the belief that the state is an adequate arbiter to resolve human conflict. Furthermore, the impact of unwritten legal tradition is not always clearly noticeable. Numerous legal devices may mask such impact. I will give a few examples.

Private lawmaking may be presented as fact, rather than as law. Value choices that are part of the oral legal tradition of a given culture are likely to be perceived as facts by the members of that culture, or they are strategically submitted as facts by their representatives. Thus rules of relevance and evidence may become applicable to the outcome of disputes, depending on whether the scope of inquiry is perceived in narrow or broad terms. Similarly, canons of interpretation and construction that govern the law of the state openly invite the influx of oral legal tradition. What actually happens is a fusion of the law of the state and unwritten legal tradition. The United States Constitution and the official laws that are promulgated under it would be anemic and could lose efficacy, but for the influx and support of unwritten private law. Participants in legal processes and scholars may think that traditional analyses of written law mandate specific outcomes of legal controversies, while their perception of written law is colored by unwritten legal traditions of which they are not necessarily fully aware. . . .

VI. Conclusion

Legal theory faces a difficult task. Is it the task of legal scholarship to engage in a pursuit of truth regardless of consequences, or is one to focus on appellate case law that, in its cumulative effect, is often more aspirational than real? There may not be a clear answer to this question, because both approaches have validity. The law of the state, as a basis of legal insight, has legitimate functions in establishing ideals and the means to render peace, if these ideals have not been met. For these purposes it does not really matter, whether the reasoning in individual cases is adequate or realistic.

As perceived from the perspective of the state, an unlimited quest for truth could have undesirable consequences, ultimately resulting in cynicism. It may lead to views, in accordance with the pre-Socratic sophists that, since no final truth can ever be established with certainty, only the power of persuasion remains. Creating an awareness of a multitude of autonomous legal systems within the realm of American law, some may argue, may lead to endless rhetoric and anarchy. The agencies of the state, including the courts, may be disinclined to acknowledge any claims of autonomy.

In application of this line of reasoning, the State of California could hardly be expected to recognize the internally generated laws of the Berkeley Penthouse Experiment. The Colonial Government of Great Britain will assume the power of its jurisdiction and the validity of English common law in Tristan da Cunha, regardless of the laws according to which the islanders actually govern themselves. The dominant countries are likely to attempt to impose their state powers on the Romani people, although realistically they may not be able to enforce every aspect of written state law. Even though any of these assertions of state power cannot be expected to be abandoned, legal scholarship traditionally has demonstrated that law is infinitely more complex than the law of the state, as promulgated by its legislators, judges, and administrators, makes it appear.

Regardless of one's feelings in these matters, the unwritten legal traditions, especially in their basic constitutional aspects, are essentially outside the control of both the state and of scholarship. Individual groups themselves have little control over their generation of law and mostly are not even conscious of this process. On the other hand, those persons who are aware of autonomous lawmaking around them have an advantage, not because they can affect unwritten law, but because they can more readily perceive strategic possibilities. Still, there is power in ignorance too because those who deny the existence of unwritten autonomous law or are unaware of it are bound to become its unwitting proponents. Thus' the substance of autonomous lawmaking is unaffected by state power and is also essentially unaffected by those with insight into how it operates.

Dawkins v. Antrobus
17 Ch. D. 615 (Ct. App. 1879)

The action in this case was brought by Colonel *Dawkins* against the trustees and committee of the *Travellers' Club,* claiming a declaration that a resolution purporting to expel him from the club was invalid, and an injunction restraining the Defendants from excluding the Plaintiff from the club, and from interfering with him in the enjoyment of the use of the buildings and property of the club.

The Plaintiff was elected a member of the club in the year 1859.

Among the rules of the club at the time when the Plaintiff joined it were the following:

"13. That the regulations for dinner, refreshment, and other details of conducting the establishment be vested in the committee, but that any alteration in the number of members or standing rules of the club be decided by a majority at a general meeting at which at least forty members must be present, to be summoned by the committee for that purpose, giving at least fourteen days' notice.

"25. That at all general meetings of the club the votes of the meeting shall be first taken by show of hands or division, provided there be forty members present, the majority to decide; but if a ballot be demanded by six members present, the proposition in debate shall be postponed until the following day, when the ballot shall be taken between the hours of three and six o'clock, or if forty members shall not be present, the proposition shall be decided the same day by ballot between the time of the adjournment of the members and six o'clock. In all cases of ballot, two thirds of the members voting to decide.

"27. That no proposition affecting the general interests of the club shall be brought forward at any general meeting without a week's notice in writing signed by six members and communicated to the secretary, and placed by him in the room."

On the 31st of May, 1875, a rule was passed at a general meeting of the club providing for the expulsion of members, in nearly the same terms as those of rule 26, hereinafter mentioned, but doubts having arisen whether the requisite number of forty members were present at the meeting, another general meeting was held on the 16th of August, 1877, in the manner prescribed by the 13th rule, at which the following rule was passed by the requisite majority, more than forty members being present:

"Rule 26. In case the conduct of any member, either in or out of the clubhouse, shall in the opinion of the committee, or of any twenty members of the club, who shall certify the same in writing, be injurious to the character and interests of the club, the committee shall be empowered (if they deem it expedient) to recommend such member to resign, and if the member so recommended shall not comply within a month from the date of such communication being addressed to him, the committee shall then call a general meeting, and if a majority of two-thirds of that meeting agree by ballot to the expulsion of such member, his name shall be erased from the list, and he shall forfeit all right or claim upon the property of the club, but his subscription for the current year shall be returned to him."

The rules were afterwards revised by a committee, and the rules as revised were submitted to a special general meeting on the 24th of June, 1878, at which forty members were present, and, with slight verbal amendments, were carried unanimously. Rule 26 was one of the rules as revised, and no exception had been taken to it by the Plaintiff or any other member of the club.

The circumstances under which the Plaintiff was expelled were shortly as follows: The Plaintiff caused to be printed and circulated a pamphlet entitled "A Farce and a Villainy—Heads I Win, Tails you Lose," in which the conduct of Lieutenant-General *Stephenson,* who was also a member of the club, was severely reflected on. A copy of this pamphlet was inclosed in a wrapper on the outside of which was printed "Dishonourable Conduct of Colonel (now Lieutenant-General) *Stephenson,*" and was sent by the Plaintiff by the post to Lieutenant-General *Stephenson,* at his official address, the Guards' Orderly Room at the Horse Guards.

This having been brought to the notice of the committee of the club, they directed a letter to be written to the Plaintiff by the secretary, asking him whether an envelope with the printed heading "Dishonourable Conduct of Colonel (now Lieutenant-General) *Stephenson,*" containing a printed paper headed "A Farce and a Villainy—Heads I Win, Tails you Lose," was sent by him or by his direction or authority.

On the 21st of January, 1879, the Plaintiff replied as follows: "I beg to acknowledge the receipt of your letter, dated the 17th of January, written by the direction of the committee of the Travellers' Club. I request you to inform the committee that I decline to give any reply whatever to the question contained therein."

On the 24th of January the secretary wrote to the Plaintiff a letter, in which, after referring to the previous correspondence, he said, "The committee, therefore, in the absence of any disavowal on your part, hold you responsible for having sent the cover and its contents. In these circumstances it becomes the duty of the committee to consider the case as it now stands before them, and after doing so with their best care and attention, they are of the opinion that in sending to a member of the club a cover with the offensive superscription set out in my former letter, and containing a printed paper or pamphlet in which disgraceful charges are made against the honour and character of certain members of the club, your conduct has been injurious to the character and interests of the club, and that the case is one which may be dealt with under the 26th rule of the club. But the committee, before taking further steps in the matter, would be glad to hear whether you have any explanation to offer on the subject. The committee wish you distinctly to understand that the matter before them only refers to the cover directed to Lieutenant-General *Stephenson,* and its inclosure, they have nothing to do with any previous disagreement between yourself and the military authorities."

On the 1st of February, 1879, the Plaintiff wrote to the secretary as follows:

"Respecting your letter of January 24th, I request you to inform the committee that I am not responsible to them in any such matters as those of which they make mention, and that if Lieutenant-General *Stephenson* or any other member of the *Travellers' Club* considers himself wronged by anybody, laws of honour direct that he should himself take notice of it, and also that those who submit to charges which in the name of the committee you describe as being against their honour and character and as involving disgrace to them, are those who are required to give an account of their conduct. And I request you to further inform the committee that under any circumstances rule 26 was never intended to settle personal disputes, nor to enable members of the *Travellers' Club* to transfer the guardianship of their honour to the committee."

On the 14th of February the secretary wrote to the Plaintiff a letter, in which he said, "I am desired to inform you that as you have failed to give any satisfactory explanation of your conduct in answer to the request of the committee, the committee deem it their duty, in accordance with the provisions of rule No. 26, to recommend you to resign your membership of the *Travellers' Club*."

The Plaintiff not having resigned, notice was given that at a general meeting to be held on the 31st of March, 1879, it would be proposed, on behalf of the committee, to expel the Plaintiff from the club. The notice was placed in the morning-room of the club, and a copy was sent to the Plaintiff. At the meeting the resolution for expelling the Plaintiff was carried by the requisite majority, the votes being taken by ballot, and the number being 108 in favour of the resolution, and 36 against it.

The resolution as entered in the minute book of the club was as follows:

"The recommendation of the committee that Lieutenant-Colonel *Dawkins* should resign his membership not having been complied with, it was moved on behalf of the committee that Colonel *Dawkins* be expelled from the club."

The minute then proceeded as follows:

"A short discussion took place, and the resolution was opposed by two or three of the speakers. A ballot was then had, and 108 appeared for the resolution and 36 against it. The resolution was therefore declared to be carried by the requisite majority in accordance with Rule 26."

On the 2nd of April, 1879, a cheque for the Plaintiff's subscription for the year 1879 was sent to the Plaintiff's bankers, but it was returned by the bankers under his instructions.

The Plaintiff alleged in his statement of claim that the resolution had been come to in an unfair, capricious, and arbitrary manner, and not *bona fide;* that notice convening the meeting at which it was carried had not been properly given; that the 26th rule had not been properly added to the rules of the club, and was not binding on the members; and he submitted that he had not been guilty of any conduct injurious to the character and interests of the Club. These charges were denied by the Defendants.

As evidence of unfairness the Plaintiff relied on the fact that of the seventeen members of the committee one was serving, and six had served, in the Brigade of Guards then under General *Stephenson's* command, and four others were serving or had served in the army; and the Plaintiff alleged that the said eleven members were liable to be influenced by General *Stephenson* to be hostile to the Plaintiff.

The action came on for trial before the Masters of the Rolls on the 23rd of June, 1879.

[The Master of the Rolls (Lord Jessel) dismissed the action. Noting that "Englishmen, and especially English gentlemen . . . are always lovers of fair play," he found that the club's rules were valid and binding on Colonel Dawkins and that the decision of the club under the rules could not be revised by a court in the absence of proof of malice or bad faith. From this decision the Plaintiff appealed.]

Brett, L.J.:

I think we ought to take great care that this Court does not by successive decisions usurp an authority in these cases for which there is no colour in point of law. In my opinion there is some danger that the Courts will undertake to act as Courts of Appeal against the decisions of members of clubs, whereas the Court has no right or authority whatever to sit in appeal upon them at all. The only question which a Court can properly consider is whether the members of the club, under such circumstances, have acted *ultra vires* or not, and it seems to me the only questions which a Court can properly entertain for that purpose are, whether anything has been done which is contrary to natural justice, although it is within the rules of the club—in other words, whether the rules of the club are contrary to natural justice; secondly, whether a person who has not condoned the departure from them has been acted against contrary to the rules of the club; and thirdly, whether the decision of the club has been come to *bona fide* or not. Unless one of those charges can be made out by those who come before the Court, the Court has no power to interfere with what has been done. It seems to me the only question in the present case is upon the last matter, viz., whether what has been done is *bona fide*.

The Court has no right, in my opinion, to consider whether what was done was right or not, or, even as a substantive question, whether what was decided was reasonable or not. The only question is, whether it was done *bona fide*. Now, it is true that an element, in considering whether a matter had been done in good faith, is the question whether what has been done is really beyond all reason. If that were so it would be evidence of want of good faith; but even where that exists, it is not a necessary conclusion that there has been a want of good faith, for, even after having come to the conclusion that a decision was wholly unreasonable, one might be convinced *aliunde* that nevertheless there was no malice— that what was done was done in good faith. Therefore the mere proof that it was contrary to reason is no sufficient ground for the interference of the Court. It is like the case of a malicious prosecution, where if there is a want of reasonable and probable cause, that is evidence to go to the jury to support the other necessary allegation that there was malice in fact, but then the jury are told, "even though there was a want of reasonable and probable cause, you must consider and decide for yourselves whether, besides that, there was malice in fact." Unless they find there was also malice in fact in such cases the propositions necessary for them to affirm are not made out. So, in this case, I wish to repeat, even though one were of opinion that the decision was wholly beyond reason, yet in such a case as this, considering the circumstances which are in evidence, and the persons against whom the charge is made, and the absolute absence of any evidence of indirect motive—even if I thought the decisions were absolutely unreasonable—I should have declined to find the decision was contrary to good faith, and should therefore have been of opinion, even though the decision were unreasonable, that there was no ground for the interference of the Court.

The first question then is whether there was anything contrary to natural justice. If a decision was come to depriving a gentleman of his position on such a charge as must be made out here, namely, that he has been guilty of conduct injurious to the character and interests of the club, in my opinion there would be a denial of natural justice if a decision was come to without his having an opportunity of being heard.

Now, in my opinion, the charge made against the Plaintiff from beginning to end was the sending the envelope through the public post to an officer in command of a regiment, on the outside of which envelope was "Dishonourable Conduct of General *Stephenson.*" That was the charge. It is true that the fact of the pamphlet being inside was mentioned, but in this case that was not the material charge; that might have been a charge in other cases, and a very fair charge, in my opinion; but in this case the substance of the charge from beginning to end was the sending the envelope. In the first letter he is informed, "We are told you have sent an envelope; we want you to answer whether that is true or not?" The gentleman will not answer, but says, "I request you to inform the committee that I decline to give any reply." They do not take that as conclusive, but they enter upon the inquiry. They have a letter in his own handwriting before them; they do that which was lawful and legitimate—they compare that with the writing on the envelope to General *Stephenson,* and they say, "We come to the conclusion it is your handwriting." They do more. They then send a letter to Colonel *Dawkins* to say we have come to a conclusion, *prima facie* no doubt, but they say having done this we ask you "Will you give any explanation?" Then he says "I deny your jurisdiction to ask me." That is telling them he will not be a party to their inquiry. It is refusing to give any explanation. It is a direct refusal to go before them, and after that it seems to me he had ample opportunity of explaining that which was in terms told to him to be a charge against him. Therefore in this case there was no want of natural justice. In my opinion he had ample opportunity before the general meeting of giving an explanation, if he chose, as to the sending that envelope, but he declined to give any explanation whatever.

Then it was urged that this matter was not carried out according to the rules, and the first ground taken was that the rule under which it was done was a void rule, because the rule had not been properly passed. I agree with the Master of the Rolls entirely in his reasoning, that the rule was properly passed. But then it was said that this was not done according to the rule, because it was said the rule had been acted upon in a sense of being applied to matters which had occurred before it was passed. The answer is, it was not so applied. It is quite true the rule ought not to be applied to matters which had happened before the rule was passed; but it was not so, it was only applied to a matter which had happened after it was passed, therefore that objection fails.

Then it was said there was malice in fact, and that the Master of the Rolls is wrong in holding there was no malice in fact. That was put upon two grounds. It was suggested—it seems to me wantonly, improperly, and indefensibly—by insinuation, and not by direct assertion, that the gentlemen whose names are here put forward as the Defendants in this case, had allowed themselves to be actuated by subservience to higher authority, and that they had come to a conclusion which they did not believe to be true, because they were dealing with matters affecting authorities at the House Guards. It is said that counsel do not suggest such things unless so instructed. All I can say is, there is not the slightest evidence to support such a suggestion. If such a suggestion had been made before me, where it would have been my duty to consider whether such a question should have been left to a jury, I should have said there is not a semblance of such evidence, and, therefore, those who have instructed counsel to make such a suggestion have done that which is contrary to every known sense of propriety.

Then it was said there is a want of reason in the decision, and that upon that the Master of the Rolls ought to have determined there was malice in fact. It seems to me that raises this proposition—Can the Court say that no reasonable men could have come to the decision that to send such an envelope to an officer in command of his regiment to his orderly room in the barracks where he has command—I care not whether he was a member of the club or not—could not reasonable men come reasonably to the conclusion that to do such a thing as that was scandalous, ungentlemanly, and inconsistent with the character and proper conduct of an officer and a gentleman? In my opinion reasonable men could come to such a conclusion. And if they have come to the conclusion that the conduct of a member of a club has been scandalous, ungentlemanly, and contrary to the proper conduct of an officer and a gentleman, it seems to me he cannot complain of their going further, and saying such conduct is injurious to the character and interests of the club.

Therefore I see no grounds for saying this is not a reasonable decision; but I wish to say further, if I thought it an unreasonable decision I should have declined to come to the conclusion that there was any malice or want of good faith in those who decided it.

United States v. Ballard
322 U.S. 78 (1944)

Mr. Justice Douglas delivered the opinion of the Court.

Respondents were indicted and convicted for using, and conspiring to use, the mails to defraud. . . . The indictment was in twelve counts. It charged a scheme to defraud by organizing and promoting the I Am movement through the use of the mails. The charge was that certain designated corporations were formed, literature distributed and sold, funds solicited, and memberships in the I Am movement sought "by means of false and fraudulent representations, pretenses and promises." The false representations charged were eighteen in number. It is sufficient at this point to say that they covered respondents' alleged religious doctrines or beliefs. They were all set forth in the first count. The following are representative:

> that Guy W. Ballard, now deceased, alias Saint Germain, Jesus, George Washington, and Godfre Ray King, had been selected and thereby designated by the alleged "ascertained masters," Saint Germain, as a divine messenger; and that the words of "ascended masters" and the words of the alleged divine entity, Saint Germain, would be transmitted to mankind through the medium of the said Guy W. Ballard;

> that Guy W. Ballard, during his lifetime, and Edna W. Ballard, and Donald Ballard, by reason of their alleged high spiritual attainments and righteous conduct, had been selected as divine messengers through which the words of the alleged "ascended masters," including the alleged Saint Germain, would be communicated to mankind under the teachings commonly known as the "I Am" movement;

> that Guy W. Ballard, during his lifetime, and Edna W. Ballard and Donald Ballard had, by reason of supernatural attainments, the power to heal persons of ailments and diseases and to make well persons afflicted with any diseases, injuries, or ailments, and did falsely represent to persons intended to be defrauded that the three designated persons had the ability and power to cure persons of those diseases normally classified as curable and also of diseases which are ordinarily classified by the medical profession as being incurable diseases; and did further represent that the three designated persons had in fact cured either by the activity of one, either, or all of said persons, hundreds of persons afflicted with diseases and ailments.

Each of the representations enumerated in the indictment was followed by the charge that respondents "well knew" it was false. After enumerating the eighteen misrepresentations the indictment also alleged:

> At the time of making all of the afore-alleged representations by the defendants, and each of them, the defendants, and each of them, well knew that all of said aforementioned representations were false and untrue and were made with

the intention on the part of the defendants, and each of them, to cheat, wrong, and defraud persons intended to be defrauded, and to obtain from persons intended to be defrauded by the defendants, money, property, and other things of value and to convert the same to the use and the benefit of the defendants, and each of them. . . .

Early in the trial . . . objections were raised to the admission of certain evidence concerning respondents' religious beliefs. The court conferred with counsel in absence of the jury and with the acquiescence of counsel for the United States and for respondents confined the issues on this phase of the case to the question of the good faith of respondents. At the request of counsel for both sides the court advised the jury of that action in the following language:

> The question of the defendants' good faith is the cardinal question in this case. You are not to be concerned with the religious belief of the defendants, or any of them. The jury will be called upon to pass on the question of whether or not the defendants honestly and in good faith believed the representations which are set forth in the indictment, and honestly and in good faith believed that the benefits which they represented would flow from their belief to those who embraced and followed their teachings, or whether these representations were mere pretenses without honest belief on the part of the defendants or any of them, and, were the representations made for the purpose of procuring money, and were the mails used for this purpose.

[T]he Circuit Court of Appeals held that the question of the truth of the representations concerning respondents' religious doctrines or beliefs should have been submitted to the jury. And it remanded the case for a new trial. It may be that the Circuit Court of Appeals took that action because it did not think that the indictment could be properly construed as charging a scheme to defraud by means other than misrepresentations of respondents' religious doctrines or beliefs. Or that court may have concluded that the withdrawal of the issue of the truth of those religious doctrines or beliefs was unwarranted because it resulted in a substantial change in the character of the crime charged. But on whichever basis that court rested its action, we do not agree that the truth or verity of respondents' religious doctrines or beliefs should have been submitted to the jury. Whatever this particular indictment might require, the First Amendment precludes such a course, as the United States seems to concede. "The law knows no heresy, and is committed to the support of no dogma, the establishment of no sect." Watson v. Jones. The First Amendment has a dual aspect. It not only "forestalls compulsion by law of the acceptance of any creed or the practice of any form of worship" but also "safeguards the free exercise of the chosen form of religion." Cantwell v. State of Connecticut. "Thus the Amendment embraces two concepts,—freedom to believe and freedom to act. The first is absolute but, in the nature of things, the second cannot be." Freedom of thought, which includes freedom of religious belief, is basic in a society of free men. West Virginia State Board of Education v. Barnette. It embraces the right to maintain theories of life and of death and of the hereafter which are rank heresy to followers of the orthodox faiths. Heresy trials are foreign to our Constitution. Men may believe what they cannot prove. They may not be put to the proof of their religious doctrines or beliefs. Religious experiences which are as real as life to some may be incomprehensible to others. Yet the fact that they may be beyond the ken of mortals does not mean that they can be made suspect before the law. Many take their gospel from the New Testament. But it would hardly be supposed that they could be tried before a jury charged with the duty of determining whether those teachings contained false representations. The miracles of the New Testament, the Divinity of Christ, life after death, the power of prayer are deep in the religious convictions of many. If one could be sent to jail because a jury in a hostile environment found those teachings false, little indeed would be left of religious freedom. The Fathers of the Constitution were not unaware of the varied and extreme views of religious sects, of the violence of disagreement among them, and of the lack of any one religious creed on which all men would agree. They fashioned a charter of government which envisaged the widest possible toleration of conflicting views. Man's relation to his God was made no concern of the state. He was granted the right to worship as he pleased and to answer to no man for the verity of his religious views. The religious views espoused by respondents might seem incredible, if not preposterous, to most people. But if those doctrines are subject to trial before a jury charged with finding their truth or falsity, then the same can be done with the religious beliefs of any sect. When the triers of fact undertake that task, they enter a forbidden domain. The First Amendment does not select any one group or any one type of religion for preferred treatment. It puts them all in that position. . . . "With man's relations to his Maker and the obligations he may think they impose, and the manner in which an expression shall be made by him of his belief on those subjects, no interference can be permitted, provided always the laws of society, designed to secure its peace and prosperity, and the morals of its people, are not interfered with." See Prince v. Massachusetts. So we conclude that the District Court ruled properly when it withheld from the jury all questions concerning the truth or falsity of the religious beliefs or doctrines of respondents. . . .

Mr. Chief Justice Stone, dissenting:

I am not prepared to say that the constitutional guaranty of freedom of religion affords immunity from criminal prosecution for the fraudulent procurement of money by false statements as to one's religious experiences, more than it renders polygamy or libel immune from criminal prosecution. See Chaplinsky v. New Hampshire; cf. Near v. Minnesota. I cannot say that freedom of thought and worship includes freedom to procure money by making knowingly false statements about one's religious experiences. To go no further, if it were shown that a defendant in this case had asserted as a part of the alleged fraudulent scheme, that he had physically shaken hands with St. Germain in San Francisco on a day named, or that, as the indictment here alleges, by the exertion of his spiritual power he "had in fact cured . . . hundreds of persons afflicted with diseases and ailments," I should not doubt that it would be open to the Government to submit to the jury proof that he had never been in San Francisco and that no such cures had ever been effected. In any event I see no occasion for making any pronouncement on this subject in the present case.

The indictment charges respondents' use of the mails to defraud and a conspiracy to commit that offense by false statements of their religious experiences which had not in fact occurred. But it also charged that the representations were "falsely and fraudulently" made, that respondents "well knew" that these representations were untrue, and that they were made by respondents with the intent to cheat and defraud those to whom they were made. With the assent of the prosecution and the defense the trial judge withdrew from the consideration of the jury the question whether the alleged religious experiences had in fact occurred, but submitted to the jury the single issue whether petitioners honestly believed that they had occurred, with the instruction that if the jury did not so find, then it should return a verdict of guilty. On this issue the jury, on ample evidence that respondents were without belief in the statements which they had made to their victims, found a verdict of guilty. The state of one's mind is a fact as capable of fraudulent misrepresentation as is one's physical condition or the state of his bodily health. . . . There are no exceptions to the charge and no contention that the trial court rejected any relevant evidence which petitioners sought to offer. Since the indictment and the evidence support the conviction, it is irrelevant whether the religious experiences alleged did or did not in fact occur or whether that issue could or could not, for constitutional reasons, have been rightly submitted to the jury. Certainly none of respondents' constitutional rights are violated if they are prosecuted for the fraudulent procurement of money by false representations as to their beliefs, religious or otherwise. . . .

Mr. Justice Jackson, dissenting:

I should say the defendants have done just that for which they are indicted. If I might agree to their conviction without creating a precedent, I cheerfully would do so. I can see in their teachings nothing but humbug, untainted by any trace of truth. But that does not dispose of the constitutional question whether misrepresentation of religious experience or belief is prosecutable; it rather emphasizes the danger of such prosecutions.

The Ballard family claimed miraculous communication with the spirit world and supernatural power to heal the sick. They were brought to trial for mail fraud on an indictment which charged that their representations were false and that they "well knew" they were false. The trial judge, obviously troubled, ruled that the court could not try whether the statements were untrue, but could inquire whether the defendants knew them to be untrue; and, if so, they could be convicted.

I find it difficult to reconcile this conclusion with our traditional religious freedoms.

In the first place, as a matter of either practice or philosophy I do not see how we can separate an issue as to what is believed from considerations as to what is believable. The most convincing proof that one believes his statements is to show that they have been true in his experience. Likewise, that one knowingly falsified is best proved by showing that what he said happened never did happen. How can the Government prove these persons knew something to be false which it cannot prove to be false? If we try religious sincerity severed from religious verity, we isolate the dispute from the very considerations which in common experience provide its most reliable answer.

In the second place, any inquiry into intellectual honesty in religion raises profound psychological problems. William James, who wrote on these matters as a scientist, reminds us that it is not theology and ceremonies which keep religion going. Its vitality is in the religious experiences of many people. "If you ask what these experiences are, they are conversations with the unseen, voices and visions, responses to prayer, changes of heart, deliverances from fear, inflowings of help, assurances of support, whenever certain persons set their own internal attitude in certain appropriate ways." If religious liberty includes, as it must, the right to communicate such experiences to others, it seems to me an impossible task for juries to separate fancied ones from real ones, dreams from happenings, and hallucinations from true clairvoyance. Such experiences, like some tones and colors, have existence for one, but none at all for another. They cannot be verified to the minds of those whose field of consciousness does not include religious insight. When one comes to trial which turns on any aspect of religious belief or representation, unbelievers among his judges are likely not to understand and are almost certain not to believe him.

And then I do not know what degree of skepticism or disbelief in a religious representation amounts to actionable fraud. James points out that "Faith means belief in something concerning which doubt is theoretically possible." Belief in what one may demonstrate to the senses is not faith. All schools of religious thought make enormous assumptions, generally on the basis of revelations authenticated by some sign or miracle. The appeal in such matters is to a very different plane of credulity than is invoked by representations of secular fact in commerce. Some who profess belief in the Bible read literally what others read as allegory or metaphor, as they read Aesop's fables. Religious symbolism is even used by some with the same mental reservations one has in teaching of Santa Claus or Uncle Sam or Easter bunnies or dispassionate judges. It is hard in matters so mystical to say how literally one is bound to believe the doctrine he teaches and even more difficult to say how far it is reliance upon a teacher's literal belief which induces followers to give him money.

There appear to be persons—let us hope not many—who find refreshment and courage in the teachings of the "I Am" cult. If the members of the sect get comfort from the celestial guidance of their "Saint Germain," however doubtful it seems to me, it is hard to say that they do not get what they pay for. Scores of sects flourish in this country by teaching what to me are queer notions. It is plain that there is wide variety in American religious taste. The Ballards are not alone in catering to it with a pretty dubious product.

The chief wrong which false prophets do to their following is not financial. The collections aggregate a tempting total, but individual payments are not ruinous. I doubt if the vigilance of the law is equal to making money stick by over-credulous people. But the real harm is on the mental and spiritual plane. There are those who hunger and thirst after higher values which they feel wanting in their humdrum lives. They live in mental confusion or moral anarchy and seek vaguely for truth and beauty and moral support. When they are deluded and then disillusioned, cynicism and confusion follow. The wrong of these things, as I see it, is not in the money the victims part with half so much as in the mental and spiritual poison they get. But that is precisely the thing the Constitution put beyond the reach of the prosecutor, for the price of freedom of religion or of speech or of the press is that we must put up with, and even pay for, a good deal of rubbish.

Prosecutions of this character easily could degenerate into religious persecution. I do not doubt that religious leaders may be convicted of fraud for making false representations on matters other than faith or experience, as for example if one represents that funds are being used to construct a church when in fact they are being used for personal purposes. But that is not this case, which reaches into wholly dangerous ground. When does less than full belief in a professed credo become actionable fraud if one is soliciting gifts or legacies? Such inquiries may discomfort orthodox as well as unconventional religious teachers, for even the most regular of them are sometimes accused of taking their orthodoxy with a grain of salt.

I would dismiss the indictment and have done with this business of judicially examining other people's faiths.

Stambovsky v. Ackley
169 A.D.2d 254 (1991)

Rubin, Justice.

Plaintiff, to his horror, discovered that the house he had recently contracted to purchase was widely reputed to be possessed by poltergeists, reportedly seen by defendant seller and members of her family on numerous occasions over the last nine years. Plaintiff promptly commenced this action seeking rescission of the contract of sale. . . .

The unusual facts of this case, as disclosed by the record, clearly warrant a grant of equitable relief to the buyer who, as a resident of New York City, cannot be expected to have any familiarity with the folklore of the Village of Nyack. Not being a "local," plaintiff could not readily learn that the home he had contracted to purchase is haunted. Whether the source of the spectral apparitions seen by defendant seller are parapsychic or psychogenic, having reported their presence in both a national publication (*Readers' Digest*) and the local press (in 1977 and 1982, respectively), defendant is estopped to deny their existence and, as a matter of law, the house is haunted. More to the point, however, no divination is required to conclude that it is defendant's promotional efforts in publicizing her close encounters with these spirits which fostered the home's reputation in the community. In 1989, the house was included in a five-home walking tour of Nyack and described in a November 27th newspaper article as "a riverfront Victorian (with ghost)." The impact of the reputation thus created goes to the very essence of the bargain between the parties, greatly impairing both the value of the property and its potential for resale. The extent of this impairment may be presumed for the purpose of reviewing the disposition of this motion to dismiss the cause of action for rescission and represents merely an issue of fact for resolution at trial.

While I agree with Supreme Court that the real estate broker, as agent for the seller, is under no duty to disclose to a potential buyer the phantasmal reputation of the premises and that, in his pursuit of a legal remedy for fraudulent misrepresentation against the seller, plaintiff hasn't a ghost of a chance, I am nevertheless moved by the spirit of equity to allow the buyer to seek rescission of the contract of sale and recovery of his down payment. New York law fails to recognize any remedy for damages incurred as a result of the seller's mere silence, applying instead the strict rule of caveat emptor. Therefore, the theoretical basis for granting relief, even under the extraordinary facts of this case, is elusive if not ephemeral.

"Pity me not but lend thy serious hearing to what I shall unfold" (William Shakespeare, Hamlet, Act I, Scene V [Ghost]).

From the perspective of a person in the position of plaintiff herein, a very practical problem arises with respect to the discovery of a paranormal phenomenon: "Who you gonna' call?" as the title song to the movie "Ghostbusters" asks. Applying the strict rule of caveat emptor to a contract involving a house possessed by poltergeists conjures up visions of a psychic or medium routinely accompanying the structural engineer and Terminix man on an inspection of every home subject to a contract of sale. It portends that the prudent attorney will establish an escrow account lest the subject of the transaction come back to haunt him and his client—or pray that his malpractice insurance coverage extends to supernatural disasters. In the interest of avoiding such untenable consequences, the notion that a haunting is a condition which can and should be ascertained upon reasonable inspection of the premises is a hobgoblin which should be exorcised from the body of legal precedent and laid quietly to rest.

It has been suggested by a leading authority that the ancient rule which holds that mere non-disclosure does not constitute actionable misrepresentation "finds proper application in cases where the fact undisclosed is patent, or the plaintiff has equal opportunities for obtaining information which he may be expected to utilize, or the defendant has no reason to think that he is acting under any misapprehension" (Prosser, Law of Torts § 106, at 696 [4th ed., 1971]). However, with respect to transactions in real estate, New York adheres to the doctrine of caveat emptor and imposes no duty upon the vendor to disclose any information concerning the premises unless there is a confidential or fiduciary relationship between the parties or some conduct on the part of the seller which constitutes "active concealment" (see 17 East 80th Realty Corp. v. 68th Associates [dummy ventilation system constructed by seller]; Haberman v. Greenspan [foundation cracks covered by seller]). Normally, some affirmative misrepresentation (e.g., Tahini Invs., Ltd. v. Bobrowsky [industrial waste on land allegedly used only as farm]; Jansen v. Kelly [land containing valuable minerals allegedly acquired for use as campsite]) or partial disclosure (Junius Constr. Corp. v. Cohen [existence of third unopened street concealed]; Noved Realty Corp. v. A.A.P. Co. [escrow agreements securing lien concealed]) is required to impose upon the seller a duty to communicate undisclosed conditions affecting the premises (contra, Young v. Keith [defective water and sewer systems concealed]).

Caveat emptor is not so all-encompassing a doctrine of common law as to render every act of non-disclosure immune from redress, whether legal or equitable. "In regard to the necessity of giving information which has not been asked, the rule differs somewhat at law and in equity, and while the law courts would permit no recovery of *damages* against a vendor, because of mere concealment of facts *under certain circumstances,* yet if the vendee refused to complete the contract because of the concealment of a material fact on the part of the other, equity would refuse to compel him so to do, because equity only compels the specific performance of a contract which is fair and open, and in regard to which all material matters known to each have been communicated to the other" (Rothmiller v. Stein [emphasis added]). Even as a principle of law, long before exceptions were embodied in statute law, the doctrine was held inapplicable to contagion among animals, adulteration of food, and insolvency of a maker of a promissory note and of a tenant substituted for another under a lease. Common law is not moribund. *Ex facto jus oritur* (law arises out of facts). Where fairness and common sense dictate that an exception should be created, the evolution of the law should not be stifled by rigid application of a legal maxim.

The doctrine of caveat emptor requires that a buyer act prudently to assess the fitness and value of his purchase and operates to bar the purchaser who fails to exercise due care from seeking the equitable remedy of rescission. For the purposes of the instant motion to dismiss the action pursuant to CPLR 3211(a)(7), plaintiff is entitled to every favorable inference which may reasonably be drawn from the pleadings, specifically, in this instance, that he met his obligation to conduct an inspection of the premises and a search of available public records with respect to title. It should be apparent, however, that the most meticulous inspection and the search would not reveal the presence of poltergeists at the premises or unearth the property's ghoulish reputation in the community. Therefore, there is no sound policy reason to deny plaintiff relief for failing to discover a state of affairs which the most prudent purchaser would not be expected to even contemplate.

The case law in this jurisdiction dealing with the duty of a vendor of real property to disclose information to the buyer is distinguishable from the matter under review. The most salient distinction is that existing cases invariably deal with the physical condition of the premises (e.g., London v. Courduff [use as a landfill]; Perin v. Mardine Realty Co. [sewer line crossing adjoining property without owner's consent]), defects in title, liens against the property, expenses or income and other factors affecting its operation. No case has been brought to this court's attention in which the property value was impaired as the result of the reputation created by information disseminated to the public by the seller (or, for that matter, as a result of possession by poltergeists).

Where a condition which has been created by the seller materially impairs the value of the contract and is peculiarly within the knowledge of the seller or unlikely to be discovered by a prudent purchaser exercising due care with respect to the subject transaction, nondisclosure constitutes a basis for rescission as a matter of equity. Any other outcome places upon the buyer not merely the obligation to exercise care in his purchase but rather to be omniscient with respect to any fact which may affect the bargain. No practical purpose is served by imposing such a burden upon a purchaser. To the contrary, it encourages predatory business practice and offends the principle that equity will suffer no wrong to be without a remedy.

Defendant's contention that the contract of sale, particularly the merger or "as is" clause, bars recovery of the buyer's deposit is unavailing. Even an express disclaimer will not be given effect where the facts are peculiarly within the knowledge of the party invoking it. Moreover, a fair reading of the merger clause reveals that it expressly disclaims only representations made with respect to the physical condition of the premises and merely makes general reference to representations concerning "any other matter or things affecting or relating to the aforesaid premises." As broad as this language may be, a reasonable interpretation is that its effect is limited to tangible or physical matters and does not extend to paranormal phenomena. Finally, if the language of the contract is to be construed as broadly as defendant urges to encompass the presence of poltergeists in the house, it cannot be said that she has delivered the premises "vacant" in accordance with her obligation under the provisions of the contract rider.

To the extent New York law may be said to require something more than "mere concealment" to apply even the equitable remedy of rescission, the case of Junius Construction Corporation v. Cohen, while not precisely on point, provides some guidance. In that case, the seller disclosed that an official map indicated two as yet unopened streets which were planned for construction at the edges of the parcel. What was not disclosed was that the same map indicated a third street which, if opened, would divide the plot in half. The court held that, while the seller was under no duty to mention the planned streets at all, having undertaken to disclose two of them, he was obliged to reveal the third.

In the case at bar, defendant seller deliberately fostered the public belief that her home was possessed. Having undertaken to inform the public at large, to whom she has no legal relationship, about the supernatural occurrences on her property, she may be said to owe no less a duty to her contract vendee. It has been remarked that the occasional modern cases which permit a seller to take unfair advantage of a buyer's ignorance so long as he is not actively misled are "singularly unappetizing" (Prosser, Law of Torts § 106, at 696 [4th ed. 1971]). Where, as here, the seller not only takes unfair advantage of the buyer's ignorance but has created and perpetuated a condition about which he is unlikely to even inquire, enforcement of the contract (in whole or in part) is offensive to the court's sense of equity. Application of the remedy of rescission, within the bounds of the narrow exception to the doctrine of caveat emptor set forth herein, is entirely appropriate to relieve the unwitting purchaser from the consequences of a most unnatural bargain. . . .

Smith, Justice (dissenting).
I would affirm the dismissal of the complaint by the motion court.
Plaintiff seeks to rescind his contract to purchase defendant Ackley's residential property and recover his down payment. Plaintiff alleges that Ackley and her real estate broker, defendant Ellis Realty, made material misrepresentations of the property in that they failed to disclose that Ackley believed that the house was haunted by poltergeists. Moreover, Ackley shared this belief with her community and the general public through articles published in *Reader's Digest* (1977) and the local newspaper (1982). In November 1989, approximately two months after the parties entered into the contract of sale but subsequent to the scheduled October 2, 1989 closing, the house was included in a five-house walking tour and again described in the local newspaper as being haunted.

Prior to closing, plaintiff learned of this reputation and unsuccessfully sought to rescind the $650,000 contract of sale and obtain return of his $32,500 down payment without resort to litigation. The plaintiff then commenced this action for that relief and alleged that he would not have entered into the contract had he been so advised and that as a result of the alleged poltergeist activity, the market value and resaleability of the property was greatly diminished. Defendant Ackley has counterclaimed for specific performance.

"It is settled law in New York that the seller of real property is under no duty to speak when the parties deal at arm's length. The mere silence of the seller, without some act or conduct which deceived the purchaser, does not amount to a concealment that is actionable as a fraud. The buyer has the duty to satisfy himself as to the quality of his bargain pursuant to the doctrine of caveat emptor, which in New York State still applies to real estate transactions." London v. Courduff.

The parties herein were represented by counsel and dealt at arm's length. This is evidenced by the contract of sale which, *inter alia,* contained various riders and a specific provision that all prior understandings and agreements between the parties were merged into the contract, that the contract completely expressed their full agreement and that neither had relied upon any statement by anyone else not set forth in the contract. There is no allegation that defendants, by some specific act, other than the failure to speak, deceived the plaintiff. Nevertheless, a cause of action may be sufficiently stated where there is a confidential or fiduciary relationship creating a duty to disclose and there was a failure to disclose a material fact, calculated to induce a false belief. However, plaintiff herein has not alleged and there is no basis for concluding that a confidential or fiduciary relationship existed between these parties to an arm's length transaction such as to give rise to a duty to disclose. In addition, there is no allegation that defendants thwarted plaintiff's efforts to fulfill his responsibilities fixed by the doctrine of caveat emptor. See London v. Courduff.

Finally, if the doctrine of caveat emptor is to be discarded, it should be for a reason more substantive than a poltergeist. The existence of a poltergeist is no more binding upon the defendants than it is upon this court.

Based upon the foregoing, the motion court properly dismissed the complaint.

Notes and Questions

1. Suppose the legislature of your state enacted a law adopting the twelve points of the Boy Scout Law and making them generally applicable to all citizens. What objections might you have?

2. In a companion case to *Randall,* the California Supreme Court unanimously affirmed the Boy Scouts' right to exclude homosexual members. The court noted that:

> Scouts meet regularly in small groups (often in private homes) that are intended to foster close friendship, trust and loyalty, and scouts are required to participate in a variety of activities, ceremonies, and rituals that are designed to teach the moral principles to which the organization subscribes. . . . [T]he Boy Scouts is an expressive social organization whose primary function is the inculcation of values in its youth members, and whose small social-group structure and activities are not comparable to those of a traditional place of public accommodation or amusement.

Curran v. Mt. Diablo Council of the Boy Scouts of America.

3. In a concurring opinion in the *Curran* case, Justice Kennard asked:

> Could the NAACP be compelled to accept as a member a Ku Klux Klansman? Could B'nai B'rith be required to admit an anti-Semite?

Did the New Jersey Supreme Court satisfactorily address these issues when it came to the exact opposite conclusion (also by a unanimous vote) in the *Dale* case?

4. Should the Boy Scouts be allowed to discriminate against potential members on the basis of race? Or gender?

5. Would you want to live under "a centralized government that does not tolerate parties of differing opinion and that exercises dictatorial control over many aspects of life"? The Random House Dictionary of the English Language (2d ed. 1987) (defining "totalitarian"). In other words, what limits (if any) would you place on the state's power to prohibit "private" association and discrimination?

6. If the New Jersey decision in the *Dale* case is upheld in the U.S. Supreme Court, what would you advise the Boy Scouts to do?

7. When is the legal system on strongest ground in regulating or intervening in the affairs of a private association? What does the *Dawkins* case suggest?

8. Suppose you belonged to a club whose rules called for the sacrificial killing of selected club members. Should the legal system intervene?

9. Should the legal system take a position on whether or not ghosts exist? Should your analysis be the same as in the previous question?

Suggestions For Further Reading

K.N. Llewellyn & E. Adamson Hoebel, The Cheyenne Way, chs. 1-2 (1941)

Bronislaw Malinowski, Crime and Custom in Savage Society, pt. 1 (1932)

Samuel D. Warren & Louis D. Brandeis, The Right to Privacy, 4 Harvard Law Review 193 (1890)

Chapter 11
Quasi-Legal Governance

Mercury Bay Boating Club v. San Diego Yacht Club
150 A.D.2d 82 (1989)

Sullivan, Justice.

This appeal is from an order which, on the basis of a determination that the defense of the America's Cup in a catamaran violated the provisions of the Deed of Gift of the America's Cup, set aside the results of the 1988 America's Cup races between the yachts of the San Diego Yacht Club and Mercury Bay Boating Club, declared Mercury Bay's challenging yacht, *New Zealand,* to be the winner of those races, and ordered San Diego, as trustee of the America's Cup, to forfeit the Cup to Mercury Bay.

The America's Cup, first won by the yacht *America* in a race around the Isle of Wight on August 22, 1851, is the corpus of a charitable trust created in the 19th century under the laws of New York. Originally donated on July 8, 1857 by *America's* six owners to the New York Yacht Club to be held in trust "as a perpetual challenge cup for friendly competition between foreign countries," the Cup was twice returned to George L. Schuyler, the sole surviving donor, after questions arose regarding the terms of the trust. The Cup was reconveyed to New York for the final time pursuant to a Deed of Gift executed on October 24, 1887 by Schuyler, as donor, and New York, as donee. Under the terms of the Deed, which has been amended by orders of the Supreme Court in 1956 and 1985, the holder of the Cup acts as sole trustee of the charitable trust, and is succeeded by whoever successfully challenges the trustee in a race for the Cup. New York served as trustee until 1983, when its defender, *Liberty,* was defeated by *Australia II,* the entry of the Royal Perth Yacht Club. Royal Perth, as successor trustee, then lost the Cup in 1987 to San Diego's *Stars & Stripes '87.*

The Deed of Gift specifies the permissible length for the competing vessels and outlines the timing and supporting documents necessary for a valid challenge. The only constraints on boat design are set forth in the Deed, which states that a challenger is entitled to a match against any "yacht or vessel," "propelled by sails only," which, if single-masted, must measure between forty-four and ninety feet on the load water-line. The challenger may determine the dimensions of its boat within this specified size range, as well as the time of the race, on condition that it provide at least ten months' notice to the defender. Races must be conducted between May 1 and November 1 in the Northern Hemisphere, and between November 1 and May 1 in the Southern Hemisphere.

The Deed of Gift also provides that America's Cup races shall be sailed under the rules of the club holding the Cup. San Diego follows the rules of yacht racing promulgated by the International Yacht Racing Union (IYRU). Under the IYRU rules, an International Jury, whose decisions are final, referees the match and decides all protests.

The Deed of Gift leaves all other details for resolution by the competitors:

> The Club challenging for the Cup and the Club holding the same may, by mutual consent, make any arrangement satisfactory to both as to the dates, courses, number of trials, rules and sailing regulations, and any and all other conditions of the match, in which case also the ten months' notice provision may be waived.

By this "mutual consent" provision, the Deed envisions the competitors' agreement on the overwhelming number of issues not controlled by the literal terms of the trust instrument. Failing such agreement, however, the Deed of Gift provides explicitly that the defender shall set the venue and the courses for the race.

The Deed of Gift is silent as to the type of boat to be used by the defender, stating only that "[t]he challenged Club shall not be required to name its representative vessel until at a time agreed upon for the start, but the vessel when named must compete in all the races, and each of such races must be completed within seven hours." Although both monohulls and multihulls were in existence at the time of its final revision in 1887, the Deed of Gift does not explicitly bar the use of a multihulled vessel or require the trustee to defend in a vessel having the same number of hulls as the challenger. Nor is there any express mandate that the competing vessels be identical or even substantially similar.

Nevertheless, until 1988, monohulls have been utilized throughout the history of the America's Cup competition since all the races were conducted under the "mutual consent" provision of the Deed of Gift. Between 1857 and 1937, New York successfully defended the America's Cup sixteen times, twice against Canadian challengers in the 1870's, and on the other fourteen occasions against challengers from British yacht clubs. In each instance, only a single challenger competed.

In the twenty years after the 1937 race there was little interest in the America's Cup, and challenges were not forthcoming. The large ocean-going yachts, known as "J-boats," which were used in the competition prior to World War II, had become too expensive to maintain, and were no longer being built. At that time, the Deed of Gift permitted only the use of boats measuring between 65 and 90 feet on the load water-line. In 1956, in an attempt to revive interest in the competition, New York successfully petitioned the court and obtained an amendment of the Deed lowering the minimum water-line length from 65 to 44 feet, so that the competition could be conducted in yachts of the International 12-Meter Class, and deleting the requirement, which had put foreign challengers at a disadvantage, that the challenger sail to the site of the match "on its own bottom." In its 1956 petition, New York argued that the greatly increased cost of both building a large racing yacht and maintaining and racing it were circumstances not anticipated by the grantor of the trust.

The first post-war match was sailed in 1958. With the exception of the 1988 match, every match since World War II has been conducted in 12-Meter yachts. As the event grew more successful and generated greater public awareness, an increasing number of challengers expressed interest in competing for the Cup.

The Deed of Gift provides that "when a challenge from a Club fulfilling all the conditions required by this instrument has been received, no other challenge can be considered until the pending event has been decided." Since this provision allows the first challenger to exclude all others, a mechanism which would accommodate multiple challengers was sought. On December 7, 1962, New York issued a memorandum stating that in the event it successfully defended the Cup in 1964, and, within thirty days, received more than one challenge for the next match, it would regard the challenges as "received simultaneously" and "after due consideration [would] determine which to accept"; that it expected to defend the Cup in 12-Meter yachts (and would give two years' notice of a change in class); and that it believed that "it would be in the best interest of the sport and of the competition for the America's Cup if such matches were not held more frequently than once every three years." New York issued a similar memorandum shortly before each subsequent defense.

Within thirty days of the conclusion of the 1967 match, New York received bids from challengers, all of whom agreed to an elimination series of races, with the winner earning the right to challenge New York for the Cup. Similar procedures were followed for each America's Cup match until 1988. Experience has shown that the elimination series enhances the quality of the competition and increases the likelihood that the best qualified challenger will win the right to sail a match for the Cup. Moreover, as the number of participants has increased with each match, it has attracted a greater level of interest around the world.

In the 1983 competition, seven foreign yacht clubs vied for the right to sail a match for the Cup and, for the first time in 132 years of competition, a challenger succeeded in wresting the Cup from New York. In late 1986, in Fremantle, Western Australia, thirteen yacht clubs representing six nations competed to determine which would challenge Royal Perth for the Cup. In the finals, *Stars & Stripes '87,* skippered by Dennis Conner and sailing under the burgee of San Diego, beat Royal Perth's defender *Kookaburra III* four races to none.

Even before the culmination of its 1987 America's Cup campaign, San Diego had intended, if successful, to conduct its first defense of the Cup in 1990 or 1991 in 12-Meter yachts, and in the familiar and traditional multiple-challenger format. Yacht clubs all around the world began preparations to compete in that event. In the midst of these preparations, Mercury Bay, by letter dated July 15, 1987, issued a notice of challenge to San Diego demanding a match less than a year later, and disclosing the dimensions of a challenging yacht of a size, 90 feet on the load water-line, that had not been built in fifty years. As noted previously, this length was the largest permitted under the Deed of Gift. Most foreign yacht clubs would be unable to compete on the terms demanded by Mercury Bay inasmuch as they were already preparing for a match in 12-Meter yachts. San Diego announced that the terms of challenge were unacceptable.

On September 2, 1987, Mercury Bay filed suit, seeking a declaration of the validity of its challenge, and for a preliminary injunction prohibiting San Diego from considering any other challenges before its own. Several days later, San Diego, as trustee of the America's Cup, commenced a second action, seeking an interpretation or amendment of the Deed of Gift to authorize a continuation of the uniform practices of the only two prior trustees. Specifically, San Diego urged the court to permit an elimination series so as to further, to the greatest extent possible, the donor's stated purpose of fostering "friendly competition between foreign countries." It was alleged that Mercury Bay sought to exclude challengers from at least nine other countries, and "to return the competition to an age when it could only be enjoyed by that handful of individuals with sufficient means to journey to the site of the competition." In opposing San Diego's application, Mercury Bay insisted that the Deed of Gift was clear and unambiguous and should be enforced according to the plain meaning of its literal terms. . . .

The court rejected San Diego's application to interpret or amend the Deed of Gift and granted the motion for a preliminary injunction, declaring that Mercury Bay's notice of challenge was valid, and holding that San Diego's options were to "accept the challenge, forfeit the cup, or negotiate agreeable terms with the challenger."

Both parties thereafter made various proposals under the mutual consent clause of the Deed, but to no avail, and San Diego proceeded with its preparations for a defense of the Cup. Although not required to name its boat until the start of the first race, in late January 1988 San Diego announced its decision to race in a multihull yacht, the dimensions of which would fall within the parameters permitted by the Deed of Gift, although it would be smaller than Mercury Bay's crew-ballasted, fin-keel monohull.

Mercury Bay sought to hold San Diego in contempt, arguing that its announced intention to meet Mercury Bay's challenge in a catamaran would deny Mercury Bay the "match" to which it was entitled under the Deed of Gift and therefore violate the court's earlier order. Mercury Bay claimed that the Deed's use of the word "match" required the defending vessel to be "like or similar" to the challenging vessel. San Diego responded that the court's prior decision had construed the Deed literally, that nothing in the Deed required similarity of vessels, and that the degree of similarity demanded by Mercury Bay was available only by consent.

By decision dated July 25, 1988, the court denied Mercury Bay's motion, holding that "[n]either this court's order, nor the terms of the deed of gift incorporated therein, so unequivocally state that multihulled boats are prohibited or that a defender must [meet] the challenger in a 'like or similar' yacht, so as to constitute contempt by San Diego if it chooses to defend in such a boat." While stating that "[n]othing in this decision should be interpreted as indicating that multihulled boats are either permitted or barred under the America's Cup deed of gift," the court concluded that the "time has come for the sailors to be permitted to participate in the America's Cup." It directed the parties "to proceed with the races and to reserve their protests, if any, until after completion of the America's Cup races." San Diego and Mercury Bay thereafter sailed a match for the America's Cup in early September 1988. San Diego's defending catamaran *Stars & Stripes* defeated Mercury Bay's monohull *New Zealand* two races to none.

Mercury Bay, arguing that San Diego's defense of the America's Cup in a multihull yacht violated the Deed of Gift and the court's prior order, moved to set aside the results of the races, and have Mercury Bay declared the winner, and for an order directing that the Cup be turned over to it. San Diego cross-moved for a declaration that its defense complied with the Deed and the court's order. Both motions addressed whether, in the absence of mutual consent, the Deed of Gift requires the trustee to defend the America's Cup in a vessel "like or similar" to the challenging vessel. Finding that San Diego had attempted "to retain the Cup at all costs so that it could host a competition on its own terms," thereby violating "the spirit of the Deed," the court held that "San Diego's defense of the America's Cup in a catamaran against Mercury Bay's monohull challenge clearly deviated from the intent of the donor" that the competing vessels be "somewhat evenly matched." San Diego's yacht was disqualified, Mercury Bay's challenger declared to be the winner of the two races, and San Diego directed to assign and transfer the America's Cup, and thus the trusteeship, to Mercury Bay. San Diego and the Attorney General appeal. We reverse. . . .

In deciding what kind of yacht or vessel to build to defend against Mercury Bay's challenge, San Diego had to rely on the written terms of the Deed of Gift, which, in the absence of mutual consent, provides a minimally restrictive class rule. In fact, Mercury Bay stated that it desired to compete in a larger yacht "utilizing modern technology outside class or rating rules."

Thus, Mercury Bay itself demanded an unrestricted design rule, without any agreement on a class or rating rule, or any system for handicapping or equalizing the competitors beyond the water-line length limitations expressly set forth in the Deed of Gift. In its first decision, on November 25, 1987, the court agreed that the Deed contained no other limitations. "Other than the size range for competing boats," it noted, "the deed of gift makes no design constraints other than that centerboards and sliding keels shall always be permitted. . . ." In its July 25, 1988 decision rejecting Mercury Bay's contempt motion, the court gave an additional indication of its view that there was no "somewhat evenly matched" rule either stated in the Deed or readily apparent from its terms. The court further stated that Mercury Bay's argument that a race between a monohull and a multihull is inherently unfair was "fundamentally shaken" by the evidence of a history of mixed racing.

Furthermore, in rejecting Mercury Bay's contempt motion, based upon what appeared to be a continuing reluctance to stray far from the terms of the Deed itself, the court gave no hint of its views on the use of a catamaran, although it did warn San Diego that in competing in such a boat it proceeded at its peril. At the very least, it had stated a second time that the water-line length limitations were the only design restrictions clearly set forth in the Deed. Moreover, the court had refused Mercury Bay's request to infer from the Deed a rule requiring some similarity between competing vessels.

Under these circumstances, it was inappropriate for the court, after the race, to engraft onto the Deed a rule so elusive as to preclude a finding of contempt eight months earlier. In any event, having refused to hold San Diego in contempt, the court should not have ordered a forfeiture on the basis of the very inference the court itself had earlier refused to draw. . . .

By exercising its rights under the Deed of Gift in accordance with the letter of that instrument, Mercury Bay was able to force San Diego into a match barely a year after it had won the Cup, despite the fact that America's Cup matches have traditionally been held three or four years apart. Mercury Bay was able to force San Diego to design and build, from scratch, a yacht that was more complex, more expensive, and riskier than those that had previously been used, when San Diego wanted to compete in yachts of the International 12-Meter Class. Finally, Mercury Bay was able to force San Diego into a one-on-one match, when San Diego wanted to continue the tradition of a multi-national challenger competition.

While a challenger, absent mutual consent, can accomplish all of this, under the Deed of Gift the defender has two important rights, viz., to decide on the type and size of boat in which it will defend—which need not be announced until the start of the match—and to name the site of the races. The argument that the Deed of Gift requires the defender, or any competitor, to attempt to compete in a boat of "inherently the same speed capability" as the challenging vessel, or "as alike as reasonably possible" to its rival, betrays a fundamental misunderstanding of the history and function of the America's Cup competition. For 140 years, challengers and defenders alike have spent fortunes and expended immeasurable effort to gain any speed advantage, however slight, to enhance their chances for victory. That is the very essence of America's Cup competition. Moreover, to compel the trustee to accept constraints upon the competition that are not specified in the trust agreement, without the mutual consent of both challenger and defender, would itself contravene the competitive scheme contemplated by the Deed of Gift.

Since the court improperly relied on extrinsic evidence to construe an unambiguous instrument, thereby creating a totally new and unworkable eligibility rule, which it belatedly used to reverse the result of a match and to justify the extreme penalty of forfeiture, its order cannot stand.

Rubin, Justice (concurring).

Upon this appeal, the court is presented with the question of whether, under the deed of trust from George L. Schuyler, dated October 24, 1887, conveying the America's Cup to the State of New York, it was permissible for the defender San Diego Yacht Club to race the catamaran *Stars and Stripes* against Mercury Bay Boating Club's monohull *New Zealand* in the 1988 competition. This statement of the issue, however, does not convey the essence of the controversy between the contenders, which extends beyond considerations of law into an area where our courts have long ago declined to venture.

Precedent may be found in the venerable case of Pierson v. Post, 3 Caines 175 (1805), which involved a remarkable dispute over title to a fox pelt. The case was brought by Lodowick Post, an aggrieved sportsman. While out with his hounds on public land hunting a fox, Mr. Pierson, with full knowledge of Post's pursuit, killed the fox and made off with the carcass. The issue, as stated on the appeal, was "whether Lodowick Post, by the pursuit with his hounds in the manner alleged in his declaration, acquired such a right to, or property in, the fox, as will sustain an action against Pierson for killing and taking him away?" The court held that it did not and reversed the judgment entered by the lower court.

Pierson v. Post is one of the first cases encountered by the neophyte law student and stands for a basic proposition of property law that no right to a wild animal is created until it is reduced to possession by so circumscribing its movement that escape is impossible. The contention between the parties, however, was not whether title to the fox had been acquired, but rather whether it was sporting for Pierson to have killed the fox when Post, in the language of the reporter, "was on the point of seizing it." The majority, confining their consideration to questions of law, stated, "However uncourteous or unkind the conduct of Pierson towards Post, in this instance, may have been, yet his act was productive of no injury or damage for which a legal remedy can be applied." It is clear that the court declined to entertain any consideration of whether Pierson's action in killing the fox was an affront to hunting etiquette or a breach of sportsmanship. Even the dissenting Justice (Livingston, J.) conceded, "This is a knotty point and should have been submitted to the arbitration of sportsmen . . . ."

There is often a marked divergence in what may be deemed sporting and what a court will uphold as legal. For instance, if a court is requested to determine whether it is permissible for a hockey player to strike an opponent with his stick, causing injury, its consideration will be confined to legal matters. Hockey is a sport known for a tendency toward violence. The court will examine such questions as whether the hockey stick constitutes a weapon and whether it was wielded with the requisite intent to constitute an assault. Against these considerations, the court will assess the extent to which the injured player may be deemed to have consented to the use of such tactics by his participation in the game or whether the assault was otherwise justifiable. However, whether such aggressive use of a hockey stick may be accepted as sporting by hockey fans, the players, the leagues or their officials and whether the general level of violence is desirable for the sport are questions simply not material to the court's deliberation.

In the matter under review, a distinction must be drawn between the parties' desire for a ruling as to 1) whether the entry of a catamaran in the America's Cup race is consistent with the terms of the deed of trust and 2) whether it constitutes good sportsmanship under the particular ethos of the yachting community to pit a catamaran against a monohull. The failure to observe such a distinction leads to confusion between what is actually stated in the deed of trust and the meaning sought to be attributed to it by reference to practices which are presently the custom in yacht racing. The practices of the sport in general and of the America's Cup competition in particular have undergone considerable change in the past and will no doubt continue to evolve in the future. The deed of trust, with some judicially sanctioned modifications, has governed the competition from 1857 to the present, from races between schooners on the New York Yacht Club's infamous "inside course" through the Narrows to contests between 12-Meter yachts on an olympic course in open water. The deed must continue to govern the contest when the 12-Meter yacht has passed into history along with the J-boat.

[U]nder the time-honored distinction of Pierson v. Post, the agreement to race boats of the 12-Meter class, which has prevailed for only about 30 years, represents merely the current assessment of the contestants as to what constitutes a sporting challenge and not what is legally permissible under the deed of trust. It constitutes a compromise between a contest which exclusively tests sailing skill (as between boats of a fixed design) and one which almost exclusively reflects sophistication of design (such as here, where the boats are built upon radically different design theories). . . .

The deed gives the contestants the widest latitude in the design of the yachts in which they choose to compete. The reference to a "yacht *or vessel* propelled by sails only" (emphasis added) constitutes the broadest possible language. Inclusion of the term "vessel" demonstrates that no limitation on design was intended, excluding even the inference that a competitor is restricted to the use of a boat customarily regarded as a "yacht." It is an inescapable conclusion that, had it been the intent of the deed of trust to exclude any type of sailboat from the competition, such expansive language would not have been employed. Moreover, it is not disputed that catamarans were known when the deed was drafted, and it would have been a simple matter for the settlor to bar them from competition by restricting eligibility to a *monohull* "yacht or vessel."

Were this court to make an assessment of whether San Diego's entry of a catamaran in the race was sporting, the result would be no different. It is apparent from the history of the race over the preceding 30 years that a 12-Meter yacht was universally regarded as the appropriate boat to race. Both Mercury Bay and San Diego departed from accepted practice by entering boats of unlimited design. Upon equitable principles, the court would therefore be constrained to consider the competitors in pari delicto and decline to assist either of them. This analysis, however, merely illustrates the shortcoming of such an approach, for it was not the rules of the sport which the competing clubs intended to circumvent but the laws of physics. . . .

In pursuing this litigation, questions have been raised which are largely beyond the courts' cavil and which, in the long and often contentious history of America's Cup competition, have never been submitted for judicial determination. If, as they contend, the parties place such great value on the quality of sportsmanship, they cannot fail to appreciate that, between true yachtsmen, victory is pursued on the water and not in the courtroom.

Kassal, Justice (dissenting).

Yachting has always been regarded as the essence of sportsmanship, and properly so. This is reflected in the spirit and venerable tradition of the America's Cup, which has long dictated that participants maintain a sense of fair play and engage in honest rivalry. These principles were violated when the San Diego Yacht Club entered a catamaran, thereby pitting a multihulled vessel against a monohull for the first time in 130 years of America's Cup competition, and virtually ensuring the latter's defeat, irrespective of the skills of its skipper and crew.

I cannot accept that such a gross mismatch was permissible under the Deed of Gift, which states that the Cup "shall be preserved as a perpetual Challenge Cup for friendly competition between foreign countries," and must therefore part company with the majority, which has dismissed this critical clause as mere "precatory" language.

The goal of fostering friendly competition is the condition upon which the Cup was donated. As such, it expresses an intent of the donor which must not be lost in the quest for victory, and which may not be measured solely through reference to physical dimensions.

In seeking to justify its entry of a vessel clearly intended not to compete, but solely to defeat, San Diego implies that the IAS court was misleading on the issue of the catamaran's eligibility when it rendered its pre-race ruling of July 25, 1988. In fact, the court's decision explicitly noted that "the issue of whether a multihulled boat is permitted to race in the America's Cup cannot properly be determined by the Court in the context of a contempt motion," and, indeed, cautioned that nothing therein "should be interpreted as indicating the multihulled boats are either permitted or barred under the America's Cup Deed of Gift." The court went on to state that "[t]he intent of the Deed seems to be that the parties must design, build and race their boats at their own risk, subject to possible disqualification and forfeiture at the conclusion of the races."

In light of the fact that San Diego did not seek declaratory relief with respect to the eligibility of its proposed vessel, the IAS court properly declined to render what would have constituted an advisory opinion on that question. At that stage in the proceedings, the court was also correct in denying Mercury Bay's premature motion to hold San Diego in civil contempt for anticipated conduct.

On this record, it is clear that San Diego was aware that the eligibility of its catamaran defender had not been determined in the earlier proceeding. Indeed, counsel for San Diego acknowledged the risk of disqualification—as well as the risk of forfeiture—when he stated, during the contempt motion hearing, "[I]f it appears . . . San Diego has not defended the cup in accordance with the deed then it would be appropriate for Mercury Bay to come into court and ask the Court to order a forfeiture of the cup." It so appears.

The 1988 America's Cup races were manifestly unfair in every sense. True sportsmanship and the integrity of this great sport demand far more, as does the very Deed of Gift by which this competition has been sponsored for over a century. For these reasons, and upon the sound opinion of the IAS court, I most respectfully dissent.

Robert's Rules of Order Revised
General Henry M. Robert

Preface

A work on parliamentary law is needed, based, in its general principles, upon the rules and practice of Congress, but adapted, in its details, to the use of ordinary societies. Such a work should give not only the methods of organizing and conducting meetings, the duties of officers, and names of ordinary motions, but also a systematic statement in reference to each motion, as to its object and effect; whether it can be amended or debated; if debatable, the extent to which it opens the main question to debate; the circumstances under which it can be made, and what other motions can be made while it is pending. Robert's Rules of Order (published in 1876, slight additions being made in 1893) was prepared with a hope of supplying the above information in a condensed and systematic form, each rule being complete in itself, or giving references to every section that in any way qualifies it, so that a stranger to the work can refer to any special subject with safety.

The fact that during these thirty-nine years a half million copies of these Rules have been published would indicate that there is a demand for a work of this kind. But the constant inquiries from all sections of the country for information concerning proceedings in deliberative assemblies that is not contained in Rules of Order, seems to demand a revision and enlargement of the manual. To meet this want, the work has been thoroughly revised and enlarged, and, to avoid confusion with the old rules, is published under the title of "Robert's Rules of Order Revised."

The object of Rules of Order is to assist an assembly to accomplish in the best possible manner the work for which it was designed. To do this it is necessary to restrain the individual somewhat, as the right of an individual, in any community, to do what he pleases, is incompatible with the interests of the whole. Where there is no law, but every man does what is right in his own eyes, there is the least of real liberty. Experience has shown the importance of definiteness in the law; and in this country, where customs are so slightly established and the published manuals of parliamentary practice so conflicting, no society should attempt to conduct business without having adopted some work upon the subject as the authority in all cases not covered by its own special rules.

While it is important that an assembly has good rules, it is more important that it be not without some rules to govern its proceedings. It is much more important, for instance, that an assembly has a rule determining the rank of the motion to postpone indefinitely, than that it gives this motion the highest rank of all subsidiary motions except to lay on the table, as in the U.S. Senate; or gives it the lowest rank, as in the U.S. House of Representatives; or gives it equal rank with the previous question, to postpone definitely, and to commit, so that if one is pending none of the others may be moved, as under the old parliamentary law. This has been well expressed by one of the greatest of English writers on parliamentary law: "Whether these forms be in all cases the most rational or not is really not of so great importance. It is much more material that there should be a rule to go by than what that rule is; that there may be a uniformity of proceeding in business, not subject to the caprice of the chairman or captiousness of the members. It is very material that order, decency, and regularity he preserved in a dignified public body."

Introduction

Parliamentary Law refers originally to the customs and rules for conducting business in the English Parliament; and thence to the usages of deliberative assemblies in general. In England these usages of Parliament form a part of the unwritten law of the land, and in our own legislative bodies they are of authority in all cases where they do not conflict with existing rules or precedents.

But as a people we have not the respect which the English have for customs and precedents, and are always ready for such innovations as we think are improvements; hence changes have been and are constantly being made in the written rules which our legislative bodies have found best to adopt. As each house adopts its own rules, the result is that the two houses of the same legislature do not always agree in their practice; even in Congress the order of precedence of motions is not the same in both houses, and the previous question is admitted in the House of Representatives but not in the Senate. As a consequence of this, the exact method of conducting business in any particular legislative body is to be obtained only from the Legislative Manual of that body.

The vast number of societies—political, literary, scientific, benevolent, and religious—formed all over the land, though not legislative, are deliberative in character, and must have some system of conducting business and some rules to govern their proceedings, and are necessarily subject to the common parliamentary law where it does not conflict with their own special rules. But as their knowledge of parliamentary law has been obtained from the usages in this country, rather than from the customs of Parliament, it has resulted that these societies have followed in part the customs of our own legislative bodies, and our people have thus been educated under a system of parliamentary law which is peculiar to this country, and yet so well established as to supersede the English parliamentary law as the common law of ordinary deliberative assemblies. . . .

How Business Is Conducted in Deliberative Assemblies

1. Introduction of Business. An assembly having been organized . . . business is brought before it either by the motion of a member, or by the presentation of a communication to the assembly. It is not usual to make motions to receive reports of committees or communications to the assembly. There are many other cases in the ordinary routine of business where the formality of a motion is dispensed with, but should any member object, a regular motion becomes necessary, or the chair may put the question without waiting for a motion.

2. What Precedes Debate. Before any subject is open to debate it is necessary, first, that a motion be made by a member who has obtained the floor; second, that it be seconded (with certain exceptions); and third, that it be stated by the chair, that is, by the presiding officer. The fact that a motion has been made and seconded does not put it before the assembly, as the chair alone can do that. He must either rule it out of order, or state the question on it so that the assembly may know what is before it for consideration and action, that is, what is the *immediately pending question.* If several questions are pending, as a reso-lution and an amendment and a motion to postpone, the last one stated by the chair is the immediately pending question. . . .

4. Motions and Resolutions. A motion is a proposal that the assembly take certain action, or that it express itself as holding certain views. It is made by a member's obtaining the floor as already described and saying, "I move that" (which is equivalent to saying, "I propose that"), and then stating the action he proposes to have taken. Thus a member "moves" (proposes) that a resolution be adopted, or amended, or referred to a committee, or that a vote of thanks be extended, etc.; or "That it is the sense of this meeting (or assem-bly) that industrial training," etc. . . .

7. Debate. After a question has been stated by the chair, it is before the assembly for consideration and action. All resolutions, reports of committees, communications to the assembly, and all amendments proposed to them, and all other motions except the Unde-batable Motions mentioned in 45, may be debated before final action is taken on them, unless by a two-thirds vote the assembly decides to dispose of them without debate. By a two-thirds vote is meant two-thirds of the votes cast, a quorum being present. In the debate each member has the right to speak twice on the same question on the same day (except on an appeal), but cannot make a second speech on the same question as long as any member who has not spoken on that question desires the floor. No one can speak longer than ten minutes at a time without permission of the assembly.

Debate must be limited to the merits of the *immediately pending question*—that is, the last question stated by the chair that is still pending; except that in a few cases the main question is also open to debate. Speakers must address their remarks to the presiding offi-cer, be courteous in their language and deportment, and avoid all personalities, never allud-ing to the officers or other members by name, where possible to avoid it, nor to the motives of members. . . .

Some Main and Unclassified Motions

40. Dilatory, Absurd, or Frivolous Motions. For the convenience of deliberative assemblies, it is necessary to allow some highly privileged motions to be renewed again and again after progress in debate or the transaction of any business, and to allow a single member, by calling for a division, to have another vote taken. If there was no provision for protecting the assembly, a minority of two members could be constantly raising questions of order and appealing from every decision of the chair, and calling for a division on every vote, even when it was nearly unanimous, and moving to lay motions on the table, and to adjourn, and offering amendments that are simply frivolous or absurd. By taking advantage of parliamentary forms and methods a small minority could practically stop the business of a deliberative assembly having short sessions, if there was no provision for such contin-gency. Congress met it by adopting this rule: "No dilatory motion shall be entertained by the speaker." But, without adopting any rule on the subject, every deliberative assembly has the inherent right to protect itself from being imposed upon by members using parliamen-tary forms to prevent it from doing the very thing for which it is in session, and which these forms were designed to assist, namely, to transact business. Therefore, whenever the chair is satisfied that members are using parliamentary forms merely to obstruct business, he should either not recognize them, or else rule them out of order. After the chair has been sustained upon an appeal, he should not entertain another appeal from the same obstructionists while they are engaged evidently in trying by that means to obstruct business. While the chair should always be courteous and fair, he should be firm in protecting the assembly from imposition, even though it be done in strict conformity with all parliamentary rules except this one, that no dilatory, absurd, or frivolous motions are allowed.

As an illustration of a frivolous or absurd motion, suppose Mr. A is to be in the city next week and a motion has been made to invite him to address the assembly at its next meeting, the meetings being weekly. Now, if a motion is made to refer the question to a committee with instructions to report at the next regular meeting, the chair should rule it out of order as frivolous or absurd.

Debate

43. Decorum in Debate. In debate a member must confine himself to the question before the assembly, and avoid personalities. He cannot reflect upon any act of the assembly, unless he intends to conclude his remarks with a motion to rescind such action, or else while debating such a motion. In referring to another member, he should, as much as possible, avoid using his name, rather referring to him as "the member who spoke last," or in some other way describing him. The officers of the assembly should always be referred to by their official titles. It is not allowable to arraign the motives of a member, but the nature or consequences of a measure may be condemned in strong terms. It is not the man, but the measure, that is the subject of debate.

If one desires to ask a question of the member speaking, he should rise, and without waiting to be recognized, say, "Mr. Chairman, I should like to ask the gentleman a question." The chair then asks the speaker if he is willing to be interrupted, or the speaker may at once consent or decline, addressing, however, the chair, through whom the conversation must be carried on, as members cannot directly address one another in a deliberative assembly. If the speaker consents to the question, the time consumed by the interruption comes out of the time of the speaker.

If at any time the chairman rises to state a point of order, or give information, or otherwise speak, within his privilege, the member speaking must take his seat till the chairman has been heard first. When called to order by the chair the member must sit down until the question of order is decided. If his remarks are decided to be improper, he cannot proceed, if any one objects, without the leave of the assembly expressed by a vote, upon which question no debate is allowed.

Disorderly words should be taken down by the member who objects to them, or by the secretary, and then read to the member. If he denies them, the assembly shall decide by a vote whether they are his words or not. If a member cannot justify the words he used, and will not suitably apologize for using them, it is the duty of the assembly to act in the case. If the disorderly words are of a personal nature, after each party has been heard, and before the assembly proceeds to deliberate upon the case, both parties to the personality should retire, it being a general rule that no member should be present in the assembly when any matter relating to himself is under debate. It is not, however, necessary for the member objecting to the words to retire unless he is personally involved in the case. Disorderly words to the presiding officer, or in respect to the official acts of an officer, do not involve the officer so as to require him to retire. If any business has taken place since the member spoke, it is too late to take notice of any disorderly words he used.

During debate, and while the chairman is speaking, or the assembly is engaged in voting, no member is permitted to disturb the assembly by whispering, or walking across the floor, or in any other way.

Legal Rights of Assemblies and Trial of Their Members

72. The Right of a Deliberative Assembly to Punish its Members. A deliberative assembly has the inherent right to make and enforce its own laws and punish an offender, the extreme penalty, however, being expulsion from its own body. When expelled, if the assembly is a permanent society, it has the right, for its own protection, to give public notice that the person has ceased to be a member of that society.

But it has no right to go beyond what is necessary for self-protection and publish the charges against the member. In a case where a member of a society was expelled, and an officer of the society published, by its order, a statement of the grave charges upon which he had been found guilty, the expelled member recovered damages from the officer in a suit for libel, the court holding that the truth of the charges did not affect the case.

73. Right of an Assembly to Eject any one from its Place of Meeting. Every deliberative assembly has the right to decide who may be present during its session; and when the assembly, either by a rule or by a vote, decides that a certain person shall not remain in the room, it is the duty of the chairman to enforce the rule of order, using whatever force is necessary to eject the party.

The chairman can detail members to remove the person, without calling upon the police. If, however, in enforcing the order, any one uses harsher measures than is necessary to remove the person, the courts have held that he, and he alone, is liable for damages, just the same as a policeman would be under similar circumstances. However badly the man may be abused while being removed from the room, neither the chairman nor the society is liable for damages, as, in ordering his removal, they did not exceed their legal rights.

74. Rights of Ecclesiastical Tribunals. Many of our deliberative assemblies are ecclesiastical bodies, and it is important to know how much respect will be paid to their decisions by the civil courts.

A church became divided, and each party claimed to be the church, and therefore entitled to the church property. The case was taken into the civil courts, and finally, on appeal, to the U.S. Supreme Court, which, after holding the case under advisement for a year, sustained the decision of the U.S. Circuit Court. The Supreme Court, in rendering its decision, laid down the broad principle that when a local church is but a part of a large and more general organization or denomination, the court will accept as final the decision of the highest ecclesiastical tribunal to which the case has been carried within that general church organization, on all questions of discipline, faith, or ecclesiastical rule, custom, or law, and will not inquire into the justice or injustice of its decree as between the parties before it.

The officers, the ministers, the members, or the church body which the highest judiciary of the denomination recognizes, the court will recognize. Whom that body expels or cuts off, the court will hold to be no longer members of that church. The court laid down the following principles:

> Where a church is of a strictly congregational or independent organization, and the property held by it has no trust attached to it, its right to the use of the property must be determined by the ordinary principles which govern ordinary associations.
>
> Where the local congregation is itself a member of a much larger and more important religious organization and is under its government and control and is bound by its orders and judgments, its decisions are final and binding on legal tribunals.
>
> Courts having no ecclesiastical jurisdiction, cannot revise or question ordinary acts of church discipline; their only judicial power arises from the conflicting claims of the parties to the church property and the use of it.

Watson v. Jones (1871).

But while the civil courts have no ecclesiastical jurisdiction, and cannot revise or question ordinary acts of church discipline, they do have jurisdiction where there are conflicting claims to church property. An independent church by an almost unanimous vote decided to unite with another independent church. A very small minority, less than ten per cent, did not wish to unite with the other church, so they were voted letters of dismission to any other church of like faith and order, against their protest. The majority then directed the trustees to transfer their property to the other church and voted themselves a letter of dismission to unite with that church. The church then voted to disband. The majority presented their letters and were received into the other church. The minority would not use their letters, but took the matter into the courts, which, of course, decided that they were the church and owned the property. According to the practice of churches of the same denomination, no member can be forced out of the church unless for neglect of his duties as a member. Letters of dismission are granted only on the request of members, and as a general rule the membership does not terminate until the letter has been used. The church could not terminate the membership of the minority, against whom there were no charges, by voting them letters without their consent. By not using their letters they soon constituted the entire membership and rescinded the order to the trustees to transfer the property to the other church. By the hasty, ill-advised action of almost the entire church the majority lost their property. In cases where property is involved, churches cannot be too careful, and it is usually best to act under legal advice.

75. Trial of Members of Societies. Every deliberative assembly, having the right to purify its own body, must therefore have the right to investigate the character of its members. It can require any of them to testify in the case, under pain of expulsion if they refuse.

When the charge is against the member's character, it is usually referred to a committee of investigation or discipline, or to some standing committee, to report upon. Some societies have standing committees whose duty it is to report cases for discipline whenever any are known to them.

In either case, the committee investigates the matter and reports to the society. This report need not go into details, but should contain its recommendations as to what action the society should take, and should usually close with resolutions covering the case, so that there is no need for any one to offer any additional resolutions upon it. The ordinary resolutions, where the member is recommended to be expelled, are (1) to fix the time to which the society shall adjourn; and (2) to instruct the clerk to cite the member to appear before the society at this adjourned meeting to show cause why he should not be expelled, upon the following charges which should then be given.

After charges are preferred against a member, and the assembly has ordered that he be cited to appear for trial, he is theoretically under arrest, and is deprived of all the rights of membership until his case is disposed of. Without his consent no member should be tried at the same meeting at which the charges are preferred, excepting when the charges relate to something done at that meeting.

The clerk should send the accused a written notice to appear before the society at the time appointed, and should at the same time furnish him with a copy of the charges. A failure to obey the summons is generally cause enough for summary expulsion.

At the appointed meeting what may be called the trial takes place. Frequently the only evidence required against the member is the report of the committee. After it has been read and any additional evidence offered that the committee may see fit to introduce, the accused should be allowed to make an explanation and introduce witnesses, if he so desires. Either party should be allowed to cross-examine the other's witnesses and introduce rebutting testimony. When the evidence is all in, the accused should retire from the room, and the society deliberate upon the question, and finally act by a vote upon the question of expulsion, or other punishment proposed. No member should be expelled by less than a two-thirds vote, a quorum voting. [The U.S. Constitution (Art. I, Sec. 5) provides that each House of Congress may "with the concurrence of two-thirds, expel a member."] The vote should be by ballot, except by general consent. The members of the committee preferring the charges vote the same as other members.

In acting upon the case, it must be borne in mind that there is a vast distinction between the evidence necessary to convict in a civil court and that required to convict in an ordinary society or ecclesiastical body. A notorious pickpocket could not even be arrested, much less convicted by a civil court, simply on the ground of being commonly known as a pickpocket; while such evidence would convict and expel him from any ordinary society.

The moral conviction of the truth of the charge is all that is necessary in an ecclesiastical or other deliberative body to find the accused guilty of the charges.

If the trial is liable to be long and troublesome, or of a very delicate nature, the member is frequently cited to appear before a committee, instead of the society, for trial. In this case the committee reports to the society the result of its trial of the case, with resolutions covering the punishment which it recommends the society to adopt. When the committee's report is read, the accused should be permitted to make his statement of the case, the committee being allowed to reply. The accused then retires from the room, and the society acts upon the resolutions submitted by the committee. The members of the committee should vote upon the case the same as other members.

If the accused wishes counsel at his trial, it is usual to allow it, provided the counsel is a member of the society in good standing. Should the counsel be guilty of improper conduct during the trial, the society can refuse to hear him, and can also punish him.

Department of the Army
The Law of Land Warfare

Basic Rules and Principles

Section I. General

1. Purpose and Scope

The purpose of this Manual is to provide authoritative guidance to military personnel on the customary and treaty law applicable to the conduct of warfare on land and to relationships between belligerents and neutral States. Although certain of the legal principles set forth herein have application to warfare at sea and in the air as well as to hostilities on land, this Manual otherwise concerns itself with the rules peculiar to naval and aerial warfare only to the extent that such rules have some direct bearing on the activities of land forces.

This Manual is an official publication of the United States Army. However, those provisions of the Manual which are neither statutes nor the text of treaties to which the United States is a party should not be considered binding upon courts and tribunals applying the law of war. However, such provisions are of evidentiary value insofar as they bear upon questions of custom and practice.

2. Purposes of the Law of War

The conduct of armed hostilities on land is regulated by the law of land warfare which is both written and unwritten. It is inspired by the desire to diminish the evils of war by:

a. Protecting both combatants and noncombatants from unnecessary suffering;

b. Safeguarding certain fundamental human rights of persons who fall into the hands of the enemy, particularly prisoners of war, the wounded and sick, and civilians; and

c. Facilitating the restoration of peace.

3. Basic Principles

a. Prohibitory Effect. The law of war places limits on the exercise of a belligerent's power in the interests mentioned in paragraph 2 and requires that belligerents refrain from employing any kind or degree of violence which is not actually necessary for military purposes and that they conduct hostilities with regard for the principles of humanity and chivalry.

The prohibitory effect of the law of war is not minimized by "military necessity" which has been defined as that principle which justifies those measures not forbidden by international law which are indispensable for securing the complete submission of the enemy as soon as possible. Military necessity has been generally rejected as a defense for acts forbidden by the customary and conventional laws of war inasmuch as the latter have been developed and framed with consideration for the concept of military necessity.

b. Binding on States and Individuals. The law of war is binding not only upon States as such but also upon individuals and, in particular, the members of their armed forces.

4. Sources

The law of war is derived from two principal sources:

a. Lawmaking Treaties (or Conventions), such as the Hague and Geneva Conventions.

b. Custom. Although some of the law of war has not been incorporated in any treaty or convention to which the United States is a party, this body of unwritten or customary law is firmly established by the custom of nations and well defined by recognized authorities on international law.

Lawmaking treaties may be compared with legislative enactments in the national law of the United States and the customary law of war with the unwritten Anglo-American common law. . . .

6. Custom

Evidence of the customary law of war, arising from the general consent of States, may be found in judicial decisions, the writings of jurists, diplomatic correspondence, and other documentary material concerning the practice of States. . . .

7. Force of the Law of War

a. Technical Force of Treaties and Position of the United States. Technically, each of the lawmaking treaties regarding the conduct of warfare is, to the extent established by its terms, binding only between the States that have ratified or acceded to, and have not thereafter denounced (withdrawn from), the treaty or convention and is binding only to the extent permitted by the reservations, if any, that have accompanied such ratification or accession on either side. . . .

These treaty provisions are in large part but formal and specific applications of general principles of the unwritten law. While solemnly obligatory only as between the parties thereto, they may be said also to represent modern international public opinion as to how belligerents and neutrals should conduct themselves in the particulars indicated.

For these reasons, the treaty provisions quoted herein will be strictly observed and enforced by United States forces without regard to whether they are legally binding upon this country. Military commanders will be instructed which, if any, of the written rules herein quoted are not legally binding as between the United States and each of the States immediately concerned, and which, if any, for that reason are not for the time being to be observed or enforced.

b. Force of Treaties Under the Constitution. Under the Constitution of the United States, treaties constitute part of the "supreme Law of the Land" (art. VI, clause 2). In consequence, treaties relating to the law of war have a force equal to that of laws enacted by the Congress. Their provisions must be observed by both military and civilian personnel with the same strict regard for both the letter and spirit of the law which is required with respect to the Constitution and statutes enacted in pursuance thereof.

c. Force of Customary Law. The unwritten or customary law of war is binding upon all nations. It will be strictly observed by United States forces, subject only to such exceptions as shall have been directed by competent authority by way of legitimate reprisals for illegal conduct of the enemy (see par. 497). The customary law of war is part of the law of the United States and, insofar as it is not inconsistent with any treaty to which this country is a party or with a controlling executive or legislative act, is binding upon the United States, citizens of the United States, and other persons serving this country.

Hostilities

Section I. Commencement of Hostilities

20. Declaration of War Required

a. Treaty Provision.

"The Contracting Powers recognize that hostilities between themselves must not commence without previous and explicit warning, in the form either of a reasoned declaration of war or of an ultimatum with conditional declaration of war."

b. Surprise Still Possible. Nothing in the foregoing rule requires that any particular length of time shall elapse between a declaration of war and the commencement of hostilities.

21. Notification to Neutrals

"The existence of a state of war must be notified to the neutral Powers without delay, and shall not take effect in regard to them until after the receipt of a notification, which may, however, be given by telegraph. Neutral Powers, nevertheless, cannot rely on the absence of notification if it is clearly established that they were in fact aware of the existence of a state of war."

23. Present Effect of Foregoing Rules

The Charter of the United Nations makes illegal the threat or use of force contrary to the purpose of the United Nations. It requires members of the organization to bring about by peaceful means adjustment or settlement of international disputes or situations which might lead to a breach of the peace. However, a nonmember nation or a member nation which violates these provisions of the Charter commits a further breach of international law by commencing hostilities without a declaration of war or a conditional ultimatum as required by the foregoing articles of Hague Convention No. III. Conversely, a State which resorts to war in violation of the Charter will not render its acts of aggression or breach of the peace any the less unlawful by formally declaring war.

24. Constitutional Provision

Article 1, section 8, clause 11, of the United States Constitution provides that "The Congress shall have power . . . to declare War." The law of war may, however, be applicable to an international conflict, notwithstanding the absence of a declaration by the Congress.

25. Enemy Status of Civilians

Under the law of the United States, one of the consequences of the existence of a condition of war between two States is that every national of the one State becomes an enemy of every national of the other. However, it is a generally recognized rule of international law that civilians must not be made the object of attack directed exclusively against them.

26. Effect on Enemy Aliens

Enemy aliens located or resident in United States territory are not necessarily made prisoners or interned en masse on the breaking out of hostilities. Such persons may be allowed to leave the United States if their departure is consistent with national interest. If the security of the United States makes it absolutely necessary, enemy aliens may be placed in assigned residence or internment. Measures of control are normally taken with respect to at least persons known to be active or reserve members of a hostile army, persons who would be liable to service in the enemy forces, and persons who it is expected would furnish information or other aid to a hostile State.

27. Expulsion

In modern practice at the outbreak of hostilities the expulsion of the citizens or subjects of the enemy is generally decreed from seaports, the area surrounding airbases, airports, and fortified places, areas of possible attack, and the actual or contemplated theaters of operation. When expulsion is decreed, the persons expelled should be given such reasonable notice, consistent with public safety, as will enable them to arrange for the collection, disposal, and removal of their goods and property and for the settlement of their personal affairs.

Section II. Forbidden Conduct with Respect to Persons

28. Refusal of Quarter

"It is especially forbidden . . . to declare that no quarter will be given."

29. Injury Forbidden After Surrender

"It is especially forbidden . . . to kill or wound an enemy who, having laid down his arms, or having no longer means of defense, has surrendered at discretion."

30. Persons Descending by Parachute

The law of war does not prohibit firing upon paratroops or other persons who are or appear to be bound upon hostile missions while such persons are descending by parachute. Persons other than those mentioned in the preceding sentence who are descending by parachute from disabled aircraft may not be fired upon.

31. Assassination and Outlawry

"It is especially forbidden . . . to kill or wound treacherously individuals belonging to the hostile nation or army."

This article is construed as prohibiting assassination, proscription, or outlawry of an enemy, or putting a price upon an enemy's head, as well as offering a reward for an enemy "dead or alive." It does not, however, preclude attacks on individual soldiers or officers of the enemy whether in the zone of hostilities, occupied territory, or elsewhere.

32. Nationals Not To Be Compelled to Take Part in Operations Against Their Own Country

"A belligerent is likewise forbidden to compel the nationals of the hostile party to take part in the operations of war directed against their own country, even if they were in the belligerent's service before the commencement of the war."

Section III. Forbidden Means of Waging Warfare

33. Means of Injuring the Enemy Limited

a. Treaty Provision.

"The right of belligerents to adopt means of injuring the enemy is not unlimited."

b. The means employed are definitely restricted by international declarations and conventions and by the laws and usages of war.

34. Employment of Arms Causing Unnecessary Injury

a. Treaty Provision.

"It is especially forbidden . . . to employ arms, projectiles, or material calculated to cause unnecessary suffering."

b. Interpretation. What weapons cause "unnecessary injury" can only be determined in light of the practice of States in refraining from the use of a given weapon because it is believed to have that effect. The prohibition certainly does not extend to the use of explosives contained in artillery projectiles, mines, rockets, or hand grenades. Usage has, however, established the illegality of the use of lances with barbed heads, irregular-shaped bullets, and projectiles filled with glass, the use of any substance on bullets that would tend unnecessarily to inflame a wound inflicted by them, and the scoring of the surface or the filing off of the ends of the hard cases of bullets.

35. Atomic Weapons

The use of explosive "atomic weapons," whether by air, sea, or land forces, cannot as such be regarded as violative of international law in the absence of any customary rule of international law or international convention restricting their employment.

36. Weapons Employing Fire

The use of weapons which employ fire, such as tracer ammunition, flamethrowers, napalm and other incendiary agents, against targets requiring their use is not violative of international law. They should not, however, be employed in such a way as to cause unnecessary suffering to individuals.

37. Poison

a. Treaty Provision.

"It is especially forbidden . . . to employ poison or poisoned weapons."

b. Discussion of Rule. The foregoing rule prohibits the use in war of poison or poisoned weapons against human beings. Restrictions on the use of herbicides as well as treaty provisions concerning chemical and bacteriological warfare are discussed in paragraph 38.

. . .

Section V. Stratagems

48. Stratagems Permissible

"Ruses of war and the employment of measures necessary for obtaining information about the enemy and the country are considered permissible."

49. Good Faith

Absolute good faith with the enemy must be observed as a rule of conduct; but this does not prevent measures such as using spies and secret agents, encouraging defection or insurrection among the enemy civilian population, corrupting enemy civilians or soldiers by bribes, or inducing the enemy's soldiers to desert, surrender, or rebel. In general, a belligerent may resort to those measures for mystifying or misleading the enemy against which the enemy ought to take measures to protect himself.

50. Treachery or Perfidy

Ruses of war are legitimate so long as they do not involve treachery or perfidy on the part of the belligerent resorting to them. They are, however, forbidden if they contravene any generally accepted rule.

The line of demarcation between legitimate ruses and forbidden acts of perfidy is sometimes indistinct, but the following examples indicate the correct principles. It would be an improper practice to secure an advantage of the enemy by deliberate lying or misleading conduct which involves a breach of faith, or when there is a moral obligation to speak the truth. For example, it is improper to feign surrender so as to secure an advantage over the opposing belligerent thereby. So similarly, to broadcast to the enemy that an armistice had been agreed upon when such is not the case would be treacherous. On the other hand, it is a perfectly proper ruse to summon a force to surrender on the ground that it is surrounded and thereby induce such surrender with a small force.

Treacherous or perfidious conduct in war is forbidden because it destroys the basis for a restoration of peace short of the complete annihilation of one belligerent by the other.

51. Legitimate Ruses

Among legitimate ruses may be counted surprises, ambushes, feigning attacks, retreats, or flights, simulating quiet and inactivity, use of small forces to simulate large units, transmitting false or misleading radio or telephone messages, deception of the enemy by bogus orders purporting to have been issued by the enemy commander, making use of the enemy's signals and passwords, pretending to communicate with troops or reinforcements which have no existence, deceptive supply movements, deliberate planting of false information, use of spies and secret agents, moving landmarks, putting up dummy guns and vehicles or laying dummy mines, erection of dummy installations and airfields, removing unit identifications from uniforms, use of signal deceptive measures, and psychological warfare activities.

52. Improper Use of Identifying Devices

"It is especially forbidden . . . to make improper use of a flag of truce, of the national flag, or of the military insignia and uniform of the enemy, as well as the distinctive badges of the Geneva Convention."

53. Flags of Truce

Flags of truce must not be used surreptitiously to obtain military information or merely to obtain time to effect a retreat or secure reinforcements or to feign a surrender in order to surprise an enemy. An officer receiving them is not on this account absolved from the duty of exercising proper precautions with regard to them.

54. National Flags, Insignia, and Uniforms as a Ruse

In practice, it has been authorized to make use of national flags, insignia, and uniforms as a ruse. The foregoing rule does not prohibit such employment, but does prohibit their improper use. It is certainly forbidden to employ them during combat, but their use at other times is not forbidden.

55. Improper Use of Distinctive Emblem of Geneva Convention

The use of the emblem of the Red Cross and other equivalent insignia must be limited to the indication or protection of medical units and establishments, the personnel and material protected by GWS and other similar conventions. The following are examples of the improper use of the emblem: Using a hospital or other building accorded such protection as an observation post or military office or depot; firing from a building or tent displaying the emblem of the Red Cross; using a hospital train or airplane to facilitate the escape of combatants; displaying the emblem on vehicles containing ammunition or other nonmedical stores; and in general using it for cloaking acts of hostility.

Remedies for Violation of International Law
Section I. Remedies and Reprisals

495. Remedies of Injured Belligerent

In the event of violation of the law of war, the injured party may legally resort to remedial action of the following types:

a. Publication of the facts, with a view to influencing public opinion against the offending belligerent.

b. Protest and demand for compensation and/or punishment of the individual offenders. Such communications may be sent through the protecting power, a humanitarian organization performing the duties of a protecting power, or a neutral state, or by parlementaire direct to the commander of the offending forces.

"A belligerent party which violates the provisions of the said Regulations shall, if the case demands, be liable to pay compensation. It shall be responsible for all acts committed by persons forming part of its armed forces."

c. Solicitation of the good offices, mediation, or intervention of neutral States for the purpose of making the enemy observe the law of war.

d. Punishment of captured offenders as war criminals.

e. Reprisals.

496. Inquiry Concerning Violations of Geneva Conventions of 1949

"At the request of a Party to the conflict, an enquiry shall be instituted, in a manner to be decided between the interested Parties, concerning any alleged violation of the Convention.

"If agreement has not been reached concerning the procedure for the enquiry, the Parties should agree on the choice of an umpire who will decide upon the procedure to be followed.

"Once the violation has been established, the Parties to the conflict shall put an end to it and shall repress it with the least possible delay."

497. Reprisals

a. Definition. Reprisals are acts of retaliation in the form of conduct which would otherwise be unlawful, resorted to by one belligerent against enemy personnel or property for acts of warfare committed by the other belligerent in violation of the law of war, for the purpose of enforcing future compliance with the recognized rules of civilized warfare. For example, the employment by a belligerent of a weapon the use of which is normally precluded by the law of war would constitute a lawful reprisal for intentional mistreatment of prisoners of war held by the enemy.

b. Priority of Other Remedies. Other means of securing compliance with the law of war should normally be exhausted before resort is had to reprisals. This course should be pursued unless the safety of the troops requires immediate drastic action and the persons who actually committed the offenses cannot be secured. Even when appeal to the enemy for redress has failed, it may be a matter of policy to consider, before resorting to reprisals, whether the opposing forces are not more likely to be influenced by a steady adherence to the law of war on the part of their adversary.

c. Against Whom Permitted. Reprisals against the persons or property of prisoners of war, including the wounded and sick, and protected civilians are forbidden. Collective penalties and punishment of prisoners of war and protected civilians are likewise prohibited. However, reprisals may still be visited on enemy troops who have not yet fallen into the hands of the forces making the reprisals.

d. When and How Employed. Reprisals are never adopted merely for revenge, but only as an unavoidable last resort to induce the enemy to desist from unlawful practices. They should never be employed by individual soldiers except by direct orders of a commander, and the latter should give such orders only after careful inquiry into the alleged offense. The highest accessible military authority should be consulted unless immediate action is demanded, in which event a subordinate commander may order appropriate reprisals upon his own initiative. Ill-considered action may subsequently be found to have been wholly unjustified and will subject the responsible officer himself to punishment for a violation of the law of war. On the other hand, commanding officers must assume responsibility for retaliative measures when an unscrupulous enemy leaves no other recourse against the repetition of unlawful acts.

e. Form of Reprisal. The acts resorted to by way of reprisal need not conform to those complained of by the injured party, but should not be excessive or exceed the degree of violence committed by the enemy.

f. Procedure. The rule requiring careful inquiry into the real occurrence will always be followed unless the safety of the troops requires immediate drastic action and the persons who actually committed the offense cannot be ascertained.

g. Hostages. The taking of hostages is forbidden. The taking of prisoners by way of reprisal for acts previously committed (so-called "reprisal prisoners") is likewise forbidden.

Notes and Questions

1. Reconsider the expression "all's fair in love and war" in light of the *Restatement of Love* and *The Law of Land Warfare*. Why might the opposing parties—even in warfare—agree on the need for *some* rules?

2. Why is it permissible under *The Law of Land Warfare* to fire upon descending paratroopers, but not upon enemy troops descending by parachute from disabled aircraft?

3. Why is it permissible to broadcast deceptive messages about troop formations, but not to feign a surrender?

Suggestions For Further Reading

Folk Law: Essays in the Theory and Practice of Lex Non Scripta (Alison Dundes Renteln & Alan Dundes eds. 1994)

Part V
Law and Morality

Though law and morality are not the same, and many things may be immoral which are not necessarily illegal, yet the absolute divorce of law from morality would be of fatal consequence . . . .[1]

It would indeed be odd and strange if the law of a society did not reflect and implement its most deep-seated moral convictions; and generally of course it does. But a defining feature of a society is the line at which it attempts to demarcate a boundary between the two.

The theme of *law and morality* may be viewed as a particularly important subset of the distinction between legal and non-legal systems for regulating social behavior. The reasons for which people actually follow rules may not coincide with the "legal" reasons for doing so; and sometimes, in fact, good moral reasons can be given for *disobeying* a legal rule.

Clearly, as the following chapters illustrate, it would not be practical for the law to take on the general task of enforcing morality. The outer limit of this principle is captured most memorably in Holmes's assertion that:

> I often doubt whether it would not be a gain if every word of moral significance could be banished from the law altogether, and other words adopted which should convey legal ideas uncolored by anything outside the law. We should lose the fossil records of a good deal of history and the majesty got from ethical associations, but by ridding ourselves of an unnecessary confusion we should gain very much in the clearness of our thought.[2]

Since Holmes wrote those words his view has decisively prevailed over that of Lord Coleridge. Yet we may still ponder whether, with our gain in "clearness of thought," something very valuable and fundamental has not also been lost—something whose loss may indeed be described without exaggeration as "of fatal consequence."

---

[1]   Regina v. Dudley and Stephens (Lord Coleridge, C.J.).

[2]   O.W. Holmes, The Path of the Law, 10 Harvard Law Review 457, 464 (1897).

Chapter 12

The Realms of Law and Morality Distinguished

The Path of the Law
Oliver Wendell Holmes

When we study law we are not studying a mystery but a well known profession. We are studying what we shall want in order to appear before judges, or to advise people in such a way as to keep them out of court. The reason why it is a profession, why people will pay lawyers to argue for them or to advise them, is that in societies like ours the command of the public force is intrusted to the judges in certain cases, and the whole power of the state will be put forth, if necessary, to carry out their judgments and decrees. People want to know under what circumstances and how far they will run the risk of coming against what is so much stronger than themselves, and hence it becomes a business to find out when this danger is to be feared. The object of our study, then, is prediction, the prediction of the incidence of the public force through the instrumentality of the courts.

The means of the study are a body of reports, of treatises, and of statutes, in this country and in England, extending back for six hundred years, and now increasing annually by hundreds. In these sibylline leaves are gathered the scattered prophecies of the past upon the cases in which the axe will fall. These are what properly have been called the oracles of the law. Far the most important and pretty nearly the whole meaning of every new effort of legal thought is to make these prophecies more precise, and to generalize them into a thoroughly connected system. The process is one, from a lawyer's statement of a case, eliminating as it does all the dramatic elements with which his client's story has clothed it, and retaining only the facts of legal import, up to the final analyses and abstract universals of theoretic jurisprudence. The reason why a lawyer does not mention that his client wore a white hat when he made a contract, while Mrs. Quickly would be sure to dwell upon it along with the parcel gilt goblet and the sea-coal fire, is that he forsees that the public force will act in the same way whatever his client had upon his head. It is to make the prophecies easier to be remembered and to be understood that the teachings of the decisions of the past are put into general propositions and gathered into text-books, or that statutes are passed in a general form. The primary rights and duties with which jurisprudence busies itself again are nothing but prophecies. One of the many evil effects of the confusion between legal and moral ideas, about which I shall have something to say in a moment, is that theory is apt to get the cart before the horse, and to consider the right or the duty as something existing apart from and independent of the consequences of its breach, to which certain sanctions are added afterward. But, as I shall try to show, a legal duty so called is nothing but a prediction that if a man does or omits certain things he will be made to suffer in this or that way by judgment of the court;—and so of a legal right.

The number of our predictions when generalized and reduced to a system is not unmanageably large. They present themselves as a finite body of dogma which may be mastered within a reasonable time. It is a great mistake to be frightened by the ever increasing number of reports. The reports of a given jurisdiction in the course of a generation take up pretty much the whole body of the law, and restate it from the present point of view. We could reconstruct the corpus from them if all that went before were burned. The use of the earlier reports is mainly historical, a use about which I shall have something to say before I have finished.

I wish, if I can, to lay down some first principles for the study of this body of dogma or systematized prediction which we call the law, for men who want to use it as the instrument of their business to enable them to prophesy in their turn, and, as bearing upon the study, I wish to point out an ideal which as yet our law has not attained.

The first thing for a business-like understanding of the matter is to understand its limits, and therefore I think it desirable at once to point out and dispel a confusion between morality and law, which sometimes rises to the height of conscious theory, and more often and indeed constantly is making trouble in detail without reaching the point of consciousness. You can see very plainly that a bad man has as much reason as a good one for wishing to avoid an encounter with the public force, and therefore you can see the practical importance of the distinction between morality and law. A man who cares nothing for an ethical rule which is believed and practised by his neighbors is likely nevertheless to care a good deal to avoid being made to pay money, and will want to keep out of jail if he can.

I take it for granted that no hearer of mine will misinterpret what I have to say as the language of cynicism. The law is the witness and external deposit of our moral life. Its history is the history of the moral development of the race. The practice of it, in spite of popular jests, tends to make good citizens and good men. When I emphasize the difference between law and morals I do so with reference to a single end, that of learning and understanding the law. For that purpose you must definitely master its specific marks, and it is for that that I ask you for the moment to imagine yourselves indifferent to other and greater things.

I do not say that there is not a wider point of view from which the distinction between law and morals becomes of secondary or no importance, as all mathematical distinctions vanish in presence of the infinite. But I do say that that distinction is of the first importance for the object which we are here to consider,—a right study and mastery of the law as a business with well understood limits, a body of dogma enclosed within definite lines. I have just shown the practical reason for saying so. If you want to know the law and nothing else, you must look at it as a bad man, who cares only for the material consequences which such knowledge enables him to predict, not as a good one, who finds his reasons for conduct, whether inside the law or outside of it, in the vaguer sanctions of conscience. The theoretical importance of the distinction is no less, if you would reason on your subject aright. The law is full of phraseology drawn from morals, and by the mere force of language continually invites us to pass from one domain to the other without perceiving it, as we are sure to do unless we have the boundary constantly before our minds. The law talks about rights, and duties, and malice, and intent, and negligence, and so forth, and nothing is easier, or, I may say, more common in legal reasoning, than to take these words in their moral sense, at some stage of the argument, and so to drop into fallacy. For instance, when we speak of the rights of man in a moral sense, we mean to mark the limits of interference with individual freedom which we think are prescribed by conscience, or by our ideal, however reached. Yet it is certain that many laws have been enforced in the past, and it is likely that some are enforced now, which are condemned by the most enlightened opinion of the time, or which at all events pass the limit of interference as many consciences would draw it. Manifestly, therefore, nothing but confusion of thought can result from assuming that the rights of man in a moral sense are equally rights in the sense of the Constitution and the law. No doubt simple and extreme cases can be put of imaginable laws which the statute-making power would not dare to enact, even in the absence of written constitutional prohibitions, because the community would rise in rebellion and fight; and this gives some plausibility to the proposition that the law, if not a part of morality, is limited by it. But this limit of power is not coextensive with any system of morals. For the most part it falls far within the lines of any such system, and in some cases may extend beyond them, for reasons drawn from the habits of a particular people at a particular time. I once heard the late Professor Agassiz say that a German population would rise if you added two cents to the price of a glass of beer. A statute in such a case would be empty words, not because it was wrong, but because it could not be enforced. No one will deny that wrong statutes can be and are enforced, and we should not all agree as to which were the wrong ones.

The confusion with which I am dealing besets confessedly legal conceptions. Take the fundamental question, What constitutes the law? You will find some text writers telling you that it is something different from what is decided by the courts of Massachusetts or England, that it is a system of reason, that it is a deduction from principles of ethics or admitted axioms or what not, which may or may not coincide with the decisions. But if we take the view of our friend the bad man we shall find that he does not care two straws for the axioms or deductions, but that he does want to know what the Massachusetts or English courts are likely to do in fact. I am much of his mind. The prophecies of what the courts will do in fact, and nothing more pretentious, are what I mean by the law.

Take again a notion which as popularly understood is the widest conception which the law contains;—the notion of legal duty, to which already I have referred. We fill the word with all the content which we draw from morals. But what does it mean to a bad man? Mainly, and in the first place, a prophecy that if he does certain things he will be subjected to disagreeable consequences by way of imprisonment or compulsory payment of money. But from his point of view, what is the difference between being fined and being taxed a certain sum for doing a certain thing? That his point of view is the test of legal principles is shown by the many discussions which have arisen in the courts on the very question whether a given statutory liability is a penalty or a tax. On the answer to this question depends the decision whether conduct is legally wrong or right, and also whether a man is under compulsion or free. Leaving the criminal law on one side, what is the difference between the liability under the mill acts or statutes authorizing a taking by eminent domain and the liability for what we call a wrongful conversion of property where restoration is out of the question? In both cases the party taking another man's property has to pay its fair value as assessed by a jury, and no more. What significance is there in calling one taking right and another wrong from the point of view of the law? It does not matter, so far as the given consequence, the compulsory payment, is concerned, whether the act to which it is attached is described in terms of praise or in terms of blame, or whether the law purports to prohibit it or to allow it. If it matters at all, still speaking from the bad man's point of view, it must be because in one case and not in the other some further disadvantages, or at least some further consequences, are attached to the act by the law. The only other disadvantages thus attached to it which I ever have been able to think of are to be found in two somewhat insignificant legal doctrines, both of which might be abolished without much disturbance. One is, that a contract to do a prohibited act is unlawful, and the other, that, if one of two or more joint wrongdoers has to pay all the damages, he cannot recover contribution from his fellows. And that I believe is all. You see how the vague circumference of the notion of duty shrinks and at the same time grows more precise when we wash it with cynical acid and expel everything except the object of our study, the operations of the law.

Nowhere is the confusion between legal and moral ideas more manifest than in the law of contract. Among other things, here again the so called primary rights and duties are invested with a mystic significance beyond what can be assigned and explained. The duty to keep a contract at common law means a prediction that you must pay damages if you do not keep it,—and nothing else. If you commit a tort, you are liable to pay a compensatory sum. If you commit a contract, you are liable to pay a compensatory sum unless the promised event comes to pass, and that is all the difference. But such a mode of looking at the matter stinks in the nostrils of those who think it advantageous to get as much ethics into the law as they can. It was good enough for Lord Coke, however, and here, as in many other cases, I am content to abide with him. In Bromage v. Genning, a prohibition was sought in the King's Bench against a suit in the marches of Wales for the specific performance of a covenant to grant a lease, and Coke said that it would subvert the intention of the covenantor, since he intends it to be at his election either to lose the damages or to make the lease. Sergeant Harris for the plaintiff confessed that he moved the matter against his conscience, and a prohibition was granted. This goes further than we should go now, but it shows what I venture to say has been the common law point of view from the beginning, although Mr. Harriman, in his very able little book upon Contracts has been misled, as I humbly think, to a different conclusion.

I have spoken only of the common law, because there are some cases in which a logical justification can be found for speaking of civil liabilities as imposing duties in an intelligible sense. These are the relatively few in which equity will grant an injunction, and will enforce it by putting the defendant in prison or otherwise punishing him unless he complies with the order of the court. But I hardly think it advisable to shape general theory from the exception, and I think it would be better to cease troubling ourselves about primary rights and sanctions altogether, than to describe our prophecies concerning the liabilities commonly imposed by the law in those inappropriate terms.

I mentioned, as other examples of the use by the law of words drawn from morals, malice, intent, and negligence. It is enough to take malice as it is used in the law of civil liability for wrongs,—what we lawyers call the law of torts,—to show you that it means something different in law from what it means in morals, and also to show how the difference has been obscured by giving to principles which have little or nothing to do with each other the same name. Three hundred years ago a parson preached a sermon and told a story out of Fox's Book of Martyrs of a man who had assisted at the torture of one of the saints, and afterward died, suffering compensatory inward torment. It happened that Fox was wrong. The man was alive and chanced to hear the sermon, and thereupon he sued the parson. Chief Justice Wray instructed the jury that the defendant was not liable, because the story was told innocently, without malice. He took malice in the moral sense, as importing a malevolent motive. But nowadays no one doubts that a man may be liable, without any malevolent motive at all, for false statements manifestly calculated to inflict temporal damage. In stating the case in pleading, we still should call the defendant's conduct malicious; but, in my opinion at least, the word means nothing about motives, or even about the defendant's attitude toward the future, but only signifies that the tendency of his conduct under the known circumstances was very plainly to cause the plaintiff temporal harm.

In the law of contract the use of moral phraseology has led to equal confusion, as I have shown in part already, but only in part. Morals deal with the actual internal state of the individual's mind, what he actually intends. From the time of the Romans down to now, this mode of dealing has affected the language of the law as to contract, and the language used has reacted upon the thought. We talk about a contract as a meeting of the minds of the parties, and thence it is inferred in various cases that there is no contract because their minds have not met; that is, because they have intended different things or because one party has not known of the assent of the other. Yet nothing is more certain than that parties may be bound by a contract to things which neither of them intended, and when one does not know of the other's assent. Suppose a contract is executed in due form and in writing to deliver a lecture, mentioning no time. One of the parties thinks that the promise will be construed to mean at once, within a week. The other thinks that it means when he is ready. The court says that it means within a reasonable time. The parties are bound by the contract as it is interpreted by the court, yet neither of them meant what the court declares that they have said. In my opinion no one will understand the true theory of contract or be able even to discuss some fundamental questions intelligently until he has understood that all contracts are formal, that the making of a contract depends not on the agreement of two minds in one intention, but on the agreement of two sets of external signs,—not on the parties' having *meant* the same thing but on their having *said* the same thing. Furthermore, as the signs may be addressed to one sense or another,—to sight or to hearing,—on the nature of the sign will depend the moment when the contract is made. If the sign is tangible, for instance, a letter, the contract is made when the letter of acceptance is delivered. If it is necessary that the minds of the parties meet, there will be no contract until the acceptance can be read,—none, for example, if the acceptance be snatched from the hand of the offerer by a third person.

This is not the time to work out a theory in detail, or to answer many obvious doubts and questions which are suggested by these general views. I know of none which are not easy to answer, but what I am trying to do now is only by a series of hints to throw some light on the narrow path of legal doctrine, and upon two pitfalls which, as it seems to me, lie perilously near to it. Of the first of these I have said enough. I hope that my illustrations have shown the danger, both to speculation and to practice, of confounding morality with law, and the trap which legal language lays for us on that side of our way. For my own part, I often doubt whether it would not be a gain if every word of moral significance could be banished from the law altogether, and other words adopted which should convey legal ideas uncolored by anything outside the law. We should lose the fossil records of a good deal of history and the majesty got from ethical associations, but by ridding ourselves of an unnecessary confusion we should gain very much in the clearness of our thought. . . .

Moral and Legal Obligation*
H.L.A. Hart

Justice constitutes one segment of morality primarily concerned not with individual conduct but with the ways in which *classes* of individuals are treated. It is this which gives justice its special relevance in the criticism of law and of other public or social institutions. It is the most public and the most legal of the virtues. But principles of justice do not exhaust the idea of morality; and not all criticism of law made on moral grounds is made in the name of justice. Laws may be condemned as morally bad simply because they require men to do particular actions which morality forbids individuals to do, or because they require men to abstain from doing those which are morally obligatory.

It is therefore necessary to characterize, in general terms, those principles, rules, and standards relating to the conduct of individuals which belong to morality and make conduct morally obligatory. Two related difficulties confront us here. The first is that the word 'morality' and all other associated or nearly synonymous terms like 'ethics', have their own considerable area of vagueness or 'open texture'. There are certain forms of principle or rule which some would rank as moral and which others would not. Secondly, even where there is agreement on this point and certain rules or principles are accepted as indisputably belonging to morality, there may still be great philosophical disagreement as to their *status* or relation to the rest of human knowledge and experience. Are they immutable principles which constitute part of the fabric of the Universe, not made by man, but awaiting discovery by the human intellect? Or are they expressions of changing human attitudes, choices, demands, or feelings? These are crude formulations of two extremes in moral philosophy. Between them lie many complicated and subtle variants, which philosophers have developed in the effort to elucidate the nature of morality.

In what follows we shall seek to evade these philosophical difficulties. We shall later identify under the heads of 'Importance', 'Immunity from deliberate change', 'Voluntary character of moral offences', and 'The form of moral pressure' four cardinal features which are constantly found together in those principles, rules, and standards of conduct which are most commonly accounted 'moral'. These four features reflect different aspects of a characteristic and important function which such standards perform in social life or in the life of individuals. This alone would justify us in marking off whatever has these four features for separate consideration, and above all, for contrast and comparison with law. Moreover, the claim that morality has these four features is neutral between rival philosophical theories as to its *status* or 'fundamental' character. Certainly most, if not all, philosophers would agree that these four features were necessary in any moral rule or principle, though they would offer very different interpretations or explanations of the fact that morality possesses them. It may indeed be objected that these features though necessary are *only* necessary and not sufficient to distinguish morality from certain rules or principles of conduct which would be excluded from morality by a more stringent test. We shall refer to the facts

*   H.L.A. Hart, The Concept of Law (Oxford: Oxford University Press, 1961), pages 163-176. © Oxford University Press 1961. Reprinted from The Concept of Law by H.L.A. Hart (1961) by permission of Oxford University Press.

on which such objections are based but we shall adhere to the wider sense of 'morality'. Our justification for this is both that this accords with much usage and that what the word in this wide sense designates, performs an important, distinguishable function in social and individual life.

We shall consider first the social phenomenon often referred to as '*the* morality' of a given society or the 'accepted' or 'conventional' morality of an actual social group. These phrases refer to standards of conduct which are widely shared in a particular society, and are to be contrasted with the moral principles or moral ideals which may govern an individual's life, but which he does not share with any considerable number of those with whom he lives. The basic element in the shared or accepted morality of a social group consists of rules of the kind which we have already described . . . when we were concerned to elucidate the general idea of obligation, and which we there called primary rules of obligation. These rules are distinguished from others both by the serious social pressure by which they are supported, and by the considerable sacrifice of individual interest or inclination which compliance with them involves. [W]e also drew a picture of a society at a stage in which such rules were the only means of social control. We noticed that at that stage there might be nothing corresponding to the clear distinction made, in more developed societies, between legal and moral rules. Possibly some embryonic form of this distinction might be present if there were some rules which were primarily maintained by threats of punishment for disobedience, and others maintained by appeals to presumed respect for the rules or to feelings of guilt or remorse. When this early stage is passed, and the step from the pre-legal into the legal world is taken, so that the means of social control now includes a system of rules containing rules of recognition, adjudication, and change, this contrast between legal and other rules hardens into something definite. The primary rules of obligation identified through the official system are now set apart from other rules, which continue to exist side by side with those officially recognized. In fact in our own, and indeed in all communities which reach this stage, there are many types of social rule and standard lying outside the legal system; only some of these are usually thought and spoken of as moral, though certain legal theorists have used the word 'moral' to designate all non-legal rules.

Such non-legal rules may be distinguished and classified in many different ways. Some are rules of very limited scope concerning only a particular sphere of conduct (e.g. dress) or activities for which there are only intermittent opportunities, deliberately created (ceremonies and games). Some rules are conceived as applying to the social group in general; others to special sub-groups within it, either marked off by certain characteristics as a distinct social class, or by their own choice to meet or combine for limited purposes. Some rules are considered to be binding by virtue of agreement and may allow for voluntary withdrawal: others are thought not to have their origin in agreement or any other form of deliberate choice. Some rules when broken may meet with no more than an assertion or reminder of the 'right' thing to do (e.g. etiquette or rules of correct speech), others with serious blame or contempt or more or less protracted exclusion from the association concerned. Though no precise scale could be constructed, a conception of the relative importance attributed to these different types of rules is reflected both in the measure of sacrifice of private interest which they demand, and the weight of social pressure for conformity.

In all societies which have developed a legal system there are, among its non-legal rules, some to which supreme importance is attached, and which in spite of crucial differences have many similarities to its law. Very often the vocabulary of 'rights', 'obligations', and 'duties' used to express the requirements of legal rules is used with the addition of 'moral', to express the acts or forbearances required by these rules. In all communities there is a partial overlap in content between legal and moral obligation; though the requirements of legal rules are more specific and are hedged round with more detailed exceptions than their moral counterparts. Characteristically, moral obligation and duty, like many legal rules, concern what is to be done or not to be done in circumstances constantly recurring in the life of the group, rather than in rare or intermittent activities on deliberately selected occasions. What such rules require are either forbearances, or actions which are simple in the sense that no special skill or intellect is required for their performance. Moral obligations, like most legal obligations, are within the capacity of any normal adult. Compliance with these moral rules, as with legal rules, is taken as a matter of course, so that while breach attracts serious censure, conformity to moral obligation, again, like obedience to the law, is not a matter for praise except when marked by exceptional conscientiousness, endurance, or resistance to special temptation. Various classifications of moral obligations and duties may be made. Some belong to relatively distinct, enduring functions or roles, which not all members of society occupy. Such are the duties of a father or husband to care for his family. On the other hand, there are both general obligations which all normal adults are conceived as having throughout life (e.g. to abstain from violence) and special obligations which any such member may incur by entering into special relations with others (e.g. obligations to keep promises or return services rendered).

The obligations and duties recognized in moral rules of this most fundamental kind may vary from society to society or within a single society at different times. Some of them may reflect quite erroneous or even superstitious beliefs as to what is required for the health or safety of the group; in one society it may be a wife's duty to throw herself on her husband's funeral pyre, and in another, suicide may be an offence against common morality. There is a diversity among moral codes which may spring either from the peculiar but real needs of a given society, or from superstition or ignorance. Yet the social morality of societies which have reached the stage where this can be distinguished from its law, always includes certain obligations and duties, requiring the sacrifice of private inclination or interest which is essential to the survival of any society, so long as men and the world in which they live retain some of their most familiar and obvious characteristics. Among such rules obviously required for social life are those forbidding, or at least restricting, the free use of violence, rules requiring certain forms of honesty and truthfulness in dealings with others, and rules forbidding the destruction of tangible things or their seizure from others. If conformity with these most elementary rules were not thought a matter of course among any group of individuals, living in close proximity to each other, we should be doubtful of the description of the group as a society, and certain that it could not endure for long.

Moral and legal rules of obligation and duty have therefore certain striking similarities enough to show that their common vocabulary is no accident. These may be summarized as follows. They are alike in that they are conceived as binding independently of the consent of the individual bound and are supported by serious social pressure for conformity; compliance with both legal and moral obligations is regarded not as a matter for praise but as a minimum contribution to social life to be taken as a matter of course. Further both law and morals include rules governing the behaviour of individuals in situations constantly recurring throughout life rather than special activities or occasions, and though both may include much that is peculiar to the real or fancied needs of a particular society, both make demands which must obviously be satisfied by any group of human beings who are to succeed in living together. Hence some forms of prohibition of violence to person or property, and some requirements of honesty and truthfulness will be found in both alike. Yet, in spite of these similarities, it has seemed obvious to many that there are certain characteristics which law and morals cannot share, though in the history of jurisprudence these have proved most difficult to formulate.

The most famous attempt to convey in summary fashion their essential difference is the theory which asserts that, while legal rules only require 'external' behaviour and are indifferent to the motives, intentions, or other 'internal' accompaniments of conduct, morals on the other hand do not require any specific external actions but only a good will or proper intentions or motive. This really amounts to the surprising assertion that legal and moral rules properly understood could not ever have the same content; and though it does contain a hint of the truth it is, as it stands, profoundly misleading. It is in fact an inference, though a mistaken one, from certain important characteristics of morals, and particularly from certain differences between moral blame and legal punishment. If someone does something forbidden by moral rules or fails to do what they require, the fact that he did so unintentionally and in spite of every care is an excuse from *moral* blame; whereas a legal system or custom may have rules of 'strict liability' under which those who have broken the rules unintentionally and without 'fault' may be liable to punishment. So it is indeed true that while the notion of 'strict liability' in morals comes as near to being a contradiction in terms as anything in this sphere, it is something which may be merely open to criticism when found in a legal system. But this does not mean that morals require only good intention, will, or motives. Indeed to argue thus is, as we show later, to confuse the idea of an *excuse* with that of a *justification* for conduct.

None the less there is something of importance caricatured in this confused argument; the vague sense that the difference between law and morals is connected with a contrast between the 'internality' of the one and the 'externality' of the other is too recurrent a theme in speculation about law and morals to be altogether baseless. Rather than dismiss it, we shall treat it as a compendious statement of four cardinal related features which collectively serve to distinguish morality not only from legal rules but from other forms of social rule.

(i) *Importance.* To say that an essential feature of *any* moral rule or standard is that it is regarded as something of great importance to maintain may appear both truistic and vague. Yet this feature cannot be omitted in any faithful account of the morality of any social group or individual, nor can it be made more precise. It is manifested in many ways: first, in the simple fact that moral standards are maintained against the drive of strong passions which they restrict, and at the cost of sacrificing considerable personal interest; secondly, in the serious forms of social pressure exerted not only to obtain conformity in individual cases, but to secure that moral standards are taught or communicated as a matter of course to all in society; thirdly, in the general recognition that, if moral standards were not generally accepted, far-reaching and distasteful changes in the life of individuals would occur. In contrast with morals, the rules of deportment, manners, dress, and some, though not all, rules of law, occupy a relatively low place in the scale of serious importance. They may be tiresome to follow, but they do not demand great sacrifice: no great pressure is exerted to obtain conformity and no great alterations in other areas of social life would follow if they were not observed or changed. Much of the importance thus ascribed to the maintenance of moral rules may be very simply explained on agreeably rationalistic lines; for even though they demand sacrifice of private interests on the part of the person bound, compliance with them secures vital interests which all share alike. It does so either by directly protecting persons from obvious harm or by maintaining the fabric of a tolerable, orderly society. But though the rationality of much social morality, as a protection from obvious harms, may be defended in this way, this simple utilitarian approach is not always possible; nor, where it is, should it be taken to represent the point of view of those who live by a morality. After all, a most prominent part of the morality of any society consists of rules concerning sexual behaviour, and it is far from clear that the importance attached to them is connected with the belief that the conduct they forbid is harmful to others; nor could such rules always be shown in fact to have this justification. Even in a modern society which has ceased to look on its morality as divinely ordained, calculations of harmfulness to others do not account for the importance attached to moral regulation of sexual behaviour such as the common veto on homosexuality. Sexual functions and feelings are matter of such moment and emotional concern to all, that deviations from the accepted or normal forms of their expression easily become invested with an intrinsic 'pudor' or importance. They are abhorred, not out of conviction of their social harmfulness but simply as 'unnatural' or in themselves repugnant. Yet it would be absurd to deny the title of morality to emphatic social vetoes of this sort; indeed, sexual morality is perhaps the most prominent aspect of what plain men think morality to be. Of course the fact that society may view its own morality in this 'non-utilitarian' way does not mean that its rules are immune from criticism or condemnation, where their maintenance is judged useless or purchased at the cost of great suffering.

Legal rules, as we have seen, may correspond with moral rules in the sense of requiring or forbidding the same behaviour. Those that do so are no doubt felt to be as important as their moral counterparts. Yet importance is not essential to the status of all legal rules as it is to that of morals. A legal rule may be generally thought quite unimportant to maintain; indeed it may generally be agreed that it should be repealed: yet it remains a legal rule until it is repealed. It would, on the other hand, be absurd to think of a rule as part of the morality of a society even though no one thought it any longer important or worth maintaining. Old customs and traditions now maintained merely for old time's sake may, indeed, once have had the status of moral rules, but their status as part of morality has evaporated together with the importance attached to their observance and breach.

(ii) *Immunity from deliberate change.* It is characteristic of a legal system that new legal rules can be introduced and old ones changed or repealed by deliberate enactment, even though some laws may be protected from change by a written constitution limiting the competence of the supreme legislature. By contrast moral rules or principles *cannot* be brought into being or changed or eliminated in this way. To assert that this 'cannot' be is not, however, to deny that some conceivable state of affairs is actually the case, as the assertion that human beings 'cannot' alter the climate would be. Instead this assertion points to the following facts. It is perfectly good sense to say such things as 'As from 1 January 1960 it will be a criminal offence to do so-and-so' or 'As from 1 January 1960 it will be no longer illegal to do so-and-so' and to support such statements by reference to laws which have been enacted or repealed. By contrast such statements as 'As from tomorrow it will no longer be immoral to do so-and-so' or 'On 1 January last it became immoral to do so-and-so' and attempts to support these by reference to deliberate enactment would be astonishing paradoxes, if not senseless. For it is inconsistent with the part played by morality in the lives of individuals that moral rules, principles, or standards should be regarded, as laws are, as things capable of creation or change by deliberate act. Standards of conduct cannot be endowed with, or deprived of, moral status by human *fiat,* though the daily use of such concepts as enactment and repeal shows that the same is not true of law.

Much moral philosophy is devoted to the explanation of this feature of morality, and to the elucidation of the sense that morality is something 'there' to be recognized, not made by deliberate human choice. But the fact itself as distinct from its explanation is not a peculiarity of moral rules. This is why this feature of morality, though exceedingly important, cannot serve by itself to distinguish morality from all other forms of social norms. For in this respect, though not in others, any social tradition is like morals: tradition too is incapable of enactment or repeal by human *fiat.* The story, perhaps apocryphal, that the headmaster of a new English public school announced that, as from the beginning of the next term, it would be a tradition of the school that senior boys should wear a certain dress, depends for its comic effect wholly on the logical incompatibility of the notion of a tradition with that of deliberate enactment and choice. Rules acquire and lose the status of traditions by growing, being practiced, ceasing to be practiced, and decaying; and rules brought into being or eliminated otherwise than by these slow, involuntary processes could not thereby acquire or lose the status of tradition.

The fact that morals and traditions cannot be directly changed, as laws may be, by legislative enactment must not be mistaken for immunity from other forms of change. Indeed though a moral rule or tradition cannot be repealed or changed by deliberate choice or enactment, the enactment or repeal of laws may well be among the causes of a change or decay of some moral standard or some tradition. If a traditional practice such as the celebrations on Guy Fawkes night is forbidden by law and punished, the practice may cease and the tradition may disappear. Conversely, if the laws require military service from certain classes, this may ultimately develop a tradition among them which may well outlive the law. So too legal enactments may set standards of honesty and humanity, which ultimately alter and raise the current morality; conversely, legal repression of practices thought morally obligatory may, in the end, cause the sense of their importance and so their status as morality to be lost; yet, very often, the law loses such battles with ingrained morality, and the moral rule continues in full vigour side by side with laws which forbid what it enjoins.

These modes of change of tradition and morality in which the law may be a causal factor must be distinguished from legislative change or repeal. For though the acquisition or loss of *legal* status due to enactment may indeed be spoken of as the enacted statute's 'legal effect' this is not a contingent causal change, as the statute's eventual effect on morals and tradition is. This difference may be simply seen in the fact that while it is always possible to doubt whether a clear, valid, legal enactment will lead to a change in morals, no similar doubts could be entertained as to whether a clear, valid, legal enactment has changed the law.

The incompatibility of the idea of morality or tradition with that of change by deliberate enactment, must also be distinguished from the immunity conferred on certain laws in some systems by the restrictive clauses of a constitution. Such immunity is not a necessary element in the status of a law as a law, for this immunity may be removed by constitutional amendment. Unlike such legal immunity from legislative change, the incapacity of morals or tradition for similar modes of change is not something which varies from community to community or from time to time. It is incorporated in the meaning of these terms; the idea of a moral legislature with competence to make and change morals, as legal enactments make and change law, is repugnant to the whole notion of morality. When we come to consider international law we shall find it important to distinguish the mere *de facto* absence of a legislature, which may be regarded as a defect of the system, from the fundamental inconsistency which, as we have stressed here, is latent in the idea that moral rules or standards could be made or repealed by legislation.

(iii) *Voluntary character of moral offences.* The old conception that morals are exclusively concerned with what is 'internal' while law is concerned only with 'external' behaviour is in part a misstatement of the two features already discussed. But it is most often treated as a reference to certain prominent characteristics of moral responsibility and moral blame. If a person whose action, judged *ab extra,* has offended against moral rules or principles, succeeds in establishing that he did this unintentionally and in spite of every precaution that it was possible for him to take, he is excused from moral responsibility, and to blame him in these circumstances would itself be considered morally objectionable. Moral blame is therefore excluded because he has done all that he could do. In any developed legal system the same is true up to a point; for the general requirement of *mens rea* is an element in criminal responsibility designed to secure that those who offend without carelessness, unwittingly, or in conditions in which they lacked the bodily or mental capacity to conform to the law, should be excused. A legal system would be open to serious moral condemnation if this were not so, at any rate in cases of serious crimes carrying severe punishments.

None the less admission of such excuses in all legal systems is qualified in many different ways. The real or alleged difficulties of proof of psychological facts may lead a legal system to refuse to investigate the actual mental states or capacities of particular individuals, and, instead, to use 'objective tests', whereby the individual charged with an offence is taken to have the capacities for control or ability to take precautions that a normal or 'reasonable' man would have. Some systems may refuse to consider 'volitional' as distinct from 'cognitive' disabilities; if so they confine the range of excuses to lack of intention or defects of knowledge. Again, the legal system may, for certain types of offence, impose 'strict liability' and make responsibility independent of *mens rea* altogether, except perhaps for the minimum requirement that the accused must possess normal muscular control.

It is therefore clear that legal responsibility is not necessarily excluded by the demonstration that an accused person could not have kept the law which he has broken; by contrast, in morals 'I could not help it' is always an excuse, and moral obligation would be altogether different from what it is if the moral 'ought' did not in this sense imply 'can'. Yet it is important to see that 'I could not help it' is only an excuse (though a good one), and to distinguish excuse from justification; for, as we have said, the claim that morals do not require external behaviour rests on a confusion of these two ideas. If good intentions were a justification for doing what moral rules forbid, there would be nothing to deplore in the action of a man who had accidentally and in spite of every care killed another. We should look upon it as we now look upon a man's killing another, when this is required as a necessary measure of self-defence. The latter is *justified* because killing, in such circumstances, is a kind of conduct which the system is not concerned to prevent and may even encourage, though it is of course an exception to a general prohibition of killing. Where someone is *excused* because he offended unintentionally, the underlying moral conception is not that this action is of a kind which it is the policy of the law to permit or even welcome; it is that when we investigate the mental condition of the particular offender, we find that he lacked the normal capacity to conform to the law's requirements. Hence this aspect of the 'internality' of morals does not mean that morals is not a form of control of outward conduct; but only that it is a necessary condition for moral responsibility that the individual must have a certain type of control over his conduct. Even in morals there is a difference between 'He did not do the wrong thing' and 'He could not help doing what he did'.

(iv) *The form of moral pressure.* A further distinguishing feature of morality is the characteristic form of moral pressure which is exerted in its support. This feature is closely related to the last and like it has powerfully contributed to the vague sense that moral is concerned with what is 'internal'. The facts which have led to this interpretation of morality are these. If it were the case that whenever someone was about to break a rule of conduct, *only* threats of physical punishment or unpleasant consequences were used in argument to dissuade him, then it would be impossible to regard such a rule as a part of the morality of the society, though this would not be any objection to treating it as part of its law. Indeed the typical form of legal pressure may well be said to consist in such threats. With morals on the other hand the typical form of pressure consists in appeals to the respect for the rules, as things important in themselves, which is presumed to be shared by those addressed. So moral pressure is characteristically, though not exclusively, exerted not by threats or by appeals to fear or interest, but by reminders of the moral character of the action contemplated and of the demands of morality. 'That would be a lie', 'That would be to break your promise'. In the background there are indeed the 'internal' moral analogues of fear of punishment; for it is assumed that protests will awaken in those addressed a sense of shame or guilt: they may be 'punished' by their own conscience. Of course sometimes such distinctively moral appeals are accompanied by threats of physical punishment, or by appeals to ordinary personal interest; deviations from the moral code meet with many different forms of hostile social reaction, ranging from relatively informal expressions of contempt to severance of social relations or ostracism. But emphatic reminders of what the rules demand, appeals to conscience, and reliance on the operation of guilt and remorse, are the characteristic and most prominent forms of pressure used for the support of social morality. That it should be supported in just these ways is a simple consequence of the acceptance of moral rules and standards, as things which it is supremely and obviously important to maintain. Standards not supported in these ways could not have the place in social and personal life distinctive of moral obligation.

Riggs v. Palmer
115 N.Y. 506 (1889)

Earl, J.

On the 13th day of August 1880, Francis B. Palmer made his last will and testament, in which he gave small legacies to his two daughters, Mrs. Riggs and Mrs. Preston, the plaintiffs in this action, and the remainder of his estate to his grandson, the defendant, Elmer E. Palmer, subject to the support of Susan Palmer, his mother, with a gift over to the two daughters, subject to the support of Mrs. Palmer, in case Elmer should survive him and die under age, unmarried, and without any issue. The testator at the date of his will owned a farm, and considerable personal property. He was a widower, and thereafter, in March 1882, he was married to Mrs. Bresee, with whom before his marriage he entered into an antenuptial contract in which it was agreed that, in lieu of dower and all other claims upon his estate in case she survived him, she should have her support upon his farm during her life, and such support was expressly charged upon the farm. At the date of the will, and, subsequently, to the death of the testator, Elmer lived with him as a member of his family, and at his death was 16 years old. He knew of the provisions made in his favor in the will, and, that he might prevent his grandfather from revoking such provisions, which he had manifested some intention to do, and to obtain the speedy enjoyment and immediate possession of his property, he willfully murdered him by poisoning him. He now claims the property, and the sole question for our determination is, can he have it? The defendants say that the testator is dead; that his will was made in due form and has been admitted to probate, and that, therefore, it must have effect according to the letter of the law.

It is quite true that statutes regulating the making, proof, and effect of wills and the devolution of property, if literally construed, and if their force and effect can in no way and under no circumstances be controlled or modified, give this property to the murderer.

The purpose of those statutes was to enable testators to dispose of their estates to the objects of their bounty at death, and to carry into effect their final wishes legally expressed; and in considering and giving effect to them this purpose must be kept in view. It was the intention of the law-makers that the donees in a will should have the property given to them. But it never could have been their intention that a donee who murdered the testator to make the will operative should have any benefit under it. If such a case had been present to their minds, and it had been supposed necessary to make some provision of law to meet it, it cannot be doubted that they would have provided for it. It is a familiar canon of construction that a thing which is within the intention of the makers of a statute is as much within the statute as if it were within the letter; and a thing which is within the letter of the statute is not within the statute unless it be within the intention of the makers. The writers of laws do not always express their intention perfectly, but either exceed it or fall short of it, so that judges are to collect it from probable or rational conjectures only, and this is called "rational interpretation"; and Rutherford, in his Institutes, says: "When we make use of rational interpretation, sometimes we restrain the meaning of the writer so as to take in less, and sometimes we extend or enlarge his meaning so as to take in more than his words express."

Such a construction ought to be put upon a statute as will best answer the intention which the makers had in view, for "qui haeret in litera, haeret in cortice" (he who considers merely the letter goes only skin deep). In Bacon's Abridgment (Statutes I, 5), Puffendorf (Law Nat. book 5, chapter 12), Rutherford (Inst. 422, 427), and in Smith's Commentaries (814), many cases are mentioned where it was held that matters embraced in the general words of statutes, nevertheless, were not within the statutes, because it could not have been the intention of the law-makers that they should be included. They were taken out of the statutes by an equitable construction, and it is said in Bacon: "By an equitable construction a case not within the letter of a statute is sometimes holden to be within the meaning, because it is within the mischief for which a remedy is provided. The reason for such construction is that the law-makers could not set down every case in express terms. In order to form a right judgment whether a case be within the equity of a statute, it is a good way to suppose the law-maker present, and that you have asked him this question, did you intend to comprehend this case? Then you must give yourself such answer as you imagine he, being an upright and reasonable man, would have given. If this be that he did mean to comprehend it, you may safely hold the case to be within the equity of the statute; for while you do no more than he would have done, you do not act contrary to the statute, but in conformity thereto." In some cases the letter of a legislative act is restrained by an equitable construction; in others it is enlarged; in others the construction is contrary to the letter. The equitable construction which restrains the letter of a statute is defined by Aristotle, as frequently quoted, in this manner: "Aequitas est correctio legis generaliter latae, qua parte deficit" (Equity is the correction of that wherein the law, by reason of its generality, is deficient). If the law-makers could, as to this case, be consulted, would they say that they intended by their general language that the property of a testator or of an ancestor should pass to one who had taken his life for the express purpose of getting his property? In 1 Blackstone's Commentaries 91 the learned author, speaking of the construction of statutes, says: "If there arise out of them collaterally any absurd consequences manifestly contradictory to common reason, they are with regard to those collateral consequences void. . . . When some collateral matter arises out of the general words, and happens to be unreasonable, then the judges are in decency to conclude that this consequence was not foreseen by the parliament, and, therefore, they are at liberty to expound the statute by equity, and only *quoad hoc* [with respect to this] disregard it"; and he gives as an illustration, if an act of parliament gives a man power to try all causes that arise within his manor of Dale, yet, if a cause should arise in which he himself is party, the act is construed not to extend to that because it is unreasonable that any man should determine his own quarrel.

There was a statute in Bologna that whoever drew blood in the streets should be severely punished, and yet it was held not to apply to the case of a barber who opened a vein in the street. It is commanded in the decalogue that no work shall be done upon the Sabbath, and yet, giving the command a rational interpretation founded upon its design, the Infallible Judge held that it did not prohibit works of necessity, charity, or benevolence on that day.

What could be more unreasonable than to suppose that it was the legislative intention in the general laws passed for the orderly, peaceable, and just devolution of property, that they should have operation in favor of one who murdered his ancestor that he might speedily come into the possession of his estate? Such an intention is inconceivable. We need not, therefore, be much troubled by the general language contained in the laws.

Besides, all laws as well as all contracts may be controlled in their operation and effect by general, fundamental maxims of the common law. No one shall be permitted to profit by his own fraud, or to take advantage of his own wrong, or to found any claim upon his own iniquity, or to acquire property by his own crime. These maxims are dictated by public policy, have their foundation in universal law administered in all civilized countries, and have nowhere been superseded by statutes. They were applied in the decision of the case of the New York Mutual Life Insurance Co. v. Armstrong. There it was held that the person who procured a policy upon the life of another, payable at his death, and then murdered the assured to make the policy payable, could not recover thereon. Mr. Justice Field, writing the opinion, said: "Independently of any proof of the motives of Hunter in obtaining the policy, and even assuming that they were just and proper, he forfeited all rights under it when, to secure its immediate payment, he murdered the assured. It would be a reproach to the jurisprudence of the country if one could recover insurance money payable on the death of a party whose life he had feloniously taken. As well might he recover insurance money upon a building that he had willfully fired."

These maxims, without any statute giving them force or operation, frequently control the effect and nullify the language of wills. A will procured by fraud and deception, like any other instrument, may be decreed void and set aside, and so a particular portion of a will may be excluded from probate, or held inoperative if induced by the fraud or undue influence of the person in whose favor it is. So a will may contain provisions which are immoral, irreligious, or against public policy, and they will be held void.

Here there was no certainty that this murderer would survive the testator, or that the testator would not change his will, and there was no certainty that he would get this property if nature was allowed to take its course. He therefore murdered the testator expressly to vest himself with an estate. Under such circumstances, what law, human or divine, will allow him to take the estate and enjoy the fruits of his crime? The will spoke and became operative at the death of the testator. He caused that death, and thus by his crime made it speak and have operation. Shall it speak and operate in his favor? If he had met the testator and taken his property by force, he would have had no title to it. Shall he acquire title by murdering him? If he had gone to the testator's house, and by force compelled him, or by fraud or undue influence had induced him to will him his property, the law would not allow him to hold it. But can he give effect and operation to a will by murder, and yet take the property? To answer these questions in the affirmative, it seems to me, would be a reproach to the jurisprudence of our state, and an offense against public policy.

Under the civil law, evolved from the general principles of natural law and justice by many generations of jurisconsults, philosophers, and statesmen, one cannot take property by inheritance or will from an ancestor or benefactor whom he has murdered. Domat's Civil Law, part 2, book 1, tit. 1, § 3; Code Napoleon, § 727; Mackeldy's Roman Law, 530, 550. In the Civil Code of Lower Canada the provisions on the subject in the Code Napoleon have been substantially copied. But, so far as I can find, in no country where the common law prevails has it been deemed important to enact a law to provide for such a case. Our revisers and law-makers were familiar with the civil law, and they did not deem it important to incorporate into our statutes its provisions upon this subject. This is not a *casus omissus* [a case not provided for]. It was evidently supposed that the maxims of the common law were sufficient to regulate such a case, and that a specific enactment for that purpose was not needed.

For the same reasons the defendant Palmer cannot take any of this property as heir. Just before the murder he was not an heir, and it was not certain that he ever would be. He might have died before his grandfather, or might have been disinherited by him. He made himself an heir by the murder, and he seeks to take property as the fruit of his crime. What has before been said as to him as legatee applies to him with equal force as an heir. He cannot vest himself with title by crime.

My view of this case does not inflict upon Elmer any greater or other punishment for his crime than the law specifies. It takes from him no property, but simply holds that he shall not acquire property by his crime, and thus be rewarded for its commission.

Our attention is called to Owens v. Owens, as a case quite like this. There a wife had been convicted of being an accessory before the fact to the murder of her husband, and it was held that she was, nevertheless, entitled to dower. I am unwilling to assent to the doctrine of that case. The statutes provide dower for a wife who has the misfortune to survive her husband and thus lose his support and protection. It is clear beyond their purpose to make provision for a wife who by her own crime makes herself a widow and willfully and intentionally deprives herself of the support and protection of her husband. As she might have died before him, and thus never have been his widow, she cannot by her crime vest herself with an estate. The principle which lies at the bottom of the maxim, *volenti non fit injuria* [one who voluntarily exposes herself to a risk is precluded from a recovery for injury resulting therefrom], should be applied to such a case, and a widow should not, for the purpose of acquiring, as such, property rights, be permitted to allege a widowhood which she has wickedly and intentionally created.

The facts found entitled the plaintiffs to the relief they seek. The error of the referee was in his conclusion of law. Instead of granting a new trial, therefore, I think the proper judgment upon the facts found should be ordered here. The facts have been passed upon twice with the same result, first upon the trial of Palmer for murder, and then by the referee in this action. We are, therefore, of opinion that the ends of justice do not require that they should again come in question.

The judgment of the General Term and that entered upon the report of the referee should, therefore, be reversed, and judgment should be entered as follows: That Elmer E. Palmer and the administrator be enjoined from using any of the personalty or real estate left by the testator for Elmer's benefit; that the devise and bequest in the will to Elmer be declared ineffective to pass the title to him; that by reason of the crime of murder committed upon the grandfather he is deprived of any interest in the estate left by him; that the plaintiffs are the true owners of the real and personal estate left by the testator, subject to the charge in favor of Elmer's mother and the widow of the testator, under the antenuptial agreement, and that the plaintiffs have costs in all the courts against Elmer.

Gray, J. (dissenting).

This appeal presents an extraordinary state of facts, and the case, in respect of them, I believe, is without precedent in this state.

The respondent, a lad of 16 years of age, being aware of the provisions in his grand-father's will, which constituted him the residuary legatee of the testator's estate, caused his death by poison in 1882. For this crime he was tried and was convicted of murder in the second degree, and at the time of the commencement of this action he was serving out his sentence in the state reformatory. This action was brought by two of the children of the testator for the purpose of having those provisions of the will in the respondent's favor canceled and annulled.

The appellants' argument for a reversal of the judgment, which dismissed their complaint, is that the respondent unlawfully prevented a revocation of the existing will, or a new will from being made, by his crime; and that he terminated the enjoyment by the testator of his property and effected his own succession to it by the same crime. They say that to permit the respondent to take the property willed to him would be to permit him to take advantage of his own wrong.

To sustain their position the appellants' counsel has submitted an able and elaborate brief, and, if I believed that the decision of the question could be effected by considerations of an equitable nature, I should not hesitate to assent to views which commend themselves to the conscience. But the matter does not lie within the domain of conscience. We are bound by the rigid rules of law, which have been established by the legislature, and within the limits of which the determination of this question is confined. The question we are dealing with is, whether a testamentary disposition can be altered, or a will revoked, after the testator's death, through an appeal to the courts, when the legislature has, by its enactments, prescribed exactly when and how wills may be made, altered, and revoked, and apparently, as it seems to me, when they have been fully complied with, has left no room for the exercise of an equitable jurisdiction by courts over such matters. Modern jurisprudence, in recognizing the right of the individual, under more or less restrictions, to dispose of his property after his death, subjects it to legislative control, both as to extent and as to mode of exercise. Complete freedom of testamentary disposition of one's property has not been and is not the universal rule, as we see from the provisions of the Napoleonic Code, from the systems of jurisprudence in countries which are modeled upon the Roman law, and from the statutes of many of our states. To the statutory restraints which are imposed upon the disposition of one's property by will are added strict and systematic statutory rules for the execution, alteration, and revocation of the will; which must be, at least substantially, if not exactly, followed to insure validity and performance. The reason for the establishment of such rules, we may naturally assume, consists in the purpose to create those safeguards about these grave and important acts which experience has demonstrated to be the wisest and surest. That freedom, which is permitted to be exercised in the testamentary disposition of one's estate by the laws of the state, is subject to its being exercised in conformity with the regulations of the statutes. The capacity and the power of the individual to dispose of his property after death, and the mode by which that power can be exercised, are matters of which the legislature has assumed the entire control, and has undertaken to regulate with comprehensive particularity.

The appellants' argument is not helped by reference to those rules of the civil law, or to those laws of other governments, by which the heir, or legatee, is excluded from benefit under the testament if he has been convicted of killing, or attempting to kill, the testator. In the absence of such legislation here, the courts are not empowered to institute such a system of remedial justice. The deprivation of the heir of his testamentary succession by the Roman law, when guilty of such a crime, plainly was intended to be in the nature of a punishment imposed upon him. The succession, in such a case of guilt, escheated to the exchequer. See Domat's Civil Law, pt. 2, bk. 1, tit. 1, § 3.

I concede that rules of law, which annul testamentary provisions made for the benefit of those who have become unworthy of them, may be based on principles of equity and of natural justice. It is quite reasonable to suppose that a testator would revoke or alter his will, where his mind has been so angered and changed as to make him unwilling to have his will executed as it stood. But these principles only suggest sufficient reasons for the enactment of laws to meet such cases.

The statutes of this state have prescribed various ways in which a will may be altered or revoked; but the very provision, defining the modes of alteration and revocation, implies a prohibition of alteration or revocation in any other way. The words of the section of the statute are: "No will in writing, except in the cases hereinafter mentioned, nor any part thereof, shall be revoked or altered otherwise," etc. Where, therefore, none of the cases mentioned are met by the facts, and the revocation is not in the way described in the section, the will of the testator is unalterable. I think that a valid will must continue as a will always, unless revoked in the manner provided by the statutes. Mere intention to revoke a will does not have the effect of revocation. The intention to revoke is necessary to constitute the effective revocation of a will, but it must be demonstrated by one of the acts contemplated by the statute. As Woodworth, J., said in Dan v. Brown: "Revocation is an act of the mind, which must be demonstrated by some outward and visible sign of revocation." The same learned judge said in that case: "The rule is that if the testator lets the will stand until he dies, it is his will; if he does not suffer it to do so, it is not his will."

The finding of fact of the referee, that, presumably, the testator would have altered his will, had he known of his grantor's murderous intent, cannot affect the question. We may concede it to the fullest extent; but still the cardinal objection is undisposed of, that the making and the revocation of a will are purely matters of statutory regulation, by which the court is bound in the determination of questions relating to these acts. Two cases in this state and in Kentucky, at an early day, seem to me to be much in point. Gains v. Gains was decided by the Kentucky court of appeals in 1820. It was there urged that the testator intended to have destroyed his will, and that he was forcibly prevented from doing so by the defendant in error or devisee; and it was insisted that the will, though not expressly, was thereby virtually revoked. The court held, as the act concerning wills prescribed the manner in which a will might be revoked, that, as none of the acts evidencing revocation were done, the intention could not be substituted for the act. In that case the will was snatched away and forcibly retained. In 1854, Surrogate Bradford, whose opinions are entitled to the highest consideration, decided the case of Leaycraft v. Simmons. In that case the testator, a man of 89 years of age, desired to make a codicil to his will, in order to enlarge the provisions for his daughter. His son having the custody of the instrument, and the one to be prejudiced by the change, refused to produce the will at testator's request, for the purpose of alteration. The learned surrogate refers to the provisions of the civil law for such and other cases of unworthy conduct in the heir or legatee, and says: "Our statute has undertaken to prescribe the mode in which wills can be revoked [citing the statutory provision]. This is the law by which I am governed in passing upon questions touching the revocation of wills. The whole of this subject is now regulated by statute, and a mere intention to revoke, however well authenticated, or however defeated, is not sufficient." And he held that the will must be admitted to probate. I may refer also to a case in the Pennsylvania courts. In that state the statute prescribed the mode for repealing or altering a will, and in Clingan v. Micheltree, the supreme court of the state held, where a will was kept from destruction by the fraud and misrepresentation of the devisee, that to declare it canceled as against the fraudulent party would be to enlarge the statute.

I cannot find any support for the argument that the respondent's succession to the property should be avoided because of his criminal act, when the laws are silent. Public policy does not demand it, for the demands of public policy are satisfied by the proper execution of the laws and the punishment of the crime. There has been no convention between the testator and his legatee, nor is there any such contractual element in such a disposition of property by a testator, as to impose or imply conditions in the legatee. The appellants' argument practically amounts to this: that, as the legatee has been guilty of a crime, by the commission of which he is placed in a position to sooner receive the benefits of the testamentary provision, his rights to the property should be forfeited and he should be divested of his estate. To allow their argument to prevail would involve the diversion by the court of the testator's estate into the hands of persons, whom, possibly enough, for all we know, the testator might not have chosen or desired as its recipients. Practically the court is asked to make another will for the testator. The laws do not warrant this judicial action, and mere presumption would not be strong enough to sustain it.

But more than this, to concede the appellants' views would involve the imposition of an additional punishment or penalty upon the respondent. What power or warrant have the courts to add to the respondent's penalties by depriving him of property? The law has punished him for his crime, and we may not say that it was an insufficient punishment. In the trial and punishment of the respondent the law has vindicated itself for the outrage which he committed, and further judicial utterance upon the subject of punishment or deprivation of rights is barred. We may not, in the language of the court in People v. Thornton, "enhance the pains, penalties, and forfeitures provided by law for the punishment of crime."

The judgment should be affirmed, with costs.

Notes and Questions

1. Why, according to Holmes, is it misleading to think of a contract as a promise?

2. What happens when you break a promise? What happens when you fail to perform a contract?

3. Would the institution of promise-keeping be improved if more people thought like lawyers?

Suggestions For Further Reading

Albert W. Alschuler, The Descending Trail: Holmes' Path of the Law One Hundred Years Later, 49 Florida Law Review 353 (1997)

Laura Carrier, Making Moral Theory Work for Law, 99 Columbia Law Review 1018 (1999)

Ronald Dworkin, The Model of Rules I, in Taking Rights Seriously 14 (1978)

Oliver Wendell Holmes, Jr., and The Path of the Law (Steven Burton ed., forthcoming)

David Luban, The Bad Man and the Good Lawyer, 72 New York University Law Review 1547 (1997)

The Path of the Law After One Hundred Years, 110 Harvard Law Review 989 (1997)

Chapter 13

Legal Implications of Personal Morality

The Invitation to Dinner Case[*]
Henry M. Hart, Jr. and Albert M. Sacks

On the way home for lunch on Friday, January 6, 1956, Mr. Patrick met Mr. David, an acquaintance of his. Mr. Patrick told Mr. David that he expected Professor Thomas for dinner and would like Mr. David to join them both for dinner and for bridge afterward. Mr. Patrick explained to Mr. David that he must be sure about coming so that there would be enough persons for bridge. Bridge, he said, was a favorite game of Professor Thomas's, and he wanted to humor the professor because he needed his help in getting a job. Mr. David asked what there would be for dinner, and Mr. Patrick promised to have planked steak, which he knew to be a favorite dish of Mr. David's. On hearing this, Mr. David promised firmly to be there at 7 p.m.

At 6:30 p.m., while Mr. David was dressing, the telephone rang. On the line was his friend, Mr. Jack, who asked him to come over for a game of poker. Mr. David agreed at once, and left soon for Jack's house, telling his wife that he was going to Patrick's.

At 9 p.m. the telephone rang in Jack's house, and a voice asked for Mr. David. Mr. David answered, fearful that it was his wife, but it was Mr. Patrick, who could hardly talk from anger. He said: "So I knew where to find you, you - - -. If you do not come over to my place at once, I'll sue you in court." Mr. David hung up the phone without answering, and told the story to Jack and his friends who had a good laugh. All of them kept on playing until the early morning hours.

Mr. Patrick was as good as his word, and his lawyer filed an action against Mr. David. He claimed damages for breach of contract, including the price of a portion of planked steak specially prepared for the defendant; $2,500 compensation for not getting a job, Professor Thomas having left in dudgeon immediately after the dinner; and $1,000 for mental suffering.

Mr. Patrick's lawyer claimed that there had been a legally binding contract, supported by consideration, and that the defendant had wilfully and maliciously failed to fulfill his

---

* Henry M. Hart, Jr. and Albert M. Sacks, The Legal Process: Basic Problems in the Making and Application of Law (Westbury, New York: The Foundation Press, Inc., William N. Eskridge, Jr. & Philip P. Frickey editors, 1994), pages 457-458.

legal and moral obligation. While acknowledging that he could find no case directly in point, he argued that the common law is elastic, and capable of developing a remedy for every wrong, especially in such a case as this where there was reliance on a promise made upon consideration, damage suffered because of malicious default, and warning to the defendant that the matter would be taken to court.

Mr. David appeared without a lawyer, telling the judge that he never thought he could be summoned to court over a social dinner invitation, and asked that the case be dismissed.

Give a reasoned judgment.

Hamer v. Sidway
124 N.Y. 538 (1891)

The plaintiff presented a claim to the executor of William E. Story, Sr., for $5,000 and interest from the 6th day of February, 1875. . . . It appears that William E. Story, Sr., was the uncle of William E. Story, 2d; that at the celebration of the golden wedding of Samuel Story and wife, father and mother of William E. Story, Sr., on the 20th day of March, 1869, in the presence of the family and invited guests, he promised his nephew that if he would refrain from drinking, using tobacco, swearing, and playing cards or billiards for money until he became 21 years of age he would pay him the sum of $5,000. The nephew assented thereto and fully performed the conditions inducing the promise. When the nephew arrived at the age of 21 years and on the 31st day of January, 1875, he wrote to his uncle, informing him that he had performed his part of the agreement, and had thereby become entitled to the sum of $5,000. The uncle received the letter and a few days later and on the sixth of February, he wrote and mailed to his nephew the following letter:

Buffalo, Feb. 6, 1875
W.E. Story, Jr.:
Dear Nephew—

Your letter of the 31st ult. came to hand all right, saying that you had lived up to the promise made to me several years ago. I have no doubt but you have, for which you shall have five thousand dollars, as I promised you. I had the money in the bank the day you was 21 years old that I intend for you, and you shall have the money certain. Now, Willie I do not intend to interfere with this money in any way till I think you are capable of taking care of it, and the sooner that time comes the better it will please me. I would hate very much to have you start out in some adventure that you thought all right and lose this money in one year. The first five thousand dollars that I got together cost me a heap of hard work. You would hardly believe me when I tell you that to obtain this I shoved a jackplane many a day, butchered three or four years, then came to this city, and after three months' perseverance, I obtained a situation in a grocery store. I opened this store early, closed late, slept in the fourth story of the building in a room 30 by 40 feet, and not a human being in the building but myself. All this I done to live as cheap as I could to save something. I don't want you to take up with this kind of fare. I was here in the cholera season of '49 and '52, and the deaths averaged 80 to 125 daily and plenty of smallpox. I wanted to go home, but Mr. Fisk, the gentleman I was working for, told me if I left then, after it got healthy he probably would not want me. I stayed. All the money I have saved I know just how I got it. It did not come to me in any mysterious way, and the reason I speak of this is that money got in this way stops longer with a fellow that gets it with hard knocks than it does when he finds it. Willie, you are 21 and you have many a thing to learn yet. This money you have earned much easier than I did, besides acquiring good habits at the same time, and you are quite welcome to the money; hope you will make good use of it. I was ten long years getting this together after I was your age. Now, hoping this will be satisfactory, I stop. One thing more. Twenty-one years ago I bought you 15 sheep. These sheep were put out to double every four years. I kept track of them the first eight years. I have not heard much about them since. Your father and grandfather promised me that they would look after them till you were of age. Have they done so? I hope they have. By this time you have between five and six hundred sheep, worth a nice little income this spring. Willie, I have said much more than I expected to. Hope you can make out what I have written. To-day is the seventeenth day that I have not been out of my room, and have had the doctor as many days. Am a little better to-day; think I will get out next week. You need not mention to father, as he always worries about small matters.

Truly yours,

W.E. Story

P.S.—You can consider this money on interest.

The nephew received the letter, and thereafter consented that the money should remain with his uncle in accordance with the terms and conditions of the letters. The uncle died on the 29th day of January, 1887, without having paid over to his nephew any portion of the said $5,000 and interest.

Parker, J.

The question which provoked the most discussion by counsel on this appeal, and which lies at the foundation of plaintiff's asserted right of recovery, is whether by virtue of a contract defendant's testator, William E. Story, became indebted to his nephew, William E. Story, 2d, on his twenty-first birthday in the sum of $5,000. The trial court found as a fact that "on the 20th day of March, 1869, . . . William E. Story agreed to and with William E. Story, 2d, that if he would refrain from drinking liquor, using tobacco, swearing, and playing cards or billiards for money until he should become twenty-one years of age then he, the said William E. Story, would at that time pay him, the said William E. Story, 2d, the sum of $5,000 for such refraining, to which the said William E. Story, 2d, agreed," and that he "in all things fully performed his part of said agreement."

The defendant contends that the contract was without consideration to support it, and therefore invalid. He asserts that the promisee, by refraining from the use of liquor and tobacco, was not harmed, but benefited; that that which he did was best for him to do, independently of his uncle's promise, and insists that it follows that, unless the promisor was benefited, the contract was without consideration. A contention which, if well founded, would seem to leave open for controversy in many cases whether that which the promisee did or omitted to do was in fact of such benefit to him as to leave no consideration to support the enforcement of the promisor's agreement. Such a rule could not be tolerated, and is without foundation in the law. The Exchequer Chamber, in 1875, defined consideration as follows: "A valuable consideration, in the sense of the law, may consist either in some right, interest, profit, or benefit accruing to the one party, or some forbearance, detriment, loss, or responsibility given, suffered, or undertaken by the other." Courts "will not ask whether the thing which forms the consideration does in fact benefit the promisee or a third party, or is of any substantial value to anyone. It is enough that something is promised, done, forborne, or suffered by the party to whom the promise is made as consideration for the promise made to him." Anson's Prin. of Cont. 63.

"In general a waiver of any legal right at the request of another party is a sufficient consideration for a promise." Parsons on Contracts, 444.

"Any damage, or suspension, or forbearance of a right will be sufficient to sustain a promise." 2 Kent, Comm. 465 (12th ed.).

Pollock in his work on Contracts, after citing the definition given by the Exchequer Chamber, already quoted, says: "The second branch of this judicial description is really the most important one. Consideration means not so much that one party is profiting as that the other abandons some legal right in the present or limits his legal freedom of action in the future as an inducement for the promise of the first."

Now, applying this rule to the facts before us, the promisee used tobacco, occasionally drank liquor, and he had a legal right to do so. That right he abandoned for a period of years upon the strength of the promise of the testator that for such forbearance he would give him $5,000. We need not speculate on the effort which may have been required to give up the use of those stimulants. It is sufficient that he restricted his lawful freedom of action within certain prescribed limits upon the faith of his uncle's agreement, and now, having fully performed the conditions imposed, it is of no moment whether such performance actually proved a benefit to the promisor, and the court will not inquire into it; but, were it a proper subject of inquiry, we see nothing in this record that would permit a determination that the uncle was not benefited in a legal sense. Few cases have been found which may be said to be precisely in point, but such as have been support the position we have taken.

In Shadwell v. Shadwell, an uncle wrote to his nephew as follows:

> My Dear Lancey:
>
> I am so glad to hear of your intended marriage with Ellen Nicholl, and, as I promised to assist you at starting, I am happy to tell you that I will pay you 150 pounds yearly during my life and until your annual income derived from your profession of a chancery barrister shall amount to 600 guineas, of which your own admission will be the only evidence that I shall require.
> Your affectionate uncle,
> Charles Shadwell

It was held that the promise was binding, and made upon good consideration.

In Lakota v. Newton, the complaint averred defendant's promise that "if you [meaning the plaintiff] will leave off drinking for a year I will give you $100," plaintiff's assent thereto, performance of the condition by him, and demanded judgment therefor. Defendant demurred, on the ground, among others, that the plaintiff's declaration did not allege a valid and sufficient consideration for the agreement of the defendant. The demurrer was overruled.

In Talbott v. Stemmons, the step-grandmother of the plaintiff made with him the following agreement: "I do promise and bind myself to give my grandson Albert R. Talbott

$500 at my death if he will never take another chew of tobacco or smoke another cigar during my life, from this date up to my death; and if he breaks this pledge he is to refund double the amount to his mother." The executor of Mrs. Stemmons demurred to the complaint on the ground that the agreement was not based on a sufficient consideration. The demurrer was sustained, and an appeal taken therefrom to the court of appeals, where the decision of the court below was reversed. In the opinion of the court it is said that "the right to use and enjoy the use of tobacco was a right that belonged to the plaintiff, and not forbidden by law. The abandonment of its use may have saved him money, or contributed to his health; nevertheless, the surrender of that right caused the promise, and having the right to contract with reference to the subject-matter, the abandonment of the use was a sufficient consideration to uphold the promise." Abstinence from the use of intoxicating liquors was held to furnish a good consideration for a promissory note in Lindell v. Rokes.

The cases cited by the defendant on this question are not in point. . . .

People v. Lafka
174 Cal. App. 2d 312 (1959)

Bray, Presiding Justice.

Defendant appeals from a judgment of conviction after jury verdict, of two felonies, violations of section 487, Penal Code, (1) theft of a diamond ring valued in excess of $200, and (2) theft of money in excess of $200. . . .

The complaining witness, Alice, met defendant in March, 1957, while both were working at a hotel. In July she started seeing him socially. After about two weeks defendant proposed marriage. The same night after saying that as they were going to get married and that everything that was his was hers, he asked her for money to go to Washington on a business deal. She gave him $300. A few days later at his request she gave him $500 more for the same trip. On August 12 she loaned him $900 in order for him to obtain a license for a bar and a lease at Bush Street and Grant Avenue. August 16, she loaned him $450 for fixtures and supplies. September 3, she loaned him $325 for a license from the Board of Equalization. September 10, she loaned him an additional $300 for the bar. These loans were to be repaid after the first of the year. When Alice informed defendant that was all the money she had, he began to admire her ring, which had cost her $290 in 1940. He told her that he could get some money for it. Defendant promised to return the ring in a week, saying that he intended to use the money from pawning it for the bar. Stating that it was necessary in order for him to be able to pawn the ring, he produced from his pocket a paper which he asked her to sign. It stated: "This is to inform anyone concerned that I have authorized J. Lafka to make a loan on this ring, and to use said monies for himself as he sees fit." Alice stated, "It isn't saying that you are using it for the bar." He again reassured her it was for the bar, that he would return the ring in a week, and that he had to word the paper that way in order to pawn the ring. Alice then signed the note and gave him the ring. Alice took a trip to Portland and was met by defendant upon her return. Thereafter he no longer visited her or talked of marriage. She called him and inquired about the ring. Toward the end of October as defendant refused to keep his promise of returning the ring, she consulted the district attorney. Alice testified that she would not have loaned defendant the money if it was not to be used for the purposes defendant described. Defendant did not testify.

It is clear that defendant used the device of pretending that he was "negotiating" for a license and a lease to deprive Alice permanently and wholly of her property, and without any intention of using it for the purposes promised. He said he was "negotiating" with the Board of Equalization for a "liquor license." Such licenses are not issued by that board but by the Department of Alcoholic Beverage Control. The department had no record of any application or "negotiations" of any sort by defendant. Moreover, the department's supervising agent testified that the department would not accept an application for a liquor license without a particular premise being specified. As to a lease, defendant called Paul Kwan who owned a store at Bush and Grant Avenue. He testified that defendant had expressed interest in renting the store for a bar but did not go so far as to discuss a lease. Kwan could not remember, however, the month in which defendant came to see him. The jury could very well have believed that it was in November or December, after Alice began to stir up trouble for defendant, that he saw Kwan in an attempt to supply proof of defendant's good faith.

Considering defendant's failure to testify, the fact that as soon as Alice's money was gone defendant's romantic interest in her also waned, the fact that defendant did not discuss a lease with Kwan, and all the other circumstances, there was sufficient evidence to amply demonstrate the defendant had no intention of using the money and ring for the purposes specified nor of repaying the money or returning the ring, and therefore extracted the money and ring by trick and device.

"Larceny amounting to grand theft can be committed by trick and device and usually results when the victim of a fraud intends not to pass complete title to his property, but that it shall be applied to a special purpose while the recipient intends to appropriate it to his own use."

It is well settled that a loan of money induced by a fraudulent representation that it will be used for a specific purpose accompanied by an intent to steal amounts to larceny by trick and device.

The elements of theft by trick or device ((1) the taking (2) asportation (3) of the property of another (4) with a fraudulent intent) are satisfied here. Clearly there was a "taking" and "asportation."

As to the "taking," applicable here is the following language in People v. Bartges:

> Without again setting forth the evidence in detail, suffice it to say that it clearly shows that appellant with a preconceived design to appropriate the money to his own use, obtain[ed] possession of it by means of fraud and trickery. The fraud vitiated the transaction and the owner is deemed still to retain a constructive possession of the property. The owner does not part with title to the alleged thief where, as here, he delivered it to appellant to be applied by the latter to a particular purpose and the recipient, having obtained possession with the preconceived intention to appropriate the money to his own use, subsequently did convert it to his own use instead of applying it to the purpose contemplated by the owner. Under the facts here present there was in contemplation of the law of larceny a "taking."

Applicable to the "asportation" is the following from the same case: "Asportation is shown by evidence that when appellant obtained delivery of the money from Mr. Simmons he did not intend to devote it to the use for which it was given him but to convert it to his own use. Upon receipt of the money he intended to keep it as his own and the conversion was then complete." No title passed. "Since the money belonged to Mr. Simmons and appellant acquired possession of it by fraud and chicanery, his holding was without right, and title thereto did not pass to him.". . .

The judgment is affirmed.

Bowers v. Hardwick
478 U.S. 186 (1986)

[After being charged with violating the Georgia statute criminalizing sodomy by committing that act with another adult male in the bedroom of his home, respondent Hardwick brought suit in Federal District Court, challenging the constitutionality of the statute insofar as it criminalized consensual sodomy. The District Court dismissed the case, and Hardwick appealed. The Court of Appeals reversed and remanded, holding that the Georgia statute violated respondent's fundamental rights.]

Justice White delivered the opinion of the Court. . . .

This case does not require a judgment on whether laws against sodomy between consenting adults in general, or between homosexuals in particular, are wise or desirable. It raises no question about the right or propriety of state legislative decisions to repeal their laws that criminalize homosexual sodomy, or of state-court decisions invalidating those laws on state constitutional grounds. The issue presented is whether the Federal Constitution confers a fundamental right upon homosexuals to engage in sodomy and hence invalidates the laws of the many States that still make such conduct illegal and have done so for a very long time. The case also calls for some judgment about the limits of the Court's role in carrying out its constitutional mandate.

We first register our disagreement with the Court of Appeals and with respondent that the Court's prior cases have construed the Constitution to confer a right of privacy that extends to homosexual sodomy and for all intents and purposes have decided this case. . . .

[W]e think it evident that none of the rights announced in those cases bears any resemblance to the claimed constitutional right of homosexuals to engage in acts of sodomy that is asserted in this case. No connection between family, marriage, or procreation on the one hand and homosexual activity on the other has been demonstrated, either by the Court of Appeals or by respondent. Moreover, any claim that these cases nevertheless stand for the proposition that any kind of private sexual conduct between consenting adults is constitutionally insulated from state proscription is unsupportable.

Precedent aside, however, respondent would have us announce, as the Court of Appeals did, a fundamental right to engage in homosexual sodomy. This we are quite unwilling to do. It is true that despite the language of the Due Process Clauses of the Fifth and Fourteenth Amendments, which appears to focus only on the processes by which life, liberty, or property is taken, the cases are legion in which those Clauses have been interpreted to have substantive content, subsuming rights that to a great extent are immune from federal or state regulation or proscription. Among such cases are those recognizing rights that have little or no textual support in the constitutional language. *Meyer, Prince,* and *Pierce* fall in this category, as do the privacy cases from *Griswold* to *Carey.*

Striving to assure itself and the public that announcing rights not readily identifiable in the Constitution's text involves much more than the imposition of the Justices' own choice of values on the States and the Federal Government, the Court has sought to identify the nature of the rights qualifying for heightened judicial protection. In Palko v. Connecticut it was said that this category includes those fundamental liberties that are "implicit in the concept of ordered liberty," such that "neither liberty nor justice would exist if [they] were sacrificed." A different description of fundamental liberties appeared in Moore v. East Cleveland, where they are characterized as those liberties that are "deeply rooted in this Nation's history and tradition."

It is obvious to us that neither of these formulations would extend a fundamental right to homosexuals to engage in acts of consensual sodomy. Proscriptions against that conduct have ancient roots. Sodomy was a criminal offense at common law and was forbidden by the laws of the original thirteen States when they ratified the Bill of Rights. In 1868, when the Fourteenth Amendment was ratified, all but 5 of the 37 States in the Union had criminal sodomy laws. In fact, until 1961, all 50 States outlawed sodomy, and today, 24 States and the District of Columbia continue to provide criminal penalties for sodomy performed in private and between consenting adults. Against this background, to claim that a right to engage in such conduct is "deeply rooted in this Nation's history and tradition" or "implicit in the concept of ordered liberty" is, at best, facetious. . . .

Nor are we inclined to take a more expansive view of our authority to discover new fundamental rights imbedded in the Due Process Clause. The Court is most vulnerable and comes nearest to illegitimacy when it deals with judge-made constitutional law having little or no cognizable roots in the language or design of the Constitution. That this is so was painfully demonstrated by the face-off between the Executive and the Court in the 1930's, which resulted in the repudiation of much of the substantive gloss that the Court had placed on the Due Process Clauses of the Fifth and Fourteenth Amendments. There should be, therefore, great resistance to expand the substantive reach of those Clauses, particularly if it requires redefining the category of rights deemed to be fundamental. Otherwise, the Judiciary necessarily takes to itself further authority to govern the country without express constitutional authority. The claimed right pressed on us today falls far short of overcoming this resistance.

Respondent, however, asserts that the result should be different where the homosexual conduct occurs in the privacy of the home. He relies on Stanley v. Georgia, where the Court held that the First Amendment prevents conviction for possessing and reading obscene material in the privacy of one's home: "If the First Amendment means anything, it means that a State has no business telling a man, sitting alone in his house, what books he may read or what films he may watch."

Stanley did protect conduct that would not have been protected outside the home, and it partially prevented the enforcement of state obscenity laws; but the decision was firmly grounded in the First Amendment. The right pressed upon us here has no similar support in the text of the Constitution, and it does not qualify for recognition under the prevailing principles for construing the Fourteenth Amendment. Its limits are also difficult to discern. Plainly enough, otherwise illegal conduct is not always immunized whenever it occurs in the home. Victimless crimes, such as the possession and use of illegal drugs, do not escape the law where they are committed at home. Stanley itself recognized that its holding offered no protection for the possession in the home of drugs, firearms, or stolen goods. And if respondent's submission is limited to the voluntary sexual conduct between consenting adults, it would be difficult, except by fiat, to limit the claimed right to homosexual conduct while leaving exposed to prosecution adultery, incest, and other sexual crimes even though they are committed in the home. We are unwilling to start down that road.

Even if the conduct at issue here is not a fundamental right, respondent asserts that there must be a rational basis for the law and that there is none in this case other than the presumed belief of a majority of the electorate in Georgia that homosexual sodomy is immoral and unacceptable. This is said to be an inadequate rationale to support the law. The law, however, is constantly based on notions of morality, and if all laws representing essentially moral choices are to be invalidated under the Due Process Clause, the courts will be very busy indeed. Even respondent makes no such claim, but insists that majority sentiments about the morality of homosexuality should be declared inadequate. We do not agree, and are unpersuaded that the sodomy laws of some 25 States should be invalidated on this basis.

Accordingly, the judgment of the Court of Appeals is reversed.

Justice Blackmun, with whom Justice Brennan, Justice Marshall, and Justice Stevens join, dissenting.

This case is no more about "a fundamental right to engage in homosexual sodomy," as the Court purports to declare, than Stanley v. Georgia was about a fundamental right to watch obscene movies, or Katz v. United States was about a fundamental right to place interstate bets from a telephone booth. Rather, this case is about "the most comprehensive of rights and the right most valued by civilized men," namely, "the right to be let alone." Olmstead v. United States (1928) (Brandeis, J., dissenting).

The statute at issue, Ga. Code Ann. § 16-6-2 (1984), denies individuals the right to decide for themselves whether to engage in particular forms of private, consensual sexual activity. The Court concludes that § 16-6-2 is valid essentially because "the laws of . . . many States . . . still make such conduct illegal and have done so for a very long time." But the fact that the moral judgments expressed by statutes like § 16-6-2 may be "natural and familiar . . . ought not to conclude our judgment upon the question whether statutes embodying them conflict with the Constitution of the United States." Roe v. Wade, quoting Lochner v. New York (1905) (Holmes, J., dissenting). Like Justice Holmes, I believe that "[i]t is revolting to have no better reason for a rule of law than that so it was laid down in the time of Henry IV. It is still more revolting if the grounds upon which it was laid down have vanished long since, and the rule simply persists from blind imitation of the past." O.W. Holmes, The Path of the Law, 10 Harv. L. Rev. 457, 469 (1897). I believe we must analyze Hardwick's claim in the light of the values that underlie the constitutional right to privacy. If that right means anything, it means that, before Georgia can prosecute its citizens for making choices about the most intimate aspects of their lives, it must do more than assert that the choice they have made is an "abominable crime not fit to be named among Christians.". . .

Georgia has provided that "[a] person commits the offense of sodomy when he performs or submits to any sexual act involving the sex organs of one person and the mouth or anus of another." Ga. Code Ann. § 16-6-2(a) (1984). The sex or status of the persons who engage in the act is irrelevant as a matter of state law. In fact, to the extent I can discern a legislative purpose for Georgia's 1968 enactment of § 16-6-2, that purpose seems to have been to broaden the coverage of the law to reach heterosexual as well as homosexual activity. I therefore see no basis for the Court's decision to treat this case as an "as applied" challenge to § 16-6-2, or for Georgia's attempt, both in its brief and at oral argument, to defend § 16-6-2 solely on the grounds that it prohibits homosexual activity. Michael Hardwick's standing may rest in significant part on Georgia's apparent willingness to enforce against homosexuals a law it seems not to have any desire to enforce against heterosexuals. But his claim that § 16-6-2 involves an unconstitutional intrusion into his privacy and his right of intimate association does not depend in any way on his sexual orientation. . . .

The Court concludes today that none of our prior cases dealing with various decisions that individuals are entitled to make free of governmental interference "bears any resemblance to the claimed constitutional right of homosexuals to engage in acts of sodomy that is asserted in this case." While it is true that these cases may be characterized by their connection to protection of the family, see Roberts v. United States Jaycees, the Court's conclusion that they extend no further than this boundary ignores the warning in Moore v. East Cleveland against "clos[ing] our eyes to the basic reasons why certain rights associated with the family have been accorded shelter under the Fourteenth Amendment's Due Process Clause." We protect those rights not because they contribute, in some direct and material way, to the general public welfare, but because they form so central a part of an individual's life. "[T]he concept of privacy embodies the 'moral fact that a person belongs to himself and not others nor to society as a whole.'" Thornburgh v. American College of Obstetricians & Gynecologists . . . .

Only the most willful blindness could obscure the fact that sexual intimacy is "a sensitive, key relationship of human existence, central to family life, community welfare, and the development of human personality," Paris Adult Theatre I v. Slaton. The fact that individuals define themselves in a significant way through their intimate sexual relationships with others suggests, in a Nation as diverse as ours, that there may be many "right" ways of conducting those relationships, and that much of the richness of a relationship will come from the freedom an individual has to *choose* the form and nature of these intensely personal bonds.

In a variety of circumstances we have recognized that a necessary corollary of giving individuals freedom to choose how to conduct their lives is acceptance of the fact that different individuals will make different choices. For example, in holding that the clearly important state interest in public education should give way to a competing claim by the Amish to the effect that extended formal schooling threatened their way of life, the Court declared: "There can be no assumption that today's majority is 'right' and the Amish and others like them are 'wrong.' A way of life that is odd or even erratic but interferes with no rights or interests of others is not to be condemned because it is different." Wisconsin v. Yoder. The Court claims that its decision today merely refuses to recognize a fundamental right to engage in homosexual sodomy; what the Court really has refused to recognize is the fundamental interest all individuals have in controlling the nature of their intimate associations with others.

The behavior for which Hardwick faces prosecution occurred in his own home, a place to which the Fourth Amendment attaches special significance. The Court's treatment of this aspect of the case is symptomatic of its overall refusal to consider the broad principles that have informed our treatment of privacy in specific cases. Just as the right to privacy is more than the mere aggregation of a number of entitlements to engage in specific behavior, so too, protecting the physical integrity of the home is more than merely a means of protecting specific activities that often take place there. Even when our understanding of the contours of the right to privacy depends on "reference to a 'place,'" Katz v. United States (Harlan, J., concurring), "the essence of a Fourth Amendment violation is 'not the breaking of [a person's] doors, and the rummaging of his drawers,' but rather is 'the invasion of his indefeasible right of personal security, personal liberty and private property.'" California v. Ciraolo . . . .

The Court's failure to comprehend the magnitude of the liberty interests at stake in this case leads it to slight the question whether petitioner, on behalf of the State, has justified Georgia's infringement on these interests. I believe that neither of the two general justifications for § 16-6-2 that petitioner has advanced warrants dismissing respondent's challenge for failure to state a claim.

First, petitioner asserts that the acts made criminal by the statute may have serious adverse consequences for "the general public health and welfare," such as spreading communicable diseases or fostering other criminal activity. Inasmuch as this case was dismissed by the District Court on the pleadings, it is not surprising that the record before us is barren of any evidence to support petitioner's claim. In light of the state of the record, I see no justification for the Court's attempt to equate the private, consensual sexual activity at issue here with the "possession in the home of drugs, firearms, or stolen goods," to which *Stanley* refused to extend its protection. None of the behavior so mentioned in *Stanley* can properly be viewed as "[v]ictimless": drugs and weapons are inherently dangerous, and for property to be "stolen," someone must have been wrongfully deprived of it. Nothing in the record before the Court provides any justification for finding the activity forbidden by § 16-6-2 to be physically dangerous, either to the persons engaged in it or to others.

The core of petitioner's defense of § 16-6-2, however, is that respondent and others who engage in the conduct prohibited by § 16-6-2 interfere with Georgia's exercise of the "right of the Nation and of the States to maintain a decent society," Paris Adult Theatre I v. Slaton. Essentially, petitioner argues, and the Court agrees, that the fact that the acts described in § 16-6-2 "for hundreds of years, if not thousands, have been uniformly condemned as immoral" is a sufficient reason to permit a State to ban them today.

I cannot agree that either the length of time a majority has held its convictions or the passions with which it defends them can withdraw legislation from this Court's scrutiny. See, e.g., Roe v. Wade; Loving v. Virginia; Brown v. Board of Education. As Justice Jackson wrote so eloquently for the Court in West Virginia Board of Education v. Barnette, "we apply the limitations of the Constitution with no fear that freedom to be intellectually and spiritually diverse or even contrary will disintegrate the social organization. . . . [F]reedom to differ is not limited to things that do not matter much. That would be a mere shadow of freedom. The test of its substance is the right to differ as to things that touch the heart of the existing order." It is precisely because the issue raised by this case touches the heart of what makes individuals what they are that we should be especially sensitive to the rights of those whose choices upset the majority.

The assertion that "traditional Judeo-Christian values proscribe" the conduct involved, cannot provide an adequate justification for § 16-6-2. That certain, but by no means all, religious groups condemn the behavior at issue gives the State no license to impose their judgments on the entire citizenry. The legitimacy of secular legislation depends instead on whether the State can advance some justification for its law beyond its conformity to religious doctrine. Thus, far from buttressing his case, petitioner's invocation of Leviticus, Romans, St. Thomas Aquinas, and sodomy's heretical status during the Middle Ages undermines his suggestion that § 16-6-2 represents a legitimate use of secular coercive power. A State can no more punish private behavior because of religious intolerance than it can punish such behavior because of racial animus. "The Constitution cannot control such prejudices, but neither can it tolerate them. Private biases may be outside the reach of the law, but the law cannot, directly or indirectly, give them effect." Palmore v. Sidoti. No matter how uncomfortable a certain group may make the majority of this Court, we have held that "[m]ere public intolerance or animosity cannot constitutionally justify the deprivation of a person's physical liberty."

Nor can § 16-6-2 be justified as a "morally neutral" exercise of Georgia's power to "protect the public environment," Paris Adult Theatre I. Certainly, some private behavior can affect the fabric of society as a whole. Reasonable people may differ about whether particular sexual acts are moral or immoral, but "we have ample evidence for believing that people will not abandon morality, will not think any better of murder, cruelty and dishonesty, merely because some private sexual practice which they abominate is not punished by the law." H.L.A. Hart, Immorality and Treason, reprinted in The Law as Literature 220, 225 (L. Blom-Cooper ed. 1961). Petitioner and the Court fail to see the difference between laws that protect public sensibilities and those that enforce private morality. Statutes banning public sexual activity are entirely consistent with protecting the individual's liberty interest in decisions concerning sexual relations: the same recognition that those decisions are intensely private which justifies protecting them from governmental interference can justify protecting individuals from unwilling exposure to the sexual activities of others. But the mere fact that intimate behavior may be punished when it takes place in public cannot dictate how States can regulate intimate behavior that occurs in intimate places.

This case involves no real interference with the rights of others, for the mere knowledge that other individuals do not adhere to one's value system cannot be a legally cognizable interest, let alone an interest that can justify invading the houses, hearts, and minds of citizens who choose to live their lives differently.

Notes and Questions

1. Suppose William E. Story, Sr., had simply promised his nephew: "I'll give you $5,000 when you're twenty-one." Why should it matter to the legal system whether a promise to pay $5,000 induces, or is induced by, a promise to give up some bad habits? In other words, why aren't promises of gifts legally enforceable?

2. Striving to "assure itself and the public that announcing rights not readily identifiable in the Constitution's text involves much more than the imposition of the Justices' own choice of values," the Supreme Court in the *Bowers* case considered whether Georgia's sodomy law violated a right "implicit in the concept of ordered liberty" or "deeply rooted in this Nation's history and tradition." In upholding the statute, the Court noted that "[t]he law . . . is constantly based on notions of morality." Do these considerations provide the sort of assurance the Court promised?

3. Writing in dissent, Justice Blackmun states that the *Bowers* case is about "the most comprehensive of rights and the right most valued by civilized men," namely, "the right to be let alone." How would you characterize the issue in *Bowers*?

Suggestions For Further Reading

Melvin Aron Eisenberg, The World of Contract and the World of Gift, 85 California Law Review 821 (1997)

Kermit L. Hall, The Magic Mirror: Law in American History, ch. 16 (1989)

Samuel D. Warren & Louis D. Brandeis, The Right to Privacy, 4 Harvard Law Review 193 (1890)

Chapter 14
Are There Affirmative Legal Duties?

Union Pacific Railway Co. v. Cappier
66 Kan. 649 (1903)

Smith, J.

This was an action brought by Adeline Cappier, the mother of Irvin Ezelle, to recover damages resulting to her by reason of the loss of her son, who was run over by a car of plaintiff in error, and died from the injuries received. The trial court, at the close of the evidence introduced to support a recovery by plaintiff below, held that no careless act of the railway company's servants in the operation of the car was shown, and refused to permit the case to be considered by the jury on the allegations and attempted proof of such negligence. The petition, however, contained an averment that the injured person had one leg and an arm cut off by the car wheels, and that the servants of the railway company failed to call a surgeon, or to render him any assistance after the accident, but permitted him to remain by the side of the tracks and bleed to death. Under this charge of negligence a recovery was had.

While attempting to cross the railway tracks, Ezelle was struck by a moving freight car pushed by an engine. A yardmaster in charge of the switching operations was riding on the end of the car nearest to the deceased, and gave warning by shouting to him. The warning was either too late, or no heed was given to it. The engine was stopped. After the injured man was clear of the track, the yardmaster signaled the engineer to move ahead, fearing, as he testified, that a passenger train then about due would come upon them. The locomotive and car went forward over a bridge, where the general yardmaster was informed of the accident, and an ambulance was telephoned for. The yardmaster then went back where the injured man was lying, and found three Union Pacific switchmen binding up the wounded limbs and doing what they could to stop the flow of blood. The ambulance arrived about 30 minutes later, and Ezelle was taken to a hospital, where he died a few hours afterwards.

In answer to particular questions of fact, the jury found that the accident occurred at 5:35 p.m.; that immediately one of the railway employees telephoned to police headquarters for help for the injured man; that the ambulance started at 6:05 p.m., and reached the nearest hospital with Ezelle at 6:20 p.m., where he received proper medical and surgical treatment. Judgment against the railway company was based on the following question and answer:

> Q. Did not defendant's employees bind up Ezelle's wounds, and try to stop the flow of blood, as soon as they could after the accident happened?

A. No.

The lack of diligence in the respect stated was intended, no doubt, to apply to the yard-master, engineer, and fireman in charge of the car and engine.

These facts bring us to a consideration of their legal duty toward the injured man after his condition became known. Counsel for defendant in error quote the language found in Beach on Contributory Negligence (3d ed.) § 215, as follows:

> Under certain circumstances, the railroad may owe a duty to a trespasser after the injury. When a trespasser has been run down, it is the plain duty of the railway company to render whatever service is possible to mitigate the severity of the injury. The train that has occasioned the harm must be stopped, and the injured person looked after, and, when it seems necessary, removed to a place of safety, and carefully nursed, until other relief can be brought to the disabled person.

The principal authority cited in support of this doctrine is Northern Central Railway Co. v. State, 29 Md. 420. The court in that case first held that there was evidence enough to justify the jury in finding that the operatives of the train were negligent in running it too fast over a road crossing without sounding the whistle, and that the number of brakemen was insufficient to check its speed. Such negligence was held sufficient to uphold the verdict, and would seem to be all that was necessary to be said. The court, however, proceeded to state that, from whatever cause the collision occurred, it was the duty of the servants of the company, when the man was found on the pilot of the engine in a helpless and insensible condition, to remove him, and to do it with proper regard to his safety and the laws of humanity. In that case the injured person was taken in charge by the servants of the railway company, and, being apparently dead, without notice to his family, or sending for a physician to ascertain his condition, he was moved to defendant's warehouse, laid on a plank, and locked up for the night. The next morning, when the warehouse was opened, it was found that during the night the man had revived from his stunned condition, and moved some paces from the spot where he had been laid, and was found in a stooping posture, dead, but still warm, having died from hemorrhage of the arteries of one leg which was crushed at and above the knee. It had been proposed to place him in the defendant's station house, which was a comfortable building, but the telegraph operator objected, and directed him to be taken into the warehouse, a place used for the deposit of old barrels and other rubbish.

The Maryland case does not support what is so broadly stated in Beach on Contributory Negligence. It is cited by Judge Cooley, in his work on Torts, in a note to a chapter devoted to the negligence of bailees, indicating that the learned author understood the reasoning of the decision to apply where the duty began after the railway employees had taken charge of the injured person.

After the trespasser on the track of a railway company has been injured in collision with a train, and the servants of the company have assumed to take charge of him, the duty, no doubt, arises to exercise such care in his treatment as the circumstances will allow. We are unable, however, to approve the doctrine that when the acts of a trespasser himself result in his injury, where his own negligent conduct is alone the cause, those in charge of the instrument which inflicted the hurt, being innocent of wrongdoing, are nevertheless blamable in law if they neglect to administer to the sufferings of him whose wounds we might say were self-imposed. With the humane side of the question courts are not concerned. It is the omission or negligent discharge of legal duties only which come within the sphere of judicial cognizance. For withholding relief from the suffering, for failure to respond to the calls of worthy charity, or for faltering in the bestowment of brotherly love on the unfortunate, penalties are found not in the laws of men, but in that higher law, the violation of which is condemned by the voice of conscience, whose sentence of punishment for the recreant act is swift and sure. In the law of contracts it is now well understood that a promise founded on a moral obligation will not be enforced in the courts. Bishop states that some of the older authorities recognize a moral obligation as valid, and says:

> Such a doctrine, carried to its legitimate results, would release the tribunals from the duty to administer the law of the land, and put in the place of law the varying ideas of morals which the changing incumbents of the bench might from time to time entertain.

Bishop on Contracts, § 44.

Ezelle's injuries were inflicted, as the court below held, without the fault of the yardmaster, engineer, or fireman in charge of the car and locomotive. The railway company was no more responsible than it would have been had the deceased been run down by the cars of another railroad company on a track parallel with that of plaintiff in error. If no duty was imposed on the servants of defendant below to take charge of and care for the wounded man in such a case, how could a duty arise under the circumstances of the case at bar? In Barrows on Negligence it is said:

> The duty must be owing from the defendant to the plaintiff, otherwise there can be no negligence, so far as the plaintiff is concerned. . . . And the duty must be owing to plaintiff in an individual capacity, and not merely as one of the general public.

> This excludes from actionable negligence all failures to observe the obligations imposed by charity, gratitude, generosity, and the kindred virtues. The moral law would obligate an attempt to rescue a person in a perilous position— as a drowning child—but the law of the land does not require it, no matter how little personal risk it might involve, provided that the person who declines to act is not responsible for the peril.

In the several cases cited in the brief of counsel for defendant in error to sustain the judgment of the trial court it will be found that the negligence on which recoveries were based occurred after the time when the person injured was in the custody and care of those who were at fault in failing to give him proper treatment.

The judgment of the court below will be reversed, with directions to enter judgment on the findings of the jury in favor of the railway company.

People v. Beardsley
150 Mich. 206 (1907)

McAlvay, C.J.

Respondent was convicted of manslaughter before the circuit court for Oakland county, and was sentenced to the state prison at Jackson for a minimum term of one year and a maximum term not to exceed five years. He was a married man living at Pontiac, and at the time the facts herein narrated occurred he was working as a bartender and clerk at the Columbia Hotel. He lived with his wife in Pontiac, occupying two rooms on the ground floor of a house. Other rooms were rented to tenants, as was also one living room in the basement. His wife being temporarily absent from the city, respondent arranged with a woman named Blanche Burns, who at the time was working at another hotel, to go to his apartments with him. He had been acquainted with her for some time. They knew each other's habits and character. They had drunk liquor together, and had on two occasions been in Detroit and spent the night together in houses of assignation. On the evening of Saturday, March 18, 1905, he met her at the place where she worked, and they went together to his place of residence. They at once began to drink, and continued to drink steadily, and remained together, day and night, from that time until the afternoon of the Monday following, except when respondent went to his work on Sunday afternoon. There was liquor at these rooms, and when it was all used they were served with bottles of whisky and beer by a young man who worked at the Columbia Hotel, and who also attended respondent's fires at the house. He was the only person who saw them in the house during the time they were there together. Respondent gave orders for liquor by telephone. On Monday afternoon, about 1 o'clock, the young man went to the house to see if anything was wanted. At this time he heard respondent say they must fix up the rooms, and the woman must not be found there by his wife, who was likely to return at any time. During this visit to the house the woman sent the young man to a drug store to purchase, with money she gave him, camphor and morphine tablets. He procured both articles. There were six grains of morphine in quarter-grain tablets. She concealed the morphine from respondent's notice, and was discovered putting something into her mouth by him and the young man as they were returning from the other room after taking a drink of beer. She in fact was taking morphine. Respondent struck the box from her hand. Some of the tablets fell on the floor, and of these respondent crushed several with his foot. She picked up and swallowed two of them, and the young man put two of them in the spittoon. Altogether it is probable she took from three to four grains of morphine. The young man went away soon after this. Respondent called him by telephone about an hour later, and after he came to the house requested him to take the woman into the room in the basement which was occupied by a Mr. Skoba. She was in a stupor, and did not rouse when spoken to. Respondent was too intoxicated to be of any assistance, and the young man proceeded to take her downstairs. While doing this, Skoba arrived, and together they put her in his room on the bed. Respondent requested Skoba to look after her, and let her out the back way when she waked up. Between 9 and 10 o'clock in the evening, Skoba became alarmed at her condition. He at once called the city marshal and a doctor. An examination by them disclosed that she was dead. . . .

In the brief of the prosecutor, his position is stated as follows:

It is the theory of the prosecution that the facts and circumstances attending the death of Blanche Burns in the house of respondent were such as to lay upon him a duty to care for her, and the duty to take steps for her protection, the failure to take which was sufficient to constitute such an omission as would render him legally responsible for her death. . . . There is no claim on the part of the people that the respondent was in any way an active agent in bringing about the death of Blanche Burns, but simply that he owed her a duty which he failed to perform, and that in consequence of such failure on his part she came to her death.

Upon this theory a conviction was asked and secured.

The law recognizes that under some circumstances the omission of a duty owed by one individual to another, where such omission results in the death of the one to whom the duty is owing, will make the other chargeable with manslaughter. This rule of law is always based upon the proposition that the duty neglected must be a legal duty, and not a mere moral obligation. It must be a duty imposed by law or by contract, and the omission to perform the duty must be the immediate and direct cause of death.

Although the literature upon the subject is quite meager and the cases few, nevertheless the authorities are in harmony as to the relationship which must exist between the parties to create the duty, the omission of which establishes legal responsibility. One authority has briefly and correctly stated the rule, which the prosecution claims should be applied to the case at bar, as follows:

If a person who sustains to another the legal relation of protector, as husband to wife, parent to child, master to seaman, etc., knowing such person to be in peril, willfully and negligently fails to make such reasonable and proper efforts to rescue him as he might have done, without jeopardizing his own life, or the lives of others, he is guilty of manslaughter at least, if by reason of his omission of duty the dependent person dies.

So one who from domestic relationship, public duty, voluntary choice, or otherwise, has the custody and care of a human being, helpless either from imprisonment, infancy, sickness, age, imbecility, or other incapacity of mind or body is bound to execute the charge with proper diligence, and will be held guilty of manslaughter, if by culpable negligence he lets the helpless creature die.

21 Am. & Eng. Enc. of Law (2d ed.) 197.

The following brief digest of cases gives the result of our examination of American and English authorities, where the doctrine of criminal liability was involved when death resulted from an omission to perform a claimed duty. We discuss no cases where statutory provisions are involved.

In Territory v. Manton, 8 Mont. 95, a husband was convicted of manslaughter for leaving his intoxicated wife one winter's night lying in the snow, from which exposure she died. The conviction was sustained on the ground that a legal duty rested upon him to care for and protect his wife, and that for his neglect to perform that duty, resulting in her death, he was properly convicted.

State v. Smith, 65 Me. 257, is a similar case. A husband neglected to provide clothing and shelter for his insane wife. He left her in a bare room without fire during severe winter weather. Her death resulted. The charge in the indictment is predicated upon a known legal duty of the husband to furnish his wife with suitable protection. In State v. Behm, 72 Iowa 533, the conviction of a mother of manslaughter for exposing her infant child without protection was affirmed upon the same ground.

State v. Noakes, 70 Vt. 247, was a prosecution and conviction of a husband and wife for manslaughter. A child of a maid servant was born under their roof. They were charged with neglecting to furnish it with proper care. In addition to announcing the principle in support of which the case is already cited, the court said:

> To create a criminal liability for neglect by nonfeasance, the neglect must also be of a personal legal duty, the natural and ordinary consequences of neglect of which would be dangerous to life.

In reversing the case for error in the charge—not necessary to here set forth—the court expressly stated that it did not concede that respondents were under a legal duty to care for this child, because it was permitted to be born under their roof, and declined to pass upon that question.

In a federal case tried in California before Mr. Justice Field, of the United States Supreme Court, where the master of a vessel was charged with murder in omitting any effort to rescue a sailor who had fallen overboard, the learned justice, in charging the jury, said:

> There may be in the omission to do a particular act under some circumstances, as well as in the commission of an act, such a degree of criminality as to render the offender liable to indictment for manslaughter. . . . In the first place, the duty omitted must be a plain duty. . . . In the second place, it must be one which the party is bound to perform by law, or by contract, and not one the performance of which depends simply upon his humanity, or his sense of justice and propriety.

United States v. Knowles, 4 Sawy. (U.S.) 517. . . .

The case of Reg. v. Nicholls, 13 Cox Crim. Cases 75, was a prosecution of a penniless old woman, a grandmother, for neglecting to supply an infant grandchild left in her charge with sufficient food and proper care. The case was tried at Assizes in Stafford, before Brett, J., who said to the jury:

> If a grown up person chooses to undertake the charge of a human creature, helpless either from infancy, simplicity, lunacy, or other infirmity, he is bound to execute that charge without, at all events, wicked negligence, and if a person who has chosen to take charge of a helpless creature lets it die by wicked negligence, that person is guilty of manslaughter.

The vital question was whether there had been any such negligence in the case designated by the trial judge as wicked negligence. The trial resulted in an acquittal. The charge of this nisi prius judge recognizes the principle that a person may voluntarily assume the care of a helpless human being, and, having assumed it, will be held to be under an implied legal duty to care for and protect such person; the duty assumed being that of caretaker and protector to the exclusion of all others.

Another English case decided in the Appellate Court, Lord Coleridge, C.J., delivering the opinion, is Reg. v. Instan, 17 Cox Crim. Cases 602. An unmarried woman without means lived with and was maintained by her aged aunt. The aunt suddenly became very sick, and for 10 days before her death was unable to attend to herself, to move about, or to do anything to procure assistance. Before her death no one but the prisoner had any knowledge of her condition. The prisoner continued to live in the house at the cost of the deceased and took in the food supplied by the trades people. The prisoner did not give food to the deceased, or give or procure any medical or nursing attendance for her; nor did she give notice to any neighbor of her condition or wants, although she had abundant opportunity and occasion to do so. In the opinion, Lord Coleridge, speaking for the court, said:

> It is not correct to say that every moral obligation is a legal duty; but every legal duty is founded upon a moral obligation. In this case, as in most cases, the legal duty can be nothing else than taking upon one's self the performance of the moral obligation. There is no question whatever that it was this woman's clear duty to impart to the deceased so much of that food, which was taken into the house for both and paid for by the deceased, as was necessary to sustain her life. The deceased could not get it for herself. She could only get it through the prisoner. It was the prisoner's clear duty at the common law, and that duty she did not perform. Nor is there any question that the prisoner's failure to discharge her legal duty, if it did not directly cause, at any rate accelerated the death of the deceased. There is no case directly in point; but it would be a slur and a stigma upon our law if there could be any doubt as to the law to be derived from the principle of decided cases, if cases were necessary. There was a clear moral obligation and a legal duty founded upon it, a duty willfully disregarded, and the death was at least accelerated, if not caused by the nonperformance of the legal duty.

The opening sentences of this opinion are so closely connected with the portion material to this discussion that they could not well be omitted. Quotation does not necessarily mean approval. We do not understand from this opinion that the court held that there was a legal duty founded solely upon a moral obligation. The court indicated that the law applied in the case was derived from the principles of decided cases. It was held that the prisoner had omitted to perform that which was a clear duty at the common law. The prisoner had wrongfully appropriated the food of the deceased and withheld it from her. She was the only other person in the house, and had assumed charge of her helpless relative. She was under a clear legal duty to give her the food she withheld, and under an implied legal duty by reason of her assumption of charge and care, within the law as stated in the case of Reg. v.

Nicholls, *supra.* These adjudicated cases and all others examined in this investigation we find are in entire harmony with the proposition first stated in this opinion.

Seeking for a proper determination of the case at bar by the application of the legal principles involved, we must eliminate from the case all consideration of mere moral obligation, and discover whether respondent was under a legal duty towards Blanche Burns at the time of her death, knowing her to be in peril of her life, which required him to make all reasonable and proper effort to save her; the omission to perform which duty would make him responsible for her death. This is the important and determining question in this case. If we hold that such legal duty rested upon respondent, it must arise by implication from the facts and circumstances already recited. The record in this case discloses that the deceased was a woman past 30 years of age. She had been twice married. She was accustomed to visiting saloons and to the use of intoxicants. She previously had made assignations with this man in Detroit at least twice. There is no evidence or claim from this record that any duress, fraud, or deceit had been practiced upon her. On the contrary, it appears that she went upon this carouse with respondent voluntarily, and so continued to remain with him. Her entire conduct indicates that she had ample experience in such affairs.

It is urged by the prosecutor that the respondent "stood towards this woman for the time being in the place of her natural guardian and protector, and as such owed her a clear legal duty which he completely failed to perform." The cases cited and digested establish that no such legal duty is created based upon a mere moral obligation. The fact that this woman was in his house created no such legal duty as exists in law and is due from a husband towards his wife, as seems to be intimated by the prosecutor's brief. Such an inference would be very repugnant to our moral sense. Respondent had assumed either in fact or by implication no care or control over his companion. Had this been a case where two men under like circumstances had voluntarily gone on a debauch together, and one had attempted suicide, no one would claim that this doctrine of legal duty could be invoked to hold the other criminally responsible for omitting to make effort to rescue his companion. How can the fact that in this case one of the parties was a woman change the principle of law applicable to it? Deriving and applying the law in this case from the principle of decided cases, we do not find that such legal duty as is contended for existed in fact or by implication on the part of respondent towards the deceased, the omission of which involved criminal liability. We find no more apt words to apply to this case than those used by Mr. Justice Field, in United States v. Knowles, *supra:*

> In the absence of such obligations, it is undoubtedly the moral duty of every person to extend to others assistance when in danger . . . and, if such efforts should be omitted by any one when they could be made without imperiling his own life, he would by his conduct draw upon himself the just censure and reproach of good men; but this is the only punishment to which he would be subjected by society. . . .

The conviction is set aside, and respondent is ordered discharged.

Pope v. State
284 Md. 309 (1979)

Orth, J.

Joyce Lillian Pope was found guilty by the court in the Circuit Court for Montgomery County under the 3rd and 5th counts of a nine count indictment, no. 18666. The 3rd count charged child abuse, presenting that "on or about April 11, 1976 . . . while having the temporary care, custody and responsibility for the supervision of Demiko Lee Norris, a minor child under the age of eighteen years [she] did unlawfully and feloniously cause abuse to said minor child in violation of Article 27, Section 35A of the Annotated Code of Maryland. . . ."

The evidence adduced at the trial established that Demiko Lee Norris, three months old, died as a result of physical injuries inflicted by his mother, Melissa Vera Norris. The abuse by the mother occurred over a period of several hours on a Sunday morning at Pope's home and in Pope's presence. Pope's involvement in the events leading to the child's abuse and death began on the preceding Friday evening when she and Melissa, with the child, were driven home by Pope's sister, Angela Lancaster, from a service held at the Christian Tabernacle Church. When they arrived at Melissa's grandparents' home, where Melissa was living, Melissa refused to enter the house, claiming that it was on fire, although in fact it was not. During the evening, Melissa had sporadically indicated mental distress. "She would at times seem caught up in a religious frenzy with a wild look about her, trying to preach and declaring that she was God. She would as quickly resume her normal self without ever seeming to notice her personality transitions." Pope agreed to take Melissa and the child into her home for the night because she did not want to put them "out on the street," and Angela would not let them stay in her home. Melissa had no money and Pope and Angela bought food and diapers for the baby. . . .

The next morning, awakened by the crying of the child, Pope fed him. Throughout the day Melissa "changed back and forth." When Melissa was "herself" she took care of her child. When Melissa thought she was God, Pope undertook the maternal duties. . . .

During a lucid period, Melissa prepared to go to church. She got a tub of water to bathe the baby. What next occurred is graphically described in the opinion of the Court of Special Appeals:

> Then, from her suddenly changed voice and appearance, [Pope] knew Melissa had changed again to "God." Calling out that Satan had hidden in the body of her son, Melissa began to verbally exorcise that spirit and physically abuse the child by punching and poking him repeatedly about the stomach, chest and privates. After she undressed the child, that which ensued was hardly describable. In her religious frenzy of apparent exorcism, Melissa poked the child's vitals and beat the child about the head. She reached her fingers down its throat, wiping mucus and blood on diapers at hand, and even lifted the child by inserting her hands in its mouth, and shook him like a rag.

Continuing to talk and stomp, Melissa began to squeeze the baby. Then, holding the child by the neck with one hand, she took him into the bathroom, acting like she did not know that Pope was present. When she first started this abuse, Melissa, in her "God voice," called Pope and asked her: "Didn't I give you eyes to see?" Pope noticed that Melissa's finger nails were "real long," and she said to Melissa: "[H]ow do you handle a baby with such long nails," but Pope did nothing. She admitted that she knew at some point that Melissa was hurting the baby and was "fearful, amazed and shocked at the 'unbelievable' and 'horrible' thing that was happening."

Melissa's frenzy diminished. Angela came to the house to take them to church. Pope did not tell Angela what happened—"I could not get it out." Angela asked her what was wrong, and Pope said: "[I]t's Melissa, the baby. . . ." She locked the door at Angela's direction so Angela's children would stay in the yard with Pope's children. Angela wrapped the child in a towel, raised him over her head and prayed.

Pope, Melissa and Angela left with the child to go to the church. At Melissa's request they stopped by her grandfather's house, arriving about 2:00 p.m. Pope told him the child was dead, but he did not believe her because all three were acting so strangely. He refused to take or look at the baby. The three women with the child then went to Bel Pre Health Center, picked up another member of the Christian Tabernacle congregation, telling her that "God has a job for you to do," and proceeded to the church. En route, they passed several hospitals, police stations and rescue squads. At the church, the child was given to, or taken by the Reverend Leon Hart, who handed him to Mother Dorothy King for her prayers. She discovered that the baby's body was cool and sent for ambulance assistance. Police and rescue personnel arrived and determined that the child was dead. There was expert medical testimony that the child had died sometime during the period of fifteen minutes to several hours after it was injured. The medical expert expressed no opinion as to whether the child could have been successfully treated if the injury had been reported sooner.

The police questioned Melissa in Pope's presence. Pope did not contradict Melissa's denial of abusing the child. In fact, Pope, in response to inquiry by the police, said that the baby did not fall, and told them that she had not seen Melissa strike the baby. She explained this untruth in subsequent statements to the police: "[I]t was her body in the flesh, but it wasn't her, because it was something else.". . .

The child abuse statute speaks in terms of a person who "has" responsibility for the supervision of a minor child. It does not prescribe how such responsibility attaches or what "responsibility" and "supervision" encompass. A doubt or ambiguity exists as to the exact reach of the statute's provision with respect to "has responsibility for the supervision of," justifying application of the principle that permits courts in such circumstances to ascertain and give effect to the real intention of the Legislature. . . .

A person may have the responsibility for the supervision of a minor child in the contemplation of § 35A although not standing in loco parentis to that child. "Responsibility" in its common and generally accepted meaning denotes "accountability," and "supervision" emphasizes broad authority to oversee with the powers of direction and decision. See American Heritage Dictionary of the English Language (1969); Webster's Third New International Dictionary (1968). As in the case of care or custody of a minor child under the child abuse law, a judicial decree is not necessary to obtain responsibility for the supervision of a minor child under that statute. Had the Legislature wished to narrow application of that law to those who had been charged with responsibility for the supervision of a child by court order, it could readily have done so in explicit language to that end. Absent a court order or award by some appropriate proceeding pursuant to statutory authority, we think it to be self-evident that responsibility for supervision of a minor child may be obtained only upon the mutual consent, expressed or implied, by the one legally charged with the care of the child and by the one assuming the responsibility. In other words, a parent may not impose responsibility for the supervision of his or her minor child on a third person unless that person accepts the responsibility, and a third person may not assume such responsibility unless the parent grants it. So it is that a baby sitter temporarily has responsibility for the supervision of a child; the parents grant the responsibility for the period they are not at home, and the sitter accepts it. And it is by mutual consent that a school teacher has responsibility for the supervision of children in connection with his academic duties. On the other hand, once responsibility for the supervision of a minor child has been placed in a third person, it may be terminated unilaterally by a parent by resuming responsibility, expressly or by conduct. The consent of the third party in such circumstances is not required; he may not prevent return of responsibility to the parent. But, of course, the third person in whom responsibility has been placed is not free to relinquish that responsibility without the knowledge of the parent. For example, a sitter may not simply walk away in the absence of the parents and leave the children to their own devices.

Under the present state of our law, a person has no legal obligation to care for or look after the welfare of a stranger, adult or child.

> Generally one has no legal duty to aid another person in peril, even when that aid can be rendered without danger or inconvenience to himself. . . . A moral duty to take affirmative action is not enough to impose a legal duty to do so.

W. LaFave & A. Scott, Criminal Law 183 (1972); see Clark & Marshall, A Treatise on the Law of Crimes § 10.02 (7th ed. 1967). The legal position is that "the need of one and the opportunity of another to be of assistance are not alone sufficient to give rise to a legal duty to take positive action." R. Perkins, Criminal Law 594-595 (2d ed. 1969). Ordinarily, a person may stand by with impunity and watch another being murdered, raped, robbed, assaulted or otherwise unlawfully harmed. "He need not shout a warning to a blind man headed for a precipice or to an absentminded one walking into a gunpowder room with a lighted candle in hand. He need not pull a neighbor's baby out of a pool of water or rescue an unconscious person stretched across the railroad tracks, though the baby is drowning, or the whistle of an approaching train is heard in the distance." LaFave & Scott at 183. The General Assembly has enacted two "Good Samaritan" statutes which afford protection to one who assists another in certain circumstances. Those statutes, however, impose no requirement that assistance be rendered.

In the face of this status of the law we cannot reasonably conclude that the Legislature, in bringing a person responsible for the supervision of a child within the ambit of the child abuse law, intended that such responsibility attach without the consent criteria we have set out. Were it otherwise, the consequences would go far beyond the legislative intent. For example, a person taking a lost child into his home to attempt to find its parents could be said to be responsible for that child's supervision. Or a person who allows his neighbor's children to play in his yard, keeping a watchful eye on their activities to prevent them from falling into harm, could be held responsible for the children's supervision. Or a person performing functions of a maternal nature from concern for the welfare, comfort or health of a child, or protecting it from danger because of a sense of moral obligation, may come within the reach of the act. In none of these situations would there be an intent to grant or assume the responsibility contemplated by the child abuse statute, and it would be incongruous indeed to subject such persons to possible criminal prosecution. . . .

[A] person may be convicted of the felony of child abuse created by § 35A as a principal in the first degree upon evidence legally sufficient to establish that the person

(1) was (a) the parent of, or (b) the adoptive parent of, or (c) in loco parentis to, or (d) responsible for the supervision of a minor child under the age of eighteen years, AND

(2) caused, by being in some manner accountable for, by act of commission or omission, abuse to the child in the form of (a) physical injury or injuries sustained by the child as the result of (i) cruel or inhumane treatment, or (ii) malicious act or acts by such person . . . .

Pope's lack of any attempt to prevent the numerous acts of abuse committed by the mother over a relatively protracted period and her failure to seek medical assistance for the child, although the need therefor was obviously compelling and urgent, could constitute a cause for the further progression and worsening of the injuries which led to the child's death. In such circumstances, Pope's omissions constituted in themselves cruel and inhumane treatment within the meaning of the statute. It follows that Pope would be guilty of child abuse *if her status brought her within the class of persons specified by the statute.* It being clear that she was neither the child's parent nor adoptive parent, and there being no evidence sufficient to support a finding that she had "the permanent or temporary care or custody" of the child so as to be in loco parentis to the child, the sole question is whether she had "responsibility for the supervision of" the child in the circumstances. If she had such responsibility the evidence was legally sufficient to find her guilty of child abuse as a principal in the first degree.

The State would have us translate compassion and concern, acts of kindness and care, performance of maternal functions, and general help and aid with respect to the child into responsibility for the supervision of the child. The crux of its argument is that although Pope was not under any obligation to assume responsibility for the supervision of the child at the outset, "once she undertook to house, feed, and care for [the mother and child], she did accept the responsibility and came within the coverage of the statute." But the mother was always present. Pope had no right to usurp the role of the mother even to the extent of responsibility for the child's supervision. We are in full accord with the view of the Court of Special Appeals that it could not "in good conscience hold that a person who has taken in a parent and child is given the responsibility for the child's supervision and protection even while the child is in the very arms of its mother." It would be most incongruous that acts of hospitality and kindness, made out of common decency and prompted by sincere concern for the well-being of a mother and her child, subjected the Good Samaritan to criminal prosecution for abusing the very child he sought to look after. And it would be especially ironic were such criminal prosecution to be predicated upon an obligation to take affirmative action with regard to abuse of the child by its mother, when such obligation arises solely from those acts of hospitality and kindness.

The evidence does not show why Pope did not intervene when the mother abused the child or why she did not, at least, timely seek medical assistance, when it was obvious that the child was seriously injured. Whether her lack of action was from fear or religious fervor or some other reason is not clearly indicated. . . . But Pope's conduct, during and after the acts of abuse, must be evaluated with regard for the rule that although she may have had a strong moral obligation to help the child, she was under no legal obligation to do so unless she then had responsibility for the supervision of the child as contemplated by the child abuse statute. She may not be punished as a felon under our system of justice for failing to fulfill a moral obligation, and the short of it is that she was under no legal obligation. In the circumstances, the mother's acquiescence in Pope's conduct was not a grant of responsibility to Pope for the supervision of the child, nor was Pope's conduct an acceptance of such responsibility. "[Pope's] concern for the child [did] not convert to legal responsibility nor parental prerogatives." We hold that the evidence was not sufficient in law to prove that Pope fell within that class of persons to whom the child abuse statute applies. Thus it is that the judgment of the trial court that she was a principal in the first degree in the commission of the crime of child abuse was clearly erroneous and must be set aside.

The mental or emotional state of the mother, whereby at times she held herself out as God, does not change the result. We see no basis in the statute for an interpretation that a person "has" responsibility for the supervision of a child, if that person believes or may have reason to believe that a parent is not capable of caring for the child. There is no right to make such a subjective judgment in order to divest parents of their rights and obligations with respect to their minor children, and therefore, no obligation to do so. . . .

The State concludes the argument in its brief:

> As is obvious from the evidence presented in this case, [Pope] witnessed a terrible event. She stood by while Melissa Norris killed her three-month old son. [Pope's] conduct during the beating . . . should be held to be culpable.

The evidence certainly showed that Pope "witnessed a terrible event" and that she "stood by" while the mother killed the child. But the culpability for her conduct during the abuse of the child must be determined strictly within the law or else the basic tenets of our system of justice are prostituted. There is an understandable feeling of outrage at what occurred, intensified by the fact that the mother, who actually beat the child to death, was held to be not responsible for her criminal acts. But it is the law, not indignation, which governs. The law requires that Pope's conviction of the felony of child abuse be set aside as clearly erroneous due to evidentiary insufficiency.

Eldridge, J., concurring in part and dissenting in part:

[I] cannot agree with the majority's restrictive interpretation of the child abuse statute, which interpretation furnishes the basis for the majority's conclusion that Pope was not guilty of child abuse as a principal in the first degree.

The child abuse statute, Maryland Code (1957, 1976 Repl. Vol.), Art. 27, § 35A(a), reaches "[a]ny parent, adoptive parent or other person who has the permanent or temporary care or custody or responsibility for the supervision of a minor child. . . ." The Court today takes the position that the statutory phrase "has responsibility for the supervision of" is ambiguous, thereby allowing the Court to "give effect to the real intention of the Legislature." The majority then states that, with regard to persons other than parents, legal custodians or individuals "in loco parentis," only those persons who have assumed responsibility for a child with the consent of the parent or guardian are covered by the statute. The majority finds it "self-evident" that "a third person may not assume such responsibility unless the parent grants it."

Thus, we are told by the majority opinion that a "person taking a lost child into his home" while an attempt is made to locate his or her parents is beyond the reach of the child abuse statute. In other words, in the Court's view, such a person may voluntarily assume full responsibility for the care of a small child, for a lengthy period of time while an effort is being made to find the parents, and during that time may batter the child unmercifully, but he would not be guilty of child abuse under Art. 27, § 35A. In my view this is a totally unwarranted narrowing of an important piece of legislation. . . .

Furthermore, even if there existed some ambiguity in the statute, I am at a loss to know why the majority finds it "self-evident" that only those persons who have been *granted* responsibility by a parent or guardian should be covered. Nothing in the statutory language indicates such a legislative purpose. I know of no public policy justifying this differentiation between a person who assumes responsibility for a child with parental consent and one who assumes just as complete a responsibility without the parent's consent. If either abuses the child, he should be held accountable under § 35A.

The majority appears to be concerned about the "good samaritans" who watch a lost child, or allow neighbors' children to play in their yards and exercise supervision, or perform "functions of a maternal nature from concern for the welfare, comfort or health of a child." However, such "good samaritans" have nothing to fear from the child abuse statute. But, if one of these same individuals assumes responsibility for the child and batters it, sexually molests it, locks it for a long period of time in a dark closet, etc., that person should be held just as accountable under the child abuse statute as someone else having responsibility for the child.

An American Tragedy[*]
Theodore Dreiser

"Oh, the sun shines bright in my old Kentucky home."

It was Roberta singing cheerfully, one hand in the deep blue water.

And then a little later—"I'll be there Sunday if you will," one of the popular dance pieces of the day.

And then at last, after fully an hour of rowing, brooding, singing, stopping to look at some charming point of land, reconnoitering some receding inlet which promised water-lilies, and with Roberta already saying that they must watch the time and not stay out too long,—the bay, south of the island itself—a beautiful and yet most funereally pine-encircled and land delimited bit of water—more like a smaller lake, connected by an inlet or passage to the larger one, and yet itself a respectable body of water of perhaps twenty acres of surface and almost circular in form. The manner in which to the east, the north, the south, the west, even, except for the passage by which the island to the north of it was separated from the mainland, this pool or tarn was encircled by trees! And cat-tails and water-lilies here and there—a few along its shores. And somehow suggesting an especially arranged pool or tarn to which one who was weary of life and cares—anxious to be away from the strife and contentions of the world, might most wisely and yet gloomily repair.

And as they glided into this, this still dark water seemed to grip Clyde as nothing here or anywhere before this ever had—to change his mood. For once here he seemed to be fairly pulled or lured along into it, and having encircled its quiet banks, to be drifting, drifting—in endless space where was no end of anything—no plots—no plans—no prac-tical problems to be solved—nothing. The insidious beauty of this place! Truly, it seemed to mock him—this strangeness—this dark pool, surrounded on all sides by those wonder-ful, soft, fir trees. And the water itself looking like a huge, black pearl cast by some mighty hand, in anger possibly, in sport or phantasy maybe, into the bosom of this valley of dark, green plush—and which seemed bottomless as he gazed into it.

And yet, what did it all suggest so strongly? Death! Death! More definitely than any-thing he had ever seen before. Death! But also a still, quiet, unprotesting type of death into which one, by reason of choice or hypnosis or unutterable weariness, might joyfully and gratefully sink. So quiet—so shaded—so serene. Even Roberta exclaimed over this. And he now felt for the first time the grip of some seemingly strong, and yet friendly sympathetic, hands laid firmly on his shoulders. The comfort of them! The warmth! The strength! For now they seemed to have a steadying effect on him and he liked them—their reassur-ance—their support. If only they would not be removed! If only they would remain always—the hands of this friend! For where had he ever known this comforting and almost tender sensation before in all his life? Not anywhere—and somehow this calmed him and he seemed to slip away from the reality of all things.

---

[*] Theodore Dreiser, An American Tragedy, Volume Two (New York: Boni and Liveright, 1925), pages 73-79.

To be sure, there was Roberta over there, but by now she had faded to a shadow or thought really, a form of illusion more vaporous than real. And while there was something about her in color, form that suggested reality—still she was very insubstantial—so very— and once more now he felt strangely alone. For the hands of the friend of firm grip had vanished also. And Clyde was alone, so very much alone and forlorn, in this somber, beautiful realm to which apparently he had been led, and then deserted. Also he felt strangely cold— the spell of this strange beauty overwhelming him with a kind of chill.

He had come here for what?

And he must do what?

Kill Roberta? Oh, no.

And again he lowered his head and gazed into the fascinating and yet treacherous depths of that magnetic, bluish, purple pool, which, as he continued to gaze, seemed to change its form kaleidoscopically to a large, crystalline ball. But what was that moving about in this crystal? A form! It came nearer—clearer—and as it did so, he recognized Roberta struggling and waving her thin white arms out of the water and reaching toward him! God! How terrible! The expression on her face! What in God's name was he thinking of anyway? Death! Murder!

And suddenly becoming conscious that his courage, on which he had counted so much this long while to sustain him here, was leaving him, and he instantly and consciously plumbing the depths of his being in a vain search to recapture it.

Kit, kit, kit, Ca-a-a-ah!

Kit, kit, kit, Ca-a-a-ah!

Kit, kit, kit, Ca-a-a-ah!

(The weird, haunting cry of that unearthly bird again. So cold, so harsh! Here it was once more to startle him out of his soul flight into a realization of the real or unreal immediate problem with all of its torturesome angles that lay before him.)

He must face this thing! He must!

Kit, kit, kit, Ca-a-a-ah!

Kit, kit, kit, Ca-a-a-ah!

What was it sounding—a warning—a protest—condemnation? The same bird that had marked the very birth of this miserable plan. For there it was now upon that dead tree—that wretched bird. And now it was flying to another one—as dead—a little farther inland and crying as it did so. God!

And then to the shore again in spite of himself. For Clyde, in order to justify his having brought his bag, now must suggest that pictures of this be taken—and of Roberta—and of himself, possibly—on land and water. For that would bring her into the boat again, without his bag, which would be safe and dry on land. And once on shore, actually pretending to be seeking out various special views here and there, while he fixed in his mind the exact tree at the base of which he might leave his bag against his return—which must be soon now—must be soon. They would not come on shore again together. Never! Never! And that in spite of Roberta protesting that she was getting tired; and did he not think they ought to be starting back pretty soon? It must be after five, surely. And Clyde, assuring her that presently they would—after he had made one or two more pictures of her in the boat with those wonderful trees—that island and this dark water around and beneath her.

His wet, damp, nervous hands!

And his dark, liquid, nervous eyes, looking anywhere but at her.

And then once more on the water again—about five hundred feet from shore, the while he fumbled aimlessly with the hard and heavy and yet small camera that he now held, as the boat floated out nearer the center. And then, at this point and time looking fearfully about. For now—now—in spite of himself, the long evaded and yet commanding moment. And no voice or figure or sound on shore. No road or cabin or smoke! And the moment which he or something had planned for him, and which was now to decide his fate at hand! The moment of action—of crisis! All that he needed to do now was to turn swiftly and savagely to one side or the other—leap up—upon the left wale or right and upset the boat; or, failing that, rock it swiftly, and if Roberta protested too much, strike her with the camera in his hand, or one of the oars free at his right. It could be done—it could be done— swiftly and simply, were he now of the mind and heart, or lack of it—with him swimming swiftly away thereafter to freedom—to success—of course—to Sondra and happiness—a new and greater and sweeter life than any he had ever known.

Yet why was he waiting now?

What was the matter with him, anyhow?

Why was he waiting?

At this cataclysmic moment, and in the face of the utmost, the most urgent need of action, a sudden palsy of the will—of courage—of hate or rage sufficient; and with Roberta from her seat in the stern of the boat gazing at his troubled and then suddenly distorted and fulgurous, yet weak and even unbalanced face—a face of a sudden, instead of angry, ferocious, demoniac—confused and all but meaningless in its registration of a balanced combat between fear (a chemic revulsion against death or murderous brutality that would bring death) and a harried and restless and yet self-repressed desire to do—to do—to do—yet temporarily unbreakable here and now—a static between a powerful compulsion to do and yet not to do.

And in the meantime his eyes—the pupils of the same growing momentarily larger and more lurid; his face and body and hands tense and contracted—the stillness of his position, the balanced immobility of the mood more and more ominous, yet in truth not suggesting a brutal, courageous power to destroy, but the imminence of trance or spasm.

And Roberta, suddenly noticing the strangeness of it all—the something of eerie unreason or physical and mental indetermination so strangely and painfully contrasting with this scene, exclaiming: "Why, Clyde! Clyde! What is it? Whatever is the matter with you anyhow? You look so—so strange—so—so— Why, I never saw you look like this before. What is it?" And suddenly rising, or rather leaning forward, and by crawling along the even keel, attempting to approach him, since he looked as though he was about to fall forward into the boat—or to one side and out into the water. And Clyde, as instantly sensing the profoundness of his own failure, his own cowardice or inadequateness for such an occasion, as instantly yielding to a tide of submerged hate, not only for himself, but Roberta—her power—or that of life to restrain him in this way. And yet fearing to act in any way—being unwilling to—being willing only to say that never, never would he marry her—that never, even should she expose him, would he leave here with her to marry her—that he was in love with Sondra and would cling only to her—and yet not being able to say that even. But angry and confused and glowering. And then, as she drew near him, seeking to take his hand in hers and the camera from him in order to put it in the boat, he flinging out at her, but not even then with any intention to do other than free himself of her—her touch—her pleading—consoling sympathy—her presence forever—God!

Yet (the camera still unconsciously held tight) pushing at her with so much vehemence as not only to strike her lips and nose and chin with it, but to throw her back sidewise toward the left wale which caused the boat to career to the very water's edge. And then he, stirred by her sharp scream, (as much due to the lurch of the boat, as the cut on her nose and lip), rising and reaching half to assist or recapture her and half to apologize for the unintended blow—yet in so doing completely capsizing the boat—himself and Roberta being as instantly thrown into the water. And the left wale of the boat as it turned, striking Roberta on the head as she sank and then rose for the first time, her frantic, contorted face turned to Clyde, who by now had righted himself. For she was stunned, horrorstruck, unintelligible with pain and fear—her lifelong fear of water and drowning and the blow he had so accidentally and all but unconsciously administered.

"Help! Help!

"Oh, my God, I'm drowning, I'm drowning. Help! Oh, my God!

"Clyde, Clyde!"

And then the voice at his ear!

"But this—this—is not this that which you have been thinking and wishing for this while—you in your great need? And behold! For despite your fear, your cowardice, this—this—has been done for you. An accident—an accident—an unintentional blow on your part is now saving you the labor of what you sought, and yet did not have the courage to do! But will you now, and when you need not, since it is an accident, by going to her rescue, once more plunge yourself in the horror of that defeat and failure which has so tortured you and from which this now releases you? You might save her. But again you might not! For see how she strikes about. She is stunned. She herself is unable to save herself and by her erratic terror, if you draw near her now, may bring about your own death also. But you desire to live! And her living will make your life not worth while from now on. Rest but a moment—a fraction of a minute! Wait—wait—ignore the pity of that appeal. And then—then— But there! Behold. It is over. She is sinking now. You will never, never see her alive any more—ever. And there is your own hat upon the water—as you wished. And upon the boat, clinging to that rowlock a veil belonging to her. Leave it. Will it not show that this was an accident?"

And apart from that, nothing—a few ripples—the peace and solemnity of this wondrous scene. And then once more the voice of that weird, contemptuous, mocking, lonely bird.

Kit, kit, kit, Ca-a-a-ah!

Kit, kit, kit, Ca-a-a-ah!

Kit, kit, kit, Ca-a-a-ah!

The cry of that devilish bird upon that dead limb—the weir-weir.

And then Clyde, with the sound of Roberta's cries still in his ears, that last frantic, white, appealing look in her eyes, swimming heavily, gloomily and darkly to shore. And the thought that, after all, he had not really killed her. No, no. Thank God for that. He had not. And yet (stepping up on the near-by bank and shaking the water from his clothes) had he? Or, had he not? For had he not refused to go to her rescue, and when he might have saved her, and when the fault for casting her in the water, however accidentally, was so truly his? And yet—and yet—

The dusk and silence of a closing day. A concealed spot in the depths of the same sheltering woods where alone and dripping, his dry bag near, Clyde stood, and by waiting, sought to dry himself. But in the interim, removing from the side of the bag the unused tripod of his camera and seeking an obscure, dead log farther in the woods, hiding it. Had any one seen? Was any one looking? Then returning and wondering as to the direction! He must go west and then south. He must not get turned about! But the repeated cry of that bird,— harsh, nerve shaking. And then the gloom, in spite of the summer stars. And a youth making his way through a dark, uninhabited wood, a dry straw hat upon his head, a bag in his hand, walking briskly and yet warily—south—south.

Notes and Questions

1. Suppose you are an Olympic gold medalist in swimming. You are hiking in a national forest and, coming through a clearing, you see a small girl swimming in a lake. As you approach, it becomes clear that the girl is floundering badly in the water and in fact is close to drowning. The water is quite shallow and you could easily rescue her. No one else is in sight, and you have just put on expensive suntan lotion that would be spoiled by the water. Should you be legally required to rescue the girl? Why or why not?

2. Suppose you live on the 31st floor of a large condominium that has a swimming pool on the ground floor. The swimming pool is clearly visible from the balconies of all the apartments in the building. Lounging on your balcony one day, you notice a small girl swimming in the pool below. As you look closer, it becomes clear that the girl is floundering badly in the water and in fact is close to drowning. The water is quite shallow and you could easily rescue her. Should you be legally required to rescue the girl? Should your analysis be the same as in the previous question?

3. In the *Pope* case, why should Pope's legal liability turn on whether or not she had been "granted" and had "accepted" responsibility for supervising the abused child? In other words, why should her relationship to the endangered child matter at all?

4. The trial judge in *An American Tragedy* instructed the jury as follows:

> Much has been said here concerning motive and its importance in this case, but you are to remember that proof of motive is by no means indispensable or essential to conviction. While a motive may be shown as a *circumstance* to aid in *fixing* a crime, yet the people are not required to prove a motive.
>
> If the jury finds that Roberta Alden accidentally or involuntarily fell out of the boat and that the defendant made no attempt to rescue her, that does not make the defendant guilty and the jury must find the defendant "not guilty." On the other hand, if the jury finds that the defendant in any way, intentionally, there and then brought about or contributed to that fatal accident, either by a blow or otherwise, it must find the defendant guilty.

Is that a correct statement of the law? Is Clyde guilty?

Suggestions For Further Reading

Hanoch Dagan, In Defense of the Good Samaritan, 97 Michigan Law Review 1152 (1999)

Samuel Freeman, Criminal Liability and the Duty to Aid the Distressed, 142 University of Pennsylvania Law Review 1455 (1994)

Steven J. Heyman, Foundations of the Duty to Rescue, 47 Vanderbilt Law Review 673 (1994)

Alison McIntyre, Guilty Bystanders? On the Legitimacy of Duty to Rescue Statutes, 23 Philosophy & Public Affairs 157 (1994)

Daniel B. Yeager, A Radical Community of Aid, 71 Washington University Law Quarterly 1 (1993)

Table of Cases
(including fictional cases)

Subject Matter Index
(references are to chapters)